Scot land the Best

PETER IRVINE

Published by Collins
An imprint of HarperCollins Publishers
Westerhill Road
Bishopbriggs
Glasgow G64 2QT
www.harpercollins.co.uk

12th edition 2016

Text © Peter Irvine 2016
Maps © Collins Bartholomew 2016

A catalogue record for this book is available from the British Library.

ISBN 978-0-00-755934-3
ISBN 978-0-00-795299-1

10 9 8 7 6 5 4 3 2 1

First published in 1993 by Mainstream Publishing
Company (Edinburgh) Ltd

First published by HarperCollins Publishers in 1997

Printed and bound in Italy

If you would like to comment on any aspect of this book,
please contact us at the above address or online.
e-mail: **scotland.best@harpercollins.co.uk**

Contents

Section 3 *Glasgow*

4

Section 4   *Regional Hotels & Restaurants*

Section 5 *Particular Places to Eat & Stay in Scotland*

Section 6 *Good Food & Drink*

Section 7 *Outdoor Places*

Section 8 *Historical Places*

Section 9 *Strolls, Walks & Hikes*

Introduction

Welcome old friends, new readers; fellow travellers. Again it's been a long labour of love; regular readers will have noticed that more than four years, not just two, have passed since the last edition. I was too preoccupied in 2013/14 ('Scotland's Big Year') with events and festivals to be able to complete the massive amount of essential field research – so much change, loads that's new. But here it is: the 12th edition of *Scotland the Best*.

Once again I've been up and down the land. Yes, people imagine this to be an enviable way of spending a summer (well, a year and a half), eating out in posh restaurants, staying in the best hotels, discovering brilliant new beaches, and so on. But I do go everywhere – the simple as well as the splendid and unfortunately there's only me on that trail; speed is of the essence on a fast as well as inside track. There's never enough time to stop and savour – until this book is done and I can consult it and use it myself, as (hopefully) you will.

For new readers please note that this is not a list of options; rather it's a highly selective personal choice in a diverse range of what I think a visitor might want to know. It's a book of impressions and opinions and, while I'm not infallible, everywhere in contention has been experienced and compared. I do believe you really can identify and ascertain what is better than the rest and over the years it seems many people agree with me. I try to be rigorous in my explorations and deliberations, comparing like with like in the categories I've determined, and also how our small country measures up in an increasingly competitive world of old and ever new destinations. Ultimately, *Scotland the Best* is a guide to the good life, not just a good country.

Hotels, restaurants and walks have their own codes and there are codes for less quantifiable aspects. ATMOS is that something that makes a place especially affecting to be in, whether it be a ruin or a restaurant, and L for LOCATION i.e. location, location, location, points up remarkable settings, whether a golf course or the terrace of a bistro overlooking a loch.

At the end of 2014, I brought out a photo book with some of Scotland's top photographers – *Scotland the Best 100 Places*. Their pictures illustrate this *genius loci*: the ineffable spirit of a place; places from Suilven to Portpatrick and from landscape to those made by extraordinary humans. The photographs are evocative and there's a digest distilled from this *Scotland the Best* that recommends where to WALK, EAT and SLEEP near to these inspiring and uniquely Scottish locations. Please see it as a companion book to this one.

And now, hurrah, finally there's an app!

Scotland the Best wouldn't be the best if I didn't receive feedback and helpful suggestions from so many people. Please send me your recommendations for new entries to **scotland.best@harpercollins.co.uk** giving brief reasons why they should be included (and directions if they're hard to find).

Pete Irvine,
Edinburgh,
January 2016

How To Use This Book

There are three ways to find things in this book:

1. There's an index at the back.
2. The book can be used by category, e.g. you can look up the best restaurants in the Borders or the best scenic routes in the whole of Scotland. Most entries have an item number in the outside margin. These are in numerical order and allow easy cross-referencing.
3. Start with the maps and see how individual items are located, how they are grouped together and how much there is that's worth seeing or doing in any particular area. Then just look up the item numbers. If you are travelling around Scotland, **I would urge you to use the maps** and this method of finding the best of what an area or town has to offer.

Top tip: as a general guide and when searching by using the maps, items numbered below 1500 generally refer to places to eat and stay.

All items have a code which gives (1) the specific item number; (2) the map on which it can be found; and (3) the map co-ordinates. For space reasons, items in Glasgow and Edinburgh are not individually marked on Map 8, although they do have co-ordinates in the margin to give you a rough idea of location. A typical entry is shown below, identifying the various elements that make it up:

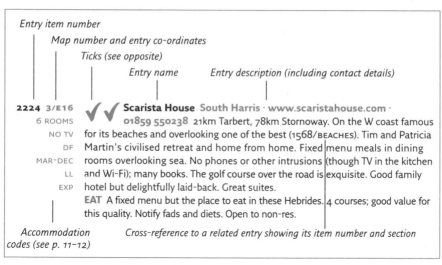

Entry item number

Map number and entry co-ordinates

Ticks (see opposite)

Entry name · Entry description (including contact details)

2224 3/E16 ✓✓ **Scarista House** South Harris · www.scaristahouse.com · 01859 550238 21km Tarbert, 78km Stornoway. On the W coast famous for its beaches and overlooking one of the best (1568/BEACHES). Tim and Patricia Martin's civilised retreat and home from home. Fixed menu meals in dining rooms overlooking sea. No phones or other intrusions (though TV in the kitchen and Wi-Fi); many books. The golf course over the road is exquisite. Good family hotel but delightfully laid-back. Great suites.
6 ROOMS / NO TV / DF / MAR-DEC / LL / EXP
EAT A fixed menu but the place to eat in these Hebrides. 4 courses; good value for this quality. Notify fads and diets. Open to non-res.

Accommodation codes (see p. 11–12)

Cross-reference to a related entry showing its item number and section

A Note On Categories

Edinburgh and Glasgow, the destinations of most visitors and the nearest cities to more than half of the population, are covered in the substantial Sections 2 and 3. You will probably need a city map or smartphone/satnav to get around. And remember, in summer 2016 there will be an STB app.

For the purposes of maps, and particularly in Section 4 (Regional Hotels & Restaurants), I have used a combination of the subdivision of Scotland based on current standard political regions and on historical ones, eg Argyll, Clyde Valley. Section 4 is meant to give a comprehensive and concise guide to the best of the major Scottish towns in each area. Some recommended hotels and restaurants will be amongst the best in the region (or even amongst the best in Scotland) and have been selected because they are the best there is in the town or the immediate area.

From Sections 5 to 11, the categories are based on activities, interests and geography and are Scotland-wide. Section 12 covers the islands, with a page-by-page guide to the larger ones.

Ticks For The Best There Is

Although everything listed in the book is notable and remarkable in some way, there are places that are outstanding even in this superlative company. Instead of marking them with a rosette or a star, they have been 'awarded' a tick.

✓   Among the very best in Scotland

✓ ✓   Among the best (of its type) in the UK

✓ ✓+   A particular commendation for Charlie Lockley of Boath House and Geoffrey Smeddle of The Peat Inn, both exceptional chefs

✓ ✓ ✓   Among the best (of its type) in the world, or simply unique

Listings generally are not in an order of merit although if there is one outstanding item it will always be at the top of the page and this obviously includes anything which has been given ticks. Ticks also indicate exceptional value for money.

The Codes

1. The Item Code
At the left-hand margin of every item is a code which will enable you to find it on a map. Thus **1126 8/N24** should be read as follows: **1126** is the item number, listed in simple consecutive order; **8** identifies the particular map at the back of the book; **N24** is the map co-ordinate, to help pinpoint the item's location on the map grid.

2. The Accommodation & Property Code
Beside each recommended accommodation or property is a series of codes, as follows:

16 ROOMS	NO KIDS
MAR-DEC	NO PETS
NO TV	DF
NO C/CARDS	LL
HS/NTS	ATMOS
MED.INX	☕

ROOMS indicates the current number of bedrooms in total (ie to give an idea of size). No differentiation is made as to the type of room.
MAR-DEC shows when the accommodation is open. No dates means it is open all year.
NO TV means there are no TVs in the bedrooms.
NO C/CARDS means the establishment does not accept credit cards.
DF denotes a place that welcomes dogs, although often with conditions. Check in advance.
L, LL, LLL indicate places in outstanding locations. **L** is set in a great location; **LL** denotes a very special setting; and **LLL** indicates a world-class spot.
ATMOS indicates a place whose special atmosphere is an attraction in itself.
NO KIDS does not necessarily mean children are unwelcome, only that special provisions are not usually made; ask in advance. In other cases, children are welcome, often with special rates.
NO PETS indicates that the hotel does not generally accept pets.
HS or **NTS** denotes a place in the care of Historic Scotland or the National Trust for Scotland.
☕ indicates a property with an exceptional tearoom.
CHP, MED.INX, MED.EX, EXP, LOTS indicates the general cost of the accommodation based on an average twin or double room rate. Many hotels change rates daily depending on occupancy

but the broad prices associated with each band are: CHP = under £80; MED.INX = £80 – 120; MED.EX = £120 – 150; EXP = £150 – 200; LOTS = £200+.

3. The Dining Codes

The price codes marked by eateries refer to the cost of an average dinner per person with a starter, main course and dessert. It excludes wine, coffee and extras. Prices are based on 2016 rates.
Where a hotel is notable also for its restaurant, this is identified by EAT on a separate line below the main accommodation description, with details following.
Within the text of an entry, LO means last orders at the kitchen. Some restaurants close earlier if they are quiet and go later on request.
10pm/10.30pm means usually 10pm Mon-Fri, 10.30pm at weekends. It's common, especially for city restaurants, to open later at weekends, particularly in Edinburgh during the Festival (August).

4. The Walk Codes

Beside each of the many walks in the book is a series of codes as follows:

3-10KM   CIRC/ XCIRC   BIKES/ XBIKES/ MTBIKES   1-A-1

3-10KM means the walk(s) described may vary in length between the distances shown.
CIRC means the walk can be circular, while XCIRC shows the walk is not circular and you must return more or less the way you came.
BIKES indicates the walk has a path which is suitable for ordinary bikes. XBIKES means the walk is not suitable for, or does not permit, cycling. MTBIKES means the track is suitable for mountain or all-terrain bikes.

The 1-A-1 Code:
First number (1, 2 or 3) indicates how easy the walk is.
1 the walk is easy.
2 medium difficulty, eg standard hillwalking, not dangerous nor requiring special knowledge or equipment.
3 difficult: care and preparation and a map are needed.
The letters (A, B or C) indicate how easy it is to find the path.
A the route is easy to find. The way is either marked or otherwise obvious.
B the route is not very obvious, but you'll get there.
C you will need a map and preparation or a guide.
The last number (1, 2 or 3) indicates what to wear on your feet.
1 ordinary outdoor shoes, including trainers, are probably okay unless the ground is very wet.
2 you will need walking boots.
3 you will need serious walking or hiking boots.
Apart from designated walks, the 1-A-1 code is employed wherever there is more than a short stroll required to get to somewhere, eg a waterfall or a monument.

Abbreviations

As well as the codes in the left hand margin, I use abbreviations within the main entries. The most common ones are:

N, S, E, W, etc – north, south, east, west, etc
TGP – time of going to press
AYR – all year round
P & P – pizza and pasta
PYO – pick your own
BYOB – bring your own bottle
J&T – jacket and tie

High Fives

A Personal Selection

Edinburgh Hotels

- The Balmoral (84)
- Prestonfield (93)
- Hotel du Vin (94)
- The Raeburn (106)
- The Dakota (129)

Glasgow Hotels

- Hotel du Vin (480)
- Radisson Blu (473)
- Blythswood Square (481)
- Citizen M (482)
- Z Hotel (488)

Edinburgh Easy Dining

- The Atelier (146)
- Bia Bistrot (147)
- Rollo (150)
- The Scran & Scallie (171)
- The Shore (174)

Glasgow Easy Dining

- Ox and Finch (506)
- Stravaigin (514, 534)
- The Vintage at Drygate (532)
- The Finnieston (533)
- Guy's Restaurant & Bar (508)

Edinburgh European Dining

- Les Escargots Bleu/Blanc (190/191)
- Nonna's Kitchen – Italian (201)
- Al Dente – Italian (203)
- Locanda de Gusti – Italian (206)
- Origano – Italian (217)

Glasgow European Dining

- Tarantino – Italian (541)
- Battlefield Rest – Italian (547)
- Le Chalet Beaumartin (563)
- Eusebi – Italian (540)
- Rioja – Spanish (604)

Edinburgh Ethnic Dining

- Mother India Café – Indian (261)
- Kalpna – Indian (244)
- El Cartel – Mexican (251)
- Kanpai – Japanese (255)
- Ting Thai Caravan – Thai (267)

Glasgow Ethnic Dining

- Mother India – Indian (571)
- Thairiffic – Thai (587)
- Loon Fung – Chinese (590)
- Hanoi Bike Shop – Vietnamese (586)
- Persia – Middle-Eastern (607)

Bracketed numbers represent entry numbers.

Edinburgh Cafés/Coffee shops

Roamin' Nose (214)

The Scottish Café (248)

Falko Konditorei (300)

Peter's Yard (301)

Artisan Roast (296)

Glasgow Cafés/Coffee shops

Saramago Café Bar (628)

Babu Bombay Street Kitchen (575)

Fish People Café (616)

Glad Café (651)

Café Gandolfi (640)

Edinburgh Pubs

Nobles (362)

Pickles (364)

Royal Dick (366)

Cumberland Bar (385)

Sofi/Boda/Joseph Pearce's/Victoria (363)

Glasgow Pubs

Òran Mór (696)

The Horseshoe (697)

Brewdog (708)

The Butterfly and the Pig (717)

Bon Accord (706)

Aberdeen Restaurants

Food Story (1001)

Chester Hotel (992)

Café 52 (1000)

Yatai Izakaya (1002)

Café Boheme (1005)

Dundee Restaurants

Jessie's Kitchen (946)

The Playwright (948)

Sol y Sombra (951)

Castlehill (949)

The Agacan (954)

Country Hotels

Monachyle Mhor, Balquhidder (1191)

Lake Hotel, Port of Menteith (835)

Gleneagles, Auchterarder (1126)

Kilberry Inn, Tarbert (1171)

The Peat Inn, St Andrews (893)

Small Town Hotels

Craigatin House, Pitlochry (910)

Ceilidh Place, Ullapool (1054)

George Hotel, Inveraray (775)

The Anchor, Tarbert (781)

Greystones, Oban (797)

Wha's
Like Us?

Famously Big Attractions

Among the 'top 10' (paid entry) and the 'top 10' (free) visitor attractions, these are the ones really worth seeing. Find them under their item numbers.
Edinburgh Castle; Holyrood Palace; Edinburgh Zoo; The National Museum of Scotland; The National Gallery; Our Dynamic Earth 417/421/420/418/425/424/MAIN ATTRACTIONS.
The People's Palace, Glasgow; The Burrell Collection; Kelvingrove; The Riverside Museum 727/725/723/MAIN ATTRACTIONS.
The Glasgow Botanic Gardens; The Gallery of Modern Art 731/732/OTHER ATTRACTIONS.
The Edinburgh Botanics 427/OTHER ATTRACTIONS.
Culzean Castle; Stirling Castle; Castle of Mey 1755/1752/1757/CASTLES.
Mount Stuart; Manderston 1814/1816/HOUSES.
Skara Brae; The Callanish Stones 1793/1795/PREHISTORIC.
Rosslyn Chapel 1842/CHURCHES.

OTHER UNMISSABLES ARE:

1 7/L24 ✓✓✓ **Loch Lomond** www.lochlomond-trossachs.org Approach via Stirling and A811 to Drymen, or from Glasgow, the A82 Dumbarton road to Balloch. Britain's largest inland waterway and a traditional playground, especially for Glaswegians; jet-skis, show-off boats. **Lomond Shores** at Balloch is the heavily retail gateway to the loch (including Jenners) and the **Loch Lomond National Park** which covers a vast area. Orientate and shop here.
The W bank between Balloch and Tarbet is most developed: marinas, cruises, ferry to Inchmurrin Island. Luss is tweeville, like a movie set (it was used in the Scottish TV soap, *High Road*) but has an OK tearoom, **The Coach House** (1411/TEAROOMS). The road is more picturesque beyond Tarbet to Ardlui; see 1285/GOOD PUBS for the less touristy Scots experience of the **Drover's Inn** at Inverarnan.
The E is more natural, wooded; good lochside and hill walks (1952/MUNROS). The road is winding but picturesque beyond Balmaha towards Ben Lomond. Hire a rowing boat at Balmaha to Inchcailloch Island: lovely woodland walks (2008/WALKS). **Cameron House,** the **Lodge on the Loch** and the **Lomond Arms** are in their different ways excellent hotel options (496/500/499/HOTELS OUTSIDE GLASGOW). Water taxis: 01301 702356; www.cruiselochlomond.co.uk.

2 5/G19 ✓✓✓ **The Cuillin Mountains** Skye This hugely impressive range in the south of Skye, often shrouded in cloud or rain, is the romantic heartland of the islands. The Red Cuillin are smoother and nearer the Portree-Broadford road; the Black Cuillin gather behind and are best approached from **Glen Brittle** (1971/WALKS; 1601/WATERFALLS). This classic, untameable mountain scenery has attracted walkers, climbers and artists for centuries. It still claims lives regularly. For best views apart from Glen Brittle, see 1622/SCENIC ROUTES; 1643/VIEWS. Vast range of walks and scrambles (see also 1658/SWIMMING). See Skye p. 387–91 for eats/sleep.

3 5/L18 ✓✓✓ **Loch Ness** Most visits start from Inverness at the N end via the Caledonian Canal. Fort Augustus is at the other end, 56km to the south. Loch Ness is part of the still-navigable Caledonian Canal linking to the W coast at Fort William. Small boats line the shores at certain points; one of the best ways to see the loch is on a cruise from Inverness: Jacobite Cruises 01463 233999, 1-6 hours; several other options, including a trip on the civilised *Royal Scot* 01320 366277. Other cruise operators from Fort Augustus: Cruise Loch Ness 01320 366277; the small, friendly Nessie Hunter from Drumnadrochit 01456 450395; and Castle Cruises 01456 450695. Most tourist traffic uses the main A82 N bank road converging on Drumnadrochit, where the Loch Ness Monster industry gobbles up your money.

If you must, the official Loch Ness Monster Exhibition is the one to choose. On the A82, you can't miss **Urquhart Castle** (1789/RUINS). But the two best things about Loch Ness are: the south road (B862) from Fort Augustus back to Inverness (1629/SCENIC ROUTES); and the detour from Drumnadrochit to Cannich to Glen Affric (20-30km) (1584/GLENS; 1978/WALKS; 1594/WATERFALLS). Best bet to drop in, eat (and stay) is the **Loch Ness Inn** at Drumnadrochit, and the top-end eat and stay is Loch Ness Lodge. Best pub grub and stay is **Glenmoriston Arms** (1181/INNS). There's also a restaurant – the only one overlooking the loch (at Fort Augustus). Abbey now The Highland Club self-catering accom.

4 8/N25   ✓✓ **The Falkirk Wheel** Falkirk · www.thefalkirkwheel.co.uk · 0870 050 0208 Halfway between Edinburgh and Glasgow, signed from the M9, M80 and locally.
The splendid wheel and deliberately dramatic massive boat-lift at the convergence of the reinstated Union and Forth & Clyde canals – the world's first coast-to-coast ship canal (to wander or plooter along). The 35-metre lift is impressive to watch and great to go on. Boats leave the visitor centre every 40 mins for the 45-min journey AYR. Great network of paths to walk and cycle from here and it links (though 8km and not so conveniently) to **The Helix** and **The Kelpies** (01324 590900; www.thehelix.co.uk), Scotland's new landmark, dramatically rearing from the canal basin beside the M9. Neither the newly created Helix Park (water, walking & family activities), nor the giant horses' heads by artist Andy Scott are easy to get to (go satnav or there's a hop on/off bus linking Grahamstown Station and Falkirk centre – the Loop Bus). Guided tours, including going inside one of the Kelpies, take 45 mins. Visitor centre and café. Both these major and iconic attractions celebrating Scotland's industrial past make the most of what is perhaps a rather undistinguished ribbon of water. Kelpies and the Helix open at all times.

▓▓▓ Favourite Scottish Journeys

5 7/J21   ✓✓ **The West Highland Line** 0845 748 4950 One of the most picturesque railway journeys in Europe and quite the best way to get to Skye from the south. Travelling from Glasgow to Fort William, you pass the biggest loch (Lomond), the longest (Awe) and the deepest (Morar), and the highest ben (Nevis), the Bonnie Prince Charlie Country (see p. 330-31) and much that is close to a railwayman's heart by viaducts (including the Harry Potter one) and tunnels over loch and down dale. It's also possible to make the same journey (from Fort William to Mallaig and/or return) by steam train from mid-May to mid-Oct (0844 850 4680; www.westcoastrailways.co.uk) on **The Jacobite** – this is generally regarded as one of the great railway journeys of the world (and it is a very busy wee train). There's a museum in the restored station at Glenfinnan with a tearoom and bunk accom. 3 trains a day leave from Glasgow Queen St for Mallaig and take about 5 hours.

6 5/H19   ✓ **Glenelg-Kylerhea** www.skyeferry.co.uk · 01599 522273 The shorter of the 2 remaining ferry journeys to Skye and definitely the best way to get there if you're not pushed for time. The drive to Glenelg from the A87 is spectacular (1618/SCENIC ROUTES) and so is this 5-min crossing of the deep Narrows of Kylerhea. Easter-Oct, every 20 mins. The ferry is run by and very much a part of the local community around Glenelg. Cute wee shack to visit before departure. This is a project worth supporting. There's an otter-watch hide at Kylerhea.

7 5/G19   ✓ **Elgol, Isle of Skye** Trips on either the *Bella Jane* (0800 731 3089) or the *Misty Isle* (01471 866288) on Loch Coruisk to see the whales, dolphins, basking sharks and, of course, the famous view (1643/VIEWS).

8 7/K25   **Wemyss Bay-Rothesay Ferry** www.calmac.co.uk · 0800 066 5000 The landmark glass-roofed station at Wemyss Bay, the railhead from Glasgow (60km by road on the A78), is redolent of an age-old terminus (refurbished 2015). The frequent (CalMac) ferry has all the Scottish traits and treats you can handle, and Rothesay (with its period seaside mansions) appears out of blood-smeared sunsets and rain-sodden mornings alike, a gentle watercolour from summer holidays past. Visit the (Victorian) toilet when you get there and **Mount Stuart** (1814/HOUSES) on beautiful Bute.

9 8/L24   **Sailing Loch Katrine** www.lochkatrine.com · 01877 376316 The historic steamship *Sir Walter Scott* (he who put it, and, at the same time, Scottish tourism on the map) and the smaller cruiser, the *Lady of the Lake*. Leave from the 'Trossachs Pier' at the end of large car park 2km off the A821 Callander/Aberfoyle Rd. This journey on Loch Katrine is a classic Trossachs experience, especially in the purple-and-golden-tinted autumn. Both do 1-hour or (to the end of the loch) 2-hour cruises. Brenachoile café/bar. Katrine Wheelz bike hire (01877 376366) in car park. Great cycling round here – you can take it on board and cycle back (22km).

10 8/P25   **The *Maid of the Forth* Cruise to Inchcolm Island** 0131 331 5000 The wee boat (though they say it holds 225 people) which leaves every day at different times (phone for details) from Hawes Pier in South Queensferry (15km central Edinburgh via A90) opposite the Hawes Inn, just under the famous railway bridge (419/ATTRACTIONS). 45-min trips under the bridge and on to Inchcolm, an attractive island with walks and an impressive ruined abbey. Much birdlife and also many seals to be seen. 1.5 hours ashore. Tickets at pier. Mar-Oct.

11 5/M18   **North & West from Inverness** 0345 748 4950 Two less celebrated (than the West Highland Line above) but mesmerising rail journeys start from Inverness. The journey to Kyle of Lochalsh no longer has an observation car in summer, so get a window seat and take a map; the last section through Glen Carron and around the coast at Loch Carron is especially fine. There are 3 trains a day and it takes 2.5 hours. Inverness to Wick (via Thurso) is a 4.5-hour journey. The section skirting the E coast from Lairg to Helmsdale is full of drama, followed by the transfixing monotony of the Flow Country. 3 trains a day in summer.

12 8/L26   **The Plane to Barra** www.hial.co.uk · 01871 890 212 Most of the island plane journeys pass over many smaller islands (eg Glasgow-Tiree, Glasgow-Stornoway, Wick–Orkney) and are fascinating on a clear day, but the daily flight from Glasgow to Barra is doubly special because the island's airport is on Cockleshell Beach in the north (11km from Castlebay) after a splendid approach. The 12-seater Otter leaves and lands according to the tide. Operated by Flybe; you can go on to Benbecula.

13 8/M26   **Paddle Steamer *Waverley*** www.waverleyexcursions.co.uk Website best for information/bookings. The last seagoing paddle steamer, built on the Clyde and recently restored, celebrates 70 years in 2016. Various trips around Western Isles and the west coast during summer months.

Great Ways To Get Around

14 **By Seaplane** www.lochlomond.seaplanes.com · 01436 675030 See Scotland from the air, landing on land and water in the more remote parts other transport can't reach. From Glasgow Science Centre to Oban and Tobermory and other west-coast destinations. Routes can be customised. You can reach Loch Lomond in 20 mins.

15 **By VW Campervan** Scoobycampers · www.scoobycampers.com There are others doing vintage campervans but Scooby were there first. They offer VW microbuses and campervans on a self-drive rental basis to see Scotland at a gentle pace and save on accom. All vehicles are refurbished classic versions with contemporary comforts. Microbuses take 6 people comfortably though not to sleep in (hire their camping equipment). Campervans take 4 – best suited to 2 adults/2 kids. Vehicles have CD radios/DVD players and satnav. 8 options, each with own name. They look cool and you'll find that folk are pleased to see you.

16 **By Classic Car** Caledonian Classic Car Rental · www.caledonianclassics. co.uk · 01259 742476 Choose a fabulous motor and take off round the byroads, experiencing that old forgotten joy of motoring. Packages are customised, but there's unlimited mileage and free delivery/collection locally for hire of 2 days or more. Short trips come with a complimentary picnic hamper. Cars include Jaguar E-type, Alfa Romeo 2000 Veloce, MGB Roadster, Austin Healey, Morgan 4/4, Triumph TR6 and VW camper. Prices from £160 a day/£1000 a week at TGP. They have their own 4-star B&B in Dollar (a good place to start).

17 **By Motorbike** Scotlandbybike · www.scotlandbybike.com · 07515 851876 Bike your way around Scotland on your own or in private or group guided tours. Scotlandbybike organises a range of tours and packages that combine accom, insurance and hire of mainly BMW, but also Triumph, Yamaha and Suzuki, including some for smaller riders; or bring your own. Tours 5 to 10 days.

18 **By Kayak** A great way to see parts of Scotland from the sea is by kayak. Bring your own or for instruction, guidance and finding spectacular routes, you couldn't do better than find **Wilderness Scotland** (0131 625 6635; www.wildernessscotland. com) who operate award-winning adventure holidays from many locations N and W; or **Seafreedom Kayaks** (01631 710173; www.seafreedomkayak.co.uk) at Connel. The coastline here offers all kinds of sea and loch possibilities, including Loch Etive and the island of Seil. Tony Hammock and his wife Olga can also offer accom at their B&B situated on the A85 overlooking the Falls of Connel.

19 **By Traditional Fishing Boat** The Majestic Line · www.themajesticline.co.uk · 01369 707951 Unique, all-inclusive holidays on traditional wooden 85-ft fishing boats, all sensitively converted to a high standard. Various itineraries of 3-6-night cruises visiting western waters from the Caledonian Canal to Skye, Mull and more. 10-day cruise to Islay, the Outer Hebrides and St Kilda, or 6-day cruise to Skye on new boat *The Glen Etive* from 2016. 6 en-suite double cabins.

20 **Under Sail** Clyde Yachts · www.clydeyachts.com · 01505 503830 W and NW Scotland offer some of the best sailing in the world. Clyde Yachts is one of the best charters with instructor/guide, operating out of Ardrossan.

The Best Annual Events

21
JAN
Up-Helly-Aa Lerwick · www.uphellyaa.org · 01595 693434 Traditionally the 24th day after Christmas, now the last Tuesday in January. A mid-winter fire festival based on Viking lore; 'the Guizers' haul a galley through the streets of Lerwick and burn it in the park; the night goes on.

22
JAN
Celtic Connections Glasgow · www.celticconnections.com · 0141 353 8000 A huge, 3-week festival of Celtic music from round the world held in the Royal Concert Hall and other city venues. Concerts, ceilidhs, workshops. Craic.

23
25 JAN
Burns Night The National Bard celebrated with supper. Increasing number of local and family celebrations. No single major event, except for recently, **The Big Burns Supper Festival** (01387 271826; www.bigburnssupper.com) in Dumfries. It is big – 5000 people in 2015. Community focused and over several days and venues. Not just about the Bard.

24
FEB
Scottish Snowdrop Festival Cambo, nr Crail · 01333 450054 Yep, a festival to celebrate the carpets of trembling snowdrops in the wondrous woods of **Cambo House** (899/FIFE). For a few weeks in early spring. Popular or what!

25
FEB
Glasgow Film Festival www.glasgowfilm.org · 0141 332 6535 Relatively recent arrival on the FF circuit but hugely popular; imaginatively programmed. Adjunct of and run through Glasgow Film Theatre.

26
MAR
Glasgow International Comedy Festival www.glasgowcomedyfestival.com · 0844 873 7353 In small and large venues, a comedy festival in the city where a comedy festival belongs.

27
MID-APR
Glasgow International www.glasgowinternational.org Biennial ('16, '18) festival presenting contemporary visual art in the city's main arts venues and unusual or found spaces; celebrating Glasgow's significance as a source and generator of cutting-edge art.

28
APR
Edinburgh International Science Festival www.sciencefestival.co.uk · 0844 557 2686 Longest established and largest science festival in the UK. Has outreached and branched out even to Abu Dhabi! Fab for kids (especially in NMS and the City Art Centre); fascinating for grown-ups.

29
APR
Melrose Sevens www.melrose7s.com · 01896 822993 This Border town is completely taken over by the tournament in their small-is-beautiful rugby ground. 7's, now global, were first played here in 1883. Lots of big lads!

30
APR
Aye Write Glasgow · www.ayewrite.com · 0141 353 8000 The city's book festival based at the Mitchell Library. It's good, but!

31
END APR
Shetland Folk Festival www.shetlandfolkfestival.com · 01595 694757 36th anniversary 2016. Britain's most northerly and one of the best folk fests, mainly in Lerwick. It never sleeps.

32
1 MAY
Beltane Edinburgh The gloriously pagan gathering on the city's Calton Hill to celebrate May Day. Full of light, fire, drumming. Wait for the dawn.

33 **Paps of Jura Fell Race** www.jurafellrace.org.uk · 01496 810254 The amazing
MAY   hill race up and down the 3 Paps (4 tops in all) on this large, remote island (2197/
       ISLANDS). About 200 runners take on the 16-mile challenge from the distillery in
       Craighouse, the village. Winner does it in 3 hours!

34 **Tweedlove Bike Festival** Peebles · www.tweedlove.com 2 weeks of cycling
MAY   for all levels, including serious international riders around the Tweed Valley. Now
       established as bike heaven.

35 **Common Ridings** The 11 Borders town festivals. Similar formats over different
MAY–AUG weeks with ride-outs (on horseback to outlying villages, etc), shows, dances and
       games, culminating on the Friday and Saturday. Total local involvement. Hawick is
       first, then West Linton, Selkirk, Peebles, Melrose, Galashiels, Jedburgh, Duns, Kelso,
       Lauder and Coldstream at the beginning of August. All authentic and truly local.

36 **Mhor Festival** www.mhor.net · 01877 384622 The fab farmhouse boutique
MAY   hotel (830/CENTRAL) hosts a hoolie and a food feast on its land overlooking the
       loch: Scottish chefs and Tom. Cooler than the Cotswolds!

37 **Ten Under The Ben** Fort William · www.nofussevents.co.uk · 01397 772899
JUN   A 10-hour mountain-bike endurance event around Ben Nevis. Good fun, though.
       Run by No Fuss Events.

38 **Edinburgh Marathon** www.edinburgh-marathon.com The UK's fastest, and
END MAY Scotland's largest and perhaps most picturesque marathon route. Also with 5km
       and 10km, junior events, etc.

39 **Moonwalk** Edinburgh · www.walkthewalk.org The big pink and hopefully
EARLY JUN moonlit walk starting at midnight through the streets of Edinburgh in aid of breast
       cancer charities. Many, many wimmin (and some guys); euphoric!

40 **Flower Shows** Edinburgh · 0131 333 0969 & Ayr · 01292 618395 Many
EARLY JUN Scottish towns hold flower shows, mainly in autumn, but the big spring show is
EARLY AUG Gardening Scotland at the Royal Highland Centre (Ingliston). The annual **Ayr show**
       in August is huge! Check local tourist information for details.

41 **Royal Highland Show** Ingliston · www.royalhighlandshow.org ·
JUN   0131 335 6207 The premier agricultural show (over 4 days) in Scotland. For the
       farming world, the event of the year. Animals, machinery, food, crafts, shopping.
       Over 180,000 attend.

42 **Mountain Bike World Cup** Fort William · www.fortwilliamworldcup.co.uk ·
JUN   01397 705825 Held at Nevis Range 5K run, around the ski gondola. Awesome
       course with international competitors over 2 days. Evening events in town. Date
       varies.

43 **Borders Book Festival** Melrose · www.bordersbookfestival.org · 01896 822644
JUN   The hugely successful and utterly appropriate (to town and times) bookfest held in
       Harmony Gardens. Intimate, friendly: reads well.

44 **The Caledonian Challenge** Fort William · www.caledonianchallenge.com ·
MID–JUN 0131 524 0350 A very big (80k) walk run by the Scottish Community Foundation,
       with teams of 4 going through various check points in Lochaber, using parts of the
       West Highland Way.

45 **Edinburgh International Film Festival** www.edfilmfest.org.uk · 0131 228 4051
LATE JUN Various screens and other locations in Edinburgh city centre. One of the world's oldest film festivals (70th anniversary year 2016). 10 days of film and movie matters. Currently restoring its serious credentials.

46 **St Magnus Festival** Kirkwall, Orkney · www.stmagnusfestival.com ·
LATE JUN 01856 871445 Midsummer celebration of the arts, founded by Sir Peter Maxwell Davies, has attracted big names for almost 40 years. Quite highbrow; the cathedral at its heart. The days are very long.

47 **Mendelssohn on Mull** www.mendelssohnonmull.com Classical but
END JUN eclectic music festival in halls and venues around the island celebrating the connection between the composer and this far-flung part of the world. And see Mull, p. 400–02.

48 **Scottish Traditional Boat Festival** Portsoy · www.stbfportsoy.com ·
EARLY JUL 01261 842951 Perfect little festival in perfect little Moray town over a weekend in early July. Old boats in old and new harbours, an open-air ceilidh and a great atmos.

49 **Scottish Game Fair** Perth · www.scottishfair.com · 01738 554826 Held in
JUL the rural and historical setting of Scone Palace, a major Perthshire day out and gathering for the hunting, shooting, fishing and shopping brigade.

50 **Insider Festival** Rothiemurchus It's small, insider and sort of secret – no
JUL website or phone. Its spiritual home is **Inshriach House and Estate** (1273/HOUSE PARTIES), growing out of 'The Outsider' held in 2007, which I instigated, on the Rothiemurchus Estate next door (it rained and I took a bath). Cool music, food and frolics here (and there) – it keeps its enigma.

51 **T in the Park** Strathallan, nr Auchterarder · www.tinthepark.com Since
JUL 1994, Scotland's highly successful pop festival owned, like much of the music business, by Live Nation. Difficulties and shortcomings of this new sylvan site 2015 (some furore) to be resolved. The T stands for Tennents, the sponsors, who are much in evidence.

52 **Hebcelt** Stornoway · www.hebceltfest.com · 01851 621234 Folk-rock format
MID-JUL festival under canvas on faraway Lewis. Celebrated 20 years in 2015. Gaelic and notable national names. Music and craic.

53 **The Great Kindrochit Quadrathlon** Loch Tay · www.
MID-JUL artemisgreatkindrochit.com The toughest one-day sporting event – swim 1.3km across the loch, run 24km (including 7 Munros), kayak 11km and cycle 54km. Then slice a melon with a sword. Jings!

54 **Merchant City Festival** Glasgow · www.merchantcityfestival.com ·
END JUL 0141 287 8985 A host of free and some ticketed events bringing life to the city's cultural quarter near George Sq. Eclectic programme.

55 **Wickerman Festival** nr Gatehouse of Fleet · www.thewickermanfestival.
END JUL co.uk · 01557 500582 Annual music fest for the SW in fields on the A755 between Gatehouse and Kirkcudbright. Under wide skies on a cool coast. They burn a huge effigy at midnight on the Saturday. Audience slow and loose.

56 **Black Isle Show** Muir of Ord · www.blackisleshow.info · 01463 870870
EARLY AUG Notable agricultural show and countryside gathering for the NE Highlands. A big family day out.

57 **Art Week** Pittenweem · www.pittenweemartsfestival.co.uk Remarkable
EARLY AUG local event where the whole of Pittenweem in Fife becomes a gallery. Over 70 venues show work: public buildings, people's houses. Refreshing!

58 **Traquair Fair** Innerleithen · www.traquair.co.uk · 01896 830323 In the
EARLY AUG grounds of **Traquair** (1817/HOUSES), a mini-Glastonbury with music, comedy and crafts. A respite from the Festival up the road in Edinburgh.

59 **Belladrum Tartan Heart Festival** nr Kiltarlity · www.tartanheartfestival.
AUG co.uk · 01463 741366 Off A862 Beauly road W of Inverness. Friendly, 2-day music fest, loyal following – sells out. Beautiful terraced site. Good for families.

60 **The Edinburgh Festivals** Since 1947 (70th anniversary 2017), Edinburgh has hosted
AUG the biggest arts festival in the world with: **The International Festival** www.eif.
co.uk · 0131 473 2000 A major programme of music, drama and dance with the **Virgin Money Fireworks** on the final Monday. **The Fringe** www.edfringe.com with hundreds of events every night in every conceivable venue, especially around the University in the Old Town (daily free performances in the Royal Mile) and around George St; the **Jazz Festival** www.edinburghjazzfestival.co.uk and (mainly for delegates on a bit of a jolly), **The TV Festival**. This is the best place to be in the world if you're into the arts. And see below.

61 **Edinburgh International Book Festival** www.edbookfest.co.uk ·
AUG 0131 718 5666 A tented village in Charlotte Sq Gardens. Same time as the above but deserving of another separate entry; uniquely engaging, superbly readable.

62 **Royal Edinburgh Military Tattoo** www.edintattoo.co.uk · 0131 225 1188 For
AUG many the main event of the August festival period and a global attraction. On the Castle Esplanade for 3 weeks. Many soldiers and marching. Always stirring stuff.

63 **The World Pipe Band Championships** Glasgow · www.theworlds.co.uk
AUG Since 1930, unbelievable numbers (3,000–4,000) of pipers from all over the world competing and seriously attuned on Glasgow Green.

64 **Cowal Highland Gathering** Dunoon · www.cowalgathering.com ·
AUG 01369 703206 One of many Highland games but this, along with **Luss and Loch Lomond Games, Inverness** in July, and **Braemar** (below) are the main events in the calendar that extends from May to September. Expect heavy events (very big lads only), dancing, pipe bands, field and track events, and much drinking and chat.

65 **Braemar Gathering** www.braemargathering.org · 01339 741098 Of many
EARLY SEP Highland games (**Aboyne** early August, **Ballater** mid-August on Deeside), this the big attraction. Go ogle the royals.

66 **Blas** Highlands & Argyll · www.blas-festival.com · 01463 783447 Across
SEP the Highlands and Argyll in a variety of venues. A rapidly expanding celebration of traditional and Gaelic music with an eclectic line up. It's a long week (9 days 2015).

67 **The Ben Nevis Race** www.bennevisrace.co.uk The race over 100 years old
SEP up Britain's highest mountain and back. The record is 1 hour 25 mins which seems
amazing. 600 runners though curiously little national, even local interest. Starts
2pm at Claggan Park off Glen Nevis roundabout.

68 **Dundee Flower & Food Festival** www.dundeeflowerandfoodfestival.com
SEP 3–6 day food fair and flower fest in the city's **Camperdown Park** (1546/PARKS;
1695/KIDS). A big Dundee day out.

69 **The Pedal for Scotland Glasgow-to-Edinburgh Bike Ride** www.
SEP pedalforscotland.org · 0141 229 5350 Fun, charity fundraiser and serious annual
bike fest. From Glasgow Green to Victoria Park with a Pasta Party at the halfway
point. 51 miles/100 miles return (or shorter versions).

70 **Wigtown Book Festival** www.wigtownbookfestival.com · 01988 403222
SEP–OCT Small, beautiful bookfest in Scotland's booktown in Galloway. In marquees in and
around the square, with great clubrooms above the shop. Edinburgh goes south.
See also 1398/1399/1400/TEAROOMS.

71 **Loch Ness Marathon** www.lochnessmarathon.com One of the UK's top
EARLY OCT marathons and a festival of running, starting midway along the SE shore of the loch
and finishing in Inverness. Also 10k races and kids' events.

72 **Tiree Wave Classic** www.tireewaveclassic.co.uk Windsurfing heaven on a
EARLY OCT faraway island (2203/ISLANDS) where beaches offer challenging wind conditions
and islanders offer warm hospitality.

73 **The Spree** Paisley · www.thespree.co.uk · 0300 300 1210 Paisley's 8-day
OCT 'National Arts Festival' in the marvellous Abbey (1880/ABBEYS) and other venues as
it prepares a bid to be UK City of Culture 2021.

74 **Tour of Mull Rally** www.mullrally.org The highlight of the national rally
OCT calendar is this racing around Mull weekend. Though drivers enter from all over the
world, the overall winner has often been a local man (well, plenty time for practice).
Accom tight, but the locals put you up.

75 **The Enchanted Forest** Pitlochry · www.enchantedforest.org.uk ·
OCT 0871 288 7655 A major month-long son et lumière and performance event
in the woodlands outside town.

76 **Perthshire Amber Festival** www.perthshireamber.com · 01350 724281 A
OCT music festival all around Perthshire. Started by musician and national treasure
Dougie MacLean, based in Dunkeld.

77 **Dundee Literary Festival** www.literarydundee.co.uk · 01382 386995 A
OCT 5-day celebration of books, reading and ideas. An initiative of Dundee University
and going from strength to strength.

78 **Botanic Lights** Edinburgh · www.rbge.org.uk · 0131 248 2909 Starting late
NOV October and for most of November, a beautiful trail of light, which makes the most
of the city's world-class Royal Botanic Gardens (427/ATTRACTIONS).

79 **St Andrew's Night** Increasingly a bigger deal than before, with government
30 NOV sponsored events. National holiday, anyone?

80   **Edinburgh's Christmas** www.edinburghschristmas.com · **0844 545 8252**

DEC   The city's 6-week Christmas illuminations, activities, fairground attractions and markets centred in E Princes St Gardens and St Andrews Sq (and the Old Town 2015). Take lotsa cash!

81   **Cromarty Film Festival** www.cromartyfilmfestival.org Cromarty on the Black

DEC   Isle (1552/VILLAGES). A small but beautiful, mainly local filmfest up north, and a refreshing weekend away.

82   **Stonehaven Fireball Festival** Stonehaven Celebrated since 1910, a traditional

31 DEC   Hogmanay fire festival that probably wouldn't get started nowadays for 'health and safety' reasons. 40 fireballers throw them around in the streets before processing to the harbour and heaving them in. Concert in the square.

83   **Edinburgh's Hogmanay** www.edinburghshogmanay.com · **0131 651 3380**

DEC-JAN   Scotland's major winter (3 days) festival; a global must-go. It's launched with a **Torchlight Procession** through the city centre. The main event is the **Street Party** on 31st. Be part of a huge, good-natured crowd; it is the Scots at their hospitable best! On worldwide TV news. On New Year's Day there's a free programme of events in the Old Town.

What The Scots Gave The Modern World...

Scotland's population is only just over 5 million, yet we discovered, invented or manufactured for the first time the following quite important things.

The Advertising Film
Anaesthesia
Ante-Natal Clinics
Antiseptics
Artificial Ice
The Alpha Chip
The Arts Festival
The ATM
Bakelite
The Bank of England
The Bicycle
Bovril
The Bowling Green
The Bus
Colour Photographs
The Compass
The Decimal Point
The Documentary
Dolly, the Cloned Sheep
Electric Light
Encyclopaedia Britannica
The Fax Machine
Fingerprinting
The Flushing Toilet
The Fountain Pen
Gardenias
The Gas Mask
Geology
The God Particle
Golf Clubs
The Golf Course
Hallowe'en
Helium
The Hypodermic Syringe
Insulin
Interferon
The Kaleidoscope
Kinetic Energy
The Lawnmower
Life Insurance
The Locomotive
Logarithms
The Mackintosh

Marmalade
The Microwave Oven
Motor Insurance
The Modern Parking Cone
The Modern Road Surface
Morphine
The MRI Scanner
Neon
The Overdraft
Paraffin
Penicillin
The Photocopier
The Pneumatic Tyre
Postage Stamps
Postcards
Quinine
Radar
Rubber Wellies
The Savings Bank
Sherlock Holmes
Sociology
The Steam Engine
Stocks and Shares
Street Lighting
Streets in blocks (as in US)
The Telegraph
The Telephone
Television
Tennis Courts
The Theory of Combustion
The Thermometer
The Thermos Flask
The Threshing Machine
Typhoid Vaccine
Ultrasound
Universal Standard Time
The US Navy
The Vacuum Flask
Video
Wave Power
Whisky
Writing Paper

...and *Auld Lang Syne*

the
Best
of Edinburgh

The Best of the Major Hotels

84 8/Q25
168 ROOMS
20 SUITES
LL
LOTS

✓✓ **The Balmoral** 1 Princes St · www.thebalmoralhotel.com · 0131 556 2414 At east end above Waverley Station. Capital landmark, its clock 3 minutes fast (except at Hogmanay), so you might catch your train. The old pile dear to owner Sir Rocco Forte's heart. 4 categories of rooms: internals quieter, all views different; only 'super deluxe' have the castle view. Some top suites. Deluxe feel to the public spaces: the Palm Court (great afternoon teas; harpist on the balcony 1429/AFTERNOON TEA). Great concierge service. Pool small (15m) but beautiful steam room and sauna. ESPA products in the spa. Few hotels anywhere are so much in the heart of things.

>£35   EAT Main restaurant, **Number One** (134/FINE DINING), is tops, and less formal brasserie, Hadrian's (good power-breakfast venue). Even the non-pretentious bar, NB, works.

85 8/Q25
241 ROOMS
NO PETS
L
LOTS

✓ **The Caledonian** Princes St · www.waldorfastoriaedinburgh.com · 0131 222 8888 An Edinburgh institution, 'The Caley' – at the west end of Princes St – a former station hotel built in 1903. Constant refurbishment under the Waldorf Astoria moniker continues to reinforce the 5-star status of Edinburgh's other landmark hotel. Good business hotel with all facilities you'd expect of the brand, including a Guerlain spa with nice pool. Endearing lack of uniformity in the rooms; castle views at a premium. Some very big bathrooms. Main restaurant, The Pompadour, for formal fine dining in an elegant setting does perhaps lack the glamour and gourmet cred of days gone by. It's run by Galvin's of London, as is the ground-floor Brasserie de Luxe. Afternoon tea in the adjoining open lounge, Peacock Alley. The Caley (whisky) bar is a famous rendezvous with an impressive – 260 and counting – whisky selection. Recently reinstating the luxe, the Caley is a capital experience.

EAT While The Pompadour does tend to remain above all that – dinner only Wed-Sun, **Galvin's Brasserie de Luxe** (0131 222 8988; www.galvinbrasseriedeluxe.com) is one of the best restaurants in the city, a perfect brasserie menu, some superior signature dishes and cosmopolitan service. Michelin Bib; we also like it a lot! 7 days lunch & dinner.

86 8/Q25
184 ROOMS
EXP

✓ **Apex Waterloo Place** 23-27 Waterloo Pl · www.apexhotels.co.uk · 0845 365 0000 As with all other hotels in this Edinburgh-based chain (also in London and Dundee 942/DUNDEE), a central location and a contemporary look. This, the newest (see others, below), opened after a major conversion of the council offices where you used to pay your council tax. Bedrooms may want for a view, the public areas (Elliot's bar and restaurant) not immediately impressive and the subterranean pool is small, but this is a well-run, modern business hotel with direct access to the back entrance of the station (Waverley).

87 8/Q25
100 ROOMS
MED.EX

✓ **Malmaison** 1 Tower Pl · www.malmaison.com · 0131 468 5000 At the Leith dock gates. This was the first Malmaison all those design-led years ago (titivation would not go amiss). All facilities that we who were once smart and young expect. Rooms have that darkish, masculine, solid yet well-lit look that has been much adopted elsewhere. Some port views. The brasserie and café-bar have stylish ambience too, and there are many very good bistro and other options adjacent, eg **Fishers** 233/SEAFOOD and **The Shore** 174/GASTROPUBS. Pity about the flats out front but the waterfront location and outside terrace is pleasant of a summer's evening. Car parking on site. It's a good 20 mins to uptown.

88 8/Q25
138 ROOMS
MED.EX

✓ **Doubletree by Hilton** 34 Bread St · www.doubletreeedinburghcity. co.uk · 0131 221 5555 This, formerly The Point, was once a Co-operative department store and was talked of as one of the great designery hotels in the world (on the cover of *Hotel Design*); there's a lot of competition now but the long corridors, cool lighting and well-laid-out rooms still offer a modern, muted and urbane city stopover. Those with castle views are best (with supplement). Café-bar, the Bread Street Brasserie, improved of late and the other on-street bar, Monboddo, is spacious and a good place to rendezvous. Expect all the Hilton efficiencies. Conference Centre adjacent with great penthouse often used for cool Edinburgh launches and parties (there's a unique view of the city: see 468/VIEWS) and they open it as a bar on the last Thursday of the month.

89 8/Q25
122/169
ROOMS
NO PETS
MED.EX

Apex City & Apex International www.apexhotels.co.uk · 0845 365 0000 Both in the middle of the Grassmarket (City at 61; International at 31-35), the picturesque but rowdy Saturday night city centre. Modern, *soi-disant* – but close to castle, club life and other bits of essential Edinburgh. More cool to roam from than in. The larger International has lots of public space, including a good bar to meet in and the Metro Bar & Brasserie overlooking the street, where you can often get a table in the otherwise busy Grassmarket. Here also is Heights restaurant on the 5th floor, which has a great view of the castle for breakfast but you can't sit on the terrace. Some castle views (rooms on 4th floor at International have balconies). The two share a small pool and minimal gym.

90 8/Q25
269 ROOMS
LOTS

The Sheraton Grand 1 Festival Sq · www.sheraton.com/grandedinburgh · 0131 229 9131 On Lothian Rd and Conference Sq, this city centre business hotel won no prizes for architecture when it opened late 1980s between Edinburgh's two most recently created squares: Festival Sq (now with BBC screen – not often on) and Conference Sq, which has never quite worked... as a square. This is a reliable stopover at the heart of the financial district, with excellent service. Many room categories: castle or non-castle views in each. Only one restaurant – called One Square – all things to all people, including afternoon tea. But the superlative feature of the Sheraton is the health club **One**, routinely identified as one of the best spas in the UK, with great indoor/outdoor pool (1260/SPAS).

91 8/Q25
238 ROOMS
NO PETS
MED.EX

Radisson Blu 80 High St · www.radissonblu.co.uk · 0131 557 9797 Modern but sympathetic building on the Royal Mile, handy for everything (especially during the Festival) and typical Radisson contemporary smart feel. Not great views but Royal Mile rooms are triple-glazed so there's minimal noise. Leisure facilities include tiny, subterranean pool and gym. Itchycoo bar/brasserie and many choices nearby. Adjacent parking handy in a hotel so central. Massive refurbishment 2016 may change some of this. Not the cheapest option but reliably Radisson!

92 8/Q25
249 ROOMS
EXP

The George 19-21 George St · www.thegeorgehoteledinburgh.co.uk · 0131 225 1251 Between Hanover St and St Andrew Sq. Owned by Principal Hayley Group, who also have the **Grand Central** in Glasgow (475/MAJOR HOTELS), with newish extension adding 50 rooms. Designed by Robert Adam and dating back to the late 18th century, this is a classy joint. Views of the Forth only from the deluxe rooms on the fourth floor in the new part. It's all a bit pricey, but you pay for the location and the Georgian niceties. Good Festival and Hogmanay hotel close to the heart of things (taken over by luvvies during TV Festival). The George has successfully shrugged off its staid, traditional image, fitting into George St's more progressive, more opportunistic present. Great on-street bar.

£25-35 **EAT** New **Printing Press Bar & Kitchen** (145/BRASSERIES) late 2015. Very Scottish menu; breakfast, lunch, dinner and late bar food till 1am.

The Best Individual & Boutique Hotels

93 8/Q25
23 ROOMS
DF
NO KIDS
ATMOS
LOTS

✓✓✓ **Prestonfield** off Priestfield Rd · www.prestonfield.com ·
0131 668 3346 3km S of city centre. I admit that the last 4 editions of
StB have been launched at Prestonfield and I, like many others, have enjoyed the
lavish hospitalities of owner James Thomson, but Prestonfield gets 3 ticks because
there's simply nowhere else like it anywhere. The Hielan' cattle in the 20-acre
grounds tell you this isn't your average urban bed for the night. A romantic, almost
other-worldly 17th-century building with period features still intact. In 2003, James,
Edinburgh's most notable restaurateur of The Tower and **The Witchery** (140/FINE
DINING), turned this old bastion of Edinburgh sensibilities into Scotland's most
sumptuous hotel. The architecture and the detail is exceptional and romantic. All
rooms (luxury/named suites and 'The Owners Suite') are highly individualistic with
hand-picked antiques and artefacts, flat screens and the usual technologies.
Prestonfield probably hosts more awards dinners and accommodates more
celebrity guests than anywhere else in town, and it itself wins more awards,
especially as a 'romantic' or 'individual' hotel. In summer, the nightly Scottish
cabaret (in the stable block) is hugely popular.

>£35   **EAT** House restaurant **Rhubarb**: a memorable experience (141/FINE DINING).

94 8/Q25
47 ROOMS
DF
MED.EX

✓✓ **Hotel du Vin** 11 Bristo Pl · www.hotelduvin.com · 0131 285 1479
The discreetly tucked-away Edinburgh link in the expanding chain of hotels
(480/BOUTIQUE HOTELS; 895/FIFE) created by imaginative and sympatico conversion
of city centre, often historic buildings – in this case, the Lunatic Asylum & Infirmary
where Robert Fergusson, one of Scotland's iconic poets and revered by Robert Burns,
died in 1774. This place was old! The hotel, however, enclosing a courtyard (with
'cigar bothy') and making maximum use of the up-and-down labyrinthine space, is
comfortable and modern. Rooms in 4 categories are all different but have the same
look. Monsoon showers in all but standard rooms. All, including suites, are well
priced. Bar (24 hours for guests), a whisky snug (250 to try) and a very bistro bistro
(170/BISTROS). As with other H du Vs, there's much to-do about wine. In busy quarter
near university and museum; heart of the Fringe.

95 8/Q25
8 SUITES
LOTS

✓✓ **The Witchery** Castlehill · www.thewitchery.com · 0131 225 5613
James Thomson's (Prestonfield, above) much celebrated and awarded
suites at the top of the Royal Mile. The Inner Sanctum, the Old Rectory and 7
others, all highly individual, indulgent, theatrical and gorgeous, and consolidated
into a uniquely Edinburgh experience above and around his restaurant and first
venture, The Witchery restaurant (140/FINE DINING). At the heart of the Old Town,
here at its most atmospheric. Join a guest list that stretches from Vivienne
Westwood (naturally) through Jack Nicholson to Catherine Zeta-Jones. You are in
good company but you will not be disturbed. You may not want to go out (breakfast
in a hamper!). Routinely regarded as among the most romantic and sexiest suites
in the world. Check the website to find out why (but this is one place you won't find
that much reviewed on TripAdvisor).

96 8/P25
42 ROOMS
DF
NO KIDS
EXP

✓✓ **The Bonham** 35 Drumsheugh Gardens · www.thebonham.com ·
0131 226 6050 Discreet townhouse in quiet West End crescent.
Cosmopolitan service and ambience a stroll from Princes St. Much favoured by
discerning celebs and writers at the Book Festival. Independent back in the day, the
Bonham is now part of the UK Starwood Group who also have the **George Hotel**
(92/MAJOR HOTELS) & **Blythswood Square** (481/BOUTIQUE HOTELS), among others.
A major refurbishment with additional rooms underway 2016: Bonham on the up!
Rooms are stylish and individual. Great views out back, over Dean Village and New
Town from second floor up.

EAT Elegant dining in calm, spacious restaurant (especially the end table by back window). Chef Maciej Szymik at the helm. No-nonsense, simple 4/5 choices described in plain English.

97 8/Q25
33 ROOMS
NO PETS
EXP

✓✓ **Tigerlily** 125 George St · www.tigerlilyedinburgh.co.uk · 0131 225 5005 Edinburgh's designtastic hotel on style boulevard by Montpeliers, who have **Rick's** nearby which has cheaper rooms (110/BOUTIQUE HOTELS). This surprisingly large hotel sits atop the never-other-than-rammed Tigerlily bar and restaurant. Rooms uniquely different but in the contemporary/ calm house style. Various categories up to the Georgian Suites. Most have walk-in showers; all have cool touches. Probably the most fashionista in town but you pay to be this close to the pulse. Downstairs in the basement is the nightclub Lulu: guests have complementary admission.
EAT Fair to say food ain't the main event – the people are – but it's fun and fast and probably better than it has to be. Big room, big atmos, some quiet corners and a cute, crowded smoking terrace. Excellent service!

98 8/Q25
69 ROOMS
NO PETS
ATMOS
EXP

✓ **The Scotsman** North Bridge · www.thescotsmanhotel.co.uk · 0131 556 5565 Deluxe boutique hotel in landmark building (the old offices of *The Scotsman* newspaper group) converted in 2001 into chic, highly individual accom with different urban views and impressive original features – stained glass, panelling and newspaper nostalgia (rooms are studies, editors' rooms, etc) and some modern touches, eg privacy locker in all rooms. Labyrinthine layout (stairs and fire doors everywhere) and slow lifts apart, this is the convenient 5-star hotel in midtown, though dining confined to the (nevertheless buzzy) North Bridge Brasserie (0131 622 2900). Spa (Aveda) below has a beautiful, low-lit steel pool, gym and treatments.

99 8/Q25
136 ROOMS
EXP

>£35

✓ **G&V Hotel** 1 George IV Bridge · www.gandvhotel.com · 0131 220 6666 Converted from an old eyesore council building and opened '09, as the first Missoni hotel in the UK, the design statement made from the start: all Italian retro and moderno, and either you like that stuff or you don't. Missoni closed the hotel group 2014 and this, without much change, became the G (after George) & V (for Victoria, i.e. Victoria St on which corner it sits). Remodelling 2016 but from the kilted doorman to the enormous rooms, 'The Original Look' is everywhere: the 5th-floor suites, categories determined by size and view. On this busy corner of the Royal Mile with its tourist tide, rooms are quiet. Cucina is rather better than Pizza Express slotted into the same building (in fact it's very good) and **Ondine** (232/ SEAFOOD) complete a strong choice for adjacent dining. The bar, perhaps a little too cool for its own good, always feels like it landed from Glasgow.
EAT Great Italian food and smart dining at a price. Report: 202/ITALIAN.

100 8/Q25
75 ROOMS
NO PETS
MED.EX

✓ **Fraser Suites** 12-26 St Giles St · http://edinburgh.frasershospitality. com · 0131 221 7200 More or less on the Royal Mile in the middle, near the Cathedral. The international chain of Aparthotels, a slightly misleading name because this is in every sense a hotel (some rooms have basic, others proper kitchen facilities) and Fraser Suites now own both the Hotel du Vin and Malmaison chains in the UK. 'Classic' and luxury rooms and one-bedroom apartments are all done to a high contemporary standard. Some great views over Princes St. Broadsheet Bistro OK but not so frequented. Though not on everyone's radar, this is a classy, very central option and not overpriced (except in August).

101 8/Q25
77 ROOMS
NO PETS
EXP

✓ **The Glasshouse** 2 Greenside Pl · www.theglasshousehotel.co.uk · 0131 525 8200 Sitting discreetly behind an old church between the Playhouse Theatre and Omni Centre. This (now) Marriott Hotel is built above the multiplex (rooms on 2 floors) and the restaurants in the mall below. Surprisingly large and labyrinthine. Main feature is the extensive lawned garden on the roof onto which most rooms look out – patios have reasonable privacy. Great views to Calton Hill and perspective on the city. Breakfast in room or the Observatory Restaurant (also open Tue-Sun for dinner) on the roof with the Calton Hill Observatory above; honesty bar. The Mall below is a disappointment; the restaurants all high-street staples but guests can use Virgin Active health facilities and spa (including 25m pool).

102 8/P25
29 ROOMS
NO PETS
EXP

✓ **Edinburgh Residence** 7 Rothesay Terrace · www. theedinburghresidence.com · 0131 226 3380 Your home in the city on an extravagant scale. 3 Victorian townhouses have been joined into an elegant apartment hotel once partly timeshare so rooms in the 3 categories – Classic, Deluxe and Townhouse – are not always available. No restaurant; breakfast is served in suite and dinner if required. 24-hour concierge (snacks & sandwiches). A discreet and distinctive stopover with views of Dean Village. Drawing room if you're feeling lonely in this quiet West End retreat; nightlife and shops are a stroll away.

103 8/Q25
18 ROOMS
NO PETS
NO KIDS
LOTS

✓ **The Howard** 34 Great King St · www.thehoward.com · 0131 557 3500 In the heart of the Georgian New Town, 3 townhouses in a splendid street imbued with quiet elegance, though only 5 mins from Princes Street. Restful drawing room, with small bar for guests. 15 spacious individual rooms (and separate mews cottage), sympatico with architecture and 3 suites downstairs with own entrances for discreet liaisons or just convenience and own drawing room for entertaining. 24-hour room service. Atholl restaurant for breakfast or dinner; and a delightful afternoon tea. Cute garden. No leisure facilities. A very Edinburgh accommodation under different ownership (Ricky Kapoor) from its creators, cachet intact!

104 8/Q25
208/140
ROOMS
DF
L
MED.INX

✓ **Motel One** www.motel-one.com/en/ & **Edinburgh-Royal** 18-21 Market St (overlooking Princes St Gardens) · 0131 220 0730 & **Edinburgh-Princes** 10-15 Princes St · 0131 550 9220 At east end of Princes St opposite the Balmoral and above the Apple shop. Part of an expanding European chain but listed here because they are very individual, hip and handy (like the Citizen M chain) and here in Edinburgh both occupy very central and convenient locations. They're also well appointed, uber-contemporary and cheap. No restaurant; breakfast in the bar (which is open 24 hours). No parking.

105 8/Q25
77 ROOMS
NO PETS
MED.INX

✓ **Ten Hill Place** www.tenhillplace.com · 0131 662 2080 Address as title on quiet square in southside near the university. Unlikely and surprising departure for the Royal College of Surgeons (429/ATTRACTIONS) who occupy the nearby imposing neoclassical building complex which fronts onto Nicolson St, and who built this unfussy, utilitarian, modern hotel that's probably the best value boutique hotel in town. Masculine, clean elegance in uniform design with 4 categories of rooms depending on size and view (some of Arthur's Seat). Small, pretty good restaurant and excellent wine bar supplied by Corney & Barrow, who have the Royal Warrant for wine. No leisure facilities; limited parking.

106 8/P25
10 ROOMS
NO KIDS
MED.EX

✓ **The Raeburn** 112 Raeburn Pl · www.theraeburn.com · 0131 332 7000 At the end of Raeburn Pl, a very Stockbridge watering hole and hotel; it's a slick operation. Rooms are 'deluxe' and upstairs 'standard'; all are individual, with muted colour schemes, tasteful and solid. On the ground floor, a spacious but bustling brasserie-style restaurant and 2 great enclosed terraces overlooking (by the time you read this) a building site or new houses. Terrace out front too. Comfy and convenient place to stay; only let-down is the fake library!

107 8/Q25
10 ROOMS
NO PETS
NO KIDS
MED.INX

✓ **Twelve Picardy Place** www.twelvepicardyplace.com · 0131 556 9908 Address as is. Once a private members' club, now a steak restaurant and a bar, with beer and skittles, and rooms above on 3 floors. Busy at street level but quiet upstairs with good urban view of Calton Hill from 3 front rooms. A stylish makeover, some great bathrooms and not so expensive. Much nightlife around you.

108 8/Q25
18 ROOMS
NO PETS
NO KIDS
MED.EX

Le Monde 16 George St · www.lemondehotel.co.uk · 0131 270 3900 Central boutique hotel on Edinburgh's designer-dressed street. Part of megabar/restaurant all themed on the world on our doorstep. Individual rooms are named after foreign cities and designed accordingly: Havana, Rome, Miami – Dublin one of the quieter ones. Serious attention to detail and very rock 'n' roll. All a tad OTT (the bar not the coolest in town) but the theme does work and beds/bathrooms/facilities would suit young professionals thrusting.

109 8/Q25
31 ROOMS
NO PETS
NO KIDS
MED.INX

Angels Share Hotel 9-11 Hope St · www.angelssharehotel.com · 0131 247 7000 Almost on Princes St, this very urban, boutique-style bedbox ain't bad value, with often good walk-in rates. It's a close cousin of Le Monde (above). Taking its name from whisky lore and a film of the same name, it pays homage to notable and honourable Scots (our 'angels') with pics of actors, sportsmen and pop stars on all walls. Rooms have their names and you sleep under an enormous Robert Carlyle, Rod Stewart, etc. You may not like your bedroom mate, but hey! Restaurant is bold, brassy and chandeliered – best prepare for breakfast!

110 8/Q25
10 ROOMS
NO PETS
NO KIDS
MED.EX

Rick's 55a Frederick St · www.ricksedinburgh.co.uk · 0131 622 7800 Very city-centre hotel and bar/restaurant in a downtown location a stone's throw from George St. By same people who have Indigo (Yard), a buzzing bistro in the West End and their other stylee hotel, **Tigerlily** (97/BOUTIQUE HOTELS). Restaurant (185/GASTROPUBS) has (loud) contemporary dining. Rooms through the bar and upstairs are surprisingly quiet. Modern, urban feel as standard (the Egyptian cotton). Book well in advance. Don't let the rooms above the bar thing put you off but get as high as you can! You know what I mean!

Excellent Lodgings

111 8/Q25
5 ROOMS
LOTS

✓✓ **One Royal Circus** www.oneroyalcircus.com · 0131 625 6669/ 07771 930816 Address as is, in the heart of the New Town at the corner of elegant Circus Place. An exclusive and sumptuous townhouse, possibly the classiest B&B in town. Like staying in a private members' club, the guestbook is a roll call of famous folk. Bookable by the day (weekends 2-day minimum). Sleeps 12.

112 8/Q25
4 ROOMS
NO PETS
EXP

✓ **21212** 3 Royal Terrace · www.21212restaurant.co.uk · 0131 523 1030 Mainly a restaurant, all lavish and urban and Michelin-starred. 4 large rooms up the Georgian staircase (no lift), comfortable and sexy with views to the (gay) cruisy gardens opposite and lush, leafy Calton Hill at the back. 2 rooms each floor: 1 front, 1 back; all spacious and loungy. No leisure facilities to work off your gorgeous dinner (137/FINE DINING) but the bedrooms are made for activities not provided for in a gym.

113 8/Q25
7 ROOMS
NO PETS
MED.EX

✓ **23 Mayfield** 23 Mayfield Gardens · www.23mayfield.co.uk · 0131 667 5806 On one of the long roads S from the city centre lined with indifferent hotels, 23, a 'boutique guest house', stands out way above the rest. Patrons Ross and Kathleen Birnie have aimed for the top, from underfloor heating, Indonesian furniture, a library of vintage books, Club Room with guest computer, Edinburgh info and Georgian chessboard to – of course – their gourmet breakfast, with its prodigious choice. They have mountain bikes; they are on the absolutely right track.

114 8/Q25 ✓ **94DR** 94 Dalkeith Rd · www.94dr.com · 0131 662 9265 As with 23
7 ROOMS Mayfield (above), this boutique guest house is one of many on a main road
NO PETS south. Once again, this is more than a cut above. Paul Lightfoot and John MacEwan
MED.EX (and the dug) have created a very calm and contemporary home from home here,
with great, no-frills attention to detail and an eye for design in everything. Rooms
in 3 'styles' are named after whiskies. Great breakfast, I'm told. Five-star friendly!
Some parking.

115 8/Q25 ✓ **Six Brunton Place** www.sixbruntonplace.com · 0131 662 0042 Address
4 ROOMS as is though actually on London Rd, the busy artery heading E from town
NO PETS eventually to London. Sue Thompson's tasteful townhouse (once the home of the
CHP guy who started the city's famous One o' Clock Gun) is consistently at the top of
B&B lists for its spacious, calm interiors, walls filled with pleasing art, bathrooms
with very mod cons and the considerate attention of its owner. A bit of a walk to
the town centre but calm respite when you get home. The garden room is superb.

116 8/Q25 ✓ **2b Cambridge Street** www.edinburghaccommodation.org.uk ·
2 ROOMS 0131 478 0005 Address as is, near the Usher Hall, Traverse Theatre and the
CHP West End. Only 2 rooms, so you'll be lucky, but Erlend and Hélène Clouston's very
individual and beautiful B&B clearly deserves a mention here. A calm in any storm:
zen-like garden, tea by the fire, particular hospitality. Media bods and creatives feel
comfortable here.

117 8/Q25 **Southside** 8 Newington Rd · www.southsideguesthouse.co.uk ·
8 ROOMS 0131 668 4422 On main street in southside where uninspiring hotels and guest
NO PETS houses stretch halfway to Dalkeith, this a surprisingly civilised haven close to town
MED.INX & gown (the university). Lynne and Franco's personal attention to decor and detail
and excellent breakfast. Nice prints, rugs, books and music. Some traffic noise, but
upstairs rooms double-glazed. There are two 4-poster rooms. Parking nearby.

118 8/Q25 **Ardmor House** 74 Pilrig St · www.ardmorhouse.com · 0131 554 4944
5 ROOMS Victorian house off (and halfway down) Leith Walk among lots of other B&Bs but
CHP this the top spot (and Michelin recommended). Individual, contemporary and
relaxed. Nice touches like home-made oatcakes and **Artisan Roast** coffee
(296/COFFEE). Proprietors Robin and Barry also have a lovely New Town apartment
for short lets. They provide you with their own Best of Edinburgh guide somewhat
following mine I think/hope.

119 8/Q25 **Queens Guest House** 45 Queen St · www.queensgh.com · 0131 226 2000
14 ROOMS Very central – in fact, in the middle of busy, arterial Queen St between Frederick
CHP and Castle Sts. Well appointed, good value and handy for all things midtown.
Access as a guest to gorgeous Queen St Gardens is a real plus.

The Best Hostels

120 8/Q25 ✓✓ **Edinburgh Central SYH** 9 Haddington Pl · www.syha.org.uk ·
71 ROOMS 0131 524 2090 Central it is, in a handy part of town though perhaps
(OVER 200 unobvious to casual visitors, i.e. it's not in the Old Town area. Haddington Pl is part
BEDS) of Leith Walk (corner of Annandale St) near theatres/bars/restaurants and gay
CHP quarter and on the way to Leith, eg, **Joseph Pearce** is across the traffic lights
(363/UNIQUE PUBS). Converted from office block with café, internet and every
hostel facility. Clean, efficient; rooms from singles to family 4-8 beds. Good for
kids. Run by the Scottish Youth Hostels Association.

121 8/Q25 ✓✓ **Smartcity Hostels** 50 Blackfriars St · www.smartcityhostels.com ·
606 BEDS   0131 524 1989 Building is enormous and also opens onto Cowgate. £10
CHP   million made this place as hotel-like as you get without completely losing the
hostel vibe. Self-service restaurant, extensive bar, facilities include a roof terrace
(with heaters and sometimes BBQ), self-catering kitchens and lots of cool things
like mobile phone charging boxes, snooker tables and internet zones; and hordes of
staying-up/out-late people. Massive number of rooms round the interior courtyard,
varying from 2 (though only 3) to 12 occupancy. Students stay here in term-time.
Good location and well smart.

122 8/Q25 ✓ **Royal Mile Backpackers** 105 High St · www.royalmilebackpackers.com ·
CHP   0131 557 6120 On the Royal Mile, near the Cowgate with its late-night bars.
Ideal central and cheap 24-hour-crash-out dormitory accom, with all the facilities
itinerant youth on a budget might look for. The original hostel in the group (30
years old 2015 and *the* first backpacker hostel in Scotland). The **High St Hostel**, 8
Blackfriars St (0131 557 3984; www.highstreethostel.com), is just across the street,
and **The Castle Rock**, 15 Johnston Terrace (0131 225 9666; www.
castlerockedinburgh.com), at the top of the Royal Mile in the old Council
Environmental Health HQ, is huge (190 beds in various dorms; 'private' rooms book
up fast) and some great views across the Grassmarket or to the castle which is just
over there. Same folk also have hostels in Fort William, Inverness, Oban, Pitlochry
and Skye, and Mac Backpacker tours so expect to be sold a trip to the Highlands.

123 8/Q25 ✓ **Argyle Backpackers Hotel** 14 Argyle Pl · www.argyle-backpackers.com ·
16 ROOMS   0131 667 9991 Quiet area and though in Marchmont there are great bars and
CHP   interesting shops nearby. 1km to centre across the Meadows (not advised for
women at night). This is a bit like living in a student flat and there are tenements
full of them all around. But it's homely with 2 kitchens, internet, lounge,
conservatory and garden. 7 rooms are double/twin.

124 8/Q25 ✓ **St Christopher Inn** 9-13 Market St · www.st-christophers.co.uk ·
160 BEDS   0131 226 1446 Couldn't be handier for the station or city centre. This (with
CHP   branches in London and other Euro cultural cities) a hostel rather than hotel with
bunk rooms, some a bit cramped, though there are single and double rooms. As
always, price depends on number sharing. Free breakfast in Belushi's café-bar on
ground floor open till 1am (food 10.30pm). A very central option, better than most
other hostels (facilities are en suite) but not so cheap.

125 8/Q25 **Budget Backpackers** 37-39 Cowgate · www.budgetbackpackers.com ·
170/170   0131 226 6351 & 2 West Port Two hostels at either end of the Grassmarket;
BEDS   great locations. The first on a corner leading up to the university area is the largest
CHP   (170 spaces with dorms of all sizes, including double/twins). The other, **Kick Ass**,
below the Castle mainly for larger parties. Both have 24-hour service and great bar-
cafés all day till late. Voted high in hostel world.

126 8/P25 **Belford Hostel** 6-8 Douglas Gardens · www.hoppo.com · 0131 225 6209
98 BEDS   Just W of the city centre near the Gallery of Modern Art. In a converted church, a
CHP   'street' of rooms artfully realised, they have ceilings so you don't look directly into
heaven. 'Private rooms' for 1 or 2 are in the basement/crypt. Friendly and dead
cheap (can be as little as £10). Heavy snorers should not apply (they have earplugs
at reception).

The Best Hotels Outside Town

127 8/R25 ✓✓ **Greywalls** Gullane · www.greywalls.co.uk · 01620 842144 In splendid gardens 36km E of Edinburgh, this is *the* country-house hotel in the region, a mecca for golfers and foodies. Report: 873/LOTHIANS.
EAT An Albert Roux suite of dining rooms. Bar meals and sublime afternoon tea.

128 8/P25
16 ROOMS
NO PETS
EXP
✓✓ **Champany Inn** nr Linlithgow · www.champany.com · 01506 834532 On A904, 3km Linlithgow on road to Forth Rd Bridge and South Queensferry. Exemplary restaurant with rooms, some overlooking lovely garden. Legendary steaks and seafood; ambience and service. Breakfast in cosy dining kitchen is excellent (nice bacon, of course!). Extraordinary wine list and cellar shop for take home (7 days noon-10pm). But veggies best not to venture here.
EAT Superb. Report: 279/BURGERS & STEAKS.

129 8/P25
132 ROOMS
DF
MED.EX
✓✓ **Dakota** South Queensferry · www.dakotahotels.co.uk · 0131 319 3690 From the people who brought us the Malmaisons and before that, 1 Devonshire Gardens (now Hotel du Vin 480/BOUTIQUE HOTELS), a bold concept, from the black metropolis-block design statement to the homage to travelling theme inside. On the edge of SQ but on main carriageway N from Edinburgh by the Forth Rd Bridge. It's all quite brilliant, a designer (Amanda Rosa) world away from anonymous others of the ilk. Rooms are calm and whisper 'understated chic'. The Grill restaurant a destination in itself (guests should book when they make a room reservation). Ken McCulloch's vision and restless energy: unceasing! See also 497/HOTELS OUTSIDE GLASGOW and a Glasgow city centre Dakota opening at TGP.
EAT Brasserie-type, daily-changing menu in signature stylish setting. Journey here!

130 8/P25
83 ROOMS
NO PETS
MED.EX
✓✓ **Norton House** Ingliston · www.handpickedhotels.co.uk · 0131 333 1275 Off A8 near the airport, 10km W of city centre. Victorian country house in 55 acres of greenery, surprisingly woody and pastoral for so close to city. Part of highly regarded Hand Picked Hotel group. 'Executive' rooms have countryside views. Labyrinthine layout with good conference/function facilities. Brasserie and small internal restaurant. Good contemporary (bedrooms) and traditional (public rooms) mix. Some rooms quite swish. Spa with pool, etc.

131 8/P25
4 ROOMS
MED.INX

£25-35
✓ **The Bridge Inn** Ratho · www.bridgeinn.com · 0131 333 1320 An old pub by an old bridge (over the Union Canal). 4 comfy, quite classy rooms above. Graham and Rachel Bucknall have transformed this waterside watering hole (along with the **Ship Inn** on the bay, 1305/GASTROPUBS, and the **The 19th Hole**, 1306/GASTROPUBS, both in Elie), into a destination gastropub – less than 30 mins from city centre via the A71 (through Sighthill) on the A8 and the Newbridge roundabout. Much to-do about boats, i.e. barges and the canal basin, beside the garden. Towpath walks.
EAT Gastropub (in an English kind of way) with same menu in bar of canalside dining room with terrace. Carefully sourced, own kitchen garden. Free-range chicken and ducks. Open 7 days. Must book weekends.

132 8/P25
17 ROOMS
NO PETS
MED.INX
✓ **Orocco Pier** 17 The High Street, South Queensferry · www.oroccopier. co.uk · 0131 331 1298 A buzzy restaurant and boutique-style hotel, in often tourist-thronged SQ with great views of the Forth and the **Bridge** (419/ATTRACTIONS). From Edinburgh take first turn-off from dual carriageway. Formerly the Queensferry Arms, but a substantial makeover has created a cool bistro and contemporary rooms above and beside (not all have views). Food in bar, restaurant or terrace. Event programme and they do conferences, weddings, etc. Parking tricky, but a great outside-town option.

The Best Fine-Dining Restaurants

133 8/Q25 ✓✓✓ **Restaurant Martin Wishart** 54 Shore · www.martin-wishart.
>£35 co.uk · 0131 553 3557 No. 5 in the *Sunday Times* Top 100 Restaurants
in Britain 2015/16 confirms Martin Wishart's discreet waterside restaurant in Leith
as top in the city, leading the clutch of 5 Edinburgh restaurants selected (there were
none in Glasgow). Room designed on simple but swanky lines, like a 1940s' cruise
ship, and calm rather than hushed or rushed; uncomplicated menu and wine list
(though not a lot in lower price ranges). Michelin-star chef Martin; reputation
obviously precedes and raises expectations, but preparation, cooking and
presentation are demonstrably a cut above the rest. Great vegetarian menu.
Unobtrusive service. A la carte and 3 tasting menus reliably superb. Martin has a
cookery school round the corner, is executive chef at **Cameron House**, Loch
Lomond (496/HOTELS OUTSIDE GLASGOW), and has **The Honours**, an uptown
brasserie (142/BRASSERIES) in Edinburgh and another at the Malmaison in Glasgow
(510/BRASSERIES). All are a treat. Lunch Tue-Fri & dinner Tue-Sat.

134 8/Q25 ✓✓ **Number One Princes Street** www.thebalmoralhotel.com ·
>£35 0131 557 6727 Though not many Edinburgers venture for a night on the
town below stairs at the Balmoral, the landmark hotel they pass every day on
Princes St, they're missing one of the best dining experiences in foodtown.
Subterranean opulence with only opaque light from the windows on Waverley
Steps. The calm, cosmopolitan ambience perfectly complements Brian Grigor's
confident cuisine. Long-standing executive chef is Jeff Bland. Michelin starred since
2003. A la carte and tasting menus with vegetarian option, from canapés to
splendid puds with pastry chef Ross Sneddon and petits fours with many mmm...
moments. Attentive, not too fussing-over-you staff: knowledgeable sommelier and
'cheeselier' can talk you through the impressive list (especially French) and board
(also especially French). 7 days dinner only. **Hadrian's Brasserie**, a lounge at
street level (grills and light choices among the mains), complements well. 7 days
lunch & dinner. **The Palm Court** for tea (1429/AFTERNOON TEA).

135 8/Q25 ✓✓ **The Kitchin** 78 Commercial Quay · www.thekitchin.com ·
>£35 0131 555 1755 Pre-eminent in the row of restaurants in front of the
Scottish government offices, you arrive in the chicest restaurant lounge in the land
and proceed to Tom Kitchin's brilliant, busy kitchen looking out on his calm,
urbane restaurant which has received much attention and many awards since it
opened in '06, including an early Michelin star. Though Tom is a TV chef fixture on
the foodfest circuit, admirably he seems omnipresent in the kitchen keeping an eye
on us as well as what we eat. Good value lunch menu (set and à la carte), 'surprise'
tasting menus and 'celebration of the season' menus in the evening, all in an
easy-to-follow ingredient-led menu; so lots of choice but all driven by impeccable
and serious sourcing of local and market ingredients. He calls it *From Nature to
Plate* (also his cookbook title). Not a large room; you do get lots of attention. Wine
list, as you would expect, is superb and the sommelier will guide you through it
(many suggestions already on the menu). Tue-Sat lunch & dinner.

136 8/Q25 ✓✓ **Timberyard** 10 Lady Lawson St · www.timberyard.co ·
>£35 0131 221 1222 Between Tollcross and the 'theatre district'. Not exactly
'fine-dining' but attention to ingredients, cooking and presentation has all the
hallmarks, and in a converted timber warehouse all stone and wood, you eat in the
city's most stylish food hall. Menu lists ingredients (in the contemporary as well as
seasonal register) in 'bites', 'smalls' (they are small), 'large' (they're not big either)
and 'sweets'. The good wine list will cost ya. Don't demur if it's big portions for
cash you're after; it's the whole deal we go for: inventive cookery, mellow but buzzy

ambience, smart service, all c/o the happy Radford family – in the kitchen (Ben), out front (Jo), Lisa (floating) and Andrew (upstairs and wondering what to do with the first floor). Best book. Tue-Sat lunch & dinner.

137 8/Q25 ✓ **21212** 3 Royal Terrace · www.21212restaurant.co.uk · 0131 523 1030
>£35 Paul and Katie Kitching's beautiful Michelin-starred restaurant, in an elegant townhouse backing onto Calton Hill. Name describes the appealing and very workable format of 3 choices for starters, mains and puds with a soupçon of soup (no choice) and a cheese plate in between (the cheese in tip-top condition). Lunch has same format with 2 choices. Food is playful and innovative, mixing surprise ingredients prepared by a small army of chefs in the shiny kitchen at the end of the sexily attired dining room. Good value wine list. This Michelin in the right hands. See also 112/LODGINGS.

138 8/Q25 ✓ **Mark Greenaway** 69 N Castle St · www.markgreenaway.com ·
>£35 0131 226 1155 On corner with Queen St opposite Martin Wishart's **The Honours** (142/BRASSERIES) which is not fine dining, but cheffy comparisons may be made. One has to admire Mr Greenaway's resilience and enterprise. In some ways he is *the* Edinburgh chef getting involved in local foodie matters and events. Here, in the muted New Town room (very Stanley Cursiter), there's quietly solicitous service and a lot going on on the plate. Signature dishes like his Loch Fyne crab 'cannelloni' smoking in the jar still wow, but as they say, it's no' cheap (reflecting the care and craft). Tue-Sat lunch & dinner ('Market Menu' lunch & 5.30-6.30pm).

139 8/Q25 ✓ **Castle Terrace** 33-35 Castle Terrace · www.castleterracerestaurant.com ·
>£35 0131 229 1222 Chef-patron Dominic Jack's smart city restaurant near the Usher Hall, Lyceum and Traverse Theatres has partnered with the city's best known chef, Tom Kitchin, and his eponymous Michelin-starred restaurant in Leith (see above). There's a no-nonsense approach and a very good dinner is to be had here (and good value lunches). The rooms, recently refreshed, are perhaps a tad corporate quiet for some, but all the fine-dining niceties are observed. Tue-Sat lunch & dinner.

140 8/Q25 ✓ **The Witchery** Castlehill · www.thewitchery.com · 0131 225 5613 I wrote
ATMOS these words some years ago. Reassuringly, they are all still true: at the top of the
>£35 Royal Mile where the tourists throng, maybe unaware that this is the city's most stylishly atmospheric restaurant, with many awards and famous names in the guest book. In 2 salons, the upper more 'witchery' and the 'Secret Garden' downstairs, a converted school playground, James Thomson has created a more spacious ambience for the (same) elegant Scottish menu. Locals on a treat, many regulars and visiting celebs pack this place out, and although they efficiently turn round the tables, you should book. The Witchery by the Castle hotel encapsulates this remarkable and indulgent ambience (95/BOUTIQUE HOTELS). The wine list is exceptional, the atmos *sans pareil*. 7 days all day. LO a very civilised 11.30pm. The theatre supper menu (5.30-6.30pm) at £19 is sensibly repeated from 10.30-11.30pm. See 331/LATE DINING.

141 8/Q25 ✓ **Rhubarb @ Prestonfield** off Priestfield Rd · www.prestonfield.com ·
ATMOS 0131 225 7800 A little out of town but the restaurant of fabulous Prestonfield
>£35 (93/BOUTIQUE HOTELS) makes 3 in a row of great restaurants for James Thomson (see above). And as above it's the whole dining experience rather than Michelin-minded menus that drives their success. Rhubarb is in the most gorgeously decadent and opulent Regency rooms at the heart of the hotel; the public rooms adjacent for before and après are superb, especially the upstairs drawing rooms. An evening of rich romance awaits. And you get your (rhubarb) desserts.

The Best Brasseries

142 8/Q25 ✓✓ **The Honours** 58a Castle St · www.thehonours.co.uk · 0131 225 2515
£25-35 A classic, brazz menu (both in content and presentation) with grill section. Prix-fixe lunch and early dinner menus (Tue-Fri). This, and The Honours in Glasgow (510/BRASSERIES), are the midtown brasserie, buzzier versions of Martin Wishart's eponymous brand (133/FINE DINING). All perfectly set and served, sourced and balanced. Hard to fault, I'd say. Where to go for smart business lunch or sophisticated supper; you'll have to book. Tue-Sat lunch & dinner.

143 8/Q25 ✓✓ **Forth Floor, Harvey Nichols** 30-34 St Andrew Sq · www.
£25-35 harveynichols.com · 0131 524 8350 On the fourth, the foodie floor: the Deli, Yo Sushi and the Chocolate Lounge with champagne and cake on the conveyor. Brasserie and more expensive (but similar) Modern-British comfort-food menus either side of the bar. Estimable chef Stuart Muir with HN since it opened. Nice just to come for cocktails and the view! 7 days lunch & dinner.

144 8/Q25 ✓ **Spoon** 6a Nicolson St · www.spoonedinburgh.co.uk · 0131 623 1752
£15-25 Upstairs opposite the Festival Theatre whose audiences it conveniently and ably serves. The entrance belies the loft-like apartment: individualist and spacious, with interesting retro furniture and lighting. Spoon is one of those places that once found you come back to time on time. Food is light, not too meaty, unassuming and good value. A reliable redoubt on the unlovely Bridges/Nicolson St bus route. Mon-Sat 10am-11pm (Sun noon-5pm).

145 8/Q25 ✓ **The Printing Press @ The George Hotel** George St · www.
£25-35 printingpressedinburgh.co.uk · 0131 240 7177 The restaurant and main bar of The George (92/MAJOR HOTELS) revamped late 2015. Intimate though keeping the grand features. Bar area and lofty top-end brasserie room, now with light streaming in (also used for breakfast). 'Bites' in the bar and brasserie-style menu are very Scottish in context and cooking – there's a posh mince 'n' tatties along with Spatchcock Border grouse, Scotch egg and a Josper Grill. Fitting, inexpensive wine list. Bar open till 1am for food – the tops-in-town late choice.

Galvin's Brasserie de Luxe The superior casual dining restaurant of the Caledonian Hotel. Report: 85/MAJOR HOTELS.

The Best Bistros

146 8/P25 ✓✓ **The Atelier** 159-161 Morrison St · www.theatelierrestaurant.co.uk ·
£25-35 0131 629 1344/0131 629 5040 This is perhaps a surprising find down Morrison St in the far West End between the Conference Centre and Haymarket station, a traffic-busy thoroughfare. Somehow chef/proprietor Maciek Zielinski and (out front) Kamila Bogut are able to produce their consistently top modern European food at very decent prices. Everything on this menu works – almost 'fine dining' for a third of the price. Here are Polish people making a real difference to dining in the capital. Great vegetarian choice. 7 days lunch & dinner.

147 8/P25 ✓✓ **Bia Bistrot** 19 Colinton Rd · www.biabistrot.co.uk · 0131 452 8453
£15-25 In a small strip of shops at the beginning of Colinton Rd near 'Holy Corner', a kind of secret spot where Irish (Roisin) and French (Matthias) Llorentes's combination of Bia (Irish for food) and Bistrot (the authentic French bistro) is a real find. The room ain't decortastic but it's unpretentious and so is the straight-talking, carefully sourced menu. These guys are cooking for Scotland and we love it the

more because it's exceptional value. Wines très reasonable, ice cream from the Chocolate Tree round the corner. This place should win awards! Tue-Sat lunch & dinner.

148 8/Q25 ✔✔ **Aizle** 107-109 St. Leonard's St · www.aizle.co.uk · 0131 662 9349 A
>£35 restaurant in the southside that opened to great acclaim in 2014: it's got concept! Ingredients are listed each month fresh as the day, seasonal and ethical by definition. Chef/proprietor Stuart Ralston with a Michelin background creates a fixed dinner menu each calendar month, though basic dietary wishes are accommodated (veg, pescatarian, gluten-free), £45 at TGP with wines to go with each course £30 (there is a wine list of BYOB but there's a £15 corkage). 2 compact candlelit rooms. Must book. Dinner only Wed-Sun.

149 8/Q25 ✔✔ **Wedgwood** 267 Canongate · www.wedgwoodtherestaurant.co.uk ·
£25-35 0131 558 8737 Just below St Mary's St. For nigh on 10 years, the compact, all-present-and-correct Old Town bistro of Paul Wedgwood. Creative, Modern-Scottish cookery with a big, loyal following and excellent lunch deals. Was included in the *Sunday Times* Britain's Top 100 Restaurants 2015/16, which made some of us remember what an asset to the tourist-thronged Royal Mile this is. 7 days lunch & dinner.

150 8/P25 ✔✔ **Rollo** 108 Raeburn Pl · www.barrollo.com · 0131 332 1232 Lovely
£25-35 Rollo is both a neighbourhood (Stockbridge) and a family affair. Ailsa, front of house, is a fashion designer, Mum and Dad Rollo are a sculptor (works on show) and an architect. It is very Stockbridge! Menu follows the bites and bowls for sharing principle, with some decent vegetarian options. Wine list short but to the point. Small converted storefront so a bit of a tight squeeze and you should book even weekdays. 7 days lunch & dinner.

151 8/Q25 ✔✔ **Sylvesters** 55-57 W Nicolson St · www.sylvestersedinburgh.co.uk ·
£15-25 0131 662 4493 Kieran Sylvester's quite brilliant and understated corner bistro near the university and George Sq serves up the best food in this quarter (good to know during the Fringe). Extraordinary how they can serve food of this quality at those prices (hence 2 ticks). Where in London, or anywhere, could you eat this well for under £25? Cooking with flair and no fuss, artfully presented. Mon-Sat lunch & dinner.

152 8/Q25 ✔✔ **The Dogs** 110 Hanover St · www.thedogsonline.co.uk ·
ATMOS 0131 220 1208 Upstairs on busy Hanover St, the first and enduring of the
£25-35 Dog pack of brusquely charming, incredibly thin and inspired patron Dave Ramsden. Lofty, busy main and smaller back room always crammed (and you are Ramsded!). Old-fashioned, simple and robust food at giveaway prices. Fidget Pie, Stargazy Pie, Devilled Ox Liver and Lardy Chips but good vegetarian too, all wearing a Michelin Bib. Great deal on wine. It all works; we go a lot! 7 days lunch & dinner.

153 8/Q25 ✔✔ **Urban Angel** 121 Hanover St · www.urban-angel.co.uk ·
£15-25 0131 225 6215 In a basement near Queen St. Gilli Macpherson's understated but well-judged café-restaurant perfectly of its time and place. Contemporary, relaxed, great value and, not surprisingly, busy and buzzing in the old flagstoned, worn-wood rooms. Organic where sensible, fair-trade and free-range; conscientiously sourced. Food is wholesome British but with a light touch and great pastry. Takeaway counter offerings of bespoke sandwiches, soup and juices. A great Sunday brunch rendezvous (341/SUNDAY BRUNCH). Sun-Wed daytime, open later Thu-Sat.

154 8/Q25 ✓✓ **The Outsider** 15 George IV Bridge · www.theoutsiderrestaurant.
ATMOS com · 0131 226 3131 The now long-established but still bright and
£15-25 contemporary dining room of maverick restaurateur Malcolm Innes. Minimalist
design with surprising view of the castle; and art! Innovative menu contrasts – the
signature beetroot coleslaw in pitta bread is almost compulsory! Daily specials. Big
helpings, pretty people. Good value lunches and great late! We go here a lot. 7 days
lunch & dinner.

155 8/Q25 ✓ **Field** 41 W Nicolson St · www.fieldrestaurant.co.uk · 0131 667 7010 &
£25-35 the newer Field 1-3 Raeburn Pl · www.fieldgrillhouse.co.uk ·
0131 332 9977 First Field, near the University, is a small parlour-like southside
bistro, invariably packed serving 'Scotland's Larder' in winning combinations. The
larger, longer grill house has the same conscientious approach, with more grilling
(it does good steaks). Strong experienced team run these places. Gordon Craig is a
creative chef. Tue-Sun lunch & dinner (Grill House closed Sun).

156 8/P25 ✓ **First Coast** 99 Dalry Rd · www.first-coast.co.uk · 0131 313 4404 I wrote
£15-25 most of this entry years ago. Reassuringly, it still applies: named after a place
in the far north where chef/patron Hector MacRae used to go on his hols, this cool
urban restaurant is also on the edge of the visited world – well, Dalry Rd. Superb
value and full of integrity. Straight-talking menu, with light food and no
bamboozling choices, and they make everything from scratch, including bread.
First Coast would grace any neighbourhood. Mon-Sat lunch & dinner.

157 8/Q25 ✓ **Iris** 47a Thistle St · www.irisedinburgh.co.uk · 0131 220 2111 In a street
£15-25 of many bistros, those that know head for Iris. Not immediately obvious,
perhaps, but expect elegant, modern rooms, and a well-judged, light and Modern-
British menu (not much vegetarian) and excellent service. Sun 'brekkies'. 7 days
lunch & dinner.

158 8/Q25 ✓ **Apiary Restaurant** 33 Newington Rd · www.apiaryrestaurant.co.uk ·
£15-25 0131 668 4999 In southside beyond the Queens Hall (handy pre & post theatre
and also for **Summerhall** 437/GALLERIES). A spacious corner building now a rather
brilliant bistro by the industrious women – Kath Byrnes and Jo Curtis – who have the
Three Birds in Bruntsfield (see page 42). A long, eclectic menu from brunch to supper
with daily specials is miraculously produced in a tiny kitchen with inventive surprises
and sharing plates; all great value. Perhaps because of its location you can usually get
in here despite its appeal, so this is a good place to know. 7 days lunch & dinner.

159 8/Q25 ✓ **Anfora** 87a Giles St · www.anforawinebar.co.uk · 0131 553 6914 In
ATMOS Leith, in the courtyard at the corner of Giles & Henderson Sts. Zak Hanif's
£25-35 remaking and revitalising of the historic 17th-century Vaults, a corner of Leith that
has seen a few restaurants come and go. This, born in 2015, seems set to stay: a
carefully selected (good organic) wine list with many by the glass, an extremely
reasonable Mod-Brit menu in the hands of a competent chef. A perfect wine-bar
setting, outdoor seating and the beautiful side room lit only by natural and, as of
old, candlelight. Closed Mon/Tue.

160 8/Q25 ✓ **New Chapter** 18 Eyre Pl · www.newchapterrestaurant.co.uk ·
£15-25 0131 556 0006 The sort of great value, buzzy bistro you would be happy to have
in your neighbourhood, this on the site of the last remaining of the once flourishing
Pierre Victoire chain. So a new chapter indeed in this north of the New Town
residential area. Careful, conscientious cookery, a well-presented Scottish meets
European menu not dissimilar to The Atelier above. Matt Korecki, chef/proprietor, was
a partner there. Any referendum would say yes to this. 7 days lunch & dinner.

161 8/Q25 ✓ **The Scotch Malt Whisky Society** 28 Queen St · www.
£25-35 thediningroomedinburgh.co.uk · 0131 220 2044 'The Dining Room' of this august yet understated private members' club – including the more atmospheric bar upstairs with its separate, more casual menu – now open to all. James Freeman's unfussy, consistently sound menu offers everything a whisky connoisseur would wish for – quality and a dram with your amuse-bouche. An oasis in traffic-unceasing Queen St, it's underused. 7 days lunch & Tue-Sat dinner.

162 8/Q25 ✓ **Three Birds** 3-5 Viewforth · www.threebirds.co.uk · 0131 229 3252 Just
£15-25 off Bruntsfield's main street. This and sister restaurant The Apiary (see page 41) are hugely popular, great value bistros with food to love. Always good vegetarian choice and lovely bites that can be starters. Three Birds ain't large so booking probably essential. 7 days lunch & dinner.

163 8/Q25 ✓ **Dine** 10 (1F) Cambridge St · www.dine.scot · 0131 218 1818 A new
£25-35 addition to city dining late 2015, a very smart metropolitan makeover of the once famed restaurant Blue above the Traverse Theatre, and a handy eaterie in theatre land (adjacent to the Usher Hall and The Lyceum). Stuart Muir, of Harvey Nichols restaurant, has created a sophisticated dining-out experience (under a tree!), and a delicious and approachable Modern-Scottish menu not expensive at this standard. Open from breakfast till supper (10am-10pm; Sun from noon). The Bar, with a great cocktail list, is open till 1am.

164 8/Q25 ✓ **Angels with Bagpipes** 343 High St · www.angelswithbagpipes.co.uk ·
>£35 0131 220 1111 In the Royal Mile opposite the cathedral, from which the slightly daft name derives – somewhere inside there's a wooden angel cradling the said bagpipe. No matter, Sylvia Hamilton's stylish, contemporary bistro is no' daft at all. Space stretched but a few tables on the Mile itself. Fraser Smith's Modern-British menus with Italian pitch and Scottish produce. Way better (but a tad more pricey) than most on the Mile, though not much for vegetarians. 7 days from noon.

165 8/Q25 **Monteiths** 61 High St · www.monteithsrestaurant.co.uk · 0131 557 0330
£15-25 Down a fairy-lit close at the tartan-clad centre of the Royal Mile, a cool, woody and clubby bar/restaurant (it's like a library) with great food, drinkies (including cocktails) and smart, sexy service. The gastropub-style menu is quite meaty. Lunch goes through to 5pm then à la carte. 7 days from noon.

166 8/P25 **Salt Café** 54 Morningside Rd · 0131 281 1885 Opposite Churchill Theatre.
£15-25 Casual diner between a café and a bistro; not so drop-in though because it's frequently full (best book evenings), this partly due to the 3 small rooms, which can seem cramped. Food's good from breakfast to dinner; sourced and seasonal. Well-selected wine and drinks list. Ambience is buzzy; recycled chic. A welcome addition to the Morningside menu. Mon-Fri from 8.30am (from 10am Sat/Sun).

167 8/Q25 **Calistoga** 70 Rose St Lane N · www.calistoga.co.uk · 0131 225 1233 In an
£15-25 unlikely back street location (between Castle & Frederick Sts) this small Californian restaurant quietly here for years thrives. This is because it's very good; we'd call it a 'real find'. Light starters, great steaks, top American wine list. Refreshingly a bit different. Amazingly, open 7 days lunch & dinner.

168 8/Q25 **Café Nom de Plume** 60 Broughton St · 0131 478 1372 This cosy
<£15 neighbourhood café-bistro, in a street well served with others, offers honest-to-goodness, home-cooked fare and is one the best value places in the street. Plants round the door, a lounge-like home and engaging service. Wide-ranging menu has many staples. Mon-Sat from 11am (Sun from noon).

169 8/Q25   **Edinburgh Larder Bistro** 1a Alva St · www.edinburghlarder.co.uk ·
£15-25   0131 225 4599 Corner of Queensferry St in the West End. Basement, very bistro kind of eaterie, sister of the Edinburgh Larder caff and takeaway in the Old Town (316/CAFFS), the one with the great Sunday breakfast (338/SUNDAY BRUNCH), so part of the Edinburgh-cool-place-to-eat family. Spread out over different rooms, best when busy. Uncomplicated not lengthy menu, very seasonal, all made from scratch. Good vegetarian choice. Tue-Sat lunch & dinner.

170 8/Q25   **Bistro du Vin** 11 Bristo Pl · www.hotelduvin.com · 0131 285 1479 Restaurant
£25-35   of the **Hotel du Vin** (94/BOUTIQUE HOTELS), entered through the sprawling and tightly fitting courtyard and reception. Though a chain, there's nothing uniform about the B du Vs, which offer classic French bistro fare. Somehow neither the room nor the food are as superior to other French places in this town as the hotel is to others of the ilk, but the all-round experience is *agréable* and the wine list, with impressive sommelier support, is excellent. 7 days lunch & dinner.

The Best Gastropubs

171 8/P25   ✓✓ **The Scran & Scallie** 1 Comely Bank Rd · www.scranandscallie.com ·
DF   0131 332 6281 Near the end of the shops etc that make up Stockbridge's
>£35   main street. This joint venture of Michelin chef Tom Kitchin (135/FINE DINING) and Dominic Jack of **Castle Terrace** (139/FINE DINING) led to an immediate scramble for tables when it opened in 2012, which has since barely abated. They only reserve some of them so it's often possible to walk in. This gastropub food is all it should be and there's a convivial and casual ambience to match. Scottish, seasonal and local throughout the menu. Daytime is very child-friendly. These *are* a hike away from pub prices! Mon-Fri lunch & dinner, all day Sat/Sun.

172 8/Q25   ✓✓ **Blackfriars** 57-61 Blackfriars St · www.blackfriarsedinburgh.co.uk ·
£25-35   0131 558 8684 Georgie Binder and Andrew Macdonald (in the kitchen) have made a top job of their restaurant, with bar adjacent, in this quiet Old Town street between the Royal Mile and Cowgate. Food conscientiously sourced, served and all made from scratch, including the bread and ice cream. Sensibly, few (ie 4) starters and mains, with a light, small all-day plate menu in the bar next door. May sometimes get forgotten in the Old Town where-to-go, but this is an excellent those-that-know choice. Wed-Sun lunch & dinner.

173 8/Q25   ✓✓ **Canny Man's** 237 Morningside Rd · www.cannymans.co.uk ·
ATMOS   0131 447 1484 Aka The Volunteer Arms on the A702 via Tollcross, 7km
£15-25   from centre. Idiosyncratic renowned eaterie in a labyrinth of snug, atmospheric rooms; a true, original gastropub. Carries a complement of malts as long as your arm and a serious wine list. There are 90 smorrebrods (soup, some seafood). Lunch 7 days & dinner Mon-Thu & Sat. Linen table cloths, nice rugs and pictures. This is a very civilised pub of good taste with a lovely patio/garden. See also 388/ALES.

174 8/Q25   ✓✓ **The Shore** 3 Shore · www.fishersbistros.co.uk · 0131 553 5080
£15-25   A long time on this shore but on a recent visit the food here was way up there in gastropub land. Run by people from **Fishers** next door (233/SEAFOOD) with a similar sympatico ambience but more pubby, less fishy. Real fire and large windows looking out to the quayside, strewn with bods on summer nights, coz when it's sunny we head to The Shore. Modern-British menu in cosy-in-winter woody bar (selective live music Tue-Thu, Sun) or in the quieter restaurant. 7 days lunch & dinner.

175 8/Q25 ✓ **The Magnum** 1 Albany St · www.themagnumrestaurant.co.uk ·
DF 0131 557 4366 Chris Graham's relaxed and reliable gastropub on the corner
£15-25 of Albany & Dublin Sts is the civilised East Village watering hole with eats. It's in my
'hood so it's a personal favourite. Bar and raised dining area. Bar menu available in
both has the pub staples (excellent tempura fish 'n' chips) and à la carte. Simple,
casual dining and great staff. Sun-Thu lunch & dinner, all day Fri/Sat.

176 8/Q25 ✓ **The King's Wark** 36 Shore · www.thekingswark.com · 0131 554 9260
£15-25 On the corner of Bernard St. Woody, candlelit, stone-walled and comfortable –
a classic gastropub, the emphasis on the food. Bar and bistro dining room.
Pub-food classics and more adventurous evening menu. Though traditional and
dark rather than pale, light and modern, this has long been one of the best bets in
Leith. Scottish slant on the big menu from a small kitchen, with excellent fish,
including their famous beer batter and chips. Mon-Sat from noon (from 11am Sun).

177 8/P25 ✓ **Caley Sample Room** 42-58 Angle Park Terrace · www.
£15-25 thecaleysampleroom.co.uk · 0131 337 7204 The CSR sells Caledonian real
ales from the nearby brewery but many guest beers (up to 16) and a plethora of
bottled craft beers. Great burgers and steaks but eclectic and full menu with daily
specials. Nice, woody ambience. Loadsa wines by the glass. Out-of-the-way
location but this is *the* west-of-the-city destination for great pub grub. A little live
music! 7 days all day.

178 8/Q25 ✓ **The Holyrood 9A** 9A Holyrood Rd · www.theholyrood.co.uk ·
DF 0131 556 5044 Round the corner at the bottom of St Mary's St towards the
£15-25 Parliament, a surprisingly bustling beer and burger den, with impressive selections of
both. Food is prepared in the tiniest kitchen and somewhere downstairs, and partaken
in the packed back room where you probably have to put your name down for a table.
Huge range of draught beers but also wines by the glass. An all-round good pub, the
first and possibly still the best of local expanding but bespoke chain, eg the **Red
Squirrel** (284/BURGERS & STEAKS). They are all different. 7 days all day.

179 8/Q25 ✓ **Under The Stairs** 3a Merchant St · www.underthestairs.org ·
ATMOS 0131 466 8550 Downstairs on the corner of small Merchant St on the road down
£15-25 to the Grassmarket from Forrest Rd and the Museum. You might call it quirky, certainly
popular with the posher student, they pack 'em in and chat levels may drown out food
appreciation murmurs. Eclectic, inventive menu, with steaks and burgers. The
drinkings include nice cocktails. Overall good atmos brings us back. 7 days all day.

180 8/Q25 ✓ **The Bon Vivant** 55 Thistle St · www.bonvivantedinburgh.co.uk ·
DF 0131 225 3275 & 4-6 Dean St · www.bonvivant-stockbridge.co.uk ·
£15-25 0131 315 3311 Similar in style, ambience and menu the 2 BVs offer cosy, convivial,
contemporary food with great wine (huge by-the-glass list) and cocktail choice.
Thistle St BV in a busy block of restaurants is dark but always full, and Stockbridge
branch, though tucked away off Raeburn Pl, is a more local secret and find. But you
should book here too. 7 days all day.

181 8/Q25 ✓ **The Blackbird** 37-39 Leven St · www.theblackbirdedinburgh.co.uk ·
£15-25 0131 228 2280 & **Hamilton's Bar & Kitchen** 16-18 Hamilton Pl · www.
hamiltonsedinburgh.co.uk · 0131 226 4199 & **Treacle** 39-41 Broughton St ·
www.treacleedinburgh.co.uk · 0131 557 0627 A local and very personally run
chain of great drop-in gastropubs, all in places you want them. Look, food, service
and cocktails different but similarly appealing. 7 days all day.

182 8/Q25 ✓ **The Ship on the Shore** 24-26 Shore · www.theshipontheshore.co.uk ·
£15-25   0131 555 0409   Midway between The Shore and The Wark (above), also with a reputation as a great quayside bistro/gastropub, specialising in seafood. Good ingredient sourcing and wine list (top by-the-glass selection, including fizz). Excellent *fruits de mer*, fish 'n' chips (Hoegaarden batter) and a buzzy ambience to enjoy them, a consistently classy joint on a quayside with many options. 7 days all day.

183 8/Q25 ✓ **Indigo Yard** 7 Charlotte Lane · www.indigoyardedinburgh.co.uk ·
£15-25   0131 220 5603   Behind Queensferry Street. For a long time one of the great West End watering holes; consummate, contemporary pubbery by the always on trend Montpelier group (see below). Breakfast, lunch and dinner in several areas, wooden-look, great lighting. Always a reliable repast. Huge list of artisan and world beers, 150 whiskies, lots of wine by the glass. 7 days all day.

184 8/Q25 ✓ **Montpeliers** 159 Bruntsfield Pl · www.montpeliersedinburgh.co.uk ·
£15-25   0131 229 3115   They call it Montpeliers of Bruntsfield and it is almost an institution S of the Meadows. Same ownership as Rick's below and similar buzz and noise levels; it's a slick operation. From breakfast menu to late supper, they've thought of everything. All the contemporary faves. Sunday roasts. Gets well mobbed. 7 days all day.

185 8/Q25 **Rick's** 55a Frederick St · www.ricksedinburgh.co.uk · 0131 622 7800
£15-25 Basement bar/restaurant along with Rick's hotel (110/BOUTIQUE HOTELS) by same people as Montpeliers (above) and **Tigerlily** (97/BOUTIQUE HOTELS). Drinking is the main activity here but they do have a variable, i.e. highs and lows, restaurant menu. Later on maybe too noisy to enjoy food, so choose time and table carefully. Inner courtyard best for dining. Up-for-it crowd (many women) enjoy champagne, cocktails and shouting. 7 days all day. Also open for breakfast from 7am (342/SUNDAY BRUNCH).

186 8/Q25 **Whighams Wine Cellars** 13 Hope St · www.whighams.com · 0131 225 8674
£15-25 On corner of Charlotte Sq. First here in 1767, Nicholas Henderson's wine bar-bistro has been discreetly dispensing the wine and the well-tried-and-tested menu (à la carte and the new 'tapas with a Scottish twist') here since 1983. Always an amiable, congenial place to return to. Great for the Book Festival in August. Live band on Sun (and sometimes Tue). Almost an institution. 7 days all day.

187 8/Q25 **The Salisbury Arms** 58 Dalkeith St · www.thesalisburyarmsedinburgh.
£15-25 co.uk · 0131 667 4518   Opposite the Commonwealth Swimming Pool, a roadhouse determined by gastropub experience perhaps more suburban than *metro urban*, though many boxes are ticked: spacious, great service, well presented. Food on the pub staple side but loads of choice. This is a well-thought-out, perennially popular GP. 7 days all day.

✓ **The Bridge Inn** Ratho   Report: 131/HOTELS OUTSIDE EDINBURGH.

The Best French Restaurants

188 8/Q25 ✓✓ **La Garrigue** 31 Jeffrey St · www.lagarrigue.co.uk · 0131 557 3032
£25-35 An airy yet intimate restaurant near the Royal Mile. Chef/proprietor Jean Michel Gauffre brings warm Languedoc to your plate. Expect your cassoulets to be spot-on. A sure foot in the Terroir. Veggies may flounder between the leggy langoustines and les lapins but meat eaters and Francophiles are très content here. Excellent Midi-centric wine list. 7 days lunch & dinner.

189 8/Q25 ✓✓ **Café Marlayne** 76 Thistle St · www.cafemarlayne.com ·
£15-25 0131 226 2230 Here a while now but this well-worn wee (we mean wee) gem is reliably the best small, authentic bistro in town. Personal, intimate and very, very French. It's like a place you find in rural France on your hols; you would say 'charmant' and you will go back. Best book! 7 days lunch & dinner.

190 8/Q25 ✓✓ **L'Escargot Bleu** 56 Broughton St · www.lescargotbleu.co.uk ·
£15-25 0131 557 1600 In a strong French field in this city, another authentic Auld Alliance bistro (and cool wine bar downstairs 364/UNIQUE PUBS) – this one un peu upmarket. Very French atmos and menu so expect tartare to mean tartare and snails to be escargots. Well-sourced ingredients mainly écossaise by Monsieur Berkmiller himself, with great French cheese selection. Michelin Bib; always busy. Menu du jour Mon-Sat, lunch & dinner. Open Sun during Festival.

191 8/Q25 ✓✓ **L'Escargot Blanc** 17 Queensferry St · www.lescargotblanc.co.uk ·
£15-25 0131 226 1890 Fred Berkmiller's upstairs bistro, à deux with L'Escargot above, though the Blanc is more fun. The loyal following love the authentic, lively atmos, the inexpensive food, fine wines, the great steaks and proper escargots (from Scotland). Street-level **Bar à Vin** wine bar has very decent wine and charcuterie. Cheery, informed staff both up and down. Mon-Sat lunch & dinner.

192 8/Q25 ✓ **Bistro Provence** 88 Commercial St · www.bistroprovence.co.uk ·
£25-35 0131 344 4295 On Leith's 'restaurant row' where, with exception of The Kitchin, restaurants do come and go. This is a breath of fresh and authentic Provençal air with Paul Malinen's confident, light touch in the kitchen, and proprietor, the très charmant Michael Fons, out front, where you can eat in the conservatory looking out to the Scottish Office. I've had some of the best French food in the city here. I hope they stay! Tue-Fri lunch & dinner. All day Sat/Sun.

193 8/Q25 ✓ **Café Saint Honoré** 34 N W Thistle St Lane · www.cafesthonore.com ·
ATMOS 0131 226 2211 Between Frederick and Hanover Sts down a lane, a classic
£25-35 bistro with French sensibilities informing an inspired Scottish menu under notable chef/proprietor Neil Forbes. Exudes atmos. Linen tablecloths, tiles and mirrors; at night in candlelight, it twinkles. Sound sourcing and a daily changing menu. Meat dishes are especially good; minimal vegetarian choice. 7 days lunch & dinner.

194 8/Q25 ✓ **Café Cassis** Salisbury Rd · www.cafecassis.co.uk · 0131 667 8991 With
£15-25 an unprepossessing entrance to the basement of an unsung hotel on a residential street between two main roads, this friendly and foodtastic bistro is a southside secret, yet frequently full. Chef Denis Guillonneau is passionate about his great value French/ Scottish menu – every dish drawing compliments from loyal and newbie diners brought here purely by word of mouth. With wife Alison out front, it's a family affair; possibly the best Auld Alliance food you'll find, so do! Tue-Sun lunch & dinner.

195 8/Q25 ✓ **Petit Paris** 38-40 Grassmarket · www.petitparis-restaurant.co.uk ·
£15-25 0131 226 2442 On busy N side of street below the castle. Tables packed together, upstairs or outside best. The terrace spreads across to the central reservation in summer. Not exactly Montmartre (stags and hens misbehaving) but authentic on atmos and ingredients (imported where appropriate). Certainly better than most of what you find in France these days. BYOB (not weekends), corkage £3.50. 7 days lunch & dinner.

196 8/Q25 ✓ **La P'tite Folie** 9 Randolph Pl · www.laptitefolie.co.uk · 0131 225 8678
ATMOS Best word for it: 'unpretentious'; maybe 'ambiente'. Mismatched furniture,
£15-25 inexpensive French *plats du jour*. Relaxed dining in a two-floor Tudoresque 'maison' in West End cul-de-sac. Great value. Many old regulars at lunch. Mon-Sat lunch & dinner. **Le Di-Vin** adjacent is a large, lofty wine bar and a surprise find behind the bistro. Great wine list and atmos (and charcuterie-style bar food). Tue-Sun all day.

197 8/Q25 ✓ **Maison Bleue** 36-38 Victoria St · www.maisonbleuerestaurant.com ·
£15-25 0131 226 1900 For 20 years now, an atmospheric, very Edinburgh café-bistro: convivial, grazing all the right notes upstairs and down. French and tapas/meze approach, building a meal from smallish dishes they call bouchées (and the brochettes!). The point is, the food here is good! 7 days all day.

198 8/Q25 ✓ **Fleur De Sel** 61 Frederick St · www.fleurdesel-creperie.co.uk ·
<£15 0131 225 7983 Julien Tesfault and Anne-Laure Roger's sweet, authentic, slightly-above-street-level crêperie sources flours from Brittany for their light crêpes and galettes (naturally gluten-free). Salades and omelettes. Simple, gentle, à point! Mon-Sat all day.

199 8/P25 ✓ **Marie Délices** 125 Comiston Rd · www.mariedelices.co.uk ·
<£15 0131 447 1909 Way up Morningside (Rd) almost into the burbs, an authentic and enthusiastic outpost of La Belle France. Everything home-made (bread from local French bakery), baking (macarons and madeleines, of course), delicious crêpes and galettes worth the extra km, I'd say. Tue-Sun daytime only.

200 8/Q25 **The (Newer) Café Marlayne** 13 Antigua St · www.cafemarlayne.com ·
£15-25 0131 558 8244 Surprisingly large and lofty eastern extension of the mini bistro above is very welcome in the strip of restaurants opposite the Playhouse Theatre. Cavernous back room means you can usually get a table when the musical punters ram this row. Few are aware that this is the best value and the most authentic – but now you are! Islay Fraser, Madame Marlayne herself (see above), in the kitchen. All-day caff menu has good home baking! 7 days all day.

 Restaurant Martin Wishart French influence on finest dining. Report: 133/FINE DINING.

The Best Italian Restaurants

201 8/Q25 ✓ **Nonna's Kitchen** 45 Morningside Rd · www.nonnas-kitchen.co.uk ·
£25-35 0131 466 6767 A personal favourite, Nonna's combines friendliness and flair to a degree that repeat custom alone means you probably have to book most evenings. The Stornaiuolo family – dad Mimmo in the kitchen, Gino out front and mama Carmela presiding, with Jimmy their trusty lieutenant (who never falters in reciting the prodigious list of daily, mainly seafood specials) all work damned hard to make this the primo easy-going Italian place in town. Pasta/pizza, long à la carte and specials. Kids' menu. You could come here for a month and not have the same thing twice. Those lucky Morningsiders. Tue-Sun lunch & dinner.

202 8/Q25 ✓ **La Cucina @ G&V Hotel** 1 George IV Bridge · www.quorvuscollection.
>£35 com · 0131 240 1666 At the Royal Mile. The upstairs spacious Italian kitchen of the first Missoni hotel, now **G&V** (99/BOUTIQUE HOTELS), where fashion, i.e. that zig-zag brand, came first. But the food here, Giorgio Locatelli- (the doyen of contemporay urban Italian cuisine) style, is excellent and not at all fancified. Ambience relaxed, chic and sexy, like the trousers and the kilts. Smart, solicitous service; good sommeliers dispense a serious Italian wine list, though cheap it ain't. 7 days all day.

203 8/Q25 ✓ **Al Dente** 139 Easter Rd · www.al-dente-restaurant.co.uk ·
£15-25 0131 652 1932 Small, discreet restaurant rather than tratt beyond the shops of Easter Rd towards Leith. Graziano Spano has built a loyal following for the genuine love of rustic regional Italian food he brings to your plate. Expect rabbit and tripe along with more familiar fare and perfectly al dente pasta. Lunch Tue/Fri/Sat only & dinner Mon-Sat.

204 8/P25 ✓ **La Bruschetta** 13 Clifton Terrace · www.labruschetta.co.uk ·
£15-25 0131 467 7464 Extension of Shandwick Pl opposite Haymarket station (regulars come by train!). Giovanni Cariello's Italian kitchen and tiny dining room in the West End. A modest ristorante with form and a following – so book. The space does not cramp their old-school style or the excellent service. Tue-Sat lunch & dinner.

205 8/Q25 ✓ **Valvona & Crolla** 19 Elm Row · www.valvonacrolla.co.uk ·
£25-35 0131 556 6066 First caff of the empire (20 years in 2015) which spread to Multrees Walk (see below) and the Jenners food hall discreetly buzzing away at the back of the legendary deli (356/DELIS). An Alexander McCall Smith kind of café much favoured by ladies who lunch. First-class ingredients and great Italian domestic cooking. It hasn't changed much in 20 years but we love it for that. It was always just right! Own bakery. One of the best and healthiest breakfasts in town (till 11.15am), favoloso lunch and afternoon tea (from 3pm). Can BYOB from shop (with corkage). 7 days daytime only.

206 8/P25 ✓ **Locanda de Gusti** 102 Dalry Rd · www.locandadegusti.com ·
£15-25 0131 346 8800 Rosario Sartore's love letter home to Naples proclaims 3 principles: 'honest, sincere, simple' and they are indeed evident here in this authentic, unpretentious neighbourhood restaurant 250m from Haymarket station. Excellent home-made pasta, seafood, etc. Small and hugely popular, so you'll have to book. Lunch Thu-Sat & dinner Mon-Sat.

207 8/Q25 ✓ **Contini Ristorante** 103 George St · www.contini.com · 0131 225 1550
ATMOS Elegant conversion by Victor and Carina Contini of a lofty, pillared Georgian
£15-25 room, towards the west end of Edinburgh's better boulevard, into the classiest restaurant on the street and the most stylish Italian joint in town. Passion for food

and good service always evident; and they are ubiquitous – they also run **The Scottish Café & Restaurant** in Princes St Gardens (248/SCOTTISH) & the **Caffe/ Gelateria** on the Royal Mile (315/CAFFS). Bar and central pizza oven, unexpected combos in a straightforward, oft-changing menu. Great people-watching strip of tables on the street. 7 days all day.

208 8/Q25
£25-35
✓ **Victor & Carina Contini Cannonball** 356 Castlehill · www.contini.com · 0131 225 1550 Bit of a mouthful but it is very much what is says on the Italian tin: the latest venture of the irrepressible Victor and Carina Contini (see above) in a place called Cannonball House, a former school at the very top of the Royal Mile by the entrance to the Castle. On 3 floors, the **Caffe** is just off the street (315/CAFFS), the gelateria is below and on the first floor is the restaurant with a Scottish-Italian menu somewhere between their other two foodie destinations. A lightsome room on the Mile with all the right ingredients, including smart service. Mon-Sat lunch & dinner, Sun noon-5pm.

209 8/Q25
£15-25
✓ **VinCaffè** 11 Multrees Walk · www.valvonacrolla.co.uk · 0131 557 0088 The downtown smart eaterie of the Valvona & Crolla dynasty (see above) in the posh-shop passage beside Harvey Nix. Café counter downstairs, restaurant above. Interesting pastas, pizzas and proper principalis. It's always busy downstairs for authentic espresso and fast snacks. Upstairs has black-and-white classic movies projected, Sunday night jazz and the occasional tea dances. A *dolce vita* kind of place. 7 days all day (closes a bit earlier on Sun).

210 8/Q25
£15-25
✓ **La Favorita** 325 Leith Walk · www.vittoriagroup.co.uk · 0131 554 2430 Tony Crolla's (of **Vittoria** and now everywhere 212/TRATTS) upmarket pizzeria halfway down the Walk where the trams may come one day. From the twin, specially imported wood-fired ovens, Tony was determined to produce 'the best pizza in Scotland' (220/PIZZA)! Gluten-free available and a menu of multifarious pastas. Family-friendly, especially on Sunday. This is many folks' favorita and good to-go from the takeaway next door, with a fleet of Favorita 500's often outside wanting to bring it to you. 7 days all day.

211 8/Q25
£15-25
Osteria Del Tempo Perso 208 Bruntsfield Pl · www.osteriadeltempoperso. info · 0131 221 1777 On a prominent corner of what locals call 'Holy Corner', a buzzy 'osteria', i.e. a tavern with good and local food (Lazio). Here is does feel authentic and home-made, with imported recipes and ingredients. Free fizz to start, not just unusual pastas (no pizza), a welcome addition here at a foodie junction. 7 days lunch & dinner.

Divino Enoteca Neither a tratt nor a ristorante: a superior wine bar with food. Report: 396/BAR FOOD.

▬▬▬ The Trusty Tratts

212 8/Q25
£15-25
✓✓ **Vittoria** 113 Brunswick St · www.vittoriagroup.co.uk · 0131 556 6171 The original (and for 45 years) on the corner of Leith Walk, also at 19 George IV Bridge · 0131 225 1740 and a newer caff by the Playhouse. For aeons Tony Crolla has provided one of the best, least pretentious Scottish-Italian café-restaurants in town. Uptown branch near the university equally full-on, with chic **Divino Enoteca** downstairs (396/BAR FOOD). Tony knows how to work the zeitgeist! Full Italian menu with classic and contemporary pastas. In Leith, outside tables on an interesting corner are great for people watching. Nice for kids (291/KIDS) and for breakfast (porridge, omelettes).

Pizzeria/ristorante further down the Walk, **La Favorita** (220/PIZZA) is the consummate pizza joint with takeaway or delivery by Fiat 500. Mon-Sat from 10am all day, from noon on Sun.

213 8/Q25 ✓✓ **Giuliano's** 18-19 Union Pl · www.giulianos.co.uk · 0131 556 6590
£15-25   Top of Leith Walk opposite Playhouse Theatre. 'Giuli's' also has the Al Fresco restaurant adjacent after the takeaway counter but it's the original that rocks; it feeds the Playhouse opposite. I've said it (many times) before: it's just pasta and pizza but it's what we like. Surprisingly good wine list and the service from staff – many of whom have been here forever but never seem to age – is top in this town. The din is loud and it's always somebody's birthday. 7 days noon-1am. Giuliano's on The Shore (0131 554 5272) on the corner of the bridge in Leith Central has the same, reliable tratt menu and is especially good for kids. 7 days all day.

214 8/Q25 ✓ **The Roamin' Nose** 14 Eyre Pl · www.theroaminnose.com ·
DF   0131 629 3135 Cheerful play on words describes this happy all-day Italian
£15-25   diner which is more a caff than a tratt, serving breakfast to supper kinda like they do in towns all over Italy. Stefano Agostini and the missus work damned hard and just about everything is home-made. The olive oil comes from home; food is light. A brilliant neighbourhood drop-in. Tue-Sat all day, daytime only Sun/Mon.

215 8/P25   **Mia** 96 Dalry Rd · www.mia-restaurant.co.uk · 0131 629 1750 Adjacent to
£15-25   **Locanda de Gusti** (206/ITALIAN), the fact the Mia is also always full attests to their success as a straight-up neighbourhood tratt where all the staples including pizza are done reliably well. Proprietor Patrick Zace runs a tight ship in very tight trousers; service here is exemplary. You'll wish you had a place like this where you live! 7 days all day.

216 8/Q25   **La Lanterna** 83 Hanover St · www.lalanternaedinburgh.co.uk ·
£15-25   0131 226 3090 One of several tratts sub-street level in this block. But this gets our vote. Though no longer owned by the same family, chef Toni Tuncay after 25 years still rules the roost. A straight-down-the-line Italian menu from an open kitchen at the back of their long, low, no-frills restaurant. Most of their customers are regulars and wouldn't go anywhere else. Well-chosen wines. Tue-Sat lunch & dinner.

The Best Pizza

217 8/Q25 ✓ **Origano** 236 Leith Walk · www.origano-leith.co.uk · 0131 554 6539 Just
<£15   down (and opposite) 'The Walk' from the original Origano, Messrs Fletcher, Blicharski and Ross have expanded into a bigger, more comfortable room, stoking the oven, plying the wine, working hard to make this our/your perfectly pitched pizzeria. Rather good salads and puds. Takeaway too, as is The Origano opposite at 227, their home delivery HQ (0131 555 1009). 7 days dinner only.

218 8/Q25 ✓ **Wildman Pizza Grill** Between Nicolson and Bristo Squares. Website and
<£15   phone number TBC at TGP. The newest venture of maestro restaurateur Malcolm Innes, who has **The Outsider** (154/BISTROS) and **Ting Thai Caravan** nearby (267/THAI), so when he says it will be the 'best pizza', it may just be. A state-of-the-art oven, which allows meat to cook too, so there's also an Argentinian grill thing. It has a terrace, it's cheap, has pizza delivery and opens at 8am for brunch. I think this may work! No reservations. 7 days all day.

219 8/Q25 ✓ **Soderberg** North Pavilion, 1 Lister Sq · www.soderberg.uk ·
£15-25 0131 228 1905 In the glass box nearest Laurieston Pl in the campus of blocks of apartments, offices, a hotel, etc, called Quartermile, where the Royal Infirmary once was. Soderberg is now the group name for Peter's Yard, their main branch is on the corner of Quartermile and Meadow Walk (301/TEAROOMS); but the cool Swedish artisan bakers and coffee shop expanded here in 2015. They're cooking up cool, crisp sourdough pizzas and salads with the bakery upstairs. Not your usual fillings. Scantly Scandic; tables in- and outside the glass. It's not Italian! 7 days till 7pm.

220 8/Q25 ✓ **La Favorita** 325 Leith Walk · www.vittoriagroup.co.uk · 0131 554 2430
£25-35 They say it's 'the best' and it's certainly the best delivery to your door (from Leith, Morningside, Blackhall and counting – www.lafavoritadelivered.com). Huge variety, great mozza and sound Italian sourcing. This pizza will travel (often to our office!) in a Fiat 500. Report: 210/ITALIAN. Opened 2015 Glasgow (Gibson St 0141 212 6070).

221 8/Q25 **Anima** 11 Henderson Row · www.anima-online.co.uk · 0131 558 2918 The
<£15 takeaway pizza section of the estimable fish 'n' chip shop **L'Alba D'Oro** next door (240/FISH & CHIPS). Definitely a slice above the rest. 3 sizes (including individual 7-inch) and infinite toppings to go. Not thin but crispy and crunchy. Also pasta, great wine to go, olive oils, Luca's ice cream and fresh OJ. This is no ordinary takeaway (see 348/TAKEAWAY)! Lunch Mon-Fri & dinner 7 days.

222 8/Q25 **Mamma's** 30 Grassmarket · www.mammas.co.uk · 0131 225 6464 Busy,
<£15 inexpensive American-style pizza. Some alternatives, eg nachos, but you come to mix 'n' match – haggis, calamari and BBQ sauce and 40 other toppings piled deep with quite chunky crust. Good local bottled beer selection: Barney's and Innis & Gunn. Outside tables on revamped Grassmarket. Stag and hen parties are not welcomed here (hurrah!). Proprietor Paul Duncan also has Gennaro's and the Mexican streetfood place El Toro Loco adjacent. 7 days from noon till 11pm (midnight Fri/Sat).

223 8/Q25 **Caprice 2 Go** Musselburgh · www.capricepizzeria.com · 0131 665 2991 Near
£15-25 the bridge. The number is for their takeaway joint round the corner which delivers to this eastern suburb of the city and other nearby E Lothian towns. The adjacent restaurant serves the same wood-fired pizza and the usual Italian fare. Ask them to crisp it but pizza here still lighter than most. Lunch (not Sun) & dinner.

224 8/Q25 **Nonna's Kitchen** 45 Morningside Rd · www.nonnas-kitchen.co.uk ·
£15-25 0131 466 6767 Like everything else here (201/ITALIAN), the pizzas are just so. Hard to choose, though, among a menu of myriad good things. Tue-Sun lunch & dinner.

The Best Mediterranean Restaurants

225 8/Q25 ✓✓ **Hanedan** 42 W Preston St · www.hanedan.co.uk · 0131 667 4242
£15-25 Small, friendly southside neighbourhood Turkish restaurant. Chef/owner Gursel Bahar a considerate, enthusiastic host. Hot and cold meze to share and shish/ kofte/musakka (sic) menu. Daily fish (those charcoal-grilled sardines!) and good vegetarian. Short pud and wine lists complement well. Tue-Sun lunch & dinner. .

226 8/Q25 ✓ **Serrano Manchego** 297 Leith Walk · www.serranomanchego.co.uk ·
£15-25 0131 554 0955 Between Dalmeny St and Iona Street. Airy corner 'tapas bar' with the exposed brick, hacked-out stone and bustling open kitchen look à la mode, with small dishes to share and graze on. Hams are good and the beer. A bueno addition to lower Leith Walk. 7 days all day.

227 8/Q25 ✓ **Tapa** 19 Shore Pl · www.tapaedinburgh.co.uk · 0131 476 6776 Great
   <£15   value, reasonably authentic and great value tapas. Tucked behind The Shore in
    Leith. Better and more satisfying by far than high-street tapas chains. Good vino
    and more Spanish beers than you knew existed. Gambas pil pil and the honey
    aubergine fritters are the moreish must! 7 days all day.

228 8/Q25 **Hanam's** 3 Johnston Terrace · www.hanams.com · 0131 225 1329 Near
   £15-25   top of the Royal Mile. A not too fancy Kurdish/Middle Eastern restaurant with
    authentic dishes and a terrace overlooking Victoria St below. Wide-ranging
    Kurdish, Lebanese, Moroccan and Saudi Arabian soul food. These folk have other
    restaurants, including **Pomegranate** opposite the Playhouse Theatre but this is
    the one. Good vegetarian choice. Lunch & dinner.

229 8/Q25 **Zucca** 15-17 Grindlay St · www.zuccarestaurant.co.uk · 0131 221 9323 Part
   <£15   of the Royal Lyceum theatre building. A few tables downstairs but mainly up,
    Zucca may get overlooked (except pre-theatre), but it's a reliable redoubt for light
    Mediterranean, mainly Italian food. Tue-Sat lunch & dinner. Open Sun/Mon during
    the Festival.

230 8/Q25 **Richmond Café** 52 W Richmond St · 0131 629 6998 Small southside corner
   <£15   caff with Dimitri's distinctive home-made pies and more familiar fare (bougatsas).
    Simplicity is the watchword here and on a summer's day with outside tables (and a
    view of Arthur's Seat), you could be in a suburb of Athens. Tue-Sun all day.

231 8/Q25 **Empires** 24 St Mary's St · www.empirescafe.co.uk · 0131 466 0100 Cosy,
   ATMOS   charming, chaotic, this tiny up-and-down restaurant is always an experience – pure
   £15-25   Turkish delight. Full of ceramics, rugs and all kinds of people. Usual and unusual
    meze; great coffee. Good for vegetarians. Service a bit mad but great atmos. Only 3
    small tables and 3 big ones to gather round. BYOB. Live Greek music on Sat. 7 days
    from noon. Closed Mon in winter.

The Best Seafood Restaurants

232 8/Q25
>£35

✓✓ **Ondine** 2 George IV Bridge · www.ondinerestaurant.co.uk · 0131 226 1888 By the G&V Hotel. Shiny, glass-encased, discreet destination upstairs and just off the Royal Mile. Chef/patron Roy Brett, who was with Rick Stein in Padstow, runs what's generally regarded as the best seafood restauarant in town, especially for shellfish. Impeccable sourcing, sure hands in the kitchen; they know their oysters; also steak tartare. Little vegetarian. Signature is their seafood platter. More casual crustaceans at the bar. Mon-Sat lunch & dinner, Sun noon-5pm.

233 8/Q25
£15-25

✓ **Fishers in Leith** 1 Shore · www.fishersbistros.co.uk · 0131 554 5666 In a uniquely special location at the foot of an 18th-century tower opposite Malmaison and right on the quay (though no boats come by). Seafood cooking with flair and commitment from small kitchen in boat-like surroundings; traditional Scots dishes get an imaginative twist – we follow the fish and lap up the soup. Some stools around bar and tables outside in summer (can be a windy corner). Often packed, so best book. 7 days all day.

234 8/Q25
>£35

✓ **Fishers In The City** 58 Thistle St · www.fishersbistros.co.uk · 0131 225 5109 Uptown version of Leith eaterie (above); this place works on all its levels (we're talking mezzanine). Fisher fan staples ('features') all here – the fishcakes, soup and blackboard specials; Leith menu but with an uptown edge. Excellent wine list and great service. Some vegetarian and meat (steaks a special). Bar stools for a drop-in bite. 7 days all day.

235 8/Q25
ATMOS
£15-25

✓ **Café Royal Oyster Bar** 19 W Register St · www.caferoyaledinburgh.co.uk · 0131 556 1884 On the corner between St Andrews Sq and the Apple shop at the east end of Princes St. Long-standing – and we do mean 'long' – a classic Victorian oyster bar. Decor is unchanged so the marble, dark wood, tiles and glass partition are all major reasons for coming here. Food has been up and down over the years and this is a Punch Tavern, but keep it simple from the classic seafood menu and you won't go wrong. 7 days all day. The bar through the partition is more fish 'n' chips but it's also a classic (370/UNIQUE PUBS).

236 8/Q25
£15-25

C-Shack 3 Pier Pl · www.cshack.co.uk · 0131 467 8628 Opposite Newhaven Harbour on the main road west. Small and, yes, shack-like seafood diner, quite the opposite of the warehouse-like Loch Fyne (see below) chain restaurant across the road. Here, personal attention to ceviche, curries, crab, etc, from chef/proprietor Stuart Lynch gives a more intimate, food-to-love experience, even as the traffic of life goes past. Many a Belgian beer! Lunch Thu-Sun & dinner Wed-Sun.

237 8/Q25
£15-25

The Loch Fyne Restaurant Newhaven Harbour · www. lochfyneseafoodandgrill.co.uk · 0131 559 3900 Large, lofty seafood canteen in excellent location on Edinburgh's secret harbour though somewhat removed from the Leith restaurant quarter. Outside tables have sunset potential. Exemplary outpost of the UK chain, this, the only one in Scotland, is at least a bit nearer to the original and its oysters (1343/SEAFOOD). Great room and very on the waterfront, but not cheap, mes amis, and a little patchy on delivery. Stick to fish and a crisp white and you'll be... fyne. 7 days all day.

238 8/Q25
£15-25

Mussel Inn 61-65 Rose St · www.mussel-inn.com · 0131 225 5979 Popular, populist cantina. In the heart of the city centre where food with integrity is hard to find, a long-standing seafood bistro specialising in mussels and scallops (kings and queens) which the proprietors rear/find themselves. Also catch of the day, some non-fish options and home-made puds. Mon-Thu offer of half kilo of mussels, chips or salad 'quickie' for £8. This formula could travel but the owners have wisely decided not to travel far – they're also in Glasgow (621/SEAFOOD). Mon-Thu lunch & dinner, all day Fri-Sun.

The Best Fish & Chips

239 8/Q25 ✓ **The Tailend Restaurant & Fish Bar** 14-15 Albert Pl · www.
tailendedinburgh.co.uk · 0131 555 3577 On the right-hand side of Leith Walk going down. Unpretentious caff where you can often get a table (only 10) though the menu, from starters (the whitebait, the smokie pâté!) to simple-choice puds, is all good stuff. Menu of fish du jour, battered, grilled and with a variety of sauces. Oh, and pizzas. Caff and takeaway counter cook to order, so fresh as it comes. A drop-in favourite! They're also in St Andrews (906/ST ANDREWS). They use animal fat. 7 days all day.

240 8/Q25 ✓ **L'Alba D'Oro** 7 Henderson Row · www.lalbadoro.com · 0131 557 2580
Near corner with Dundas St. Large selection of deep-fried goodies, including many vegetarian savouries. Since 1975, Filippo Crolla's chipper has been way above the ordinary – as several plaques on the wall attest (including *StB*!); the pasta/pizza counter **Anima** next door is also a winner (221/PIZZA; 348/TAKEAWAY). Luca's ice cream. Vegetable oil, though like everywhere else they do fry some meaty things in it. 7 days evenings only.

241 8/Q25 **The Deep Sea** 2 Antigua St · www.deepseaedinburgh.co.uk · 0131 557 0276
Opposite the Playhouse. Open late and often has queues but these are quickly dispatched. The haddock has to be of a certain size and is famously fresh (via Something Fishy in Broughton St nearby). Traditional menu and the deep-fried Mars Bar. Now there's also kebabs but stick to one of the most reliable fish suppers in town and feed your impending hangover (there's a pharmacy of pills alongside the Irn Bru). Open till 2am-ish (3am Fri-Sat).

242 8/Q25 **Cafe Piccante** 19 Broughton St · www.cafepiccante.com · 0131 478 7884 &
7 E Norton Pl · 0131 652 6221 It's the original that still rocks: takeaway and café with tables on the black 'n' white tiles. Near the Playhouse Theatre, this is the clubbers' chippy (occasional DJs) with unhealthy lads purveying delicious, unhealthy food to the flotsam of the Pink Triangle and club world. Including deep-fried Mars Bars (you'd need to be well out of it). Can sit in. Open till 2am (3am weekends).

The Best Vegetarian Restaurants

243 8/Q25 ✓✓ **David Bann's** 56-58 St Mary's St · www.davidbann.com ·
£15-25 — 0131 556 5888 Bottom of the street off Royal Mile – slightly off the tourist track – but always a busy restaurant and not only with non-meaters, because this is one of the best 'healthy' restaurants in the city and for vegetarian food in the UK: mood lighting, non-moody staff and no dodgy stodge. A creative take on round-the-world dishes, changing seasonally. Light meal selection; lovely tartlets and 'parcels'. Oh, and nice chips! Vegan selection, gluten-free, etc, and no ostentatious 'organics' (there are vegetarian wines), just honest-to-goodness good. David only sometimes chefs, but a great kitchen and out-front team. 7 days.

244 8/Q25 ✓✓ **Kalpna** 2-3 St Patrick Sq · www.kalpnarestaurant.com ·
£15-25 — 0131 667 9890 They say 'you do not have to eat meat to be strong and wise' and they are of course right. Maxim taken seriously in this lovely Indian restaurant in the southside for over 30 years, one of the best vegetarian menus in the UK; ever-dependable, vegetarian or not. The thali gives a good overview. The butter masala is the definitive dosa. Lovely, light and long may it prevail. 7 days lunch & dinner. See also 260/INDIAN.

245 8/Q25 ✓✓ **Henderson's** 94 Hanover St · www.hendersonsofedinburgh.co.uk ·
ATMOS — 0131 225 2131 Edinburgh's original and trailblazing basement vegetarian
<£15 self-serve café-cum-wine bar. A national treasure! Canteen seating to the left, candles and nightly live music down a few stairs to the right (pine interior is retro-perfect). Happy wee wine list and organic real ales. Those salads, hot main dishes and famous puds will go on forever. Mon-Sat all day.
Farm Shop upstairs with a deli and takeaway and, round the corner in Thistle St, The Bistro (see below) for crêpes, nutburgers. There is also a self-service outpost: Henderson's @ St John's, underneath St John's church, at the Lothian Rd corner of Princes St. And remember: Henderson's (organic) oatcakes are *the* best.

246 8/Q25 ✓ **Henderson's Bistro** 25c Thistle St · www.hendersonsofedinburgh.co.
£15-25 — uk · 0131 225 2605 Adjacent to the Deli and Restaurant (see above). In 2015, the Bistro went vegan – Edinburgh's first proper go at dairy-free. Non-purists should not be put off – the food here is delicious and inventive (despite what the *Guardian* said), as well as nutritious, guilt-free and (some) gluten-free. A good burger and lovely creamless puds. 7 days from noon.

247 8/Q25 ✓ **The Mosque Kitchens** There are two Mosque Kitchens; the one on the
ATMOS — original site (no website or phone), through an archway in W Nicolson
<£15 St is the totally stripped-back streetfood version, with some seats upstairs behind the Mosque and a tented section in the lane. You order in the kitchen and can eat for under a fiver. The more substantial 31-33 Nicolson Sq · www.mosquekitchen.com · 0131 667 4035 on a prominent corner is a big, bright canteen with various vegetarian (but also lamb and chicken) curries and naans. Self-serve with paper plates and also incredibly cheap. Downstairs buffet at weekends with plates and cutlery for £10. No frills authentic food, though not much atmos. 7 days. Closed for Friday prayers 12.50-1.50pm.

✓✓✓ **Restaurant Martin Wishart** 54 Shore · www.martin-wishart.
co.uk · 0131 553 3557 Not, of course, a vegetarian restaurant, but does have a vegetarian menu. Food, ingredients and presentation are taken seriously here, so this is where to go for *the best* vegetarian food in Scotland. Report: 133/FINE DINING.

✓✓ **The Atelier** Excellent value bistro with great vegetarian choice. Report: 146/BISTROS.

The Best Scottish Restaurants

248 8/Q25 ✓ **The Scottish Café & Restaurant** The Mound · www.
L thescottishcafeandrestaurant.com · 0131 225 1550 Below and very much
£15-25 part of the National Gallery. Victor and Carina (of the **Contini** group 207/ITALIAN)
have cast their magic dining dust over the hard-to-get-right gallery caff genre and
now this comfort zone of great Scottish cooking is a destination in itself. You enter
from Princes St Gardens which the windows overlook (heart of Christmas in
winter); you walk past their cute herb garden and map of their Scottish suppliers.
Cullen skink, mac cheese, Victoria sponge: your faves are all here! 7 days daytime
only (till 7pm Thu). Sun from 10am (340/SUNDAY BRUNCH).

249 8/Q25 ✓ **The Grain Store** 30 Victoria St · www.grainstore-restaurant.co.uk ·
ATMOS 0131 225 7635 For an impressive 25 years this revered bistro in an interesting
£25-35 street near the Royal Mile has regulars and discerning tourists climbing the stairs
for a great value grazing lunch menu or innovative à la carte in the candlelit night.
A laid-back, first-floor eaterie in a welcoming stone-walled labyrinth. Good for
groups. Perhaps more Modern British than simply Scottish. Chef/proprietor Carlo
Coxon and the team are serious about quality. Hunting/shooting/fishing
ingredients like roe deer and woodcock, along with your proper oysters. Mon-Sat
lunch & dinner 7 days.

250 8/Q25 **Whiskirooms** 4-7 N Bank St · www.whiskirooms.co.uk · 0131 225 7224 Just
£15-25 off the Royal Mile at the top of the Mound. All-round homage to the national drink
aimed at both passers-by and aficionados, but all – the shop (0131 225 1532, open
daytime only), the bar and the restaurant – rather sympathetically done. Stone,
wood and whisky in the glass (and throughout the menu, eg Ardbeg sauce with
your steak). They're also at 119 High St (www.whiskibar.co.uk) down the hill with
Whiski Bar & Restaurant, their pub bang on the money and the Mile.

 The Witchery Top restaurant that really couldn't be anywhere else but
Scotland. Report: 140/FINE DINING.

The Best Mexican Restaurants

251 8/Q25 ✓ **El Cartel** 64 Thistle St · www.elcartelmexicana.co.uk · 0131 226 7171
£15-25 Tiny cantina in mid-Thistle St proclaiming its street and Mexicana cred.
Endorsed by esteemed food critic Joanna Blythman who gave it 9/10, extolling the
virtue of their authentic 'pliant' tortillas and the taqueria sauce, ceviche, and just
about everything. Service rapido so no hanging about but gorge on the small plates
as they come, trying not to overeat or heat. No booking. Owned by the Bon Vivant
folk across the street (180/GASTROPUBS). 7 days all day.

252 8/Q25 ✓ **Viva Mexico** Anchor Close, Cockburn St · www.viva-mexico.co.uk ·
£15-25 0131 226 5145 Since 1984 the pre-eminent Mexican bistro in town. Judy
Gonzalez's menu still innovates, although all the expected dishes are here.
Genuine originals, famously good calamares and fajitas; lovely salad sides. Lots of
seafood. Reliable venue for those times when nothing else fits the mood but
proper fajitas and limey lager. 2 floors; nice atmos even downstairs. Mon-Sat lunch
& dinner 7 days.

253 8/Q25 ✓ **The Basement** 10a-12a Broughton St · www.basement-bar-edinburgh.
£15-25　　co.uk · 0131 557 0097　Established long before every second doorway in Broughton St led to a café or bar, this subterranean stalwart was rebooted in 2012. Tequila central (35 varieties) and late-night revelries but a surprisingly imaginative sound and spicy Mexican menu in restaurant section and bar. The *best* guacamole mixed at your table Look no further for your enchilada! 7 days all day.

254 8/Q25 ✓ **Mirós Cantina Mexicana** 184 Rose St · www.miroscantinamexicana.
<£15　　com · 0131 225 4376　In the western block of a street of bars and indifferent dining, a cute, usually crowded Mexican bistro which, though I've never been, seems a lot like a caff down Mexico way. Seafood stew and big-portion comfort food. 7 days all day.

The Best Japanese Restaurants

255 8/Q25 ✓✓ **Kanpai** 8-10 Grindlay St · www.kanpaisushi.co.uk · 0131 228 1602
£15-25　　Along from the Lyceum Theatre. Probably the smartest Japanese restaurant in town; staff flow, food arrives. Open kitchen where the magic happens. Numerous nigiri; the dragon rolls. Good sake list (and a Hakushu malt). Tue-Sun lunch & dinner.

256 8/Q25 ✓ **Bonsai** (the original) 46 W Richmond St · www.bonsaibarbistro.co.uk ·
£15-25　　0131 668 3847 & 14 Broughton St · 0131 557 5093　The first is on a discreet street in the southside, a café/bistro (actually feels like a Japanese pub) where Andrew and Noriko Ramage show a deft hand in the kitchen. Unlike the sushi crop that has sprung up in Edinburgh (and everywhere), this is at least Japanese owned, so the freshly made sushi/yakitori and teppanyaki are the real McCoy. No conveyor belt in sight, just superb value in downbeat neighbourhood café setting. Broughton St (near the top) is a buzzier Bonsai but has a similar menu and approach. The Bento boxes for under a tenner are a winner. And the sake sorbet. Both 7 days from noon.

257 8/P25 ✓ **Sushiya** 19 Dalry Rd · www.sushiya.co.uk · 0131 313 3222　100m from
£15-25　　Haymarket station. Smart sushi bar in the West End, little brother of Kanpai (above). Surprisingly extensive menu, paper-thin dumplings; all delicious. More drop-in than night out but this place works for aficionados as well as newbies. Tue-Sun lunch & dinner.

258 8/Q25 **Harajuku Kitchen** 10 Gillespie Pl · www.harajukukitchen.co.uk ·
£15-25　　0131 281 0526　On the main road between Tollcross and Bruntsfield opposite the Church. Kaori Simpson's delightfully simple, authentic diner with a lengthy menu of all the usuals and many dishes that are not: dumplings, curries, salads with the sushis, rolls and miso. Dinner only Tue-Thu, all day Fri-Sun.

259 8/Q25 **Hakataya** 120-122 Rose St S Lane · 0131 629 3320　Just off Rose St in western
£15-25　　section. Small, unassuming Japanese kitchen: sushi, sashimi and loadsa noodles. Asahi/Sapporo beers and sakes. Bento boxes and takeaway. Sun-Fri lunch & all day Sat.

260 8/Q25 ✓✓ **Kalpna** 2-3 St Patrick Sq · www.kalpnarestaurant.com ·
£15-25   0131 667 9890   The original Edinburgh Indian veggie restaurant and still very much the business. Favourites remain on the Gujarati menu and the thalis are famous, but also unique dishes and dosas to die for. Report: 244/VEGETARIAN.

261 8/Q25 ✓✓ **Mother India Café** 3 Infirmary St · www.motherindia.co.uk ·
£15-25   0131 524 9801   Off S Bridge. That rare thing: a restaurant successfully transferred from Glasgow (572/INDIAN), this the eastern outpost in Monir Mohammed's Indian empire. Has all the things that made it work in Glasgow's West End: neighbourhood feel, great value, small tapas-like dishes to share (40 to choose from), some specials; great service. We always go back to Mum. Mon-Thu lunch dinner, all day Fri-Sun.

262 8/P25 ✓ **Indian Cavalry Club** 22 Coates Crescent · www.indiancavalryclub.co.uk ·
£15-25   0131 220 0138   Off the main Glasgow road between Haymarket and Princes St. For 30 years Shahid Chowdry's Cavalry Club has unobtrusively been serving some of the best and most conscientiously prepared northern and southern Indian food in the city. It's more upmarket than most on this page: with smart waiters and linen cloths, the CC has always attracted the West End suits, especially at lunchtime. Good buzz here and food always pukka, served in small copper tureens: confident Indian cooking. Good vegetarian. An unlikely carry-out place, but they do, and it's one of the best to your door. 7 days lunch & dinner.

263 8/Q25 ✓ **Kebab Mahal** 7 Nicolson Sq · www.kebab-mahal.co.uk · 0131 667 5214
<£15   Near Edinburgh University and Festival Theatre. Since 1979, Zahid Khan's slightly misnamed Indian diner (kebabs figure only slightly on a mainly curry menu) has been a word-of-mouth winner. As a no-frills Indo-Pak halal café it attracts Asian families, as well as students and others who long for Asia. Great takeaway selection of pakoras, samosas, etc. One of Edinburgh's most cosmopolitan restaurants. It's open late! 7 days all day. Prayers on Fri (1-2pm). A no-alcohol zone.

264 8/Q25 **Tanjore** 6-8 Clerk St · www.tanjore.co.uk · 0131 478 6518   In southside near
<£15   Queens Hall. Unobtrusive South Indian restaurant with loyal following for Mrs Boon Ganeshram's inexpensive, authentic and distinctive cuisine, with lighter curries and lovely breads (big dosas). BYOB with no corkage. All easy on the pocket and digestion. Good vegetarian choice. 7 days lunch & dinner.

265 8/Q25 **Khushi's** 10 Antigua St · www.khushis.com · 0131 558 1947   In the row of
£15-25   restaurants opposite the Playhouse Theatre and feeding its punters. Khushi's through its various locations is the city's longest established Indian diner. There have been a few, now only this one. Many are its loyal clientele. Personally, I'm not an avid fan after recent disappointing visits, but it's regularly crammed, so it's lively and it continues to curry favour. BYOB with no corkage is a big attraction. 7 days all day.

10 To 10 In Delhi   Chai shop. Report: 318/CAFFS.
Punjabi Junction   Report: 320/CAFFS.

The Best Thai & Asian Restaurants

266 8/Q25 ✓✓ **Dusit** 49 Thistle St · www.dusit.co.uk · 0131 220 6846 In the
£25-35   continuing proliferation of Thai restaurants in Edinburgh, this one still
gets the gold orchid. Elegant though a little cramped interior, excellent service and
food that's good in any language but just happens to be exquisite Thai cuisine.
Tantalising combinations with atypical, i.e. Scottish ingredients; strong signature
dishes with charming names: Two Brothers, A Loving Couple, Fleeing Fish! Decent
wine list. 7 days lunch & dinner.

267 8/Q25 ✓✓ **Ting Thai Caravan** 8 Teviot Pl · 0131 225 9801 Buzzing like Bangkok, a
NO C/CARDS   Thai streetfood café. Boxes and bowls at long tables, rice noodle dishes
<£15 and curries. At busy times you might queue for half an hour (but you do; no
reservations). Food comes as it's ready; snappy, friendly service. It's Thai without
the fat! Alcohol choice similarly stripped down. You're back on Koh Phangan many
moons ago! 7 days all day from 11.30am. Cash only.

268 8/Q25 ✓ **Passorn** 23 Brougham Pl · www.passornthai.com · 0131 229 1537
£15-25   Unpretentious, innovative Thai bistro in Tollcross. Cindy Sirapassorn's
enthusiasm and creativity evident in every mouthful (and to Michelin – it has a
Bib). Great tempuras, massaman & panang curries. Tue-Sat lunch & dinner 7 days.
Passorn Brasserie (0131 225 1430, 97 Hanover St). Larger, more downtown
version opened late 2015 attesting to popularity and Thai cooking cred. Perhaps
pricey, but methinks justified.

269 8/Q25 ✓ **Nanyang Restaurant** 3-5 Lister Sq · www.nanyangrestaurant.com ·
£15-25   0131 629 1797 In the middle of the Quartermile (the old Royal Infirmary)
development, on a recently created square with other restaurants. Cold as glass,
not like Edinburgh, but not unlike Singapore; this is the best Asian fusion
restaurant in town. A rich, seductive menu to roam through, with Thai, Malay,
Chinese influences. A ripping rendang! 7 days lunch & dinner.

270 8/Q25 ✓ **Thai Lemongrass** 40-41 Bruntsfield Pl · www.thailemongrass.net ·
£15-25   0131 229 2225 Smart but intimate, not too tiddly Thai eaterie by the people
who have the estimable **Jasmine** (275/CHINESE) and a few other Thais to boot. This
one has a nice, solid, woody ambience, charming waitresses (Thai and Chinese)
and food that's well loved by traditional Thai aficionados. Can BYOB (hefty £7
corkage) though has good wine list. Mon-Thu lunch & dinner, all day Fri-Sun.

271 8/Q25 **Phuket Pavilion** 8 Union St · www.phuket-pavilion.co.uk · 0131 556 4323
£15-25 Near the Playhouse Theatre and Omni Cinemaplex. When other restaurants
in this busy area are full, you can often get a table at Bill Parkinson's roomy,
unpretentious Thai place that just never lets you down. Decor nothing to write
home from Phuket about but friendly Thai staff and just the right sprinkle of holy
basil. 7 days dinner only.

272 8/P25 **Vietnam House** 3 Grove St · www.vietnamhouse.co.uk · 0131 228 3383 This
<£15 tiny, minimalist but charming Vietnamese café is a long way from its 'parent' in
Saigon but is delightful in every way from proprietor Jodie Nguyen, and its pictured
menu featuring phos (pronounced fuh), rice-noodle soups, through its single sticky
rice-cake dessert to a small bill at the end. Go west for this corner of the East. Can
BYOB (£1.50). 7 days dinner only.

The Best Chinese Restaurants

273 8/Q25 ✓ **Karen's Unicorn** 8b Abercromby Pl · www.karensunicorn.com ·
£15-25   0131 556 6333 On a very New Town crossroads, a decades-established, fairly
traditional Cantonese restaurant in three calm, grey-toned dining rooms that
nevertheless bustle with loyal customers and many waiters. Decent wine selection,
predictable but well-presented menu. Tue-Sun lunch & dinner. Also in St Stephen
St (closed Tue).

274 8/P25 ✓ **Chop Chop** 248 Morrison St · www.chop-chop.co.uk · 0131 221 1155
ATMOS   Near Haymarket station. Authenticity and simplicity are the watchwords in
<£15 Madame Wang's Chinese diners (the other in Glasgow). Stripped down and bright,
and easy on the eye and pocket. Company makes dumplings wholesale and
supplies Sainsbury's so they're de rigueur here; there's a vast selection, as with
everything else. All come in small dishes when ready. It's a sharing, daring,
dumpling experience; full of people on the go as in China. Note though that much
as we love it, there are not so many Chinese people in the room. 7 days lunch &
dinner.

275 8/Q25 ✓ **Jasmine** 32-34 Grindlay St · www.jasminechinese.co.uk · 0131 229 5757
£15-25   Opposite Lyceum Theatre. Long-established restaurant with big following and
the only Chinese restaurant of the Chinese owners of the locally owned Thai chain
(Thai Lemongrass, above, and the one next door in Grindlay St). Pre- and
post-theatre menus and good service to match (though it can be brusque). Seafood
a speciality (Cantonese style). May need to book or queue in tiny doorway. Some
memorable dishes await. Mon-Thu lunch & dinner, all day Fri-Sun.

276 8/Q25 ✓ **Edinburgh Rendezvous** 10a Queensferry St · www.
£15-25   edinburghrendezvous.co.uk · 0131 225 2023 An upstairs restaurant you
could walk past for years, but look up – this is one of the city's best and longest
serving: from 1956! Curiously calm and aesthetic here; old style that's become
contemporary. All Cantonese cooking credentials in place. Lunch & dinner
Mon-Sat, Sun dinner only. LO 10pm.

277 8/Q25 **Loon Fung** 2 Warriston Pl · www.loonfungedinburgh.co.uk · 0131 556 1781
£15-25 This place has been a destination diner since 1972. Famous lemon chicken and
crispy duck signature dishes in a traditional neighbourhood restaurant specialising
in Cantonese food. Good dim sum. Mon-Thu from noon, weekends from 2pm.

278 8/Q25 **Kweilin** 19-21 Dundas St · www.kweilin.net · 0131 557 1875 After over
£25-35 25 years this is still a destination for imaginative Cantonese cooking (and other
regions). Good seafood and genuine dim sum in pleasant though uninspired New
Town setting. But this is a more genteel old China. Lunch Tue-Sat & dinner 7 days.

The Best Burgers & Steaks

279 8/P25
ATMOS
>£35
£25-35
✓✓ **Champany Inn** nr Linlithgow · www.champany.com · 01506 834532 On A904, Linlithgow to S Queensferry road (3km Linlithgow) near M9 at junction 3. Accolade-laden restaurant (and 'Chop and Ale House') different from others below because it's out of town (and out of some pockets). Superbly surf 'n' turf. Live lobsters. The best Aberdeen Angus beef hung 3 weeks and butchered on premises. Good service, huge helpings (Americans may feel at home). Top wine list (and wine cellar shop). The Chop House also has great home-made sausages. C&A: 7 days. Restaurant: closed Sun. Rooms adjacent (128/HOTELS OUTSIDE TOWN).

280 8/Q25
>£35
✓✓ **Leith Chop House** 102 Constitution St · www.leithchophouse.co.uk · 0131 629 1919 On the road to Leith. Arrived late 2015, a great addition to eating out in the restaurant quarter though a bit offshore. Messrs Fraser and Spink have created a smart, very à point, always buzzing bar and eaterie, in which to celebrate or savour steak. The meat is properly hung in the cabinet. All is explained and comes with sides and trimmings. By no means only steak on the menu (fish & burgers), but it is superlative here. 8 cask ales on the bar. 7 days lunch & dinner.

281 8/Q25
£15-25
✓ **Bells Diner** 7 St Stephen St · 0131 225 8116 Edinburgh's small but celebrated burger joint, the antithesis of the posh nosh. No seasonal/locally sourced/slow food or organic nonsense here. Nothing has changed in 35 years except the annual paint job and (with an unusually low turnover) the gorgeous staff. Some people go to Bells *every* week in life and why? For perfect burgers, steaks, shakes and coincidentally, one of the best veggie (nut) burgers in town. Bill ain't running the shop anymore but his presence still looms... well, large! 7 days.

282 8/Q25
DF
£15-25
✓ **The Holyrood 9A** 9A Holyrood Rd · www.theholyrood.co.uk · 0131 556 5044 Along from the Cowgate and round the corner at the bottom of St Mary's Street. Quite simply some of the best burgers and the best artisan draught beer selection in town, in hugely popular if slightly out-of-the-way location. 15 kinds of burger to choose from, some starters and calorific puds. All good. 7 days all day. Report: 178/GASTROPUBS.

283 8/Q25
£15-25
Smoke Stack 53-55 Broughton St · www.smokestack.org.uk · 0131 556 6032 The Smoke Stack has long been an E Village staple. Reliable, good value and friendly service. Carnivores will come here forever and dig into burgers no matter how many other buns there are on this block. Lunch Mon-Sat & dinner 7 days.

284 8/Q25
£15-25
Red Squirrel 21 Lothian Rd · www.redsquirreledinburgh.co.uk · 0131 229 9933 A perhaps surprisingly good main street bar/diner on traffic-cluttered Lothian Rd which has only recently been thought of for food. So it's good that this mainly burger place by the people who brought us Holyrood 9A (above) has opened and, in keeping with its 'West End' location, it's handily open late for theatre-goers. The burgers, the beers and the service are great. 7 days all day from 9am.

285 8/Q25
<£15
Burger Meats Bun 1 Forth St · www.burger-meats-bun.co.uk · 0131 556 7023 A leading example of the new ('14/15) gastroburger explosion: the shiny brioche, paper trays and utility tin dishes for sides. Straight up, simple menu of burgers, chick wings and a 'nae meat' option. No booking, often very busy. Tue-Sun from noon.

286 8/Q25
£25-35
Kyloe 1-3 Rutland St · www.kyloerestaurant.com · 0131 229 3402 At the corner of the west end of Princes St by the Caledonian Hotel. Prominent position with big upstairs Edinburgh watching windows for this steak joint from Aberdeen, with its Aberdeen Angus meat rack an homage to the cow. Other dishes do figure (smoked eels, Loch Etive mussels) but it's really meat we come to eat. They do know their cuts. Good wine rack too.

Kid-Friendly Places

287 8/P25 ✓ **Luca's** 16 Morningside Rd · www.s-luca.co.uk · 0131 446 0233 The
£15-25 ice-cream kings (1445/ICE CREAM) from Musselburgh brought this modern ice creamery and café to 'Holy Corner' where kids with dads will enjoy their spag and their sundae Sundays. Big cups of capp. Crowded and clamouring upstairs, especially at weekends. Daytime snacks and family evening meals. Food not fab but gorgeous ice cream at all times. BYOB. 7 days all day.

288 8/Q25 ✓ **Reds** 254 Portobello High St · www.reds4families.com · 0131 669 5558 In main street, along from the shops, a purposefully kid-friendly café (Derek and Louise have 4 kids themselves). A camera projects the rear playing/climbing area to a plasma screen in front. Kids get their portions from the adult menu, which is freshly and conscientiously prepared, so a no-nugget zone. 7 days.

289 8/Q25 ✓ **The Beach House** Portobello · www.thebeachhousecafe.co.uk · 0131 657 2636 In the middle of the Prom, a shelter from the storm and those searing hot days on the beach and confirming 'Porty's' credentials as one of the best parts of town to bring, or bring up, kids. Simple and ethical sustenance for buggy-pushing parents and their bairns. 7 days daytime only.

290 8/Q25 ✓ **Joseph Pearce's** 23 Elm Row · www.bodabar.com · 0131 556 4140 Leith Walk below London St. Because they've thought of everything that a vibrant and vital pub should (363/UNIQUE PUBS), they've also thought about the kids of their living-the-life clients. Bar but also a delightfully informal café-restaurant. Kids are made welcome till 5pm. And kept amused!

291 8/Q25 ✓ **Vittoria** 113 Brunswick St · www.vittoriagroup.co.uk · 0131 556 6171 Excellent Italian all-rounder that can seat 200 people, including outside on the pavement on a people-watching corner. Kids eat for £1 which is donated to a kids' charity (under 12s till 5.30pm only). And they get a balloon and crayons and stuff. Now that's friendly. Report: 212/TRATTS.

292 8/Q25 ✓ **Café Tartine** 72 Commercial St · www.cafetartine.co.uk ·
DF 0131 554 2588 In 'restaurant row' of Leith, facing the Scottish Office off Dock
£15-25 Place, Michael Graham and Joanne Ramsay's spacious 'French café wine bar' buzzing from breakfast to night. Crêpes, tartines, quite cheffy specials and wine. Very family and dog friendly, especially in the loungy conservatory. 7 days.

293 8/P25 ✓ **The Scran and Scallie** 1 Comely Bank Rd · www.scranandscallie.com · 0131 332 6281 At the north end of Stockbridge's main street. Top gastropub that welcomes, feeds and entertains kids. Report: 171/GASTROPUBS.

294 8/R25 ✓ **Goblin Ha' Hotel** Gifford · www.goblinha.com · 01620 810244 35km
£15-25 from town in neat E Lothian village. A restaurant with (6) rooms. Good woodland walking (455/WALKS). The garden, busy in summer, is nice for kids and there's pizza. 7 days lunch & dinner.

295 8/P25 **The Bridge Inn** Ratho · www.bridgeinn.com · 0131 333 1320 16km W of
DF centre via A71, turning right opposite Dalmahoy Golf Club. Waterside pub by canal
£25-35 basin with walks and barge watching which can be a thrill for kids; occasional canal cruises (must book). Proper food for kids and grown-ups. 7 days.

Skylark Report: 321/CAFFS.

The Best Coffee

296 8/Q25 ✓✓ **Artisan Roast** 57 Broughton St · www.artisanroast.co.uk ·
07858 884756 A honeypot/coffeepot for Broughton St society and
possibly the best coffee in town. Pioneers of the stand-up service – the guy stands
by the machine, there's no counter. Most of the very laid-back seating is in the
back room, like someone's pad (not so cool for private meets). 2 blends: the earthy
Janszoon and the lighter Primavera have different proportions of Brazilian and
Sumatran beans. No paninis in sight, though there is cake. 7 days. Branch in
Glasgow, see 634/COFFEE.

297 8/Q25 ✓ **Brew Lab** 6-8 S College St · www.brewlabcoffee.co.uk · 0131 662 8963
In a quiet street between 'The Bridges' and the university, they brew. Certainly
a lot of calculation and refinement has gone into it in the three designer-distressed
rooms where we sample and measure their caffeinated concoctions. Soup by
Union of Genius nearby, cakes by Lovecrumbs: it's a good formula (and a great
coffee, by the way). 7 days daytime only.

298 8/Q25 ✓ **Fortitude** 3C York Pl · www.fortitudecoffee.com · 0131 557 3063 A few
steps up where the tram turns along from the National Portrait Gallery. Matt
Carroll's cool little coffee stop with just the right ingredients: Lovecrumbs' cakes,
proper strombolis and a cuppa coffee many consider tops, though he does change
his brews. Guest espressos. Mon-Sat daytime only.

299 8/P25 **The Caffeine Drip** 10 Melville Pl · www.thecaffeinedrip.com ·
0131 538 9579 The extension of Queensferry St in the West End. Kind of quirky
three-level caff through a door on busy road. Up to the tiny lounge, down to the
basement bar and counter. Christopher Wedge brings a South African twist to the
cosmo snack menu which includes breakfast tortillas, lovely germagrain bread, and
harissa & sweet potato salad washed down with the drip of Matthew Algie coffee.
Folk swarm to this discreet doorway. 7 days daytime only.

The Best Tearooms

300 8/Q25 ✓✓ **Falko Konditorei** 185 Bruntsfield Pl · www.falko.co.uk ·
ATMOS   0131 656 0763 End of Bruntsfield, beginning of Morningside, an exquisite
teashop – some would say the Morningside matrons are too well served – but Falko
(who are also in Gullane 1377/TEAROOMS) is baking at its best (from the
'Meisterhand'). Well known for their artisan bread (at the Farmers' Market); the
tortes are practically irresistible (to me, anyway). Great tea list; soup at lunchtime.
Wed-Sun daytime only.

301 8/Q25 ✓✓ **Peter's Yard** 27 Simpson Loan · www.petersyard.com ·
0131 228 5876 & 3 Deanhaugh St · 0131 332 2901 The first on Middle
Meadow Walk, the pedestrian path through the Meadows, part of the new
Quartermile project that was once the Edinburgh Royal Infirmary. Light, airy
bakery/deli/café that feels not like Edinburgh. Soup, salads, artisan bread and
non-cream-laden cakes: big on baking. It gets very busy and the ordering system is
a bit annoying, but... you wait! Nice outside people-watching patio. Same
ambience in Stockbridge: the breads, bakery and other classy and branded stuff
(those crispbreads!). A new takeaway (a few tables) opened 2015 in Queensferry St:
see **Soderberg** (219/PIZZA). There's no stopping these Swedes; the crispbreads are
everywhere! Both 7 days daytime only.

302 8/Q25 ✓ **Lovecrumbs** 155 W Port · www.lovecrumbs.co.uk · 0131 629 0626 In what has endearingly been dubbed the 'Pubic Triangle' – there's a lap-dancing bar opposite. Whilst many on this page may be genteel Edinburgh tearooms, Lovecrumb positively hums. Boho chic, cables over the ceiling, students from the Art School nearby scoffing enormous numbers of their enormous cakes. No hot food, just tea & scones and chat. 7 days daytime only.
Twelve Triangles 90 Brunswick St · www.twelvetriangles.co.uk · 0131 629 4664 Just off Leith Walk, the lower-key, more savoury version near the Lovecrumbs bakery, with daily bread, doughnuts and probably Edinburgh's best brioche. Cosy and friendly. 7 days.

303 8/P25 ✓ **Gallery of Modern Art (Modern One) Café** Belford Rd · www. nationalgalleries.org · 0131 624 6200 Unbeatable on a fine day when you can sit out on the patio on the lawn, with sculptures around (430/ATTRACTIONS), have some wine and a plate of Scottish cheese and oatcakes. Hot dishes are good – always 2 soups, meat/fish and vegetarian baked potatoes. Cakes and stuff! Lunch dishes usually gone by 2.30pm. **Café Newton** at Modern Two (431/ATTRACTIONS) across the main road and the gardens is a smaller, more interior café by the same people (Heritage Portfolio much less corporate catering than you might expect). Soup, sandwiches and 2 hot lunch dishes. Paolozzi's *Vulcan* towers above. Both 7 days daytime only.

304 8/P25 ✓ **Henri** 48 Raeburn Pl · www.henriofedinburgh.co.uk · 0131 332 8963 In the midst of main street, a deli with wine bar/café behind that's just perfect for foodie Stockbridge. Soup with sourdough, scrumptious salads, charcuterie and unusual cheeses. Even the floor looks good! All to takeaway. 7 days daytime (open late on Fri).

305 8/Q25 ✓ **Colonnades @ The Signet Library** Parliament Sq · www. thesignetlibrary.co.uk/colonnades · 0131 226 1064 On the Royal Mile behind the Cathedral. The classiest tearoom in town in the august, lofty ambience of a classic Georgian library – real books, real colonnades – you are at the heart of Edinburgh: World Heritage site. Daytime only for soup and light snacks and most notably for afternoon tea which can be booked. The corporate hospitality aspect (by Heritage Portfolio) easily tholed in these surroundings. Sun-Fri daytime only.

306 8/Q25 ✓ **Porto And Fi** 47 Newhaven Main St · www.portofi.com · 0131 551 1900 On the corner of Craighall Rd, Trinity, set back from the busy shoreline road. Light, just right room, where Fi's home cooking and baking hits the spot for the ladies (and others) who lunch. Orkney ice cream, Black Isle ales. Great cakes and sometimes the sunset over there. 7 days.

307 8/Q25 ✓ **Mimi's** 63 Shore · www.mimisbakehouse.com · 0131 555 5908 They call it a bakehouse and they do with a big selection of home-baked goodies coming out of their small kitchen and into their sprawling, multi-chambered tearooms always packed with cake eaters. 'Award-winning' and from mini to massive, who would think there are so many folk not watching their figures as they work through the tiers. Great for kids and birthdays. Open breakfast till teatime, and though the meals are perhaps less successful than the bakes, at last foodie Leith has a cupcake to call its own. **Mimi's Picnic Parlour** has more recently arrived on the Royal Mile at 250 Canongate (0131 556 6632).

308 8/Q25 ✓ **Fruitmarket Café** 45 Market St · www.fruitmarket.co.uk · 0131 226 1843 Attached to the Fruitmarket Gallery, a cool, spacious place for coffee pastries or a light lunch. Big salads, home cooking, deli plates and 2/3 daily specials. It attracts a mix of tourists, art-baggers and Edinburgers who meet and know that this is where to hang out as well as eat. The rest of the world goes by outside those big windows! 7 days daytime only.

309 8/Q25 ✓ **G&T (Glass & Thompson)** 2 Dundas St · 0131 557 0909 An original and definitive New Town coffee shop and deli for foodies before 'foodies' existed. Many 'ladies who latte', a phrase coined by Alexander McCall Smith, whom you'd expect to see with a notepad in a corner seat. Great antipasti, soups, salads, sandwiches to go; Very fine cakes, non-creamy and some gluten-free, and Au Gourmand artisan breads. Food 7 days daytime only.

310 8/Q25 ✓ **Clarinda's** 69 Canongate · www.clarindastearoom.co.uk · 0131 557 1888 At the bottom of the Royal Mile near Holyrood Palace and the Parliament building. Small but with total tearoom integrity. Hot dishes and snacks worth the sit-down stop on the tourist trail and some of the best home baking in town. Inexpensive; run by good Edinburgh folk (Maggie Hetherington and team) who work that tiny kitchen. Takeaways possible. Outside tables overlook the garden. 7 days daytime only. For nearly 40 years, the best apple pie in town. Believe it! No debit/credit cards.

311 8/Q25 ✓ **The Pantry** 1-2 N W Circus Pl · www.thepantryedinburgh.co.uk · 0131 629 0206 On the road to Stockbridge. Laid-back, conscientious café-dining with home-made hot food and proper baking. A hang-out and a I'm-writing-a-book kind of place! Sun-Tue daytime only, open till 9pm Wed-Sat.

312 8/Q25 **The Elephant House** 21 George IV Bridge · www.elephanthouse.biz · 0131 220 5355 Near libraries and Edinburgh University, a rather self-conscious but elephantine, i.e. large, and well-run coffee shop with light snacks and big choice. If there's a queue it's because J.K. Rowling (1912/LITERARY PLACES) once sat here: they say 'the birthplace of Harry Potter'; they make a lot of their literary connections. Counter during day, waitress service evenings. Cakes/pastries are bought in but can be taken out. View of graveyard and castle to dream away a student life in Edinburgh. 7 days all day.

313 8/P25 **Botanic Gardens** www.rbge.org.uk There are 3 coffee-shop options in these famous and fabulous gardens (427/ATTRACTIONS). Firstly, the small snack-bar café at the Inverleith Rd entrance. Then the Terrace by 'The House' (where there are regular exhibitions; enter by Arboretum Place): this self-service food operation though corporate ain't bad but the outside tables and view of the city are why we come here (and the cheeky, not-red squirrels!). And there's the Gateway Restaurant atop the shop in the landmark John Muir Gateway on Arboretum Place. Waited service for breakfast, lunch and afternoon tea. 7 days daytime only. The gardens are always to love!

The Best Caffs

Also see Best Takeaway Places, p. 70.

314 8/Q25 ✓ **The Broughton Deli** 7 Barony St · 0131 558 7111 Just round the corner from Broughton St. Takeaway counter and some deli items (great bread & free-range eggs), but mostly frequented as a caff and takeaway (347/TAKEAWAY). Soups, tarts, hot dishes and imaginative salads. Their cheese scone is a staple of my diet! My local lunchbox. Open for early supper till 6/7pm. BYOB (no corkage).

315 8/Q25 ✓ **Contini Caffe (Royal Mile Café)** 365 Castlehill · www.contini.com · 0131 225 1550 At the very top of the Royal Mile by the Castle gateway. This, the drop-in café of a 3-storey Scottish/Italian food, well, story by Victor and Carina Contini, Edinburgh's esteemed restaurateurs. The actual restaurant above (207/ITALIAN) is probably the most Scottish element, the caffe here and gelateria below are full of delicious ice cream and more familiar Italian fare (though the pasta is a maccy cheese). Light dishes from breakfast. 7 days. Gelateria noon-4pm.

316 8/Q25 ✓ **The Edinburgh Larder** 15 Blackfriars St · www.edinburghlarder.co.uk · 0131 556 6922 Off the middle part of the Royal Mile. Deli, caff and takeaway food stop. Certainly more than a soup 'n' sandwich place, with home-made specials and a foodie approach. A wee Scottish gem, probably missed by the tourists around here who are looking for one. Its sister restaurant, Edinburgh Larder Bistro, is similarly good (169/BISTROS). 7 days daytime (338/SUNDAY BRUNCH).

317 8/Q25 ✓ **Zulu Lounge** 366 Morningside Rd · www.thezululounge.com · 0131 466 8337 Tiny, tucked-away South African tea shack run by Natalie & Anthony Dodson who took over from the enterprising Wedges. Soups, sandwiches, including Boerewors (SA sausages) sandwiches, great home-made muffins. Miele bread and biltong and their signature espresso made from red Rooibos tea. What they produce from that miniscule kitchen is kinda miraculous. 7 days daytime only.

318 8/Q25 ✓ **10 To 10 In Delhi** 67 Nicolson St · www.10to10indelhi.co.uk · 07536 757770/0131 510 4746 Near Nicolson Sq and university. A mini maharajah's tent in the southside, homage to Bollywood (movies on TV) and sweet memories of India. Chai and Pekoe teas (including Masala tea), soups and chef Alieu's curries and daal. Chilled vibe, nice people. A no-alcohol zone. 7 days.

319 8/P25 ✓ **Luca's** 16 Morningside Rd · www.s-luca.co.uk · 0131 446 0233 In-town version of legendary ice-cream parlour in Musselburgh (1445/ICE CREAM). Ice cream and snacks downstairs, more family food parlour up. Cheap and cheerful. Great for kids. 7 days. 287/KIDS.

320 8/Q25 ✓ **Punjabi Junction** 122-124 Leith Walk · www.punjabijunction.org · 0131 553 4737 A real taste of Punjab in a simple caff run by local women from the diverse ethnic minorities of Leith. Snacks (pakoras, samosas), daals and curries (Friday is 'curry day'). Inexpensive thali and genuine sweet desserts. The real deal and great value. They have cookery classes. Closed Sun.

321 8/Q25 **Skylark** 241-243 Portobello High St · www.theskylarkportobello.com · 0131 629 3037 E beyond the main traffic lights in the main road through Portobello. Café/bistro/bar and all-round neighbourhood hang-out, the feel changing through the day. Buggy junction daytime, with soups and salads; candlelit dinner, organic beers and wines at night. Reclaimed furniture; all easy-going. Closed Tue.

322 8/Q25　**Forest Café** 141 Lauriston Pl · 0131 229 4922　At corner of Brougham St at the main Tollcross crossroads. Busy drop-in café run by volunteers (they're a registered arts charity) from morning to night. Internet and/or Fringe vibe (which is where they came from). Good vibes! All food is vegetarian.

323 8/Q25　**Mademoiselle Macaron** 22 Grindlay St · www.mademoisellemacaron.co.uk · 0131 228 4059　Opposite Lyceum. Holding her own in the macaroon explosion; here they are very good. There are also choux pastries and crêpes but not a cupcake in sight. So French! All are to go, but there are a few tables. Tue-Sun daytime.

324 8/Q25　**Cuckoo's Bakery** 150 Dundas St · www.cuckoosbakery.co.uk · 0131 556 6224 & 116 Bruntsfield Pl · 0131 228 6100　Cupcake central and cakes at large – definitely among the best in town. Soups, ciabattas, doorstep sandwiches, big scones. Many ladies, the odd office chap. More chai than coffee in the cups. Tue-Sun daytime.

325 8/Q25　**Chocolate Tree** 123 Bruntsfield Pl · www.choctree.co.uk · 0131 228 3144　Crafty chocolatiers are everywhere, but these guys are thought by many to be at the top of the tree. Their organic products made in E Lothian are widely for sale; this is the only place you buy on their premises and have a hot choco and churros or their delicious ice cream. 7 days 10am-7.30pm.

326 8/P25　**Maxi's** 33 Raeburn Pl · 0131 343 3007　Serving Stockbridge, as it says, since 1997, in the middle of the main street and the midst of many (subsequent) other caffs. Still Maxi's does what it says on the sign, as indicated by its frequent full house. Its signature tiled walls are old and chipped; the soup, salad and baking is fresh and there are no chips in sight. A reliable redoubt. 7 days daytime only.

327 8/Q25　**MUM'S Great Comfort Food** 4a Forrest Rd · www.mumsgreatcomfortfood. co.uk · 0131 260 9806　There will always be a place for comfort food in our hearts and in our stomachs. This place does exactly what it declares. It's not a chain so somebody's mum has a lot to do with this. Pies, stews, sausages of the day, mash and crumble. What exactly is not to like? 7 days all day.

328 8/Q25　**Café Renroc** 91 Montgomery St · www.caferenroc.co.uk · 0131 629 3727　Cool neighbourhood caff on the corner ('renroc' backwards) with outside tables and more downstairs, beside the Nevo Health suites (acupuncture, massage and other treatments). A popular hang-out. Breakfasts, ciabattas, strombolis, nice coffee, fresh OJ. Sat-Wed daytime only, till 8pm Thu & 11pm Fri.

329 8/Q25　**Sprio** 39 St Stephen St · 0131 226 7533　Tiny, authentic Italian coffee shop – a splash of Milano style in old St Stephen St. Few tables but you can take away. Paninis, piadines (northern Italian unleavened bread), cured meats, cakes and locally the *best* espresso. 7 days daytime only.

330 8/Q25　**Drill Hall Arts Café** 34 Dalmeny St · www.outoftheblue.org.uk · 0131 555 7100　Off Leith Walk. A drill hall right enough, turned into a vibrant and vital arts centre and neighbourhood social hub by Out of the Blue (an arts & education trust). Collectivism and community arts very much alive here; it buzzes, especially on Saturdays at the Flea (last Saturday of the month), at the vintage markets or the ping pong nights. Studios, dance classes, workshops, music at the heart of this eco/fair-trade/creative food kitchen. Soups, sandwiches & big for brunch. Mon-Sat daytime only. The beating heart of Leith.

The Best Late-Night Restaurants

331 8/Q25
ATMOS
£25-35
✓ **The Witchery** Castlehill · www.thewitchery.com · 0131 225 5613 Top of Royal Mile near the Castle. Excellent value post- (and pre-) theatre menu from one of the city's best restaurants, which means there's somewhere civilised to eat late. 2 courses only £19 at TGP. Worth it for the atmos alone. See also 140/FINE DINING. 7 days lunch & LO **11.30pm**.

332 8/Q25
£15-25
✓ **Giuliano's** 18-19 Union Pl · www.giulianos.co.uk · 0131 556 6590 Leith Walk opposite Playhouse Theatre. Buzzing Italian tratt day and night. Report: 213/TRATTS. Till **1am**.

333 8/Q25
£15-25
✓ **El Cartel** 64 Thistle St · www.elcartelmexicana.co.uk · 0131 226 7171 Really good Mexican streetfood. No booking. Till **11.45pm weekends** (10pm during the week). Report: 251/MEXICAN.

334 8/Q25
DF
£15-25
✓ **The Holyrood 9A** 9A Holyrood Rd · www.theholyrood.co.uk · 0131 556 5044 Round the corner from the bottom of St Mary's St. Like other Fuller Thomson bar/restaurants (The Red Squirrel above and The Southern (0131 662 8926), in the southside, at 22 S Clerk St), this, their original, serves food – a burger based menu – all day till **11pm**. Report: 178/GASTROPUBS.

335 8/Q25
£15-25
Red Squirrel 21 Lothian Rd · www.redsquirreledinburgh.co.uk · 0131 229 9933 In the West End. Burgers and beers done well and great ambience. Only place hereabouts to eat after theatre or film. Till **11.30pm**. Report: 284/BURGERS & STEAKS.

✓ **The Printing Press** At the George Hotel. Till **1 am**. Report: 145/BRASSERIES.

Good Places For Sunday Brunch

336 8/Q25
✓ **Peter's Yard** 27 Simpson Loan · www.petersyard.com · 0131 228 5876 & 3 Deanhaugh St · 0131 332 2901 Two of the best places in town for the civilised non-fry breakfast; they're the real brioche. From **9am**. Report: 301/TEAROOMS.

337 8/Q25
✓ **Joseph Pearce's** 23 Elm Row · www.bodabar.com · 0131 556 4140 Near the top of Leith Walk. Up-and-down corner bar, good for many reasons and in the way they know what people want, a top Sunday breakfast/brunch till 4pm, including Swedish/classic healthy versions and every way with eggs. From **11am**. Report: 363/UNIQUE PUBS.

338 8/Q25
✓ **Edinburgh Larder Café** 15 Blackfriars St · www.edinburghlarder.co.uk · 0131 556 6922 This is where to go for Sunday brekkies near the Royal Mile as the queue will attest. From **9am**. Report: 316/CAFFS.

339 8/Q25
✓ **The Broughton Deli** 7 Barony St · 0131 558 7111 Neighbourhood café/deli. Daily bread and other fresh baking. Breakfast from **10am**. Report: 314/CAFFS.

340 8/Q25
✓ **The Scottish Café & Restaurant** The Mound · www.thescottishcafeandrestaurant.com · 0131 225 1550 Below the National Gallery; enter via Princes St Gardens. The definitive Scottish breakfast of course, but many variations. Great location for easing into Sunday, and upstairs there's very good art. From **10am** Sun. Report: 248/SCOTTISH.

341 8/Q25 ✓ **Urban Angel** 121 Hanover St · www.urban-angel.co.uk · 0131 225 6215
Convivial, contemporary breakfast from porridge and top granola to eggs
Benedict. Freshly made croissants and the potato scones (153/BISTROS)! Saturday
night a distant memory. From **9am**.

342 8/Q25 ✓ **Rick's** 55a Frederick St · www.ricksedinburgh.co.uk · 0131 622 7800
The buzzing café-bar with rooms (110/BOUTIQUE HOTELS) opens early as
well as late; an excellent spot for laid-back or power breakfast brunch 7 days,
including unusually early start on Sundays. Eclectic, contemporary menu. Open
7 days from **7am**.

343 8/Q25 **City Café** 19 Blair St · www.thecitycafe.co.uk · 0131 220 0125 It's been here
   DF for decades now but it keeps on (as they used to say) truckin'. BIG for breakfast
(carnivore or veggie), few places in the city beat it for content or American-diner
atmos. Slow to get going; most of the clientele have been up very late (here there
are DJs), but it does! From **9am**.

344 8/Q25 **King's Wark** 36 Shore · www.thekingswark.com · 0131 554 9260 On busy
corner for traffic, but calm and comforting inside. Dining room or bar. No early
start (**11am**), but a civilised brunch on the waterfront.

345 8/Q25 **The Broughton St Breakfast** There's lots of choice in the main street of
Edinburgh's East Village. From the top down: Lovely-looking **Treacle** kicks in from
10am with upmarket gastropub choices. **Artisan Roast** has the best coffee from
10am. **The Basement** also does Tex-Mex brex from **noon** and regulars attest
to its ability to hit the spot. Further down on the corner with people-watching
windows is **The Barony** with breakfast and papers **12.30-3.30pm** (live music early
Sun evenings); **The New Town Deli** on the corner of Barony St is neither a deli nor
a café but has a few seats, the papers and is open from **9am**. The NTD is also at 23
Henderson Row (355/TAKEAWAY). And special mention for:

346 8/Q25 **The Olive Branch** 91 Broughton St · www.theolivebranchscotland.co.uk ·
0131 557 8589 The definitive **Broughton St Breakfast**: big windows, outside
tables. Med menu and breakfast fry-ups. This place is routinely packed. On Sundays
you pray for a table. From **10am**.

✓ **Wildman Pizza Grill** Between Nicolson and Bristo Squares. In heart of
University campus and, in August, the Fringe. A top spot, they get 'brunch'.
From **8am**. Report: 218/PIZZA.
Earthy Southside From **10am**. Report: 359/DELIS.
Milk Café One of the earliest openers and a healthy start. From **8am**. Report:
349/TAKEAWAY.

The Best Takeaway Places

347 8/Q25 ✓ **The Broughton Deli** 7 Barony St · 0131 558 7111 Neighbourhood café/deli with daily fresh bread and baking, including cakes. Soup, tart, frittata and a hot dish all to go. See 314/CAFFS.

348 8/Q25 ✓ **Anima** 11 Henderson Row · www.anima-online.co.uk · 0131 558 2918 Adjacent and part of **L'Alba D'Oro** (240/FISH & CHIPS). Smart, busy Italian hot 'n' cold takeaway. 'Italian soul food' includes great pizza and freshly prepared pastas made to order. Excellent wine selection, some desserts. A welcome expansion from chips – our soul food – to theirs. Lunch Mon-Fri & 7 days evenings.

349 8/P25 ✓ **Milk Café** 232 Morrison St · www.cafemilk.co.uk · 0131 629 6022 Original home of Milk Caff and takeaway that has now gone on to provide sustenance for visitors to the two coolest art venues – the **Collective** at the City Observatory on Calton Hill 439/GALLERIES and the silver caravan at **Jupiter Artland** 2131/GALLERIES. Far from bland, Milk's menu includes world food from all over: Brazil, Morocco, Thailand. Great brunch menu, including burritos. Creative cuisine unusual in a takeaway, and a pale, calm place to graze. 7 days daytime only.

350 8/P25 ✓ **Cucina LC** 68 Haymarket Terrace · 0131 467 2671 LC the initials of proprietor Lucina Crolla, a takeaway that's just better than the many clustered around the station, though a 200m walk away. 2 soups, 2 quiches and 4 specials daily. Those that know are in the lunchtime queue here. Mon-Fri daytime.

351 8/Q25 ✓ **The Social Bite** 131 Rose St · www.social-bite.co.uk · 0131 220 8206 In the heart of the consumer throng, this is a food stop with heart. All the profits go to charity (the homeless) of this (1 of 4 in Scotland) 'social business' where the menu is created by a Michelin chef. Expect innovative bespoke sandwiches and comforting hot dishes. George Clooney was here. 'I can do stew', he said, and we swooned! Mon-Fri 7am-3pm. Also in Shandwick Pl.

352 8/Q25 ✓ **The Edinburgh Larder** 15 Blackfriars St · www.edinburghlarder.co.uk · 0131 556 6922 Off the Royal Mile. The café and takeaway of the Larder Duo (the Bistro is at 1a Alva Street). High-quality home cooking here, in the tiny kitchen behind the counter. Simple and seasonal soups, salads, cakes 'n' all. 7 days daytime.

353 8/Q25 ✓ **Kebab Mahal** 7 Nicolson Sq · www.kebab-mahal.co.uk · 0131 667 5214 For 30 years this unassuming but cosmopolitan Indian diner and takeaway has occupied a fond place on the edge of the university quarter for snacks, curries, babas, kulfi and lassis. 7 days from noon till late (2am Fri/Sat).

354 8/Q25 **Embo** 29 Haddington Pl · 0131 652 3880 Halfway down Leith Walk. Mike Marshall's neighbourhood hang-out and takeaway is a step up from the rest. Bespoke sandwiches, wraps, etc. Excellent coffee and smoothies. Few seats in and a couple of tables on the step. Nice cakes. Local sourcing. Good to know. Mon-Sat.

355 8/Q25 **The New Town Deli** 42 Broughton St & 23 Henderson Row · www. thenewtowndeli.com · 0800 073 1211 These slightly misleadingly named soup 'n' sandwich places are not delis but great local takeaways. Open daytime for sandwiches, rolls and focaccia. Big window for people watching. There's another branch in Deanhaugh St, the main street of Stockbridge, which is mainly a sit-in coffee shop.

The Best Delis

356 8/Q25 ✓✓✓ **Valvona & Crolla** 19 Elm Row · www.valvonacrolla.co.uk ·
ATMOS 0131 556 6066 Near top of Leith Walk. Since 1934 an Edinburgh
institution, the perfect provisioner for the good things in life. I wrote this report
years ago and like V&C itself there's no reason to change it now! Full of smells,
genial, knowledgeable staff and a floor-to-ceiling range of cheese, meats, oils,
wines and artisan bread. Superlative fresh produce, irresistible cheese counter,
on-premises bakery, great café-bar (205/ITALIAN). Demos, tastings and a Fringe
venue – it's a national treasure. They were first – still first! 7 days daytime only.

357 8/Q25 ✓✓ **I.J. Mellis** 30a Victoria Street, 330 Morningside Rd & 6 Baker's
Place, Stockbridge · www.mellischeese.co.uk Started out as the
cheese guy, now more of a very select deli for food that's good and 'slow'. Coffees,
hams, sausages, olives and seasonal stuff, like apples and mushrooms (branches
vary); smells mingle. Branches also in Glasgow (668/DELIS) and St Andrews.
Times vary. See also 1478/CHEESES. He's still the cheese guy.

358 8/P25 ✓✓ **George Mewes** 3 Dean Park St · www.georgemewescheese.co.uk ·
0131 332 5900 End of Raeburn Pl. Further extending Stockbridge's food
quarter, late 2015 George arrives from Glasgow's West End where for 6 years, he's
been the Cheese King (669/DELIS). Taking cheese to the next level, this
temperature controlled, bespoke shop is both chilled and chilled. New Town dinner
parties just got a new cheeseboard. 7 days daytime only.

359 8/Q25 ✓✓ **Earthy** 33-41 Ratcliffe Terrace · 0131 667 2967 & 1-6 Canonmills
Bridge · 0131 556 9696 · www.earthy.uk.com Tucked-away kitchen,
garden and lifestyle emporium in southside. An ambitious 2-floor shop and café
(that feels like a market) with plants outside. Kind of co-op of like-minded
gardeners and growers passionate about food, so all suppliers are hand-picked
along with most of the fruit and veg (source countries noted). Related to
Phantassie, the organic farm in E Lothian. Local, fair-trade and seasonal are the
watchwords. Superb range of everything (even the oatcakes). Initially not easy to
find, but you will do. The much-loved sister deli/restaurant **Earthy Canonmills** is
under some threat from development at TGP but seems likely to prevail. Same
ethic. See 160/BISTROS.

360 8/Q25 ✓✓ **181 Delicatessen** 181 Bruntsfield Pl · 0131 229 4554 Slap-bang on the
foodie strip near 'Holy Corner', a deli that takes a lot of care to get it right.
Conscientiously sourcing from local producers and shelves with trusted labels.
Bread from Patrick's and baking on the premises. The Billinghursts there for chat
on their goodies. Couple of tables for soups, platters and scones. Mon-Sat daytime.

361 8/P25 ✓ **Herbie of Edinburgh** 66 Raeburn Pl · www.herbieofedinburgh.co.uk ·
0131 332 9888 Notable originally for cheese (that Brie!) and other cold-
counter irresistibles (1481/CHEESES). There's always a queue in their packed-from-
floor-to-ceiling emporium of good things. Excellent artisan bread and scrumptious
munchies. Mon-Sat daytime only.

Unique Edinburgh Pubs

362 8/Q25
DF
✓ **Nobles** 44a Constitution St · www.noblesbarleith.co.uk · 0131 629 7215
Over the last 5 years Nobles has consolidated itself into the definitive
neighbourhood and go-to Leith pub. Comfortably occupying an elegant Victorian
room: lofty, beautiful and civilised. People like it here, so it's always busy. Not your
usual pub grub either, though there is a decent burger. Full of life! Food served all
day (Fri/Sat brunch 10am-4.30pm).

363 8/Q25
DF
✓ **Sofi/Boda/Joseph Pearce's/Victoria** Leith · www.bodabar.com 4 pubs
all in the Leith area where the Christophersons have built a very particular little
empire that could only happen in Edinburgh. All have been transformed from old,
defunct pubs and are fresh, quirky, laid-back, mix 'n' match and full of individual
touches. Sofi is the smallest, in a Leith backstreet (Henderson St); JP the largest on
a busy corner (Elm Row) at the top of Leith Walk (with good pub-grub menu and
outside tables, Scrabble nights, 'language café', a jogging club – you get the
picture?); the others are on corners on the Walk and dogs are welcome in all.
There's also **Hemma** in Holyrood Rd, near the Parliament, and in 2015 the super
Swedes opened **Akva**, a big 2-floor very uptown bar (408/OUTDOORS).

364 8/Q25
DF
✓ **Pickles** 56a Broughton St · www.getpickled.co.uk · 0131 557 5005
Below L'Escargot Bleu, Jonny Bristow's perfectly sympatico wine bar is a local
secret though nevertheless much commended on TripAdvisor. Selected wines,
cheese and charcuterie platters (conveniently available late if you can get a table).
Feels like a comfy bohemian parlour or salon. A few outside tables under the stairs.
My local hang-out so I have an interest in keeping it quiet. Do not come here!

365 8/Q25
DF
ATMOS
✓ **Port o' Leith** 58 Constitution St · 0131 554 3568 The legendary Leith bar
on the busy road to what used to be the docks is perhaps not what it once was
when Mary Moriarty was Madame, but some aura still remains. Always good music.
It's still a port in the storm for a' sorts but winds of change blow at TGP.

366 8/Q25
DF
✓ **The Royal Dick at Summerhall** 1 Summerhall · www.summerhall.co.uk ·
0131 560 1572 Close to the Meadows, a bar in the corner of the central
courtyard of the extraordinary independent art and cultural centre, Summerhall, a
huge complex of creative types, where anything is possible. Formerly the Royal Dick
Veterinary College, the bar maintains the theme. They say it's a bar-bistro and
though the food is a bit hit and miss, it's always good to hang out here, indoors or
in the yard, whether you're at a gig, exhibition, festival or the Fringe, where it is a
major venue. Unique! Food from noon till 10pm.

367 8/Q25
✓ **Bramble Bar** 16A Queen St · www.bramblebar.co.uk · 0131 226 6343
At Hanover St. A discreet, hidden-away corner basement; cool, comfy and big
(internationally big) on cocktails. Mike Aikman and Jas Scott have made a
discerning drinkers' haven, so great voddies, whiskies and over 60 gins. Nice Gen X
(and Y and Z) people in the mix(ology) and non-compromising soundtrack rather
than fluffy lounge music. They get through a lotta limes! DJs Fri/Sat.

368 8/Q25
ATMOS
✓ **Bennets Bar** 8 Leven St · 0131 229 5143 By King's Theatre. Stand at the
back and don't watch the sports, watch light stream through the stained glass
like it always did. Same era as Café Royal and similar ambience, mirrors and tiles.
Decent food at lunch and early evening (400/BAR FOOD).

369 8/Q25 ✓ **Sandy Bells** Forrest Rd · www.sandybellsedinburgh.co.uk ·
ATMOS 0131 225 2751 Near the university and Greyfriars Kirk; it seems like it's been there as long. Mainly known as a folky/traditional music haven (live 7 nights), it reeks (though the smoke has gone) of atmos (it should be given a dispensation). Soup 'n' pies.

370 8/Q25 ✓ **Café Royal** 19 W Register St · www.caferoyaledinburgh.co.uk ·
ATMOS 0131 556 1884 Behind the Apple shop at the east end of Princes Street, one of Edinburgh's longest-celebrated pubs. Unrelated to the London version, though there is a similar Victorian/Baroque elegance. Through the partition is the **Oyster Bar** (with perfect atmos for oysters and all, 235/SEAFOOD). Central counter and often standing room only. Bar food till 10pm.

371 8/Q25 **Barony Bar** 81-85 Broughton St · 0131 558 2874 East Village venue with a mixed clientele and a good vibe. Belgian and guest beers. Newspapers to browse over a Sunday brunch. Bert's band and others on early Sunday evenings one of the best pub-music nights in town though somewhat curtailed of late because of noise complaints.

372 8/Q25 **The Basement** 10a-12a Broughton St · www.basement-bar-edinburgh. co.uk · 0131 557 0097 Years down the line, The Basement is still a happening sort of, er, basement bar, with perennially popular Mex-style food served by smiley staff (253/MEXICAN). At night, the punters are well up for it – late, loud and still alive.

373 8/Q25 **Kay's Bar** 39 Jamaica St · www.kaysbar.co.uk · 0131 225 1858 Tucked away
ATMOS in a corner of the New Town, a true original, remodelled in the 1970's from a wine & spirit merchants. They care for the beer (393/ALES) and do nice grub at lunchtime (anything that goes with HP Sauce). A gentleman would be happy here.

374 8/Q25 **Mathers Bar** 1 Queensferry St · 0131 225 3549 Edinburgh's West End has a complement of 'smart' bars that cater for people with ties and no (domestic) ties. The alternative is here – a stand-up space for old-fashioned pubbery, slack coiffure and idle talk (384/ORIGINAL PUBS). Wimmin rarely venture and men drink in peace. There are pies.

375 8/Q25 **The Stockbridge Tap** 2 Raeburn Pl · 0131 343 3000 On a corner. A definitive
DF local – i.e. Stockbridge – pub in understated Edinburgh style. Good selection of cask ales, many whiskies, decent grub. They take care here. A CAMRA Pub of the Year 2015. Lunch & dinner.

376 8/Q25 **City Café** 19 Blair St · www.thecitycafe.co.uk · 0131 220 0125 25 years on,
DF the retro Americana chic has aged gracefully. The comfy banquettes, the chrome and the customers look good. All-day diner food, decent coffee. A hip Edinburgh bar that has stood the test of mind-altering time. DJs weekends; and see 343/ SUNDAY BRUNCH. Food till 10pm.

377 8/Q25 **The Sheep Heid Inn** Duddingston · www.thesheepheidedinburgh.co.uk ·
ATMOS 0131 661 7974 18th-century inn 6km from city centre behind Arthur's Seat and reached most easily through the Queen's Park. Village and nearby wildfowl loch should be strolled around if you have time. Food gets mixed reviews but can be al fresco; also comfy upstairs room. Atmos and history is why we come. Food served all day (book weekends).

378 8/Q25   **The Dome** 14 George St · www.thedomeedinburgh.com · 0131 624 8624 Edinburgh's first megabar (and not a Wetherspoon) in truly impressive former bank, and grandiose in a way that only a converted temple to Mammon could be. The main part sits 15m under an elegant domed roof with an island bar and raised platform at back (**The Grill**) for determined diners. Big chandeliers, big, big flower arrangements: you come for the surroundings more than the victuals, perhaps. Adjacent and separate **Club Room** is more intimate, more clubby, better for a blether. 'Garden' patio bar at back (in good weather) – enter via Rose Street. Final bit, downstairs: **Why Not?** – a nightclub for over-25s still lookin' for lurve (Fri/Sat). Food till 10pm.

379 8/Q25   **The Doric** 15-16 Market St · www.the-doric.com · 0131 225 1084 Long-serving and mixed fortunes as a bistro, i.e. the food, but the upstairs wine bar is Edinburgh in a nutshell. The window tables looking over the town to the Balmoral offer one of the defining views of the city. Bar also on street level. Food till late.

▬▬▬ The Best Original Pubs

380 8/P25   ✓ **The Diggers** 1-3 Angle Park Terrace · 0131 337 3822 Officially the Athletic
     DF   Arms, a Jambo pub *par excellence*, stowed with the Tynecastle faithful before and after games. Still keeps a great pint of locally brewed 'The Diggers' 80/- (by esteemed Stewart Brewing). Food basic, i.e. pies at lunch (can be with beans).

381 8/Q25   ✓ **The Royal Oak** Infirmary St · www.royal-oak-folk.com · 0131 557 2976
  ATMOS   Tiny upstairs and not much bigger down. During the day, pensioners sip their pints (couple of real ales), downstairs 'lounge' from 9pm. Has surprisingly survived the smoking ban. Mainly known as a folk-music stronghold (live music every night for 50 years!) and home of the 'Wee Folk Club', they definitely don't make 'em like this any more. Gold-carat pubness. 7 days till 2am.

382 8/P25   ✓ **Roseburn Bar** 1 Roseburn Terrace · www.roseburnbar.co.uk ·
      0131 337 1067 On main Glasgow road out W from Haymarket and one of the nearest pubs to Murrayfield Stadium. Wood and grandeur and red leather; bonnie wee snug. A fine pint, and wall-to-wall rugby, of course. Heaving and heaven before internationals. It is a man's bar.

383 8/Q25   **Oxford Bar** 8 Young St · www.oxfordbar.co.uk · 0131 539 7119 Downhill from George St. No time machine needed – just step in the door and find one of Edinburgh's most celebrated non-reconstructed bars. Inspector Rebus wuz here. Be prepared to be scrutinised when you come in. Some real ales but they're as beside the point. No accoutrements, not even a pie.

384 8/Q25   **Mathers Bar** 1 Queensferry St · 0131 225 3549 Not only a reasonable real-ale pub but almost worth visiting just to look at the ornate fixtures and fittings – frieze and bar especially. Unreconstructed in every sense since 1903. Men quietly drinking. Pies all day. 50 malts. Report: 374/UNIQUE PUBS. There's another, unrelated, Mathers in Broughton St which is managing to keep its head in the city's grooviest street by remaining pub-like and unpretentious. Football on the telly.

    ✓ **Bennets Bar** Report: 368/UNIQUE PUBS.

    ✓ **Sandy Bells** Report: 369/UNIQUE PUBS.

385 8/Q25 ✓ **The Cumberland Bar** 1–3 Cumberland St · www.cumberlandbar.co.uk ·
DF 0131 558 3134 Corner of Dundonald St. After work, this New Town bar
attracts its share of suits, but later the locals (and droves of posh students) claim it.
Long a CAMRA (Campaign for Real Ale) redoubt but now, as well as 8 real-ale taps,
an impressive selection of lagers and ciders on tap and bottles aplenty. Nicely
appointed, decent pub lunches (including the Sunday roast), unexpected beer
garden (noon-evening Sat/Sun; 409/OUTDOORS).

386 8/Q25 ✓ **The Bow Bar** 80 W Bow · www.thebowbar.co.uk · 0131 226 7667
DF Halfway down Victoria St. They know how to treat drink in this excellent wee
bar. Traditional selection of 8 ales, many bottles and whiskies (over 270 malts) – no
cocktails! One of the few places in the Grassmarket area an over-25-year-old might
not feel out of place. Pie 'n' pint at lunch.

387 8/Q25 ✓ **Cloisters** 26 Brougham St · www.cloistersbar.com · 0131 221 9997 This
DF is a drinker's paradise: 19 taps and 70 whiskies with 35ml measures and many
wines by the glass in this simple and unfussy bar with wooden floors and laid-back
approach. Good pub grub though mostly burgers like everywhere else these days!
Food for lunch & till 9pm (Sat/Sun all day from midday). 9 casks, 8 on rotation. Bar
closes midnight (1am Fri/Sat). Both pubby and clubby; girls go too! The same
people own the Bow Bar (above) and the **Stockbridge Tap** (375/UNIQUE PUBS) on
the corner of busy Raeburn Pl. Good neighbourhood spot.

388 8/Q25 ✓ **Canny Man's** 237 Morningside Rd · www.cannymans.co.uk ·
ATMOS 0131 447 1484 Officially the Volunteer Arms but everybody calls it the Canny
Man's. Many smorrebrods at lunch (7 days) and evenings (Mon-Thu & Sat only).
Report: 173/GASTROPUBS. A wide range of real ales and myriad malts. Clubby and
civilised, this much-loved family fiefdom is one of the city's most convivial pubs

389 8/Q25 ✓ **The Guildford Arms** 1 W Register St · www.guildfordarms.com ·
0131 556 4312 Behind Apple shop at east end of Princes St on same block as
the **Café Royal** (370/UNIQUE PUBS). Forever in the same family. Lofty, ornate
Victorian hostelry with loadsa good ales, typically 7 Scottish, 3 English (and 16
wines by the glass). There are some you won't find anywhere else in the city. Pub
grub available on 'gallery' floor as well as bar. Big wallpaper and carpet (don't drink
too much). Lunch & dinner, and Sunday brunch from 10am.

390 8/Q25 ✓ **Blue Blazer** 2 Spittal St · 0131 229 5030 Opposite **Doubletree Hilton**
(88/MAJOR HOTELS). No frills, no pretensions, just wooden fixtures and fittings
and all sorts in this fine howff that carries a huge range of real ales. Regularly a
CAMRA pub of the year with 8 ales on tap. Extraordinary rum and gin list and then
the malts. Much more soul than its competitors nearby.

391 8/Q25 ✓ **The Beer Kitchen** 81-83 Lothian Rd · www.thebeerkitchen.co.uk ·
0131 228 6392 New in 2015 and part of the renaissance of dodgy old Lothian
Rd, this 'vibrant' and, well, noisy pub is more bar than kitchen, a purveyor of local
artisan brewery Innis and Gunn (who own the joint), a superb product and a stack
of selected others. Food served till 9.30pm.

392 8/Q25 ✓ **Brewdog** 143 Cowgate · www.brewdog.com · 0131 220 6517 The
Edinburgh Brewdog barking louder for craft beers than others round here. All
their estimable strong, very strong and pale and interesting are here served with
their signature strut and spirit and Punk IPA. It's come a long way from Fraserburgh
(and their crowdfunded brewery up north in Ellon).

393 8/Q25   **Kay's Bar** 39 Jamaica St · www.kaysbar.co.uk · 0131 225 1858 Off India St in
ATMOS   the New Town. Go on an afternoon when gentlemen of a certain age talk politics,
history and rugby over pints of porter. The knowledgeable barman patiently serves.
All red and black and vaguely distinguished with a tiny snug: the Library. Comfort
food simmers in the window (lunch only). Report: 373/UNIQUE PUBS.

394 8/Q25   **Starbank Inn** 64 Laverockbank Rd · www.starbankinn-edinburgh.co.uk ·
0131 552 4141 A Belhaven house on the seafront road W of Newhaven Harbour.
8 different ales on offer. Great place to sink a pint and watch the sun sink over the
Forth. The pub-grub food is fine (till 9pm).

395 8/Q25   **Cask & Barrel** 115 Broughton St · 0131 556 3132 & 24-26 W Preston St ·
0131 667 0856 A real pub with a great selection of ales (8) and a couldn't-care-
less crowd at the foot of gay and groovy Broughton St. Here they prefer a good pint
and the football. Outside tables on a windy corner. Southside version has many
ales too, integrity & the TV.

Bars With Good Food

Also see Gastropubs, p. 43. These below are not so high-falutin' foodwise but
nevertheless are worth going to for food as well as drink.

396 8/Q25 ✓ **Divino Enoteca** 5 Merchant St · www.divinoedinburgh.com ·
0131 225 1770 This is the downstairs of **Vittoria** (212/TRATTS), the wine and
food bar of maestro Tony Crolla. You can descend through the restaurant from
George IV Bridge but you usually enter at ground level off the Cowgate.
Atmosphere of dark materials and fairy-lit garden, designed to make you love
Italian wine. Small plate/grazing menu and more substantial dishes. The fancy
machinery keeps the wines pristine (16 white, 16 red, including some superior
vintages). Closed Sun.

397 8/Q25 ✓ **The Compass** 44 Queen Charlotte St · 0131 554 1979 Corner of
Constitution St opposite Leith Police Station. This well-run 'bar & grill' is a
popular Leith haunt, maybe missed by uptown grazers. Stone and woody look with
mix-match furniture; food better and more ambitious than you might first think,
and all home-made. Some very good deals, eg steak and a bottle of wine for <£30
on Thursdays. Bar kicks in later. Food till 10pm.

398 8/Q25 ✓ **Cambridge Bar** 20 Young St · www.thecambridgebar.co.uk ·
DF   0131 226 2120 On the W extension of Thistle St. Discreet doorway to
Edinburgh institution. Sporty in a rugger kind of way and notable for its
gastroburgers, probably among the best in town. Huge in size and huge choice,
including vegetarian (bean burgers); Mackie's estimable ice cream to follow. Sadly,
only a handful of tables but at the quiet end of the street so you can often get one.
Food till 10pm.

399 8/Q25 ✓ **Roseleaf** 23/24 Sandport Pl · www.roseleaf.co.uk · 0131 476 5268
Corner of Quayside between The Shore and busy Commercial St. They see
themselves as a 'cosy wee hidden treasure' and they're not wrong. Food definitely
the thing here, with everything home-made, including an afternoon tea on a tier
(pre-order). Small it is and perfectly formed. Kid-friendly – they have games.
Weekends you'd better book. Food till 9.30pm.

400 8/Q25 ✓ **Bennets Bar** 8 Leven St · 0131 229 5143 Next to the King's Theatre. Since
ATMOS 1875, an Edinburgh standby, listed for several reasons (368/UNIQUE PUBS), not
least its honest-to-goodness (and cheap) pub lunch. A la carte (stovies, steak pie,
etc) and daily specials under the enormous mirrors. And 2015 a restaurant **La
Petite Mort** (0131 229 3693; www.lapetitemortedinburgh.co.uk) round the back
(down the side) with chef Neil Connor.

401 8/P25 ✓ **The Fountain** 131 Dundee St · www.thefountainbar.co.uk ·
DF 0131 229 1899 Opposite the soulless Cineworld Mall (that only comes alive
during the International Film Festival). At last a place to eat and hang out in
faraway Fountainbridge. Mix 'n' match vibe. Daily menu and à la carte. Home-
made grub, some tables on the street. Nice peeps come here. Lunch & LO 9.20pm.

402 8/Q25 ✓ **The Espy** Portobello · 0131 669 0082 At the foot of Bath St on the said
DF Esplanade. The original place for pub grub in Porty (the Portobello seaside
suburb) with slouchy couches in the lounge area and a fair few tables (including in
the window), with a view of the sea and the surprising beach. Usually full. Food all
fresh and cooked to order; good burgers. Occasional live music. Some tables
outside. Food till 9.30pm.

403 8/Q25 ✓ **Guild Of Foresters** 40 Portobello High St · www.forestersguild.co.uk ·
DF 0131 669 2750 Arrived (the makeover) 2014 at the west (city) end of the main
road through Porty – at last, a contemporary bar-bistro. It just hits the spot:
selected ales & beers, 'beer garden' with huts – yes, huts! Food is fair.

404 8/Q25 ✓ **Hector's** 47-49 Deanhaugh St · www.hectorsstockbridge.co.uk ·
DF 0131 343 1735 On the corner of Stockbridge's main street, Raeburn Place. A
Mitchells & Butlers pub but long a distinctive Stockbridge destination for beers on
tap (12), bottled beers (expensive) and all-day decent pub grub (2 courses, £10). Just
a lot better than Wetherspoons.

405 8/Q25 **Cross and Corner** 1 Canonmills · www.crossandcorner.co.uk · 0131 558 7080
DF & **The Other Place** 2-4 Broughton Rd · www.theotherplaceedinburgh.com ·
0131 556 1024 Two bars on opposite corners of busy crossroads that arrived at
the same time and with a very similar set-up. C&C more bistro than bar; OP more
spacious and big on beer (8 on tap, 130 bottled varieties), burgers and dogs. Both
good though; can't say which – cross & check! Both all-day menus till 9/10pm.

406 8/Q25 **Woodland Creatures** 260-262 Leith Walk · www.woodlandcreatures.co.uk ·
DF 0131 629 5509 Halfway down the Walk, the delightfully named and nurtured
Woodland Creatures is quietly becoming a secret bower of good bar food: eclectic
and imaginative menu with Asian aromas, good vegetarian, puds and decent
cheese. And there is a secret beer garden. Find the path! Food till 10/11pm.

407 8/Q25 **The Abbotsford** 3 Rose St · 0131 225 5276 A doughty remnant of Rose St
drinking days of yore, and still the best pub lunch near Princes St. Fancier than it
used to be but still grills and bread-and-butter pudding. Huge portions. Restaurant
upstairs more cuisine. Lunch & LO 9.45pm.

The Best Places To Drink Outdoors

408 8/Q25 ✓ **Akva** 129 Fountainbridge · www.bodabar.com · 0131 290 2500 & 150m from Lothian Rd On the canal basin of the Union Canal, 'Edinburgh Quay', a surprising watery corner of the city, this is an ambitious venture by the sure-footed Swedes, the Christophersons, who have a clutch of cool bars in Leith (363/UNIQUE PUBS). 2 spacious floors and waterfront terrace, signature smorrebrod and all-day menu, including great brunch. Many social activities, eg dancing and ping pong.

409 8/Q25 ✓ **The Cumberland Bar** 1-3 Cumberland St · www.cumberlandbar.co.uk · 0131 558 3134 Some tables by the door but more space in the beer garden below, packed on summer evenings (till 10pm). Report: 385/ALES.

410 8/Q25 ✓ **The Pleasance Courtyard** The Pleasance & George Square Gardens · www.pleasance.co.uk Open during the Festival only. Major Fringe venues, one a large, open courtyard and the other in the heart of the university and the new south-centred Fringe. If you're here, you're on the Fringe, so to speak.

411 8/Q25 ✓ **The Shore** 3 Shore · www.fishersbistros.co.uk · 0131 553 5080 Excellent place to eat (174/GASTROPUBS), some tables just outside the door, but it's fine to wander over to the quayside and sit with your legs over the edge. Do try not to fall in. 7 days from noon.

412 8/Q25 ✓ **Malmaison** 1 Tower Place · www.malmaison.com · 0131 468 5000 Just along from The Shore (above), this hotel (part of the chain) has more proper seating; a terrace. If you can ignore the nearby flats, it's a great Leith vantage point.

413 8/Q25 DF **Teuchters Landing** 1c Dock Pl · www.aroomin.co.uk · 0131 554 7427 Another very good Leith eaterie but with waterside tables and spread over adjacent pontoons. Mugs of prawns, stovies, etc in half- or full-pint portions. Great wine list – 20 by the glass. Outside open 10.30am-10pm (inside till 1am).

414 8/Q25 **Pear Tree** 38 W Nicholson St · www.pear-tree-house.co.uk · 0131 667 7533 Adjacent to parts of Edinburgh University so real student style with large beer garden. Serried ranks of tables and refectory-style food. Sports screens everywhere. Stage for occasional live music, and BBQ. Good malt list.

415 8/Q25 **The (Café) Hub** Castlehill · www.thehub-edinburgh.com · 0131 473 2067 The café-bar of the International Festival Centre. Unfortunately, food so-so. Great enclosed terrace for people watching. Brollies and heaters extend the possibilities. OK for kids. 7 days 9.30am-10pm (till 6.30pm Sun).

416 8/Q25 DF **The Street** 2b Picardy Pl · www.thestreetbaredinburgh.co.uk · 0131 556 4272 Great people-watching potential on busy corner. Gay in and out. General locations: **Greenside Pl** (**Theatre Royal** and **Café Habana**), bars in **The Grassmarket**. All rise (or sit down) to pavement café culture when the sun's out.

✓ **The Royal Dick at Summerhall** Courtyard bar. Report: 366/UNIQUE PUBS.

Guild Of Foresters In the beer garden...there are huts. Report: 403/BAR FOOD.
The Bridge Inn In Ratho. Report: 131/HOTELS OUTSIDE EDINBURGH.

The Main Attractions

417 8/Q25
ADMISSION
HS
LLL

✓✓✓ **Edinburgh Castle** www.edinburghcastle.gov.uk · 0131 225 9846
Go to Princes St and look up! Extremely busy all year round and yet the city's must-see main attraction does not disappoint. St Margaret's 12th-century chapel is simple and beautiful; the rolling history lesson that leads up to the display of Scotland's crown jewels is fascinating; the Stone of Destiny is a big deal to the Scots (though others may not see why). And, ultimately, the Scottish National War Memorial is one of the most genuinely affecting places in the country – a simple, dignified testament to shared pain and loss. The Esplanade is a major concert venue just before the International Tattoo in July, the single major event of the Festival in August. Last entry 1 hour before closing. 9.30am-5/6pm.

418 8/Q25
FREE

✓✓✓ **The National Museum of Scotland** Chambers St · www.nms.ac.uk · 0300 123 6789 After an almost £50-million refit, the fully integrated and effectively reinvented NMS opened to huge acclaim in 2011. A new basement entrance (and restaurant), the restored-to-former-Victorian-grandeur atrium, thousands of objects in state-of-the-art displays and interactivity, and integration with the adjacent Museum of Scotland (opened in 1999), make this a uniquely special homage and celebration of the ingenuity, industry and influence of a small country that changed the world. Not to forget the big animals and all that went before! With the Riverside Museum in Glasgow, Scotland has 2 paeans to its proud cultural and entrepreneurial past that are in themselves everything to be proud of. 7 days 10am-5pm. A roof terrace reveals the city skyline. The independently run Tower Restaurant is rather good.

419 8/P25

✓✓✓ **The Forth Bridge** www.forth-bridges.co.uk 20km W of Edinburgh via A90. First turning for S Queensferry from dual carriageway; don't confuse with signs for road bridge. Or train from Waverley to Dalmeny, and walk 1km. The mighty bridge was 100 in 1990. The Road Bridge – 50 years old in 2014 and celebrated with spectacular firework displays – is to be followed by another, the Queensferry Crossing. At TGP it remains to be seen how they all relate but the Rail Bridge will always be *the* Forth Bridge. An international symbol of Scotland, it should certainly be seen, but go to the N side: S Queensferry's very crowded and a bit tacky though improving these days (shame on Tesco for spoiling the view from the road bridge approach and well done the **Dakota** for dramatising it 129/HOTELS OUTSIDE EDINBURGH). There is also a good hotel-restaurant in S Queensferry (132/HOTELS OUTSIDE TOWN) with views of the bridge.

420 8/P25
ADMISSION

✓✓✓ **Edinburgh Zoo** Corstorphine Rd · www.edinburghzoo.org.uk · 0131 334 9171 4km W of Princes St; buses from Princes St Gardens side. Opened in 1909, this is no ordinary zoo. Apart from being fun and educational and all that, its conservation work and serious zoology is highly respected (hence The Giant Pandas). Penguins parade at 2.15pm daily in summer months and there are many other old friends and favourites, as well as new ones: the Sumatran tigers, the only UK koalas and the beavers – there are many animals here to love and cherish. And you will not be able to miss the pandas – unless there's a pregnancy! Timed tickets. Check the website. Open AYR 7 days (even Christmas Day!). Apr-Sep 9am-6pm, reduced hours in winter. See also 1679/KIDS.

421 8/Q25
ADMISSION

HS

✓✓ **Palace of Holyroodhouse** www.royalcollection.org.uk · 0131 556 5100 Foot of the Royal Mile, the Queen's North British timeshare – she's here for a wee while late June/early July. Large parts of the palace are dull (Duke of Hamilton's loo, Queen's wardrobes) and only a dozen or so rooms are open, most dating from the 17th century with a couple from the earlier 16th. Lovely cornices abound. Anomalous Stuart features, adjacent 12th-century abbey ruins quite interesting. Courtyard and conservatory café one of the nicest in town. Apr-Oct: 9.30am-6pm (last ticket 4.30pm) daily. Nov-Mar: 9.30am-4.30pm (last ticket 3.15pm) daily. Also... **The Queen's Gallery** 0131 556 5100 Visually appealing addition opposite the Parliament building with separate entrance. By architect Ben Tindall (who also did The Hub at the top of the Royal Mile, though this is better). Beautiful, contemporary setting for changing exhibits from Royal Collection every 6 months which include art, ceramics, tapestries, etc. Shop stuffed with monarchist mementos. Apr-Oct 9.30am-5pm (last ticket), reduced hours in winter.

422 8/Q25 ✓✓ **The Royal Mile** www.edinburgh-royalmile.com The High Street, the medieval main thoroughfare of the capital follows the trail from the volcanic crag of Castle Rock and connects the castle and palace (above). Heaving during the Festival but if on a winter's night you chance by with a frost settling on the cobbles and no one is around, it's magical. Always interesting with its wynds and closes (Whitehorse Close, Dunbar's Close, the secret garden opposite Huntly House), but lots of disgraceful, made-in-China tartan shops too. Central block closed to traffic and during the Festival Fringe it's the best street-performance space in UK. See the Mile on a walking tour: there are several, especially at night (ghost/ghouls/witches, etc). Mercat Tours (0131 225 5445), Cadies & Witchery Tours (0131 225 6745) and City of the Dead (0131 225 9044) are pretty good.

The Real Mary King's Close 0131 225 0672 Part of a medieval street under the Royal Mile. Daily tours. Enter by Warriston's Close near City Chambers. **Scottish Poetry Library** is in Crichton's Close on right between St Mary's St and the Parliament. Great collections, lovely contemplative space. Endorses Edinburgh's status as City of Literature. www.scottishpoetrylibrary.org for opening hours after major renovations.

423 8/Q25 ✓✓ **The Scottish Parliament** Royal Mile · www.scottish.parliament.uk ·
ADMISSION 0131 348 5200 Adjacent to Holyroodhouse (above) and Our Dynamic Earth (below). Designed by Catalan architect Enric Morales who died long before it opened, this building was mired in controversy after first First Minister, the late Donald Dewar, laid the first stone. We got over it, though it is still is loved and hated in equal measure. However, it's used publicly a lot and in my view it should not be missed – it is the finest modern building in the city (it won the 2005 Stirling Prize, the UK's premier architectural award). Tour (including a visit to the Debating Chamber) times vary; best book in advance.

424 8/Q25 ✓✓ **Our Dynamic Earth** Holyrood Rd · www.dynamicearth.co.uk ·
ADMISSION 0131 550 7800 Edinburgh's Dome, an interactive museum/visitor attraction, made with Millennium money. For kids really; good for a family outing. Now within the orbit and campus of the Parliament building. Salisbury Crags rise above. Vast restaurant and outside, an amphitheatre. Secret and inexpensive car park from which to explore the area.

425 8/Q25 ✓✓ **Scottish National Gallery** The Mound · www.nationalgalleries.org ·
FREE 0131 624 6200 Neoclassical buildings housing a superb collection of Old Masters in a series of hushed salons. Many are world famous but you don't emerge goggle-eyed as from the National in London. The building in front, the **Royal Scottish Academy**, often has blockbuster exhibitions. Daily 10am-5pm, Thu 7pm. Extended hours during Festival. Very good caff, **The Scottish Café & Restaurant** (248/SCOTTISH) and Contini Espresso offer high-quality choices with views.

426 8/Q25
ADMISSION
✓✓ **Royal Yacht *Britannia*** Leith · www.royalyachtbritannia.co.uk · 0131 555 5566 In the docks, enter by Commercial St at end of Great Junction St. Berthed outside Conran's shopping mall, the Ocean Terminal. Done with ruling the waves, the royal yacht has found a permanent home as a tourist attraction (and prestigious corporate night out). Check out the Royal Deck Tea Room. Close up, the Art Deco lines are surprisingly attractive, while the interior was one of the sets for our best ever soap opera. Booking advised in Aug.

✓✓✓ **Rosslyn Chapel** Roslin Famous, infamous, fabulous. Report: 1842/ CHURCHES.

■■■■■ The Other Attractions

427 8/P25
ADMISSION
FOR GLASS-
HOUSES;
OTHERWISE
FREE
🖳
✓✓✓ **Royal Botanic Garden** Inverleith Row · www.rbge.org.uk · 0131 248 2909/0131 552 7171 3km Princes Street. Enter from Inverleith Row or the landmark John Muir gateway in Arboretum Place. 70 acres of ornamental gardens, trees and walkways; a joy in every season. Tropical Palm House, landscaped rock and heath garden, the more recent 'Chinese Garden' and space just to wander. Precocious squirrels everywhere. The Botanics have talks, guided tours, events, including 'Botanic Lights' in Nov (info 0131 248 2968). They also look after other important outstanding gardens in Scotland. Gallery with occasional exhibitions and 3 separate cafés, one with an outdoor terrace for afternoon teas (313/TEAROOMS), and views. Total integrity and the natural high. Houses the National Biodiversity Interpretation Centre and garden. Open 7 days AYR.

428 8/Q25
ATMOS
FREE
🖳
✓✓ **Scottish National Portrait Gallery** 1 Queen St · www. nationalgalleries.org · 0131 624 6200 Sir Robert Rowand Anderson's fabulous, custom-built neo-Gothic pile holds paintings and photos of the good, great and merely famous. Alex Ferguson hangs out next to the Queen Mum, and Nasmyth's familiar Burns pic is here. Good venue for photo exhibitions, beautiful atrium with star-flecked ceiling and frieze of (mainly) men in Scottish history, from a Stone Age chief to Carlyle. The caff does a good cheese scone! 7 days 10am-5pm (7pm Thu). Extended hours during Festival.

429 8/Q25
ADMISSION
✓✓ **Surgeons' Hall Museum** Nicolson St · www.museum.rcsed.ac.uk · 0131 527 1711 Housed in the landmark Playfair building (1832) this museum is the real deal, integrity writ large and full of fascinating stuff. With recent major renovations, for over 500 years the Royal College of Surgeons has set and tested the standards of their craft and this museum records the growth of scientific medicine and Edinburgh's extraordinary contribution to it. Some key collections and changing exhibitions but wonder and wince through the Pathology Museum and get your teeth into the Dentistry Collection, both the finest in the UK. 7 days 10am-5pm (4pm last entry).

430 8/P25
FREE
🖳
✓ **Scottish National Gallery of Modern Art One** 75 Belford Rd · www. nationalgalleries.org · 0131 624 6200 Between Queensferry Rd and Dean Village (nice to walk through). Best to start from Palmerston Pl and keep left; or see below (Modern Two). Former school with permanent collection from Impressionism to Emin; the Scottish painters alongside and a growing collection of the conceptual art in which Scotland is notably strong (see the Douglas Gordon on the staircase and see if you can find my name – I couldn't!). All in all, an intimate space where you can fall in love (with paintings or each other). Around 3 major temporary exhibitions annually. Excellent café (303/TEAROOMS). Charles Jencks art in the landscape piece outside is stunning. 7 days. Open longer during Festival.

431 8/P25 ✓ **Scottish National Gallery of Modern Art Two** 73 Belford Terrace ·
FREE www.nationalgalleries.org · 0131 624 6200 Across the road from Modern
One (above). Originally built as a grand orphan hospital with high windows children
cannot see out of, there is plenty of light but no distractions in this mansion of
intimate spaces. Cool coffee shop, large gardens to wander. Superb 20th-century
collection; many surreal moments. Great way to approach both galleries is by
Water of Leith walkway (444/WALKS). No miracles here but there is magic. 7 days.

432 8/Q25 **Museum of Childhood** 42 High St · www.edinburghmuseums.org.uk ·
FREE 0131 529 4142 Shrine to the dreamstuff of tender days where you'll find
everything from tin soldiers to Lady Penelope on video. Full of adults saying, 'I had
one of them!' Child-size mannequins in upper gallery can be very spooky if you're
up there alone. Mon-Sat 10am-5pm, Sun from noon.

433 8/Q25 **St Giles' Cathedral** Royal Mile · www.stgilescathedral.org.uk ·
FREE 0131 225 9442 Not really a cathedral anymore, though it was once: the High
Kirk of Edinburgh, Church of Scotland central since the 16th century and heart of
the city since the 9th. The building is mainly medieval with Norman fragments
encased in a Georgian exterior. Lorimer's oddly ornate chapel and the 'big organ'
are impressive. Simple, austere design and bronze of John Knox set the tone
historically. Holy Communion daily; short worship service 12-12.10pm Mon-Sat,
requiring peace and quiet. Candlelit concert on 31st Dec is part of Edinburgh's
Hogmanay. Mon-Fri 9am-7pm (till 5pm in winter), Sat 9am-5pm, Sun 1-5pm.

434 8/Q25 **The Georgian House** 7 Charlotte Sq · www.nts.org.uk · 0131 226 3318 Built in
ADMISSION the 1790s, Robert Adam's masterpiece of urban architecture is full of period furniture
NTS and fittings. Not many rooms, but the dining room and kitchen are drop-dead
gorgeous – you want to eat and cook there. Delightful ladies from the National Trust for
Scotland answer your queries. New 20-min roof tour (£6). Times vary. Closed Jan/Feb.

Arthur's Seat Report: 445/WALKS.
The Pentlands Report: 448/WALKS.
The Scott Monument/Calton Hill Report: 470/466/VIEWS.
Newhailes House Report: 1818/HOUSES.
Dr Neil's (Secret) Garden Report: 1515/GARDENS.

The Best Independent Galleries

435 8/Q25 ✓✓ **Ingleby Gallery** 15 Calton Rd · www.inglebygallery.com ·
0131 556 4441 Light exhibition rooms behind Waverley Station for this
important contemporary gallery. Shows work by significant UK artists and the
Scots, eg Callum Innes and Alison Watt, with a refreshing and innovative approach
to the constantly changing exhibition programme. Mon-Sat 10am-6pm.

436 8/Q25 ✓✓ **The Fruitmarket Gallery** Market St · www.fruitmarket.co.uk ·
0131 225 2383 Behind Waverley Station and opposite City Art Centre. A
2-floor, warehousey gallery showing international work, retrospectives,
installations; this is the city's most contemporary art space. Excellent bookshop.
Always interesting. Cate (308/TEAROOMS) highly recommended for meeting, eating
and watching the world (and the art world) go by. Mon-Sat 11am-6pm, Sun
noon-5pm.

437 8/Q25 ✓✓ **Summerhall** 1 Summerhall · www.summerhall.co.uk · 0131 560 1581
By SE corner of the Meadows. Unlike anywhere else in the UK, with little
or no public funding, a multi-arts centre with several non-conventional gallery
spaces and a prodigious number of (free) exhibitions. Especially vibrant during
August. Open all hours. Café and 366/UNIQUE PUBS (The Royal Dick).

438 8/Q25 ✓ **The Printmakers' Workshop & Gallery** 23 Union St · www.
edinburghprintmakers.co.uk · 0131 557 2479 Workshop-studio and gallery
with exhibitions of work by contemporary printmakers and shop where prints from
many of the notable names in Scotland are on sale at reasonable prices. Good
courses. A local treasure moving to major new art complex in Fountainbridge 2018.

439 8/Q25 ✓ **The Collective Gallery** City Observatory & City Dome, Calton Hill ·
www.collectivegallery.net · 0131 556 1264 Installations and exhibition of
Scottish and other young contemporary trailblazers. Installed here on top of the hill
with panoramic views of the city. Now embedded in the Edinburgh World Heritage
site; exciting plans ahead for this airy location. Open-air caff. Events programme.

440 8/Q25 ✓ **The Scottish Gallery** 16 Dundas St · www.scottish-gallery.co.uk ·
0131 558 1200 Guy Peploe's influential New Town gallery. Excellent exhibitions.
Where to go to buy something painted, sculpted or crafted by up-and-comers or
established names – from affordable jewellery to Joan Eardleys. Or just look.

441 8/Q25 ✓ **Dovecot Studios** 10 Infirmary St · www.dovecotstudios.com ·
0131 550 3660 Altogether fascinating centre for contemporary art and craft
built around functioning tapestry studio of international repute. Good caff and
shop where a sampler loom can be got! Gallery & shop Mon-Sat.

442 8/Q25 ✓ **Stills** 23 Cockburn St · www.stills.org 0131 622 6200 Bang in the city
centre and 40 years old in 2017, this is Scotland's original photography gallery
with facilities, courses and year-round exhibitions. 7 days.

443 8/Q25 ✓ **Gayfield Creative Spaces** 11 Gayfield Sq · www.gayfield.co.uk
DF Brainchild of energetic John Ennis, embraces a wide and diverse creative
design portfolio. Significant talks, events, workshops.

The Best Walks In The City

See p. 12 for walk codes.

444 8/P25
1-15KM
XCIRC
BIKES
1-A-1
✓✓ **Water of Leith** www.waterofleith.org.uk The indefatigable wee river that runs from the Pentlands through the city and into the docks at Leith can be walked for most of its length. The longest section is from Balerno 12km outside the city, through Colinton Dell to the Blue Goose car park on Lanark Rd (4km from city centre). The dell itself is a popular glen walk (1-2km). All in all a superb urban walk. The Water of Leith Visitor Centre is worth a look. (0131 455 7367). Open 7 days 10am-4pm AYR (closed Christmas/New Year). **STARTS** (A) A70 to Currie, Juniper Green, Balerno; park by the high school. (B) Dean Village to Stockbridge: enter through a marked gate opposite the hotel on Belford Rd (combine with a visit to the art galleries 430/431/ATTRACTIONS). (C) Warriston, past the spooky old graveyard to The Shore in Leith (plenty of pubs to repair to). Enter by going to the end of the cul-de-sac at Warriston Cres in Canonmills; climb up the bank and turn left. Most of the Walkway (A, B and C) is cinder track and good for cycling.

445 8/Q25
1-8KM
CIRC
MTBIKES
(RESTRICTED
ACCESS)
2-B-2
✓✓ **Arthur's Seat** Of many walks, a good circular one taking in the wilder bits, the lochs and great views (467/VIEWS) starts from St Margaret's Loch at the far end of the park from Holyrood Palace. Leaving the car park, skirt the loch and head for the ruined chapel. After 250m, in a dry valley, the buttress of the main summit rears above you on the right. Keeping it to the right, ascend over a saddle joining the main route from Dunsapie Loch which appears below on the left. Crow Hill is the other peak crowned by a triangular cairn – both can be slippery when wet. From Arthur's Seat head for and traverse the long, steep incline of Salisbury Crags. Paths parallel to the edge lead back to the chapel. Just cross the road by the Palace and head up. No mountain bikes. For info on the Ranger service and special events through the year, call 0131 652 8150. **PARK** There are car parks beside the loch and in front of the Palace (paths start here too, across the road). **START** Enter park at Palace by the Parliament. Cross the main road or follow it and find your path, eg via the ruined chapel.

446 8/P25
1/3/8KM
XCIRC
BIKES
1-A-1
Cramond The charming village (though not so the suburb) on the Forth at the mouth of the Almond with a variety of great walks. (A) To the right along the prom; the traditional seaside stroll. (B) Across the causeway at low tide to Cramond Island (1km). Best to follow the tide out; this allows 4 hours (tides are posted). People have been known to stay the night in summer (oh yes they have!). (C) Past the boathouse, up the River Almond Heritage Trail which goes eventually to the Cramond Brig restaurant on the A90 and thence to the old airport (3-8km). Though it goes through suburbs and seems to be on the flight path of the London shuttle, the Almond is a real river with a charm and ecosystem of its own. 500m along is the **Cramond Falls Café** (0131 312 8408) for hot food and cakes till 5pm (Closed Wed). **The Cramond Gallery Bistro** (0131 312 6555) at the start is a pleasant quayside caff (open 7 days) and **The Cramond Inn** (0131 336 2035) is a proper inn with grub all day till 8.30pm (Sun 6.30pm). **START** Leave centre by Queensferry Rd (A90), then right following signs for Cramond. Cramond Rd N leads to Cramond Glebe Rd; go to end. **PARK** Large car park off Cramond Glebe Rd to right. Walk 100m to the sea.

447 8/P25
1-7KM
CIRC
Corstorphine Hill www.corstorphinehill.org.uk W of centre, a knobbly, hilly area of birch, beech and oak, criss-crossed by trails. A perfect place for the contemplation of life's little mysteries and mistakes. Or walking the dog. It has a

radio mast, a ruined tower, a boundary with the wild plains of Africa (at the zoo) and a vast redundant nuclear shelter that nobody's supposed to know about. See how many you can spot. If it had a tearoom in an old pavilion, it would be perfect. **START** Leave centre by Queensferry Rd and 8km out turn left at lights, signed Clermiston. The hill is on your left for the next 2km.
PARK Park where safe, on or near this road (Clermiston Rd).

Easy Walks Outside The City

448 8/P26
1-20KM
CAN BE CIRC
MTBIKES
2-B-2

The Pentlands www.pentlandhills.org · 0131 445 3383 A serious range of hills rising to almost 600m, remote in parts and offering some fine walking. Many paths up the various tops and round the lochs and reservoirs. (A) A good start in town is made by going off the bypass at Colinton, follow signs for Colinton Village, then the left fork up Woodhall Rd. Go left (signed Pentland Hills Regional Park). Go as far as you can (2km) and park by the gate leading to the hill proper where there is a map showing routes. The path to Glencorse is one of the classic Pentland walks. (B) Most walks start from signposted gateways on the A702. There are starts at Boghall (5km after Hillend ski slope); on the long straight stretch before Silverburn (a 10km path to Balerno); from Habbie's Howe about 18km from town; and from the village of Carlops, 22km from town. (C) The most popular start is probably from the visitor centre behind Flotterstone Inn, also on the A702, 14km from town (decent pub grub); trailboard and ranger service. The more remote tops around Loganlea Reservoir are worth the extra mile. (D) Lower slopes can be enjoyed from Swanston village (with R.L. Stevenson connections 1911/LITERARY PLACES) where quaint thatched white cottages are passed en route to the T-wood and a relatively easy climb to a great city view to the north. Car park next to Swanston Golf Club – good tea and scones.

449 8/Q25
1-4KM
CAN BE CIRC
XBIKES
1-A-1

Hermitage of Braid www.edinburgh.gov.uk Strictly speaking, still in town, but a real sense of being in a country glen. Main track along the burn is easy to follow and you eventually come to Hermitage House visitor centre; any paths ascending to the right take you to the ridge of Blackford Hill. From the windy tops of the Braid Hills there are some marvellous views back over the city. In snowy winters there's a great sledging place over the first bridge up to the left across the main road. Nearest caffs are in Morningside.
START Entrance on Braid Rd, just yards beyond junction with Hermitage Drive.

450 8/Q26
1-8KM
XCIRC
BIKES
1-A-1

Roslin Glen www.midlothian.gov.uk Spiritual, historical, enchanting and famous with the chapel **Rosslyn** (1842/CHURCHES), a ruined castle and woodland walks along the River Esk, though the map at the new visitor centre isn't that helpful and there's little waymarking.
START A701 from Mayfield, Newington or bypass: turn-off Penicuik, A702 then left at Gowkley roundabout and other signed roads. Park near chapel 500m from Main St/Manse Rd corner, or follow B7003 to Rosewell (also marked Rosslynlee Hospital) and 1km from village the main car park is to the left.

451 8/N25
2-8KM
CIRC
MTBIKES
1-A-1

Beecraigs & Cockleroy Hill nr Linlithgow · www.beecraigs.com · 01506 844516 Another country park S of Linlithgow with trails and clearings in mixed woods, a deer farm and a fishing loch. Great adventure playground for kids. Best is the climb and extraordinary view from Cockleroy Hill, far better than you'd expect for the effort – from Ben Lomond to the Bass Rock; and the gunge of Grangemouth in the sky to the east. New visitor centre and bistro 2016. The hill never closes.
START M90 to Linlithgow (26km), through town and left on Preston Rd. Go on 4km, park is signed, but for hill you don't need to take the left turn. The hill, and nearest car park to it, are on the right. 7 days. Summer 9am-8pm, winter 10am-4pm.

452 8/Q26 **Borthwick & Crichton Castles** nr Gorebridge · www.borthwickcastle.com ·
7KM 01875 820514 & Pathhead · www.historic-scotland.gov.uk · 01875 320017
XCIRC Takes in 2 impressive castles, the first a posh-ish hotel, the other an imposing ruin
XBIKES on a ridge overlooking the Tyne. Walk through dramatic Border country steeped in
1-B-1 lore. From Borthwick follow the old railway line. From Crichton, start behind the
ruined chapel. In summer vegetation can be high and may defeat you.
START From Borthwick: A7 S for 16km, past Gorebridge, left at N Middleton;
signed. From Crichton: A68 almost to Pathhead, signed then 3km past church.
Park and walk 250m.

Woodland Walks Near Edinburgh

453 8/P27 ✓ **Dawyck Gardens** nr Stobo · www.rbge.org.uk · 01721 760254 10km W
ADMISSION of Peebles on B712 Moffat road. Outstation of the Edinburgh Botanics. Tree
planting here goes back 300 years. Sloping grounds around the Scrape Burn which
trickles into the Tweed. Landscaped woody pathways for meditative walks. Famous
for shrubs, fungi and blue Himalayan poppies. Visitor centre, café, studio and shop.
Last entry 1 hour before gardens close. 7 days. Apr-Sep 10am-6pm, Mar and Oct
10am-5pm, Nov and Feb 10am-4pm. Closed Dec-Jan.

454 8/Q25 ✓ **Dalkeith Country Park** Dalkeith · www.dalkeithcountrypark.co.uk ·
ADMISSION 0131 654 1666 15km SE by A68. Part of the Buccleuch Estates, these wooded
policies of Dalkeith House (enter at end of Main St) just got a whole lot more
interesting. Along the river banks and under these stately deciduous trees, are
carpets of bluebells, daffs and snowdrops, primroses and wild garlic, according to
season. Most extensive preserved ancient oak forest in southern Scotland. A
'redevelopment' plan is developing as we write. Open 7 days 10am-5.30pm.

455 8/R26 ✓ **The Yester Estate** Gifford Large estate, in which there are some beautiful
woodland walks. Hard to find (and I won't tell you how) is the legendary Goblin
Ha', the bad-fairy place (the hotel in the village takes its name 878/LOTHIANS). Access
from the village: 100m beyond Tweeddale Arms, turn left; various lanes lead to Park
Rd. Go to end (500m), small car park and a gate in the wall, or 4km along the B6365
road, foot of steep tree-lined hill, on bend. Park by house, Danskine Lodge, and go
through marked gate. 3km back to village, it's 2km to Goblin Ha' itself.

456 8/Q26 **Humbie Woods** nr Aberdour 25km SE by A68 turn-off at Fala; signed for
church. Beech woods past car park. Churchyard a reassuring place to be buried; if
you're set on cremation, come and think of this earth. Follow path from churchyard
wall past cottage.

457 8/P25 **Cammo Estate** www.edinburgh.gov.uk · 0131 529 2401 On N edge of the city
via road to Forth Bridge. After Barnton roundabout, left on Cammo Rd, past the
gatehouse (and visitor centre) to the car park. A lungful of fields and woods close
to home.

458 8/R25 **Smeaton Nursery Gardens** East Linton · www.smeatonnurserygardens.
co.uk · 01620 860501 2km from village on N Berwick road (signed Smeaton).
Up a drive in an old estate is this early 19th-century walled garden. An additional
pleasure is the Lake Walk halfway down the drive through a small gate in the
woods. A 1km stroll round a secret finger lake in magnificent woodland. Garden
Centre hours Mon-Sat 9.30am-4.30pm, Sun from 10.30am; phone for winter
hours. Tearoom OK 10.30am-4pm (2195/GARDEN CENTRES). Lake walk 10am-dusk.

459 8/Q26   **Vogrie Country Park** nr Gorebridge · www.midlothian.gov.uk 25km S
by A7 then B6372 6km from Gorebridge. Small country park well organised for
'recreational pursuits'. 9-hole golf course, tearoom and country-ranger staff.
01875 821716 for events and opening times. Busy on Sundays, but a spacious corral
of countryside on the very edge of town. Open 7.30am-sunset.

460 8/Q27   **Cardrona Forest/Glentress** nr Peebles · www.7stanesmountainbiking.com ·
01721 721180   40km S to Peebles, 8km E on B7062 and similar distance on A72.
Cardrona on same road as **Kailzie Gardens** (1522/GARDENS). Forestry Commission
woodlands so mostly regimented firs, but Scots pine and deciduous trees up
the burn. Glentress (on A72 to Innerleithen) has become a major destination for
mountain bikers, but tracks also to walk. Consult at the visitor centre. See 2084/
CYCLING. The **Gypsy Glen** walk from Glen Rd via Springhill Rd, across the Tweed
Bridge from the High St in Peebles, is signed and a very decent amble with a wee
climb at the end.

The Best Beaches

461 8/R25   ✓ **Seacliff** North Berwick The best: least crowded/littered, perfect for picnics,
beachcombing and rock-pool gazing. Old harbour good for swimming. 50km
from Edinburgh off the A198 to or from N Berwick, 3km from **Tantallon Castle**
(1787/RUINS). At a bend in the road and a farm (Auldhame) is an unsigned road to
the left. 2km on there's a barrier, costing £2 (2 x £1 coins) for cars. Car park 1km
then walk. From A1, take E Linton turn-off, go past Whitekirk towards N Berwick.

462 8/R25   ✓ **Tyninghame Beach & St Baldred's Cradle** Also off A198. Going towards N
Berwick from the A1, it's the first (unmarked) turning on the right after
Tyninghame village. 1km then park, walk to left through gate 1km, past log cabin on
clifftop which you can hire for parties (as I have); great wild camping and the beach
magnificent. Nice caff in Tyninghame village with courtyard seating and Luca's ice
cream (9.30am-4.30pm, Sun 10.15am-5pm). And nearer N Berwick beyond the
Glen Golf Club off the A198 to Tantallon is gorgeous little Canty Bay.

463 8/Q25   **Portobello** www.porty.org.uk Edinburgh's town beach, 8km from centre by
London Rd. When sunny – chips, lager, bad ice cream and hordes of people, like
Bondi, minus the surf. When miserable – soulful dog-walkers and the echo of
summers past. Arcades, mini-funfair, long prom and pool. **The Espy** and the **Guild
of Foresters** (402/403/BAR FOOD) both great for a seaside drink and food. And **The
Beach House** caff 289/KIDS.

464 8/R25   **Yellowcraigs** nr Dirleton Another E Lothian splendour 35km from town. A1 or
bypass, then A198 coast road. Left outside Dirleton for 2km, park and walk 100m
across links to fairly clean strand and sea. Gets busy, but big enough to share.
Hardly anyone swims, but you can. Many a barbie has braved the indifferent
breeze, but on summer evenings, the sea slips ashore like liquid gold. See also
1686/KIDS. Scenic. Gullane Bents, a sweep of beach, is nearby and reached from
village main street. Connects westwards with Aberlady Reserve.

465 8/P25   **Silver Sands** Aberdour Over Forth Bridge on edge of charming Fife village (1558/
VILLAGES). Train from Edinburgh (nice station). Also cliff walk.

The Best Views Of The City

466 8/Q25 ✓✓ **Calton Hill** www.edinburgh.gov.uk Great view of the city easily gained by walking up from east end of Princes St by Waterloo Place to the end of the buildings and then up the stairs on the left. The City Observatory and Greek-style folly lend an elegant backdrop to a panorama (unfolding as you walk round) where the view up Princes St and the sweep of the Forth estuary are particularly fine. At night the city twinkles. Popular cruising area for gays; take care if you do. Home of the Hogmanay Festival *Son et Lumière* (30 Dec) and the **Beltane Fire Festival** (30 Apr) 83/32/EVENTS. Now of the **Collective Gallery** 439/GALLERIES.

467 8/Q25 ✓✓ **Arthur's Seat** E of city centre. Best approach through Holyrood Park from the foot of Canongate by Holyrood Palace. The igneous core of an extinct volcano with the precipitous sill of Salisbury Crags presiding over the city and offering fine views for the fit. Top is 251m; on a clear day you can see 100km. Surprisingly wild considering proximity to city. Report: 445/WALKS.

468 8/Q25 **Penthouse of the Point Hotel (as it is still known locally)** 34 Bread St · www.doubletreeedinburghcity.co.uk · 0131 221 5555 Unadvertised spot but the penthouse function space of the cool, design-driven Point Hotel (now the **Hilton Doubletree** 88/MAJOR HOTELS) offers a unique perspective of the city. They may allow you up if there's nothing booked in but it opens as a public bar on the first Thursday of the month.

469 8/Q25 **The National Museum of Scotland Terrace** Chambers St · www.nms.ac.uk · 0300 123 6789 6th floor of the fabulous recreated museum (418/ATTRACTIONS) has a beautiful terrace planted all round and offering revealing city skyline views and a great castle perspective. Andy Goldsworthy sculptures.

470 8/Q25 ADMISSION **Scott Monument** Princes St · www.edinburghmuseums.org.uk · 0131 529 4068 Design inspiration for Thunderbird 3. This 1844 Gothic memorial to one of Scotland's best-kent literary sons (1910/LITERARY PLACES) rises 61.5m above the main drag and provides scope for the vertiginous to come to terms with their affliction. 287 steps mean it's no cakewalk; narrow stairwells weed out claustrophobics too. 4 landings to catch the breath and view. Those who make it to the top are rewarded with fine views. Underneath, a statue of the mournful Sir Walter gazes across at Jenners. 7 days AYR.

471 8/Q25 ADMISSION **Camera Obscura & World of Illusions** 549 Castlehill · www.camera-obscura.co.uk · 0131 226 3709 At very top of the Royal Mile near the castle entrance, a tourist attraction that, surprisingly, has been there for over a century. You ascend through a shop, photography exhibitions and interactive gallery to the viewing area where a continuous stream of small groups are shown the effect of the giant revolving periscope thingy. An Alice in Wonderland room, a revolving tunnel of light, hall of mirrors: plenty to distort your view of reality! 7 days.

472 8/R25 1-A-1 **North Berwick Law** The conical volcanic hill, a 170m-high beacon in the E Lothian landscape easily reached from downtown N Berwick. **Traprain Law** nearby (signed from the A1 S of Haddington) is higher, more frequented by rock climbers but has major prehistoric hill-fort citadel of the Goddodin and a definite aura. Both are good family climbs. Allow 2-3 hours. For refreshments – Steampunk – brilliant coffee shop, restaurant and fish 'n' chips in N Berwick (883/LOTHIANS).

The Pentlands/Hermitage Report: 448/449/WALKS.
Edinburgh Castle Ramparts Report: 417/ATTRACTIONS.

the
Best
of Glasgow

The Best of the Major Hotels

473 8/M26
250 ROOMS
NO PETS
EXP

✓✓ **Radisson Blu** 301 Argyle St · www.radissonblu.com/hotel-glasgow · 0141 204 3333 Probably the best of the big city centre hotels, which is why there's nearly always a do on upstairs on the mezzanine – awards ceremonies, etc. Frontage makes major modernist statement; lifts the coolest in town. Leaning to minimalism but rooms have all you need, poster art from Glasgow's cultural events, though no great views; some face the internal 'garden'. All in all, a sexy urban bed for the night. Good rendezvous bar in large, open foyer. Collage, the only restaurant, is curiously small. Fitness facilities by direct lift in basement include a small pool (15m). No parking.

474 8/M26
72 ROOMS
NO PETS
MED.EX

£25-35

✓ **Malmaison** 278 W George St · www.malmaison.com · 0141 572 1000 Sister hotel of the ones in Edinburgh, Aberdeen and elsewhere; this chain of good design hotels under new ownership 2015. Well-laid-out rooms (though mostly small, the 4 duplex suites are great spaces), with DVDs, cable, etc – though the central location affords no great views. However, this is reliable, stylish and discreet. Great restaurant and bar with top casual dining, craft beers, etc. No leisure facilities or parking.
EAT Martin Wishart's **Honours** brasserie is one of the city's best restaurants (510/ BRASSERIES).

475 8/M26
230 ROOMS
NO PETS
L
MED.EX-EXP

✓ **Grand Central** 99 Gordon St · www.thegrandcentralhotel.co.uk · 0141 240 3700 Beside and very much on Central Station. A Principal Hayley hotel, who also have **The Blythswood** (481/BOUTIQUE HOTELS), extensively (£20 million) refurbished in 2010, restoring its position as an iconic hotel and gathering place (there are many function suites) for the city. The famously long corridors still go on forever but rooms are all that they should be (at this price). Champagne bar à la Grand Central NYC overlooks the station concourse. You could miss your train! Tempus so-so for food, the Deli a caff on the go. Out there, the station and the full-on Saturday night. Parking a pain but you'd arrive by train, wouldn't you? You're in the heart of Glasgow!

476 8/M26
164 ROOMS
NO PETS
L
MED.EX

Hilton Garden Inn Finnieston Quay · www.glasgowcitycentre.hgi.com · 0141 240 1002 Modern block by the big crane near the SECC makes most of its Clydeside location with deck (a long frontage) and very urban views. Rooms are a cut above the usual though not large. Uniformity throughout but thought-out. The City Café bar/restaurant on the ground floor extends outside over the walkway to a riverside terrace under the purple-lit-at-night Clyde Arc ('Squinty') Bridge: it's a good spot! IMAX TV and computer facilities in all rooms, small gym. Elevated from the economy travel lodge to the designer (though not quite boutique) hotel, really because of the river (though it is a bit of a hike into 'town').

477 8/M26
116 ROOMS
NO PETS
MED.EX

The Millennium Hotel 50 George Sq · www.millenniumhotels.co.uk · 0141 332 6711 Modest landmark hotel situated on the square, which is the municipal heart of the city, and next to Queen St Station (trains to Edinburgh and points north). Glasgow will be going on all about you and there's a conservatory terrace, serving breakfast and afternoon tea, from which to watch. Bedrooms vary (you can ask for front room overlooking square) in 3 categories. No parking or leisure facilities. Restaurant so-so but many nearby.

478 8/M26
319 ROOMS
EXP

Glasgow Hilton 1 William St · www.hilton.co.uk/glasgow · 0141 204 5555 Approach from the M8 slip road or from city centre via a less straightforward route. It has a forbidding Fritz Lang/Metropolis appearance and the entrance via the underground car park is grim. Though this hotel could be in any city anywhere, with motorways scything around it, it's possibly the most metropolitan hotel in Scotland. Dated now, its huge atrium, bars, restaurant and 20 floors of rooms (3 are 'Executive') makes it good for business, less so for happy hols. Views from some rooms to the west are stunning. Leisure facilities include small pool. Breakfast room and restaurant are interior; you'd eat here because you couldn't be bothered going into town. The other Hilton, the **Grosvenor** (0141 339 8811), on Gt Western Rd at junction with Byres Rd (97 rooms), has no more charm but is opposite the lovely **Botanic Gardens** (731/ATTRACTIONS) and close to many bars and restaurants.

479 8/M26 **Crowne Plaza** Congress Rd · www.crowneplazaglasgow.com ·
283 ROOMS 0141 306 9988 Beside the SECC on the Clyde, this towering, glass monument
EXP to the 1980s is another urban edifice which serves its business bedbox purpose but wouldn't cut it in many of the world's emerging cities. The Science Centre and Tower gleam and twinkle on the opposite bank near the BBC HQ; there's a footbridge across. Some good river views from the 16 floors (pay the premium for the corner suites!). The Mariner Restaurant in the lobby has a carvery and some ringside seating for river-gazing. Somewhat removed from city centre (about 3km, which you wouldn't want to walk), it's especially handy for the SECC and Hydro concerts, conferences, etc.

The Best Individual & Boutique Hotels

480 8/L25 ✓✓ **Hotel du Vin** 1 Devonshire Gardens · www.hotelduvin.com ·
49 ROOMS 0141 339 2001 Long Glasgow's no. 1 boutique hotel (as One Devonshire
DF Gardens, one of the first in the UK), now part of the small but beautiful Hotel/
ATMOS Bistro du Vin chain. This hotel probably offers the most individual experience, and
LOTS the smartest, most solicitous service in town. Five townhouses, the whole of a West End terrace, integrated into an elegant and sumptuous retreat a world away from Glasgow's wilder West End (centred on Byres Rd, a 12-min walk). Even parking is easy. House 1 has the bistro, bar, etc and House 5 the function rooms, but each retains character with fabulous stained glass, staircases and own doors to the street (though enter by reception in House 3). Cosy sitting rooms everywhere. Rooms large, as are beds, bathrooms, drapes, etc. Great bar (especially late) with malt list and, as you'd expect, well-chosen wines. No spa or pool, small gym. Long after its original conception, this is an enduring oasis of style.
£25-35 **EAT** Chic dining under chef Barry Duff in elegant salons with fastidious service and excellent wine list. See also 504/TOP-END DINING.

481 8/M26 ✓✓ **Blythswood Square** 11 Blythswood Sq · www.blythswoodsquare.
100 ROOMS com · 0141 248 8888 Along one side of a serene square (one of
EXP Glasgow's dear green places) in the city centre. A huge and sympathetic conversion of the historic building that was home to the RSAC Club; the motoring theme is everywhere. The restaurant buzzes, the upstairs salon bar is a civilised rendezvous for cocktails and afternoon tea, and the seductive, state-of-the-art, chilled-out spa is almost too busy to keep its calm (1263/SPAS). Original classic features (that lobby floor) and contemporary furnishings (acres of marble in the rooms and Harris Tweed big lamps) throughout. Rooms, all in house style, vary in size and amount of light – larger in the original section while others round an internal courtyard can be dark but are quiet. Parking a bit of a pain but, all in all, a great urban hotel.
£25-35 **EAT** Restaurant/brasserie menu reflects classic and contemporary theme. Always busy, it's the most buzzing of hotel dining in town.

482 8/M26   ✓ **Citizen M** 60 Renfrew St · www.citizenm.com · 0141 404 9485 Between
198 ROOMS   the Theatre Royal and the Pavilion Theatre – not that most of the clientele
CHP   would be seen dead in the latter. This is a very superior bed (or identical pod) box,
very good value boutique hotel. Part of an international chain and its first in the UK
– spot-on for Glasgow. Rooms solid, sexy and for once not just ergonomic but also
well designed. No restaurant, but café/bar (till 3am) and 24-hour tuck shop. Online
check in, EasyJet-style, you can only pay by card. Public space extensive (ground &
first floor) and relaxing. Great breakfast. Room controls (temperature, blackout, TV)
by iPad. TV films (including adult) free. Ubiquitous exhortations to 'Get Together'
and slogans surround you. Total brand immersion a bit gagging, but this is way
ahead of Ibis/Yotel and a host of urban-chic arrivistes. Parking 250m.

483 8/M26   ✓ **Abode Glasgow** 129 Bath St · www.abodeglasgow.co.uk · 0141 221 6789
59 ROOMS   Smart, contemporary Edwardian townhouse hotel, with wide, tiled stairwell
NO PETS   and funky lift to 3 floors of individual rooms (so size, views and noise levels vary a
MED.INX   lot). Fab gold embossed wallpaper in the hallways, notable stained glass and some
OK art. Part of the Andrew Brownsword Hotel Group, which specialises in
sympathetic conversions of notable old buildings. Heart of Bath St so very
downtown location, with many good restaurants adjacent and nearby.

484 8/M26   ✓ **15 Glasgow** 15 Woodside Pl · www.15glasgow.com · 0141 332 1263
5 ROOMS   Elegant and superbly appointed townhouse in a quiet street overlooking a
MED.INX   private garden at the western end of Sauchiehall St, beyond Charing Cross and the
M8. Contemporary Farrow & Ball kind of decor; the rooms are large so you probably
don't even need to use the guest lounge. Good for exclusive-use house parties.
Laura and Shane McKenzie your discreetly solicitous hosts: Tunnock's teacakes and
flowers! A very superior B&B in a city where good ones are few and far between.

485 8/M26   ✓ **Hotel Indigo** 75 Waterloo St · www.hotelindigoglasgow.com ·
94 ROOMS   0141 226 7700 Another smart, mid-price, very urban boutique hotel in a UK
MED.INX   chain (another in Edinburgh). Sympathetic conversion of historic building in a
former power station, in Glasgow's downtown financial district. The city is
referenced throughout: portraits of well-kent 'Weegies' in bar, themed floors
(theatre, Clyde, etc). Uniform but high design values. Well priced.
EAT Marco Pierre White's presence looms large in 'sophisticated' street-level
restaurant (512/BRASSERIES).

486 8/M26   ✓ **The Brunswick Hotel** 106-108 Brunswick St · www.brunswickhotel.co.
18 ROOMS   uk · 0141 552 0001 Contemporary, minimalist hotel that emerged back in the
CHP   90s as part of the new Merchant City. Time, perhaps, for titivation but rooms make
use of tight space and are good value. Bold colours. Good base for nocturnal forays
into pub- and clubland. Restaurant **Brutti Ma Buoni** (525/BISTROS) enduringly and
rightly popular. Pleasant breakfast, especially Sundays. Penthouse suite often used
for parties. No parking.

487 8/M26   ✓ **Artto Hotel** 37-39 Hope St · www.arttohotel.com · 0141 248 2480
50 ROOMS   Surprising, boutique-ish hotel very centrally situated beside Central Station on
CHP   busy-with-buses Hope St, though its rooms are double-glazed and quiet. Facilities
basic but this place is good value. Restaurant adjacent, Bombay Blue, features an
Indian buffet. Breakfast is continental/cooked buffet.

488 8/M26
104 ROOMS
CHP

✓ **Z Hotel** 36 N Frederick St · www.thezhotels.com · 0141 212 4550 The latest version (2015) of the emerging cool, urban budget hotel chain that started as the cheapest decent stopover in Covent Garden. Stripped to basics (some rooms have no windows) but all you need for a short stay. Good breakfast, helpful staff and handy location 100m from George Square, close to Queen St Station.

489 8/M26
5 ROOMS
NO TV
CHP

✓ **Babbity Bowster** 16-18 Blackfriars St · www.babbitybowster.com · 0141 552 5055 This much-loved 18th-century townhouse was pivotal in the redevelopment of the Merchant City and is famous for its bar (710/ALES), where you get breakfast, and for its beer garden. Schottische restaurant upstairs (weekends only); rooms are above, with pleasing, simple facilities. No TV. A very Glasgow hostelry and popular, so book ahead.

490 8/M26
12 ROOMS
CHP

✓ **Alamo Guest House** 46 Gray St · www.alamoguesthouse.com · 0141 339 2395 By Kelvingrove Park. A Victorian (1880s) grand house in a quiet residential area overlooking the tennis courts of the park and beyond to **Kelvingrove Art Gallery & Museum** (724/ATTRACTIONS). The Benzies run a very individual and hospitable house. No evening meal but innumerable good restaurants nearby. Only 5 rooms with en suite but aesthetics intact (Grade A listed).

491 8/M26
104 ROOMS
MED.INX

✓ **Apex Glasgow** 110 Bath St · www.apexhotels.co.uk · 0845 365 0000 Upgraded and completely refurbished, very downtown hotel by Edinburgh's Apex group (86/89/EDINBURGH HOTELS; 942/DUNDEE). Haven't stayed at TGP but expect contemporary efficiencies. Light bites and self-service food in lounge and many food and drink prospects along Bath St.

492 8/M26
8 ROOMS
CHP

The Pipers' Tryst Hotel 30-34 McPhater St · www.thepipingcentre.co.uk · 0141 353 5551 Opposite the top of Hope St and visible from dual carriageway near *The Herald* HQ at Cowcaddens. Circuitous route to the street by car. Hotel upstairs from café-bar of the adjacent piping centre and whole complex a nice conversion of an old church and manse. Centre has courses, conferences and a museum, so staying here is to get close to Highland culture. Small restaurant.

493 8/M26
8 ROOMS
CHP-MED.INX

Cathedral House Cathedral Sq · www.cathedralhousehotel.co.uk · 0141 552 3519 Opposite Glasgow Cathedral. Rooms above the bar; their main appeal is the outlook to the edifice, i.e. the cathedral, and **Necropolis** (1863/GRAVEYARDS). Functional and friendly though needs TLC. A walk to the Merchant City. **Drygate** nearby a great bar/restaurant (532/GASTROPUBS).

The Best Hostels

494 8/M26
110 BEDS
ROOMS

✓ **Glasgow SYH** 8 Park Terrace · www.syha.org.uk · 0141 332 3004 Oddly quiet and upmarket location, in an elegant terrace in posh West End, overlooking Kelvingrove Park. Was, until 1992, the Beacons Hotel, which was where rock 'n' roll bands used to stay in the 80s. Dorms for 4 6 (some larger) and the public rooms are common rooms with TV, games, etc. All rooms en suite.

495 8/M26
365 BEDS

Euro Hostel Glasgow 318 Clyde St · www.eurohostels.co.uk · 0141 222 2828 A very central (2 mins Central Station), independent hostel block at the bottom of Jamaica St and almost overlooking the river. Mix of single, twin or dorm accom, but all en suite and clean. Breakfast included in price. Kitchen and laundry. Games and TV room. The ground-floor bar, **Mint & Lime** (they see themselves as a hot pre-, even après-club/gig bar), is open to the public. A good all-round spot, especially if you're with a bunch of mates. 24-hour desk.

The Best Hotels Outside Town

496 7/L25
132 ROOMS
NO PETS
LOTS

✓✓ **Cameron House on Loch Lomond** nr Luss · www.qhotels.co.uk · 01389 755565 A82 via West End or Erskine Bridge and M8. 45km from city centre. Deluxe hotel complex with excellent leisure facilities in 100 acres of open grounds on the loch's bonnie banks. Recent changes of ownership. Interiors plush, sombre, urbane; you swish. Sports include 9-hole golf by the hotel ('the wee demon') as well as the 18-hole Carrick, 2 pools (1 with chutes for kids), tennis, snooker and lots to do on the loch including windsurfing and cruising (and you can arrive by seaplane). Casual dining at poolside or the Cameron Grill (not great for vegetarians – the meat is visibly well-hung) and notably Martin Wishart, the western outpost of Scotland's best urban restaurant (502/TOP-END DINING). The Spa with a huge range of treatments and pamperings has outdoor deck and pool, bar/restaurant. All this ain't cheap, but as they say, 'this is the life': they're not wrong.

>£35   **EAT** 4 restaurants to choose from, including Michelin-starred Martin Wishart's (lunch Thu-Sun & dinner Wed-Sun) make this the best dining prospect W of the city.

497 8/M26
92 ROOMS
NO PETS
MED.EX

✓✓ **Dakota** EuroCentral · www.dakotahotels.co.uk · 01698 835444 24km from centre on the M8. Like the South Queensferry version (129/HOTELS OUTSIDE EDINBURGH) this is a chip off the new (black granite, smoked glass) block and similarly situated overlooking the highway, in the spot of regenerating Lanarkshire they call EuroCentral. Behind the severe exterior is a design-driven roadhouse that is a paean to travel and elegantly rises to meet the requirements of modern travellers. You come off the thrashing M8 into an oasis of subdued colour, wood and brick – a perfect antidote. Another hotel hit for the pioneering McCulloch/Rosa team. Another Dakota in Glasgow city centre (Pitt St) 2016.
EAT The Grill is superb: way the best motorway caff in the UK?

498 8/L25
53 ROOMS
NO PETS
EXP

✓✓ **Mar Hall** Earl of Mar Estate, Bishopton · www.marhall.com · 0141 812 9999 M8 junction 28A/29, A726 then A8 into Bishopton. 5-star luxury a convenient 10 mins from the airport and 25 mins from central Glasgow, in 240 acres of wooded estate. Impressive conversion of imposing, *très elegant* baronial house with grand though slightly gloomy public spaces, including the central grand hall where you congregate and rooms that vary (some huge) but all with 5-star niceties. (Decleor) spa/leisure club adjacent with 15m pool, gym and fitness programme: it's a lift and a wee walk away. The Cristal, with long windows onto the gardens, is the fine-dining restaurant and Italian suppers in the hall! Opulent though it is, Mar Hall is very much part of the local Erskine community. And there's the 18-hole golf course. Close but far enough away from the city.

499 7/L24
14 ROOMS +
7 COTTS
DF
MED.EX

✓ **Loch Lomond Arms Hotel** Luss · www.lochlomondarmshotel.com · 01436 860420 Well smart and empathetic hotel in village sometimes thought to be on the twee side of cute. This (main) roadside inn does not reach to the loch or overreach itself; rooms are tastefully done. Restaurant, cosy pub-like pub and beer garden. Loch Lomond tourist trail is the better for this.

500 7/L24
47 ROOMS
EXP

✓ **The Lodge on Loch Lomond** www.loch-lomond.co.uk · 01436 860201 Edge of Luss on A82 N from Balloch; 40 mins to Glasgow's West End. In a linear arrangement that makes the most of a great lochside setting. This hotel, ignored by the posher guides, is a good prospect. Wood-lined rooms (the Corbetts), with balconies and saunas, overlook the bonnie banks; then there's the Grahams and, in the adjacent, newer, higher block, the Munros – it's a Scottish hill thing. Spa, nice pool, weddings; and once, Bill Clinton. Colquhoun's restaurant has the view and the terrace and is surprisingly good; book at weekends.

The Best Top-End Restaurants

501 8/M25
ATMOS
£25-35

✓✓ **Ubiquitous Chip** 12 Ashton Lane · www.ubiquitouschip.co.uk ·
0141 334 5007 The pioneering creation of one Ronnie Clydesdale, now in the hands of son and chef Colin (with Brian Finnie) and his wife Carol, moves onwards and upwards. Its essential characteristic – smart and friendly service and unpretentious fine dining, with conscientiously sourced ingredients under the skylights and vines – is much in evidence. 45 years on, The Chip remains the destination restaurant in the West End. The upstairs Brasserie has a lighter, less expensive menu. Beyond that, commandeered mainly by smokers, is a rooftop terrace. See also **Stravaigin** (514/BISTROS) and **Hanoi Bike Shop** (586/VIETNAMESE): all these chips off the old block open late. 7 days. Bar till 1am

502 7/L25
>£35

✓✓ **Martin Wishart at Loch Lomond** www.mwlochlomond.co.uk ·
01389 722504 This not-in-Glasgow Michelin-starred restaurant is probably the best restaurant in Glasgow. Martin Wishart (of the watery logo) here on the lochside at **Cameron House** (496/HOTELS OUTSIDE TOWN) from the water (of Leith) side location in Edinburgh (133/FINE DINING). Though the man himself is not stationed here, under his direction chef Graeme Cheevers produces its 6/8-course tasting menu and vegetarian version (and à la carte) with expected purpose and panache. Fans of Martin, of which I am one, will love this simply stylish refurbished room by the loch, with a distant mountain view. Lunch Thu-Sun & dinner Wed-Sun. The hotel's Cameron Grill is also VG on the grill drill.

503 8/M26
£25-35

✓ **Le Chardon D'Or** 176 W Regent St · www.brianmaule.com ·
0141 248 3801 Brian Maule's midtown eaterie. Meaning 'Golden Thistle' in English, with contemporary spin on Auld Alliance as far as the food's concerned: impeccable ingredients, French influence in the prep. A delightfully simple, unpretentious menu and a tranquil room remains one of Glasgow's temples to culinary excellence and you're in good hands. Brian takes cooking ingredients and seasonality seriously. This is honest, fine-in-the-right-way dining. Smart, not too solicitous service. Vegetarian and very good deal pre-theatre menus. An exemplary, easy-to-follow wine list. After 15 years, Le Chardon D'Or is still the business. Lunch (Mon-Fri) & LO 9.30pm. Closed Sun.

504 8/L25
£25-35

✓ **Bistro du Vin** 1 Devonshire Gardens · www.hotelduvin.com ·
0141 339 2001 Glasgow's oldest and, well, best boutique hotel (480/BOUTIQUE HOTELS) has, since it opened, had one of the city's classiest dining rooms. The salons in House 5 in this elegant row are comfortable, rather than fawning and formal, happy rather than merely hushed: like dining in your club. Presentation and service exemplary under chef Barry Duff and not expensive at this level. If you don't want the whole number there's a great bar menu (11am-10pm) where you get the kitchen's accomplishments for gastropub prices. A top spot in the West End. 7 days.

505 8/M26
ATMOS
>£35

£15-25

✓ **Two Fat Ladies At The Buttery** 652-654 Argyle St · www. twofatladiesrestaurant.com · 0141 221 8188 Can be tricky to find; just W of the M8. Under Ryan James and his team, the Buttery, aeons ago *the* best restaurant in Glasgow, did come back, does remain *the* posh night out and is the flag-waving Fat Lady. Mahogany-dark, discreetly sumptuous surroundings, gorgeous period tableware in a calm Victorian salon. Chef's table in a glass box in the kitchen where Stephen Johnson still leads a well-oiled team. Lotta fish, some vegetarian.
Shandon Belles, the Ladies' thinner sister round the corner is the below-stairs parlour and bistro; cosier, less costly. Indeed, not just less; the Belles packs 'em in with 2-courses-for-£16 and 3-for-£19 menus. And some careful attention to detail (the side plates!); the wine! Both open 7 days.

The Best Brasseries

506 8/M26 ✓✓ **Ox and Finch** 920 Sauchiehall St · www.oxandfinch.com ·
£25-35 0141 339 8627 In the heart of Glasgow's new eating-out quarter between the Park and Finnieston's restaurant row, Jonathan MacDonald and Mano Podolo's hugely popular, airy corner diner. Small plate menu (good helpings, so no more than 2 or 3 per person) both global and local. Good service turns the tables. Buzzy atmos. Faultless Ox and Finch is the one you want to get into. 7 days from noon.

507 8/M26 ✓✓ **Rogano** 11 Exchange Pl · www.roganoglasgow.com · 0141 248 4055
ATMOS Between Buchanan and Queen Sts. A Glasgow institution since the 1930s.
>£35 Decor replicating a Cunard ship, the *Queen Mary*, is the major attraction. A flagship restaurant for the city, serving contemporary surf (those oysters) and turf (that steak) brasserie-style menu, with classic dishes of reassuringly high quality. Spacious and perennially fashionable, the buzzing old-style glamour still holds. Downstairs, Café Rogano is the cheaper alternative. Outdoor heated 'terrace' is pure dead Glasgow, though the surrounding 'hedges', being plastic, never actually die. Restaurant: lunch & LO 10.30pm. Café Rogano: 7 days (LO 11pm).

508 8/M26 ✓✓ **Guy's Restaurant & Bar** 24 Candleriggs · www.guysrestaurant.co.
ATMOS uk · 0141 552 1114 This intimate and busy Merchant City restaurant does
£15-25 'real food' really well and is unquestionably one of the best restaurants in the quarter. The menu is long and diverse and never disappoints. In a welcoming, old-style room, the eponymous Guy and family serve you Scottish staples like mince 'n' tatties and prawn cocktail (and sushi), their signature 'Glasgow Tapas' with a bit of everything, and particularly good pasta. It's all home-made. Wines vary from good house to Cristal Rosé at £600 a bottle. Live but sympatico music Thu-Sat and Sun afternoons. 7 days all day. There's a **Wee Guy's** snack bar near George Sq daytime only (693/TAKEAWAY).

509 8/M26 ✓✓ **Hutchesons** 158 Ingram St · www.hutchesonsglasgow.com ·
£25-35 0141 552 4050 Landmark building near George Sq, looking down Hutcheson St. Converted by James Rusk to very high spec into a 2-storey (and private dining up top) café-bar and brasserie. Clubby, though ceiling high, and spacious. Open 7 days early till late. Excellent rep though some say pricey. A great chef (Andrew Doherty) surfs the turf.

510 8/M26 ✓✓ **The Honours @ The Malmaison** 278 W George St · www.
£25-35 thehonours.co.uk · 0141 572 1001 Michelin chef Martin Wishart's city-centre brasserie, in the basement of the Malmaison (474/MAJOR HOTELS). Not fine dining here but, as in Edinburgh (142/BRASSERIES), exemplary cooking under the direction of chef-director Paul Tamburrini. A little lacking in atmos but polished service of a light à la carte and prix-fixe menu, and a welcome addition to the city's menu in late 2014. 7 days lunch & dinner. **The Bar** adjacent and from same kitchen with stripped-down pub menu and craft beers from noon till 10pm.

511 8/M26 ✓ **Urban Bar & Brasserie** 23-25 St Vincent Pl · www.urbanbrasserie.
£25-35 co.uk · 0141 248 5636 Very central (off George Sq), urban as they say and very Glasgow. Great brasserie atmos; it just works, as you might expect from notable Glasgow restaurateur Alan Tomkins. Clubby atmos and linen tablecloths, etc, in different seating areas; outside terrace for people-watching. Bar and congenial à la carte and lunch menu (many ladies do). 7 days lunch & dinner.

512 8/M26
>£35

✔ **Marco Pierre White** 75 Waterloo St · www.mpwsteakhouseglasgow. co.uk · 0141 226 7726 The restaurant of the **Hotel Indigo** (485/BOUTIQUE HOTELS). They call it a steak house and there's plenty of meat on the menu (28 day dry-aged, etc) but it's a mixed brasserie offering (even token vegetarian). The governor looms large over this urban sophisticated room that doesn't feel too much like being in a hotel, and we know that MPW is never really there. Expectations are high, hence mixed opening reviews, but technically (and on a good night) it's pretty good. Possibly best stick the 'Market Menu' if you're not stuck on steak and can come 'pre-theatre', 7 days lunch & dinner.

513 8/M26
£15-25

✔ **The Restaurant Bar & Grill** Princes Sq · www. therestaurantbarandgrill.co.uk · 0141 225 5620 Upstairs in this long-established but no longer exclusively upmarket mall on Glasgow's principal shopping street, one of many restaurants and the best bet. Huge number of tables, including balcony overlooking mall, but often busy, attesting to its appeal. Contemporary British menu with Scottish sourcing. 7 days.

▰▰▰ The Best Bistros

514 8/M26
ATMOS
£15-35

✔✔ **Stravaigin** 28 Gibson St · www.stravaigin.co.uk · 0141 334 2665 This indispensable bar/restaurant, along with the **Ubiquitous Chip** (501/ TOP-END DINING), exemplifies the feel-good attitude to food of Colin and Carol Clydesdale. The original restaurant is downstairs – food served in both bar areas (no apologies for flagging it up also in 534/GASTROPUBS). In standards, Stravaigin sets a high bar. Mixes cuisines, especially Asian and Pacific Rim: the mantra 'think global, eat local'. Excellent, affordable food without the formalities and open later than most. All areas can be cramped but it buzzes brilliantly. Open 7 days all day (till 1am). The Clydesdales also have the excellent **Hanoi Bike Shop** nearby in Ruthven Lane (586/VIETNAMESE).

515 8/L25
ATMOS
£15-25

✔✔ **Cafezique** 66 Hyndland St · www.delizique.com · 0141 339 7180 The original location for Mhairi Taylor's landmark deli (which moved 2 doors up, then became a deli/café 652/CAFFS), is still the definitive West End grazing spot and hugely popular (book at weekends). Convivial is the word and though cramped, the ground floor and mezzanine hum along nicely day and night. Light, easy food with top ingredients, Mediterranean with apple crumble. From the best (all-day) breakfast, including home-made potato scones, to civilised last orders at 10.30pm, you can only wish you had an eaterie (and caff up the street) like this in your neighbourhood. But then it's probably a Hyndland thing! Perfect pitch! 7 days 9am-midnight (day menu till 5pm).

516 8/M26
£25-35

✔✔ **The Gannet** 1155 Argyle St · www.thegannetgla.com · 0141 204 2081 In the strip of Argyle St towards the West End, first put on the foodie map by Crabshakk opposite. From its opening in 2014, its look (wood and metal), its atmos (casual and buzzy), its clientele and its Mod-Scot menu have been a must à la mode. Chef/proprietors Ivan Stein and Peter McKenna leave their well-sourced Scottish ingredients to speak for themselves. Narrow bar-like front section leads to raised dining room through the back. A contemporary Glasgow hotspot! Small plates available till 6.30pm. Tue-Sat lunch & dinner, Sun 1-7.30pm. Closed Mon.

517 8/L26
£25-35

✔✔ **No. Sixteen** 16 Byres Rd · www.number16.co.uk · 0141 339 2544 Joel Pomfret and Gerry Mulholland's well-loved No. 16 at the Partick end of Byres Rd. Small upstairs and ground-floor bistro one of the most consistently good spots for unpretentious, inexpensive contemporary food. I'm a fussy guy but every time I go, I want everything on the menu. Irresistible, indispensable! Cramped, perhaps, but calm. 7 days lunch & dinner.

518 8/M25
£25-35
✓ **Turnip & Enjoy** 393-395 Great Western Rd · www.turnipandenjoy.co. uk · 0141 334 6622 Near Kelvinbridge. This amusingly entitled restaurant (once it was just Enjoy) gets very good press and under chef Martin Connor they're really going for it: fine-ish dining in a 5 starter/5 main choice menu. Good detail, innovative cooking in a light, airy room with big windows. A calm, non-pretentious and polite place. Wed-Sun lunch & dinner.

519 8/L25
£15-25
✓ **Epicures of Hyndland** 157 Hyndland Rd · www.epicuresofhyndland.co. uk · 0141 334 3599 I've revised my opinion of Epicures. This very Hyndland coffee shop/bistro in the heart of the territory is simply a great place to hang out, graze or just eat. Breakfast, lunch and snacks and dinner on the airy ground floor, more intimate mezzanine or outside terrace. 7 days all day.

520 8/M26
£25-35
✓ **The Western Club** 32 Royal Exchange Sq · www.theclubrestaurant.co. uk · 0141 248 2214 Behind the Gallery of Modern Art in a corner close to George Sq. First-floor stylish restaurant, part of the long-established private members' Western Club (but open to the public) by estimable restaurateur Alan Tomkins. Well-sourced classic dishes in a reassuringly comfortable and stylish setting. 7 days.

521 8/M26
£15-25
✓ **The Left Bank** 33-35 Gibson St · www.theleftbank.co.uk · 0141 339 5969 Laid-back, stylish, all-round and all-day eaterie, a West End safe bet near the university. From the same stable as The Two Figs in Byres Rd and The Bungo at 17 Nithsdale Rd in the southside, I reckon this is the one to love. From healthy, imaginative breakfast (that granola!) to great value snack and main meal menu 9am-10pm (from 10am Sat/Sun), this is a grown-up Glasgow place to hang out and graze with your cooler friends. Good vegetarian.

522 8/M26
£15-25
✓ **Ian Brown Food & Drink** 55 Eastwoodmains Rd · www. ianbrownrestaurant.co.uk · 0141 638 8422 A neighbourhood restaurant (albeit an affluent one): it's a long way from town but this is probably the best meal in the southside; discriminating southsiders know it! Over 20 years head chef of the Ubiquitous Chip and Ronnie Clydesdale's right-hand man, so expectations were high when he and the missus opened in this modest room in '10. Unpretentious, excellent-value, confident cooking ensured packed houses ever since. Ian's always there, visible in the kitchen and talks round the tables: you can see, he cares. Tue-Sat lunch & LO 9.30pm. Sunday roast 12.30-9.30pm.

523 8/M26
£15-25
✓ **Fanny Trollopes** 1066 Argyle St · www.fannytrollopes.co.uk · 0141 564 6464 Discreet presence on this once unloved but now booming boulevard, and a narrow room, but Fanny's has always been a dining and much-loved destination. Unpretentious, and great value and flair in the kitchen from chef/patron Gary Bayless make this is a Glasgow fave. Franco-Scottish menu with lovely puds. Lunch (not Sun) & dinner. Closed Mon.

524 8/M26
£15-25
✓ **Riverhill** 3 W Nile St · www.riverhillcafe.com · 0141 248 3495 Round the corner from their coffee bar which blew in from Helensburgh (the original caff and now the **Courtyard Restaurant** 842/CENTRAL). It's not a long story. In fact, it all happened fairly quickly; people just love what these Macdonalds do: light, eclectic, creative cookery from chef/co-proprietor Johnny Aitken, a seasonal, often inspired menu in an easy to drop in but not large bistro setting. Brill breakfast. 7 days all day. The caff takeaway is at 24 Gordon St.

525 8/M26 ✓ **Brutti Ma Buoni at The Brunswick Hotel** (486/BOUTIQUE HOTELS) &
<£15 ✓ **Brutti Compadres** www.brutticompadres.com · 0141 552 1777 At 43
Virginia St through the arch. Two sympatico Mediterranean-menu (brutti, a light
pizza) joints by Stephen Flannery and Michael Johnson who just slice it right.
Grazing food, good vibe. Both have outside tables.

526 8/M26 ✓ **Tibo** 443 Duke St · www.cafetibo.com · 0141 550 2050 Angus Macleod
£15-25 and Usman Shaikh's neighbourhood cool caff/bistro, now 10 years down the
line. Kinda funky and kinda rustic-in-the-city. Full-on menu but can graze and
great for breakfast. It's an East End thing – the food and the slower vibe! 7 days.

527 8/L26 ✓ **Art Lover's Café** Bellahouston Park · www.houseforanartlover.co.uk ·
£15-25 0141 353 4779 Near the artificial ski slope and the walled garden, on the
ground floor of House for an Art Lover, a building based on drawings left by
Mackintosh. Bright room, crisp presentation and a counterpoint to wrought iron,
purply, swirly Mockintosh caffs elsewhere. This is unfussy and elegant. Soup 'n'
sandwiches and light à la carte, all beautifully presented; a serious and aesthetically
pleasing lunch spot. Great terrace looks on the Park. 7 days daytime only.

528 8/L25 ✓ **Wee Lochan** 340 Crow Rd · www.an-lochan.com · 0141 338 6606
£25-35 A reworking of An Lochan, the previous restaurant here, by Aisla and Rupert
Staniforth. A neighbourhood café, just a short diversion from the West End food
belt, this wee lochan is worth diving into. A Mod-Brit menu, affable staff. Reports
tell me food is fab here. 7 days lunch & dinner.

529 8/M26 **Tribeca** 102 Dumbarton Rd (the original), 144 Park Rd (the smartest) &
£15-25 1 Fenwick Rd (southside) · www.tribecabarandgrill.com · 0844 357 7777
Note: you pay for the privilege of phoning them! Somewhere between a coffee
shop and a diner/bistro, there's definitely a NYC feel to this Glasgow chain of
individual eateries. Big local followings from breakfast to supper. In their separate
ways they're all winners (though southside very suburban). Expect Americana food
and portions. All open 7 days all day.

530 8/M26 **Pelican Bar & Bistro** 1377 Argyle St · www.thepelicancafe.co.uk ·
£15-25 0141 334 7330 Directly across the street from the splendid edifice of Kelvingrove
Art Gallery & Museum. Well-situated and well-run bistro. Small plates, delish
salads, Scottish staples, big burger and steak choice and some vegetarian. Suppliers
are listed. Particularly good wine list. Closed Tue/Wed till 5pm.

531 8/L25 **Sisters Jordanhill** 1a Ashwood Gardens · www.thesisters.co.uk · 0141 434 1179
£15-25 Off Crow Rd, and a little out of the ordinary, a great Scottish eaterie by sisters
Pauline and Jacqueline O'Donnell. Great atmos, proudly home-cooked from fine
ingredients. Loyal clientele. Phone for directions if you've never been beyond the
bright lights of Byres Rd. Closed Mon. Another Sisters in Kelvingrove 0141 564 1157.

✓✓ **Café Gandolfi** Now and forever. Report: 640/TEAROOMS.

✓✓ **The Finnieston** Gastropub or bistro? See report below.

✓ **Roastit Bubbly Jocks** Brother to Fanny Trollope's. Report: 564/SCOTTISH.

✓ **Firebird** Well-loved West End corner bistro. Report: 555/PIZZA.

The Best Gastropubs

532 8/M26 ✓✓ **The Vintage at Drygate** 85 Drygate · www.drygate.com ·
£15-25 **0141 212 8815** In East End below the Necropolis, part of the Tennent's
Brewery. The Drygate site itself is rambling and impressive: a relatively large-scale
microbrewery you look into (with tours 2/5pm Sundays), an outdoor terrace up top,
an event hall (comedy show every second Friday), a bottle shop with an
extraordinary selection of bottled craft beers, and knowledgeable and enthusiastic
advice on what to drink, and the Vintage part (a bar/restaurant transported from
Leith in Edinburgh) is a great beerhall restaurant with gastropub staples but also
creative cookery using all the right ingredients. If you like beer or casual good food
or just a great place to hang out, Drygate is about it. 7 days all day.

533 8/M26 ✓✓ **The Finnieston** 1125 Argyle St · www.thefinniestonbar.com ·
£25-35 **0141 222 2884** In the West End restaurant mile of Argyle St, a bar rather
than a gastropub, perhaps. Specialises in seafood; famed for its oysters. Cosy and
low-ceilinged, always busy, and excellent service. Fish of the day comes as you like;
top chips. Generally classy menu. You should book! 7 days all day.

534 8/M26 ✓✓ **Stravaigin** 28 Gibson St · www.stravaigin.co.uk · 0141 334 2665
ATMOS Excellent pub food upstairs in doubled-up rooms from one of the best
£15-25 restaurants in town. Doors open onto sunny Gibson St. Mezzanine gallery above.
Often packed, but inspirational grub; no pretence. Must have the busiest, most
exercised waiters in town. Nice wines. 7 days till late. Report: 514/BISTROS.

535 8/M26 ✓ **Bar Gandolfi** 64 Albion St · www.cafegandolfi.com · 0141 552 6813
<£15 Above Merchant City landmark **Café Gandolfi** (640/TEAROOMS) in a light, airy
upstairs garret with a congenial atmos and classy comfort food served till 10pm.
Bar 11.45pm. Good veggie choice (same menu) and pizzas. Great rendezvous spot.

536 8/L25 ✓ **The Bar @ Hotel du Vin** 1 Devonshire Gardens · www.hotelduvin.com ·
£15-25 **0141 339 2001** Alongside Great Western Rd. Not really a gastropub or even a
pub but mentioned here because one of the best restaurants in town – **Bistro du
Vin** (504/TOP-END DINING) – has an adjacent cosy lounge with a simple bar menu
done typically and stylishly well. Burgers, etc; no dinner frills. LO 11pm.

537 8/M26 ✓ **The Grumpy Goat** 90 Old Dumbarton Rd · www.
DF thegrumpygoatglasgow.co.uk · 0141 237 4730 What a delightful pub/
£15-25 restaurant just behind Argyle St near Kelvingrove Art Gallery & Museum. By the
Matteos (Dad has the estimable City Merchant, which was the best spot in the
Merchant City for years). Straight-up, decent gastropub food. Terrace gets sun all
day (when it's about). Great conversion of a historic house. 7 days all day.

538 8/M26 ✓ **MacSorley's** 42 Jamaica St · www.macsorleys.com · 0141 248 8581
£15-25 Originally from the makers of the legendary Sub Club, a reinvigoration of a
great old Glasgow pub (from 1899) with mahogany bar and old-world style and
atmos. Celebrating music and food: live bands and a seasonal, Scottish-centric
menu; tables on mezzanine. Some quite fancy cooking, artisan cheeses – a
contemporary menu with pies amid the old wood and the old rock 'n' roll. 7 days.

539 8/M26 **The Salisbury** 72 Nithsdale Rd · www.salisburybar.com · 0141 423 0084
£15-25 Once, as Cookie, this was a destination café/restaurant in the southside with the
je ne sais quoi. The Salisbury (which does sound like a pub) is avowedly a bar with
food, with which they do make an effort and some atmos remains, but to my mind
it ain't got the *quoi* any more. Worth a mention still for contemporary gastropub
food. It is rated, so often busy; you can feel cramped. 7 days.

The Best Italian Restaurants

540 8/M26 ✓✓ **Eusebi Deli** 152 Park Rd · www.eusebideli.com · 0141 648 9999 On
£15-25 a prominent Woodlands corner opposite the park, by Gibson St. The West
End deli of the industrious Eusebi family, a takeaway, *traiteur* but also a perfect and
popular Italian eaterie. After 15 years in Shettleston (the East End original 670/DELIS),
Edmund and Giovanna opened this demonstrably authentic and heartfelt aria to
Italian food. The tomatoes are from Calabria, the passata from a farmer they know
back home. An impressive range of food made on the premises – the Sicilian pastry
chefs start downstairs in the kitchen from 5am; the pasta made for all to see; the
pizza or pinsa dough (ancient Rome version) rises for 72 hours. Not a lot of tables, so
the queue merges with the counter queue – it's all worth the wait. 7 days.

541 8/M26 ✓✓ **Tarantino** 914-916 Sauchiehall St · www.tarantinoristorante.co.uk ·
£25-35 0141 237 3902 In the emerging Finnieston food quarter (next to Ox and
Finch), this is the go-to Italian. Title is the name of the proprietor, not a Hollywood
director. Together with chef Giovanni Giglio they have created a genuinely top slice
of the Italian pie (not pizzas you understand). Familiar faves from Puglia and Sicily.
Good Italian wine list. Not large, so book. 7 days.

542 8/M25 ✓✓ **La Parmigiana** 447 Great Western Rd · www.laparmigiana.co.uk ·
£25-35 0141 334 0686 Long-established top ristorante in Kelvinbridge by the
Giovanazzi brothers (Sandro here). They're always mentioned (though not starred)
in Michelin. No great surprises but reliably excellent. Traditional, solicitous service,
authentic ingredients and contemporary Italian cooking meld into a seamless
performance. Carefully chosen wine list. La P up there with the best! 7 days.

543 8/M26 ✓ **La Lanterna** 35 Hope St · www.lalanterna-glasgow.co.uk · 0141 221 9160
£15-25 A basement restaurant near Central Station, surprisingly spacious and busy
with a loyal clientele – well, it has been here 45 years. Tightly yet informally run,
with meticulous attention to detail and service, it strikes a comfortable balance
between a tratt and a ristorante, traditional and contemporary: friendly service but
linen tablecloths and sparkling glasses. Missed in previous editions of *StB*, to my
shame. Italian foodies alerted me; we're all happy now. Closed Sun.

544 8/M26 **The Italian Caffe** 92 Albion St · www.theitaliancaffe.co.uk · 0141 552 3186
£15-25 Modelled on an enoteca (a wine bar with small tapas-like plates of food), it's too
sophisticated to see itself as a mere tratt. Well located and usually packed. Some
flair and attention in the kitchen; a lotta risotto, and cute pizzas, frittatas. Good
wine selection. 7 days. Sister place **Paesano** in Miller St does only pizza – good but
(558/PIZZA).

545 8/M26 **Barolo** 92-94 Mitchell St · www.barologrill.co.uk · 0141 221 0971 From the
£25-35 decades-old, pure Glasgow L'Ariosto, an arriviste in the brash style of an arriviste
and an instant success (2011) on this still developing foodie street near Central
Station. Part of the Di Maggio group, there's a similar big-scale pasta/pizza
operation in Edinburgh (Amarone). Here in the heartland it seems to work better,
the banquettes always abrim (they muffle the noise levels), the calorific carbs
coming! Some no' cheap Barolos on the wine list. 7 days all day.

546 8/M26 **Piccolo Mondo** 344 Argyle St · www.piccolomondo.co.uk · 0141 248 2481
£25-35 In the midtown, along from the Radisson Hotel. A proper, quite posh Italian joint
with a long, happy following. Despite being a wee bit out of the restaurant zones,
it's invariably packed. Classic Tuscan fare and ingredients. A safe bet! Closed Sun.

547 8/M26 ✓✓ **Battlefield Rest** 55 Battlefield Rd · www.battlefieldrest.co.uk ·
£15-25 0141 636 6955 In southside opposite the old Victoria Infirmary, in a
landmark pavilion building, a former tram station on a traffic island. 22 years on,
this is probably still the best tratt in town. Huge menu from solid staples to
surprising specials. 'Event' express menu when there's something on at
Hampden up the road. Marco Giannasi at the helm. Family-run, lovingly
home-made, great Italian atmos. Small, with good daylight, this place
unquestionably is one of the most convivial places to eat in the southside. You
should book! Closed Sun.

548 8/M26 ✓ **Michaelangelo's** 9 Helena Pl · www.michaelangelosglasgow.co.uk ·
£15-25 0141 638 7772 In Clarkston, in the southside, at the roundabout on Busby Rd.
For years they had Roma Mia nearer town, now dad Massimo Onorati has handed
the pasta tongs to son Michaelangelo who's set up a simple, contemporary and
delightful restaurant/tratt. Folk are travelling across the burbs and from town to
visit. Some beautiful, imaginative cooking. 7 days all day.

549 8/M26 ✓ **Fratelli Sarti** 133 Wellington St · 0141 248 2228, 121 Bath St ·
ATMOS 0141 204 0440 & 42 Renfield St · 0141 572 7000 · www.fratelli-sarti.
£15-25 co.uk For over 20 years Glasgow's famed *Impero d'Italia* combining a deli/wine
shop in Wellington St, wine shop in Bath St and bistro in each. Great, bustling
atmos (eating upstairs in deli has more atmos). Good pizza, specials change every
day, *dolci* and *gelati* in supercalorific abundance. 7 days all day (560/PIZZA). The
restaurant at 42 Renfield St (corner of W George St) is more like dining; an elegant
room with exceptional marble tiling and wine list. Same menu as others, but more
ristorante specials.

550 8/M26 ✓ **Celinos** 620 Alexandra Parade · www.celinos.com · 0141 554 0523 Way
£15-25 out E on the long Parade (but hey, it's not so far) a brilliant, very
neighbourhood deli counter and tratt that's always busy. An Italian Aladdin's cave.
Big menu in different combos. Great value wines and seafood. 7 days all day.

551 8/M26 ✓ **Bella Napoli** 83 Kilmarnock Rd · www.bellanapoliglasgow.com ·
£15-25 0141 632 4222 Fabulously full-on family tratt on main road through the
southside, a restaurant that's a' things to a' body (ie universal appeal). Big hams in
the cold counter may amuse the kids. Bright presence on the street, inside the
space goes on forever. Linen tablecloths in the back section and you can see them
kneading the dough; it all goes like a Glasgow fair. 7 days all day.

552 8/M26 **Lamora** 1166-1170 Argyle St · www.lamorakitchen.co.uk · 0141 560 2070
£15-25 At the east end of the Finnieston strip of restaurants. Family-run, father and
son Silviano and Luciano Mora. Italian home cooking, handy for the Hydro.
Known for takeaway pizzas (adjacent shop counter). Very friendly service; recent
refurbishment. Folk rave about this place. 7 days lunch & dinner.

553 8/M26 **Panevino** 1075 Argyle St · www.panevino.co.uk · 0141 221 1136 Wine bar/
£15-25 enoteca kind of tratt with big windows onto Finnieston's restaurant row. Sister
of Little Italy, a Byres Rd staple, this is the upscale Sardinian version with decent
regional wine list and fastidious service. Closed Mon.

554 8/M26
<£15
Buongiorno 1012 Pollokshaws Rd · www.buongiornobistro.com ·
0141 649 1029 In Shawlands. P & P straight-up. Some home-made desserts.
Conveniently there are 3 good tratts within 100m of each other near these corners:
Di Maggio's, the **Brooklyn** (660/CAFFS) and this smallish Buongiorno. All often full.
This one, Marco and Angela's, is the one I'd choose. Takeaway menu. 7 days.

Coia's Café Report: 655/CAFFS.

The Best Pizza

555 8/M26
£15-25
✓ **Firebird** 1321 Argyle St · www.firebirdglasgow.com · 0141 334 0594
Big-windowed, spacious bistro at the far west end of Argyle St. Mixed modern
menu and everything covered, but notable for their light, imaginative Neapolitan
pizzas and pastas (big on gluten-free). Firebird is a perennially popular West End
hang-out and still a key spirit-of-Glasgow spot. 7 days all day.

556 8/M26
<£15
✓ **Brutti Ma Buoni at The Brunswick Hotel** 106-108 Brunswick St · www.
brunswickhotel.co.uk · 0141 552 0001 The not-large, usually bustling bar
and restaurant of this hip-ish hotel in the Merchant City (486/BOUTIQUE HOTELS) has a
big reputation for its brutti bread, a delicious, thin pizza – the star on a grazing/sharing
menu turned out from a gantry kitchen. 7 days. Sister restaurant **Brutti Compadres** in
a courtyard in Virginia St does the same good stuff in an enticingly convivial room.

557 8/M26
<£15
✓ **Republic Bier Halle** 9 Gordon St · www.republicbierhalle.com ·
0141 204 0706 Near Buchanan St. Notable for its mind-boggling and
presumably mind-altering selection of beers from all over the world, they also do a
great pizza. Apparently permanent 2-for-1 'offers' (though they are £15 a pop).
Noon-midnight; pizza till 10pm (there are other things on the menu).

558 8/M26
<£15
✓ **Paesano Pizza** 94 Miller St · www.paesanopizza.co.uk · 0141 258 5565
Related to the estimable **Italian Caffe** further into the Merchant City (544/
ITALIAN), this 2015 addition and very on-Glasgow-trend strips away the pasta in a
pizza only menu, that's as cheap as, well, chips. Some hoo-ha about the ovens,
imported from Italy and costing a fortune, turning out the classic sourdough
Neapolitan... they still ain't thin and crispy enough for me! 7 days all day.

559 8/M25
<£15
Inn Deep 445 Great Western Rd · www.inndeep.com · 0141 357 1075
Formerly the Big Blue which made a point of its pizzas. This downstairs, off-the-
street pub for craft and cask beers still fires out the pizzas (and burgers, etc). They
ain't bad. The main thing here as always is the outside terrace overlooking the
Kelvin where you can eat them. 7 days all day.

560 8/M26
£15-25
Fratelli Sarti 133 Wellington St, 121 Bath St & 42 Renfield St ·
www.fratelli-sarti.co.uk Excellent, thin-crust pie, buffalo mozzarella and freshly
made *pomodoro*. 7 days, hours vary. It's the ingredients that count here, the pizza
dough on the chunky side. Report: 549/TRATTS.

561 8/M26
CC's Pizzas 685 Clarkston Rd · www.ccspizza.co.uk · 0141 637 8883 They
take their several awards seriously here – as you would to draw both attention and
the pizza nuts this far into the south lands. It is (and as far as I can see) 'the only
wood-fired pizza in town'. It's simple, straight-up and straight out of the oven.
Takeaway and delivery only (to these burbs) 7 days 5-10pm. Deliveries Fri/Sat/Sun.

✓ **The Clutha** Great pub, great pizza. Report: 700/UNIQUE PUBS.

✔✔ **Le Chardon D'Or** Not a French restaurant *per se* but Monsieur Maule worked with the Roux brothers (a while back now) and the French gastronomy prevails here more than most. Report: 503/TOP-END DINING.

562 8/M26
£25-35

✔ **Côte** 41-43 W Nile St · www.cote-restaurants.co.uk · 0141 248 1022 Downtown Glasgow edition of the Côte story, expanding across the UK, and though *StB* doesn't often champion chains, Glasgow has precious few French restaurants and this well-laid-out and presented contemporary brasserie is à la mode and jolly good too. From breakfast till late, it's very Parisien and very on trend (London).

563 8/M25
<£15

✔ **Le Chalet Beaumartin** 518 Great Western Rd · www. lechaletbeaumartin.co.uk · 0141 237 3363 The West End little brother of the midtown bistro (sadly closed 2016) and the coolest spot for French bonhomie in town. This wee place in the West End is transplanted from Savoie and the ski-zone with a non-cheffy, cook-at-the-table approach: raclette, fondues, charcuterie. Some licensing problems at TGP hopefully sorted so we can park our skis in the snows of Kelvinbridge and enjoy this très charmant caff. Dinner only Tue-Fri. All day on Sat. Closed Sun/Mon. No debit/credit cards at TGP.

The Best Scottish Restaurants

564 8/L26
£15-25
✓ **Roastit Bubbly Jocks** 450 Dumbarton Rd · www.roastitbubblyjocks. com · 0141 339 3355 Far up in the West End but for over 13 years we have beaten our way to this Partick dining room where Mo Abdulla runs a seriously good kitchen at admirably good value. Comforting, creative, unpretentious Scottish fare make for one of the best dinners (or 'teas' as we may call them) in the West End. You'll have to book at weekends. It's very Scottish, by the way! 7 days.

565 8/M26
£25-35
✓ **City Merchant** 97-99 Candleriggs · www.citymerchant.co.uk · 0141 553 1577 This long-established Merchant City restaurant has an enduring appeal and high standards. Seafood, game, steaks, focusing on quality Scottish produce with Italian flair. Lovely oysters; top fish platter. Daily and à la carte menus in warm bistro atmos. Good biz restaurant or an intimate rendezvous. Closed Sun.

566 8/M25
£25-35
✓ **Cail Bruich** 725 Great Western Rd · www.cailbruich.co.uk · 0141 334 6265 Near Byres Rd junction. The name means 'eat well' and you do in this small bistro with a light ambience. Chef/proprietor Chris Charalambous creates a 'modern style of Scottish cuisine influenced by classical techniques', with seasonal ingredients from named sources. Occasional guest chefs with their 'Madklubben' events. Lunch is good value. 7 days.

567 8/M26
<£15
✓ **Babbity Bowster** 16-18 Blackfriars St · www.babbitybowster.com · 0141 552 5055 Listed as a pub for real ale and as a hotel (there are rooms upstairs), their all home-made food is mentioned mainly for its authentic Scottishness (haggis and stovies) and all-day availability. It's pleasant to eat outside on the patio/garden in summer. Reports: 710/ALES; 489/INDIVIDUAL HOTELS.

568 8/M26
ATMOS
<£15
✓ **The Horseshoe** 17 Drury St · www.thehorseshoebarglasgow.co.uk · 0141 248 6368 A classic pub to be recommended for all kinds of reasons, and on this page because it serves the epitome of the Scottish pub 'bar lunch'. And there is a particularly good deal upstairs in the lounge, with 3 courses for £4.50 at TGP: old favourites on the menu like mushy peas, macaroni cheese, jelly and (not fresh) fruit. High tea till 7.45pm (not Sun) then... the karaoke. Report: 697/UNIQUE PUBS.

569 8/M26
£15-25
✓ **The Black Sheep Bistro** 10 Clarendon Rd · www.blacksheepbistro.co. uk · 0141 333 1435 Off the start (eastern end) of Great Western Rd, a little off the (foodie) map. Not proclaiming itself as a particularly Scottish restaurant, but it is. A neighbourhood diner where Angela Loftus with nae bother prepares an extensive menu including all the faves your ma made: lentil soup, traditional prawn cocktail, haggis, beef olives. Honest scran with all the trimmings. Closed Mon.

570 8/M25
£15-25
The Bothy 11 Ruthven Lane · www.bothyglasgow.co.uk · 0141 334 4040 Off Byres Rd. Part of a Scottish chain of (various) restaurants so somewhat contrived and no individual passion here, but a corporate and comfortable version of Scottish contemporary safe choices and obvious sourcing. Nevertheless, you tourists, there is Scottishness! 7 days all day.

The Best Indian Restaurants

571 8/M26
ATMOS
£15-25
✓✓ **Mother India** 28 Westminster Terrace · www.motherindia.co.uk · 0141 221 1663 Monir Mohammed's mothership restaurant; it's *sans pareil*! Different dining experiences on each of 3 floors though the straightforward, not absurdly long menu with old and new favourites is the same in each. Ground floor more clubby with panelling and leather benches, the larger (more asked for) upstairs room intimate, candlelit, and downstairs a more contemporary ambience (Fri/Sat only). It's all stylish, solid and quite the best Indian restaurant in town (Mother's also in Edinburgh 261/INDIAN). House wine and Kingfisher beer but for £2.50 corkage you can BYOB. Best book. Lots of vegetarian choice. Lunch (not Mon-Thu) & dinner 7 days. Takeaway too.

572 8/M26
£15-25
✓ **Mother India Café** 1355 Argyle St · www.motherindia.co.uk · 0141 339 9145 Opposite **Kelvingrove Museum and Art Gallery** (724/ATTRACTIONS). Rudely healthy progeny of Mother (above) and cousin to Wee Curry House (below); a distinctive twist here ensures another packed house at all times. Menu made up of 40 thali or tapas-like dishes (4/5 for a party of 2), so just as we always did, we get tastes of each other's choices – only it's cheaper! Fastidious waiters (do turn round the tables). Miraculous tiny kitchen. Can't book – you may wait! 7 days.

573 8/M26
£15-25
✓ **Dining In With Mother India** 1347 Argyle St · www.motherindia.co.uk · 0141 334 3815 Right next door to Mother India Café, a more intimate dining in. Somewhere between Mother herself and the tapas-driven caff is this more laid-back place also known as The Den, with hot (ie temperature) and cold dishes. You can dine here or take it home. The usual signature irresistible curries and breads. 7 days. Can BYOB and exclusive hire.

574 8/M26
<£15
✓ **Ranjit's Kitchen** 607 Pollokshaws Rd · www.ranjitskitchen.com · 0141 423 8222 They say 'homemade Panjabi food' ('Pan' not 'Pun'), in this southside caff and takeaway high on ethnic integrity, which was a hit from the weekend it opened in 2015. Ranjit in the kitchen, friendly young staff on the counter. Great value. No alcohol; superb lassis. Closed Mon.

575 8/M26
<£15
✓ **Babu Bombay Street Kitchen** 186 W Regent St · www.babu-kitchen.com · 0141 204 4042 On corner of Blythswood St and opposite (in every sense) the **Blythswood** (481/BOUTIQUE HOTELS). A downstairs relaxed but lively caff and takeaway (Tiffin boxes) with great counter service, and top value and tastin' cold and hot streetfood. Joanna Blythman, the *Sunday Herald* food critic who knows her red onions, gave it 10/10. Those 4 tablefuls would agree. So not much room but open from spicy breakfast till suppertime. BYOB (£3 wine, 75p beer). Closed Sun.

576 8/M26
£15-25
✓ **Nakodar Grill** 13 Annfield Pl · www.nakodargrill.com · 0141 556 4430 On the little park and visible from Duke St this North Indian diner wins awards and has a far and wide loyal following but is still a bit of a Dennistoun secret. Great tandoori menu and the 'Golden Oldies' and vegetarian. It is a winner! 7 days.

577 8/M26
<£15
✓ **The Wee Curry Shop** 7 Buccleuch St · 0141 353 0777 & Ashton Lane · 0141 357 5280 · www.weecurryshopglasgow.co.uk Tiny outposts of Mother India above, 2 neighbourhood home-style-cooking curry shops, just as they say. Cheap, always cheerful. Stripped-down menu in small, if not micro rooms. Buccleuch St 8 tables; Ashton Lane the bigger, with 2 sittings (7 & 9pm) at weekends. House red and white and Kingfisher but can BYOB (1 bottle wine only, £3.50). Lunch & dinner. Sun lunch Byres Rd only. No credit cards.

578 8/L26 ✓ **The Little Curry House** 41 Byres Rd · www.littlecurryhouse.co.uk ·
£15-25   0141 339 1339 Little it is and all the better for it, the mezzanine overlooking the kitchen and its aromas. This is close to real streetfood. A former head chef from Mother India; compact menu all enticing. Must book weekends. 7 days.

579 8/M26 ✓ **Balbir's** 7 Church St · www.balbirs.co.uk · 0141 339 7711 Round the
£15-25   corner at the bottom end of Byres Rd, the grandee Glasgow proprietor, Balbir Singh Sumal, oversees with his son, Neki, in this cavernous, chandelier-chic, routinely packed restaurant. Both regular and innovative dishes from the subcontinent that Glasgow has taken to its heart (though low-cholesterol rapeseed oil is used instead of ghee) and stomach. Good vegetarian, with some recipes from Balbir's wife Paramjit. 7 days dinner only.

580 8/M26 **Shish Mahal** 60-68 Park Rd · www.shishmahal.co.uk · 0141 334 7899 First-
£15-25   generation Indian restaurant that still, after (unbelievably) over 50 years, remains one of the city's faves. Modernised some years back but not compromised and still feels like it's been here forever. Menu of epic size. Many different influences in the cooking, and total commitment to the Glasgow curry (and chips). The Shish Mahal's great claim to fame is that it actually invented chicken tikka masala, the UK's favourite curry. Mon-Thu lunch & dinner, Fri/Sat all day, Sun dinner only.

581 8/M26 **Banana Leaf** 76 Old Dumbarton Rd · www.thebananaleaf.co.uk ·
ATMOS   0141 334 4445 Across Argyle St from Kelvingrove Art Gallery, up Regent Moray
<£15   St, turn left. Discreet doorway into 2 tiny South Indian living rooms in a Glasgow tenement. Some chicken and lamb dishes but mostly vegetarian and loadsa dosas. Disarmingly real, cheap as chapatis; even the slightly chaotic service and mad kitchen is reminiscent of downtown Cochin. The takeaway operation can be a bit offhand. 7 days.

582 8/M26 **Dakhin** 89 Candleriggs · www.dakhin.com · 0141 553 2585 Upstairs, out
£15-25   of sight and a good find for lovers of southern Indian food. Same owners as The Dhabba (below) but menu is a subcontinent away. Lighter and saucier with coconut, ginger and chilli and light-as-a-feather dosas make essential difference to the tandoori/tikka-driven menus of most other restaurants in this category. Signature dish: must-have paper-thin dosa. 7 days lunch & dinner.

583 8/M25 **Ashoka Ashton Lane** 19 Ashton Lane · 0141 337 1115 & Ashoka West End
£15-25   at 1284 Argyle St · 0141 339 3371 · www.ashokarestaurants.com Part of the Harlequin Restaurants chain, they have always been good, simple and dependable places to go for curry and have kept up with the times. Argyle St is *the* original. Nothing surprising about the menus, just sound Punjabi via Glasgow fare. Good takeaway service. Both open 7 days till late.

584 8/M26 **The Dhabba** 44 Candleriggs · www.thedhabba.com · 0141 553 1249 Mid-
£15-25   Merchant City curry house serving slow-cooked North Indian cuisine in big-window diner. Complemented by sister restaurant Dakhin (above); often busy. Methinks it's not as good as it thinks it is but is overall a decent Merchant City choice. 7 days.

585 8/M26 **The Alishan Tandoori** 250 Battlefield Rd · www.alishantandoori.co.uk ·
£15-25   0141 632 5294 Southsiders and many from further afield swear by this Mount Florida Indo-Pak restaurant that's especially good for veggie and other diets. It's been here for almost 30 years, with honesty and integrity in their mix of spices on a very long menu. 7 days dinner only. Takeaway too.

Spice Garden Report: 673/LATE DINING.

586 8/M25 ✓ **The Hanoi Bike Shop** 8 Ruthven Lane · www.thehanoibikeshop.co.uk ·
£15-25 **0141 334 7165** From the makers of the **Ubiquitous Chip** (501/TOP-END DINING) and **Stravaigin** (514/BISTROS), a different proposition but still the same innovative, contemporary approach, with appropriate well-sourced ingredients, subtle flavours and authentic combos: phos and banh mi, home-made tofu and salads. Fish oil used instead of seasoning. A refreshing offshoot of the Clydesdales' eclectic approach to food. Like their other restaurants, you can eat here late. 7 days.

587 8/M26 ✓ **Thairiffic** 303 Sauchiehall St · www.thairifficrestaurant.com ·
£15-25 **0141 332 3000** Upstairs on the corner with Pitt St, above Antipasti. Thai restaurants often have daft names, this one is little difficult to live up to, perhaps, but actually it comes close. At last Glasgow has a Thai place with good food in a great room. Though not big on atmos, it overlooks the 'Sauchiehall Street of Dreams' (and the ABC venue opposite with its punters milling in and out) and the young staff are enthusiastic and friendly. Delicious dishes in all fish, meat and vegetarian departments. Mon-Sat lunch & dinner, Sun dinner only.

588 8/M26 ✓ **Thai Lemongrass** 24 Renfrew St · www.thailemongrass.net ·
£15-25 **0141 331 1315** Noticing perhaps that Glasgow has far fewer good Thai restaurants than Edinburgh (see p. 59) TL opened up here, near the Concert Hall and opposite Cineworld; years later there are few rivals and it is one of the best in town. Contemporary (those banquettes) while still cosy. Good service and presentation of the ubiquitous Thai faves. 7 days lunch & dinner.

589 8/M26 **Thai Siam** 1191 Argyle St · www.thaisiamglasgow.com · 0141 229 1191
£25-35 Traditional, low-lit atmos but a discerning clientele forgive the decor and get their heads down into fragrant curries et al. All-Thai staff maintain authenticity (same chef for years). What it lacks in style up front it makes up for in the kitchen. 7 days.

The Best Chinese Restaurants

590 8/M26
£15-25

✓ **Loon Fung** 417-419 Sauchiehall St · 0141 332 1240 Through a long hall off the night-time (western) end of the legendary street, a legendary Cantonese restaurant risen from the ashes of a fire in 2010. Remade in a lovely interior spacious room that feels like China, this is the real deal as the regular Chinese clientele attest. 7 days.

591 8/M26
£25-35

✓ **Ho Wong** 82 York St · www.ho-wong.com · 0141 221 3550 Inconspicuous location for a discreet, urbane Pekinese/Cantonese restaurant which relies on its reputation and makes few compromises. Calm, quite chic room with mainly upmarket clientele; an ambience you either love (a lot) or hate. Good champagne list. Reassuringly expensive. Notable for seafood and duck. / days.

592 8/M26
£15-25

✓ **Sichuan House** 345-349 Sauchiehall St · www.sichuanhouse.co.uk · 0141 333 1788 A great addition (2014) to the city's Chinese (and Malay) menu. May seem a bit chain-like and it's big, but it's a Glasgow one-off. It's spicy; a lavish picture menu offers exotic choices. This very good value place is just a little 'hotter' than the rest of the pack. 7 days all day.

593 8/M26
£25-35

✓ **Dragon-i** 311-313 Hope St · www.dragon-i.co.uk · 0141 332 7728 Refreshingly contemporary Chinese/Pan-Asian opposite Theatre Royal. Thai/Malaysia and rice/noodle/tempura dishes with sound non-MSG. Often unlikely Scottish ingredients make for fusion at its best. Proper puds. Chilled-out room, creative Chinese cuisine, smart service and handy for theatre. Closed Sun.

594 8/M26
£25-35

✓ **Amber Regent** 50 W Regent St · www.amberregent.com · 0141 331 1655 Elegant Cantonese restaurant that prides itself on courteous service and the quality of its cuisine, especially seafood. Chung family here almost 30 years. The menu is traditional, as is the atmos. Influences from Mongolia to Malaysia. Creditable wine list, quite romantic at night and a good biz lunch spot. The only Glasgow Chinese restaurant regularly featured in both AA and Michelin. Lunch & dinner Mon-Sat, Sun dinner only.

595 8/M25
£15-25

✓ **Chow** 98 Byres Rd · www.chowrestaurant.co.uk · 0141 334 9818 Away from other Chinese restaurants clustered downtown, this is the contemporary, smarter and buzzy West End version. Broad menu is imaginative and different. Good vegetarian choice. Can be a tight squeeze down or up. Takeaway and delivery. Good value, especially lunch. Lunch (not Sun) & dinner.

596 8/M26
ATMOS
<£15

✓ **Asia Style** 185-189 St George's Rd · 0141 332 8828 Near Charing Cross. Discreet, authentic and exceptionally good value, this makes for an excellent late-night rendezvous though they make no compromises to a Scottish/Chinese palate. Bright canteen with banter to match. Traditional Chinese without MSG. Malaysian dishes and a reputation for shellfish. Think old Singapore! 7 days dinner only (till 1.30am). Cash only. Report: 674/LATE DINING.

597 8/M26
<£15

Dumpling Inn 325 Sauchiehall St · 0141 332 5053 Here the name says it all – you drop in for dumplings. Fast, simple, authentic food, smallish room, cheery young staff. And dumplings: boiled, grilled, in soup, cold, with noodles. Genuinely good stuff. 7 days all day.

598 8/M26
£15-25

Banana Leaf 67 Cambridge St · www.bananaleafglasgow.com · 0141 333 9994 Near the Concert Hall and Buchanan Bus Station, below the Easy Hotel. Perhaps in accord with the digs upstairs, this is a backpackery or folk-on-a-budget cosmopolitan diner, Singapore style. Big menu, everything you could want with rice or noodles. Family run, good buzz. 7 days all day. No relation to Banana Leaf (Indian) above.

The Best Japanese & Fusion Restaurants

599 8/M26
£15-25

✓ **Rumours** 21 Bath St · 0141 353 0678 From an elevated first-floor position at the corner of W Nile and Bath Sts, this Malaysian caff (or kopitiam) eschews the style dictates of the restaurant/bar culture further along Bath St and is the better for it. Odd name but the word on the street is that this is the real deal: fusion/Malaysian cooking that is fresh and authentic and a long, unusual, non-alcoholic drinks list (though also Tiger, Singha and wine). 7 days.

600 8/M26
£15-25

✓ **Opium** 191 Hope St · www.opiumrestaurant.co.uk · 0141 332 6668 City centre corner location for this Hong Kong-style fusion restaurant regularly lauded for its dim sum. But chef Kwan Yu Lee's mainly Chinese menu ranges aromatically over the continent and is much to our taste; good fish and prawn choices, decor is Malaysian minimalist with calm lighting. Alluring but non-addictive. 7 days lunch & dinner.

601 8/M26
£15-25

Pickled Ginger 512 St Vincent St · www.pickledgingerfinnieston.co.uk · 0141 328 8941 Out west, corner of Pembroke St. Happy sushi in this flavour-of-2015, clean-cut Japanese diner and takeaway. They show you how to eat it. Wide choice of ingredients, including octopus, clams, sizzling beef and all the usuals. Beers to go with. 7 days all day.

602 8/M26
£15-25

Ichiban 50 Queen St · 0141 204 4200 & 184 Dumbarton Rd, Partick · 0141 334 9222 · www.ichiban.co.uk Queen St: a noodle bar based loosely on the Wagamama formula. Fundamental food, egalitarian presentation, some technology. Ramen, udon, soba noodle dishes; also chow meins, tempuras and other Japanese snacks. Long tables, eat-as-it-comes 'methodology'. Partick version more Asian fusion, here amid the West End restaurant culture. Light, calm, modern. Near Byres Rd, it is possibly the better of the 2, but a healthy option in both quarters. Both open 7 days.

603 8/M26
£15-25
£25-35

Yen 28 Tunnel St · www.yenrotunda.com · 0141 847 0220 In the landmark Rotunda building near the SECC, so often busy with pre- or après-concert audiences. First-floor 'oriental' i.e. Cantonese/Japanese/Thai noodle restaurant (the ground floor is Italian). Location and convenience the thing here. 7 days.

Other Ethnic Restaurants

SPANISH

604 8/M26
£15-25
✓ **Rioja** 1116 Argyle St · www.riojafinnieston.co.uk · 0141 334 0761 In heart of Finnieston food quarter, this avowedly Spanish vinoteca doesn't let the side down, i.e. contemporary Spanish cuisine which, despite its renaissance, is not so well represented in this or any UK city. Classic and reconstructed tapas, an appealing example of small plate sharing/grazing. In Barcelona/Madrid style, it's open unusually late. Tue-Sun noon till 1am.

605 8/M26
<£15
✓ **Tinto Tapas Bar** 138 Battlefield Rd · www.tintotapasbar.co.uk · 0141 636 6838 In the southside near the Victoria Infirmary. Sliver of a restaurant serving tapas and specials all day, with good, inexpensive Spanish wine selection. 10 years on, this is not only the original of a now expanding Glasgow chain but also the first of the tapas/small plate menus that have spread like Spanish flu. Battlefield Rd still has the most authentic Iberian vibe. Newer branches at 39-41 Hyndland St in the West End (0141 337 3135), 105 Main St in Uddingston (01698 801383), and (in 2016) the Merchant City. 7 days all day from 10am.

606 8/M25
8/M26
£15-25
Café Andaluz 2 Cresswell Lane · 0141 339 1111 & St Vincent Pl · 0141 222 2255 · www.cafeandaluz.com The original is a basement on corner of Cresswell (the less heaving of the Byres Rd lanes) where folks gather of an evening (outside benches are cool). Nice atmos encased in ceramica, with a wide choice of passable tapas and mains (also vegetarian). Owned by Di Maggio (Italian) chain. St Vincent Pl also busy but because of location perhaps rather than as a destination. 7 days all day. In Aberdeen too, but Edinburgh Andaluz is possibly best of the four.

GREEK/MIDDLE-EASTERN

607 8/M25
£15-25
✓ **Persia** 665 Great Western Rd · 0141 237 4471 No kebab or hummus house here, but a restaurant that presents authentic Iranian traditional and contemporary dishes, and some of the best Middle-Eastern food in our mid-west. Start with a glass of refreshing doogh (yoghurt, fizzy water & mint), then choose from the tantalising range of dishes you've probably never had before. Lovely, light bread from the tandoor. A strong vegetarian list. Many rices; more herbs than spices. 7 days all day from noon.

608 8/M26
£15-25
Athena Greek Taverna 141 Elderslie St · www.athenataverna.co.uk · 0141 339 3895 In the streets between Charing Cross and Finnieston/Kelvingrove Park, an unassuming little Greek restaurant that acerbic, hard-to-impress critic A.A. Gill found and loved; TripAdvisors concur. Light on plate (though generous portions) and pocket, with much ado about meze, small-plate style or à la carte, this is where to go in Glasgow to relive your hols and eat meze and Med. 7 days all day from noon.

609 8/M26
£15-25
Elia 24 George Sq · www.eliagreekrestaurant.com · 0141 221 9988 Slap bang on the city's landmark square (Queen St side), a surprising location for an authentic Greek family-run bistro (cf. Jamie Oliver's or Browns mainstream operations overby). Menu in Greek and English. Mythos and Keo beers and good Boutari. Italian and Spanish too but mainly the reasonably real Greek. 7 days.

The Best Burgers & Steaks

610 8/M26
\>£35

✓✓ **The Butchershop Bar & Grill** 1055 Sauchiehall St · www. butchershopglasgow.com · 0141 339 2999 Near the Art Gallery & Museum. This high-end, very well-conceived and presented restaurant is in some ways as it says, a shop. It sells the cow, the animal: its parts and cuts frame the menu. Of the other places on this page and all over the city, this is where you can be sure the meat is hung, quartered and cooked to the modern taste – actually the NYC style, as is envisioned by proprietor James Rusk, who's also behind **Hutchesons** (509/BRASSERIES). There are other meaty options (pork, lamb) and a decent fish curry, but it's the cow the regular clientele really come for, in two smart, urban dining rooms, always buzzing and with personal, attentive servers. There are burgers at lunch. 7 days lunch & dinner.

611 8/M26
£25-35

✓✓ **Porter & Rye** 1131 Argyle St · www.porterandrye.com · 0141 572 1212 By the guys with The Finnieston next door, restaurants that have blazed a trail on Glasgow's foodie map, this has the meatier métier. Carcasses from the cabinet next to the kitchen counter from which perfectly cooked steaks emerge (any stray vegetarians should eat upstairs). Nice touches; amuse-bouche. Booths, bar stools and mezzanine. There is also a reduced but great late menu 11pm-1am. Report: 671/LATE DINING.

612 8/M26
£15-25

✓ **Ad Lib** 11 Hope St · 0141 248 6645 & 33 Ingram St · 0141 552 5736 · www.adlibglasgow.com American-style diners, Hope St since 1998 ('the first burger joint in the city') still pumping it out; the soul music, soul food and a burger hard to beat (and long before there were 'gourmet' burgers). Steaks very reasonably priced. Ingram St room much roomier. Hope St open till 3am with DJs and dancin' Fri/Sat. Owner Billy McAneney has opened an Ad Lib on the other side – of the hemisphere – in Malawi, in southern Africa, a country kind of adopted by Scotland. See you there in your gap or senior years!

613 8/M26
£25-35

✓ **Alston Bar & Beef** Central Station · www.alstonglasgow.co.uk · 0141 221 7627 In the left corner at the main entrance, also opening onto Gordon St. A great diner and bar to have in a station... well, underneath it. Alston, though part of a national chain company, is individual, innovative and smart. Apparently this was once Alston St. Though subterranean, it's light and bright. Great tiled floor; there is stylish life under the archways. A live departure board reminds you where you are. Good gin and wine selection, ones for the road or rail. And very good steaks, cool starters and imaginative burgers. Eat here, you don't even need to go into Glasgow! Food till 10pm.

✓ **Marco Pierre White Steakhouse, Bar & Grill** Report: 512/BRASSERIES.

THE BURGERS OF WEST REGENT STREET

614 8/M26
£15-25

Jacker de Viande 111 W Regent St · www.jackerdeviande.co.uk · 0141 243 2405 Somewhat secreted away but those that swear it's best beat the path there. More loungy than others of the ilk, though Jackson Pollock blood-splattered walls may quease the veggies (OK then, they probably won't be here – though there is a side of maccy cheese). Lunch & dinner. Closed Mon/Tue.

615 8/M26
£15-25

Meat 142 W Regent St · www.themeatbar.co.uk · 0141 204 3605 Pulls no punches, this one, in name or delivery. Somewhat heavy metal, they take their meat seriously. It is a bar with food. By no means only burgers, indeed some imaginative things with chicken, pork, etc. Good cocktails and beers. It's quite rock 'n' roll down here. Noon-10pm. Bar later.

The Best Seafood & Fish Restaurants

616 8/M26
£25-35
✓✓ **The Fish People Café** 350 Scotland St · www.thefishpeoplecafe. co.uk · 0141 429 8787 Next to Shields Rd subway station. In fact, you walk out the station onto their 'terrace'. This is S of the river (about 1km) near the junction of the M8 and M74, and not that easy to find so best to go by train. 'Fish People' because the fishmonger is right next door – the wholesaler of choice to many of Glasgow's top-end restaurants. Here in the caff, head chef John Gillespie has the pick of the daily (sustainable) catch; expect simple but innovative cookery. This place is a real treat for fish people. Closed Mon.

617 8/M26
£25-35
✓✓ **Gamba** 225a W George St · www.gamba.co.uk · 0141 572 0899 In basement at corner of W Campbell St, a seafood bistro which for a long time now has been one of the best restaurants of any in the city. Lowlight, understated – a grown-up kind of ambience. A great maître d' and the service to follow. Simplicity and sourcing are the watchwords here and chef/proprietor Derek Marshall doesn't put a finger wrong. His signature fish soup with prawn dumplings is always there but menu changes around every 8 weeks. One meat, one vegetarian choice and the brilliant value 'Market Menu'. Exemplary wine list includes halves. Gamba unlike many, open on Monday. They take the sustainable fishing code seriously like we should. Lunch (not Sun) & dinner.

618 8/M26
£25-35
✓✓ **Gandolfi Fish** 84-86 Albion St · www.cafegandolfi.com · 0141 552 9475 Adjacent the much-loved caff and bar, this big-windowed Merchant City diner has a good location, stylish look, good proprietorship (Seumas MacInnes) and a direct link to the West Coast, Skye and Hebridean fishing grounds (Seumas is from Barra) through the estimable Fish People (above). Brilliant fish 'n' chip shop adjacent (622/FISH & CHIPS). Always busy and buzzing, even midweek (a good sign in Glasgow). 7 days lunch & dinner.

619 8/M26
ATMOS
£25-35
✓✓ **Two Fat Ladies** 88 Dumbarton Rd · 0141 339 1944 & 118 Blythswood Sq · 0141 847 0088 · www.twofatladiesrestaurant.com The landmark West End restaurant and its city extension. Everything selectively sourced; both tiny kitchens produce delicious dishes with a light touch for packed-in discerning diners. Splendid puds. Similar, though not same menus. 7 days lunch & dinner. More Ladies also at the brilliant **Buttery** (505/TOP-END DINING).

620 8/M26
ATMOS
£15-25
✓✓ **Crabshakk** 1114 Argyle St · www.crabshakk.com · 0141 334 6127 John Macleod's tiny, 3-floor caffshakk, pioneering straight-up seafood since 2009, once the destination food stop hereabouts. Now there are many good options in this humming section of Argyle St, including, a couple of doors down, **Table 11**, Crabshakk's even smaller, more intimate room, which can be exclusively booked. Here they do for oysters what Crabshakk does for lobsters and crab, though in the shakk itself expect squid, moules marinière and fab fish 'n' chips, though most notably the meat of shell and claw, in a drop-in, grab-a-seat kind of atmos. Both Tue-Sun all day from noon.

621 8/M26
£15-25
✓ **Mussel Inn** 157 Hope St · www.mussel-inn.com · 0141 572 1405 Downtown location for light, bright bistro (big windows) where seafood is serious but fun. From cold waters up north. Mussels, scallops, oysters, catch-of-the-day-type blackboard specials; also vegetarian options. Mussels in variant concoctions; kilo pots are the thing, of course. As in Edinburgh (238/SEAFOOD), this formula is sound; the owners are to be commended for keeping it real. Mon-Fri lunch & dinner. All day Sat/Sun.

✓✓ **Rogano** Report: 507/BRASSERIES.

✓✓ **The Finnieston** West End bar and seafood restaurant with great
ambience and attention to detail. Report: 533/GASTROPUBS.

The Best Fish & Chips

622 8/M26 ✓ **Gandolfi Fish To Go** 84-86 Albion St · www.gandolfifish.com ·
0141 552 9475 The takeaway (and a few tables) bit of Gandolfi Fish in 'the
Gandolfi World' at this Merchant City crossroads. Same quality and conscientious
approach. Haddock (breaded or battered), cod, salmon, sea bass, as well as
Stornoway black pudding and proper Cullen skink. Best in the quarter by far. 7 days
from noon.

623 8/L26 ✓ **Catch** 186 Fenwick Rd · www.catchfishandchips.co.uk · 0141 638 9169
In the deep S but you might want to sail over here for the smartest, most
thought-through F&C shop/café in town. Seasoned restaurateurs behind this 2015
venture on a suburban strip (you could see it spreading). Starters from Cullen skink to
salt & chilli squid, through to lemon posset, via all the fish in the sea (maccy cheese
with lobster, anyone?). They pride themselves on the batter; they're not wrong! Good
for the family tea. Use rapeseed oil. Mon-Sat from noon, Sun from 1pm.

624 8/M25 **Philadelphia** 445 Great Western Rd · 0141 339 2372 Adjacent to **La
Parmigiana** (542/ITALIAN), owned by same family. Since 1930, a Glasgow fixture
and fresher fryer than most. Open 7 days (Fri/Sat till 2am).

625 8/M25 **Old Salty's** 337 Byres Rd · 0141 334 3334 & 1126 Argyle St, Finnieston
· 0141 357 5677 · www.oldsaltys.co.uk Reconstructed big-scale chippies,
designer-distressed but traditional fare nevertheless. Range of fish (veg oil used)
and 'old school suppers': mince and peas, macaroni pies. Open early should you
not be able to face the day without a fry-up. Tables and takeaway. Both open 7
days early till late.

626 8/M26 **Merchant Chippie** 155 High St · www.amoreglasgow.co.uk · 0141 552 5789
At corner of High & Ingram Sts. A chippie that does try harder and wins awards.
Long seafood list, including whiting and calamari, together with 'chip shop
classics', including pizza and haggis. Unusually, they use palm oil. Open 7 days
(Fri/Sat till 1am).

627 8/M26 **Mario's** 3 Fenwick Rd · 0141 633 1760 Another southside chippie (see Catch
above). Mario's more established, how shall we say, 'old-style'. Still a Giffnock go-
to for great fish, great chips – what more do you want out there? Well, pizzas and
kebabs which they also have. They use vegetable oil. Mon-Fri lunch & evenings,
Sat/Sun evenings only.

The Best Vegetarian Restaurants

628 8/M26
<£15
✓✓ **Saramago Café Bar** 350 Sauchiehall St · www.cca-glasgow.com/saramago-caf · 0141 352 4920 The café-bar of the CCA arts & exhibition centre. In the midst of the wild west end of Sauchiehall St and its probably unhealthy nightlife, a calm, laid-back restaurant which takes its foodie and vegan credentials seriously. A lofty atrium space and nice people either side of the counter. Small plates, great soups and salads. Best vegetarian in town? 7 days.

629 8/M26
ATMOS
<£15
✓✓ **Stereo** 22-28 Renfield Lane · www.stereocafebar.com · 0141 222 2254 Unobtrusive (some might say scruffy) in this lane off Renfield St near Central Station, Stereo nevertheless happily occupies a notable building, the former *Daily Record* printing works, designed by Charles Rennie Mackintosh (see p. 136), and built in 1900. Sits above street level with a music venue downstairs and is crowded at weekends. Menu is all vegetarian, some vegan and basically organic. Much to graze; daily specials. Hand-made and more delicious than the somewhat grungy surroundings may suggest. 7 days. Opposite, the **Old Hairdresser's**, is a cool bar, exhibition and event space evenings & weekends.

630 8/M26
<£15
✓ **Mono** Kings Court · www.monocafebar.com · 0141 553 2400 In odd no-man's land between the Merchant City and East End behind Parnie St, a cool hang-out in an alternative world! PC in a 'people's collective' kind of way; the antithesis of Glasgow's manufactured style. Great space with art, music (and a vinyl & CD store, Monorail), occasional performance and interesting totally vegan food served with few frills by friendly staff. Organic ales/wines. 7 days.

631 8/M26
<£15
✓ **The 78** 10-14 Kelvinhaugh St · www.the78cafebar.com · 0141 576 5018 Round the corner from (and preceding) the 'Finnieston Strip'. Mix 'n' match laid-back bar/café from the stable as Stereo and Mono above. Rory Forbes the chef here. Some great daily specials adding to the veggie burgers, wraps, nachos of the à la carte. Some organic. Pub-like ambience. 7 days.

632 8/M26
<£15
Tapa Bakehouse 21 Whitehill St · www.tapaorganic.com · 0141 554 9981 **& Tapa Coffee** 721 Pollokshaws Rd · www.tapacoffee.com · 0141 423 9494 Two organic caffs: the original in the East End, producing their artisan bread and bakes and with a smattering of seats, and the larger laid-back deli and proper café way down Pollokshaws Rd in the southside. Soups and meze are here and cakes. Both dispense some of the best coffee in Glasgow and good for breakfast. 7 days.

633 8/M26
<£15
The 13th Note 50-60 King St · www.13thnote.co.uk · 0141 553 1638 Old-style veggie hang-out – a good attitude/good vibes café-bar; live music downstairs. Menu unexceptional but honest, from veggie burgers to Indian, Greek meze dishes. Some dairy, otherwise vegan. Organic booze and Glasgow bevvy. 7 days.

Tchai-Ovna Old-style vegetarian caff; truly boho. Report: 649/TEAROOMS.

Restaurants serving good but not exclusively vegetarian food.

Mother India Reports: 571/572/INDIAN.
Café Gandolfi Report: 640/TEAROOMS.
Banana Leaf Report: 581/INDIAN.
Persia Report: 607/ETHNIC.
Balbir's Report: 579/INDIAN.
Nakodar Grill Report: 576/INDIAN.
The Hanoi Bike Shop Report: 586/VIETNAMESE.

The Best Coffee

634 8/M26 ✓✓ **Artisan Roast** 15-17 Gibson St · www.artisanroast.co.uk · 07776 428409 Follow that aroma that blew over from Edinburgh where they dispense the same indispensable coffee in a similar neighbourhood (296/ COFFEE). A bit fancier and snackier here, with more tables and a mezzanine, but the same blend and stripped-back offering. Probably the best coffee in the West (End). 8am-8pm (till 6.30pm weekends).

635 8/M25 ✓ **Papercup** 603 Great Western Rd · www.papercupcoffeecompany. bigcartel.com · 0141 339 7822 Heart of artisan coffee culture, frequently said to be 'the best flat white'. Much ado about beans and individual brewing. Unusual snacks, good chat. For aficionados and those that just need the fix. 7 days daytime only.

636 8/M26 ✓ **Tapa Coffee** 721 Pollokshaws Rd · www.tapacoffee.com · 0141 423 9494 & **Tapa Bakehouse** 21 Whitehill St, Dennistoun · www.tapaorganic. com · 0141 554 9981 Quality, integrity, artisan: all the right words apply. Great, organic bread they wholesale. A full, cool menu in the southside (ie Pollokshaws Rd). Mon-Fri 8am-7pm (till 6pm Sat/Sun).

637 8/M25 ✓ **Avenue G** 291 Byres Rd · www.avenue.coffee · 0141 339 5336 & **Avenue G Speciality Coffee House** 321 Great Western Rd · 0141 339 1334 Arrived late after the new breakfast dawn of artisan coffee but they're passionate about their brew which they roast in Great Western Rd. You really can smell the coffee. Nice home-made snacks. 7 days daytime only.

638 8/M26 **Coffee, Chocolate & Tea** 944 Argyle St · www.coffeechocolateandtea.com · 0141 204 3161 Among many others, this stands out: they make the chocolates, they blend and roast their own coffee (5 different beans) and there's munchies from **Bakery 47** (688/TAKEAWAY). 40 teas and unquestionably good cuppas of C, C & T.

639 8/M25 **Tinderbox** 189 Byres Rd · 0141 339 3108 & 118 Ingram St · 0141 552 6907 & at Paperchase, Princes Sq Stylish, shiny coffee shops. Snacks and great people-watching potential, especially at Byres Rd, the original. Better sandwiches and cakey things than others of this ilk. Daily soups, pies, etc. A great made-in-Glasgow brand now widespread. Branch times vary.

The Best Tearooms

640 8/M26 ✓✓ **Café Gandolfi** 64 Albion St · www.cafegandolfi.com · 0141 552 6813
ATMOS For decades now, Seumas MacInnes's definitive and landmark meeting/eating place has occupied a pivotal corner of the Merchant City. A bistro menu, but the casual, boho ambience of a tearoom or coffee shop. Long ago now the stained glass and heavy, over-sized wooden furniture created an ideal ambience that has withstood the vagaries of Glasgow style. The food is light and imaginative and served all day. You may have to queue. Mon-Sat all day from 9am, Sun from noon (680/SUNDAY BRUNCH). The **Bar** upstairs (535/GASTROPUBS), **Fish** restaurant (618/SEAFOOD) and takeaway next door (622/FISH & CHIPS) contribute to a unique and exemplary Glasgow experience.

641 8/M25 ✓✓ **Kember & Jones** 134 Byres Rd · www.kemberandjones.co.uk · 0141 337 3851 A deli with well-sourced nibbles and the stuff of the good life. Of all those places with piles of pies and meringues, this is the real deal. They roast the coffee, they bake the bread. Tables outside and on the mezzanine. Great sandwiches, honey-toasted granola, and the best tartes and pecan perfect tortes in town. How they do all that baking from that small kitchen is a triumph of cookability. 7 days.

642 8/M26 ✓✓ **Hidden Lane Tearoom** 1103 Argyle St · www. thehiddenlanetearoom.com · 0141 237 4391 The lane next to Tesco leads to another lane then at the end, as it says, the Hidden Tearoom. There's a new Kirsty here since the original cake-maker, but Kirsty Webb carries on the tradition of the traditional afternoon tea. Small downstairs and upstairs parlour quiet and civilised. Sandwiches, soup and top cakes especially combined in the tier of mouth-watering morsels. Good gluten-free selection. Mon-Sat 10am-6pm (Sun from noon).

643 8/M26 ✓ **Montgomery's** 9-11 Radnor St · www.montgomeryscafe.co.uk · 0141 357 1666 Near Kelvingrove Art Gallery & Museum out west between Argyle St and Sauchiehall St. It calls itself a café but Montgomery's is much more. It starts with Colin Montgomery, a damned good baker and it has become an easy-going, light and lofty room for breakfast, lunch, afternoon tea and dinner at weekends. Lovely, light grub. Sun-Wed daytime only, Thu-Sat till 10pm.

644 8/M25 ✓ **Sonny & Vito's** 52 Park Rd · 0141 357 0640 On a West End corner between Great Western Rd and Gibson St, a daytime deli-caff with excellent home baking, light menus and tarteletes to eat in or take away. Not many tables, always busy; those outside have interesting urban aspects. Nice for breakfast. Mon-Sat 9am-6pm, Sun from 10am.

645 8/M26 ✓ **Martha's** 142A St Vincent St · www.mymarthas.co.uk · 0141 248 9771 In the heart of dirty old midtown a standout fast-food place that's fresh, healthy and kind of pure. They have their 'Hero' ingredients: beetroot, kale, mackerel, etc. Takeaway or eat-in wraps, salads, soups, super smoothies and cakes. And proper spicy hot dishes. You feel better here! Mon-Fri 7.30am-7pm, Sat 9am-4pm.

646 8/M25 **Cup Tea Room** 311 Byres Rd · www.cupglasgow.co.uk · 0141 357 2525 A caff in the middle of busy Byres Rd where 'cup' refers to what you eat rather than what you drink out of. They have survived the cupcake explosion and the confection is here in its multi-iced and festooned glory. Sandwiches, soup, afternoon tea. They've expanded into a fabulous room downtown (below). 7 days 9am-6pm.

647 8/M26 **Cup Tea Lounge** 71 Renfield St · www.cupglasgow.co.uk · 0141 353 2959 Corner of W Regent St. The upmarket version of The Cup above, these cupcakes have perhaps gone as far as they can go. Main thing here though is the stunning lofty, ornate room, once the Bank of India – so an appropriate place to take tea (and possibly gin). Mon-Sat 9am-6pm, Sun from 11am.

648 8/M26 **Once Upon A Tart** 45 King St · www.onceuponatart.co.uk · 0141 552 0305 An art-end-of-Merchant-City tearoom, big on cakes but also ciabattas, soups and the apple tart. Very pink, shabby kitsch with mix 'n' match furniture and laid-back lassies. Great daily selection of cakes under the domes. Ladies who lunch and laugh off the calories. Mon-Fri 8am-5pm, Sun from 9.30am.

649 8/M26 **Tchai-Ovna** 42 Otago Lane · www.tchaiovna.com · 0141 357 4524 For 15 years now, a 'house of tea' hidden away off Otago St on the banks of the Kelvin. A decidedly gap-year tearoom which could be Eastern Europe, North Africa or

Kathmandu but the vibe mainly Middle Eastern. Hookahs are smoked. 70 kinds of tea, soup, organic sandwiches and cakes from the tiny kitchen. Impromptu performances likely. A real find but suits and ladies who lunch may not be quite so chilled out here. 7 days all day from 11am. May be moving 2016.

650 8/M26 **The Tearooms** 151 Bath St · www.thebutterflyandthepig.com/thetearooms · 0141 243 2459 Upstairs and part of The Butterfly and The Pig, this very tea kind of room has fully embraced the T-comeback. But it's on the go from breakfast (traditional with twists) through soup and super 'sanner' lunch to the all-important tier of afternoon tea, then, of course, high tea. All very much in-period, and in the vibe of **The B&P** (717/BAR FOOD). Mon-Sat 8.30am-8pm (Sun from 10am).

The Best Caffs

651 8/M26 ✓✓ **The Glad Café** 1006A Pollokshaws Rd · www.thegladcafe.co.uk · 0141 636 6119 Door in a wall of shops and restaurants (including Glad Rags, the vintage clothes bit) opposite the park in arterial Pollokshaws Rd. You enter a different, more civilised world and an arterial route for the life blood of the southside's (and the city's) roots cultural scene. There are books (and they have their own newspaper), music, theatre and performance and, of course, café food and drink for more corporeal sustenance. Rachel Smillie has done a very good thing here. Event space through another door. 7 days all day.

652 8/L25 ✓✓ **Delizique** 70-72 Hyndland St · www.delizique.com · 0141 339 2000 Down from Cottiers, an adorable and convivial daytime café, with in-house bakery (top breads). Complements **Cafezique**, their original corner restaurant two doors away (515/BISTROS), perfectly. Confusingly, not so much a deli, more a caff mixing up the good ingredients of life. Gorgeous food to go includes the daily bread, salads, tarts, sourdough pizzas and scrumptious cakes; sit-in to eat from bowls or boards. 7 days 9am-7pm.

653 8/M26 ✓✓ **University Café** 87 Byres Rd · 0141 339 5217 People have been ATMOS coming here for generations to sit at the 'kneesy' tables and share the salt and vinegar. Run by the Verecchia family who administer advice, sympathy and pie, beans and chips with equal aplomb. And have done apparently since 1918! 6 booths only; it resists all change. BYOB (no corkage). There's trifle! 9am-10pm. Closed Sat.

654 8/M26 ✓✓ **Trans Europe Café** 25 Parnie St · www.transeuropecafe.co.uk · 0141 552 7999 Easy-going classic caff near Glasgow Cross off Trongate with neighbourhood atmos and home-made food individually prepared in Tony Sinclair's mad gantry kitchen. Light food, especially bespoke sandwiches and more meal-like at night (Fri/Sat only). Could be Europe? Naw, this could only be Glasgow! 7 days.

655 8/M26 ✓ **Coia's Café** 473 Duke St · www.coiascafe.co.uk · 0141 554 3822 Since 1928, Coia's has been supplying this East End high street with ice cream, great-deal breakfasts and the kind of comforting lunch that any neighbourhood needs. Some years back a substantial makeover and expansion turned this caff into a full-blown food operation with deli counter, takeaway and restaurant. So now it's traditional grub and ice cream along with the olive-oil niceties. They still do the Havana cigars. 7 days.

656 8/M25 ✓ **North Star** 108 Queen Margaret Drive · 0141 946 5365 Up from the Botanic Gardens, long a fave caff in the West End. Under Maurizio and Ester it's become a real hang-out even though there are only a few tables and when, as often, it's busy, it's a bit chaotic at the counter. Soup, hot specials, their great 'hot rolls' and a big gluten-free choice. It's amazing how they keep it all coming from the tiniest kitchen. 7 days daytime only.

657 8/M25 ✓ **Smile Café** 102 Queen Margaret Drive · 07528 661275 No website or landline as befits a cool local caff which my friends, in this bordering on the affluent neighbourhood, swear by. It is a smiley, laid-back nook of the Italian deli plate, sandwich and cake world, charmingly and creatively done. 7 days daytime only.

658 8/M26 ✓ **McCune Smith** 3-5 Duke St · www.mccunesmith.co.uk · 0141 548 1114 The very beginning of Duke St heading E off the High St and the Merchant City. There's a Scottish Enlightenment thing going on here: it's named after the 19th-century African-American abolitionist 'as somebody who embodies both Glasgow's complicity in slavery and the fortunes its merchants made and the abolitionist movement which sprang from Enlightenment'. It's a heady and fascinating connection and it runs through the look and the menu of this very cool caff, with imaginative sandwiches and salads. And an 'enlightened' breakfast. Open daytime. Closed Sun.

659 8/M26 **Singl-end** 265 Renfrew St · 0141 353 1277 In a basement along from Glasgow School of Art. A re-opening (of a loved but short-lived diner) at TGP so not reviewed, but in here because it's the same indie/retro space and augurs well. Reports, please.

660 8/M26 **Brooklyn Café** 21 Minard Rd · 0141 632 3427 Here just off Pollokshaws Rd since 1931, the kind of all-purpose caff any neighbourhood would be proud of. More tratt perhaps than caff, with pasta/pizza, risottos, salads and the ice cream (the Pelosi family still make their own vanilla recipe). It will, of course, never die, like their Empire biscuits. Can BYOB. 7 days.

661 8/M25 **Matilda's** 378-380 Byres Rd · www.matildaspatisserie.co.uk · 0141 339 8809 Top end of Byres Rd with its multitude of caffs and bars. Matilda's stands out here because of its very good take on cakes, not standard patisserie but somewhere between Scottish and French, and an excellent brownie. Stone-baked pizza, baguettes, omelettes, waffles. The genuine article. 7 days.

662 8/L26 **Siempre** 162 Dumbarton Rd · www.siemprebicyclecafe.com · 0141 334 2335 West by the subway station. Good example of the trend for bike shops seeing the opportunity to extend their community by serving food for thought as well as bikes to ride. Siempre, a bike-lover's hive, has good, light cooking, vintage as well as new bikes and a garden! Mon-Fri daytime only, Sat/Sun till 10pm.

Kid-Friendly Places

663 8/L26 ✓ **Rio Café** 27 Hyndland St · 0141 334 9909 A kid-friendly caff that's cool – cool for parents that is – with decent food and service for both, from all-day breakfast fry-ups to sustaining suppers. Also DJs, 'spoken word' nights, jazz on Wednesdays, poker on Sundays, and sweeties, sweeties, sweeties! An all-round neighbourhood place for all Jock Tamson's bairns. 7 days. No kids after 8pm.

664 8/M26 **Tramway Café** 25 Albert Drive · www.tramway.org · 0141 276 0953 Caff at Tramway arts and Turner Prize 2015 venue in the southside. Venue itself cavernous and contemporary, with changing programme always worth visiting. Caff well run with some healthy grub (mainly vegetarian) and facing onto the **Hidden Gardens** (1528/GARDENS). Play area. Snack bags for kids, freshly made fruit and vegetable juices.

665 8/M26 **Brooklyn Café** 21 Minard Rd The unassuming, long-established southside (off Pollokshaws Rd) caff where families are very welcome for the carbs and the cones and the jars of sweeties on the shelf. Report: 660/CAFFS.

666 8/M26 **Princes Square** Buchanan St Glasgow's downtown mall almost taken over by eateries with 'outside' tables, especially on the bottom floor, with many options. There's a central mosaic piazza in the basement where kids can run around.

The Best Delis

667 8/M25 ✓✓ **Roots & Fruits** 451-457 Great Western Rd · www.rootsfruitsandflowers.com · 0141 339 3077 Main branch (see 690/TAKEAWAY) of the all-round, all-good-things-in-life provisioner of the West End: the flower shop, the deli and the fruit and veg together offering a superlative service. Makes you wonder why all things can't be as good as this. 7 days daytime only.

668 8/M25 ATMOS ✓✓ **I.J. Mellis** 492 Great Western Rd · www.mellischeese.net · 0141 339 8998 Started out as *the cheese guy*, now more of a very select deli for food that's good and 'slow'. Coffees, Iberico hams, sausages, olives and seasonal stuff like apples and mushrooms (branches vary), so smells mingle. Irresistible! Branches also in Edinburgh (357/DELIS), St Andrews and Aberdeen. 7 days though times vary. See also 1478/CHEESES. He *is* the cheese guy!

669 8/M25 ✓✓ **George Mewes** 106 Byres Rd · www.georgemewescheese.co.uk · 0141 334 5900 Well, there was Ian Mellis (above, since 1993), then there was a George Mewes (2009) and his beautifully chilled (hence the woolly-hatted staff) and fragrantly smelly shop in Byres Rd, giving Mellis a run, well, a runny cheese for his money. Great presentation and range (Scottish selection seasonal), Poilâne bread, top organic eggs. 7 days. George also in Edinburgh (358/DELIS).

670 8/M26 ✓✓ **Eusebi Deli** 793 Shettleston Rd · www.eusebideli.com · 0141 763 0399 Folk travel here from way beyond the neighbourhood. Great Italian wine and deli ranges but especially notable for Giovanna Eusebi's home-made food to go. A real *traiteur*; a passion for food and for Italy written all over it. Tue-Sat 9am-6pm. The new (2015) West End deli and restaurant rocks (540/ITALIAN).

The Best Late-Night Restaurants

671 8/M26
£25-35
✓✓ **Porter & Rye** Excellent at any time for steaks and the rest but a stripped-down menu 11pm-**1am**: steak, sauce, chips just hits the spot. Great for Glasgow, post-Hydro, etc. Report: 611/BURGERS & STEAKS.

672 8/M26
£25-35
✓✓ **Stravaigin** Worth remembering that this excellent restaurant (514/BISTROS; 586/VIETNAMESE) has last orders at **10.45pm**.

673 8/M26
£15-25
✓ **Spice Garden** 11-17 Clyde Pl · www.spicegardenglasgow.com · 0141 429 4422 Just over Glasgow (Jamaica St) Bridge on S side of Clyde. For years the late-night hang-out, now possibly better than ever. Jaz and Raj keep a great Indian restaurant going... and going. Great for the late-night lot, for those in a show (as many pics on the walls attest) and those who have just been to one. *Daily Record* likes it too! Good at any time but this is Glasgow's latest-opening proper restaurant. 7 days 5pm-**3am** (**4am** Fri/Sat).

674 8/M26
ATMOS
<£15
✓ **Asia Style** 185-189 St George's Rd · 0141 332 8828 Simple, authentic Chinese and Malaysian café/canteen with familiar sweet 'n' sour, curry and satays, 4 kinds of noodle, exotic specials and 5 kinds of porridge. Only open evenings. 7 days 4.30pm-**1.30am**. Report: 596/CHINESE.

675 8/M26
<£15
The Noodle Bar 482 Sauchiehall St · 0141 333 1883 The stripped-down noodle bar in Sauchiehall St where and when you need it. Authentic, fast, no-frills Chinese (ticket service and eezee-kleen tables). The noodle is 'king'; but cooking *is* taken seriously. 7 days till 4am.

676 8/M26
£15-25
Browns 1 George Sq · www.browns-restaurants.co.uk · 0141 221 7828 The tried and tested UK chain comfort food in huge two-floor café-bar on corner of George Sq. Mentioned because it is open till **midnight Fri/Sat**, and **11pm midweek**, and you can always get a table. **Jamie Oliver's** adjacent is similar in every respect but closes an hour earlier.

✓✓ **Ubiquitous Chip** Best late choice in the West End. 7 days till **11pm**. Report: 501/TOP-END DINING.
✓✓ **Guy's Restaurant & Bar** Best late choice in the Merchant City. **11.30pm Fri/Sat**. Report: 508/BRASSERIES.
✓ **Rioja** Great tapas and, of course, rioja. Open surprisingly late. Tue-Sun noon till **1am**. Report: 604/ETHNIC.

Good Places For Sunday Brunch

677 8/L26
ATMOS
✓✓ **Cafezique** 66 Hyndland St · www.delizique.com · 0141 339 7180 This award-winning, hard-to-fault, two-level bistro/caff (515/BISTROS) opens at **9am** every day for snacking or more ambitious breakfast. A very civilised start to the day; fills up quickly. **Delizique** adjacent 652/CAFFS also from **9am**.

678 8/M26
✓✓ **Stravaigin** 28 Gibson St · www.stravaigin.co.uk · 0141 334 2665 Same care and flair given to their famous brunch menu as the rest (514/BISTROS). Cramped maybe, but reflects appetite for Sunday breakfast, from home-made granola to French toast and the Ayrshire bacon. Served till 5pm. From **11am**.

679 8/M26 ✓ **The Left Bank** 33-35 Gibson St · www.theleftbank.co.uk · 0141 339 5969
Classy and popular café-bar-restaurant in student and luvvyland. From great
granola to eggs mornay and beans on toast. 521/BISTROS. From 9am weekdays,
Sat/Sun from **10am**.

680 8/M26 ✓ **Café Gandolfi** 64 Albion St · www.cafegandolfi.com · 0141 552 6813
ATMOS   Breakfast here an institution in itself in an atmospheric room, with daylight
filtering through stained glass and comforting, oversized wooden furniture. See
also 640/TEAROOMS. All breakfast variants are here, including eggs Florentine,
Benedict or 'Hebridean'. With the chat, the coffee and the papers, what better start
to a lazy Sunday? From **9am**.

681 8/M25 ✓ **Sonny & Vito's** 52 Park Rd · 0141 357 0640 Much-loved West End brunch
rendezvous. A deli-caff with home baking from scones and muffins to
Mediterranean platefuls. Outside tables and takeaway. 644/TEAROOMS. From **noon**.

682 8/M26 ✓ **Coia's Café** They've been doing breakfast here for over 85 years. Goes like a
fair and still damned good. The full-fry monty lasts all day (vegetarian too). The
East End choice. From **10am**. Report: 655/CAFFS.

683 8/M26 ✓ **Tribeca** The three Tribeca diners (Dumbarton Rd, Park Rd and Fenwick Rd in the
southside) all do a roaring breakfast trade. From **8am**. Report: 529/BISTROS.

684 8/L25 ✓ **Epicures of Hyndland** Definitive West End coffee house and more is perfect
for a buzzing brunch any day of the week. On Sundays you may need to wait to
join this congregation. From **9am** (brunch till 3pm). Report: 519/BISTROS.

685 8/M25 ✓ **North Star & Smile Café** Adjacent excellent caffs in Queen Margaret Dr in
the West End. Reports: 656/657/CAFFS. Both open from **10am**.

The Best Takeaway Places

686 8/L25 ✓✓ **The Kitchen Window** 187 Hyndland Rd · 0141 339 3303 Small but brilliant. A few tables and the 'window' but Pauline King's cookery skills are evident in their (with partner Eileen Campbell) home-made everything, including the bread. Usually 3 soups, salads, and other irresistibles. 7 days.

687 8/M25 ✓✓ **Cottonrake Bakery** 497 Great Western Rd · www.cottonrake.com · 07910 282040 Michelin-experienced Stefan Spicknell's superlative bakery brings proper patisserie and top takeaway tarts, real croissants and the sausage roll extraordinaire to Glasgow's West End. You better be quick! 7 days.

688 8/M26 ✓✓ **Bakery 47** 76 Victoria Rd · www.bakery47.com · 0141 237 9470 (opening hours hotline) In the 'scruffy' (Ron Mackenna) end of Victoria Rd. Anna and Sam Luntley set up shop and oven here in 2015. A true artisan operation, they make bread, croissants, cakes, etc, and you can sit in on Wed and Sun. Also workshops and pop-ups. It's very nice to be there!

689 8/M26 ✓✓ **Cherry and Heather** 7 North Gower St · www.cherryandheather. co.uk · 0141 427 0272 Just off Paisley Rd West, next to Bellahouston Post Office. A perfect wee takeaway, with food of integrity and a great range of soups, casseroles and truly gourmet sandwiches. Artisan bread, unusual combos. A few stools. Cherry is for Japan (where the cook comes from) and Heather is for Scotland, where she and her Indonesian partner have settled; a happy combination. Closed Sat/Sun.

690 8/M25 ✓ **Roots & Fruits** 451-457 Great Western Rd · 0141 339 3077 & 1137 Argyle St · 0141 229 0838 · www.rootsfruitsandflowers.com In Great Western Rd, a row of wholefood shops near Kelvinbridge, famously where to go for fruit & veg in the West End (and a lovely flower shop). A *traiteur* section, with some seats, but the delicious home-made food (paellas, tortillas, salads) and bakery (bread from Tapa) is mainly to take home. Argyle St is mainly a deli. Opening hours vary.

691 8/M25 ✓ **Juice Garden** 223 Byres Rd · 0141 339 6275 & 23 Renfield St · 0141 221 3876 · www.juicegarden.org The two original JG's on busy streets with lots of unhealthy eating around them, so their juices, smoothies, salads and some hot dishes (curries, falafel and spinach burgers) seem even more fresh and refreshing. More branches are in the making. Their signature 'Leafy Greens': apple, kale and ginger juice is a joy. 7 days.

692 8/M26 ✓ **Piece** 1056 Argyle St · www.pieceglasgow.com · 0141 221 7975 Neat and nifty, hard-working sandwich bar that started here and is proliferating piece by piece as we write. Bespoke fillings (all better than most), daily soup and rather good tartes. 8am-5pm (some branches close earlier).

693 8/M26 ✓ **The Wee Guy's** 51 Cochrane St · www.guysrestaurant.co.uk · 0141 552 5338 The Wee Guy is the wee guy, Guy, of **Guy's**, (508/BRASSERIES), here catering for offices and passers-by. Hot food here or to go, soups, great home-made wee pies. 7 days.

694 8/L26 ✓ **My Home Bakery** 59 Hyndland St Corner-shop counter, and bakery in the back where two real baker guys turn out the daily rolls, bread and big range of savoury (4 kinds of big sausage rolls) and big cakes. Less choice later on. 7 days.

695 8/M26 ✓ **Where The Monkey Sleeps** 182 W Regent St · www.monkeysleeps.com · 0141 226 3406 Lo-fi, below stairs, Gen X caff and takeaway. 2 soups, 2 stews, mean panini and bagels. It's a vibe! Mon-Fri 7am-3pm.

Unique Glasgow Pubs

696 8/M25 ✓✓ **Òran Mór** 731 Great Western Rd · www.oran-mor.co.uk · 0141 357 6200 This is the epitome of all the things you can do with a pub; you could spend your (Glasgow) life here. A huge and hugely popular emporium of drink and divertissements in a converted church on a prominent West End corner, the always evolving vision of Colin Beattie. Drinking on all levels (and outside) but also decent pub food and separate brasserie, the only bit which for some reason has not set the heather alight. Big entertainment programme from DJs to comedy in the club, and is home of the brilliant 'A Play, a Pie and a Pint'. From lunch till very late, this is a hostelry of happiness and hope. 7 days till midnight (club later).

697 8/M26 ✓✓ **The Horseshoe** 17 Drury St · www.thehorseshoebarglasgow.co.uk · 0141 248 6368 A mighty pub since the 19th century in a small street between W Nile and Renfield Sts near Central Station. Early example of this style of pub, dubbed 'gin palaces'. Island rather than horseshoe bar ('longest in the UK'), impressive range of alcohols and an upstairs lounge where they serve lunch and high tea and karaoke till midnight (no, really!). Food is amazing value (568/ SCOTTISH). All kinds of folk. Daily till midnight.

698 8/M26 ✓✓ **The Winged Ox @ St Luke's** 17 Bain St · www.stlukesglasgow.com · 0141 552 8378 Round the corner from the Barrowlands, heart of an emerging East End. In an impressively no-expense-spared conversion of Glasgow's third oldest church (1836), a bar/restaurant and venue for all kinds of gigs, receptions, launches, etc. Michael and Tony Woods have taken a bold step East. Music, food and drink for the soul and a great new Glasgow place to go.

699 8/M26 ✓✓ **Scotia Bar** 112 Stockwell St · www.scotiabar.net · 0141 552 8681 Probably Scotland's oldest continuously running pub, established 1792. Tudor-style with a low-beamed ceiling and intimate, woody snugs. Long the haunt of folk musicians, writers and raconteurs. Music and poetry sessions, folk and blues Thu-Sun. A must-visit for true pub lovers though it will never be the same now the smoke has gone.

700 8/M26 ATMOS ✓ **The Clutha & Victoria Bar** 167-169 Stockwell St · 0141 552 7400 Corner with Broomielaw opposite bridge to the Gorbals. These historic riverside pubs merged after the tragic, much-reported helicopter crash in November 2013. Reopened (though memorial part will remain closed) by owner Alan Crossan in 2015. A pub of memories but great live music 7 nights in the 'beer garden' and very good pizzas.

701 8/M26 ATMOS ✓ **Corinthian** 191 Ingram St · www.thecorinthianclub.co.uk · 0141 552 1101 Mega makeover of impressive listed building to form a restaurant and comfy lounge/cocktail bar, The Gaming Room casino and a night club downstairs, all in glorious surroundings. Awesome ceiling in main room. The flagship unit of the mighty (Glasgow-based) G1 Group, this in both senses mirrors Glasgow perfectly (see me!). More or less all of the day and all of the night.

702 8/M26 ATMOS **The Saracen Head (aka the 'Sarry Heid')** 209 Gallowgate · www. saracenhead.com · 0141 552 1660 Close to Barrowland. If ever the word 'legendary' could be legitimately used for a pub this might be it! At one time across the road, the SH dates from 1755. Often said to be haunted, it's home to the skull of the last witch to be executed in Scotland. It's featured in films (most recently in *The Legend of Barney Thomson*, directed by and starring Robert Carlyle, his homage to the

East End of Glasgow, where he grew up). But it's whenever Celtic play at home that it comes into its own (sea of green); you're better to be with them than against! Low on gentrification, high on Glasgow! Craft beers, naw! Open when you are.

703 8/M26   **The Baby Grand** 3 Elmbank Gardens · www.babygrandglasgow.com · 0141 248 4942 By Charing Cross station in the shadow of a high-rise Premier Inn. One of the first and fully conceived operations of serial restaurateur Billy McAneney. Piano player, food, the urban melancholy, the this-could-only-be-Glasgow. I just like the Baby Grand. Sun-Wed till midnight, Thu-Sat till 1am.

704 8/L26   **The Lismore** 206 Dumbarton Rd Named after the long island off Oban. Great
ATMOS   neighbourhood (Partick) bar that welcomes all sorts. There's just something about this place from the stained glass to the floor and the walls that's good to be in. Gives good atmos, succour and malts. Occasional music.

705 8/M26   **Ben Nevis** 1147 Argyle St · 0141 576 5204 Owned by the same people as Lismore and Òran Mór (above) but run by others. A great look and feel to this bar in contemporary but not faux-Scottish style. Small and pubby, the Deuchars is spot-on and great malt list. A calm and civilised corner of the West End. 'Killie pies' and 'Belter bridies' (from Kilmarnock daily). And 230 whiskies to choose from.

✓ **Republic Bier Halle** Bewildering selection of beers from all over the sodden world, and a top pizza. Report: 557/PIZZA.

The Best Real-Ale & Craft Beer Pubs

706 8/M26   ✓ **Bon Accord** 153 North St · 0141 248 4427 Over 40 years on the road above the motorway near the Mitchell Library. One of the first real-ale pubs in . Glasgow. Good selection of malts and up to 12 beers; always Deuchars and IPA plus many guest ales on hand pump. Food from 11am till 7.45pm (LO). Light, easy-going atmos but they do take their ale to heart. Quiz night on Wed, live band on Sat.

707 8/M26   ✓ **WEST** Templeton Building, Glasgow Green · www.westbeer.com ·
DF   0141 550 0135 First find the **People's Palace** (727/ATTRACTIONS) then gaze at the fabulous exterior of the Templeton edifice, where on the bottom corner, the UK's first German brewery brews its award-winning beers (4 ingredients only: water, malt, hops and yeast). 8 in total in a beerhall setting and garden overlooking the Green. St Mungo for starters and a massive selection of imports. 'Simple, hearty' food with a German slant till 9pm. Decent wine list. There's also a West End extension, a bar/restaurant **West on the Corner** at 160 Woodlands Rd (0141 332 0540), which somehow lacks atmos but the beer and the German(ish) grub also here.

708 8/M26   ✓ **Brewdog** 1397 Argyle St · www.brewdog.com · 0141 334 7175 Opposite Kelvingrove Art Gallery & Museum in a prominent corner site. The Glasgow Brewdog of the fast proliferating pack unleashed on a sober public in 2007 from Fraserburgh and now the flag-bearers of the craft-beer revolution. All their cute and trashily named beers present, including their not-so-strong ones. Food, games, live music. Martin and James just get it right. 7 days till midnight.
The Doghouse Corner of Hutcheson and Garth Sts in the Merchant City. A 'new concept' Brewdog, with a focus on food, self-service select, BBQ/smoked meats. Interesting but methinks they should stick to beer. 11 draughts here from 0.5% to 9.2%, including their signature Punk IPA. And there's a bottleshop.

709 8/M26   ✓   **The State Bar** 148-148A Holland St · www.comedyatthestate.co.uk ·
ATMOS   0141 332 2159   Off Sauchiehall St at the west end. Uncompromising, old-style pub, all wood and old pictures. 8 guest ales. No fancy extras. Will probably outlive the many makeovers around here. Food at lunchtime. Some music and stand-up.

710 8/M26   **Babbity Bowster** 16-18 Blackfriars St · www.babbitybowster.com ·
0141 552 5055   In a pedestrianised part of the Merchant City and just off the High St, a now classic Glasgow pub/restaurant/hotel (489/INDIVIDUAL HOTELS); but the pub comes first. Caledonian, Deuchars, IPA and well-chosen guests. Many malts and cask cider. Food all day (567/SCOTTISH), occasional music, and outside 715/OUTDOORS.

711 8/M26   **The Horseshoe** 17 Drury St · www.thehorseshoebarglasgow.co.uk ·
0141 248 6368   Great for lots of reasons (697/UNIQUE PUBS), not the least of which is its range of beers in exactly the right surroundings to drink them. Sky Sports. Always rammed (but not quite men only).

   ✓ ✓   **Drygate** Mega microbrewery with own bottle shop, bar/café. Bottled beers from next door and all over, and draught. Report: 532/GASTROPUBS.
     ✓   **Republic Bier Halle** Midtown beer heaven. Report: 557/PIZZA.

Inn Deep With terrace overlooking the Kelvin. Connected to William Brothers Brewery. Alternatively kegs and cask ales. Report: 559/PIZZA.
Brel Belgian beer central but great craft collection from New Zealand, USA and Scotland. Report: 714/OUTDOORS.

▬▬▬ Places To Drink Outdoors

712 8/L25   **Cottiers** 93 Hyndland St · www.cottiers.com · 0141 357 5825   First on the left after the swing park on Highburgh Rd (going west) and the converted church is on your right, around the corner. Heart of West End location. Think a cold beer on a hot day sitting in the leafy shade of a churchyard.

713 8/M25   **Booly Mardy's** 28 Vinicombe St · www.boolymardys.com · 0141 560 8004   Booly's (an anagram of Bloody Marys), a much smaller and personally run (Mark Tracey) bar has outdoor seating with great people-watching potential and inside a cool, unforced ambience. A good crowd come here. Food till 8pm.

714 8/M25   **Bar Brel & others in Ashton Lane** As soon as the sun comes out, so do the punters. With numerous watering holes, benches suddenly appear and Ashton Lane becomes a cobbled, al fresco pub. The nearest Glasgow gets to Euro or even Dublin drinking. Brel has the best in-house al fresco.

715 8/M26   **Babbity Bowster** 16-18 Blackfriars St · www.babbitybowster.com ·
0141 552 5055   Unique in the Merchant City for several reasons (710/ALES; 567/SCOTTISH), but in summer certainly for its napkin of garden in an area bereft of greenery. Though enclosed by surrounding streets, it's a concrete oasis. Good craic.

Inn Deep Outside terrace overlooks the Kelvin. Report: 559/PIZZA.
McPhabbs Back 'n' front. Report: 719/BAR FOOD.
Chinaski's Conservatory and courtyard. Report: 721/BAR FOOD.

Bars With Good Food

See also Gastropubs, p. 100.

716 8/M26 ✓✓ **Drygate** 85 Drygate · www.drygate.com · 0141 212 8815 In East End, part of Tennent's brewery. Reported as others in 532/GASTROPUBS but a special mention here – a unique food, microbrewery, bottleshop and live venue.

717 8/M26 ✓ **The Butterfly and The Pig & B&P @ The Corona**
www.thebutterflyandthepig.com · 153 Bath St · 0141 221 7711 & @ The Corona 1039 Pollokshaws Rd · 0141 632 6230 Two very different spaces, though same look and feel. Among many come-and-go, style-heavy bars and eateries, the original B&P in Bath St is here to stay. Kitschy and cosy but more real than just recherché and cooler than merely contrived. Colloquial food descriptions but what comes is imaginative and fun to eat. They do proper afternoon tea upstairs in the proper Tearooms (650/TEAROOMS). The southside venture is bigger and newer but still mix 'n' match everything (lights, crockery, furniture), with restaurant area through the back, slouching out front (plus a proper bar). Derived from the makers of the legendary Buff Club, hence DJs and bands at night, B&P is a great socially engaging concept and very Glasgow.

718 8/M26 ✓ **Vroni's** 47 W Nile St · www.vronis.co.uk · 0141 221 4677 Not a pub by any means, rather a dark but welcoming wine bar from the days when wine bars were where we went after work. So, great list, champagne and interesting 'small plates' to snack and graze. From suits to ladies lingering over a Sancerre.

719 8/M26 ✓ **McPhabbs** 22 Sandyford Pl · www.mcphabbsglasgow.com · 0141 221 8176 Sauchiehall St W of Charing Cross. Long-standing great Glasgow pub with loyal following. Tables in front garden and on back decks. Standard home-made pub-grub menu and great specials. Food till 9pm.

720 8/M26 ✓ **Bar Soba** 11 Mitchell Lane (the original) · 0141 204 2404, 116-122 Byres Rd (the big one) · 0141 357 5482 and the newest one at TGP 79 Albion St · 0141 237 1551 · www.barsoba.co.uk, opening into corner of Merchant Sq is another huge Soba style operation. The first, cosier Soba is up the narrow lane off Buchanan St, next to the Lighthouse design centre, a bright, contemporary room. The expanded 'vibrant' vision is in the West End. Menus same fusion of Asian 'streetfood'. Cocktails a big feature, including mixology demos and music.

721 8/M26 ✓ **Black Sparrow** 241 North St · www.theblacksparrow.co.uk · 0141 221 5530 & **Chinaski's** 239 North St · www.chinaskis.com · 0141 221 0061 Two great pubs for food and atmos, both with homages to Charles Bukowski (the American cult novelist and drinker). Moody interior and at Chinaski's outdoor seating that goes on and on. Bukowski would doubtless approve.

722 8/M25 **Brel** Ashton Lane · www.brelbar.com · 0141 342 4966 Always-busy bar in West End lane where teams of students and the rest of us teem, especially at weekends. Pots of moules/frites help the many euro-brews go down. Popular, stuff-your-face type of lunches and serried ranks of outside tables up the back. Lunch & food till 9.45pm (10.30pm weekends). Out back is the hill (714/OUTDOORS).

Babbity Bowster Reports: 710/ALES; 715/OUTDOORS.
Republic Bier Halle Report: 557/PIZZA.

The Main Attractions

723 8/L26
FREE
✓✓✓ **Riverside Museum** 100 Pointhouse Rd · www.glasgowlife.org. uk · 0141 287 2720 Across the Clyde from Govan. Glasgow's newest and most spectacular attraction, the Zaha Hadid-designed relocated and reborn Museum of Transport. Entirely at home here. 3,000 objects from trains and trams to paddle steamers and prams are skilfully and imaginatively arranged and displayed in the big, battleship-grey wavy shed. A 'Tall Ship' on the river and the New Glasgow emerging in the distance and getting closer. Given Scotland's and in particular Glasgow's pre-eminence in the invention and manufacture of so many forms of transport, it's heartening that this museum is such an impressive showcase. Like much of its contents, it's world class! Not just for boys! 7 days.

724 8/M26
ATMOS
FREE
✓✓ **Kelvingrove Art Gallery & Museum** Argyle St · www.glasgowlife. org.uk · 0141 276 9599 Huge Victorian sandstone edifice with awesome atrium. On the ground floor is a natural history/Scottish history museum. The upper salons contain the city's superb British and European art collection. A prodigious success, with literally millions of visitors since it reopened '06 after major refurb. Endless interest and people-friendly presentations. Excellent online and digital pre- and post-visit extras. See the world from a Glasgow point of view! (You go through 'Glasgow Stones' to get to 'Ancient Egypt'). And it's all free, folks! Cheap car park. 10am-5pm (from 11am Fri & Sun).

725 8/L26
FREE/
ADMISSION
NTS
✓✓ **The Burrell Collection & Pollok Park** 2060 Pollokshaws Rd · www. glasgowlife.org.uk · 0141 287 2550 S of the river via A77 Kilmarnock Rd (over Jamaica St Bridge from the city centre), or M77, well signed. Set in rural parkland, this award-winning modern gallery was built to house the eclectic acquisitions of Sir William Burrell. Closing for major refurbishment 2016 for up to 4 years. **Pollok House** www.nts.org.uk · 0141 616 6410 (with works by Goya, El Greco and William Blake) is worth a detour and has, below stairs, the better tearooms. Gardens to the river. 7 days 10am-5pm. See also 742/WALKS.

726 8/M26
FREE
✓ **Glasgow Cathedral** www.historic-scotland.gov.uk · 0141 552 8198 & **Provand's Lordship** www.glasgowlife.org.uk · 0141 276 1625 Both on Castle St Across the road from one another, they represent what remains of the oldest part of the city, which (as can be seen in the People's Palace below) was, as late as the early 18th century, merely a ribbon of streets from here to the river. The present cathedral, though established by St Mungo in AD 543, dates from the 12th century and is a fine example of very real, if gloomy, Gothic. The house, built in 1471, is a museum which strives to convey a sense of late medieval life. Don't get run over when you re-emerge into the 21st century and try to cross the street. In the background, the Necropolis piled on the hill invites inspection and offers a viewpoint and full Gothic perspective (though maybe don't go alone). Easy to do all these and St Mungo's Museum (below) together; allow half a day. **Vintage at Drygate** nearby for food and drink for the soul (532/GASTROPUBS). Cathedral 7 days; Provand's Lordship Tue-Sun.

727 8/M26
ATMOS
FREE
✓ **The People's Palace** www.glasgowlife.org.uk · 0141 276 0788 Approach via Glasgow Cross and London Rd, then turn right into Glasgow Green. This has long been a folk museum *par excellence* wherein, since 1898, the history, folklore and artefacts of a proud city have been gathered, cherished and displayed. But this is much more than a mere museum; it is part of the heart and soul of the city and, together with the Winter Gardens adjacent, shouldn't be missed if you want to know what Glasgow's about. Tearoom in the Tropics, among the palms and ferns of the Winter Gardens. Microbrewery and café-bar **WEST** nearby (707/ALES). Closed Mon.

728 8/M26 ✓ **Glasgow Science Centre** 50 Pacific Quay · www.
ADMISSION glasgowsciencecentre.org · 0141 420 5000 On south side of the Clyde by the BBC and opposite the SECC. Built with Millennium dosh. Approach via the Clyde Arc ('Squinty') Bridge or walk from SECC complex by Bell's Bridge. Impressive, titanium-clad mall, IMAX cinema and 127m-high tower. 4 floors of interactive exhibitions, planetarium and theatre. Separate tickets or combos. Book slot for the on-again, off-again tower (closed on windy days). 7 days 10am-5pm. Check website for winter opening hours.

729 8/M26 **St Mungo Museum of Religious Life & Art** 2 Castle St · www.glasgowlife.
FREE org.uk · 0141 276 1625 Part of the lovely and not-cherished-enough cathedral precinct (see above), this houses art and artefacts representing the world's 6 major religions arranged tactfully in an attractive stone building with a Zen garden in the courtyard. 3 floors, 4 exhibition areas. The assemblage seems like a good and worthwhile vision not quite realised, but in a time and place where sectarianism is still an issue and a problem, this is a telling and informative display. 7 days.

730 8/M26 **Hunterian Museum & Art Gallery** University Avenue · www.gla.ac.uk/
FREE hunterian · 0141 330 4221 On one side of the street, Scotland's oldest public museum with geological, archaeological and social history displayed in a venerable building. The **University Chapel** and cloisters should not be missed. Across the street, a modern block holds part of Glasgow's exceptional civic collection: Rembrandt to the Colourists and the Glasgow Boys, as well as one of the most complete collections of any artist's work and personal effects to be found anywhere, viz. that of Whistler. Fascinating stuff, even if you're not a fan. There's also a print gallery and superb **Mackintosh House** (769/MACKINTOSH). Closed Mon.

The Other Attractions

731 8/M25 ✓✓ **Botanic Gardens & Kibble Palace** 730 Great Western Rd · www.
FREE glasgow.gov.uk · 0141 276 1614 Smallish park close to River Kelvin with riverside walks (740/WALKS), and pretty much the 'Dear Green Place'. Kibble Palace (built 1873; major renovation 2006) is the distinctive domed glasshouse, with statues set among lush ferns and shrubbery from around the (mostly temperate) world. Killer Plant House especially popular. Main range arranged through smell and colour and seasonality. A wonderful place to muse and wander. Heritage Trail. New tearoom. Gardens open from 7am till dusk. Palace 10am-6pm (4.15pm in winter).

732 8/M26 ✓✓ **Gallery of Modern Art** Royal Exchange Sq · www.glasgowlife.org.
FREE uk · 0141 287 3050 Central, accessible and housed in former Stirling's Library, Glasgow's big visual arts attraction opened in a hail of art-world bickering in 1996 though it now more reflects Glasgow's eminence as a provenance of cutting-edge or conceptual work (all those Turner Prize nominees and winners?). It should definitely be on your Glasgow hit list. Late opening on Thu.

733 8/M26 ✓ **The Barras** East End The sprawling street and indoor market area around the Gallowgate. Over 20 years ago when I first wrote this book, the Barras was pure dead brilliant, a real slab of Glasgow life, and across the street the legendary **Sarry Heid** and the recently arrived **St Luke's** (702/698/UNIQUE PUBS). Its glory days are over but, as with all great markets, it's full of character and characters and it's still just about possible to find bargains, if not collectables. Everything from clairvoyants to the latest scam. Sat/Sun 10am-5pm.

734 8/M26 **The Tenement House** 145 Buccleuch St · www.nts.org.uk · 0141 333 0183
ADMISSION Near Charing Cross but can approach from near the end of Sauchiehall St and over
NTS the hill. Typical 'respectable' Glasgow tenement, kept under a bell jar since 'Our
Agnes' moved out in 1965. She had lived there with her mother since 1911 and
wasn't one for new-fangled things. It's a touch claustrophobic when busy and is
distinctly voyeuristic, but, well... your house would be interesting, too, in 50 years if
the clock were stopped. Reception on ground floor. Opening times vary.

735 8/M26 **Sharmanka Kinetic Theatre** 103 Trongate · www.sharmanka.com ·
ADMISSION 0141 552 7080 (limited times) A small and intimate experience like most others
on this page, but an extraordinary one. The gallery/theatre of Russian émigré
Eduard Bersudsky shows his meticulous and amazing mechanical sculptures. Short
performance (40 mins) Wed-Sun 3pm (4.15pm also on Sat). Full performances Thu
7pm, Sun 7pm. Closed Mon/Tue. For info best to email info@sharmanka.com.

736 8/M26 **Greenbank Garden** Clarkston · www.nts.org.uk · 0141 616 5126 10km SW
ADMISSION of centre via Kilmarnock Rd, Eastwood Toll, Clarkston Toll and Mearns Rd, then
NTS signposted (3km). A spacious oasis in the suburbs; formal gardens and 'working'
walled garden, parterre and woodland walks around elegant Georgian house.
Very Scottish. Gardens open AYR 9.30am-dusk; shop/tearoom Apr-Oct 11am-5pm,
Nov-Mar Sat/Sun 1-4pm.

737 8/M26 **City Chambers** George Sq · www.glasgow.gov.uk · 0141 287 4018 The hugely
impressive building along the whole east side of Glasgow's municipal central
square. This is a wonderfully evocative monument of the days when Glasgow was
the Second City of the Empire. Guided tours Mon-Fri 10.30am and 2.30pm (subject
to availability).

738 7/L25 **Finlaystone Country Estate** Langbank · www.finlaystone.co.uk ·
ADMISSION 01475 540505 Signed off the dual carriageway just before Port Glasgow.
Delightful gardens and woods around mansion house with many pottering places
and longer trails (and ranger service). Estate open AYR 10am-5pm. Visitor centre
and the Finlaystone tearoom. Spectacular bluebells and voluptuous peonies in May,
colour therapy in autumn. Visitor Centre & shop 11am-5pm (till 4pm Oct-Mar).
Tearoom 10am-5pm weekends and during school holidays.

739 8/M26 **The Waverley** www.waverleyexcursions.co.uk · 0845 130 4647 'The World's
ADMISSION Last Seagoing Paddle Steamer' which plied the Clyde in the glorious 'Doon the
Watter' days had a £7-million lottery-funded refit. Definitely the way to see the
West Coast. Sailings from Glasgow's Science Centre to Rothesay, Kyles of Bute,
Arran. Other days, leaves from Ayr or Greenock, many destinations. Call for
complex timetable of late June to August. Bar, restaurants, live bands: it's a party!

Paisley Abbey Reports: 73/EVENTS; 1880/ABBEYS.
Glasgow School of Art Report: 767/MACKINTOSH.
The Lighthouse Report: 771/MACKINTOSH.

The Best Walks In The City

See p. 12 for walk codes.

740 8/M26
2-13+KM
XCIRC
BIKES
1-A-1

Kelvin Walkway A path along the banks of Glasgow's other river, the Kelvin, which enters the Clyde unobtrusively at Yorkhill but first meanders through some of the most interesting parts and parks of the NW city. Walk starts at Kelvingrove Park through the university and Hillhead district under Kelvin Bridge and on to the celebrated **Botanic Gardens** (731/ATTRACTIONS). The trail then goes N, under the Forth & Clyde Canal (see below) to the Arcadian fields of Dawsholm Park (5km), Killermont (posh golf course) and Kirkintilloch (13km from start). Since the river and the canal shadow each other for much of their routes, it's possible, with a map, to go out by one waterway and return by the other (e.g. start at Great Western Rd, return Maryhill Rd).
START Usual start at the Eildon St (off Woodlands Rd) gate of Kelvingrove Park or Kelvin Bridge. Street parking only.

741 8
ANY KM
XCIRC
BIKES
1-A-1

Forth & Clyde Canal Towpath www.scottishcanals.co.uk The canal, opened in 1790, reopened 2002 as the Millennium Link. Once a major short-cut for fishing boats and trade between Europe and America, it provides a fascinating look round the back of the city from a pathway that stretches on a spur from Port Dundas just N of the M8 to the main canal at the end of Lochburn Rd off Maryhill Rd, and then E all the way to Kirkintilloch and Falkirk (**Falkirk Wheel** 08700 500208 4/ATTRACTIONS), and W through Maryhill and Drumchapel to Bowling and the Clyde (60km). A good option is go as far as Croy and take the very regular train service back. Much of the route is through the forsaken or redeveloped industrial heart of the city, past waste ground, warehouses and high flats, but there are open stretches and curious corners and, by Bishopbriggs, it's a rural waterway. More info from Scottish Canals (0141 332 6936).
START (1) Top of Firhill Rd (great view of city from **Ruchill Park**, 100m further on 753/VIEWS). (2) Lochburn Rd (see above) at the confluence from which to go E or W to the Clyde. (3) Top of Crow Rd, Anniesland where there is a canalside pub, Lock 27, with tables outside, real ale and food (noon-evening). (4) Bishopbriggs Sports Centre, Balmuildy Rd. From here it is 6km to Maryhill and 1km in other direction to the country churchyard of Cadder or 3km to Kirkintilloch. All starts have some parking.

742 8/L26

Pollok Country Park www.glasgow.gov.uk The park that (apart from the area around the gallery and the house 725/ATTRACTIONS) most feels like a real country park. Numerous trails through woods and meadows. The leisurely guided walks with the park rangers can be educative and more fun than you might think (0141 276 0924 for details). Burrell Collection and Pollok House & Gardens are obvious highlights. The better (old-fashioned) tearoom is in the basement of the latter, serving an excellent range of hot, home-made dishes, soups, salads, sandwiches, as well as the usual cakes and tasties. 7 days 10am-5pm (0844 493 2202). Enter by Haggs Rd or by Haggs Castle Golf Course. Well signed for cars including from Pollokshaws Rd and then to the car park in front of the Burrell.

743 8/L25
5-20KM
CAN BE CIRC
BIKES
1-A-2

Mugdock Country Park Craigallian Rd, nr Milngavie · www.mugdock-country-park.org.uk · 0141 956 6100 Not technically within the city, but one of the nearest and easiest escapes. Park, which includes Mugdock Woods (a SSSI) and 2 castles, is NW of Milngavie. Regular train from Queen St Station takes 20 mins, then follow route of the West Highland Way for 4km across Drumclog Moor to S edge of the park. By car to Milngavie by A81 park is 5km N. Well signed. 5 car parks; the main one includes Craigend Visitor Centre, Stables Tearoom, craft gallery and theatre. There's also a garden centre and farm shop. Many trails marked out and further afield rambles. This is a godsend between Glasgow and the Highland hills.

Cathkin Braes S edge of city with views. Report: 751/VIEWS.

See p. 12 for walk codes.

744 **8/M25**
10+KM
CAN BE CIRC
MTBIKES
2-B-2

Campsie Fells nr Glasgow 25km N of city best reached via Kirkintilloch or Cumbernauld/Kilsyth. Encompasses area that includes the Kilsyth Hills, Fintry Hills and Carron Valley between. **START** (1) Good approach from A803, Kilsyth main street up the Tak-me-Doon (*sic*) road. Park by golf club and follow path by the burn. It's possible to take in the two hills to left as well as Tomtain (453m), the most easterly of the tops, in a good afternoon; views to the E. (2) Car park on the south side of the B818 to Fintry at the W end of the Carron Valley reservoir opposite the access road to Todholes Farm and the wind farm. Follow tracks along reservoir to ascend Meikle Bin (570m) to the right. (3) The bonnie village of Fintry is a good start/base for the Fintry Hills and Earl's Seat (578m). (4) Campsie Glen – a sliver of glen in the hills. Approach via Clachan of Campsie on A81 (**Campsie Glen Coffee Shop** 01360 313049 for food stop) or from viewpoint high on the hill on B822 from Lennoxtown to Fintry; the easy Campsie introduction.

745 **8/L26**
2-10KM
CAN BE CIRC
MTBIKES
1-A-2

Gleniffer Braes Paisley · www.renfrewshire.gov.uk Ridge to the south of Paisley (15km from Glasgow) has been a favourite walking-place for centuries. M8 or Paisley Rd West to town centre then S via B774/B775 (Causeyside St then Neilston Rd) and sharp right after 3km to Glenfield Rd. Park/start at Robertson Park (signed). Here there are superb views and walks marked to E and W. 500m along Glenfield Rd is a car park/ranger centre (0141 884 3794). Walk up through gardens and formal parkland and then W along marked paths and trails.

746 **7/K25**
15/16KM
CIRC
MTBIKES
1-B-2

Greenock Cut www.clydemuirshiel.co.uk 45km W of Glasgow. Can approach via Port Glasgow but simplest route is from A78 road to Largs. Travelling S from Greenock take first left after IBM, brown-signed Loch Thom. Lochside 5km up winding road. Park at Greenock Cut Centre (01475 521458). Walk left along lochside road to Overton (5km) then path is signed. The Cut, an aqueduct built in 1827 to supply water to Greenock and its 31 mills, is now a historic monument. Great views from the mast along the Cut, though it is a detour. Another route to the right from the centre leads through a glen of birch, rowan and oak to the Kelly Cut. Both trails described on board at the car park.

747 **7/L26**

Clyde Muirshiel www.clydemuirshiel.co.uk General name for vast area of Inverclyde W of city, including Greenock Cut (see above), Lochwinnoch, Castle Semple Country Park and Lunderston Bay, a stretch of coastline near the Cloch Lighthouse on the A770 S of Gourock for littoral amblings. Best wildish bit is around Muirshiel Centre itself, Muirshiel Country Park (01505 614791), with trails, a waterfall and Windy Hill (350m). Nothing arduous, but a breath of air. The hen harrier hunts here. From M8 junction 29, take A737 Lochwinnoch, then B786 to top of Calder Glen Rd. Follow brown signs.

748 **8/L25**
2-A-2

Dumgoyne nr Blanefield Close to Glasgow and almost a mountain, so a popular non-strenuous hike. Huge presence, sits above A81 and Glengoyne Distillery (open to public). Approach from Strathblane War Memorial via Campsie Dene road. 7km track, allow 3-4 hours (or take the steep way up from the distillery). Refresh/replenish in Killearn (1318/GASTROPUBS) or **The Beech Tree Inn** in Dumgoyne, with global menu and play area for kids.

749 8/L25
5KM
CIRC
XBIKES
NO DOGS
1-A-1

The Whangie On A809 N from Bearsden about 8km after last roundabout and 2km after the Carbeth Inn, is the car park for the **Queen's View** (752/VIEWS). Once you get to the summit of Auchineden Hill, take the path that drops down to the west (a half right angle) and look for crags on your right. This is the 'back door' of The Whangie. Carry on and you'll suddenly find yourself in a deep cleft in the rock face with sheer walls rising over 10m on either side. The Whangie is more than 100m long and at one point the walls narrow to less than 1m. Local mythology has it that The Whangie was made by the Devil, who lashed his tail in anticipation of a witchy rendezvous somewhere in the north, and carved a slice through the rock, where the path now goes.

750 8/M26
2-8KM
CIRC
BIKES
1-A-2

Chatelherault nr Hamilton · www.slleisureandculture.co.uk Junction 6 off M74, well signposted into Hamilton, follow road into centre, then bear left away from main road where it's signed for A723. The gates to the 'château' are about 3km outside town. A drive leads to the William Adam-designed hunting lodge of the Dukes of Hamilton, set amid ornamental gardens with a notable parterre and extensive grounds. Tracks along the deep, wooded gorge of the Avon (ruins of Cadzow Castle) lead to distant glades. Good walks and ranger service (01698 426213). House open Mon-Thu and Sat 10am-4.30pm (Sun noon-4.30pm); walks at all times. Café, gift shop, visitor centre. The circular walk from the visitor centre is about 8km.

The Best Views Of The City & Beyond

751 8/M26

Cathkin Braes The southern ridge of the city on the B759 from Carmunnock to Cambuslang, about 12km from centre. Go S of river by Albert Bridge to Aikenhead Rd which continues S as Carmunnock Rd. Follow to Carmunnock, a delightfully rural village, and pick up the Cathkin Rd. 2km along on the right is the Cathkin Braes Golf Club and 100m further on the left is the park. Marvellous views to N of the Campsies, Kilpatrick Hills, Ben Lomond and as far as Ben Ledi. Walks on the Braes on both sides of the road. Refresh in **Laura's** in Carmunnock (15 Busby Rd, 0141 644 5657).

752 8/L25
1 A-1

Queen's View Auchineden Not so much a view of the city, more a perspective on Glasgow's Highland hinterland, this short walk and sweeping vista to the north has been a Glaswegian pilgrimage for generations. On A809 N from Bearsden about 8km after last roundabout and 2km after the Carbeth Inn, a very decent pub to repair to. Busy car park attests to popularity. The walk, along a path cut into ridgeside, takes 40-50 mins to the cairn, from which you can see **The Cobbler** (1929/HILLS), that other Glasgow favourite, Ben Ledi and sometimes as far as Ben Chonzie 50km away. The fine views of Loch Lomond are what Queen Victoria came for. Further on is **The Whangie** (749/WALKS).

753 8/M25

Ruchill Park Glasgow An unlikely but splendid panorama from this overlooked but well-kept park to the N of the city near Possilpark housing estate. Go to top of Firhill Rd (past Partick Thistle football ground) over **Forth & Clyde Canal** (741/WALKS) off Garscube Rd where it becomes Maryhill Rd. Best view is from around the flagpole; the whole city among its surrounding hills, from the Campsies to Gleniffer and Cathkin Braes (see above), becomes clear.

754 8/M25
1-A-2

Bar Hill Twechar, nr Kirkintilloch 22km N of city, taking A803 Kirkintilloch turn-off from M8, then the low road to Kilsyth, the B8023, bearing left at the black-and-white bridge. Next to Twechar Quarry Inn, a path is signed for Bar Hill and the Antonine Wall. Steepish climb for 2km; ignore the strange dome of grass. Over to left in copse of trees are the remains of one of the forts on the Roman wall which was built across Scotland in the 2nd century AD. Ground plan explained on a board. This is a special place with strong history vibes and airy views over the plain to the city which came a long time after.

755 8/N27 **Black Hill** nr Lesmahagow 28km S of city. Another marvellous outlook, but in
1-A-2 the opposite direction from above. Take junction 10/11 on M74, then off the B7078 signed Lanark, take the B7018. 4km along past Clarkston Farm, head uphill for 1km and park by Water Board mound. Walk uphill through fields to right for about 1km. Unprepossessing hill that unexpectedly reveals a vast vista of most of east-central Scotland.

756 8/L26 **Paisley Abbey** Paisley · www.paisleyabbey.org.uk · 0141 889 7654 M8 to Paisley; frequent trains from Central Station. Abbey Mon-Sat 10am-3.30pm. Every so often on Abbey 'open days', the tower of this amazing edifice can be climbed. The tower (restored 1926) is 50m high and from the top there's a grand view of the Clyde. This is a rare experience, but phone the tourist information centre (0141 889 0711) or abbey itself (mornings) for details; it could be your lucky day. Guided tours by arrangement. Regular events. Café. See also 1880/ABBEYS.

757 7/K25 **Lyle Hill** Gourock Via M8 W to Greenock, then round the coast to relatively genteel old resort of Gourock where the Free French worked in the yards during the war. A monument has been erected to their memory on the top of Lyle Hill above the town, from where you get one of the most dramatic views of the great crossroads of the Clyde (Holy Loch, Gare Loch and Loch Long). Best vantage-point is further along the road on other side by trig point. Follow British Rail station signs, then Lyle Hill. There's another great view of the Clyde further down the water at **Haylie, Largs**, the hill 3km from town reached via the A760 road to Kilbirnie and Paisley. The Isle of Cumbrae lies in the sound and the sunset.

758 8/M26 **Top of the Lighthouse** 11 Mitchell Lane · www.thelighthouse.co.uk · 0141 276 5365 Off Buchanan St. Viewing platform atop the six-floor Mackintosh and Design Centre, reached by 136 steps or lift for views across a great city. See also 771/MACKINTOSH.

759 8/M25 **Ubiquitous Chip Terrace** 12 Ashton Lane · www.ubiquitouschip.co.uk · 0141 334 5007 The almost secret roof terrace on top of one of Glasgow's top restaurants has surprising views of the urban neighbourhood of the vibrant and wonderful West End. 501/TOP-END DINING.

Campsie Fells & Gleniffer Braes Reports: 744/745/WALKS.

The Best Independent Galleries

Apart from those listed in Main Attractions and Other Attractions, the following galleries are always worth looking into. The Glasgow Gallery Guide, free from any of them, lists current exhibitions.

760 8/M26 ✓✓ **Glasgow Print Studio** Trongate 103 · www.glasgowprintstudio. co.uk · 0141 552 0704 Influential and accessible gallery in Glasgow's contemporary-art centre, with print work on view and for sale from many of Scotland's leading and rising artists. Gallery open Tue-Sun; Workshop Tue-Sat.

761 8/M26 ✓✓ **Transmission Gallery** 18 King St · www.transmissiongallery.org · 0141 552 2540 Cutting-edge and often off-the-wall work from contemporary Scottish and international artists. Reflects Glasgow's importance as a hot spot of conceptual art. Stuff you might disagree with. Closed Sun/Mon.

762 8/M26 ✓✓ **The Modern Institute** 14-20 Osborne St · www. themoderninstitute.com · 0141 248 3711 The original gallery and exhibition space at 3 Aird's Lane nearby. Scotland's leading gallery/art space for commercial and conceptual contemporary art. International reputation for cutting-edge art ideas and occasional events. MI shows at London's pre-eminent, highly selective Frieze Art Fair. Gallery Thu-Sat noon-5pm.

763 8/M26 ✓ **Mary Mary** 6 Dixon St · www.marymarygallery.co.uk · 0141 226 2257 Cool, always interesting gallery showing the kind of work that keeps Glasgow pre-eminent as a UK centre of edgy, contemporary work. Tue-Sat noon-6pm. Closed Aug.

764 8/M26 ✓ **Compass Gallery** 178 W Regent St · www.compassgallery.co.uk · 0141 221 6370 Glasgow's oldest established commercial contemporary art gallery. Their New Generation exhibition in Jul-Aug shows work from new graduates of the art colleges and has heralded many a career. Combine with the other Gerber gallery (see below). Closed Sun.

765 8/M26 ✓ **Cyril Gerber Fine Art** 178 W Regent St · www.gerberfineart.co.uk · 0141 221 3095 British paintings and especially the Scottish Colourists and 'name' contemporaries. Gerber and the Compass (see above) were created by the legendary and lovely Cyril Gerber, who probably did more for young Scottish artists over the last 50 years (and many have become well known and collectable) than anyone else. He passed away in 2012 and the gallery is now run by his similarly informed and enthusiastic daughter Jill. They have summer and Christmas exhibitions where small, accessible paintings can be bought for reasonable prices. Closed Sun.

766 8/M26 **Street Level Photoworks** 103 Trongate · www.streetlevelphotoworks.org · 0141 552 2151 Glasgow's photography place; for artists and public to see and do in lens-based media. Prints for sale. Tue-Sat 10am-5pm, from noon Sun. Open till 8pm first Thursday of the month.

The Mackintosh Trail

Architect and designer Charles Rennie Mackintosh (1868-1928) had an extraordinary influence on contemporary design. Visit www.crmsociety.com

767 8/M26
ATMOS
✓✓✓ **Glasgow School of Art** 167 Renfrew St · www.gsa.ac.uk · 0141 353 4500 Mackintosh's supreme architectural triumph and one of Europe's favourite buildings as evinced by the response to the fire that engulfed it and decimated its priceless library in 2014. It's enough almost to admire it from the street (and maybe best – it's very much a working college) but there are daily guided tours (0141 353 4526). You may wonder if the building itself is partly responsible for its remarkable output of acclaimed artists. The complementary 2014 Reid building by US architect Steven Holl, though also full of students, has a superb permanent exhibition of the workings and influence of the Art School, temporary exhibitions, and a great café-bar open to all.

768 8/M25
ADMISSION
✓✓ **Queen's Cross Church** 870 Garscube Rd · www.mackintoshchurch.com · 0141 946 6600 Built 1896-99. Calm and simple, the antithesis of Victorian Gothic. If all churches had been built like this, we'd go more often. The HQ of the Charles Rennie Mackintosh Society which was founded in 1973.

769 8/M26
ADMISSION
✓✓ **The Mackintosh House** 82 Hillhead St · www.gla.ac.uk/hunterian · 0141 330 4221 Opposite and part of the **Hunterian Museum & Art Gallery** (730/ATTRACTIONS) within the university campus. The master's house has been transplanted and methodically reconstructed from the next street (they say even the light is the same). If you've ever wondered what the fuss is about, go and see how innovative and complete an artist, designer and architect he was, in this inspiring yet habitable set of rooms. Tue-Sat 10am-5pm.

770 8/M26
ATMOS
FREE
✓✓ **Scotland Street School Museum** 225 Scotland St · www.glasgowlife.org.uk · 0141 287 0500 Opposite Shields Rd underground station; best approach by car from Eglinton St (A77 Kilmarnock Rd over Jamaica St Bridge). Entire school (from 1906) preserved as museum of education through Victorian/Edwardian and wartimes. Original, exquisite Mackintosh features, especially tiling, and powerfully redolent of happy school days; a uniquely evocative time capsule. Café and temporary exhibitions. Closed Mon. Brilliant café **The Fish People** over the road (616/SEAFOOD).

771 8/M26
ADMISSION
✓✓ **The Lighthouse** 11 Mitchell Lane · www.thelighthouse.co.uk · 0141 276 5360 Glasgow's legacy from its year as UK City of Architecture and Design. Changing exhibitions in Mackintosh's 1893-95 building for *The Herald* newspaper. It houses, over 6 floors, a shop and books, a café-bar, an interpretation centre and exhibition space. Fantastic rooftop views. 7 days. See also 758/VIEWS.

772 7/K25
ATMOS
ADMISSION
NTS
✓✓ **The Hill House** Helensburgh · www.nts.org.uk · 01436 673900 Take Sinclair St off Princes St (at Romanesque tower and tourist information centre) and go 2km uphill, taking left into Kennedy Dr and follow signs. A complete house incorporating Mackintosh's typical total unity of design, built for publisher Walter Blackie in 1902-04. Much to marvel over and wish that everybody else would go away and you could stay for the night (in that fabulous bedroom). There's a library full of books (though not to touch). Tearoom; gardens and shops. Apr-Oct 1.30-5.30pm. Helensburgh is 45km NW of city centre via Dumbarton (A82) and A814 up the N Clyde coast.

the
Best
Regional Hotels
& Restaurants

The Best Hotels & Restaurants In Argyll

773 7/J22
11 ROOMS +
COTTAGE
DF
EXP

✓✓ **Airds Hotel** Port Appin · www.airds-hotel.com · 01631 730236
32km N of Oban, 4km off A828. For a reassuringly long time, Airds has been one of the foremost northern hostelries and a legendary gourmet experience. Shaun and Jenny McKivragan have continued this tradition and, with care and attention, ongoing refurbishment and a great team, Airds remains a 'civilised escape in a hectic world'. Contemporary-cosy might describe bedrooms and lounges (and conservatory dining room). Dinner is the culmination of a hard day on the croquet lawn or gazing over the bay. Unobtrusive service and the creativity of chef Chris Stanley. Tasting menu and à la carte. 2 elegant suites: one with patio, one with balcony. Port Appin is one of Scotland's most charming places. The **Lismore** passenger ferry is 2km away (2208/ISLANDS). Bring a bike (or hire locally) and come home to Airds!
EAT Has always been one of the best meals in the North, a destination in itself.

774 7/H24
20 ROOMS
DF
LL
EXP

>£35/£15

✓✓ **Crinan Hotel** Crinan · www.crinanhotel.com · 01546 830261 8km off A816. On coast, 60km S of Oban (Lochgilphead 12km) at head of the Crinan Canal which joins Loch Fyne with the sea. Nick Ryan's (and family's) landmark hotel in a stunning setting and some of the best sea views in the UK. Rooms do vary. This hotel has long housed one of the UK's great seafood restaurants. Nick's wife's (notable artist Frances Macdonald) pictures of these shorelines and those of son, Ross, are hung around you and are for sale; the rooftop lounge regularly shows other curated pictures from significant Scottish artists and there's the piano first played by Dave Brubeck that I never noticed before. The perfect sunset setting for your aperitif. Beautiful flowers.
EAT Choice of Westward dining room, Lock 16 up top with 'the view' (not always open), or perfect pub grub in Seafood Bar.

775 7/J24
25 ROOMS
DF
ATMOS
MED.INX-MED.
EX

✓✓ **George Hotel** Inveraray · www.thegeorgehotel.co.uk · 01499 302111 On the main street of a historic town on Loch Fyne with credible attractions both here (castle) and nearby, The George gets 2 ticks because this ancient inn (1770), still in the capable and friendly hands of the Clark family (since the 1860's), has fantastic atmos, especially in the bars. Rooms refurbished tastefully in a Highland-chic kind of way. Downstairs open fire, great grub; all Scottish towns on the visitors' map should have a place like this. The First House adjacent (actually the first house in the town) has 8 of the 25 rooms, with some great loch views. Very much part of the local community, the main bar is surprisingly cosmopolitan: memories of Scotland are made of this!
EAT Gastropub grub in multi-chambered stone and wood setting and conservatory. Good ales, wines and staple/classic-led menu. Music Fri/Sat.

776 7/H26
5 ROOMS
DF
MAR-OCT
MED.EX

✓✓ **The Kilberry Inn** nr Tarbert · www.kilberryinn.com · 01880 770223
Small Knapdale roadside inn with famously good food. Simple, stylish cottage-courtyard rooms. Beautiful drive out on B8024 off the Tarbert-Lochgilphead coast road. 2-tick gastropub food as good as it gets. Michelin agree. David out front, Clare in the kitchen. Hotel deal includes dinner. Secret beaches nearby to wander. Report: 1302/GASTROPUBS.

777 7/J22
4 ROOMS
NO PETS
NO KIDS
MED.EX

✓✓ **Ardtorna** Barcaldine · www.ardtorna.co.uk · 01631 720125 Just off the A828 18km N of Oban. A deluxe B&B where the O'Byrnes have thought of everything, from the scones on arrival, the guest fridges in the room to the whisky liqueurs. Great views over Loch Creran in a new-build house with underfloor heating, and decor coordinated around the light fittings! Communal breakfast, guest lounge. Pleasant walking nearby (2012/WALKS). A top stopover!

778 7/J25
16 ROOMS +
BY THE NIGHT
MED.INX-MED.
EX

£15-25

✓✓ Portavadie Marina Portavadie · www.portavadie.com · 01700 811075 Off the B8000. The surprisingly shiny sheltered marina that's popped up at the mouth of Loch Fyne opposite Tarbert, with a steel and glass restaurant and yachty complex with rooms, lodges, cottages; leisure centre with infinity pool and outdoor tubs. Bit like landing on a space station in backwoods Argyll, but it works – it so works!
EAT A marina-side café-bar with mezzanine restaurant, a café-restaurant as you come in and a pizza caff in the leisure centre. All-day dining.

779 7/H24
25 ROOMS
DF
FEB-DEC
MED.INX

✓ Loch Melfort Hotel Arduaine · www.lochmelfort.co.uk · 01852 200233 30km S of Oban on the beautiful road between Oban and Campbeltown. Landmark hotel, which owners Calum and Rachel Ross are still restoring; still upping the game. You get the view of Loch Shuna from most rooms (including all those in extension that come with either balcony or patio). Those in the main mansion are more traditional but are pleasantly large; 2 suites. Same view dominates the dining room and the Chartroom II bar with pub-food menu (seafood specials). Hotel has the same access road as **Arduaine**, an extraordinary back garden in which to wander (1516/GARDENS).

780 7/H23
11 ROOMS
MED.EX

✓ The Manor House Oban · www.manorhouseoban.com · 01631 562087 On S coast road out of town towards Kerrera ferry, overlooking bay where the big ferries come and go. Understated elegance in contemporary style and a restaurant that serves (in an intimate dining room) probably the most fine-dining dinner in town. Daily changing menu. Bedrooms small but cosy: it is a civilised lodging. More delightful than merely deluxe. Nice bar.

781 7/H25
12 ROOMS
NO PETS · L
MED.INX-MED.
EX

✓ The Anchor Hotel Tarbert · www.lochfyne-scotland.co.uk · 01880 820577 A fine wee town much favoured by messers-about-on-boats. The Anchor is not only on the harbour, it is also in the harbour – 4 of the contemporary, well-appointed rooms are on a boat. Here you really do wake up at sea level. You definitely feel at one with this town on the water.
EAT The Sea Bed Restaurant, the best bet in Tarbert. Seafood slant.

782 7/H23
12 ROOMS
MAR-NOV
CHP

✓ Glenburnie Hotel Oban · www.glenburnie.co.uk · 01631 562089 In the middle of a broad sweep of hotels overlooking the bay, this the most notable. Amiable Graeme Strachan's a natural innkeeper so everything in his seaside mansion is welcoming and easy on the eye. Great detail: home-made muesli and fruit for breakfast; nice furnishings. No dinner but good advice of where to go.

783 7/J25
11 ROOMS
NO KIDS
FEB-DEC
MED.EX-EXP

✓ The Royal Hotel Tighnabruaich · www.theroyalanlochan.co.uk · 01700 811239 Long live the Royal! Keith and Christine Bettis found it a few years back (you may have seen their search on *Relocation, Relocation*) and restored the name of this grand old seaside mansion. Lovely rooms, many looking over to Bute, comfy furnishings and a plethora of pictures. Lots of public space and the lovely wee Shinty Bar with pics of decades of the team (it's gay heaven). Food in bar or conservatory. Time moves slowly in Tighnabruaich!

784 7/J25
8 ROOMS
NO TV
DF
L
MED.INX

✓ Kilfinan Hotel Kilfinan · www.kilfinan.com · 01700 821201 13km from Tighnabruaich on B8000. A much-loved, historic (well, 300 years) inn on the beautiful single-track road that skirts Loch Fyne. The Wyatts run what is still a quiet getaway inn (quiet as the adjacent graveyard) with amazingly long-standing manager and people person, Madalon. Relaxing rooms, great cooking from Helen Wyatt in dining room or bar; sensible wine list. For a not-too-expensive retreat on a quiet peninsula, this is a good bet. They make a virtue of the poor mobile-phone and TV reception (no TVs in the rooms). A nice place to bring kids. There are weddings. 1143/KIDS.

785 7/J23
3 ROOMS
CHP

✓ **Roineabhal** nr Kilchrenan · www.roineabhal.com · 01866 833207
Another great place to stay near Kilchrenan (see **Ardanaiseig** 1132/COUNTRY-HOUSE HOTELS) deep in the Loch Awe interior (10km from A85, near Taynuilt). This is a good deal less expensive. Roger and Maria Soep call this a Highland country house (pronounced Ron-ay-val) – it is a gorgeous guest house in a family home; good pictures (they're quite arty). Intimate (you eat round the same table) but all in excellent taste; set-menu dinner (you don't have to have it but you should). And there's an excellent breakfast (that porridge!). Wine provided but you can BYOB.

786 7/G28
22 ROOMS
L
MED.EX

✓ **Machrihanish Dunes** nr Campbeltown · www.machrihanishdunes.com · 01586 810000 Over the wide ocean from America came a new golf course and resort adjacent to the time-honoured and Old Tom Morris-designed Machrihanish; same dunes, same strand. Here we are talking about **The Ugadale Hotel** by the first tee of the Machrihanish Golf Club (the actual Dunes course is 5km away), with rooms, cottages and a spa. Part of the same group, the refurbished **Royal Hotel** in Campbeltown brings a new standard of accom to this town at the end of the road.

787 7/J24
67 ROOMS
MED.INX

Loch Fyne Hotel Inveraray · www.crerarhotels.com · 01499 302980 A surprisingly large and decent hotel in this charming town. On main A83 towards Lochgilphead overlooking loch. Part of the Crerar Group; this one of their best. Pleasing, simple design makeover with a touch of tartan. Bistro OK. Pool and modest spa facilities. But they do take coach parties.

788 7/H21
11 ROOMS
DF
MED.EX

Kilcamb nr Strontian · www.kilcamblodge.co.uk · 01967 402257 A country-house hotel just outside the hamlet of Strontian. A comfortable, welcoming place and base from which to explore glorious Ardnamurchan and Morvern. Good outlook with lawns to Loch Sunart, great woodland walking nearby (2007/WALKS). The brasserie restaurant strong on seafood. It is calm!

789 7/H25
32 ROOMS
DF
L
MED.INX

Stonefield Castle Hotel Tarbert · www.bespokehotels.com · 01880 820836 Just outside town on the A83, a castle evoking the 20th more than preceding centuries. Splendid luxuriant gardens leading down to Loch Fyne. Rhoddies in spring, hydrangeas in summer. Dining room with baronial splendour and splendid views. Friendly, flexible staff; overall, it seems quintessentially Scottish and OK, especially for families. 4 principal rooms, but standards with loch views (you pay a premium) are fine.

790 7/J25
4 ROOMS
CHP

Wellpark Hotel Tighnabruaich · www.wellparkhotel.co.uk · 01700 811921 In a substantial mansion along the front at the very end of the village, a hotel and especially restaurant that's one of those secret spots adored by all who find it. Have to admit I've only been once when it was closed, looking through the windows. Public rooms seem elegant and stylish, the lawn overlooks the Kyles. What more can I say – reports, please.

✓✓ **Isle of Eriska** Ledaig 20km N of Oban. Report: 1127/COUNTRY-HOUSE HOTELS. And see Restaurants below.

✓✓ **Ardanaiseig Hotel** Kilchrenan Report: 1132/COUNTRY-HOUSE HOTELS.

✓ **Kames Hotel** nr Tighnabruaich Report: 1176/INNS.

THE BEST RESTAURANTS IN ARGYLL

791 7/J24 ✓✓ **Inver Restaurant** Strathlachlan, Loch Fyne · www.inverrestaurant.
£25-35 co.uk · 01369 860537 S of Strachur on scenic B8000, a cottage bar/ bistro overlooking loch and ruins of Castle Lachlan (nice 40-min walk along the shore). Rob Latimer and Pam Brunton (in the kitchen with a great team) have transformed the old Inver Cottage and, to some extent, eating out in Argyll. This truly is *the* destination restaurant in the region. Food is foraged, found, grown and sourced locally and made into something simple; beautiful to look at and to eat. Bar (by the fire) menu or in the caff area. Many awards coming, I suspect. Downstairs the occasional 'Boat House Sessions' (music). Pam has a hearty laugh. That pleasure is on the plate too. A real find! Weekends only Nov/Dec & closed Jan/Feb.

792 7/J25 ✓ **Portavadie Marina** Portavadie · www.portavadie.com · 01700 811075
£15-25 On the edge of Loch Fyne and the known world, the surprising super-yachty and all-round leisure complex with 3 restaurant options. Report: 778/ARGYLL.

793 7/K23 ✓ **Loch Fyne Oysters** Clachan · www.lochfyne.com · 01499 600264 On the
£15-25 A83 near Arrochar, the one that started it all and still a fine place to stop for seafood and sustenance. Report: 1343/SEAFOOD.

794 7/J22 ✓ **The Deck @ Isle of Eriska** Ledaig · www.eriska-hotel.co.uk ·
£15-25 01631 720371 Isle of Eriska Hotel is evermore with a great fine-ish dining room. The Deck is the light and casual alternative café/restaurant in the spa overby. Possibly overlooked for a drop-in lunch or high tea but definitely a good option between Oban and Ballachulish. The spa has treatment rooms and its own pampering menu, the restaurant overlooks the golf course with a wide terrace/ deck and serene views over the greens to the loch. Familiar food done well; a pleasant detour. See also 1127/COUNTRY-HOUSE HOTELS.

795 7/J24 ✓ **Samphire** Inveraray · www.samphireseafood.com · 01499 302321
£25-35 Andrew Maclugash came home to Inveraray, that most beguiling of Argyll
CLOSED JAN towns, crafting his skills in some top kitchens to open this seafood restaurant in the main street that leads to Loch Fyne. An intimate bistro where ethical supply and simple presentation has proven to be a winning fishy formula. Best book!.

796 7/K25 **Livingstone's** Dunoon · 01369 703991 In its previous incarnation as Chatters,
£25-35 this was *the* place to eat and now under chef/proprietor Jackie Coutts, well, it still is. Haven't tried but all reports have been good. Nice garden. If you are down this water, the Cowal Peninsula awaits your explorations (and **Younger/Benmore Gardens** 1501/GARDENS). Mon-Sat lunch & dinner.

If you're in Oban...

WHERE TO STAY

797 7/H23
5 ROOMS
NO PETS
NO KIDS
MED.EX

✓ **Greystones** www.greystonesoban.co.uk · 01631 358653 At the end of a cul-de-sac, an imposing house with splendid views over the town out front, and below **McCaig's Folly** (1837/MONUMENTS) behind (lit at night). Once again (they were once out of town) architects Mark and Suzanne McPhillips have created a superb, calm, aesthetic luxury B&B. Makes Oban all the nicer if you can get one of their spacious, airy rooms (with the view!).

59 ROOMS
DF
MED.EX

Caledonian Hotel www.obancaledonian.co.uk · 01764 651844 In the centre of things, the port and the people, so it can be noisy but this has long been a landmark hotel. Under new management 2015. Shake-up is expected (and due). Reports, please.

✓ **The Manor House** www.manorhouseoban.com · 01631 562087 S of centre and ferry terminal. Quietly posh. Report: 780/ARGYLL.

✓ **Glenburnie Hotel** Corran Esplanade From tea and shortbread on arrival and lovely rooms, it's clear this is a superior bed for the night. Report: 782/ARGYLL.

S.Y. Hostel www.syha.org.uk · 01631 562025 Good location on the front.

Oban Backpackers & Backpackers Plus Report: 1159/HOSTELS.

WHERE TO EAT

L
£25-35

✓ **Ee-Usk** www.eeusk.com · 01631 565666 & **Piazza** 01631 563628 · North Pier These 2 adjacent contemporary steel-and-glass restaurants on the corner of the bay are both the ambitious creation and abiding passion of the Macleod family; Calum now presides. They epitomise the open and up-for-it Oban; a new hotel is planned nearby. Ee-Usk is a bright, modern seafood café with great views. Halibut, haddock and cod locally sourced (they know its origins and the fishermen personally), hand-cut chips; home-made starters and puds. Piazza purveys standard though rather good standard Italian fare. Both pack 'em in. You need look no further out to sea. Open AYR. 7 days lunch & dinner.

£25-35

✓ **The Waterfront** www.waterfrontoban.co.uk · 01631 563110 In the port, by the station, in the midst of all, a place that's serious about seafood. 'From pier to pan' is about right. Blackboard (well, TV-screen) menu and the usuals à la carte. Big on oysters and scallops. An airy upstairs diner whose busyness attests to popularity and down the more recent:
YuWu www.yuwu.co.uk · 01631 563338 A Chinese restaurant UK style in colour, tone and menu that quickly filled a niche. Many locals, many tourists. Both are open lunch & dinner AYR.

£25-35

✓ **Coast** www.coastoban.co.uk · 01631 569900 Main street on corner of John St. Richard (in the kitchen) and Nicola (out front) Fowler have since 2004 run the best (non-seafood) restaurant in Oban. Modern-British menu by a pedigree chef in contemporary, laid-back room. Excellent value for this quality, especially their 'Light Bite' menu, and no fuss. Seasonal menu. Open AYR.

>£35

✓ **The Manor House** Gallanach Rd The best hotel dining room in town. Creative cuisines and fresh seafood in an elevated location. Report: 780/ARGYLL.

<£15

✓ **Fish & Chips In Oban** Oban has called itself the 'seafood capital of Scotland' and for good reason. Not only is there a choice of seafood restaurants, there are 4 good fish 'n' chip shops, 3 with cafés: **Nories**, the related **Oban Bay Fish Bar**, the **Oban Fish & Chip Shop** and the **George Street Fish & Chip Shop**. See 1353/FISH & CHIPS to find out who tops the list.

<£15 ✓ **Julie's Coffee House** www.juliescoffeehouse.co.uk · 01631 565952
Opposite Oban Whisky Visitor Centre. No Julie, rather Janet and Ann, who bake and make it Oban's best home-style coffee shop. Only 10 tables, so fills up. Nice approach to food (excellent home baking, soups and snacks) and customers. Good Elektra coffee; my fave drop-in coffee & cake stop. Closed Sun/Mon.

APR-SEP ✓ **Kerrera Tea Garden (& Bunkhouse)** Isle of Kerrera · www.
<£15 kerrerabunkhouse.co.uk · 01631 566367 An Oban secret and an open secret, this tea garden rather than tea room comes at the end of a wee adventure i.e. the 3-min ferry from Gallanach pier (2km along the coast beyond the big ferry terminal) and then a 2km walk (or from the quay by the Piazza restaurant in the bay then a lovely though longer walk). A garden below ruined Gylen Castle and a cosy, decorated barn. Martin and Aideen's cool retreat is simply a great place to be. Fresh, local home cooking, including bread. Apr-Sep, 7 days 10.30am-4.30pm.

£15-25 ✓ **Maatchi** www.maatchi.co.uk · 01631 358080 Overlooking the bay. An upstairs Indian restaurant from the people who've covered the waterfront (the eponymous restaurant and YuWu above) and the ethnic menu in Oban; it's done well for locals and tourists alike. This is a very passable Indian restaurant with all the saags, masalas and bhoonas we are used to. 7 days lunch & dinner.

£15-25 **The Seafood Temple** www.obanseafood.com · 01631 566000 Along the bay adjacent to Oban Sailing Club. Great location with dreamy views. Yes, it is about the seafood and the view! Eilidh Smith and family make/bake everything. Probably have to book. Dinner only Tue-Sat (2 sittings 6.15/8.15pm).

<£15 **Oban Chocolate Coffee Shop** www.obanchocolate.co.uk · 01631 566099
The place to go for coffee, cake and, of course, chocolate. And they do go; it's usually packed. Chocs are made on the premises. You can have the hot variety. Croissants for breakfast. Waffles whenever. 7 days. Closed Jan.

<£15 **The Kitchen Garden** www.kitchengardenoban.co.uk · 01631 566332
Oban's deli-café; you may have to queue for the upstairs gallery caff. Not a bad cup of coffee; sandwiches and hot dishes. Plethora of cheese and whisky.

£15-25 **Cuan Mor** www.cuanmor.co.uk · 01631 565078 On the bay, very central and busy bar-bistro attached to Oban Brewery. They say 'contemporary Scottish' and that's about right. It is very well done, extensive additional bar upstairs at the back. Perfectly good pit or quay stop. 7 days all day.

MAY-SEP **Waypoint Bar & Grill** Isle of Kerrera · www.waypointbarandgrill.com ·
<£15 01631 565888 Another caff on Kerrera (see above), this one just over there at the (Oban) marina on the island, 8 mins away by a free ferry from the North Pier (by Piazza, 10 mins past the hour). Casual dining, seafood and sandwiches. Fun but not as fab now it's not al fresco. 7 days noon-6.30pm (LO).

Tourist Information Centre 3 North Pier · 01631 563122 Open AYR.

798 7/K28
149 ROOMS +
6 LODGES
LL
LOTS

✓✓ **Turnberry** Turnberry · www.turnberry.co.uk · 01655 331000 Not just a splendid hotel on the Ayrshire coast, more a way of life centred on golf. Looks over the 2 celebrated courses (home to the Open '09) and Ailsa Craig, the enigmatic lump of rock in the sea (2038/GOLF). But in 2016, after a closure, the stylish old place returns decidedly trumped: and now the Trump Turnberry Resort. At TGP there was no chance to be impressed (or not) with its transformation; a huge amount of loot will have been spent (on chandeliers alone). But let us not prejudge, and we know at least that there will be spectacular views of the Ailsa and Kintyre Courses and the coast. Every day a different sunset!

799 8/L28
22 ROOMS +
2 COTTS
DF
L
MED.EX

✓✓ **Dumfries House** nr Cumnock · www.dumfrieshouselodge.co.uk · 01290 429920 On the A70 25km E of Ayr. The conservation and spectacular transformation of the House and extensive grounds is unquestionably due to the successful intervention of Prince Charles, much done in the name of the Prince's Trust. Around a courtyard near the House, the Lodge is a luxury GH, with self-catering cottages. As with all else, rooms are in very good taste. The Woodlands Restaurant and adjacent sawmill are social and educational projects (Thu-Sat from 5pm & Sun lunch); the Coach House Café open 7 days from 10am. Wonderful walks await 1505/GARDENS.

800 8/L27
4 ROOMS
DF
MED.INX
£25-35

✓✓ **The Sorn Inn** Sorn · www.sorninn.com · 01290 551305 8km E of Mauchline on the B743 off the A76. Traditional inn in rural setting and pleasant village in deepest Ayrshire. The Grant family have established a big reputation for food with a continuing clutch of awards, including consecutive Michelin Bib Gourmands. There are 4 simple, great-value rooms with Wi-Fi, etc. **EAT** People travel from miles around to eat here. Restaurant and pub meals. Craig Grant a nice guy in the kitchen. See 1301/GASTROPUBS.

801 7/K28
6 SUITES +
LODGES
NO PETS
APR-OCT
LL
LOTS

✓ **Culzean Castle** nr Maybole · www.culzeanexperience.org · 01655 884455 18km S of Ayr, this accom in the suites of Culzean (1755/CASTLES), including the famous and lavishly refurbished Eisenhower apartment, not so much a hotel but, in any case, a bed for the night rarely comes as historically posh. The second floor (you enter by the original 1920s lift and there's a very grand staircase) has some fabulous views. Rates are expensive but include afternoon tea. Dinner is available. Bookable for individual or exclusive use (where you won't find strangers in the drawing room) 1276/HOUSE PARTIES. The clifftop setting, the gardens and the vast grounds are superb.

802 7/L27
32 ROOMS
NO PETS
MED.EX

✓ **Lochgreen House** Troon · www.lochgreenhouse.com · 01292 313343 Top hotel of the Bill Costley group which is so pre-eminent in this neck of the woods. Lochgreen (adjacent to and overlooking Royal Troon Golf Course) is a comfortable, spacious yet homely country house with big bedrooms looking out to the green. Andrew, the younger Costley, is in executive charge (and all those below) of the smart brasserie-type menu in chandeliered but clubbable dining room; lounges can be tight pre/après. The **Brig o' Doon** at Alloway is the romance-and-Rabbie Burns hotel (01292 442466), with a fabulous self-catering house, **Doonbrae**, opposite (1278/HOUSE PARTIES) in gorgeous gardens, while **Highgrove** (01292 312511), more intimate and with great coastal views, is just outside Troon. All operate at a high standard. The Costleys also have the **Ellisland Hotel** in Ayr

(808/AYR) and 2 excellent roadside inns, the **Cochrane** at Gatehead (1321/GASTROPUBS) and **Souter's Inn** in Kirkoswald (1312/GASTROPUBS).

>£35   **EAT** Lochgreen: The top restaurant here but consistently high quality throughout the group. The consummate Costleys cater for all.

803   **7/K28**
11 ROOMS
NO PETS
MED.INX

£25-35

✓ **Wildings Hotel & Restaurant** Maidens · www.wildingshotel.com · 01655 331401 The family of the late consummate restaurateur Brian Sage run this 'restaurant with rooms' with love and respect for him and their customers. Contemporary and comfortable rooms overlook a serene harbour in this coastal village near Turnberry (and a fraction of the cost of the course).

EAT A beautiful spot and excellent gastropub-style menu in 2 large, buzzing rooms. They come from all over the county, so book at weekends.

804   **7/K27**
37 ROOMS
DF
MED.EX

Piersland Hotel Troon · www.piersland.co.uk · 01292 314747 Opposite Portland Golf Course, which is next to **Royal Troon** (2039/GOLF). Mansion house of character and ambience much favoured for weddings. Wood-panelling, open fires, lovely gardens only a 'drive' away from the courses (no preferential booking on Royal, but Portland usually possible); lots of great golf nearby. 15 rooms in the house, 14 in 'cottages' around the building and 9 lodges. Eat in the Red Bowl Restaurant. Local reputation also for bar meals.

✓✓ **Glenapp Castle** nr Ballantrae Discreet and distinguished. A jewel in the Scottish crown in fabulous grounds and gardens in deepest South Ayrshire. Report: 1128/COUNTRY-HOUSE HOTELS.

THE BEST RESTAURANTS IN AYRSHIRE & THE CLYDE VALLEY

805   **7/K26**
>£35

✓✓ **Braidwoods** nr Dalry · www.braidwoods.co.uk · 01294 833544 Simplest approach is from the section of A78 N of Irvine; take B714 for Dalry. Cottage restaurant discreetly signed 5km on left. Michelin-star dining doesn't get more casually accomplished and they've had that star for over 20 years. Keith and Nicola Braidwood here since 1994 with their impeccable sourcing (long before it was de rigueur); they use selected local suppliers and naturally everything is made on the premises (bread, chocolates). With its own quiet dignity, Braidwoods remains the best meal in the shire; you'll go a long way to find this quality at these prices. Lunch Wed-Sat & dinner Tue-Sat. Sun lunch in winter.

806   **7/K26**
£15-25

Nardini's Largs · www.nardinis.co.uk · 01475 675000 On the Esplanade. This legendary seaside salon came back after a million-dollar refit, trading somewhat on its glory days. Still, in a town now hoaching with eateries, I'm with the new Nardini, though it has nowt to do with the original family. Its big rooms usually packed; the cafeteria and Tony Macaroni trattoria. Snowdrifts of ice cream.

807   **7/K26**
<£15

Rare Flour West Kilbride · 01294 822099 Just off the main A78 S of Largs. Haven't been here but foodie spies in Ayrshire rave about their pizzas. Tue-Sun 5-11pm. Reports, please.

✓✓ **MacCallums of Troon Oyster Bar** Report: 1335/SEAFOOD.

The Catch @ Fins Fairlie, nr Largs Report: 1344/SEAFOOD.

GASTROPUB GRUB IN AYRSHIRE

Ayrshire has many good gastropubs. All routinely packed with happy Ayrshire eaters. Book at weekends.

✓✓ **The Sorn Inn** Sorn Report: 1301/GASTROPUBS.

✓ **Souter's Inn** Kirkoswald Report: 1312/GASTROPUBS.

Cochrane Inn Gatehead Report: 1321/GASTROPUBS.
The Wheatsheaf Inn Symington Off main A77. Report: 1314/GASTROPUBS.

If you're in Ayr...

WHERE TO STAY

808 7/K27
44 ROOMS
MED.INX

Fairfield House Hotel www.fairfieldhotel.co.uk · 01292 267461 1km centre on the front. Solid, decent, suburban. 'Deluxe' facilities include pool/sauna/steam, and conservatory brasserie. 5 rooms have sea view.

9 ROOMS
MED.EX

The Ellisland www.ellislandhouse.com · 01292 260111 On road to Alloway. Another success story by the Costley group who have Lochgreen and many bar/restaurant options (see above). Rooms vary but mostly large and well appointed. Very decent restaurant with their irresistible comfort food.

✓✓ **The Sorn Inn** Sorn 25km E. Once again we're sworn to the Sorn: top gastropub with rooms. Reports: 1301/GASTROPUBS; 800/AYRSHIRE.

✓ **Savoy Park** Racecourse Rd Interesting period mansion run by the hard-working Hendersons. Very Scots, very Ayrshire. Report: 1212/SCOTTISH HOTELS.

✓✓ **Lochgreen House** Troon White seaside mansion near famous golf courses. Flagship hotel of Costley family (see below and all over Ayrshire). Report: 802/AYRSHIRE.

Piersland Hotel Troon 12km N of Ayr. Report: 804/AYRSHIRE.

WHERE TO EAT

£15-25
Saffy's www.saffys-ayr.com · 01292 288598 Opposite the Mercure Hotel. Honest, home-made, do-the-lot cookery: seafood, meat, game and good vegetarian. Ayr is the better for this restaurant by the splendid Smith family. Open from 9.30am till late.

<£15
The Lido Troon · www.lido-troon.co.uk · 01292 310088 Contemporary Italo-American café-bar that buzzes from breakfast to supper. Massive-choice menu and a stylish spot by the Blairs who have their finger completely on the button around here. 7 days from 8.30am. They also have:

£15-25
Scott's Troon · www.scotts-troon.co.uk · 01292 315315 In the marina about 2km from Troon centre. A self-consciously stylish but seriously well-thought-out contemporary bar/restaurant upstairs overlooking the surprisingly packed marina. Owners, the Buzzworks Group, have another Scott's in Troon, **Elliots** in Prestwick, The Lido (above) and the less interesting **Treehouse** in Ayr. Food OK, bling in evidence. 7 days from 8.30am.

£15-25
Cecchini's 72 Fort St · 01292 263607 & Prestwick & Clyde Marina, Ardrossan · www.cecchinis.com Excellent Italian and Med restaurants run by the estimable Cecchinis. It's dependable! In Ardrossan where the Arran ferry comes in. Mon-Sat lunch & dinner.

£15-25   **Ayr India** Alloway Place · 01292 261026 & Seafield Rd · 01292 263731 · www.ayrindia.com Cleverly named, serviceable Indian restaurants in the centre and seafront.

£15-25   **The Rupee Room** www.therupeeroom.com · 01292 283002 Ordinary-looking restaurant on the square serving the denizens of Ayr; they do fish 'n' chips but also rather good Indian food that's exactly what they want. 7 days lunch & dinner.

✓✓ **MacCallums of Troon Oyster Bar** This faraway dock on the bay has both the best restaurant hereabouts and also the best fish 'n' chip takeaway in the **Wee Hurrie** (see below). Report: 1335/SEAFOOD.

✓✓ **The Wee Hurrie** Troon The best fish 'n' chips on the coast. See **MacCallums** (above) and report: 1351/FISH & CHIPS.

Tourist Information Centre 22 Sandgate · 01292 290300 Open AYR.

The Best Hotels & Restaurants In The South West

809 9/J31
10 ROOMS
DF
LL
LOTS
>£35

✓✓ **Knockinaam Lodge** Portpatrick · www.knockinaamlodge.com · 01776 810471 Tucked away on a dream cove, a historic country house full of fresh flowers, great food, sea air and sympatico service. Sian and David Ibbotson balance a family home and a top-class get-away-from-it-all hotel. Rooms traditional but top-drawer, especially the famous Churchill suite. Family suite with high tea for kids at 6pm. 1131/COUNTRY-HOUSE HOTELS.
EAT Best meal in the South from an outstanding and long-established chef, Tony Pierce. Fixed menu – lots of unexpected treats.

810 9/N30
6 ROOMS
DF
NO KIDS
MED.INX

✓ **Cavens** Kirkbean · www.cavens.com · 01387 880234 20km S Dumfries via A710, Cavens is signed from Kirkbean. This elegant mansion in 20 landscaped acres has been converted by Angus and Jane Fordyce into a homely, informal Caven-haven of peace and quiet – a great base for touring the SW and Angus your personal tour guide. Lots of public space so you can even get away from each other. Honest, good cooking using locally sourced ingredients: lots from **Loch Arthur** (1462/FARM SHOPS), including the excellent granola for breakfast. Gardens to wander: cottage garden supplies dinner. Inexpensive to take over the lot 1281/HOUSE PARTIES.
EAT Best food in the quarter and so reasonably priced. Straightforward daily-changing menu like going to a dinner party but without having to get on with the guests.

811 9/N29
14 ROOMS
DF
MED.INX

✓ **Buccleuch & Queensberry Arms Hotel** Thornhill · www.bqahotel.com · 01848 323101 At the crossroads of charming Thornhill 25km N of Dumfries on the A76. A very civilised billet operating in partnership with **Drumlanrig Castle** 6km N (1529/PARKS). Tasteful, contemporary bedrooms. Bar and dining room. Great for the hunting/shooting/fishing crowd and the rest of us.

812 9/M29
6 ROOMS
DF
CHP

✓ **The Clachan Inn** St John's Town of Dalry · www.theclachaninn.co.uk · 01644 430241 Main street of this wee town N of New Galloway on the A702 to Moniaive and Thornhill (and on the A713 to Ayr), also a major stop on the **Southern Upland Way** (1967/WALKS), so geared to walkers, cyclists and outdoorists generally; and drinkers. Open fires, cheery folk, a haven on the way as you'd hope. Good food, ales and simple, inexpensive rooms above.

813 9/N31
20 ROOMS
DF
FEB-NOV
LL
EXP

✓ **Balcary Bay** nr Auchencairn · www.balcary-bay-hotel.co.uk · 01556 640217 20km S of Castle Douglas and Dalbeattie. Off A711 at end of shore road and as close to the shimmering Solway as you can get. I haven't stayed here for years but on a recent visit, it's obvious that this is a well-cared-for and well-loved (by its regulars) hideaway and romantic retreat (as the weekend magazines like). Ideal for walking, bird-watching, outdoor pursuits (dogs welcome). Kitchen continues a strong commitment to local produce. 100-strong wine list. Afternoon tea by the sea in lounge or conservatory. Location, location!

814 9/M31

✓ **Good Spots in Kirkcudbright** Pronounced Cur-*Coo*-Bree. A gem of a town. On a High Street filled with posh B&Bs, the Cowans' **Gladstone House** www.kirkcudbrightgladstone.com · 01557 331734 stands out. Only 3 (lovely attic) rooms so book well ahead.

815 9/L30
17 ROOMS
FEB-DEC
LOTS

Kirroughtree Hotel Newton Stewart · www.kirroughtreehousehotel. co.uk · 01671 402141 On A712. Built 1719, Rabbie Burns was once here. Extensive and private country house draped and plushed, run in the same manor and manner by new owners 2015. For a long time now the standout hotel in the region. Original panelled hall and stairs, some spacious rooms the epitome of traditional country-house living; nice grounds. Gracious dining. No leisure facilities.

816 9/M31
16 ROOMS
MED.INX

Selkirk Arms www.selkirkarmshotel.co.uk · 01557 330402 Much more your 'proper hotel', in very good private hands. They set out to turn this Kirkcudbright townhouse into the best hotel and dining in the district – they did! 16 of the best medium-expensive rooms in this most interesting of SW towns. EAT Dining with strong local menu; informal bar-bistro and garden. Best food in Kirkcudbrightshire.

817 9/J30
11 ROOMS
DF
LL
ATMOS
MED.EX

Corsewall Lighthouse Hotel nr Stranraer · www.lighthousehotel.co.uk · 01776 853220 A718 to Kirkcolm 3km, B738 to Corsewall 6km (follow signs). Wild location on clifftop. Cosily furnished, clever but snug – don't say cramped – just go with someone you like. The adjacent fully functioning lighthouse (since 1817) makes for surreal evenings. 3 suites are outside the lighthouse and 2 are further away. All suites have the sea and sky views (though only half the hotel rooms do). Small dining room. Food just OK but it's a long way to the chipper.

818 9/N30
15 ROOMS
DF
MED.INX

Clonyard House Colvend · www.clonyardhouse-hotel.co.uk · 01556 630372 On Solway Coast road near **Rockcliffe** and **Kippford** (1556/VILLAGES; 2025/WALKS) but not on sea. Extension to house provides 11 somewhat utilitarian bedrooms adjacent patio garden, though shaded. Friendly family, good for kids; decent pub grub. The old building has old-style charm; now with the Goldies.

819 9/N30
6 ROOMS
DF · L · CHP

Anchor Hotel Kippford · www.anchorhotelkippford.co.uk · 01556 620205 Very seaside hotel in cute village 3km off main A710. Basic accom but great pub atmos and extensive food operation; seafood menu (local lobster, pints of prawns). See 1325/GASTROPUBS, though 'gastro' it ain't.

Cally Palace Gatehouse of Fleet Report: 1146/KIDS.

THE BEST RESTAURANTS IN THE SOUTH WEST

820 8/M28
7 ROOMS
DF
£25-35

Blackaddie Hotel Sanquhar · www.blackaddiehotel.co.uk · 01659 50270 This foodie destination hotel is as far-flung as it's sensible to be; first find Sanquhar then left at gas station (Glasgow end of village), through a small industrial estate; surprisingly, it's on a river (the Nith). Notable once-Michelin chef/ patron Ian McAndrew (a mentor to many others) carries the cook's blowtorch here with dogged determination. Hotel itself very adequate if not quite in the league of the cooking but this is a bold bothy in unforgiving hills (Wanlockhead and Leadhills are also worth discovering). Hail to the chef! Amazing **Crawick** nearby (2133/ART).

821 9/P30
£15-25

Del Amitri Annan · www.delamitrirestaurant.co.uk · 01461 201999 Off the beaten track, perhaps, though only 10km from the A74(M) N of Carlisle, this sweet little restaurant is worth a detour. Traditional Scottish-Euro cooking sound in seasonal (monthly) changing menu, presentation and service. It's a find but definitely best to book. So inexpensive! Tue-Sat dinner only & Sun lunch.

822 9/M30
<£15

Galloway Lodge Preserves Gatehouse of Fleet · www.galloway-lodge. myshopify.com · 01557 814001 On a corner of the main street. A shop for pressies, ceramics and stuff in jars but also a great self-service comfort-food and home-baking station, I mean, café. It's better than the rest for some miles. 7 days.

823 9/M30 ✓ **Carlo's** Castle Douglas · www.carlosrestaurant.co.uk · 01556 503977
£15-25 Here nearly 30 years, the Bignami family restaurant with Carlo in the kitchen is your absolute best option in this self-designated 'food town'. Bustling tratt atmos – probably the best Italian food in the South. Open Tue-Sat dinner only.

824 9/M30 **The Masonic Arms** Gatehouse of Fleet · www.masonicarms.co.uk ·
£15-25 01557 814335 This place always had a reputation for food but some changes of management later it's hard to say where it's going. Always a good local atmos. Garden & conservatory. Sunday carvery.

825 9/J30 **Campbell's** Portpatrick · www.campbellsrestaurant.co.uk · 01776 810314
£15-25 Robert and Diane Campbell's quayside restaurant since 1998. Unpretentious fishy fare with something for everyone, including vegetarians. Crab and lobster from their boat a good, fresh bet. Invariably gets a Michelin mention. Tue-Sun lunch & dinner.

826 9/J30 **The Crown** Portpatrick · www.crownportpatrick.com · 01776 810261
L Harbourside hotel and pub with better-than-average grub. Goes like a fair in
£15-25 summer. 7 days. Competition from the Waterfront next door. The Crown has better atmos and decidedly better seafood. The **Chip Ahoy** chip van on the opposite side of the harbour does what it says on the van. 7 days.

827 9/M29 **Piccola Italia** Moniaive · 01848 200400 High St of lovely village N of Dumfries
<£15 and E of New Galloway. Surprisingly good Italian menu and wood-fired pizza from Serbian chef/proprietor. Summer 7 days dinner only. Closed Mon/Tue winter.

828 9/N29 **Green Tea House @ The Club House, Thornhill Golf Club** www.green-
<£15 teahouse.co.uk · 01848 330546 2km from town from the crossroads. Once in Moniaive, Catherine Braid has taken her tea house to a club house, with her top cake-baking and comfort-food-making skills; it is worth the detour from town on that road N or S to Dumfries. Overlooks serene greens. BYOB (no corkage). 7 days daytime and supper weekends.

✓✓ **Kitty's Tearoom** New Galloway A definitive tearoom in the definitive Galloway town. Report: 1381/TEAROOMS.

✓ **Thomas Tosh** Thornhill Great selective shopping. Lovely caff. Report: 2168/ SHOPS.

✓ **The Schoolhouse** Ringford An excellent, there-forever roadside (A75) café/ bistro. Report: 1397/TEAROOMS.

Caffs in Wigtown 3 to choose from in Wigtown, the Book Town. Report: 1398/1399/1400/TEAROOMS.

If you're in Dumfries...

WHERE TO STAY

829 9/N30
71 ROOMS
MED.INX

Holiday Inn www.hidumfries.com · 01387 272410 Edge of town in the Crichton Estate (signposted from centre), a surprising 100-acre campus of listed sandstone buildings including a conference centre. We don't do chain hotels as a rule in *StB* but this is the best stay in Dumfries. Contemporary-furnished hotel with brasserie. Modern facilities and OK food. 20-min walk to/from centre.

32 ROOMS
NO PETS
MED.INX

Station Hotel www.stationhoteldumfries.co.uk · 01387 254316 Charming address (Lovers Walk) but actually right by the station. Functional, old-fashioned but does have atmos. 'Courtyard Bistro'. A Best Western and best in town centre.

Cavens Kirkbean Report: 810/SW HOTELS. And very civilised dining!

WHERE TO EAT

£15-25
Hullabaloo www.hullabaloorestaurant.co.uk · 01387 259679 At the Robert Burns Centre, also home to an arthouse cinema. Hard to reach by car, so walk across the bridge over the river. Lighter food by day. Some say it's not as good as you'd wish. Summer Sunday BBQs a nice idea! Times vary.

£15-25
Bruno's www.brunosrestaurant.co.uk · 01387 255757 Off Annan Rd. Very long-established old-style Italian eaterie. Many folks attest to this being the most reliable albeit old-style eating-out in town. Wed-Mon dinner only.

<£15
Balmoral 01387 252583 Chippy adjacent, Bruno's (family related); the best in or out choices are next to one another. Interior (they close the blinds) but home cooking and real. Wed-Mon dinner only. See 1358/FISH & CHIPS.

£15-25
Pizzeria Il Fiume www.pizza-pasta.co.uk · 01387 265154 Near St Michael's Bridge, underneath Riverside pub. Usual Italian menu but this town's best pizzas. (Last time I was here, the family were out unloading the logs). Cosy tratt atmos. A long-standing Italian gem. 7 days dinner only.

<£15
Globe Inn 56 High St · www.globeinndumfries.co.uk · 01387 252335 Historic (17th-century) pub internationally famed as Robert Burns' howff (1906/LITERARY PLACES). Decent lunches and suppers by arrangement. Best found on foot.

<£15
Kings Coffee & Books 12 Queensberry St · www.kings-online.co.uk · 01387 254444 Central coffee shop with well good coffee and (mostly Christian) books. And snacks. Starbucks ambience without the Starbucks! Open daytime.

Cavens Kirkbean In a town not tops for eating out, Cavens is only 20 mins away. Report: 810/SW HOTELS.

Kilnford Barns Café Edge of town on A75. Report: 1470/FARM SHOPS.

The Best Hotels & Restaurants In Central Scotland

830 8/L23
14 ROOMS
LL
ATMOS
LOTS

✓✓ **Monachyle Mhor** nr Balquhidder · www.mhor.net · 01877 384622
Along the ribbon of road that skirts Loch Voil 7km beyond the village (which is 4km) from the A84 Callander-Crianlarich road. Relatively remote (1191/ GET-AWAY HOTELS), the Braes a splendid backdrop for this informal and pink farmhouse hotel with great food, fabulous sexy, contemporary rooms and altogether good vibes. An urbane back of beyond. I've sent lots of people here, even to get married; we all go back and back. It's the mothership in a constellation of top Scottish foodie destinations (see below).

>£35 **EAT** It's a long way for dinner but some of the best dining in Scotland is to be had here. The wee bar before for the craic, dinner in the conservatory, drawing room dram after. Tom Lewis and team out back; Black Betty and Angel in attendance.

831 8/L23
7 ROOMS
DF
ATMOS
MED.INX

✓✓ **Mhor 84** nr Balquhidder · www.mhor.net · 01877 384646 On the A84 near Strathyre and Balquhidder. After MM above, came another sure-fire hit hotel - actually and really a motel - which you see from the road on the right as you hurtle for Oban, Fort William and the North West. You should stop and, if you're lucky, stay (there are only 7 rooms). Purposefully a budget stopover with few frills in the comfy bedrooms, it's the whole friendly bar/restaurant, where locals become fellow travellers, that makes this as rock 'n' roll as Route 66.

832 8/M24
15 ROOMS
DF
ATMOS
LOTS

✓✓ **Roman Camp Hotel** Callander · www.romancamphotel.co.uk · 01877 330003 Through a chink in Callander's main street to a more refined world, nothing much changes - or needs to - in Eric and Marion Brown's top-of-the-Trossachs hotel, away from the tourist throng and set in extensive gardens on the River Teith, with Roman ruins nearby. The house, built for the Dukes of Perth, has been a hotel since the war. Highly individual rooms; some snug. Magnificent period furnishings. Candlelight and log fires! In the old building corridors do creak. Delightful drawing room and conservatory. Oval dining room very sympatico. Private chapel should a prayer come on and, of course, some weddings. Rods for fishing - the river swishes past the lawn.

>£35 **EAT** Dining room effortlessly the best food in town with a great and long-standing chef - Ian McNaught. Nice for Sunday lunch.

833 8/M24
10 ROOMS
5 SUITES
DF
L
LOTS

✓✓ **Cromlix House** nr Dunblane · www.cromlix.com · 01786 822125 3km from A9 and 4km from town on B8033; follow signs for Perth, then Kinbuck. A leisurely drive through old estate with splendid mature woods to this spacious mansion both sumptuous and homely and, since 2014 and a major revamp, 'Andy Murray's hotel', part of the estimable ICMI collection. No leisure facilities - except, of course, tennis - but woods to walk and 3,000 acres of meadows and fishing lochs. House Loch is serenity itself. Private chapel. Cromlix has long been one of Scotland's great and true country-house hotels.

>£35 **EAT** As with other ICMI hotels, the menu is under the Albert Roux brand (brasserie-style) with great service (and signature soufflé). All light and delicious.

834 8/M23
5 ROOMS
MED.EX

✓ **Creagan House** Strathyre · www.creaganhouse.co.uk · 01877 384638 End of the village on main A84 for Crianlarich. Gordon and Cherry Gunn's very personally run Creagan farmhouse is the place to eat in Rob Roy and Callander country. Rooms are small and inexpensive in an old-fashioned home from home. Traditional and quirky, you might say. You eat in an impressive baronial dining room (stone fireplace, vaulted ceiling). There are many hills to walk and forest trails start in the garden (1931/HILLS).

EAT Gordon's been in that kitchen creatively cooking for about 30 years. They do take Wed/Thu nights off (which I think we can allow).

835 8/M24
16 ROOMS
LL
MED.EX

✓ **Lake Hotel** Port of Menteith · www.lake-hotel.com · 01877 385258
A very lakeside hotel on the Lake of Menteith in the Trossachs' purple heart. A good centre for touring, walking and fishing (adjacent; 01877 385664): the lake swarms with fishermen in floaty boats. The **Inchmahome** ferry leaves from nearby (1893/MARY). A kind of New England feel pervades (they also have a hotel on Chesapeake Bay, and another on the way). Conservatory restaurant for sunset supper or lazy lunch; also bar menu. All rooms are light and quiet; some overlook the dreamy lake. A great hotel if you're in love with Scotland or each other.

£15-25 **EAT** Different menus in bar and conservatory, all stylish and well done.

836 8/M24
3 ROOMS
DF
CHP

✓ **The Cross Keys** Kippen · www.kippencrosskeys.com · 01786 870293
Main St of loved little village above the Forth flood plain 15km from Stirling. 3 pleasant, airy rooms above a homely pub with a great reputation for a warm welcome and excellent food (1304/GASTROPUBS).

837 8/M24
200 ROOMS
DF
MED.EX

✓ **Doubletree Dunblane** Dunblane · www.doubletreedunblane.com ·
01786 825800 One of the huge hydro hotels left over from the last health and holiday-at-home boom, refurbished at vast expense (£12m) in 2009 by Hilton to create a massive urban edifice on the edge of a small town. Nice views for some and a long walk down corridors for most. Leisure facilities include pool.

£15-25 **EAT** Celebrity chef Nick Nairn has created a couthy contemporary menu in the Kailyard restaurant. His 'signature dishes' at very reasonable prices under executive chef Steven Campbell are a vast improvement on hydrocatering of yore.

838 8/M24
4 ROOMS
DF
MED.INX

The Inn at Kippen Kippen · www.theinnatkippen.co.uk · 01786 871010 In the middle of the village, a village-inn experience in contemporary stylee, with 4 good-value rooms above and an extensive food operation, which has had a mixed reception over recent years but now becoming an eating out destination again.

839 7/K23
14+16
ROOMS
L
ATMOS
CHP

Inverarnan Hotel/The Drover's Inn & Lodge Inverarnan · www.
thedroversinn.co.uk · 01301 704234 N of Ardlui on Loch Lomond and 12km S of Crianlarich on the A82. Much the same now as when it was pub of the year in 1705: bare floors, open fires and heavy drinking (1285/GOOD PUBS). The lodge on the other side of the road is, let's say, more modern. Highland hoolies here much recommended (live music Saturdays). Bar staff wearing kilts look like they're meant to. Rooms highly individual: traditional in the hotel, uniform and contemporary in the lodge. Some surprises (1 room in hotel, 5 in lodge house have jacuzzis and 4-posters). A wild place in the wilderness. Expect atmos not service. Neither places have phones, only a couple have TVs and mobiles probably don't work. Hey, you're away!

840 8/N24
40 ROOMS
NO PETS
MED.EX

Colessio Stirling · www.hotelcolessio.com · 01786 448880 On the road to Stirling Castle (250m), therefore historic (actually Victorian) and in a central location. Stirling's new trying-very-hard (to be boutiquey) hotel, a tad blingy for my taste and it might date rather quickly but quite happening at TGP: the restaurant, the bar, afternoon tea. Bedrooms exude 'opulence'. Certainly, it is Stirling's most contemporary hotel; service is good.

✓✓ **Cameron House on Loch Lomond** nr Luss Report: 496/HOTELS OUTSIDE GLASGOW.

✓ **The Lodge on Loch Lomond** Loch Lomond Report: 500/HOTELS OUTSIDE GLASGOW.

THE BEST RESTAURANTS IN CENTRAL SCOTLAND

841 8/N24 ✓ **Jam Jar** Bridge of Allan · www.jamjarcafe.co.uk · 01786 831616 Bustling
<£15 all-day café-bistro where they've thought of you. Various eating areas including terraces on the street and out back with a stove. From ingredients to trimmings to the wine list, it's all good. Home-made cakes, excellent breakfasts, Highland 'Wagyu' beef. Definitely worth coming over the bridge from Stirling.

842 7/K25 ✓ **Riverhill Courtyard Restaurant & Bar** Helensburgh · www.riverhillcafe.
£15-25 com · 01436 676730 This was the first (well, the second as they started up the hill) of the Riverhills (see 524/BISTROS). A converted boxing gym, now a great place to eat, drink and hang out. All-day menus; lunch till 6pm. Steak frites, maccy cheese. A but also proper evening dining. Great room, great formula.

843 8/N24 **Allan Water Café** Bridge of Allan · www.allanwatercafe.co.uk ·
<£15 01786 833060 Caff that's been here forever at end of the main street in BoA with big brassy, glassy extension. Original features and clientele still remain in the old bit. It's all down to fish 'n' chips and the family ice cream (Bechelli's). 1452/ICE CREAM. Mon-Sat 8am-8.30pm (Sun from 9am).

844 8/M24 **Callander Meadows** Callander · www.callandermeadows.co.uk ·
£15-25 01877 330181 Bang in the middle of the tourist-thronged main street, this is your best bet by far for home-made, well-presented contemporary food. The Parkes preside over 3 townhouse dining rooms; some nice local girls. Excellent puds. Lunch & dinner. Closed Tue/Wed (and Mon in winter).

✓ **The Greengrocer** Stirling Report: 845/STIRLING.

✓ **The Hideaway** Bridge of Allan Report: 845/STIRLING.

✓ **The Woodhouse** nr Kippen Report: 1474/FARM SHOPS.

✓ **The Cross Keys** Kippen Report: 1304/GASTROPUBS.

✓ **Lion & Unicorn** Thornhill Report: 1322/GASTROPUBS.

✓ **Delivino** Auchterarder Report: 934/PERTHSHIRE.

If you're in Stirling...

WHERE TO STAY

845 8/N24 **Cook's** www.cooksofstirling.co.uk · 01786 430890 In the centre of the town
7 ROOMS and its hard-to-fathom road system, a former bank transformed some years back,
MED.INX but decor fresh and the busy brasserie, probably Stirling's finest.

9 ROOMS **Park Lodge** www.parklodge.net · 01786 474862 Quite posh hotel in
MED.INX Victorian/Georgian town (they say country) house near King's Park and golf course. Objets and lawns. Med menu in restaurant; Michelin-mentioned. Some weddings.

4 ROOMS
MED.INX **Portcullis Hotel** www.theportcullishotel.com · 01786 472290 Jim and Lynne Walker's pub with rooms in one of the best locations in town, no more than a cannonball's throw from the castle. Unpretentious, basic accom near the tourist magnet. Pub and pub food; 4 rooms upstairs.

100 ROOMS
NO PETS
MED.INX **Stirling Court Hotel** www.stirlingcourthotel.com · 01786 466000 On main road between Stirling and Bridge of Allan, 7km town centre. Part of the university campus, near the National Swimming Academy, and in the shadow of the Wallace Monument (some views). Run by Sodexo, the catering management people. No atmos but a good business-like option on a budget.

S.Y. Hostel www.syha.org.uk · 01786 473442 On road up to the castle in a great location is this well-appointed hostel, still very SYH (1152/HOSTELS) **Willy Wallace Hostel**, 77 Murray Pl (01786 446773) is more funky. Upstairs in busy centre with caffs and pubs nearby. Unimposing entrance but bunkrooms for 54.

WHERE TO EAT

<£15 ✓ **The Hideaway** Bridge of Allan This truly is hidden away so listen up: find Fountain Rd to the left of the main street as you come in from Stirling (opposite the Royal Hotel). 80m on left, 25m down Fountain Mews, in an old telephone exchange, a permanent pop-up kind of café with great people, baking, breakfast and their delicious gelato. Closed Sun.

<£15 ✓ **The Greengrocer** 81 Port St · 01786 479159 Through a pend, boxes of fruit & veg outside. Shameful, I know, but I didn't find (wasn't alerted, I guess) this hidden deli/café gem until this edition. Intimate, friendly, efficient and great home-made, deli-driven food. Apologies, guys, for the late recognition – they've been here cool as, for 20 years! Open daytime.

£25-35 ✓ **Hermann's** www.hermanns.co.uk · 01786 450632 After many a year, probably still Stirling's best. A house on road up (and very close) to the castle. Hermann Aschaber's corner of Austria, where schnitzels and strudels figure along with Scottish fare. 2-floor, ambient, well-run rooms (conservatory best). 7 days.

<£15 **Corrieri's** Causewayhead · www.corrieris.co.uk · 01786 472089 On the road to Bridge of Allan at Causewayhead. Since 1934 this excellent café/restaurant near busy corner below the Wallace Monument has been serving pasta/pizza and ice cream probably as it should be. A genuine family caff. LO 9.30pm. Closed Tue.

£15-25 **La Cucina** Bridge of Allan · www.lacucinabridgeofallan.co.uk · 01786 834679 On the main (Henderson) street. Contemporary, reasonably authentic Italian place. Once again, BoA is where 2 eat! 7 days lunch & dinner.

£15-25 **Birds & Bees** Causewayhead · www.thebirdsandthebees-stirling.com · 01786 473663 Between Stirling and Bridge of Allan at Causewayhead. Going towards Stirling from BoA it's first on the right (Easter Cornton Rd). A local secret and a hugely popular pub-grub destination in the burbs. This unlikely roadhouse occasionally hosts *pétanque* (boules to you!). Good for kids. Terrace. 7 days.

Tourist Information Centre Old Town Jail, St John St · 01786 475019 Open AYR.

The Best Hotels & Restaurants In The Borders

846 8/R27
20 ROOMS
DF
MED.EX

£15->£35

✓ **Burt's** Melrose · www.burtshotel.co.uk · 01896 822285 In Market Sq/ main street; some (double-glazed) rooms overlook. Busy bars, especially for food; it's easy to see why. The dining room (chef Trevor Williams) is where to fine dine in this part of the Borders. Cosy in winter, it looks out to the garden and is summery in summer. Traditional but comfortably modernised small-town hotel, though some rooms also feel small. Convenient location for Borders roving (1884/ ABBEYS; 1947/HILL WALKS; 1521/GARDENS). Where to stay for the **Sevens** or the **Book Festival** (if you can get in) 29/43/EVENTS.
EAT The bar, routinely a pub of the year, serves very decent grub. It and the main restaurant together are, in a good way, an institution!

847 8/R27
11 ROOMS
MED.EX

✓ **The Townhouse** Melrose · www.thetownhousemelrose.co.uk · 01896 822645 The long-standing (4 decades) Burt's (above) spawned a stylish little sister across the street some years back. Charming and boutique-ish with a coherent, elegant look by Michael Vee Decor (from down the street); it's very Melrose! In the whole of the Borders, this is probably the only hotel you could call contemporary. Dining room and busy brasserie confidently positioned between the fine dining of Burt's and its gastrogrub bar. The Hendersons (James) here and over the road (Nick) continue to put their town on the map.

848 8/S27
22 ROOMS
MED.EX

✓ **Roxburghe Hotel** nr Kelso · www.roxburghe-hotel.net · 01573 450331 *The* consummate country-house hotel in the Borders. Owned by the Duke and Duchess of Roxburghe, who have a personal input, but now managed by the efficient but sympatico ICMI Group (Inverlochy, etc). Rooms distinctive, all light with garden views. Owls hoot at night and once – no, twice, a crow fell down my chimney (the Bowmont Suite). This was good luck! The 18-hole golf course has major appeal – it's challenging, championship-standard and in a beautiful riverside setting. Non-res can play (2058/GOLF). 2 treatment rooms and health and beauty suite in the courtyard for golf widows. Game, meat and fish from the estate inform the menu. Compared with other country-house hotels, the Roxburghe is good value. Beautiful conservatory, whisky bar, serene garden, perfect policies!

849 8/Q27
6 ROOMS
DF
MED.INX
>£35

✓ **Windlestraw** Walkerburn · www.windlestraw.co.uk · 01896 870636 On A72, up discreet driveway overlooking the Tweed Valley. A beautiful historic house and garden; more a restaurant with rooms than merely a boutique B&B. Wood panelling, comfortable lounge and destination dining (non-res if space).
EAT Chef/proprietor John Matthews builds on the reputation of this long-standing exclusive lodging. Borders sourcing and from the greenhouse and garden. Book!

850 8/P26
12 ROOMS
DF
LOTS

✓ **Cringletie House** Peebles · www.cringletie.com · 01721 725750 Privately owned and carefully tended country-house hotel 5km from town just off A703 Edinburgh road (35km). Late-19th-century Scottish baronial house in 28 acres. Quintessential Peeblesshire: comfortable and civilised with an imperturbable air of calm. Well-loved local art. Restful garden view from every room. Top disabled facilities, including a lift! Conservatory, lounges up and downstairs; gracious dining room. Walled kitchen garden.

851 8/R27
19 ROOMS
DF · MED.INX

✓ **Buccleuch Arms** St Boswells · www.buccleucharms.com · 01835 822243 Here forever on the A68 where the road turns into St B. I've passed it all my life. Recently things have definitely looked up; the busy bar and bistro a local magnet and rooms above simple but contemporary. A convivial roadstop.

£15-25 **EAT** Informal dining in back bistro; gastropub in front.

852 8/S27
3 ROOMS
NO PETS
APR-DEC
L
MED.INX

>£35

✓ **Edenwater House** Ednam, nr Kelso · www.edenwaterhouse.co.uk · 01573 224070 Find Ednam on Swinton road B6461 from Kelso, 4km. Discreet manse-type house beside old kirk and graveyard overlooking Eden Water, the lovely garden and tranquil green countryside. Bucolic is the word. You have the run of the home of Jeff and Jacqui Kelly. Jacqui's flair in the kitchen and Jeff's carefully wrought wine list (he has a wine shed in the old coach house and he will suggest) make this the secret Borders dinner destination.
EAT Best cook in the counties? Jacqui Kelly is long-standing, unassuming and underestimated. Food lighter of late, from wintering in Australia. Candlelit overlooking the garden. Non-res must book.

853 8/P26
8 ROOMS
NO PETS
MED.INX

£25-35

✓ **Horseshoe Inn** Eddleston, nr Peebles · www.horseshoeinn.co.uk · 01721 730225 On the A703 (8km Peebles, 35km Edinburgh), a recreated reconstructed coaching inn and a convivial and contemporary stopover with destination good food from chef Alistair Craig and a strong team. Rooms in the old village school behind are peaceful and, well, plain, but you can stumble back there replete after dinner.
EAT Dining room on the formal side. Dinner's the thing! Tasting menu and à la carte; but gloriously gastro. Lunch & dinner Wed-Sun.

854 8/Q27
14 ROOMS +
3 LODGES
DF
MED.EX

Philipburn Selkirk · www.bw-philipburnhousehotel.co.uk · 01750 720747 1km from town centre. Excellent, privately owned Best Western 'Plus' hotel for families, walkers, a weekend away from it all; Selkirk a good Borders base. Bar with great malt selection and decent bistro. Comfy rooms, some more luxurious than others (the 'garden' rooms).

855 8/S27
32 ROOMS
MED.INX

Ednam House Kelso · www.ednamhouse.com · 01573 224168 Overlooking River Tweed; a majestic Georgian mansion with very old original features, including some of the guests, who quietly get on with the main business of fishing and dozing in an old armchair. After being owned by the same family for 70 years, the august Ednam changed hands, so upgrading is underway. The Garden Restaurant conservatory is the main attraction: a stunning setting. Half the bedrooms have a view. In contrast to this old-style ambience, the new Pharlanne deli and coffee shop at the gateway is bright and contemporary. Open lunch till 4pm.

856 8/R27
5 ROOMS
MED.INX

Clint Lodge nr St Boswells · www.clintlodge.co.uk · 01835 822027 On B6356 (1627/SCENIC ROUTES) between **Dryburgh Abbey** (1082/ABBEYS) and **Smailholm Tower** (1841/MONUMENTS). Small country guest house in great border country with tranquil views from rooms. Nice conservatory pre dinner. Very good home cooking and service from Bill and Heather Walker, and daughter Suzie (& Toots the Border Terrier) in attendance. A splendid Borders breakfast.

857 8/R27
3 ROOMS
DF
CHP

Fauhope Gattonside, nr Melrose · www.fauhopehouse.com · 01896 823184 Borders house in sylvan setting overlooking Tweed. Lovely front rooms, terrace and terraced lawns. Only 3 rooms but in more guides than mine (*Best B&Bs*, *Michelin*, etc), so must book. They have a treatment room! Family dogs much in evidence.

858 8/R28
4 ROOMS
DF · CHP

Hundalee House Jedburgh · www.accommodation-scotland.org · 01835 863011 1km S of Jedburgh off A68. Lovely old manor house in 15-acre garden. For over 30 years, brilliant value; great base, views of Cheviot hills. Near the famously old Capon Tree. Closed Mar.

✓ **The Wheatsheaf** Swinton Report: 1311/GASTROPUBS.

✓ **Traquair Arms** Innerleithen Report: 1179/INNS.

THE BEST RESTAURANTS IN THE BORDERS

859 8/R27
<£15

✓✓ **Main Street Trading Company** St Boswells · www.
mainstreetbooks.co.uk · 01835 824087 Main Street, as they say, and
an all-round affirmation of life emporium, bookshop and caff. Eat before/after
browsing/walking, etc. Great home baking. Hot dishes noon-3pm. Closed Mon.
Report: 2165/SHOPS.

860 8/Q27
£15-25

✓ **Coltman's** Peebles · www.coltmans.co.uk · 01721 720405 Bridge end of
main street. A light, contemporary deli and café, with restaurant through the
back and bar upstairs. Karen and Kenny Coltman set up shop here in 2010;
Peebles-wise it's the bee's knees. Exudes confidence and class. Weekly changing
menus. Dining area small, so book. Lovely breakfasts and puds. Deli counter out
front with café tables. Sun-Wed 10am-5pm, Thu-Sat 10am-10pm.

861 8/Q27
£15-35

✓ **Osso** Peebles · www.ossorestaurant.com · 01721 724477 Ally McGrath's
perfectly judged and effective bistro/tearoom/restaurant changes through the
day from lightsome lunch to scones and cakes to superb comfort-food dining-out
experience at night. With local staff and no city prices or pretensions, Osso, with a
Michelin Bib, is perfectly Peebles. Lunch 7 days through to dinner (Thu-Sat).

862 8/R27
£15-25

✓ **Marmions** Melrose · www.marmionsbrasserie.co.uk · 01896 822245
Near the abbey. Local fave since yon time – one of the first 'bistros' in
Scotland; original formula and atmos reassuringly unchanged. Open for breakfast,
lunch and dinner in a brasserie-type room with bistro-type menu. Good vegetarian.
A reliably good repast in the Borders foodie capital. Mon-Sat lunch & dinner.

863 8/R27
£25-35

✓ **Chapters** Gattonside, nr Melrose · www.chapters-bistro.co.uk ·
01896 823217 Over the River Tweed (you could walk by footbridge as quickly
as going round by car). A surprising bistro taken over 2015 by estimable
restaurateurs Roger (chef) and Bea (out front) McKie. They were just settling in
when we called, but track record suggests this will be a great addition to the
Melrose menu du jour. Huge choice from à la carte and daily seafood specials in a
seasonal menu. Lunch Fri-Sun & dinner Wed-Sun.

864 8/R27
£15-25

✓ **Pub Food in Melrose: Burt's** www.burtshotel.co.uk · 01896 822285 &
The Townhouse www.thetownhousemelrose.co.uk · 01896 822645 On
opposite sides of main square (see hotels above). Burt's often wins pub food of the
year. But locals also swear by:
The Kings Arms www.kingsarms-melrose.co.uk · 01896 800335 Further
down the street. Great atmos and good grub; food-themed nights. The Kennedys in
capable charge. 7 days lunch & dinner.

865 8/P26
<£15

✓ **Whitmuir, the Organic Place** nr West Linton · www.
whitmuirtheorganicplace.co.uk · 01968 661908 Off A701, 15 mins from
Peebles. Ambitious farm shop (1466/FARM SHOPS), food hall, gallery and café/
restaurant in contemporary build on a real farm in the best kind of middle of
nowhere. Food is taken seriously on a light, largely organic menu with fish, meat
and vegetarian. Make things better; we need more farms like this! Open 7 days.

866 8/R26 ✓ **Firebrick Brasserie** Lauder · www.firebrickbrasserie.co.uk ·
£15-25 01578 718915 In the market place, the main street. Chef David Haetzman and pastry chef Amanda Jordan brewing 'simply special food' and well, great pastry and puddings in the northern gateway to the Borders (only 30 mins from Edinburgh bypass on the A68). Local sourcing, top ingredients but nothing too fancy. 45-day hung meat and the *best* chips. Light lunches and the Eccles cake! Joanna Blythman gave it 10/10! 11am-9.30pm. Closed Mon.

867 8/R28 ✓ **Damascus Drum Café & Books** Hawick · www.damascusdrum.co.uk ·
ATMOS 0786 7530709 Near tourist office. Chris and Frances Ryan's surprisingly
<£15 contemporary, laid-back second-hand bookshop and caff in a Hawick backstreet. A love letter to (old) Damascus (he wrote a book, on sale here). Comfy seats. Home made soups, quiche and bagels (1330/VEGETARIAN)... and rugs. Closed Sun.

868 8/R28 ✓ **Turnbull's** Hawick · www.turnbullshop.com · 01450 372020 By 'the
<£15 Horse', this foodie oasis is thought by some to be the best thing to happen to Hawick in a while. This may be true. Open 7 days. Report: 1457/DELIS. And they're now in Galashiels, 8 High Street, 01896 750577 (though I haven't been) with evening meals Fri/Sat.

869 8/R27 **The Hoebridge Inn** Gattonside · www.thehoebridgeinn.com · 01896 823082
£15-25 At Earlston end of village, signed towards the river (or from Melrose by footbridge). Newly stylish (2015) superior bistro. Wed-Sat dinner only. Not been.

870 8/R27 **Monte Cassino** Melrose · www.montecassinomelrose.co.uk · 01896 820082
£15-25 Up from the main square in the old station and station master's house. Probably Melrose's biggest and buzziest restaurant. Cheerful, non-pretentious and popular Italian – Neapolitan – with pasta/pizza staples and the odd OK special. The place is packed; it tells you something! Tue-Sun lunch & dinner.

871 8/Q27 **Saffron** Innerleithen · www.saffronauthenticindianrestaurant.co.uk ·
£15-25 01896 833466 The food here is authentic and surprising at that, on this street of traffic and bikes such a long way from, well, India. Smallish room, longish menu. Some say this is the best ethnic food in the Borders. 7 days 4-11pm.

872 8/S27 **The Cobbles Inn** Kelso · www.thecobbleskelso.co.uk · 01573 223548 Off the
£15-25 main square behind the Cross Keys. Popular local pub-grub (more grub than pub) restaurant. The Meiklejohns run a tight, friendly ship and care about their (mostly local) suppliers. Everything here is home-made: the bread, the chips, even the beer (Tempest Ales, 7 varieties). Bar and restaurant menu (evenings). 7 days.

Giacopazzi's www.giacopazzis.co.uk · 01890 750317 **& Oblò's** · www. oblobar.com · 01890 752527 · **Eyemouth** Great fish 'n' chips and ice cream (which is now everywhere). Upstairs bistro near harbour. Report: 1367/FISH & CHIPS.

✓**Woodside** nr Ancrum Report: 1386/TEAROOMS.

✓ **The Ancrum Cross Keys** Ancrum · www.ancrumcrosskeys.com · 01835 830242 By the village green, a village pub with great grub.
✓ **The Craw Inn** Auchencrow Report: 1182/INNS.

✓ **No1 Peebles Road Coffee House** Innerleithen Report: 1404/COFFEE.

Laurel Bank Main Street, Broughton Report: 1415/TEAROOMS.

The Best Hotels & Restaurants In The Lothians

See Section 2 for Edinburgh Hotels & Restaurants just outside the city.

873 8/R25
23 ROOMS
NO PETS
LL
ATMOS
LOTS

✓✓ **Greywalls** Gullane · www.greywalls.co.uk · 01620 842144 Outside the village on the North Berwick road 36km E of Edinburgh, a classic country-house hotel in 6 superb acres of garden. Especially convenient for golfing: there are 12 courses nearby, including 3 championship (2044/2042/GOLF) and the hotel overlooks Muirfield (though no right of access). No grey walls here but warm sandstone and light, summery (cosy in winter) rooms: a manor house designed by Lutyens, the garden by Gertrude Jekyll – a rather winning combination. The roses are legendary and what could be nicer than afternoon tea... well, dinner probably, in the Albert Roux-managed (and very branded) restaurant. Unsurprisingly expensive, the hotel and adjacent Colonel's House can be taken for exclusive use. There's a tennis court, croquet. 5 garden rooms look seaward. The evening light from the western sky on the terrace pre- or postprandial is priceless.

>£35 **EAT** Dining rooms, drawing rooms and conservatory for bar and à la carte menu; both it and the wine list characteristically (of Roux outstations) good value.

874 8/P25
16 ROOMS
NO PETS
NO KIDS
MED.EX

✓✓ **Champany Inn** nr Linlithgow · www.champany.com · 01506 834532 Excellent restaurant with rooms near M9 junction 3, 30 mins from Edinburgh city centre, 15 mins from the airport. Anne and Clive Davidson's long-established roadhouse hotel, and, across the courtyard, their nationally famous restaurant (128/HOTELS OUTSIDE EDINBURGH), especially for those who want their meat properly hung (3 weeks, butchered on the premises) and presented. Superlative wine list, especially South African vintages also available to buy from The Cellar (noon-10pm, 7 days).

>£35
£25-35 **EAT** Accolades confirm the best meal in West Lothian. More casual dining in the Chop 'n' Ale House. Angus beef, home-made sausages, the right oysters.

875 8/R25
12 ROOMS
MED.INX

✓ **Open Arms** Dirleton · www.openarmshotel.com · 01620 850241 Under careful and conscientious private ownership for some time, the OA is a cosy and countrified hotel in this quintessentially East Lothian village opposite ancient ruins. If this were in France it might be a Hôtel de Charme. Location means it's a golfers' haven. Nice public rooms and lounging space. Deveau's Restaurant.

876 8/R25
12 ROOMS
MED.EX

✓ **Nether Abbey** North Berwick · www.netherabbey.co.uk · 01620 892802 On the Coastal Trail. Long-established, well-managed family seaside hotel and a major drop-in bar/restaurant operation – the Fly-Half Bar and Grill (locally and well-sourced dishes). Busy downstairs, comfy up.

877 8/R25
6 ROOMS
CHP

✓ **The Linton Hotel** East Linton · www.thelintonhotel.co.uk · 01620 860202 Family-run small country village hotel; friendly and welcoming. Simple, quiet rooms and notable locally for bar meals and dining. Unusual upstairs walled garden. A cosy corner of the county; unusually good value. **EAT** Honest pub food (with steaks); and upstairs restaurant onto a garden.

878 8/R25
7 ROOMS
MED.INX

✓ **Goblin Ha' Hotel** Gifford · www.goblinha.com · 01620 810244 A restaurant with rooms in a much-loved village 7km from Haddington on the road to Lammermuirs (good walking and on the village's **Yester Estate** 455/WALKS). Always busy restaurant especially good for families (beer garden). A Punch Tavern, very personally run. **EAT** Extensive menu. Exemplary village pub grub in an exemplary village.

879 8/R25   **Castle Inn** Dirleton · www.castleinndirleton.com · 01620 850221 Close
5 ROOMS to the castle ruins on the corner of the green in the lovely wee village 4km from
NO PETS Gullane and 30 mins from Edinburgh. Only a few rooms; refurbished 2015 – you do
L · MED.INX feel like you're in an inn – and decent food downstairs, in this village well-placed
for county affairs.

£15-25 **EAT** Comfortable gastropub/bistro busy and buzzing, so book weekends. Outside
terrace. Daily and seasonal. Mon-Fri lunch & dinner, all day Sat/Sun.

880 8/R25   **Marine Hotel** North Berwick · www.macdonaldhotels.co.uk ·
83 ROOMS 01620 897300 The old seaside hotel of North Berwick extensively remodelled
MED.EX by the Macdonald Group into a corporate hotel, spa and conference centre. Done
in the sombre/elegant style à la mode with lots of public space and everywhere
(except the leisure area) the great views of the Links and the sea. There are 20
golf courses on your doorstep. Fine-ish dining in the plush restaurant. Links bar
less formal and there's a drawing room for that afternoon tea. Pool and other vital
facilities. It's all very North Berwick sitting there with your tea or your G&T, the
lawn, the links and serene grey sea!

881 8/R25   **The Rocks** Dunbar · www.therocksdunbar.co.uk · 01368 862287 Not signed
12 ROOMS but at the E end of Dunbar (take a right at Marine Rd), with great views across to
CHP the rocky harbour area, a hotel with big local reputation for food. Rooms vary but
most have a view.

£15-25 **EAT** They come from across the county to Jim Findlay's gastropub but it's a
Dunbar thing. Seafood and the rest in various rooms. Old-style food and service.
Always best to book.

✓✓ **Dakota** South Queensferry Designed for travellers. Report: 129/
HOTELS OUTSIDE EDINBURGH.

✓ **Orocco Pier** South Queensferry Boutique on the water. And the bridge.
Report: 132/HOTELS OUTSIDE EDINBURGH.

THE BEST RESTAURANTS: EAST LOTHIAN

882 8/R25   ✓✓ **La Potinière** Gullane · www.la-potiniere.co.uk · 01620 843214 On
>£35 the main street of a golfing mecca, this small, discreet restaurant has
been an East Lothian destination for decades. Keith Marley and Mary Runciman,
who share the cooking, have guarded its reputation since 2003. The simple room is
not bustling, but is just right for gentle, perhaps genteel, appreciation of their
nurtured excellent 2-choice, locally sourced menu. By far the best dining in East
Lothian. I wrote this for a previous edition. After a recent visit I still stick by it word
for word. Lunch Wed-Sun & dinner Wed-Sat (also Sun in summer). Closed Jan.

883 8/R25   ✓✓ **Steampunk** North Berwick · www.steampunkcoffee.co.uk ·
<£15 01620 893030 Parallel small road to main street (49A Kirk Ports). Well, it
is only a coffee shop, but two ticks because it's a perfect wee coffee shop
permanently established but with a pop-up (as in Shoreditch) atmos. Great coffee
is roasted, blended and brewed here in an old joinery warehouse, with comfy seats
upstairs and some outside. Great cakes, most especially the brownies. People do
come from Edinburgh. Open 7 days daytime only.

884 8/R25   ✓ **Fenton Barns Farm Shop** nr Drem · www.fentonbarnsfarmshop.com ·
<£15 01620 850294 Farm shop/deli but also a great café with delicious food
home-made from the mainly local produce they sell; hot dishes till 3.30pm then
scrumptious cake. Not licensed. Open 7 days. See 1471/FARM SHOPS.

885 8/R25
£25-35

✓ **Creel** Dunbar · www.creelrestaurant.co.uk · 01368 863279 Logan Thorburn's meticulously run but informal bistro on a corner of old Dunbar near the harbour; from a tiny kitchen he produces sound and simple, almost rustic menus. Local, of course (crab and Eyemouth-landed haddock & whiting), and not just seafood. Close-up and personal. Lunch Thu-Sun & dinner Wed-Sat.

886 8/R25
£15-25

✓ **Osteria** North Berwick · www.osteria-no1.co.uk · 01620 890589 A classic Italian restaurant in downtown small town out of Edinburgh's legendary Cosmo. Angelo & family run it with old-fashioned values yet it is comfortably urbane in both menu and service. North Berwick's most consistently good restaurant. Good Italian wine list. Closed Sun & Mon lunch.

887 8/R25
£25-35

✓ **The Herringbone** North Berwick · www.theherringbone.co.uk · 01620 890501 Arrived à la mode and perfectly formed in 2014, a bar (great by-the-glass wine list and all the right bottled and draught beers) and restaurant on the cool Edinburgh side of casual dining. You could almost be at the Brighton seaside, though it is more calm and retiring outside.

888 8/R25
£15-25

✓ **The Old Clubhouse** Gullane · www.oldclubhouse.com · 01620 842008 Behind main street, on corner of Green. Large, woody clubhouse; a bar/bistro serving a long menu (of the burgers/pasta/nachos variety) and daily specials all day till 9.30pm. Obliging, reliable. Great busy atmos. Surprising wine selection.

889 8/R25
DF
L
£15-25

Waterside Bistro Haddington · www.watersidebistro.co.uk · 01620 825674 Long a food find on the Tyne (over the bridge by St Mary's – the big church), of mixed fortunes but under new ownership 2015. It is a classic waterside bistro. Separate chambers and ambience options, same menu throughout. Perfect on a summer's eve with the ducks plashing.

THE BEST RESTAURANTS: WEST LOTHIAN

890 8/N25
£15-25

✓ **Livingston's** Linlithgow · www.livingstons-restaurant.co.uk · 01506 846565 Through arch at east end of High St, now sitting a bit uncomfortably behind a brash but serviceable tratt (Barleo). Cottage conversion with conservatory and garden – a bistro with imaginative modern Franco-Scottish cuisine (4 starters, mains, desserts) holding on to its reserve and still the best in town and shire. Straightforward menu; good vegetarian. Tue-Sat lunch & dinner.

891 8/P25
£15-25

✓ **The Boathouse** South Queensferry · www.theboathouse-sq.co.uk · 0131 331 5429 Enter from main street or down steps to terrace overlooking shingly beach and excellent views of the Bridge (419/ATTRACTIONS). Bistro serving all day from noon and restaurant room in evenings. Nothing too fancy, mainly seafood in a lucky location.

 ✓ ✓ **Champany Inn** nr Linlithgow · 01506 834532 See *Hotels In The Lothians*, above.

✓ ✓ **Dakota** South Queensferry Report: 129/HOTELS OUTSIDE EDINBURGH.

✓ **Orocco Pier** South Queensferry Report: 132/HOTELS OUTSIDE EDINBURGH.

The Best Hotels & Restaurants In Fife

892 8/R23
109 ROOMS
35 SUITES
NO PETS
LL
LOTS

✓✓ **Old Course Hotel** St Andrews · www.oldcoursehotel.co.uk · 01334 474371 Arriving in St Andrews on the A91, you come to the Old Course and this world-renowned hotel first. An elegant presence on the hallowed greens, it's full of golfers coming and going. It was designed by NY architects with Americans in mind. Rooms, most overlooking the famous course and sea, are immaculate and tastefully done, with no facility or expense spared, as with the Sands Grill and fine-dining Road Hole Restaurant up top. Bar here also for lingering views and a big choice of drams. Truly great for golf, but anyone could unwind here, towelled in luxury. Excellent Kohler (the hotel's US owners) water spa with 20m pool, thermal suite and some top treatments (1261/SPAS). No preferential deal on the Old Course adjacent but there are 11 courses nearby; hotel has its own course, Dukes, 5km away. Hotel of The Open 2015.

>£35
£25-35

EAT Road Hole Restaurant for spectacular dinner, especially on late, light summer nights. Sands is a grill, but an all-round casual dining menu. Nice afternoon tea.

893 8/Q24
8 ROOMS
NO PETS

✓✓ **The Peat Inn** nr St Andrews · www.thepeatinn.co.uk · 01334 840206 A luxurious restaurant with rooms at a historic crossroads 20 mins from St Andrews (by Leven road or Strathkinness Rd). Long a foodie destination. Geoffrey and Katherine Smeddle have upgraded the rooms and transformed The Residence into a comfortable, very contemporary and quiet retreat, rather than just a place to kip so you don't have to drive anywhere after dinner. 7 of the rooms over 2 floors, breakfast discreetly delivered (from pre-order) to your upstairs dining room so you start your day relaxed. Flowers in the room which look out to the flowers in the serene gardens.

EAT Very special. This is Fife's top dining experience (see below).

894 8/R23
24 ROOMS +
3 LODGES
L
LOTS

✓✓ **Rufflets** St Andrews · www.rufflets.co.uk · 01334 472594 4km from centre along Strathkinness Low Rd. The Murray-Smiths' calm, elegant country-house hotel on edge of town is the epitome of comfort and I have to declare that I love it for its tranquillity and simple good taste. The celebrated topiary gardens leading down to the burn (you can walk to downtown St A in half an hour) are not just a joy, they're among the most beautiful hotel grounds in the land. Garden-restaurant fine dining; lovely lounges, especially for afternoon tea. Cosy rooms, half overlook garden: 3 lodges in the garden and a conference/wedding suite in a separate building (so serenity remains intact). New whisky bar with French windows to the lawn demonstrates the pleasing balance of traditional and contemporary that a superb management team achieve here.

895 8/R23
37 ROOMS
DF
LOTS

✓✓ **Hotel du Vin** St Andrews · www.hotelduvin.com · 0844 748 9269 Overlooking sea to W of the West Sands. It's a measure of the seemingly unstoppable sophisticating of hotels and restaurants in St A that H du V set up shop here after Glasgow & Edinburgh (480/94/BOUTIQUE HOTELS), before anywhere else in Scotland. Usual sympathetic conversion, this time an old hotel; understated opulence. Corporate, golfy & masculine style.

EAT Bistro du Vin out front, al fresco terrace out back.

896 8/R23
209 ROOMS +
2 LODGES
L
LOTS

✓ **Fairmont St Andrews (aka St Andrews Bay)** nr St Andrews · www.standrewsbay.com · 01334 837000 8km E on A917 to Crail overlooking eponymous bay. Smart modern edifice in rolling greens by international hotel group. Soulless perhaps, but every facility a golfing family could need. It does have a championship course and service at the Fairmont is top. There's an eclectic approach to the menu in The Squire, a brasserie-type restaurant in an immense atrium (feels a bit like a municipal leisure facility but for the bold clashing carpet). La Cucina is the Italian job and the Clubhouse on the green has its signature fish 'n' chips. There is, of course, the course! And afternoon tea.

897 8/Q24
31 ROOMS
DF
EXP

>£35

✓ **Balbirnie House** Markinch, nr Glenrothes · www.balbirnie.co.uk · 01592 610066 Signed from the road system around Glenrothes (3km) in surprisingly sylvan setting of Balbirnie Country Park. One of the most sociable and comfortable country-house hotels in the land, with high, if traditional, standards in service and decor, overseen by the Russell family. Library Bar leads to tranquil garden. Lots of luxury space. Choice of dining and a good wine list. No leisure facilities. Nice wedding/honeymoon destination (many of). Good golf in the park. **EAT** Surprisingly good (in Glenrothes) in Orangery or the downstairs Bistro.

898 8/R23
8 ROOMS
MED.INX

✓ **The Old Station** nr St Andrews · www.theoldstation.co.uk · 01334 880505 On B9131 (Anstruther road) off A917 from St Andrews. It's different, the Old Station – Colin and Fiona Wiseman's individualist contemporary makeover of an old station with themed rooms. Great consideration for guests: library, putting green, snooker, ping pong. Conservatory breakfast room, comfy lounge. 2 garden suites in a railway carriage, where I stayed last time; curiously comfy! Nice for kids. B&B only.

899 8/R24
45 BEDS
L
VARIES

Cambo Estate nr Crail · www.camboestate.com · 01333 450054 2km E of Crail on A917. Huge country pile in glorious gardens on the St Andrews–Crail coastal road. Hugely individual, even quirky self-catering, B&B (communal-style breakfast in enormous morning room) and 2 yurts (May-Oct) (1248/GLAMPING). Rooms arranged in apartments (and 3 cottages). This is home-stay in the grand manner, especially for groups (1280/HOUSE PARTIES). A real period piece and not so expensive. Grounds are superb, especially in spring (the snowdrops!); an event programme makes the most of the gardens (24/EVENTS). Lovely plant shop and tearoom in the yard and an interesting gift shop indoors. Great walks and **Kingsbarns** golf, distillery and beach adjacent (2052/GOLF). Rattle around, pretend you're house guests and be grateful you don't have to pay the bills. Many grounds to love Cambo!

For accommodation in St Andrews, see p. 166.

THE BEST RESTAURANTS IN FIFE

900 8/Q24
ATMOS

>£35

✓ ✓+ **The Peat Inn** nr St Andrews · www.thepeatinn.co.uk · 01334 840206 Legendary restaurant (with 8 suites; see above) at the eponymous crossroads. Geoffrey and Katherine Smeddle have made it one of the great Scots dining-out experiences. A tasting menu, seasonal à la carte and good-value menu du jour offer loads of toothsome choice. Unlike some top chefs, Michelin-starred chef-patron Geoffrey Smeddle is always there (*and* somehow writes a column in the *Sunday Herald*). Handily close to St Andrews, it is still the top spot in an area not short of foodie options. Superb wine list, especially French. Tue-Sat lunch & dinner.

901 8/R24
£25-35

✓ ✓ **East Pier** St Monans · www.eastpier.co.uk · 01333 405030 Arrive at the front in St Monans and look left, by the harbour: the big, blue shed. Inside, and on the roof in summer, Fife's most effortlessly cool place to eat. Shellfish and fish from the sea that laps (or crashes) below. Superbly matched wines and home-made cakes. Upstairs tables in and out. A rosé on the terrace on a summer's eve with dolphins over there is not the Fife we used to know. Apr-Oct.

902 8/R24 ✓ **The Cellar** Anstruther · www.thecellaranstruther.co.uk · 01333 310378
ATMOS   Off a courtyard behind the Fisheries Museum in this busy East Neuk town
>£35   (1557/VILLAGES). You'd never think it was a restaurant from the approach but inside
is a comforting oasis of epicurean delight, one that has put Anstruther on the
foodie map for 40 years. Now under chef/patron Billy Boyter, a new chapter is
being written. I haven't managed to eat here at TGP (hence only 1 tick) but all
reports are good, and The Cellar is Scotland's latest Michelin-starred restaurant.

903 8/Q23 ✓ **Ostler's Close** Cupar · www.ostlersclose.co.uk · 01334 655574 Down a
£25-35   close off the main street, Amanda and Jimmy Graham quietly and
conscientiously run a bistro/restaurant that has been on the gastronomic map and
a reason for coming to Cupar for 35 years. Intimate, cottagey rooms. Amanda out
front also does puds, Jimmy a star in the kitchen. Long before it was de rigueur they
pioneered local and personal sourcing. Often organic and from their garden, big on
mushrooms and other wild things, lots of fish choice – the handwritten menu
sums up their approach. This is a place that deserves more recognition and your
discovery. Cupar is only 20 mins from St Andrews. Go to it! Must book.

904 8/P25 ✓ **The Wee Restaurant** North Queensferry · www.theweerestaurant.
£25-35   co.uk · 01383 616263 Just over the Road Bridge from Edinburgh and in the
shadow of the **Rail Bridge** (419/ATTRACTIONS). It's a wee restaurant (in a quiet wee
town) with only a few tables up a few stairs from the street, but it's a sparkling wee
gem. Award-winning owner/chef Craig Wood and missus, Vikki, live through the
back, bake the bread in the morning and prepare their no-fuss menu with
commitment (to good food) and aplomb (and awards!). There's nowhere as good as
this anywhere nearby except Edinburgh. Neat wine list. Tue-Sun lunch & dinner.

905 8/Q23 **The View** Wormit · www.view-restaurant.co.uk · 01382 542287 On the main
£15-25   road in or out of Wormit next to the PO, it has a great view right enough (of the Tay
Bridge and bonnie Dundee). Steve and Karen Robertson's lovely café/restaurant over
the water with non-city but almost urban dining. The menu all day, from breakfast
through lunch and tea and cakes to light bites and dinner. There ain't nothing like it
in Dundee so come on over. Lunch & dinner but check hours. Closed Mon.

<£15   **Fish & Chips In Fife: Valente's, The Anstruther Fish Bar, The Wee Chippy,
The Pittenweem Fish & Chip Bar** 4 great fish 'n' chip shops in Fife; queues every
day, and all very good and a change from the fancier foodie places above. Report:
1361/1366/FISH & CHIPS.

✓✓ **The Ship Inn** Elie Report: 1305/GASTROPUBS.

✓✓ **The Adamson** St Andrews Eat in St Andrews, p. 167–68.

✓✓ **The 19th Hole** Earlsferry Report: 1306/GASTROPUBS.

✓ **The Grange Inn** St Andrews Report: 1308/GASTROPUBS.

✓ **The Vine Leaf** St Andrews Eat in St Andrews, p. 167–68.

Craig Millar @ 16 West End St Monans Report: 1338/SEAFOOD.

If you're in St Andrews...

Many of the places below are listed in Scotland- or Fife-wide categories.

WHERE TO STAY

906 8/R23 ✓✓ **Old Course Hotel** Report: 892/FIFE.

✓✓ **Hotel du Vin** Report: 895/FIFE.

✓✓ **Rufflets** Report: 894/FIFE.

✓ **Fairmont (St Andrews Bay)** Report: 896/FIFE.

✓ **The Old Station** Report: 898/FIFE.

68 ROOMS
DF
LOTS
Rusacks www.macdonaldhotels.co.uk · 0344 879 9136 Long-standing golfy hotel near all courses and overlooking the 1st and 18th of the Old. You're at the heart of the matter here. Nice sun lounge and breakfast overlooking the greens. Jack Nicklaus looms large. Reliable and quite classy Macdonald Hotel. Offering much improved, with Rocca dining (see below) and gastropub The One Under.

36 ROOMS
MED.INX
Ardgowan Hotel www.ardgowanhotel.co.uk · 01334 472970 Long-standing notable but modest hotel (incorporating the Pilmour adjacent) and restaurant, Playfair's (does a very good steak). Simple, serviceable rooms.

22 ROOMS
NO PETS
MED.EX
Albany Hotel www.albanyhotelstandrews.co.uk · 01334 477737 Townhouse hotel with surprising number of rooms and secret back garden. All rooms are individually (though not in a boutique sense) done; 3 suites. Bar and basement breakfast room, The Garden. A very St Andrews kind of a hostelry.

13 ROOMS
MED.INX
Ogstons On North Street www.ogstonsonnorthst.com · 01334 473387 Corner of Murray Park where there are numerous guest-house options. Boutique-ish rooms above restaurant and often-busy bar. Club room in basement, the Oak Rooms on street level is quite civilised café-bar. Comfy, contemporary rooms, perhaps best for students and their mates, rather than their parents (club kicks in from 10pm at weekends, though soundproofed).

20 ROOMS
NO PETS
NO KIDS
MED.INX
Greyfriars www.greyfriarshotel-standrews.co.uk · 01334 474906 Immediately adjacent to Ogstons (above), another bar/restaurant with rooms above and a similar offering. Perhaps even more self-consciously contemporary: a more recent makeover. Restaurant not bad; a busy, sports-on-TV kind of billet.

8 ROOMS
MED.EX
Dunvegan Hotel www.dunvegan-hotel.com · 01334 473105 If you like golf you'll like the Dunvegan and if you're on that kind of a holiday, this, a stroll to both town and greens, is for you (of a modest budget). The Willoughbys run a tidy and friendly house, bar and (The Claret Jug) restaurant.

7 ROOMS
NO PETS
NO KIDS
MED.INX
Five Pilmour Place www.5pilmourplace.com · 01334 478665 Adjacent 18th green of Old Course (and Dunvegan Hotel, above). Contemporary-style and well-TripAdvised guest house with lounge. The Wrights have got it, well... right, and are notably obliging. Great breakfast choice.

WHERE TO EAT

>£35 ✓✓ **The Adamson** www.theadamson.com · 01334 479191 Together with its new cocktail bar adjacent (2015), The Adamson has brought a truly urban-contemporary look and feel to St Andrews dining & drinking. Always busy but smart, sympatico service. And the food, Modern British, seasonal and locally sourced is somehow even better than you'd expect from this level of turnover and noise. Along with The Vine Leaf next door (and almost the polar opposite), this is probably the most fine, though not *fine* dine in town. 7 days.

£25-35 ✓ **The Vine Leaf** www.vineleafstandrews.co.uk · 01334 477497 Inauspicious entrance belies what has been for a very long time St A's best all-round restaurant. Incredibly long and varied eclectic menu covers all bases, including vegetarian and wines. Morag and Ian Hamilton look after you and know what you like (especially for pud). How they manage to turn out such consistently high-quality food of this variety remains a mystery; they pick the leaves in their garden, they bake many breads. Somebody give these guys an award or I will. David Joy's calming pictures around the walls are for sale. Tue-Sat dinner only.

>£35 ✓ **Rocca** www.roccarestaurant.com · 01334 472549 The main restaurant of Rusacks hotel. In what must be one of the best views of the Green in golf, with lavish dining rooms, Executive Chef Davey Aspin produces top food at far from top prices. Not Michelin fancy and the better for that (3 AA Rosettes). I had a great meal here and a sunset over the West Sands. 7 days lunch & dinner.

£15-25 ✓ **Little Italy** www.littleitaly.org.uk · 01334 472595 Behind the church in South St, down the lane from Pizza Express. Here the pizzas, pastas and all things tratt are better. Hidden from view it is perhaps surprising that this is one of St A's busiest restaurants. 7 days noon-10.30pm (open later than most). Best book.

£15-25 ✓ **Steak Barn @ Balgove Larder** www.balgove.com · 01334 898145 2km town on the A91 beyond the Old Course Hotel. Beside the farm shop, one of the most innovative and interesting diners in the land – a lofty barn with crates for walls, serving great steaks and burgers. Al fresco but undercover, it's a bit like a great long B&Q. Luvians ice cream. Rough, ready and rather good. 7 days daytime.

<£15 ✓ **The Tailend Restaurant & Fish Bar** www.thetailend.co.uk · 01334 474070 The original of the Tailends (in Edinburgh though different owners & 2015 in Dundee) and still the commitment to good F&C served sizzlingly fresh. Contemporary design, takeaway out front, surprisingly spacious caff through the back and outside terrace. Many choices but it's haddock/cod 'n' chips, ain't it?

<£15 ✓ **Cromars 'Classic' Fish & Chips** www.cromars.co.uk · 01334 475555 At corner with Market St. Café/takeaway & delivery (winter only). 'Classic', so they use lard but everything fresh and, yes, so tasty. They also do Cullen skink, maccy cheese and Jannetta's ice cream. St A has two, not one, great chippies. 7 days.

The following 3 'House' restaurants, all made in St Andrews, now part of Scotland's expansive G1 Group (www.g1group.co.uk):

£15-25 **The Doll's House** www.dollshousestandrews.co.uk · 01334 477422 Very central café/restaurant that caters well for kids (and their parents). Eclectic range, smiley people and tables outside in summer.

£15-25 **The Grill House** www.grillhousestandrews.co.uk· 01334 470500 A real townhouse with 3 different rooms and young staff grilling.

£15-25 **The Glasshouse** www.glasshousestandrews.co.uk · 01334 473673
Contemporary building with few tables downstairs and a few up. Bright, buzzy
surroundings of metal, brick and glass. Recent refurbishment. All 'Houses' open 7
days noon-10pm.

The G1 group also has:
The Vic www.vicstandrews.co.uk · 01334 476964 This is possibly the funkiest
of the bunch. Spacious upstairs eaterie.
Mitchell www.mitchellsdeli.co.uk · 01334 441396 A deli and, along with
Forgan's adjacent, a café-bar with all the right contemporary civilities. St A has
been well and truly G1'd. 7 days early till late.

£25-35 **Balaka Bangladeshi Restaurant** www.balaka.com · 01334 474825 One
of those 'Best Curry in Scotland' winners. But as good as many in Edinburgh or
Glasgow. Celebrated herb and spice garden out back which supplies others in St
Andrews. Handily open later than most (midnight at weekends).

<£15 **North Point** 01334 473997 Top of the street. Great little caff. Coffee, salads,
home-made stuff – soup, scones, hot dishes; good vibe. Open daytime.

✓ ✓+ **The Peat Inn** 01334 840206 15km SW. Only 20 mins to the best meal
around. Report: 900/FIFE.
✓ **The Seafood Restaurant** 01334 479475 Top seafood, top view (Old Course
and the sea). Report: 1337/SEAFOOD.
✓ **The Grange Inn** 01334 472670 4km E off Anstruther road A917. Popular
country pub with big local reputation. Report: 1308/GASTROPUBS.
Jannetta's Popular caff. 7 days till 10pm. Report: 1447/ICE CREAM.

The Best Hotels & Restaurants In Perthshire & Tayside

907 8/N22
26 ROOMS
DF
LOTS

✓✓ **Fonab Castle Hotel** Pitlochry · www.fonabcastlehotel.com · 01796 470140 Above town and Loch (Faskally), grounds edged by A9 but reached via road behind Festival Theatre. Somebody (Jed Clark) spent a lot of money and a lot of time on this extraordinary contemporary hotel, unique in the county. Rooms in the 'Castle' itself and two separate extensions all to very high spec; spacious and comfortable. Some balconies. Brasserie or fine-dining restaurants, spa overby, with 4 treatment rooms and 15m pool. None of this is cheap but it is a well-shorn cut above the rest.
EAT Paul Burns oversees fine-dining Sandemans (dinner only Tue-Sat), and the Brasserie; views & terrace. Hotel picks up and taxis back to Pitlochry.

908 8/P21
17 ROOMS
DF
L
MED.EX-LOTS

✓✓ **Dalmunzie Castle** Spittal of Glenshee · www.dalmunzie.com · 01250 885224 3km from Perth–Braemar road close to Glenshee ski slopes and good base for Royal Deeside without Deeside prices. 9-hole golf course for fun and the air. Highland-lodge feel: tasteful, comfortable, great attention to detail; a semi-chic retreat! Hills all around and burn besides; a truly peaceful outlook. Food mention in Michelin and many good reports, notable wine list, bar-billiards room, great whisky bar. A fire in the hall!

909 8/M23
11 ROOMS
DF
MED.EX

✓ **The Royal Hotel** Comrie · www.royalhotel.co.uk · 01764 679200 Central square of cosy town, a surprisingly stylish small-town hotel in the capable hands of the Milsom family. Excellent restaurant with good light, a bar and also a pub out back with ale and atmos. Lovely gardens for both hotel and pub. Bar food menu available all over and à la carte and specials in the dining room. Nice rugs and pictures. A pleasing touch of understated class in the county bit of the country. Both restaurant and bar food till 9pm.

910 8/N21
14 ROOMS
NO PETS
NO KIDS
MED.INX

✓ **Craigatin House** Pitlochry · www.craigatinhouse.co.uk · 01796 472478 Gorgeous boutique B&B in, as they say, Highland Perthshire, on main street (but the road N) of this tourist town. The house and courtyard (1820s) transformed into a smart contemporary and comfortable retreat from Pitlochry's less tasteful aspects. Martin and Andrea Anderson are your obliging and constantly upgrading hosts. Rooms in both mansion and courtyard; great bathrooms. Breakfast and guest lounge built around a wood-burning stove. Patio and serene garden. Great value at this standard.

911 8/N22
98 ROOMS
EXP

✓ **(Hilton) Dunkeld House** Dunkeld · www.hilton.co.uk/dunkeld · 01350 727771· Former home of Duke of Atholl, a very large, impressive country house on the banks of the Tay in beautiful grounds (some time-share) outside Dunkeld. Leisure complex with good pool, etc, and many other activities laid on, eg. quad bikes, clay pigeons. Traditional dining. Fine for kids. Pleasant walks. Not cheap but often deals available. Rooms in old house best. Weddings.

912 8/N22
13 ROOMS
DF
EXP

✓ **East Haugh House** nr Pitlochry · www.easthaugh.co.uk · 01796 473121 On S approach to Pitlochry from A9, a mansion house built in the 18th century; part of the Atholl estate. Notable for hunting/shooting and especially fishing breaks, and for very decent food in dining room or Cosy Fisherman's bar. Family-run with chef/proprietor Neil McGown. Nice fishing fly themed rooms especially up top, romantic with it (3 rooms have four-posters). A top retreat near the Tay.
EAT Food taken seriously here. Fish/game: good sourcing; seasonality. Bar or larger bistro, same menu.

913 8/N21 ✓ **Killiecrankie Hotel** Killiecrankie · www.killiecrankiehotel.co.uk ·
10 ROOMS 01796 473220 5km N of Pitlochry off A9 on B8079 signed Killiecrankie; near
DF Blair Castle. Roadside inn long known for food and cosy rooms. Delightful garden
MAR-NOV supplying kitchen. Conscientiously run with a simple good taste. Henrietta
L Ferguson's cottage home from home will also be yours, though, alas, since she got
MED.EX here and despite my good intentions, it hasn't at TGP been mine.
EAT Bar and conservatory seasonal menus and dining room with daily à la carte
menu. All proper good food from chef Mark Easton.

914 8/N22 ✓ **Errichel** Aberfeldy · www.errichel.co.uk · 01887 829562 4km from
4 ROOMS Aberfeldy in the hills overlooking the valley, even Schiehallion, a farm
homestead with self-catering cottages and boutique-type rooms in the farmhouse.
Great location and rural setting with a duck pond and a notable restaurant open
Thu-Sat for dinner (they also run a cook school).
EAT Thyme at Errichel: great reports and food with views.

915 8/N21 ✓ **Knockendarroch** Pitlochry · www.knockendarroch.co.uk ·
12 ROOMS 01796 473473 On Higher Oakfield, above the town via E Moulin Rd. The
NO PETS Lothian family moved from Torrdarach (see below) to this larger mansion also
NO KIDS overlooking the town and transformed it into a contemporary top stay with a
MED.INX destination dining room. Comfortable, friendly, classic Perthshire accom.
EAT Haven't tried but solid local reputation.

916 8/N21 ✓ **Torrdarach House** Pitlochry · www.torrdarach.co.uk · 01796 472136
7 ROOMS The big pink house above town (via Larchwood Rd off N main street) and
NO PETS almost in the country: they have their own wee woody glen. Complete
NO KIDS contemporary makeover of old established B&B: light, modern rooms; lots of
MED.EX pictures. Free-range hens in garden and eggs for breakfast in beautiful room
overlooking garden & gorge. Golfy guy Graeme Fish your enthusiastic host.

917 8/N23 ✓ **Yann's** Crieff · www.yannsatglenearnhouse.com · 01764 650111
4 ROOMS Yannick and Shari Grospellier's restaurant with rooms: a bistro and a small
DF mansion-house hotel on the Perth road out of town. This really is where to eat
MED.INX around here. Very French (Yann from Chamonix). A la carte, specials, grill menu and
savoyard specials, raclette & fondue and, well,... steak frites. Rooms lovely and not
expensive. Dinner Wed-Sun & Sun lunch. Best book!

918 8/N21 ✓ **The Old Mill Inn** Pitlochry · www.theoldmillpitlochry.co.uk ·
12 ROOMS 01796 474020 Mill Lane behind the main bus stop on the main street
MED.EX (opposite Fishers Hotel). Extraordinary conversion to create this restaurant with
rooms, done to a high spec. There is an old mill wheel and a busy bar/restaurant
around it, with OK contemporary food. Rooms are surprisingly fresh, urban and
relaxing. Priced accordingly, they are still good value and right in the centre of
town.

919 8/P22 ✓ **Ballathie House** Kinclaven, nr Perth · www.ballathiehousehotel.com ·
25+16+12 01250 883268 A true country-house hotel on the Tay that you can fall in love
ROOMS with, especially if you hunt, shoot, fish. Comfortingly old-style, the river and the
DF astonishing trees are the thing. Great fishing, though you can't necessarily get on
L the river; good for a weekend away. 'Riverside' rooms are over the lawn (150m walk
MED.EX-LOTS for breakfast) and uniform but you taste the Tay. Also cheaper, motel-like
Sportsman's Lodge adjacent main house. Love the approach: red squirrels, copper
beeches, golden corn.
>£35 **EAT** Chef Scott Scorer. Local and estate produce, especially beef/lamb.

920 8/P23
34 ROOMS
NO PETS
MED.INX

Huntingtower Hotel nr Perth · www.huntingtowerhotel.co.uk ·
01738 583771 Crieff road (1km off A85, 3km W of ring route A9 signed). Elegant, modernised mansion house outside town. Good gardens with spectacular copper beech and other trees. The tartan carpet. Subdued, panelled restaurant with traditional menu (OK lunch) and wine list. Business-like service.

921 8/N21
29 ROOMS
DF
MED.INX

Pine Trees Hotel Pitlochry · www.pinetreeshotel.co.uk · 01796 472121 A safe and sophisticated haven in visitor-ville – it's above the town and above all that (there are many mansions here). Take Larchwood Rd off N end of main street. Woody gardens, woody interior. Valerie and Robert Kerr the owners. Very traditional but with taste (nice rugs). Annex and Coach House have added more standardised but high-spec rooms (short walk).

922 8/M22
10 ROOMS
EXP

Fortingall House nr Aberfeldy · www.fortingall.com · 01887 830367 Historic roadhouse hotel on the road to gorgeous Glen Lyon, 8km from Aberfeldy, one of the most beautiful Arts and Crafts villages in Scotland. Refurbished to a boutique-style standard. Adjacent the kirkyard and famous Fortingall Yew, the oldest tree in Europe. It has long had a reputation for food (in 2 dining rooms). The Ewe Bar at the side is a sympatico spot. Sunday lunch.

923 8/Q21
10 ROOMS
NO PETS
L
CHP

Glen Clova Hotel www.clova.com · 01575 550350 Near end of Glen Clova, one of the great Angus glens (1589/GLENS) on B955 25km N of Kirriemuir. A walk/climb/country-retreat hotel; very comfy. Superb walking nearby. Often full. Also bunkhouse accom behind. 3 luxury lodges out back have hot tubs and fluffy downies. This place a very civilised Scottish inn in the hills and great value.

924 8/N22
7 ROOMS
DF
CHP

Dalshian Guest House nr Pitlochry · www.dalshian.co.uk · 01796 472173 Historic house in lovely gardens just off the A9, 2km S towards Ballinluig (GH signed). Martin and Heather Walls' old hoose and their hospitalities make for a very civilised retreat. Good fishing prospect. Logierait Inn (below) & East Haugh (above) nearby for dinner. Family friendly. Great breakfast by the fire. Very good value.

925 8/P22
17 ROOMS
DF
MED.INX

Atholl Arms Hotel Dunkeld · www.athollarmshotel.com · 01350 727219 On main street by the bridge. Decent hotel in a great Perthshire town with great walking, fishing, etc. Good that there's somewhere to recommend here. Simple rooms of different sizes (2 with river view). Pub & Riverview Restaurant have good reputation.

✓✓✓ **Gleneagles** Auchterarder Report: 1126/COUNTRY-HOUSE HOTELS.

✓✓✓ **Crieff Hydro** Superb. These ticks especially for family holidays. Quintessentially Scottish. Report: 1133/KIDS.

✓✓ **Kinloch House** nr Blairgowrie Quintessential Perthshire comfort and joy. Report: 1129/COUNTRY-HOUSE HOTELS.

✓✓ **The Bield at Blackruthven** Tibbermore, nr Perth Report: 1254/RETREATS.

✓✓ **The Barley Bree** Muthill, nr Crieff Report: 1170/INNS.

✓ **The Inn on the Tay** Grandtully Report: 1178/INNS.

THE BEST RESTAURANTS IN PERTHSHIRE & TAYSIDE

926 8/N24
>£35

✓✓✓ **Andrew Fairlie at Gleneagles** Auchterarder · www.gleneagles.com · 01764 694267 I have perhaps been mealy-mouthed about not giving Andrew Fairlie's consistently 2 Michelin-starred restaurant (the only one in Scotland) 3 ticks, the *StB* designation for 'among the best in the world'. Being by common consensus at a different level to all the other 2-tick restaurants, I had compromised with two and a half to recognise this. But now, on balance, in view of the setting (Gleneagles is obviously a world-class destination) and Andrew's international accolades, unassuming dedication to food, to good cooking and to Scotland, 3 ticks it is. Deep in the hotel's interior, well laid out and lit, a room where we come to experience as well as eat ingredients that seem both effortlessly and masterfully matched, dish after dish. Tasting menus and à la carte. Perfectly judged, mouth-watering morsels, pre and après. The new kitchen garden supplies superb salad & veg. Despite wider commitments, Andrew is usually there, both in the kitchen and on the wall in a portrait among the Archie Forrests. Dinner only. Closed Sun and Jan.

927 8/P23 ✓✓ **63 Tay Street** Perth · www.63taystreet.com · 01738 441451 On the
>£35 riverside road and walk. Graeme Pallister from Parklands hotel (see Perth) where there is another 63, presides over Perth's premier foodie haven; well sourced, seasonal and, as they say, 'local, honest, simple'. Tasting menu and à la carte fine dining. Must book weekends. Tue-Sat lunch & dinner.

928 8/R22 ✓✓ **Gordon's** Inverkeilor · www.gordonsrestaurant.co.uk ·
£25-35 01241 830364 Halfway between Arbroath and Montrose on the main street. A restaurant with rooms (5) which has won loadsa accolades for Gordon and son Garry in the kitchen. It's been here for 30 seriously good years! Splendid people doing good Franco-Scot cooking. Seasonal menu. It is the best meal for miles. Closed Mon (except for residents).

929 8/P23 ✓ **The Roost** Bridge of Earn · www.theroostrestaurant.co.uk ·
£25-35 01738 812111 About 5km from Perth and less from the M9, 1km from Bridge of Earn main street (signed) and at the gates of Kilgraston School, a superb little cottage bistro that has eluded me till now (it's been here since 2008); my loss. Tim and Anna Dover have created a secret food oasis in the Perth hinterland. Great local sourcing: Perthshire pigeon & roe deer, gorse flower ice cream, French-style cooking in a small, usually full parlour. Go book! Lunch Tue-Sun, dinner Thu-Sat.

930 8/P23 ✓ **Deans @ Let's Eat** Perth · www.letseatperth.co.uk · 01738 643377
£25-35 Long-established and popular but perhaps no longer a pre-eminent Perth eaterie, this is decent contemporary dining and great value. Must book. Chef/ patron Willie Deans very much in charge. Tue-Sat lunch & dinner. Sun noon-5pm.

931 8/R22 ✓ **The But 'n' Ben** Auchmithie · www.butnbenauchmithie.co.uk ·
LL 01241 877223 2km off A92 N from Arbroath, 8km to town, or 4km by clifftop
£15-25 walk. Village on that clifftop where a ravine leads to a cove and quay. Adjacent cottages converted into a cosy restaurant. All very Scottish and informal, emphasising fresh fish, seafood and the smokies. The brilliant couthy creation of Margaret Horn; after 35 years, still in the family – Angus (in kitchen) and Margo out front assuring a warm welcome and consistency for a huge loyal following. Lunch & dinner. Famous Sunday high tea, sittings at 4pm & 5.30pm. Closed Tue. Book!

932 8/M23 ✓ **Deil's Cauldron** Comrie · www.deilscauldron.co.uk · 01764 670352 On
£15-25 bend of the A85 main road through town and corner of the Glen Lednock road. For over a decade Katy and Brian Healy have run their cottage restaurant quietly and effectively. A hugely popular destination for lunch, dinner (especially steaks) and the eclectic tapas menu in the wine bar. Seriously good wine list; cosy ambience and just possibly boules out the back. Tue-Sun lunch & Tue-Sat dinner.

933 8/Q22
<£15
✓ **88° Kirriemuir** · 07449 345089 & **Forfar** · 07449 343099 The original in Kirriemuir is on main square. Johanna and Philip Woodhead's labour-of-love deli-cafés are very welcome find hereabouts. Artisan food, chocolates, hand-made specials and great coffee. Hot food and deli platters all conscientiously done. Kirriemuir: 9.30am-5pm (10am-4pm Sun). Closed Mon/Tue. Till 9pm every other Fri. Forfar (really a café): Tue-Sat 9am-3pm.

934 8/N23
£15-25
✓ **Delivino** www.delivino.co.uk · **Crieff** · 01764 655665 & **Auchterarder** · 01764 660033 The original branch (Crieff) is just off the main street. Jamie Stewart's perfectly judged deli counter and wine bar, but mainly an Italian bistro where ladies may lunch. Great thin, crispy, wood-oven pizza. In Auchterarder, less deli, more vino. Takeaways too. Opening times vary.

935 8/N22
<£15
Logierait Inn nr Ballinluig · www.logieraitinn.co.uk · 01796 482423 8km S of Pitlochry. An inn (and self-catering lodges) by the River Tay 2km from the main A9 on A827 to Aberfeldy. Reputation for food is such that it keeps its own particular opening hours but its many rooms are always busy, so book. Excellent gastropub grub, all with a very traditional Scottish slant, piled high, chips & coleslaw with almost everything (home-made though). Wed-Fri dinner only, Sat/Sun 12.30-8.30pm.

936 8/N23
£15-25
Lounge (aka Wee Yann's) Crieff · www.loungeincrieff.co.uk · 01764 654407 West end of main street. As it says, a lounge, an uptown extension of Yann's (see Hotels, above) – his sister Delphine keeping even more Perthshire people happy and well fed. Here you come to graze and sup, not pig out. Has that comfy wine-bar look. Another good thing for Crieff. Closed Sun/Mon.

937 8/P22
£15-25
Cargills Blairgowrie · www.cargillsbistro.com · 01250 876735 The fact that Lesley and Ronny McDonald's bistro, tucked away behind the square, not quite on the riverside, has been here for over 15 years and has survived, never mind thrived, says a lot. It clearly works and on a recent visit I liked everything on its classic bistro blackboard. Wed-Sun 10.30am-9pm (LO).

938 8/N22
DF
£25-35
Port-na-Craig Pitlochry · www.portnacraig.com · 01796 472777 Just by the Pitlochry Theatre, cottage-style bistro with courtyard in a 17th-century inn and 3 nice, very individual rooms. Informal and friendly with a Modern-European menu. Especially handy pre- and post-theatre.

939 8/N21
£15-25
The Auld Smiddy Inn Pitlochry · www.auldsmiddyinn.co.uk · 01796 472356 A long time here, great of late, the Auld Smiddy dispenses reliable grub that remarkably is all (the chips, the bread, the ice cream) home-made. In downtown Pitlochry look no further. 7 days lunch & dinner.

940 8/P22
£15-25
Little's Blairgowrie · www.littlesrestaurant.co.uk · 01250 875358 On the corner of the main square and the Braemar road. Willy Little's mainly fish bistro may be a long way from the sea but it's among the best up river in the shire. Casual dining, no airs, a bit of a find on your way to the Glenshee slopes or Royal Deeside, or you're just in Blairgowrie. Lunch Fri/Sat & dinner Tue-Sat.

941 8/N22
£15-25
3 Lemons Aberfeldy · www.threelemons.co.uk · 01887 820057 East end of main street. Along with the Good Food Takeaway adjacent, eating out or in got a whole lot smarter end of 2014, with this all-round bar/restaurant, pizzas to-go place. Original features, good contemporary dining, whiskies and cocktails. I haven't actually eaten here, so reports please. Closed Mon/Tue.

The Best Places To Stay In & Around Dundee

942 8/Q23
151 ROOMS
NO PETS
MED.EX

✓ **The Apex** www.apexhotels.co.uk · 01382 202404 There are 4 Apex hotels in Edinburgh (86/89/MAJOR HOTELS), 3 in London, and new one in Glasgow 491/MAJOR HOTELS, and they're all good 4/5-star business and leisure options. Here in Dundee, this contemporary waterfront edifice, overlooking both bridge and dock has good detail in its modern facilities, including the Yu Spa and pool. As a business stopover it's good value compared to elsewhere. Metro restaurant so-so, but options in the adjacent quarter. Rooms facing the firth and out to sea are best. Big waterfront developments are in progress, including the much-heralded V&A. Apex will service all you new visitors. The beauty of the Apex location is its urban serenity with dreamy views of a non-bustling waterfront. New extension 2016/17.

943 8/Q23
91 ROOMS
L
MED.EX

✓ **Malmaison** www.malmaison.com · 0844 693 0661 On the roadways bordering the waterfront and the recent public space developments, including the V&A. So, a great location near the station and downtown Dundee. No expense spared in the 2014 'Mal-ing' up of this old hotel building, though the plush purple and grey drapes and decoration may feel a tad OTT (or dare we suggest... already passé). Rooms overlook the river or the city. Original windows so not a lot of light. First-floor brasserie, with classic brazz menu, does overlook the developments. Breakfast not a strong point. Malbar (the bar) but no leisure facilities or parking (though car park adjacent). Rooms often surprisingly good value.

944 8/Q23
26 ROOMS
NO PETS
MED.INX

The Fort Hotel Broughty Ferry · www.fort-hotel.com · 01382 737999 On street leading to the waterfront, 'The Ferry' is 20 mins from downtown Dundee but it's just possibly where you want to be: low rise, low noise and the village boasts a lovely riverfront & esplanade and lots of good restaurant/café choices. This is TV's *Bob Servant* (the small-minded local bigot played by Brian Cox) territory but actually the Ferry is rather genteel. This hotel has a good bar (and restaurant) and a very good Italian dining room (see below). Rooms either above (11) or along the street (15) are pleasant, contemporary and quiet.

945 8/Q23
12 ROOMS
ATMOS
CHP

Fisherman's Tavern Broughty Ferry · www.fishermanstavern-broughtyferry.co.uk · 01382 775941 Not a hotel, it's a pub but an old and interesting one at that, down by the river and the sea. These modest 17th-century fishermen's cottages were converted into a pub in 1827. Rooms above and adjacent cottages are contemporary and very decent for the price. Excellent real ales and pub menu, but also near **The Ship Inn** (956/DUNDEE) and many other eats.

✓ **Dundee Backpackers Hostel** 71 High St · www.hoppo.com/dundee · 01382 224646 A very central and well-appointed billet for the night in historic building. May just be the best value accom in the city. Some doubles and en suite.

The Best Places To Eat In & Around Dundee

946 8/Q23
<£15

✓✓ **Jessie's Kitchen** Broughty Ferry · 01382 778488 20 mins direct from city centre via Dundee Rd or Victoria Rd. Part of **Turriff's** (2189/GARDEN CENTRES) which has been in the grounds of this suburban Victorian house for decades. But Jessie's, which takes up the ground floor of the very lived-in mansion, has only been going a few years. 2 ticks in this book because for what it is – a café – it is so brilliantly couthy and comforting; good home baking and cooking, and very Dundonian. All rooms on the go at once. Excellent cakes, of course. Local lassies. Granny Jessie not there now, but the family still live upstairs. 7 days.

947 8/Q23
£15-25
✓ **Jute at Dundee Contemporary Arts** www.jutecafebar.co.uk ·
01382 909246 Jute, the downstairs bar/restaurant of Dundee's acclaimed arts centre, DCA, is the most convivial place in town to eat – still no contest. Chef Chris Wilson offers a menu far superior to any old arts venue, especially one which is all things to all people. Bar and restaurant: your rendezvous in Dundee. A good kids' menu. Very pleasant outdoor terrace on a warmer day. Book weekends.

948 8/Q23
£15-25
✓ **The Playwright** Tay Sq · www.theplaywright.co.uk · 01382 223113 On the square adjacent and taking its point of reference from the estimable Dundee Rep Theatre, this upstairs bistro has long plugged the informal but informed contemporary-dining gap in Dundee and invariably gets good notices from public and critics alike. Dundee's Brian Cox has pride of place (and he does, too). Good Modern-British cookery under chef David Anderson. Mon-Sat.

949 8/Q23
>£35
✓ **Castlehill Restaurant** 22-26 Exchange St · www.castlehillrestaurant. co.uk · 01382 220008 Not on a hill at all (there is an explanation) but since 2014 this has been Dundee's downtown fine diner. Graham Campbell's straight-talking 4 starters/4 mains, listing 3/4 ingredients menu plays to an enthusiastic audience. Best to book (I couldn't get myself in but I take the word of foodie friends who eat here regularly). Intimate & unpretentious. Tue-Sat lunch & dinner.

950 8/Q23
£25-35
✓ **The Tayberry** Broughty Ferry · www.tayberryrestaurant.com · 01382 698280 On the front. Adam Newth (a young chef of the year and from Castlehill above) opened Tayberry to great local acclaim 2015. Haven't been at TGP but foodies have flocked. Straight-talking menu. Closed Sun eve & Mon.

951 8/Q23
£15-25
✓ **Sol y Sombra** Broughty Ferry · 01382 776941 On corner with King St. An upstairs authentic and decidedly good tapas bar; yes, probably one of the best in Scotland. Fixed, daily changing selection of hot and cold dishes: 12 for lunch and 16 for dinner (you will eat them!). Very good value (£21.50 dinner at TGP). *Postres* (Santiago almond or Turron cake – yum!). This place definitely worth the 20 mins from city centre. 7 days lunch & dinner.

952 8/Q23
£15-25
✓ **Kobee** www.kobee.co.uk · 01382 221811 Overlooks the waterfront area (though not the water itself). The new Dundee had to have a Japanese restaurant and this one (with token Thai and an Indonesian rendang curry) is a pretty good go at the genre. Tepanyaki, with performing chefs (though not on Mon), a roomy though rather atmos-less room. A welcome break from Italy & India. 7 days lunch & dinner.

953 8/Q23
£15-25
✓ **Manchurian** 15A Gellatly St · www.manchuriandundee.com ·
01382 228822 In an unprepossessing street between the waterfront and main street and above an Oriental supermarket, one of the best restaurants for dim sum in any Scottish downtown. Huge menu. Spacious room; from both outside and in, this feels like Chinatown. 7 days lunch & dinner.

954 8/Q23
£15-25
✓ **The Agacan** 113 Perth Rd · www.agacan.co.uk · 01382 644227 Since 1983 Dundee's fabled bistro for Turkish eats and wine (and beer). Brilliantly boho with much (rotated) art, chosen by Zeki Agacan and his once art lecturer wife, on the walls. You smell the meat (veggies go meze). Tue-Sat dinner only.

955 8/Q23
£25-35
✓ **Piccolo** 210 Perth Rd · www.piccolodundee.co.uk · 01382 207149 An intimate dining experience (only 9 tables) with chef/patron Athol Shepherd in the hot kitchen, cramped but civilised out front. Many regulars though newbies may feel this place is a bit, well, up-itself. Definitely more ristorante than mere tratt. Well-priced wine list. Tue-Sun dinner only.

956 8/Q23
L
ATMOS
£15-25
✓ **The Ship Inn** Broughty Ferry · www.theshipinn-broughtyferry.co.uk · 01382 779176 There's nowt nicer than heading down 'The Ferry' and on the front, weathered by the River Tay since the 1800s, this cosy pub that has sustained smugglers, fishermen and foodie folk alike. Bar and upstairs restaurant; no-nonsense Scottish menu and a fabulous picture window overlooking the Tay. Bar food and upstairs restaurant (best book). 7 days. See 1316/GASTROPUBS.

957 8/Q23
<£15
✓ **T. Ann Cake** 27 Exchange St · 01382 203950 In a street of good food options (Castlehill above and the Cheesery), this charmingly named caff (owned by Ann, of course) has good cred and good crit, both savoury and sweet. Individual and cool as. Closed Sun/Mon.

958 8/Q23
<£15
✓ **Fisher & Donaldson** 12 Whitehall St · www.fisheranddonaldson.com · 01382 223488 The best traditional bakers in Scotland (1432/BAKERS) with busy tearoom and 2 other Dundee branches. Snacks and all their fine fare from maccy cheese to chocolates. Mon-Sat 8am-4.45pm (shop till 5.15pm).

959 8/Q23
£15-25
Malabar 304 Perth Rd · www.malabardundee.co.uk · 01382 646888 More than a few Indian restaurants in Dundee, but for authenticity and sympatico service and surroundings, the Chacko family's Malabar (for nigh on 10 years) has the (soft) edge. Avowedly south of the subcontinent, and though not as vegetarian as might be expected, mellow sauces and good seafood curries. Wed-Sun 5.30-10pm.

960 8/Q23
<£15
Visocchi's Broughty Ferry · www.visocchis.co.uk · 01382 779297 Following from the original Kirriemuir caff (now no relation): a busy tratt and ice-cream parlour. Over 3 generations they've made mouth-watering Italian ice creams (amaretto, cassata, etc.) and ice-cream cakes, alongside home-made pasta (and less good pizza) and snacks. Hard work and integrity evident here. Lovely prints on the walls by Leon Morrocco, and dad Alberto. Closed Mon.

961 8/Q23
<£15
The Parlour West Port · www.theparlourcafe.co.uk · 01382 203588 Opposite the Globe Bar, this wee caff at the end of the row of shops is easily missed but loyal locals and students pack it for home-made light food, tortes/tortillas, soups, salads and big slabs of cakes. Lunch & LO 5pm, 7pm Sat. Closed Sun. Good vegetarian; and... they have their own cookbook.

962 8/Q23
<£15
Folk Café 118 Nethergate · 01382 228794 The downtown cousin of The Parlour; same approach & menu on a prominent corner. 7 days.

963 8/R23
L
£15-25
The Glass Pavilion Broughty Ferry · 01382 732738 Overlooking the Tay but tricky to find; easier to walk E from Broughty Ferry Castle and harbour, about 1km. Food so-so but the glass pavilion is a modern reconstruction of an Art Deco gem. Pictures of old Broughty Ferry beach and Esplanade are worth the trip alone (2037/WALKS). Nice coffee and terrace. 7 days 9.30am-10pm.

The Best Tratts:

964 8/Q23
£15-25
Borgotaro Broughty Ferry · www.fort-hotel.com · 01382 737999 Part of the Fort Hotel and at TGP just possibly the best (though small) of the pasta/pizza parlours. A top spot in 'The Ferry'! 7 days from 5pm till late.

965 8/Q23
£15-25
Italian Grill City Sq · www.italiangrill.net · 01382 690600 Brasserie-style contemporary spacious room and terrace on Dundee's classy central square. Grills and the P & P! 7 days lunch & dinner.

966 8/Q23
£15-25
True Kitchen Whitehall Crescent · 01382 225023 A 2-floor pizza parlour and tratt by the waterfront, the former their speciality (thin & crispy) with a great maccy cheese. **Jam Jar** adjacent is a refreshingly urbane cocktail bar and hang-out.

967 8/Q23
£15-25
Don Michele Perth Rd · www.donmichele.co.uk · 01382 660600 Over 10 years many folks' fave. Home cooking from the Lochis. 7 days lunch & dinner.

968 8/Q23
£15 25
Ciao Sorrento Union St · www.ciaosorrentodundee.co.uk · 01382 221760 Well-regarded midtown tratt which does everything it says on the tin (or pizza box or website). Standard fare, though. Lunch Fri/Sat only, dinner Tue-Sun.

The Best Tearooms & Coffee Shops:

969 8/Q23
Avery & Co S Tay St · www.averyandco.co.uk · 01382 201533 Cool caff near Dundee Rep with lunch & dinner menus. Fresh, natural, local. 7 days.

970 8/Q23
Express Oh! (aka Pacamara) Perth Rd Quite far up Perth Rd, a convivial coffee shop and great cuppa, soups, paninis, etc. 7 days.

971 8/Q23
The Palais Union St · 07842 155730 Downtown, off Nethergate. Cosy, retro tearoom where Tanja and Jacqueline serve tea and cake (mum and gran also bake) and breakfasts, soups, etc. Nice soundtrack. Open daytime.

972 8/Q23
The Camperdown House Tea Room Camperdown Country Park · www.dundeeandangus.ac.uk/tearoom · 01382 834834 Summer tearoom in the lofty, glorious atrium and library of the big hoose in Camperdown Park. Closed for decades, reopened 2014. 3 sittings for afternoon tea. A social enterprise by Dundee City Council and Dundee & Angus College. Check website for opening.

If you're in Perth...

WHERE TO STAY

973 8/P23
15 ROOMS
DF
MED.EX
✓ **Parklands** www.theparklandshotel.com · 01738 622451 Near station overlooking expansive green parkland of South Inch. Reasonable town mansion hotel with a reputation for food under chef/proprietor Graeme Pallister who also cooks at **63 Tay Street** (927/PERTHSHIRE).
EAT Smaller, 63 @ Parklands for fine dining. Closed Tue/Wed. The larger room, No. 1 The Bank, has eclectic menu; fusion going on. Top hotel dining in this town.

34 ROOMS
NO PETS
MED.INX
Huntingtower Hotel nr Perth · www.huntingtowerhotel.co.uk · 01738 583771 Crieff road (1km off A85, 3km W of ring route A9 signed). Decent modernised mansion-house hotel outside town. Good gardens (that copper beech!). Subdued, panelled restaurant; decent menu (folk come for lunch) and wine list. Business-like service (and weddings!).

39 ROOMS
MED.INX
The Royal George www.theroyalgeorgehotel.co.uk · 01738 624455 By Perth Bridge (lit at night) over the Tay to the A93 to Blairgowrie. Georgian proportions and nostalgic niceties, all unapologetically old style. Big on high tea, especially on Sundays. Weddings and functions. Perth does gather here.

WHERE TO EAT

<£15 ✓✓ **Small Talk** High St · 01738 634770 A tearoom, proudly traditional (no website, lots of word of mouth). Best place to eat during the day but you'll have to wait or book. 7 days daytime only. Report: 1379/TEAROOMS.

£15-25 ✓ **Pig'Halle** www.pighalle.co.uk · 01738 248784 Paula and Herve Tabourel's very French bistro; some standards, some innovation. Poisson du jour, trotters in filo. Good service & wine list. Best downtown choice in a town well served by la cuisine française. 7 days lunch & LO 9/9.30/10pm.

£15-25 ✓ **Santé** www.sante-winebar.co.uk · 01738 449710 A wine bar/restaurant that gives Perth a chic place to hang out and graze. Open all day, brasserie-style, from coffee to nightcap (great by-the-glass selection) and excellent plats, plats du jour and a tapas menu with Spanish chefs. 7 days morning till late.

£15-25 ✓ **Grand' Italia** www.granditaliaperth.co.uk · 01738 626016 Iris and Mario's excellent ristorante in the town centre does all that it says on the tin, i.e. the menu outside. Better than La Lanterna opposite and possibly the best Italian food in the shire. 7 days noon-9.30/10pm.

£25-35 **Café Tabou** www.cafetabou.co.uk · 01738 446698 Central corner of a pedestrianised square (one day they'll get City Hall sorted); from outside and in, it feels like an unassuming *café de la place*; locals go. French staff, French wine and a reasonable pass at French country food. 7 days lunch & dinner.

£15-25 **Breizh** www.cafebreizh.co.uk · 01738 444427 Breizh (pronounced Brez), the Breton name for Brittany, is a buzzy eaterie: galettes galore, salads, grillades, good pizza and home-made puds. Good food all-round. 7 days from 9am till 9/9.30pm.

£15-25 **Reids** www.reidscafe.com · 01738 636310 Next to Breizh, another good cafe/restaurant but with a Scottish – and unlike others in this town, an authentic Scottish – flavour. Food though is eclectic, including Italian, and all home-made, including the bread (which is for sale). Great casual dining! 7 days.

£15-25 **Tabla** www.tablarestaurant.co.uk · 01738 444630 Credible Indian under the Kumars. North and south cuisine. Farm-grown spices from family in India. Open kitchen. A big plus for ethnic eating in Perth. Lunch (not Sun) & dinner.

<£15 **Holdgate's Fish & Chips** 01738 636922 Here for over 100 years! A classic with reconstructed caff through the back. Well-sourced haddock; their fritters! Veg oil. Noon-8.30pm (Sun 3-8pm).

 ✓✓ **63 Tay Street** Report: 927/PERTHSHIRE.

✓ **Deans @ Let's Eat** Report: 930/PERTHSHIRE.

Tourist Information Centre High St · 01738 450600 Open AYR.

The Best Hotels & Restaurants In The North East

Excludes Aberdeen (except Marcliffe); see p. 182. Speyside listings on p. 187.

974 6/S19
35 ROOMS
7 SUITES
DF
MED.EX-LOTS

✓✓ **Marcliffe at Pitfodels** Pitfodels · www.marcliffe.com · 01224 861000 En route to Royal Deeside, 5km from Union St. On the edge of town, a successful mix of intimate and spacious, the old (mansion house) and the newer wing are still personally run by the Spence family: Stewart Spence the consummate hotelier; his son Ross is head chef. Their many pics on the piano with the famous (both Margarets – the princess and Mrs Thatcher; and that other T, The Trump) attest to this hotel's enduring primacy. Excellent restaurant and breakfast in light conservatory with nice courtyard and terrace overlooking gardens. Spa facilities (no pool). Honeymoon suites are fab; there are many weddings and rollicking Aberdonian functions. This understated hotel caters for all and is unquestionably one of the best all-round hotels in Scotland. To wide concern and disappointment there was a wobble in 2014 when this grand old Deeside Duchess might have been unseated. Happily, there's no keeping those Spences out of the palace.

975 6/R20
18 ROOMS
DF
ATMOS
MED.EX

✓✓ **Raemoir House** Banchory · www.raemoir.com · 01330 824884 5km N from town via A980 off main street. Romantic, quirky country mansion with old-fashioned, very individual comfy rooms given contemporary details. Flowers, pictures, candles at night. The Ha' Hoose (from 1715) behind predates the hotel. Extensive grounds (helicopter pad). Owner Neil Rae is very hands-on, with a great team; you will be looked after. From the kitchen uncomplicated, delicious dining (new chef since I was there). There's lots of public space to slouch in. Staff largely local and all friendly! This place has the perfect peace and quiet and is decidedly Deeside!

976 6/S18
29 ROOMS
DF
MED.EX-EXP

✓✓ **Meldrum House** Oldmeldrum · www.meldrumhouse.com · 01651 872294 1km from village, 30km N of Aberdeen via A947 Banff road. Immediately impressive chunk of Scottish baronial set amid new 18-hole golf course (private membership, but guests can use) and a lake with swans. Rooms large with atmos and nice furnishings; many original antiques and period pictures. Lodge with contemporary rooms in stable block, and in 2016 another expansion will almost double the accom. A lot of cash has gone into restoring this landmark Aberdeenshire hotel to its former glory: the deluxe choice for business (especially whisky industry) and the golfing fraternity. Expect weddings – increasingly big weddings. Nice afternoon tea.

977 6/R20
8 ROOMS
DF
MED.INX

✓✓ **The Boat Inn** Aboyne · www.theboatinnaboyne.co.uk · 01339 886137 Behind the prominent green, off the road connecting to the South Dee road. Recent refit and big uplift of long-serving riverside inn, with comfy, contemporary, inexpensive rooms, and a great bar and food operation downstairs. Eileen and David Haywood and a good team have floated this boat and made it a Deeside destination for good gastropub food, including on Tue (pie night), Wed (fish) and Thu (local produce). They are known for their fish & chips. Same menu in bar and restaurant. There is simply nowhere else to eat of an eve; thankfully it's as good as it is.

978 6/R19
27 ROOMS
L
EXP

✓ **Pittodrie House** nr Inverurie · www.macdonaldhotels.co.uk · 01467 681444 A large family mansion house on an estate in one of the best bits of Aberdeenshire with **Bennachie** above (1943/HILLS). 30km Aberdeen; well signed. Comfortable rooms look out on verdant lawns and topping trees. Exquisite walled garden 500m from house and many walks around. A Macdonald hotel (possibly their best) with very individual rooms in old house and a new extension out back. Period pictures, great whisky bar. Afternoon tea a treat (and includes a 'gentleman's' version). Many weddings!

979 6/S20
28 ROOMS
DF
MED.EX

✓ **Banchory Lodge** Banchory · www.banchorylodge.co.uk · 01330 822625 Downhill from the main town crossroads, the B974 to Strachan, S Dee and the Falls of Heugh. Recent makeover of riverside hotel in suburban Banchory (well, it's all suburban really and a caravan lurks behind the hedge on the long driveway) transformed it into a major food (though not foodie) spot: a restaurant, in the bar, a dining room and outside deck (same menu). Rooms fine (refurbished in the separate Cobbleheugh building behind at TGP). The river setting here is superb.

980 6/T17
20 ROOMS
L
MED.INX

✓ **Tufted Duck Hotel** St Combs, nr Fraserburgh · www.tuftedduckhotel. co.uk · 01346 582481 Here's a surprise: though 'only 40 mins from Aberdeen', this very well-appointed boutique-style hotel, 8km S of Fraserburgh by the B9033, is a real find. You go a fair way for contemporary accom and cool, casual dining on this coast. Tiny village, lovely views and some serenity, with Loch of Strathbeg Nature Reserve nearby. I do confess I haven't been but the Duck gets rave reviews from readers. More reports please.

981 6/R17
5 ROOMS
DF
MED.INX

£15-25

✓ **The County Hotel** Banff · www.thecountyhotel.com · 01261 815353 Eric and Vida Pantel's love letter from France. Notable mainly for food in dear sleepy Banff. Bistro (L'Auberge) restaurant and bar (lunches and bar suppers Mon-Sat). Menu has tartiflette, proper terrine and salade champêtre. Burgers et al in the bar but the food here is quite something; an appreciative letter from Alex Salmond is one of many flapping on the noticeboard by the door. Rooms basic; charmant secret garden. **EAT** Where to eat on this long coast. Eric makes and bakes everything.

982 6/S18
6 ROOMS
CHP

✓ **The Red Garth** Oldmeldrum · www.redgarth.com · 01651 872353 This family-run (the Singers) inn (signed from main road system) has only 6 rooms but it's great value; food is very popular locally. Stuart does everything, including the garden. View of Bennachie. Nice flowers. Very Aberdeenshire.

983 6/Q20
7 ROOMS
DF
MED.INX

✓ **The Auld Kirk** Ballater · www.theauldkirk.com · 01339 755762 On Braemar road heading out of town. It is indeed an auld kirk and Peter Graydon and Tony Fuell make the most of the ecclesiastical shapes and ambience. Bedrooms (2 standards) are tasteful, contemporary boutique-style. B&B only.

984 6/R18
18 ROOMS
NO PETS
MED.INX

Castle Hotel Huntly · www.castlehotel.uk.com · 01466 792696 Behind the spooky ruin of Huntly Castle; take the B9022 off the A96 for 2km, then signed. Former dowager house of the Dukes of Gordon, family-run and not bad value for the faded grandeur (with recent titivations) and the setting. Nice period feel.

THE BEST RESTAURANTS IN THE NORTH EAST

985 6/S18
>£35

✓✓ **Eat On The Green** Udny Green · www.eatonthegreen.co.uk · 01651 842337 Former pub, now a restaurant on a cute village green. Folk come from miles for this celebratory, unpretentious food that's great value. Chef/proprietor Craig Wilson has cooked for Alex Salmond, Sir Sean and often Scotland but he's still always here to cook for you. This is one of Scotland's premier country restaurants, with recent expansions upstairs (2 private dining rooms) and out the back into the garden, attesting to its destination status. Metropolitan decor is a long way from publand. Food elegant, simple. Craig talking of book at TGP, ambitions undimmed on the distant green (only 30 mins from Aberdeen); you'll be pushed to get in at weekends. Wed-Fri & Sun lunch & dinner Wed-Sun.

986 6/S20 ✓ **The Cow Shed** Banchory · www.cowshedrestaurantbanchory.co.uk ·
£15-25   01330 820813 Just outside this expanding Deeside hub on Raemoir Rd,
essentially in the country – you look to the hills. Graham Buchan's light, big-windowed restaurant and cook school has a no-frills menu. Some chefs just accord with one's taste and Graham does. I could eat just about everything on this light and easy-to-love menu. Local and lovely! Lunch 7 days & dinner Wed-Sat.

987 6/S20 ✓ **Buchanan's** Banchory · www.buchananfood.com · 01330 826530 Turn
£15-25   right at Tesco as you enter town from Aberdeen; 1km signed. Adjacent Woodend Barn arts centre (home to an eclectic, quality mix of music, theatre and film), the bistro in the barn is a contemporary, urbane, informed eaterie on the edge of Banchory, the prospering heart of Royal Deeside. Val and Calum Buchanan have an enlightened grow-your-own approach (there are allotments out back) and this airy bistro demonstrates the best kind of rural re-creation. Their daily breads are fantastic. I could eat here every day (and would be so much healthier!). 7 days.

988 8/S20 ✓ **The (Art Deco) Carron Restaurant** Stonehaven · www.carron-
£25-35   restaurant.co.uk · 01569 760460 Discreet location off main street in a fantastic and faithfully restored Art Deco building, under new ownership 2015. The lighting could be softer but they don't make 'em like this any more. A Modern-Scottish menu, and friendly and efficient service. Closed Mon/Tue.

989 6/S20 ✓ **Milton Restaurant** Crathes · www.miltonbrasserie.com · 01330 844566
£15-25   On A93 Royal Deeside road, 4km E of Banchory, opposite the entrance to **Crathes** (1502/GARDENS; 1826/HOUSES). Contemporary restaurant in old steading adjacent craft village, event field and railway (sic). Light and pleasant space. Rather fine brasserie menu for lunch & dinner, daytime snack menu in the Conservatory. With the art gallery, the Wee Boorachie furnishings, decor and craft shop, this is an all-round good diversion (even the kids' playground by the river is lovely). Brasserie: lunch 7 days (Sun noon-5pm) & dinner Fri-Sat. Conservatory: 7 days 9.30am-4pm.

990 6/S19 **Echt Tandoori** Echt · www.echttandoori.co.uk · 01330 860601 On the B9119
<£15   N of Banchory and 24km W of Aberdeen via Westhill. An unlikely outpost of Nepal, perhaps, but here is where to find what many consider to be the best Indian food in the city or shire. Crisp linen, candlelight, roses. Extensive menu, big portions; tandoori dishes best. Krishna Gurung a modest (and much-loved locally) chef/proprietor. Tue-Sun lunch & dinner.

991 6/T19 **Cock & Bull** Balmedie · www.thecockandbull.co.uk · 01358 743249 On A90,
DF   20km N of Aberdeen. Atmospheric roadside pub long a fixture here but increasing
L   reputation for grub and winning awards; a strong team in the kitchen. A lot of
£15-25   Aberdeen Angus. Very pubby and intimate, oak beams, etc. Always busy. 7 days.

✓ **The Tolbooth** Stonehaven Report: 1341/SEAFOOD.

✓ **The Lairhillock Inn** nr Netherley, Stonehaven Reports: 1006/ABERDEEN.

✓ **The Black-Faced Sheep** Aboyne Report: 1384/TEAROOMS.

✓ **The Creel Inn** Catterline, nr Stonehaven Report: 1313/GASTROPUBS.

✓ **Raemoir Garden Centre** Banchory Report: 2193/GARDEN CENTRES.

The Best Places To Stay In Aberdeen

✓✓ **Marcliffe at Pitfodels** Pitfodels Aberdeen's premier hotel: nothing else is close for old-style comfort and service. Report: 974/NE HOTELS.

992 6/S19
54 ROOMS
NO PETS
MED.EX

✓✓ **The Chester Hotel** Queen's Rd · www.chester-hotel.com · 01224 327777 A complete and high-spec refurbishment of previous hotel on this site, 2km from Union St (adjacent to Malmaison below). 'Luxurious' but often inexpensive (oil business seeping from Aberdeen, perhaps), with good-value classic and grand rooms. Restaurant and bar in adjoining building; both are night-out destinations. Small gym & spa.
EAT Well-laid-out bar (casual food menu) and extensive restaurant – the city's most flash. Kevin Dalgleish executive chef, seafood bar, Josper oven. Top-notch nosh at TGP. Lunch & dinner. Bar food noon-9pm.

993 6/T19
185 ROOMS
NO PETS
MED.EX

✓ **Park Inn By Radisson** Justice Mill Lane · www.parkinn.co.uk/hotel-aberdeen · 01224 592999 Though we don't do chains in the main, for location, style and convenience, this has to get a mention. Just behind the west end of Union Street, in an area of some of the city's best bars and restaurants. Contemporary and efficient. No pool, small gym, parking adjacent.

994 6/T19
39 ROOMS
NO PETS
MED.INX

✓ **Bauhaus Hotel** Langstane Place · www.thebauhaus.co.uk · 01224 212122 Excellent downtown location for a *soi-disant* boutique hotel. Not exactly an homage to Le Corbusier and the Modernists but good quality, no fuss and nice furniture. 3 standards of room all good value. B&B only; good bars and restaurants adjacent (see below). Parking 100m.

995 6/S19
79 ROOMS
MED.EX
£25-35

✓ **Malmaison** Queen's Rd · www.malmaison.com · 01224 327370 2km from centre, a welcome find in Aberdeen, though perhaps a little tired now. Usual design values of the brand here put to notably good use. Ambient, accessible. ESPA spa, no pool. Rooms cosy and cool; you might say seductive.
EAT Large, well-laid-out brasserie: you dine surrounded by wine; meat in the larder and animals on the walls, so veggies pass by. They like their steak here!

996 6/T19
7 ROOMS
NO PETS
NO KIDS
CHP

✓ **The Globe Inn** 13 N Silver St · www.theglobeinn-aberdeen.co.uk · 01224 624258 Rooms above the Globe, the civilised pub in a street off Golden Sq. Pub has good reputation for ales, food (and live music Tuesday and weekends, so no early to bed). Accom is reasonably priced. Breakfast is continental and comes on a pre-packed tray with flasks – not a strong point. Since decent value and individuality are hard to find in Aberdeen, book ahead. Parking is cheap in nearby square.

997 6/S20
40 ROOMS
NO PETS
L
MED.EX

Maryculter House Hotel Maryculter · www.maryculterhousehotel.com · 01224 732124 Excellent setting on banks of Dee: riverside walks and an old graveyard and ruined chapel in the priory. The hotel is on the site of a 13th-century preceptory. Newer annex; rooms overlook river. Poacher's Bar is special, dining room not; food not a strong point. At weekends this hotel can be a wedding factory! Fishing rights on Dee (though further up river).

998 6/T19
14 ROOMS
NO PETS
CHP-MED.INX

City Centre Hotel Belmont St · www.aberdeencitycentrehotel.co.uk · 01224 658406 Beneath and part of Siberia (a fairly full-on bar with great deck overlooking Union Terrace Gardens) in a busy street off Union St. Opened '09, an upmarket bedbox for urban sophisticates and whoever you meet in the night. All subterranean. Voddy-fuelled sessions up; breakfast down(stairs).

999 6/T19
83 ROOMS
MED.INX

The Caledonian Hotel Union Terrace · www.thehotelcollection.co.uk · 01224 640233 Victorian edifice, one of several city centre hotels off Union St, The Caley, an institution and time-tested, always seems the easiest to deal with; the most likely to be calm and efficient. Taken over in 2015 by The Hotel Collection group. Dining room and on-street bar/brasserie. Some nice suites overlooking the gardens. Location's the thing!

The Best Places To Eat In Aberdeen

1000 6/T19
ATMOS
£15-25

✓ **Café 52** The Green · www.cafe52.net · 01224 590094 Below the east end of Union St in the 'Merchant Quarter': go down the steps or approach via Market St. A sliver of a cosy bistro with outside terrace. It has a kind of boho chic. Chef/owner Steve Bothwell keeps customers happy with unusual dishes but comforting combinations prevail. Mum does the puds and supplies herbs and leaves from her organic garden. Café 52 is still the biz! Busy at (good-value) lunch. Lunch then tapas and dinner. LO 9.30pm (4pm Sun). Bar till midnight.

1001 6/T19
<£15

✓ **Food Story** Thistle St · www.foodstorycafe.co.uk Food Story's story is a great Aberdeen story. From small takeaway beginnings they expanded into larger premises nearby, then knocked them into what is now a spacious always ambient café to hang out in and eat ethically and heartily. A couple of meaty items but mostly vegetarian and vegan. Creative approach to lounging, living and lunch. Lara and Sandy have done a good thing here. Closed Sun.

1002 6/T19
£25-35

✓ **Yatai Izakaya** Langstane Place · www.yatai.co.uk · 01224 592355 West end of Union St opposite Bauhaus Hotel (above), adjacent to Orchid (below) and Dusk cocktail bars, none of which are chains, so a cool Aberdonian corner. Any city would be pleased to have this Japanese eaterie with tapas-style eating (Omakase) in ambient rooms up and down (Japanese restaurants often minimal, even clinical), with superior sakes, beers and wine list. And credible edibles.

1003 6/T19
£25-35

✓ **Adelphi Kitchen** 28 Adelphi · www.theadelphikitchen.co.uk · 01224 211414 In a lane off Union St. Chris Tonner's breakout bistro La Stella morphed into a charcoal grill and seafood restaurant, which literally went up in (some) flames in 2015. We haven't been since but we know it will be perfectly judged and routinely full. Big-choice grill menu with many (mainly fish) specials. From amuse-bouche to petit fours, this is fine bistro dining at great prices.

1004 6/T19
£25 35

✓ **Fusion Bar & Bistro** N Silver St · www.fusionbarbistro.com · 01224 652959 Fusion has been an Aberdeen foodie fixture since, well, fusion became a buzzword. Restaurateur Mark Cavanagh's flagship fine diner and still a place to eat and be seen. Cocktails, interesting wine and an eclectic menu; straightforward 3 choices changing monthly. Not fusion food in the conventional sense but diverse and creative. Good value. Closed Sun/Mon.

1005 6/T19
ATMOS
£15-25

✓ **Le Café Bohème** Windmill Brae · www.cafebohemerestaurant.co.uk · 01224 210677 Authentic French bistro, atmos and food in an area that gets drunk at weekends. Here, all is calm with style and good service. Food proper French from chef John Pattillo, à la carte and plats du jour (especially seafood). Best place to eat by far in this part of the city centre. Closed Sun/Mon.

1006 6/S20 ✓ **The Lairhillock Inn** nr Netherley, Stonehaven · www.lairhillock.co.uk ·
ÁTMOS 01569 730001 Not in the city at all but a 200-year-old roadside inn at a
£15-25/ country crossroads to the S. Head S on A92, turn off at Durris then 5km. Long
£25-35 famous for food and informal atmos in conservatory lounge and bar (same menu).
The **Crynoch** adjacent available for functions. Inn 7 days lunch & dinner.

1007 6/T19 ✓ **Silver Darling** Pocra Quay · www.thesilverdarling.co.uk · 01224 576229
LLL Didier Dejean still on the stoves in this exemplary seafood bistro in a perfect
ATMOS spot. Not so easy to find: head for Beach Esplanade, the lighthouse and harbour
>£35+ mouth (Pocra Quay). The light winks and ghostly boats glide past. Upstairs dining
room not large and you so want to be by the window. Menus vary with catch and
season. Apposite wines; every one a winner. Due desserts. Long-serving but still
the best and most dynamic location of any seafood restaurant in the land. Long
may it ride these waves (though for sale at TGP). Closed Sun.

1008 6/T19 ✓ **Moonfish** Connection Wynd · www.moonfishcafe.co.uk · 01224 644166
£15-25 Down steps from east end of Union St. Discreet location in 'Merchant Quarter'
and still a bit of an Aberdeen secret, this easy-on-the-eye, informal caff/restaurant.
Highly rated local, with chef Brian McLeish, turns out simple good food with some
panache. Usually 4 starters/mains/puds, each with 4 listed ingredients. Tue-Sat.

1009 6/T19 ✓ **Number 1 Bar & Grill** Queen's Terrace · www.number1restaurant.co.
£25-35 uk · 01224 611909 Parallel to Albyn Pl, the west end extension of Union St.
Basement bar and grill related to Fusion (above), highly regarded hereabouts because
quite simply it's a classy joint with good, contemporary food and smart, friendly
service. Nice conservatory at the back. The 'donians dig it! Mon-Sat lunch & dinner.

1010 6/S19 ✓ **The Broadstraik Inn** Elrick, Westhill · www.broadstraikinn.co.uk ·
ATMOS 01224 743217 Not in the city but on the main A944 to Alford at Elrick near
£15-25 Westhill, about 12km city centre. Roadside pub since 1905, gastrofied and civilised,
and a destination with a reputation for good food and smart service. Great for
families early evening. 7 days lunch & dinner.

1011 6/T19 **Howie's** Chapel St · www.howies.uk.com · 01224 639500 Follows successful
£15-25 formula once made in Edinburgh in classic/contemporary bistro style, this
discreetly fronted restaurant presses all the right Aberdonian buttons (including the
price!). A reliable redoubt. 7 days lunch & dinner.

1012 6/S19 **Café Cognito** St Swithin St · 01224 209727 In the West End. Unlikely sharing of
£15-25 premises with a nail bar, where ladies have their nails done in a kind of pod at the
side. Doesn't detract though from this buzzy, popular café from breakfast through
lunch to supper. So busy it is that sometimes a tad cramped through the back (I say
get rid of the nails!). One of the few places you can get an actual Aberdeen buttery
(you must try) for your brekkie (better than croissants). 7 days.

1013 6/T19 **Angus & Ale** Schoolhill · www.angusale.com · 01224 643324 Bang in the
£15-25 centre. Can't fail formula of decent burger and a craft ale in 'studentville'; by people
who know what Aberdeen wants. Much better here than the gastroburger chain
thing. 7 days 11am-11pm.

ITALIAN

1014 6/T19 — **Rustico** Union Row · www.rustico-restaurant.co.uk · 01224 658444 If this
£15-25 — were French I'd say it had the *je ne sais quoi*, but it is most definitely Italian (Sicilian
actually). Tony and Nikos' love for Sicily evident (their brill photos on the walls)
though Nikos is Greek. And the food is well above the tratt average: everything
home-made, including the puds. A happy crew here (always a good sign). 7 days.

1015 6/T19 — **Carmine's Pizza** Union Terrace · 01224 624145 A tiny slice of a room for *the*
<£15 — best pizza in town and behind, slaving over a hot stove, the eponymous, much-
loved, curvy Carmine. Take away (to the gardens opposite). Real pasta in basic
spag/tag/penne variants in no-frills caff. Brill! Lunch & dinner. Closed Sun.

EASTERN

1016 6/T19 — **Yorokobi by CJ** Huntly St · www.yorokobibycj.co.uk · 01224 566002
£15-25 — Authentic Japanese/Korean restaurant by chef/proprietor Jang – that's Chef Jang to
you and me. Sushi, sashimi and maki rolls, this is a share-and-savour kind of place
but there are teriyakis and even curry. Setting perhaps less inspired than the food.
Closed Sun/Mon.

1017 6/T19 — **Jewel In The Crown** Crown St · www.thejewelaberdeen.com · 01224 210288
£15-25 — Way down the street on corner with Affleck St. The Ahmeds have been serving up
great North Indian food for over 30 years, home-made and authentic. Recent flash
makeover; some say the best curry in town – always arguments about that (see
below), though not from the sons of Farooq Ahmed who work like a football team
to make this a top spot. Mon-Sat lunch & LO 11pm, Sun 2.30pm-10.30pm.

1018 6/T19 — **Shri Bheema** Belmont St · www.shribheemas.co.uk · 01224 645555 A
£15-25 — doorway in busy with bars Belmont St, up unpromising stairs and through a door
into the Bheema, apparently the people's choice for curry (there's another branch
in Balgownie Rd, Bridge Of Don 01224 821155). You wouldn't think of this place
until you asked around as I did, but it consistently comes tops for a straight-up
curry. 7 days lunch & dinner.

1019 6/T19 — **Nargile** Skene St · www.nargileaberdeen.co.uk · 01224 636093 Turkish
£25-35 — survivor that has made regulars happy for 30 years. But the newer **Rendezvous @
Nargile**, 106-108 Forest Ave (01224 323700), is the lighter, brighter version on a
suburban corner whose constant buzz attests to destination status. Ms Iridag, wife
of the original owner, cooks here. Both do definitive and enormously popular meze.
Both open 7 days. Times vary.

✓✓ **Hammerton Store** Great Western Rd Report: 2164/SHOPS.

✓ **The Tippling House** Belmont St See below.

The Best Bars In Aberdeen

1020 6/T19
ATMOS
✓ **The Prince of Wales** St Nicholas Lane · www.princeofwales-aberdeen. co.uk · 01224 640597 St Nicholas Lane, just off Union St at George St. An all-round great pub (by Belhaven) always mentioned in guides and one of the best places in the city for ale: Old Peculier, Caledonian 80/ and guests. Very cheap self-service food till 8.30pm. Wood, flagstones, booths. Large and very pub-like; gets very crowded.

1021 6/T19
ATMOS
✓ **Ma Cameron's** Little Belmont St · www.macamerons-aberdeen.co.uk · 01224 644487 Labyrinthine old pub (dating back 300 years and the oldest in the city), named after the wife who took it over in 1937. Plenty of different spaces to eat and sup: intimate snugs and the busy main bar; there is even a beer garden on the roof. Pub grub classics till 9pm. A Belhaven pub with 3 changing ales.

1022 6/T19
ATMOS
✓ **The Grill** Union St · www.thegrillaberdeen.co.uk · 01224 573530 Here in the middle of the main street, i.e. Union St, since 1870. Historic, atmospheric, solid, and a great place to drink. Mahogany gantry of superb whisky range (served in a Glencairn Glass), ales and craft beers. Integrity is intact and evident. No ladies served here until 1973; their other principles have endured.

1023 6/T19
✓ **Under the Hammer** N Silver St Time-served basement bar. Forever and a day favourite (and certainly mine) in Aberdeen. No snooker, no sports, no food. Candlelight, ales, open-mic nights and the mellow vibe.

The first four pubs above are old style. The next three are new style.

1024 6/T19
✓ **Orchid** Langstane Place · www.orchidaberdeen.com In West End behind Union St. Stylish bar for hipsters and discerning drinkers in relaxed and contemporary ambience. Big on cocktails, served by knowledgeable mixologist types. Open late so a good crowd after 11. 7 days 6pm (Fri 5pm) till 2am (3am Fri/Sat).

1025 6/T19
✓ **The Tippling House** Belmont St · www.thetipplinghouse.com Through a door by an interesting window and down a few stairs in busy-with-riff-raff Belmont St into a more calm and cool with itself world. More of a restaurant/ cocktail bar than mere pubbery here. Small plates and sharing platters, with imaginative combos. And great 'sliders' (burgers). Food served until 1 hour before bar closes so this is the place to eat late. Bar 4pm-2am (3am Fri/Sat). From 1pm Sat.

1026 6/T19
The Albyn Albyn Place · www.thealbyn.com · 01224 211666 All-round, full-on, very Aberdonian night out kind of place W of Union St. You can dine, drink extensively, even dance. There's a big outside terrace/garden when on one afternoon and in a civilised way we watched Wimbledon on the big TV. Live bands Fri/Sat. 11am-1am (2am Fri/Sat).

✓ **The Globe Inn** N Silver St Report: 996/ABERDEEN.

✓ **The Lairhillock Inn** nr Stonehaven Report: 1006/ABERDEEN.

✓ **Cock & Bull** Balmedie Report: 991/NE RESTAURANTS.

The Best Hotels in Speyside

1027 6/P17
15 ROOMS
DF
MED.EX

✓ **Knockomie** nr Forres · www.knockomie.co.uk · 01309 673146 Well placed for the Moray Coast, Inverness and your golfing and Speyside meanderings. Gavin and Penny Ellis are discreet, fastidious hosts in this comfortable but contemporary mansion house, which is more a gastro inn with rooms than a stuffy manor with manners. Informal dining, nice whisky-oriented bar. Comfortable in its tree-surrounded country self, though the suburbs have arrived.

1028 6/Q18
28 ROOMS
NO PETS
L
MED.EX

✓ **The Craigellachie Hotel** Craigellachie · www.craigellachiehotel.co.uk · 01340 881204 The quintessential Speyside hotel, off A941 Elgin to Perth. A major refurbishment 2014 returned Craigellachie to much of its past glory; it is the pre-eminent (actually on) Speyside hotel. Good for fishing, walking (**Speyside Way** at the bottom of the garden 1968/WALKS) and distillery visits (1497/WHISKY). Public rooms very hotel-like; bedrooms OK – you want one overlooking the river. The food is sufficient and the Quaich bar is for lovers of the dream and the dram.

1029 6/P18
11 ROOMS
L
MED.INX

✓ **Archiestown Hotel** Archiestown · www.archiestownhotel.co.uk · 01340 810218 Main street of village in the heart of Speyside near **Cardhu Distillery** (1498/WHISKY). Over the years I've warmed to Jane and Alan Hunter's village inn/hotel with comfortable rooms and bistro, which comes with a long-standing reputation for good food. In fact I've decided it's quite the epitome of the good village inn. All very lived-in, especially by fishers. A plethora of armchairs to lounge in and take a dram (many to choose from).

1030 6/Q18
5 ROOMS
MED.INX

The Mash Tun Aberlour · www.mashtun-aberlour.com · 01340 881771 Off main street behind the church by a lovely river meadow park. A restaurant/pub with rooms above (all named after whiskies). This is a very Malt Trail destination that's boutique standard, informal and better value than most. 2 of the 5 rooms are higher spec. Pub has nice ambience and good grub.

1031 6/Q18
19 ROOMS
MED.INX

Aberlour Hotel Aberlour · www.aberlourhotel.co.uk · 01340 871287 On main street of whisky (and Walkers Shortbread town). Recent refurbishment has rendered it serviceable if soulless. Large restaurant. Town bar. Decent value.

1032 6/P17
23 ROOMS
NO PETS
MED.EX

Mansion House Elgin · www.mansionhousehotel.co.uk · 01343 548811 This mansion house in grounds below the monument to the last Duke of Gordon is also overshadowed by a 24-hour Tesco, in a suburb somewhat encroaching on its serenity. Comfy enough and all the public rooms, except the very interior bistro, are lovely. Leisure facilities include a small pool and gym. Best in Elgin.

1033 6/Q18
16 ROOMS
MED.INX

Dowans Hotel Aberlour · www.dowanshotel.com · 01340 871488 Above river and charming town signed off the A95 to/from Grantown. Solid mansion and solid Speyside hospitality, though oddly you approach from the back. Inside all is pleasant and comfortable. 150 malts in the bar. Fishermen- and whisky-corporates-friendly. Inexpensive. Scottish menu in bistro or posher dining room.

The Best Hotels In The Highlands

See also Inverness, p. 198; Skye, p. 387-89; Outer Hebrides, p. 396-97.

1034 7/K21
17 ROOMS +
LODGE
DF
LL
ATMOS
LOTS

✓✓ **Inverlochy Castle** Torlundy · www.inverlochycastlehotel.com ·
01397 702177 5km from Fort William on A82. Scotland's long-established
flagship Highland hotel is filled with sumptuous furnishings, elegant decor and
occasional film stars, luminaries and royalty. Owner Mr KC Chai insists on old-style
hospitality in this, the anchor hotel of expanding ICMI group; Inver Lodge, Lochinver
– see both below; and **Greywalls** near Edinburgh (873/LOTHIANS). As you sit in the
atrium after dinner, perhaps with someone tinkling the piano, marvelling at the
ceiling and stylish people swishing up and down the staircase, you know this is no
ordinary country-house hotel. And it has all you expect of a castle; the epitome of
grandeur and service. Huge comfortable bedrooms, the antlered billiard room, acres
of rhododendrons, trout in the lake, tennis and a lovely terrace; though no spa or
pool. Dog kennel. The big Ben is over there.
EAT A dining destination open to non-res. Michelin-starred Philip Carnegie many
years on these sacred stoves. J&T a must for dinner in an old-style setting.

1035 5/H16
7 ROOMS
NO KIDS
ATMOS
LOTS

✓✓ **Pool House Hotel** Poolewe · www.pool-house.co.uk · 01445 781272
Once owned by Osgood MacKenzie who founded the nearby gardens
(1500/GARDENS). With immaculate style and determination the Harrisons have
transformed this Highland home into one of Scotland's must-do stopovers. The
new lavish Chinese suite adds to the others, fastidiously themed around the ships
who sailed from here when the house was a WWII HQ; the Boathouse overlooking
the river mouth and the bay, all tweedy and cosy with a woodstove; HMS Diadem
with Titanic memorabilia (they will explain). All rooms are meticulously assembled
and hand-painted by daughter Liz. Bathrooms are fabulous. This has been a labour
of love for the whole family and for this standard, is great value. Dinner is a treat
here and on summer Sundays there may be a BBQ in the pavilion in the kitchen
garden. Home-baked afternoon tea on request. Go luxuriate in their remarkable
achievement. They close Mon.

1036 6/N17
8 ROOMS
LOTS

✓✓ **Boath House** Auldearn, nr Nairn · www.boath-house.com ·
01667 454896 Signed from A96 3km E of Nairn. A small country-house
hotel in a classic, immaculately restored mansion: Don and Wendy Matheson's
family home with superb landscaped grounds, and Michelin-starred dining. Comfy
public rooms with local artists' pics. Bedrooms (3 woodland, 2 lake, 2 downstairs
with their own conservatory and a cottage overby) are home from home with great
bathrooms. Chef Charlie Lockley's 6-course (the full experience) or 3-course (no
choice, so declare diet first) dinner is the finest (and in no way overstated) dining in
the north, much of it foraged and farmed nearby. You'll have had your afternoon
tea (1428/AFTERNOON TEA). Service impeccable; friendly and local. Delightful
grounds include Wendy's immaculate walled garden (from whence your salad &
veg), a lake where deer come to drink and a big heron waits motionless for its
dinner; you watch while having yours. Beautiful **Brodie** nearby (1754/CASTLES).

>£35 **EAT** Mr Lockley: intuitive, great judgement, Michelin-starred and 4 AA rosettes.
Cooking: organic, slow and from the kitchen garden. Set menu. The Boath
experience: this dinner, those gardens. Good life in a nutshell.

1037 4/J14
5 ROOMS
NO PETS
NO KIDS
MAR-DEC

✓✓ **The Albannach** Lochinver · www.thealbannach.co.uk ·
01571 844407 2km up road to Baddidarach as you enter Lochinver on the
A837. Lesley Crosfield and Colin Craig's uniquely beautiful boutique hotel in the
north: ancient splendid landscape around you, contemporary splendid comfort to
return to. The Byre suite overlooks the Croft from its own conservatory and hot tub.

LL
LOTS

The Loft has its own terrace. Colin has put these immaculate rooms together with admirable DIY determination. Your stay revolves around Lesley's 5-course fixed (so declare diets up front): locally sourced, seasonal and fabulous (especially seafood). Non-res can also dine. Suilven is the big mountain over there as you linger in the conservatory or on a relatively midge-free terrace, contemplating its grandeur. They also have the **Caberfeidh** in the village (1082/HIGHLANDS).

EAT Maybe the smallest team (Lesley and Colin) and smallest kitchen in the Michelin galaxy, so even more remarkable. Laid-back and inexpensive for this standard.

1038 5/M18
11 ROOMS
NO PETS
LOTS

Rocpool Reserve Inverness · www.rocpool.com · 01463 240089
Above the town, a determinately urbane hotel now owned by the people who have Inverlochy (above). Though look and feel are poles apart, service is similarly top. Room categories somewhat off-putting ('extra decadence', anyone? See 1097/INVERNESS) but they do exceed expectations.

EAT Albert Roux's no-nonsense French food brilliantly done for a fraction of what you'd pay in London. See *Best Places To Eat In Inverness, p. 199–200*.

1039 5/M18
30 ROOMS
LOTS

Glenmoriston Townhouse Inverness · www.
glenmoristontownhouse.com · 01463 223777 Along the riverside
opposite Eden Court Theatre. No expense was spared in the conversion of 2 adjacent buildings into a chic boutique and urban hotel in the early 21st-century ascendance of Inverness. Rooms split 50/50 between main hotel and adjacent Windsor House, the latter refurbished to urban-chic standard, with rooms overlooking the river; the old building more traditional. Piano bar and bistro/brasserie, **Contrast**, where breakfast is served, overlooks the river. All a smart, well-oiled operation. See *Best Places To Eat In Inverness, p. 199 200*.

1040 5/M18
28 ROOMS
DF
LL
LOTS

Culloden House Inverness · www.cullodenhouse.co.uk ·
01463 790461 5km E of town near A9, follow signs for Culloden village
not the battlefield. Easiest approach from A96 Nairn road, turn right at first roundabout after the mall. Hugely impressive Georgian mansion and lawn a big green duvet on edge of suburbia and, of course, history. Near town and airport. Demonstrates that sometimes old style is the best style. Lovely big bedrooms overlooking the policies. Some fab suites in main and separate garden house. Elegant dining in beautifully conserved room under long-serving chef Michael Simpson. Garden House is adjacent to an immaculately restored 4-acre walled garden, yours to wander. Fabulous trees include redwoods. Tennis courts. A true country house (but close to town) courtesy of Culloden's caring American owners.

1041 5/M20
8 ROOMS
NO PETS
FEB-DEC
MED.INX

The Cross Kingussie · www.thecross.co.uk · 01540 661166 Off main
street at traffic lights 200m uphill then left. Tasteful hotel and long-regarded restaurant in converted tweed mill by the river which gurgles outside most windows. Comfy rooms. Derek and Celia Kitchingman continue the reputation of this slightly out-of-the-way discreet find.

EAT Deal probably includes dinner which is so what you want, but also open to non-res. Imaginative, even ambitious, menu.

1042 5/L17
4 ROOMS
APR-OCT
MED.EX

The Dower House nr Muir of Ord · www.thedowerhouse.co.uk ·
01463 870090 On A862 between Beauly and Dingwall, 18km NW of
Inverness and 2km N of village after the railway bridge. Charming, personal place; you are the house guest of Robyn (in the kitchen) and Mena Aitchison, your empathetic hosts. Cottagey-style, lived-in, small country house (an Editor's Choice, *The Good Hotel Guide 2015*), with comfy public rooms and lovely garden with pond for G&T moments. Packed lunch for those fishing. Lovely dinner (residents only).

1043 4/K14 ✓ **Blar Na Leisg at Drumbeg House** Drumbeg · www.blarnaleisg.com ·
4 ROOMS + 1   01571 833325 No signage to help you find this fabulous restaurant with rooms
CHALET behind the Drumbeg Hotel in the village between Kylesku and Lochinver (1621/SCENIC
NO PETS ROUTES). Eddie and Anne Strachan keep out of sight but foodies beat a path to their
MAR-OCT kitchen door. Have to admit I still haven't eaten but all reports tell me this is good,
MED.EX very good. Fixed 4-course menu so discuss fads up front. Eddie's small but selective
wine list. You eat round the expandable table. Good contemporary art surrounds you
(some of it Eddie's); rooms are modest and modish. A stylish home from home in the
back of a beautiful beyond (with otters, pine marten and deer).

1044 5/N16 ✓ **Glenmorangie House** Cadboll, nr Fearn · www.theglenmorangiehouse.
6 ROOMS + 3   com · 01862 871671 S of Tain 10km E of A9. Old mansion in open grounds
COTTS overlooking a distant sea. Owned, like the distillery, by Moët Hennessy-Louis
NO PETS Vuitton (LVMH) so expect some luxury (understated in public areas but all-
LOTS embracing in bedrooms). No leisure facilities but no shortage of distractions
around (the 'seaboard villages', the dolphins, **Anta Factory** and **Tain Pottery**
2145/2146/SCOTTISH SHOPS). Open fires and communal, house-party atmos.
Afternoon tea; fixed dinner round one table, honesty bar; great service.

1045 4/J15 ✓ **The Summer Isles Hotel** Achiltibuie · www.summerisleshotel.com ·
13 ROOMS   01854 622282 40km from Ullapool with extraordinary views over the isles;
DF Stac Polly and Suilven are close by. A long-established romantic retreat on the
APR-OCT strand at Achiltibuie, with a range of comfortable, contemporary rooms in the main
LL hotel and adjacent cottage conversions. Local sourcing here means scallops from
LOTS the bay, lamb and beef from own croft, veg and salad leaves from a hydroponic
garden. You couldn't get fresher and lighter than this. Fixed menu with their famous
cheeseboard of mainly Scottish cheeses (all in perfect condition; they offer a cheese
flight with selected libations) in a fixed 6-course menu. Adjacent pub offers similar
quality food at half the price (1303/GASTROPUBS). Lots to do outdoors, including boat
trips and don't miss some of the best views of Scotland nearby (1640/VIEWS).
EAT Great fine dining with a view. Fixed (truly individual) menu and a celebrated
cheeseboard. And the sunset over the Isles. Bar menu is great value.

1046 4/N15 ✓ **Royal Marine Hotel** Brora · www.royalmarinebrora.com · 01408 621252
21 ROOMS +   Turn-of-century mansion house by Robert Lorimer overlooking the harbour
APARTS and self-catering apartment block newly built overlooking the golf course. Great for
DF golfers, a civilised stopover for the rest of us. Contemporary public rooms;
MED.EX bedrooms vary. Spa has very decent pool. 3 dining options including 'fine', with
complementary atmospheres.

1047 4/N16 ✓ **Royal Golf Hotel** The First Tee, Dornoch · www.royalgolfhoteldornoch.
22 ROOMS   co.uk · 01862 810283 Comfy, not-too-golfy golfing hotel by Dornoch's
MED.EX famously fabulous golf course. On a much more human scale than others of the ilk
further S. Casual dining, whisky bar and conservatory restaurant overlooking course
and distant waves.

1048 4/J14 ✓ **Inver Lodge** Lochinver · www.inverlodge.com · 01571 844496 Here a
21 ROOMS   long time on the hill overlooking the bay and the harbour but not in *StB* until
DF taken over by the never-less-than-excellent ICMI group, who have **Inverlochy**
MAR-OCT **Castle** and **Greywalls** (1034/HIGHLANDS; 873/LOTHIANS) in an expanding
LL collection. House here is a bit austere though comfortable, but it's dinner and that
EXP view that you probably come for. Albert Roux's menu and the estimable manager
Nicholas Gorten hereabouts these 20 odd years. Lovely 'bar bites' till 6pm. No
leisure facilities but there's a surprising sauna.

1049 7/K21
7 ROOMS
DF
LL
LOTS

✓ **Glencoe House Hotel** Glencoe · www.glencoe-house.com ·
01855 811179 By Glencoe village, a Victorian estate house and once the local
maternity hospital. Between a country-house and an apartment hotel. Deluxe suites
with open fires and Highland views (some with private terraces and hot tubs).
Welcoming hall but no public rooms. Breakfast and dinner served en suite.
Inexpensive honesty bars but your privacy comes at a price. Glen Coe walks close by.

1050 5/M18
11 ROOMS +
2 COTTS
DF
EXP

✓ **Loch Ness Country House Hotel** Inverness · www.
lochnesscountryhousehotel.co.uk · 01463 230512 6km SW of town on
A82. Formerly Dunain Park, now rebranded with the magic Loch Ness moniker, the
old-style mansion-house, refurbished to a fairly high standard is a good alternative
to hotels in town. Gorgeous gardens; real countryside beyond. The Park restaurant
in various (3) cosy dining rooms with sound Scottish menu. Excellent wine and
malt list. Enviro-friendly garden (where the cottages are) and a great deck/terrace
for that warmer evening. Weddings at weekends in adjacent suite.

1051 5/M18
16 ROOMS
DF
EXP

✓ **Bunchrew House Hotel** nr Inverness · www.bunchrewhousehotel.com ·
01463 234917 On A862 Beauly road only 5km from Inverness yet completely
removed from town; on the wooded shore of the Beauly Firth. A historic and
atmospheric billet, but it mainly functions as a wedding hotel (so midweek stays
are more likely). Lovely dark public rooms and the light on the water.

1052 4/P12
14 ROOMS
MED.EX

✓ **Forss House Hotel** Forss, nr Thurso · www.forsshousehotel.co.uk ·
01847 861201 Georgian mansion house set in 20 (rare in these parts)
woodland acres by the meandering River Forss. This stretch of the river and the
foot of the lawn with its perfect pool and waterfall is yours to contemplate and (if
fortunate) to fish. It's quite exceptional and the main reason for the *StB* tick.
Rooms are spacious and comfortable (4 in separate River House, 2 in cottages),
conservatory is nice and the bar has an impressive malt list. Though long the only
decent hotel in the NE corner, it is a bit set in its ways: dinner 7-9pm (LO 8.30pm),
bar no later than 11pm. But fishermen will always throw a line into this river and if
you, passing-through tourist, toe theirs, you can enjoy their well-located if
inconsistent hospitality.

1053 7/J21
20 ROOMS +
5 LODGES
DF
MED.EX

✓ **Holly Tree Hotel** Kentallen · www.hollytreehotel.co.uk · 01631 740292
On A828 Fort William (Ballachulish)-Oban road, 8km S of Ballachulish Bridge.
On road and sea and once the railway; it was formerly a station. Convenient
location and superb setting on Loch Linnhe with views from all bedrooms (some
balconies) and dining room. Appropriate location for surf 'n' turf menu. Nice for
kids. Surprising pool and the jetty on the sea outside. 1144/KIDS.

✓✓ **The Torridon** Glen Torridon, nr Kinlochewe · www.thetorridon.
com · 01445 700300 At the end of Glen Torridon in immense scenery.
Highland Lodge atmos, big hills to climb. Now with adjacent **Torridon Inn**
(inexpensive, with bar and bistro). Report: 1192/GET-AWAY HOTELS.

✓✓ **Ackergill Tower** nr Wick Now stay by the night. Very special. Report:
1269/HOUSE PARTIES.

✓✓ **House Over-By at The Three Chimneys** Colbost, Skye Report: 2239/
SKYE.

✓✓ **Eilean Iarmain** Sleat, Skye Report: 2239/SKYE.

✓✓ **Kinloch Lodge** Sleat, Skye Report: 2239/SKYE.

✓✓ **Scarista House** South Harris Report: 2224/ISLAND HOTELS.

The Best Less Expensive Highland Hotels

1054 4/K15
13 ROOMS +
20 BUNKS
NO TV
ATMOS
CHP-MED.EX

✓✓ **The Ceilidh Place** Ullapool · www.ceilidhplace.com · 01854 612103 'Books, Music, Art' and Life: Jean Urquhart's oasis of hospitality, craic and culture in the Highlands, with daughter Rebecca in charge as Jean has many other matters N and S to attend to. What started out in the 1970s as a coffee/exhibition shop in a boat shed, spread along the row of cottages, now comprises a restaurant, bookshop, café/bar (and performance) area with bedrooms upstairs. Bar and restaurant go all day from famously good breakfast to dinner menu from 6.30pm (LO 9pm). Though it's hardly changed a bit, it's still on the button. Bunkhouse across the road offers cheaper accom: stay 'luxuriously rough'. Live music and events through the year (check the website) or you can simply sit in the cosy downstairs parlour or, if you're a hotel guest, in the lounge upstairs with honesty bar or on the terrace overlooking Ullapool where the boats come in.

£25-35 **EAT** Bar and restaurant areas in one big, happy room. All-day menu then supper. Puts the craic into casual dining.

1055 4/L12
7 ROOMS
DF
MAY-OCT
L
MED.INX

✓✓ **Mackay's** Durness · www.visitdurness.com · 01971 511202 In the centre and at the heart of a straggled-out township. Small but perfectly conceived and formed hotel at the corner of NW Scotland (literally where the road turns S again). In the Mackay family for generations. Fiona and Robbie have transformed this solid old house into a cool spot in this northern hemisphere where in summer the light lingers forever. Recently visited mid-summer – oh boy! Wood and slate. Discreet but efficient service. Comfy beds in calm, stylish rooms. No bar/restaurant; eat at the Sango Sands Oasis pub. Many interesting distractions nearby (2147/SCOTTISH SHOPS; 1561/BEACHES; 2073/GOLF; 1834/MONUMENTS, Smoo Cave, etc). As well as the adjacent bunkhouse (1162/HOSTELS), they now have 2 fabulous state-of-play new-build eco-cottages at Lade, 9km E, overlooking **Loch Eriboll** (1614/LOCHS). Sex, romance, nature. Go treat yourself in splendid isolation.

1056 5/M20
5 ROOMS
CHP

✓ **Coig na Shee** Newtonmore · www.coignashee.co.uk · 01540 670109 Road out of Newtonmore (which is just off the A9) for Fort William. Mansion house with light, contemporary feel and furnishings. Nice breakfast (they have free-range hens) and evening meals on request. **The Letterbox** (01540 673231) in the village also has good food, or repair to the **Silverfjord** (pronounced locally as Silfird!), 01540 661292. Back at CNS, the Bords are friendly and will tell you where else you can go. Exceptional value.

1057 7/J20
14 ROOMS
NO TV
DF
MAR-OCT
LL · ATMOS
MED.INX-EXP

✓ **Glenfinnan House Hotel** Glenfinnan · www.glenfinnanhouse.com · 01397 722235 Victorian mansion with lawns down to Loch Shiel and the Glenfinnan Monument over the water. No shortbread-tin twee or tartan carpet here; instead a warm welcome from the MacFarlanes, and managers, the Gibsons. Everything is just right here. Bar with atmos, craic and music (Thu); eat in bar or dining room. Cruise on the stunning loch (01687 470322). Great for kids and quintessentially Scottish. 1211/SCOTTISH HOTELS.

1058 5/M17
9 ROOMS
ATMOS
MED.INX

✓ **The Anderson** Fortrose · www.theanderson.co.uk · 01381 620236 Main street of town in the middle of the Black Isle. Restaurant, bar and reasonable rooms in very individual hotel notable for an extraordinary bottled ales and whisky collection and then the food. Rooms have a certain and well-chosen charm; in fact this place exudes boho-chic with a tartan trim. US owners diligent in their pursuit of approvals. Many accolades, including mine.
EAT Anne Anderson manages a perhaps unfeasibly long daily-changing menu (smokes the venison, makes the black pudding and just about everything else) in atmospheric bar and dining room. It's a find!

1059 5/L19
28 ROOMS
MED.INX

✓ **The Lovat** Fort Augustus · www.thelovat.com · 01456 490000 On edge of town, on the road to Fort William. Refurbished and very effectively run by the family of the people who brought us **Torridon** (1192/GET-AWAY HOTELS). A contemporary, comfortable roadside hotel, unquestionably the best hereabouts. Brasserie menu and lovely, light dining rooms for 5-course dinner. Good looks and smart service in the heart of the Great Glen.

1060 7/K20
4 ROOMS
NO PETS
APR-OCT
L
CHP

✓ **Corriechoille Lodge** Spean Bridge · www.corriechoille.com · 01397 712002 4 (riverside) km out of Spean Bridge on the small road by the station. Justin and Lucy Swabey's hideaway house facing the mountains. Beautiful corner of the country with spectacular views to the Grey Corries and Aonach Mor. Lovely set dinner, very simple cosy rooms. (No kids under 7 years). 2 turf-roofed self-catering chalets overby. Great walks begin here. Also 1201/GET-AWAY HOTELS.

1061 5/L18
12 ROOMS
NO PETS
MED.INX

✓ **The Loch Ness Inn** nr Drumnadrochit · www.staylochness.co.uk · 01456 450991 1km from the monster mash of Drumnadrochit. A functional roadhouse hotel, quite the best in the area and with a notable restaurant that's invariably full. The estimable Judy Fish from the **Applecross Inn** (1200/GET-AWAY HOTELS) has a hand in this and supplies the langoustines, etc.
EAT Lewiston Restaurant, the best casual meal between Inverness and Fort Augustus – may have to book; separate bar menu; the beer garden is out the back.

1062 7/J21
9 ROOMS
MED.INX

✓ **The Lime Tree** Fort William · www.limetreefortwilliam.co.uk · 01397 701806 At the roundabout as you come from the south. Regional and local art gallery (owner David Wilson's work for sale) with rooms above and a very good restaurant that makes you feel better about Fort William. Simple, convivial, contemporary atmos in the usually buzzing restaurant and the 2 comfy lounges of the Old Manse.

1063 7/K20
8 ROOMS
MED.INX

✓ **Old Pines** nr Spean Bridge · www.oldpines.co.uk · 01397 712324 3km Spean Bridge via B8004 for Garlochy at **Commando Monument** (1836/MONUMENTS). Open-plan pine cabin with wood stove, neat bedrooms and a huge polytunnel (where bits of your dinner come from). A very comfy, unpretentious hotel with great food; à la carte menu open to non-res lunch and dinner. Chickens run, the pines are old! And see 1142/KIDS.

1064 5/K20
26 ROOMS
APR-OCT
L
MED.EX

✓ **Glengarry Castle** Invergarry · www.glengarry.net · 01809 501254 A family-run hotel for over 50 years, in the charge of the younger MacCallums (mum still does the flowers and the scones!). Rhoddies, honeysuckle as you walk to the loch. Magnificent trees, and a newly restored castle in the grounds, the stronghold of the Macdonells: you may remember the famous portrait by Raeburn – the epitome of the fashionable Highland chief. 2 rowing boats at your disposal (and the brown trout). A romantic destination in every way. Big rooms.

1065 5/H17
11 ROOMS
DF
CLOSED JAN
LL
MED.EX

✓ **Tigh an Eilean** Shieldaig · www.tighaneilean.co.uk · 01520 755251 Chris and Cathryn Field's cosily furnished hotel on waterfront overlooks Scots pine island on loch (sea eagles swoop). Coastal Kitchen pub, transformed with upstairs bistro and deck overlooking the loch, is adjacent. Live music weekends. Dining room and the Kitchen busy with people, pizzas and specials. A good spot at the heart of a Highland village.

1066 5/M20
3 ROOMS
NO KIDS
FEB-NOV
CHP

✓ **The Rumblie** Laggan, nr Newtonmore · www.rumblie.com · 01528 544766 Off the A9 on the A86 midway between Dalwhinnie and Newtonmore to this eco-friendly and people-friendly B&B which takes its green agenda seriously. Organic breakfast and evening meal by arrangement. Nice garden; bike hire nearby at Wolftrax.

1067 5/H18
14/15 ROOMS
MED.INX

The Plockton Inn www.plocktoninn.co.uk · **01599 544222 & The Plockton Hotel** · www.plocktonhotel.co.uk · **01599 544274** Two stays in perfect Plockton (1549/VILLAGES) though the village is why we come. The Inn is away from the front. Some good cask ales in bar. Very basic rooms – 7 in hotel and 7 in more contemporary annex over the street. Bistro in labyrinth of rooms: mainly seafood. Tables on terrace in summer, back garden for kids; probably best for food. The Plockton Hotel is by the water's edge and is busier and buzzier, with better bedrooms. Pub and pub meals; always packed. May be noisy weekends.

1068 6/N19
34 ROOMS
MED.INX-EXP

Boat Hotel Boat of Garten · www.boathotel.co.uk · **01479 831258** Centre of village overlooking the steam train line and near golf course (2065/GOLF). Great old-style (Victorian/1920s) hotel, with a variety of rooms. There are also 6 chalet-type garden rooms: OK and quiet. Decent food in very pleasant bar, bistro and dining room: woody, tasteful and timeless.

1069 4/N16
24 ROOMS
MED.INX-EXP

Dornoch Castle Hotel Dornoch · www.dornochcastlehotel.com · **01862 810216** Main street of delightful Sutherland town with nice beaches, great golf and a cathedral made famous by Madonna who once got married here. Very castle-like (from 15th century), up-and-down building where rooms vary hugely, as do prices. Garden Restaurant (yes, on the garden) is up and down (for food) too. Great lounge bar for whisky and ales. Overall there is charm.

1070 5/N17
42/14 ROOMS
NO PETS
MED.EX
MED.INX

Hotels in Nairn: The Golf View www.crerarhotels.com · **01667 452301 & The Clubhouse** www.clubhousenairn.co.uk · **01667 453321** Both in suburban Seabank Rd, off the A96. Comfy Golf View, often busy, has 'The View' (of the sea). Clubhouse is the brasher arriviste with slightly lurid decor that may date quickly – inexpensive though, and the restaurant gets good local reports.

1071 5/L18
33 ROOMS
DF
MED.EX

Lovat Arms Beauly · www.lovatarms.com · **01463 782313** In lovely wee priory town 20 mins from Inverness. They say 'home away from home' and this old-style hotel run by the Fraser family for over 25 years is definitely that kind of thing. Rooms in hotel and 22 in separate townhouse behind. Good pub. All very Highland.

1072 4/M13
19 ROOMS
MED.INX

Tongue Hotel Tongue · www.tonguehotel.co.uk · **01847 611206** One of 2 hotels in Tongue at the centre of the N coast where Ben Loyal rises. The Hooks' hotel on the main road, the more presentable at present though a little more expensive. Nicely turned-out rooms. Lounge bar and candlelit dining room. Very Highland. The Brass Tap pub downstairs has atmos and many locals. Worth noting that **The Craggan Hotel** nearby at Melness, though with very basic rooms, is where locals eat (1096/HIGHLANDS).

1073 5/K18
8 ROOMS
DF
L
MED.INX

Tomich Hotel Tomich · www.tomichhotel.co.uk · **01456 415399** The inn of a quiet conservation village, part of an old estate on the edge of Guisachan Forest. Odd fact: the Golden Retriever breed was invented here! Near fantastic **Plodda Falls** (1594/WATERFALLS) and **Glen Affric** (1584/GLENS). Rooms pleasant and cosy. Use of pool nearby in farm steading; especially good for fishing holidays. 25km from Drumnadrochit by A831. Nice bar; personally run.

1074 4/K16
10 ROOMS
DF
CHP

The Arch Inn Ullapool · www.thearchinn.co.uk · **01854 612454** On the shore of Loch Broom along from the ferry, heart of the town and especially its music scene and festivals (Loopallu and Fèis). Most rooms have a view and may be on the street. Great pub food (no bookings taken); busy at weekends. An all-round good base and you sleep by the sea.
EAT Long-established, locally popular pub for food, with patio, and upstairs their restaurant notable for seafood (dinner only).

The Best Restaurants In The Highlands

1075 7/H22
MAR–OCT
L
£25-35

✓✓ **The Whitehouse Restaurant** Lochaline, Ardnamurchan · www.thewhitehouserestaurant.co.uk · 01967 421777 Sits above the ferry port as the Mull boats come in, a restaurant adjacent the village shop with all the right/best principles: local produce, organic, imaginative cooking. Ingredients from Mull and Lochaber – bay, woods and hedgerow. Sarah and Jane's award-winning, back-of-beyond bistro under chef Michael Burgoyne is a true destination in itself; often fully booked. Quiet days in Ardnamurchan begin here. Home-made everything and Scottish cheeses. Tue-Sat 11am-afternoon tea-dinner.

1076 4/M12
MAY–SEP
>£35

✓✓ **Côte du Nord** nr Bettyhill · www.cotedunord.co.uk · 01641 521773 This small (very small, precisely 10 seats) Highland croft bistro (ie French-influenced cooking) has something of a legendary status among foodies. Ingredients for the 8-course, no-choice menu really are sourced mostly locally on the far N coast. For Chris Duckham, also the local GP, cooking is a hobby. Sadly, I've never been but friends who have describe this 'experience' only in superlatives. May-Sep dinner only. Obviously, you must book. *Sans pareil* – it has to be 2 ticks!

1077 6/P17
<£15

✓✓ **The Bakehouse** Findhorn · www.bakehousecafe.co.uk · 01309 691826 Follow the one-way system round end-of-the-road village – you can't and mustn't miss it. Jan Boultbee and David Hoyle run this brilliant coffee shop/restaurant where you eat ethically and well. Home-made/home-grown/organic, naturally, part of the slow-food movement; all individually prepared. Mostly vegetarian though they do great burgers and breakfasts. 7 days 10am-4pm. Famous locally for David's bread (1439/BAKERS) and their Fri/Sat pizza nights Book!

1078 5/H18
MAR–OCT
L
<£15

✓ **Walled Garden Restaurant** Applecross · www.applecrossgarden.co.uk · 01520 744440 In N Applecross along the strand, 'The Potting Shed', at the back of a gorgeous walled garden. Ongoing restoration after years of neglect – enter via a pergola of roses (in summer). A destination coffee shop/restaurant like the Inn (1200/GET-AWAY HOTELS), making that harrowing drive worthwhile. Everything home-made and often from the garden or the sea over there. Breakfast, full-menu lunch and dinner. 7 days 'early till evening'.

1079 5/H18
L
£15-25

✓ **Plockton Shores** Plockton · www.plocktonshoresrestaurant.com · 01599 544263 Shores and village stores! On the foreshore of lovely little Plockton, an all-purpose eatery with fine home cooking making the most of location and hinterland (for ingredients). Decent vegetarian choice. Closed Mon; Mon/Tue in winter.

1080 5/M17
L
£15-25

✓ **Sutor Creek** Cromarty · www.sutorcreek.co.uk · 01381 600855 Near the seafront. An end-of-the-road (across the Black Isle) diner in Cromarty (1552/VILLAGES). Both a destination and a neighbourhood caff, conscientiously run by the Foxes, with focus on seasonal- and local-produce specials. Wood-fired oven turning out their quite famous crispy pizza. Noon-9pm. Winter hours vary. See **Couper's Creek** 1387/TEAROOMS.

1081 5/H18
LL
ATMOS
£25-35

✓ **Waterside Seafood Restaurant** Kyle of Lochalsh · www.watersideseafoodrestaurant.co.uk · 01599 534813 Not quayside, more platform-side by the busy port, off the road to Skye, that bridge in the distance. *Brief Encounter* location; being actually on the platform at the end of the line lends distinction to Jann and Neil MacRae's long-standing destination. Seafood from Kyle/Mallaig/Skye, i.e. very local. A la carte and blackboard. Mon-Sat dinner.

1082 4/J14   ✓ **The Caberfeidh** Lochinver · www.thecaberfeidh.co.uk · 01571 844321
£15-25   Main St as you come into the village. An old, now dining pub on the (sea)loch run by the estimable Lesley Crosfield and Colin Craig, from the landmark Highland hotel, the **Albannach**, up the road (1037/HIGHLANDS). Here, a pub (on the street) and a dining room overlooking the loch. Mainly small plates; tapas-style menu, with their impeccable seasonal sourcing policy. Lochinver's well served for folk who love their grub – this is a must eat. Closed Mon & Tue/Wed lunch in winter.

1083 4/P15   ✓ **La Mirage** Helmsdale · www.lamirage.org · 01431 821615 A bright little
£15-25   gem up Sutherland way and once a homage to Barbara Cartland, the romantic novelist, who lived nearby in this gorgeous wee village by the sea and strath. Snacks of every kind all day and great home cooking and baking from Don, son-in-law of Nancy Sinclair who famously put this caff on the map (her pic is on the wall). Great fish and chips (can takeaway). Open AYR.

1084 7/K20   ✓ **The Smiddy House** Spean Bridge · www.smiddyhouse.com ·
L   01397 712335 Near junction of A82 for Skye on A86 for Laggan, Messrs
£15-25   Bryson and Russell's carefully run restaurant with (4) rooms (and cottage apartment). Excellent, unpretentious fare all home made. Fish selection and great chargrill steaks. Especially good for vegetarian food and diets. Best in a wide area (including Fort William). Afternoon tea in light lounge with great choice of teas and tier of tea things (1430/AFTERNOON TEA). Best book.

1085 4/K14   ✓ **Kylesku Hotel** nr Kylestrome · www.kyleskuhotel.co.uk · 01971 502231
MAR-NOV   On A894, tucked down by Loch Glencoul where the boat leaves to see Britain's
LL   highest waterfall (1602/WATERFALLS). Tanja and Sonia's small quayside pub/hotel
£15-25   (8 relaxing, basic rooms, 4 with loch views and Willie's Hoose annex) serves great seafood in fabulous waterside setting with mighty **Quinag** behind (1927/HILLS). Food in bar or residents-only dining room. Noon-9pm. See also 1315/GASTROPUBS.

1086 5/N19   **Mountain Café** Aviemore · www.mountaincafe-aviemore.co.uk ·
<£15   01479 812473 On the main street above an outdoor shop, one of the better bets for food in this activity hub town. Great for breakfast and home baking (especially bread). Good vegetarian: they make everything and have own-branded deli. Big, big helpings for hungry outdoorsy types. But they ain't open for dinner. 7 days.

1087 6/N19   **Anderson's** Boat of Garten · www.andersonsrestaurant.co.uk ·
£15-25   01479 831466 On the main road to/from Aviemore and Carrbridge. The Andersons' family-run restaurant (Steve in the kitchen), a welcome dine-out around here where there are lots of visitors and not much good food on the go. Laudably, all home-made, including bread and many ice creams. Nothing fancy but an eclectic choice. Lunch & dinner. Great Sun lunch. Closed Mon/Tue in winter.

1088 4/N16   **Luigi** Dornoch · www.luigidornoch.com · 01862 810893 On the way into
£15-25   town. Smart-looking café/restaurant, a welcome find in dreamy Dornoch. Drop-in snack place by day with good Lavazza coffee; Euro Scottish menu in evenings. Open AYR from 10am. Dinner 7 days in summer.

1089 4/M16   **Crannag Bistro** Bonar Bridge · www.crannag.com · 01863 766111 Brill bistro,
£15-25   where you might least expect one in faraway Sutherland. Scottish, local as usual these days but with more than a soupçon of spice: Ian and Kathy Smith also have the Caledonian Curry Co., so venison etc with a twist. Might say 'a culinary oasis'; and in this quarter there's nowhere else. Must add: this is all based on hearsay – I've visited but never eaten. Tue-Sat dinner only.

1090 5/M17 **The Storehouse** nr Evanton · www.thestorehouseathome.com ·
<£15 **01349 830038** Roadside farm shop/deli and destination diner on A9 N of
Inverness, overlooking the firth. Locally sourced meats and various olives/haggis/
and mugs! (you get the picture). However, there's no doubting that they've got the
food just right – the self-service restaurant goes like a fair with all things irresistible
to the Scots and their kin (though not necessarily good for you). Often queues.
Lashings of cream. 7 days daytime only.

1091 6/P17 **The 1629** Lossiemouth · www.1629lossiemouth.co.uk · **01343 813743** Only
L found this beachfront taverna recently though it's been here dispensing pasta,
£15-25 pizza (and more recently tapas) to the Moray masses for 37 years. More informal
La Caverna tratt below. Nice outlook. The locals (always) know best! 7 days 10am-
9.45pm (LO). 1629 evenings only.

1092 5/N17 **The Classroom** Nairn · www.theclassroombistro.com · **01667 455999** At
<£15-25 top end of main shopping street in Cawdor St, a continuation. Contemporary
makeover (though some time ago now) in this conservative, golfy town. An airy
bar/restaurant; almost feels like a real brasserie. Good for kids, for afternoon tea
and grown-up dinner. 7 days morning to night.

1093 4/J14 **Riverside Bistro** Lochinver · www.lochinverlarder.co.uk · **01571 844356** On
<£15-25 the way into town on A837. This Lochinver larder is notable mainly for the vast
array of Ian Stewart's superb home-made pies (www.piesbypost.co.uk) and calorific
cakes (1435/BAKERS). The banoffi pie here is truly wicked. You can eat in or take
away. Conservatories out front and back. Bistro on riverside serves very popular
meals at night; using local seafood, venison and vegetarian. ·

1094 5/N16 **The Oystercatcher** Portmahomack · www.the-oystercatcher.co.uk ·
APR–OCT **01862 871560** On promontory of the Dornoch Firth (Tain 15km), this hidden
L seaside village (the only east-coast village that faces west) may bring back
£25-35 beach-plootering memories. Restaurant (a bistro by day – they switch rooms)
is a destination in itself, the wine list and malt choice truly extraordinary. Food
is inventive, multi-ingredient, always interesting. Bistro does 'hearty' or 'ample'
portions. A la carte and prix fixe menu for dinner. Closed Mon/Tue. Book.

1095 5/J18 **Carron Restaurant** Strathcarron · www.carronrestaurant.com ·
£15-25 **01520 722488** On A890 round Loch Carron (joins A87 Kyle of Lochalsh road) near
Strathcarron. A long-standing roadside diner and with new owners – the McGales
– since my last visit. A welcome location on this long road in great scenery, 2km to
Attadale Gardens (1526/GARDENS). Reports, please!

1096 4/M13 **Craggan Hotel** Melness, nr Tongue · www.thecraggan.co.uk · **01847 601278**
£15-25 Melness, a straggly township, in spectacular N coast scenery (1653/VIEWS). 6km
from the causeway W of Tongue. The 4 non-en-suite bedrooms are basic and very
inexpensive but folk come from far (and for 40 years) for their honest, entirely
home-made food. The real deal!

The Best Places To Stay In & Around Inverness

1097 5/M18
11 ROOMS
NO PETS
LOTS

√√ **Rocpool Reserve** Culduthel Rd · www.rocpool.com · 01463 240089
Looking down on the centre from above (great view from terrace) this self-consciously presented boutique hotel is owned by the expanding superlative ICMI group who have **Inverlochy Castle** (1034/HIGHLANDS) and **Greywalls** (873/LOTHIANS). Each room a design statement, divided into Hip, Chic or Decadent, and, er, ... Extra Decadent. You may feel you have to live up to the titles. 2 rooms have hot tubs on outdoor decks. Probably best to have someone to shag in these circumstances. As with others in the group, a restaurant under Albert Roux who has assembled a great team, and a great menu, which is most definitely worth sampling, even as a non-res. Solicitous and great room service; a top stay.

8 ROOMS
MED.INX

√ **The Heathmount** www.heathmounthotel.com · 01463 235877
Kingsmills, then centre (from Eastgate Mall). Fiona Newton's stylish boutique-style hotel – an Inverness secret stopover – with popular, and at weekends very busy, bar/restaurant. High standard of mod con; rich boudoir decor with personal attention to detail. Good value and friendly service.

82 ROOMS
DF
MED.INX

Columba Hotel Ness Walk · www.columbahotelinverness.com ·
01463 231391 An excellent central location overlooking the main bridge over the Ness and across the river to the castle. Pleasant and friendly. Rooms vary, some small, a little worn-down last time I visited (me, too!); you will want a river view. Very nice bar with good grub and outside tables.

84 ROOMS
DF
L
MED.EX

Royal Highland Hotel Academy St · www.royalhighlandhotel.co.uk ·
01463 231926 Literally on top of the station. Nice staircase and a recherché charm but rooms rather average. A surreal start to the day in the very interior breakfast room. Very much in the centre of things; definitely more functional than flash. Many of the old bods in the central foyer seem like they've been waiting for that train forever! A Rubens behind the desk sets a higher tone (no, not a real one!).

6 ROOMS
MED.INX

Moyness House Bruce Gardens · www.moyness.co.uk · 01463 233836
Accolade-gathering and TripAdvisor-rated suburban guest house over bridge S of river but 10-min walk to centre; on-street parking. Jenny Jones's friendly family house. B&B only. Writer Neil Gunn lived here; rooms named after his canon.

√√ **3 Good Hostels: S.Y. Hostel** Victoria Drive · www.syha.org.uk ·
01463 231771 Large official hostel (SYHA). More funky are the **Student Hostel** 8 Culduthel Rd (01463 236556) and **Bazpackers** (01463 717663).

√√ **Glenmoriston Townhouse** Ness Bank Smart riverside hotel. Independently owned and personally run with excellent service. Good brasserie. Report: 1039/HIGHLANDS.

√√ **Culloden House** 5km E near (but not adjacent to) the battlefield. Gracious living, splendid grounds. Report: 1040/HIGHLANDS.

√ **Loch Ness Country House Hotel** 6km SW on A82 Fort William road. Comfy country house just outside town. Report: 1050/HIGHLANDS.

√ **Bunchrew House Hotel** nr Inverness 4km N on the road to Beauly on the firth shore. Atmospheric and refined, often a wedding hotel but weekdays possible. Report: 1051/HIGHLANDS.

The Best Places To Eat In Inverness

>£35 ✓ ✓+ **Boath House** Auldearn, nr Nairn Well out of town off A96 3km E of Nairn, 30 mins from Inverness. 2-plus ticks from me to make the distinction that in the Highlands Michelin-star chef Charlie Lockley is cooking at another level. Report: 1036/HIGHLANDS.

1098 5/M18 ✓ ✓ **Rocpool** Ness Walk · www.rocpoolrestaurant.com · 01463 717274
£15-25 Corner of main bridge over river. Steven Devlin is a consummate host in this stylish bright, buzzy diner with accent on inexpensive daytime and eclectic evening menu. Still the consistently good place to eat in the centre of Inverness. Look no further – if you can get in! Forerunner of the Reserve (below). Mon-Sat.

£15-25 ✓ ✓ **Café One** Castle St · www.cafe1.net · 01463 226200 Over 10 years now that Norman MacDonald has been running one of the most in-tune-with-its-clientele restaurants in Scotland. With wine bar out front and 2 spacious rooms, it's quite apparent that this is Inverness's number one choice for an affordable dinner out. On a recent midweek visit, it was packed, when restaurants all around were empty. Seasonally changing menu, superb well-informed wine list (with huge by-the-glass choice) at good prices. Café One and Rocpool are the par excellence eateries in this ville. Closed Sun.

£25-35 ✓ ✓ **Rocpool Reserve Chez Roux** Culduthel Rd · www.rocpool.com · 01463 240089 3 rooms, private dining and terrace overlooking town. The Albert Roux experience: classic French à la carte at great prices. The 3-course dinner is good value and includes his signature floating soufflé. He ain't here of course (though he phones every week and comes several times a year) but the kitchen team are top. 7 days lunch & dinner.

£15-25 ✓ **Contrast** Ness Bank · www.glenmoristontownhouse.com · 01463 223777 Part of the Glenmoriston Townhouse (above), this bistro/brasserie quite French, informal and a light à la carte. Outside tables overlook the river. 7 days lunch & dinner.

£15-25 ✓ **The Mustard Seed** Fraser St · www.mustardseedrestaurant.co.uk · 01463 220220 Catriona Bissett's cool restaurant in architectural riverside room with good attitude and buzz. Contemporary menu, OK wine. A restaurant that emerged with Inverness foodtown in the noughties and is still packing them in. 7 days lunch & dinner.

£15-25 ✓ **Girvans** Stephens Brae Behind M&S. Fast-turnover food for all folks. Home-made and on the button. All towns should have an easy drop-in, reliable eaterie like this. 7 days. Report: 1370/CAFÉS.

£15-25 **Fig & Thistle** Stephens Brae · 01463 712422 New 2015 and immediately flavour of the season, the F&T is a 2-floor, contemporary wee bistro opposite the Eastgate shopping centre. By lovely Karen Smith and chef partner Steven Dewart, who once had a Pig & Whistle in Portugal. Light and bright it is; Mod-Brit/Scot menu. Lunch Tue-Sat & dinner Mon-Sat. Closed Sun.

<£15 **The Kitchen** Huntly St · www.kitchenrestaurant.co.uk · 01463 259119 In a glassy building on the river almost opposite its parent, The Mustard Seed (see above). On 3 floors so waiters work hard up and down those staircases as does the kitchen which you can watch on screen. Often all floors (though small) are packed. It's coz of the exceptional value (and a good burger). 7 days lunch & dinner.

£25-35 **Riva Restaurant** Ness Walk · www.rivarestaurant.co.uk · 01463 237377
Prominent (by main bridge) restaurant and (upstairs) tratt. Probably best in town. By
the Girvans (above). Contemporary room overlooking riverside. Decent Italian menu.
Riva lunch & dinner, outside tables, upstairs evenings only (P & P); lively room.

£25-35 **Riverhouse Restaurant** Greig St · www.riverhouseinverness.co.uk ·
01463 222033 Over the pedestrian bridge. Intimate restaurant with contemporary
food (mainly fish) from Allan Little, who knows his oysters, in an open kitchen. Gets
busy so can feel cramped but excellent reputation. Lunch Tue-Sat & dinner Tue-
Sun. Closed Sun in winter.

£15-25 **Riverside Restaurant** Bank St · www.riversiderestaurant.info ·
01463 714884 On town side of the river near pedestrian bridge. Small, friendly
café/restaurant – a high-tea kind of place. Solid and unpretentious evening menu
and ladies who lunch. Home-made and good value. Closed Sun/Mon.

£15-25 **Little Italy** Stephens Brae · 01463 712963 Up the brae from the Eastgate
Centre end of main street. Small, we do mean small, family-run (the De Vitas) tratt
that Inverness folk like. Authentic menu of everything you'd want that ends in a
vowel. Outside tables. Closed Sun.

£15-25 **Rajah** www.rajahinverness.com · 01463 237190 Downstairs in the lane
(between Church and Academy Sts, behind Queensgate), one of the best of several
curry houses. Here since 1982 and usually packed. Says it all! Will probably see off
all the nouveau Indians.

£15-25 **Sams** Church Street (next to Hootananny) · www.samscuisine.com ·
01463 713111 And this is the other (more recent) one. Invernessians swear by one
or the other.

£15-25 **La Tortilla Asesina** Top of Castle St · www.latortillaasesina.co.uk ·
01463 709809 Near castle and hostels. Reasonably authentic Spanish restaurant
serving the UK version of tapas, i.e. 2/3 portions as a meal. All the faves and some
variants are here with lots of *platos del día*. Rioja and the beers, of course. 7 days.

✓ **Castle Restaurant** Castle St Legendary caff of the Highlands. Hardest-
working kitchen in the North? Report: 1369/CAFÉS.

WHERE TO STAY

1099 7/J21
9 ROOMS
MED.INX

✓ **The Lime Tree** www.limetreefortwilliam.co.uk · **01397 701806** As you come from S the last hotel of many near the end of main street. Combines regional art-gallery space in the old manse, with (Victorian) rooms above and a (modern/rustic) newer extension. Bar/restaurant with open kitchen and terrace. David Wilson (his art on the walls) and Charlotte Wright run a convivial, cosmopolitan inn.

3 ROOMS
NO PETS
NO KIDS
MAR-NOV
MED.INX

✓ **The Grange** www.grangefortwilliam.com · **01397 705516** Overlooks the loch and the main road S. Look for Ashburn House on main A82 turning into Ashburn Lane. Joan and John Campbell have been running this superlative, contemporary B&B in bereft Fort William for years. Discreet, almost suburban house but great views from garden terrace and fresh, modern rooms with great bathrooms. **Ashburn House** (01397 706000) on the main road and water's edge has 7 rooms and gets a Michelin mench.

20 ROOMS
NO PETS
MED.EX

✓ **Nevis Bank Inn** www.nevisbankinn.co.uk · **01397 705721** On the main A82 to Inverness near the roundabout and road into Glen Nevis. Extensively refurbished hotel in contemporary style: neutrals, browns, stone and wood. Busy bistro. Better by far than several very dated stopovers in this town.

S.Y. Hostel Glen Nevis · www.syha.org.uk · **01397 702336** 5km from Fort William by picturesque but busy Glen Nevis road. The Ben is above. Grade 1. Many other hostels in area, especially **FW Backpackers** www.fortwilliambackpackers.com · **01397 700711** · Alma Rd.

Achintee Farm Glen Nevis · www.achinteefarm.com · **01397 702240** On approach to Ben Nevis main route and adjacent Ben Nevis Inn (see below). Guest house/self catering and bunkhouse in walkers' haven.

WHERE TO EAT

✓✓ **Inverlochy Castle** Torlundy 5km out on A82. In the forefront of hotels in Scotland. Victorian elegance, classically stylish; impeccable service. Restaurant is open to non-res but this is not casual dining. Report: 1034/HIGHLANDS.

MAR-OCT
L
£25-35

✓ **Lochleven Seafood Café** North Ballachulish From the A82 15km S at Ballachulish, take the lochside road to this award-winning seafood caff. Simply worth the drive. Report: 1334/SEAFOOD.

£15-25

✓ **The Smiddy House** Spean Bridge Busy bistro dining at busy Highland corner. Good vegetarian. Reports: 1430/AFTERNOON TEA; 1084/HIGHLANDS.

£15-25

✓ **The Lime Tree** www.limetreefortwilliam.co.uk · **01397 701806** At roundabout as you arrive from S or the S end of the main street. Restaurant of boutiquey hotel (see above) with good atmos, open kitchen and terrace. 4 starters/mains/desserts. Local sourcing; Scottish cheeses; neat wine list.

£15-25

✓ **Browns @ Nevis Bank Inn** www.nevisbankinn.co.uk · **01397 705721** The stylish bistro/brasserie of the Nevis Bank Inn (above), near the Glen Nevis turn-off. A place to eat à la mode in FW.

L
£15-25

Crannog Restaurant www.crannog.net · **01397 705589** Finlay Finlayson's long-established landmark restaurant on the waterfront. Freshly caught seafood mainly (one meat/one vegetarian) in informal bistro setting. Good wine list. Open AYR. 7 days lunch & dinner.

ATMOS **Ben Nevis Inn** Achintee · www.ben-nevis-inn.co.uk · 01397 701227 On main
<£15 approach to the Ben itself. Reach across river by footbridge from visitor centre or by
road on right after Inverlochy/Glen Nevis roundabout on A82 (marked Claggan and
Achintee; 3km). Excellent atmospheric inn in converted farm building. Good grub/
ale and walking chat. LO 9pm; bar 10.45pm. Thu-Sun in winter.

<£15 **The Grog & Gruel** www.grogandgruel.co.uk · 01397 705078 In downtown
Fort William, a long-established pub known for its ales and atmos, also does very
decent home-cooked Scottish pub grub. Upstairs restaurant. 7 days.

If you're around Wick & Thurso...

WHERE TO STAY

1100 4/P13 ✓ **Ulbster Arms Hotel** Halkirk · www.ulbsterarmshotel.co.uk ·
13 ROOMS 01847 831641 In middle of village off A9 10km S of Thurso. By the river which
MED.INX is there to be fished (the hotel has 13 beats). Refurbished to comfy and country-
stylish standard, unusually contemporary up Caithness way. Dining more
traditional in atmospheric bar or dining room.

4/Q12 **Natural Retreats** John o' Groats · www.naturalretreats.co.uk ·
0844 384 3166 Top of the North/end of the road inn (John o' Groats House Hotel)
of apartments and lodges, café and store. Self-catering but night stays possible.
Haven't been, didn't get that far. Reports please.

✓ **Forss House Hotel** nr Thurso · www.forsshousehotel.co.uk ·
01847 861201 8km W to Tongue off A836. Mansion by a magic river in woody
policies in a region where you may long for a tree. Report: 1052/HIGHLANDS.

WHERE TO EAT

✓✓ **Captain's Galley** Scrabster · www.captainsgalley.co.uk ·
01847 894999 The best dinner to be had on this coast. Seafood with
simplicity and integrity. Report: 1332/SEAFOOD.

1101 4/P12 ✓ **The Tempest Café** Thurso · www.cafetempest.vpweb.co.uk ·
<£15 01847 892500 On the harbour, a damned good café/tearoom, the best this
side of the waves. The MacInnes's make, bake and keep it real. All-day menu and
specials of comfort food in the north where the sea comes in. Closed Sun.

1102 4/P12 **Le Bistro** Thurso · 01847 893737 On the main road through at the end of the
<£15 pedestrianised main street. If you have to eat in Thurso, this is the long-established
local choice. A' things to a' folk, they have a bit of everything. Tue-Sat.

Thurso Tourist Information Centre Old Town Hall, High St · 01847 893155 &
Wick Tourist Information Point McAllans, 66 High St · 01955 602547 Both
open AYR.

Gay Scotland the Best!

EDINBURGH

1103 8/Q25 ✓ **The Street** www.thestreetbaredinburgh.co.uk · 0131 556 4272 Corner of Broughton St and Picardy Pl on the big roundabout by the Playhouse Theatre, a crossroads, as it were, of the gay village. Great people-watching, i.e. all kinds of people, with outside tables and big windows. Trendy Wendy made this over 12 years ago and it is still the spot to gather and gossip, and later, downstairs, dance (3am Fri/Sat). Quizzes, cabaret and food till 9pm.

1104 8/Q25 ✓ **CC Bloom's** Greenside Lane · www.ccbloomsedinburgh.com · 0131 556 9331 CC's is the city's longest-enduring gay nightspot. Once described as wonderfully cheesy, it's now more likely to serve wonderful cheese on its food menu. Only becomes gay gay later on; till 9/10pm it's a civilised pre-theatre rendezvous (it's next to the Playhouse). There's even an all-day breakfast. Late night, however, it's fun and frolics and deafening disco. 2 floors. Cruisy, of course. Queue weekends. 7 days. Bar 11pm-3am.

1105 8/Q25 ✓ **The Regent** Corner of Abbeyhill · www.theregentbar.co.uk · 0131 661 8198 A great neighbourhood bar for many reasons gay but not by design. Adjacent well-known cruising gardens. Friendly locals, relaxed, straight-friendly. They have many ales (Deuchars, Cally 80/ and guests). 7 days till 1am.

1106 8/Q25 **Planet** 6 Baxter's Place · 0131 556 5551 A happy, clappy place on the gay strip. Clubby and pre-club crowd dominate later but an unthreatening vibe in this long bar below the Playhouse. Karaoke and gals out to play. 7 days till 1am.

1107 8/Q25 **Café Habana** 22 Greenside Lane · 0131 558 1270 Adjacent CCs above and Playhouse Theatre. Banging music. Young crowd. Quite tiny really, so usually rammed. Line-up on the mezzanine so coming in is like arriving on the beach at Mykonos (i.e. you are immediately checked out, probably dismissed, then you can relax). Outside tables. 7 days noon-1am.

1108 8/Q25 **Café Nom de Plume** 60 Broughton St · 0131 478 1372 Very gay-friendly proper <£15 café-bistro with changing à la carte home-made food and nice people sitting around at the heart of the village! 7 days noon-9.30/10pm food, bar later.

1109 8/Q25 **Steamworks** Broughton Market · 0131 477 3567 At the end of Barony St, off Broughton St. Modern, Euro-style wet and dry areas. Cubies and lockers. Café. Dark room and cruise area. Mixed crowd. Part of the Village Apartments (see below). 7 days 11am-10pm.

1110 8/Q25 **No. 18** 18 Albert Place · 0131 553 3222 Sauna for gentlemen (mainly older). Discreet doorway halfway down Leith Walk. Dark room. Mon-Thu noon-10pm; Fri-Sun till 11pm. Cheaper after 8pm.

1111 8/Q25 **Ardmor House** 74 Pilrig St · www.ardmorhouse.com · 0131 554 4944 Quiet 5 ROOMS mix of contemporary and original design in a stylish guest house run by Robin, Barry MED.INX and Vera the schnoodle. Family room, so straight-friendly.

1112 8/M26 **Village Apartments** Broughton Market · www.villageapartments.co.uk · 4 ROOMS 0131 556 5094 Attached to Steamworks (above), 4 well-turned-out rooms (2 CHP 'deluxe'), central especially for the gay village (between the New Town and CC's). It is very gay accom though I have never stayed (well, I live along the street). Men only.

GLASGOW

1113 8/M26 ✓ **Delmonica's** 68 Virginia St · 0141 552 4803 Del's has been in this quiet lane at the heart of the Merchant City gay quarter for over 25 years (can it be that long?). Glasgow-stylish pub with long bar and open plan. Pleasant and airy by day but busy and sceney at night, especially weekends. It's nice if your face fits. Themed nights, karaoke, quizzes. 7 days till midnight (then the PL, below).

1114 8/M26 ✓ **Polo Lounge** 84 Wilson St · www.pologlasgow.co.uk · 0845 659 5905 Similarly long-established late-night venue with stylish decor. Smart service, themed nights downstairs. Gents' club meets Euro-lounge ambience. From 11pm, 3am licence; otherwise till 1am. Downstairs disco (with admission).

1115 8/M26 ✓ **Waterloo Bar** 306 Argyle St · 0141 248 7216 Scotland's oldest gay bar and it tells. But an unpretentious down-to-earth vibe, refreshing in its way. Long-in-the-tooth, like its clientele, very LGBT friendly. Good soundtrack, Sunday bingo! You might not fancy anybody but they're a friendly old bunch. 7 days noon-midnight.

1116 8/M26 ✓ **Underground** 6a John St · www.underground-glasgow.com · 0141 553 2456 In basement opposite Italian Centre, in the heart of the Merchant City. Civilised subterranea. Free juke box, pool, ale. Some uniform nights. Big on karaoke, or 'queeraoke' but most of the men will be men. 7 days all day to midnight.

1117 8/M26 ✓ **The Pipeworks** 5 Metropole Lane · www.thepipeworks.com · 0141 552 5502 E of St Enoch Centre, near Slater Menswear, down an unlikely lane. Scotland's most full-on (and modern) sauna labyrinth. 7 days (all night Fri/Sat).

1118 8/M26 **The Lane** 60 Robertson St · 0141 221 1802 Near Waterloo (above), across Argyle St, lane on right. You look for the green light. Sauna, private club with dark room. You wouldn't call it upmarket. 7 days, afternoons till 7/8pm.

ABERDEEN

1119 6/T19 **Cheerz** 2 Exchange St · www.cheerzbar.co.uk · 01224 582648 Evening gay bar and (next door) club later on. A cheeky z but a cheery kind of (local) gay as gay bar. Aberdeen's only LGBT (how can that be?). 6pm-midnight. Club till 2/3am.

1120 6/T19 **Wellman's Health Studio** 218 Holburn St · www.wellmans-health-studio.co.uk · 01224 211441 Through the archway halfway down Holburn St, west end of Union. A sauna to saunter: jacuzzi, steam, sauna and cabins. Very cruisy! 7 days.

DUNDEE

1121 8/Q23 **Out** 124 Seagate · 01382 200660 Bar and dance floor. Everybody knows everybody else, but not you. This may have its advantages. Wed-Sun till 2.30am. Also ...

1122 8/Q23 **B4OUT** 2 St Andrews Lane · 01382 200660 Behind and above Out (above). A pre-club bar on disco nights (reduced tickets available at bar). Till midnight.

1123 8/Q23 **The Klozet** 73 Seagate · www.klozetdundee.co.uk · 01382 226840 Mixed, mainly gay bar close to Out (above). Make a night of it.

1124 8/N24 **Number 11** 11 Princes St · www.number11.net · 01382 451986 Smallish steam, sauna and roaming bits. Noon-10pm (till 6pm Mon, 8pm Tue).

1125 8/Q23 **Salty Dog** 9 Crichton St, nr Nethergate Cosy (very cosy), good fun pub. Mixed but very gay-friendly. 2pm-midnight.

the
Best
Places to Eat & Stay

Superlative Country-House Hotels

1126 8/N24
232 ROOMS
DF
L
LOTS

✓✓✓ **Gleneagles** Auchterarder · www.gleneagles.com ·
01764 662231 Off A9 Perth-Stirling road and signed. Scotland's
truly luxurious resort hotel. For facilities on the grand scale; others pale into
insignificance. This is an international destination. Though it runs like a well-
oiled and beautiful machine, it is surprisingly human and welcoming – they make
you feel special from arrival (I'm sure this is not just me). In new hands 2015,
contemporising will follow! Sport and leisure activities include: shooting, riding,
fishing, gun-dog school, off-roading (even kids' jeeps), in my view Scotland's best
suite of swimming pools (one for lengths) with outdoor tub, and for inactivity the
spa is gorgeous (1264/SPAS). Gleneagles golf (3 courses plus 1 9-hole) is world-
renowned; the Ryder Cup was here 2014. Rooms both trad/luxe and contemporary
in the main house; the new wing Braid House contemporary and remote (in the
'handset to control temperature, lights, curtains and fireplace' sense). Strathearn
Restaurant is a foodie (if formal) heaven, though still has a bustling brasserie feel,
with state-of-the-sector service.
EAT Casual dining in Deseo: lighter, brighter Mediterranean. The Clubhouse
(200m) has an informal, top gastropub menu and Andrew Fairlie's intimate dining
room is Scotland's only 2 Michelin-star restaurant (926/PERTHSHIRE). Gleneagles
could be anywhere but it is quintessentially Scottish. It has airs and graces but it's
still a friendly old place. It is more than all right!

1127 7/J22
25 ROOMS +
2 COTTS
DF
FEB-DEC
LL
LOTS

✓✓ **Isle of Eriska** Ledaig · www.eriska-hotel.co.uk · 01631 720371
20km N of Oban (signed from A85 N of Benderloch). Hotel, spa and they do
say, island! As you drive over the Victorian iron bridge, you enter a more tranquil and
gracious world. Its 300 acres are a sanctuary for wildlife; you are not the only guests.
The famous badgers come to the door of the conservatory bar for their milk and
peanuts. This comfortable baronial house with fastidious service and facilities goes
from strength to strength, Beppo Buchanan-Smith developing it into a first-class
rural hotel resort; it has been in his family for 40 years. Rooms (named after islands)
are very individual. Two 2-bedroom and five 1-bedroom suites in spa outbuilding are
more contemporary, with private terraces and hot tubs. 2 (soon to be more) Hilltop
lodges are above all that; comfy, private and not expensive. Picturesque 9-hole golf,
great 17m pool and gym excellent in summer when it opens on to the garden. In the
spa, ishga and ESPA treatment rooms. Dining, with a distinctly Scottish flavour from
a rich backyard and bay, in elegantly remodelled dining rooms; the **Deck
Restaurant** above, overlooking the golf course has great casual dining (794/ARGYLL).
EAT Under Paul Leonard and Ross Stovold. Michelin star though delightfully
informal. Good value wine list; top cheeseboard (lots of Scottish interest).

1128 9/J29
17 ROOMS
DF
APR-DEC
LOTS

✓✓ **Glenapp Castle** nr Ballantrae · www.glenappcastle.com ·
01465 831212 Relais & Châteaux luxury in South Ayrshire S of Ballantrae.
Very discreet entrance (first right turn after village): no sign, and entryphone
system. From the oaklined cloakrooms on either side of the main entrance, even
before you go up the staircase to the lounges, you sense a soft enveloping
opulence. Home of Inchcape family for most of 20th century; opened as a hotel in
first year of 21st. New owners 2015, with ambitious plans to add new rooms (7 on
the unused top floor) and develop the stable block but keep the laid-back luxe.
Excellent and considerate service, top-notch food, impeccable interiors. The rooms
are all individually beautiful, the suites enormous. Quality costs but the price
includes just about everything, so relax and join this effortless house party. Kids
can have separate high tea. Tennis, lovely walks in superb grounds (especially May

and September) kept by almost as many gardeners as there are chefs. A southern secret though with many accolades and more to come, I suspect.
EAT Dinner commensurate with surroundings in 2 elegant dining rooms. Afternoon tea also for non-res by appointment.

1129 8/P22
15 ROOMS
DF
LOTS

✓✓ **Kinloch House** nr Blairgowrie · www.kinlochhouse.com · 01250 884237 5km W on A923 to Dunkeld. Quintessential rural Scottish comfort and joy. Beautiful mansion among the green fields and woods of Perthshire, home to exemplary, welcoming hosts and consummate hoteliers, the Allen family. Open fires, oak-panelled hall and portrait gallery. Comfy rooms and informal but sure service. Nice conservatory. Bucolic south-facing views.
EAT Excellent food: Graeme Allen and Steven MacCallum in the kitchen. Top wine list (especially French). Classy dining.

1130 8/M24
15 ROOMS
LOTS

✓✓ **Cromlix House** Dunblane · www.cromlix.com · 01786 822125 5km from Dunblane following signs and just through Kinbuck on the B8033. A long-established and favourite country-house hotel, taken over by Andy Murray's family (who famously hail from Dunblane), discreetly modernised, managed by the premier ICMI Group and reopened in 2014. All mod cons, as you'd expect, with some fittings and fixtures from before. No spa/leisure but 2 tennis courts, fishing lochs and 3000 acres of a beautiful wooded estate to wander. Private chapel, open fires, nice terrace.
EAT Brasserie-style restaurant in conservatory is Albert Roux, who does, as with the other Scottish franchises, take a close interest. Light, contemporary cuisine.

1131 9/J31
10 ROOMS
DF
LL
LOTS

✓ **Knockinaam Lodge** Portpatrick · www.knockinaamlodge.com · 01776 810471 An ideal place to lie low; a historic Victorian house nestled on a cove. The Irish coastline is the only thing on the horizon, apart from discreet service and excellent food. Winston Churchill was once very comfortable here, too! (His room the top suite). Superb wine (especially French) and whisky list. 15km S of Stranraer, off A77 near Lochans but get directions. Further report: 809/sw HOTELS.
EAT Tony Pierce – one of Scotland's great chefs. Tasting set menu (advise requirements). Understated foodie fabulousness.

1132 7/J23
16 ROOMS
DF
FEB-DEC
LL
ATMOS
LOTS

✓ **Ardanaiseig Hotel** Loch Awe · www.ardanaiseig.com · 01866 833333 16km from Taynuilt signed from main A85 to Oban down a beautiful winding road and 7km from Kilchrenan. Overlooking the enchanting loch, in sheltered landscaped gardens dotted with ongoing sculpture project to complement this rambling gothic mansion's collection of selected antiques (proprietor owns antique business in London). Peaty water on tap, splendid trees on the grounds, the omnipresent loch; deer wander and bats flap at dusk. This is pure romance. Chef Colin Cairns gets it just right. The Boatshed suite, with its boat and its loch, is simply idyllic. Not surprisingly, some posh weddings.

✓✓ **Raemoir House** Banchory 5km N from town via A980. A gem in the NE. Historical with contemporary comforts and excellent dining. Report: 975/NE HOTELS.

✓✓ **Monachyle Mhor** nr Balquhidder More farmhouse than country house; certainly more laid-back than many of the above. A top rural relax. Report: 1191/GET-AWAY HOTELS.

✓ **Ballathie House** Kinclaven, nr Perth Superb situation on River Tay. Handy for Perth. Report: 919/PERTHSHIRE.

✓ **Glencoe House** Luxe loveliness in magnificent surroundings. 1049/ HIGHLANDS.

Hotels That Welcome Kids

1133 8/N23
214 ROOMS +
51 LODGES
MED.INX-EXP

✓✓✓ **Crieff Hydro** Crieff · www.crieffhydro.com · 01764 655555 A national institution, still a family business and a truly splendid family hotel that moves with the times. They strike the perfect balance between relaxation and activity (of which there is a staggering range of choice). Hence, 3 ticks, i.e. among the best in the world. And it is so very much in and of Scotland, a vast Victorian pile still run by the Leckies from hydropathic beginnings. The continuous refurbishments include the fabulous winter gardens, the sports hall (the Hub), café and kids' centre and the rooms. Formal chandeliered dining room (Meikle's) and the Brasserie (best for food Med-style; open all day). There are 6 dining choices. Activities all day and all around: great tennis courts, riding school, 2 pools including the Victorian pool (and spa) for adults only. Tiny cinema shows family movies; nature talks, donkey rides. Kids entertained (even while you eat) with a high tea (4.30-6pm) just for them. Chalets in the grounds are among the best in Scotland. Great for family get-togethers. Despite the many bairns, it's also brilliant for adults on their own. Populism with probity and no preciousness: when in doubt, resort to this resort!

1134 7/J25
16 ROOMS
MED.INX-MED.
EX

✓✓ **Portavadie Marina** Portavadie · www.portavadie.com · 01700 811075 End of the road, very contemporary, very yachty leisure and activity complex on Loch Fyne, across from Tarbert. Much ado about boats but lots of other activities inside and out. Restaurant choices and different types of accom by night or week. Report: 778/ARGYLL.

1135 3/E14
6 ROOMS
NO TV
DF
MAY-SEP
LLL
MED.INX

✓✓ **Baile-Na-Cille** Timsgarry, West Lewis · www.bailenacille.co.uk · 01851 672242 Far, far into the sunset on the W of Lewis. 60km from Stornoway so a plane/ferry and drive to somewhere you and the kids can leave all your other baggage behind. Exquisite, vast beach and many others nearby, garden, tennis, games room. Wi-Fi in the lounges. Plenty books. Rooms basic. Good places nearby for lunch (2242/HEBRIDES). Dinner (closes one night a week) is excellent value, with good wine list. The kids will keep this place in their hearts.

1136 3/E16
6 ROOMS
NO TV
DF
MAY-DEC
LL
EXP

✓✓ **Scarista House** South Harris · www.scaristahouse.com · 01859 550238 20km S of Tarbert on W coast of South Harris, just over an hour to Stornoway. Big, comfortable former manse overlooking amazing beach (1568/BEACHES); and golf course (2061/GOLF). Lots of other great countryside around. The Martins having had 3 kids of their own will welcome yours and are happy to do a separate supper at 6pm. And a famously good dinner for grown-ups. A laid-back, far from Alton Towers experience.

1137 7/J27
36 ROOMS
MED.INX

✓ **Auchrannie Spa Hotel** Brodick, Arran · www.auchrannie.co.uk · 01770 302234 Much expanded from the original house, the new block is perfect for a family holiday. You may have the run of both. Loadsa activities on tap, including 2 pools, racquet court, spa and outdoor stuff (c/o Arran Adventures out back) on rivers, trails and hills. Many rooms can take 2 adults and 2 kids. Main restaurant is a bit motorway services but 2 other options in the original hotel, including very decent dining in remodelled eighteen69 (phone-monitoring service; hotel can arrange babysitting). Kids will begin their lifelong love of Arran here.

1138 7/J21
59 ROOMS
DF · L
MED.INX

✓ **Isles of Glencoe Hotel** Ballachulish · www.islesofglencoe.com · 01855 811602 Beside the A82 Crianlarich to Fort William: a modern hotel and leisure centre jutting out onto Loch Leven. Adventure playground outside and nature trails. Conservatory restaurant overlooks the water. Lochaber Watersports next door have all kind of boats from pedalos to kayaks, and bikes. 10% off for hotel guests. Hotel has small pool. Almost 50% are family rooms. Snacks in the restaurant all day. Glen Coe and 2 ski areas nearby. The loch is the thing!

1139 7/F23
17/27 ROOMS
APR-OCT
MED.INX

Argyll Hotel www.argyllhoteliona.co.uk · 01681 700334 & **St Columba Hotel** www.stcolumba-hotel.co.uk · 01681 700304 · **Iona** The 2 Iona hotels owned by local people on this charmed and blessed little island. Holidays here are remembered forever. Argyll has more atmos, St Columba is basic but more spacious, both child- and people-in-general-friendly. Unhurried, hassle-free; beautiful organic gardens; kids run free. Both Apr-Oct.

1140 7/J20
14 ROOMS
NO TV
DF
MAR-OCT
LL
ATMOS
MED.INX-EXP

Glenfinnan House Hotel Glenfinnan · www.glenfinnanhouse.com · 01397 722235 Just off the Road to the Isles (the A830 from Fort William to Mallaig 1631/SCENIC ROUTES). Very large Highland hoose with so many rooms and such big gardens you can let them loose (or stick them in front of a DVD in the mini-playroom – no, let them loose). Great introduction to the Highland heartland; music, scenery and local characters. Comfy rooms: no phone or TV but fresh flowers. The loch's at the foot of the lawn; the midge-eater in the garden is welcome. Report: 1057/HIGHLANDS.

1141 8/Q27
132 ROOMS
DF
MED.EX

Peebles Hydro Peebles · www.peebleshydro.co.uk · 01721 720602 One of the first Victorian hydros (1881, rebuilt 1907) and a complete resort for families; it has that well-worn look but it doesn't matter too much if they run amok. Huge grounds, corridors (you get lost) and floors of rooms. Taken over 2015 by Crieff Hydro (see above) who will know how to make this Hydro thrive again. Improvements in progress, eg the pool; hopefully they'll keep it traditionally wholesome and refreshingly untrendy. Dining room is vast and, well, hotel-like. Many family rooms. Peebles area is great for active kids!

1142 7/K20
8 ROOMS
MED.INX

Old Pines nr Spean Bridge · www.oldpines.co.uk · 01397 712324 3km Spean Bridge via B8004 for Gairlochy at Commando Monument. A ranch-like hotel in a good spot N of Fort William. This hotel has long had a big reputation not only for food but also for welcoming kids. The Dalleys have 2 kids too and welcome yours. Separate mealtimes with Imogen's proper family-food menu, then a great dinner for the adults. Very safe, easy environment with chickens and woods (those pines!) to run. Nice stroll to the old Spean Bridge.

1143 7/J25
8 ROOMS
NO TV
DF
L
MED.INX

Kilfinan Hotel Kilfinan · www.kilfinan.com · 01700 821201 N of Tignabruaich on B8000 close to but not on Loch Fyne, in the country heart of Cowal and Argyll. On a quiet road, a 300-year-old coaching inn with a good reputation for hospitality (and now food). The Wyatts have 3 kids and there's a proper kids' menu and early supper times. Lots of chickens and ducks and a fairy bridge; wild walks nearby (they loan their dogs out). A relaxing and easy place for the whole bunch.

1144 7/J21
20 ROOMS +
5 LODGES
DF
MED.EX

Holly Tree Hotel Kentallen · www.hollytreehotel.co.uk · 01631 740292 On A828 Fort William–Oban road S of Ballachulish. Long-established roadside and seaside hotel in great setting. All rooms have the view. Garden on the shore with pier. Former railway station. Surf 'n' turf restaurant with children's menu, bar and surprising swimming pool (though not shallow).

1145 8/N22
6 ROOMS
DF · MED.INX

The Inn on the Tay Grandtully · www.theinnonthetay.co.uk · 01887 840760 Road and riverside inn in small village near Aberfeldy. This stretch of river famous for its rapids so usually plenty of raft and canoe action. Josie and Geoff keep this place family-friendly. Some rooms have 3 beds (kids £20 at TGP). 4 overlook and you are soothed to sleep by the river. Nice lounge and café/bar with river deck. The brilliant chocolate shop is opposite (1391/TEAROOMS).

1146 9/M30
56 ROOMS
DF
MED.INX

Cally Palace Gatehouse of Fleet · www.mcmillanhotels.co.uk ·
01557 814341 The big, all-round family and golf hotel in the SW, in charming
village with safe, woody walks in the grounds. Old-style ambience (let's not say
tired); a piano is played at dinner. Leisure facilities include pool and tennis. 500
acres of forest good for cycling (bike hire can be arranged). There are allegedly red
squirrels. Kids' tea at 5pm. Nice beach nearby at **Sandgreen** (1583/BEACHES) and,
of course, **Cream o' Galloway** (1446/ICE CREAM). See also 1517/GARDENS.

1147 5/N19
175 ROOMS
MED.INX-EXP

Hilton Coylumbridge nr Aviemore · www.hiltonaviemore.com ·
01479 810661 8km from Aviemore Centre on B970 to ski slopes and nearest hotel
to them. 2 pools of decent size, sauna, flume, etc. Plenty to do in summer and
winter (1704/KIDS) and enough to do when it rains. Best of the often-criticised
Aviemore concrete blocks. Huge shed with kids' play area (the Funhouse). Majority
are family rooms. Whole hotel a playground in school hols.

✓✓ **Comrie Croft** Hostel accom on a working farm with basic or quite posh
camping in the woods in beautiful Perthshire setting. Report: 1148/HOSTELS.
✓✓ **Lazy Duck** nr Nethy Bridge Report: 1149/HOSTELS.

Stonefield Castle Hotel Tarbert On A83 on slopes of Loch Fyne with wonderful
views. A real castle in 60 acres of woody grounds. Report: 789/ARGYLL.

The Best Hostels

1148 8/N23

✓✓ **Comrie Croft** nr Comrie · www.comriecroft.com · 01764 670140
On A85 Comrie-Crieff/Perth road, Andrew Donaldson's Perthshire
landmark stopover. 2 self-contained buildings: the Farmhouse, and the Lodge and
courtyard of a working farm in beautiful countryside, which includes a millpond and
a mountain. Excellent facilities: shop, kitchen, lounges. Mountain bikes for hire/sale.
Bike trails, 'squirrel trails' and a wee hike up the road. Eco-friendly camping in the
woods, including 5 Swedish katas for hire, with wood-burning stoves. Cool for kids,
great for grown-ups! Tea garden, cakes and snacks (Easter-Oct).

1149 6/P19
L

✓✓ **Lazy Duck Hostel, Hut & Lodge** nr Nethy Bridge · www.lazyduck.
co.uk · 01479 821642 'Tiny hostel' (8 beds), eco-hut for 2, facing across
the moor to Cairngorm and 'The Duck's Nest', a beautifully elemental lodge on the
waterfowl pond. And a 4-pitch camping ground. 2km from Nethy Bridge off the
B970 towards the A939 to Tomintoul. Idyllic, romantic; all that and not expensive.
In same family, in both senses as **The Dell of Abernethy** www.holiday-
cairngorm.co.uk · 01479 821643, a Georgian lodge for 8, and 5 self-catering
cottages in another part of the woods. All so sylvan.

1150 3/E13
LL

✓✓ **The Blackhouse Village** Gearrannan, Lewis · www.gearrannan.
com · 01851 643416 At the road end (3km) from A858, the W coast of
Lewis, an extraordinary reconstruction of several blackhouses, the traditional
thatched dwelling of the Hebrides, now 4 separate houses/cottages. Authentic and
atmospheric, basic but not spartan. Township on a cove, so sunsets and the wild
Atlantic foam. Sleeping 2/14 and 2 for 4/5. No Sunday arrivals.

1151 7/F23

✓ **Iona Hostel** Iona · www.ionahostel.co.uk · 01681 700781 Bunkhouse in
N, 2km hike from ferry on John Maclean's farm. Feels like the edge of the
world looking over to Staffa and beyond; beach besides. Beautiful open-plan space
with wood stove. Open AYR. 5 rooms, sleeps 22, and Shepherd's Bothy more
secluded, for 2. **Iona**, of course, is very special (2198/ISLANDS).

1152 8/N24 ✓ **Stirling SYH** Stirling · www.syha.org.uk · 01786 473442 Modern conversion in great part of town, close to castle, adjacent ancient graveyard and with fine views from some rooms. One of SYHA's hotel-like hostels with student-hall standard and facilities. Many oldies and international tourists. Breakfast included or self-catering. Access till 2am.

1153 5/N19 ✓ **Aviemore Bunkhouse** Aviemore · www.aviemore-bunkhouse.com · 01479 811181 Main road into Aviemore from S (A95) near station and by the river. Part of **Old Bridge Inn** (1307/GASTROPUBS) so great food adjacent. En-suite rooms for 6/8 and family rooms available. Can accommodate 44. Open AYR.

1154 4/K14 ✓ **Inchnadamph Lodge** Assynt · www.inch-lodge.co.uk · 01571 822218
LL 25km N of Ullapool on A837 road to Lochinver and Sutherland. Well-appointed mansion house for individuals or groups in geology-gazing, hill-walking, mountain-rearing Assynt. Kitchen, canteen (dinner not provided but self-service breakfast). Commune with nature, then with each other. Some twin rooms.

1155 8/Q21 ✓ **Prosen Hostel** Glen Prosen · www.prosenhostel.co.uk · 01575 540238
LL Glen Prosen, the gentlest, most beautiful and wooded of the Angus glens (1589/GLENS). 10km from start of glen at Dykehead and part of Prosen village (well, church) at the end of the road. An SYH 'green' hostel; wood-burning stove, internet. Rooms for 4 and 6; 18 beds. Grassy sward, lovely terrace and red squirrels.

1156 5/M20 ✓ **Pottery Bunkhouse** Laggan Bridge · www.potterybunkhouse.co.uk · 01528 544231 On A889 near Loch Laggan. Homely bunkhouse: 3 'dorms' for 6, 2 family rooms, great home-bakes caff (1395/TEAROOMS). Lounge overlooks hills and has TV; wood stove, hot tub on deck. Open AYR.

1157 3/E16 ✓ **Am Bothan** Harris · www.ambothan.com · 01859 520251 At Leverburgh
L in the S of South Harris, a bunkhouse hand-built and personally run – a bright, cool building with well-lived-in feel. Good disabled facilities. 18 beds. Caff & shop nearby. Look for the *Free Spirit*!

1158 5 ✓ **Hostelling in the Hebrides** www.syha.org.uk Simple hostelling in the
LL crofting communities of Lewis, Harris and the Uists. Run by a trust to
ATMOS maintain standards of Highland hospitality; local crofters act as wardens. Lewis, Harris, North and South Uist. The Blackhouse cottages on Lewis at Gearrannan (above) are exceptional. Check local tourist info centres for details.

1159 7/H23 ✓ **Hostels in Oban** As well as a relatively grand SYH Hostel on the seafront, there are 2 cosy independent hostels in Oban. One of them, **Backpackers Plus** www.backpackersplus.com · 01631 567189 · Breadalbane St has 3 separate dorm areas – the main one in the United Free Church. They have the most private rooms. Continental breakfast. **Oban Backpackers** www.obanbackpackers.com · 01631 562107 across the street is probably the more chilled. All close to the main street and the port.

1160 1/Q9 ✓ **Bis Geos Hostel & Cottages** Westray, Orkney · www.bisgeos.co.uk · 01857 677420 Remote and fabulous: this is how this traditionally rebuilt croft
L is described, because I still haven't been. Sounds like perhaps 2 ticks may be due. Exceptional standard with nautical theme. Conservatory overlooks the wild ocean. Minibus from the ferry. Sleeps 12. 2 cottages.

1161 5/G20 ✓ **The Glebe Barn** Eigg · www.glebebarn.co.uk · 01687 482417 On
    L   fabulously good Eigg, a haven in a haven (sailings from Mallaig and Arisaig 2200/ISLANDS). Civilised, comfy, wood-burning, well-furnished; duvets and linen provided. Just what you and the island needs. Apr-Oct. Exclusive use possible.

1162 4/L12 ✓ **Lazy Crofter Bunkhouse** Durness · www.durnesshostel.com ·
07803 927642 Adjacent (and with the same owners as) **Mackay's Hotel** (1055/HIGHLANDS). A small, laid-back woody chalet (sleeps 12 in 4 rooms) in good location for exploring Durness, Cape Wrath, etc (2023/2033/WALKS; 1561/BEACHES); caff at **Balnakeil** nearby (2147/SCOTTISH SHOPS). No pub/dining in the hotel. Kitchen and outdoor terrace. Open AYR.

1163 5/G17 ✓ **Dun Flodigarry** nr Staffin, Skye · www.hostelflodigarry.co.uk ·
 APR-OCT   01470 552212 In far N, 32km from Portree in big, big scenery beside
    LL   Flodigarry Country House Hotel, which has a bistro/pub with a great view. Overlooks sea. Bunkrooms for 6-8 and 3 doubles (holds up to 30) and great refectory. Very green credentials; entirely run on wind power.

1164 5/M18 **Inverness Student Hostel** 8 Culduthel Rd · www.invernessstudenthotel.
com · 01463 236556 Best independent hostel in town uphill from town centre. Run by same folk who have the great Edinburgh one (122/HOSTELS) with similar laid-back atmos and camaraderie. **Bazpackers** 100m downhill, similar vibe.

1165 7/L24 **Rowardennan SYH** Loch Lomond · www.syha.org.uk · 01360 870259 The hostel at the end of the road up the E (less touristy) side of Loch Lomond from Balmaha and Drymen. Large, well managed and modernised, and on a waterside site. On West Highland Way and obvious base for climbing **Ben Lomond** (1952/MUNROS). Good all-round activity centre and lawns to the loch of your dreams. Rowardennan Hotel boozer nearby. 62 beds; some private rooms.

1166 7/G22 **Tobermory SYH** Mull · www.syha.org.uk · 01688 302481 Looks out to Tobermory Bay. Central, very pink, highly rated hostel; very busy in summer. 5/6 bunks in 7 rooms (4 on front). Kitchen. Internet. Sweet garden terrace. Near ferry to Ardnamurchan; main Oban ferry 35km away (1554/VILLAGES). Mar-Oct. The new **Craignure Bunkhouse** www.craignure-bunkhouse.co.uk · 01680 812043 is handy for the Oban ferry. Rooms 4 or 6 only.

1167 7/J26 **Lochranza Youth Hostel SYH** Lochranza · www.syha.org.uk · 01770 830631 On left coming from south. Refurbished Victorian house overlooking fab bay, castle ruins. Swans dip at dawn. Full self catering. Comfortable sitting room. Mar-Nov. Nice bistro, **Stags Pavilion**, nearby (2240/ARRAN).

1168 7/K22 **Glencoe SYH** Glencoe · www.syha.org.uk · 01855 811219 Deep in the glen
    L   itself, 3km off A82, 4km by back road from Glencoe village and 33km from Fort William. Modern timber house near river; especially handy for climbers and walkers. Laundry, good drying room. **Clachaig** pub, 2km for good food and craic. See 1617/SCENIC ROUTES; 1914/ENCHANTING PLACES; 1889/BATTLEGROUNDS; 1287/GOOD PUBS; 1973/WALKS.

The Best Roadside, Seaside & Countryside Inns

1169 5/F17
6 ROOMS
LOTS

✓✓ **The Three Chimneys** Colbost, Skye · www.threechimneys.co.uk · 01470 511258 7km W of Dunvegan on B884 to Glendale. The Chimneys: smokin' now and forever! Accom is in a new build, **The House Over-By** across yard from the much-loved, much-awarded Three Chimneys restaurant (2239/SKYE). Roadside, yes, but only the traffic of local life and you, and there's the smell of the sea. Calm and contemporary split-level rooms with own doors to the sward. Little treats and nice touches. Breakfast room doubles as a pre-dinner lounge in the evening. Many destination inns up north now, this the first. Book for dinner!

1170 8/N23
6 ROOMS
ATMOS
MED.INX

✓✓ **The Barley Bree** Muthill, nr Crieff · www.barleybree.com · 01764 681451 Stylish, excellent-value restaurant with rooms above on main road. Great food; tasteful, comfortable rooms. Chef/patron Fabrice Bouteloup a great chef and patron and all-round nice guy. Bar/restaurant open Wed-Sun for lunch & dinner. A top Sunday lunch. Not much to do in Muthill itself but the amazing **Drummond Castle Gardens** are nearby (1506/GARDENS) and the walk along the **Earn** (1989/RIVER WALKS).

1171 7/H26
5 ROOMS
DF
MAR-OCT
MED.EX

✓✓ **The Kilberry Inn** nr Tarbert, Argyll · www.kilberryinn.com · 01880 770223 Halfway round the Knapdale peninsula on the single-track B8024 (1633/SCENIC ROUTES), the long and breathtaking way to Lochgilphead. Homely roadside inn with simple, classy rooms and excellent cooking (1302/GASTROPUBS) that comes fresh and local. Michelin Bib Gourmand. Lunch Fri-Sun, dinner Tue-Sun. Open Nov/Dec at weekends.

1172 5/H18
7 ROOMS
NO TV
DF
LL
MED.INX

✓✓ **Applecross Inn** Applecross · www.applecross.uk.com/inn · 01520 744262 The end of the legendary road to a definitive seaside inn on the Applecross strand. Spectacular journey to get here (1619/SCENIC ROUTES) and not for the faint-hearted driver; hit the shoreline and settle in (though only 7 small rooms). They all face the sea, which is what you want here. Then eat at Judy Fish's seafood table and get forever Applecrossed. Report: 1200/GET-AWAY HOTELS.

1173 5/H19
7 ROOMS
DF
L
APR-OCT
ATMOS
MED.EX

✓✓ **Glenelg Inn** Glenelg · www.glenelg-inn.com · 01599 522273 At the end of that great road over the hill from Shiel Bridge on the A87 (1618/SCENIC ROUTES)... well, not quite the end because you can drive further round to ethereal Loch Hourn. This halt has always been a civilised hostelry and often a whole lot of fun. Great home-cooked food in warm, cosy bar. Good drinking, snug lounge. Garden with tables and views. Sheila Condie and a great team keep this quintessential village pub at the heart of a thriving community that makes you very welcome. From Glenelg, take the best route to Skye (6/JOURNEYS). Winter: bar only.

1174 7/H21
6 ROOMS
DF
MED.INX

✓ **Glenuig Inn** Glenuig · www.glenuig.com · 01687 470219 Just off A861 between Lochailort on the Road to the Isles from Fort William (1631/SCENIC ROUTES) and Kinlochmoidart, a perfect Highland road and seaside inn. Refurbished to high standard in the green tourism code (sustainable materials, solar-powered, etc). Light and contemporary. New bunkhouse sleeps groups of up to 20. Good base for sea kayaking, biking and boating. Locally sourced and organic grub.

1175 7/F23
17 ROOMS
NO TV
APR-OCT

✓ **Argyll Hotel** Iona · www.argyllhoteliona.co.uk · 01681 700334 On beautiful, turquoise bay between Iona and Mull on road between ferry and abbey. Day trippers come and go; you should stay! A charming hotel on a remarkable island. Cosy rooms quite fabulous (1 suite and singles in the 'annex').

LL
MED.EX
All-home-made food (especially vegetarian) from organic garden. Real peace and quiet and that's just sitting in the sun lounge or on the bench outside. It's Colourist country and this is where they would have stayed too. Nice for kids (1139/KIDS).

1176 7/J25
10 ROOMS
L
ATMOS
MED.EX
✓ **Kames Hotel** Tighnabruaich · www.kames-hotel.com · 01700 811489
Frequented by passing yachtsmen (hotel has its own free moorings) who can pop up for lunch. Great seaside setting overlooking the Doon-the-Watter shore, Argyll's secret coast, and atmospheric bar busy with locals. Owners Shelley and Pat at the helm: a calming colour scheme, friendly staff; nice photos on the walls. Simply, reasonably stylish and a good local vibe.

1177 7/K22
32 ROOMS
MED.EX
✓ **Bridge of Orchy Hotel** Bridge of Orchy · www.bridgeoforchy.co.uk · 01838 400208 Unmissable on the A82 (the road to Glen Coe, Fort William and Skye) 11km N of Tyndrum. A great stopover for motorists and walkers; it's on the **West Highland Way** (1965/WALKS). 10 rooms in hotel and 3 new blocks, with simple, contemporary motel-like rooms – 3 price structures; good à la carte menu and specials in pub/conservatory. Good spot for the malt or a munch on the Way.

1178 8/N22
6 ROOMS
DF
MED.INX
✓ **The Inn on the Tay** Grandtully · www.theinnonthetay.co.uk · 01887 840760 Contemporary conversion of roadside inn that also has a commanding position on the riverbank where rapids tax legions of helmeted rafters and canoeists; so constant entertainment. Café/bar with good food, residents' lounge, outside deck and comfortable modern bedrooms – some with 3 beds.

1179 8/Q27
14 ROOMS +
6 COTTS
DF
MED.INX
✓ **Traquair Arms** Innerleithen · www.traquairarmshotel.co.uk · 01896 830229 100m from the A72 Galashiels–Peebles road towards Traquair. An old roadside inn, deep in Border and biking country. Notable for bar meals (Scottish emphasis), real ale and family facilities. Rooms refurbished to a decent standard. David and Jane Rogers making a fair go of it here. Lovely beer garden out back. Much cycling nearby; and the Tweed.

1180 7/J22
12 ROOMS +
COTTAGE
DF
LL
MED.INX
✓ **The Pierhouse Hotel** Port Appin · www.pierhousehotel.co.uk · 01631 730302 Inn at the end of the road (minor road that leads off A828 Oban-Fort William) and at end of the pier where the tiny Lismore passenger ferry leaves (2208/ISLANDS). A mainly seafood restaurant (1350/SEAFOOD) in a great setting. Comfy adjacent rooms (more expensive overlook the sea and island). Sauna and showers. Good place to take kids and a great yachty stop.

1181 5/L19
10 ROOMS
FEB-NOV
MED.INX
✓ **Glenmoriston Arms Hotel** Invermoriston, Loch Ness · www. glenmoristonarms.co.uk · 01320 351206 On main A82 between Inverness (45km) and Fort Augustus (10km) at the Glen Moriston corner, a worthwhile corner of Scotland to explore. Busy local bar, fishermen's tales. Food under Ailsa McInnes and a real chef; and extensive malt list – certainly a good place to drink them. Inn-like bedrooms with 3 cottagey rooms overby.

1182 8/S26
5 ROOMS
MED.INX
The Craw Inn Auchencrow · www.thecrawinn.co.uk · 01890 761253 4km A1 and well worth the short detour into Berwickshire countryside. Quintessential inn with cosy pub and dining room. Funky furniture, simple rooms. Food decent, wines extraordinary. Lunch & dinner. 1309/GASTROPUBS.

1183 5/F17
5 ROOMS
NO TV
DF · L
CHP-MED.INX
The Stein Inn Waternish, Skye · www.steininn.co.uk · 01470 592362 Off B886, the Dunvegan-Portree road, about 10km Dunvegan. In row of cottages on the shore of Loch Bay. The over 200-year-old 'oldest inn on Skye' with great pub (open fire, OK grub lunch and dinner). Rooms above are cottagey, small and cosy and Waternish is a very special spot. Top seafood restaurant adjacent (1342/SEAFOOD).

1184 5/H16
18 ROOMS
DF
MED.INX

Old Inn Gairloch · www.theoldinn.net · 01445 712006 Southern approach on A832, tucked away by river and old bridge. Excellent pub for food in bar, lounge and restaurant and tables by the river. Nice, simple rooms. The pub goes like a fair; recommended in pub guides. Their ale is good (including 4 of their own: Mike's Mild, the Bees Knees). Regular live music.

1185 8/P21
6 ROOMS
DF
CHP

Glenisla Hotel Kirkton of Glenisla · www.glenisla-hotel.com · 01575 582223 20km NW of Kirriemuir via B951 at head of secluded story-book glen. A home from home: hearty food, real ale and local colour. Fishers, stalkers, trekkers and walkers (a stopover on the **Cateran Trail** 1969/WALKS) come by for grub, grog and a chat along the way (pub closed Mon). Simple rooms and the countryside.

1186 8/P22
18 ROOMS
DF
CHP

Bridge of Cally Hotel Bridge of Cally · www.bridgeofcallyhotel.com · 01250 886231 Wayside pub on a bend of road between Blairgowrie and Glenshee/ Braemar (ski zone and Royal Deeside). Cosy and inexpensive between gentle Perthshire and the wilder Grampians. Another staging post on the **Cateran Trail** (1969/WALKS). See also Glenisla above. Rooms quiet, pleasant and good value. Restaurant and bar meals.

1187 8/P22
5 ROOMS
DF
MED.INX

Meikleour Hotel Meikleour · www.meikleourarms.co.uk · 01250 883206 1km A93 Perth-Blairgowrie road (on B984) by and behind famously high beech hedge (a Perthshire landmark). Roadside inn in sweet village with quiet accom and 4 cottages; food in dining room or (more convivially) the bar. Woody, not foodie.

1188 5/J19
13 ROOMS +
BUNKHOUSE
DF · L
CHP-MED.EX

Cluanie Inn Glenmoriston · www.cluanieinn.com · 01320 340238 On road to Skye 15km before Shiel Bridge, a traditional inn surrounded by mountain summits (they say 21 Munros within reach) that attract walkers and travellers: 5 Sisters, Ridge and Saddle (1975/WALKS). Clubhouse adjacent has some group accom while inn rooms vary (one has a sauna, one a jacuzzi). Dining room and bar food all wholesome. Friendly staff.

1189 7/K21
23 ROOMS
DF · L
ATMOS
MED.INX

Clachaig Inn Glencoe · www.clachaig.com · 01855 811252 Basic accom but you will sleep well, especially after walking/climbing/drinking, which is what most people are doing here. Great atmos both inside and out; wood stoves aplenty. Food (very basic too) available bar/lounge and dining room till 9pm. Ales aplenty 1287/ GOOD PUBS. 4 lodges out back. Harry Potter crew were once here.

1190 8/N21
15 ROOMS
DF
ATMOS
CHP

Moulin Hotel Pitlochry · www.moulinhotel.co.uk · 01796 472196 Kirkmichael Rd; at the landmark crossroads on the A924. Basic rooms above (2 cottages overby) and beside notable pub for food and especially ales – they brew their own out back. (1297/REAL-ALE PUBS) Not sure about the taxidermy over breakfast!

✓✓ **Mhor 84** nr Balquhidder On the A84 from Stirling to Argyll. A top roadside bar/restaurant and rooms above – a motel even! Report: 831/CENTRAL.
✓✓ **The Sorn Inn** Sorn Report: 1301/GASTROPUBS.

✓ **Buccleuch & Queensberry Arms Hotel** Thornhill Charming inn on main street. Report: 811/SW HOTELS.
✓ **The Harbour Inn** Bowmore, Islay Waterfront inn on faraway Islay. Report: 2233/ISLAND HOTELS.
✓ **The Clachan Inn** St John's Town of Dalry Report: 812/SW HOTELS.

Anchor Hotel Kippford Solway setting. Report: 819/SW HOTELS.

The Best Restaurants With Rooms

√ √+ **The Peat Inn** nr St Andrews Brilliant restaurant under Michelin chef Geoffrey Smeddle. Swish suites. Report: 900/FIFE.

The following all have 2 ticks:

The Sorn Inn Sorn 8km E of Mauchline on the B743, 30 mins from Ayr. Report: 800/AYRSHIRE.

The Three Chimneys Colbost, Skye State-of-the-art dining and contemporary rooms far away in the west. Report: 2239/SKYE.

The Barley Bree Muthill, nr Crieff French guy in the kitchen, Scots partner on design have put sleepy village on the map. Report: 1170/INNS.

The Cross Kingussie Rooms upstairs in converted tweed mill. Best restaurant and wine list in the region. Report: 1041/HIGHLANDS.

The Cross Keys Kippen Long-established gastropub with rooms in foodie village main street. Report: 1304/GASTROPUBS.

The Kilberry Inn nr Tarbert, Argyll Report: 1171/INNS.

The Ship Inn Elie On the bay, on the money. Report: 1305/GASTROPUBS.

The Boat Inn Aboyne Perfect Deeside stopover. Report: 977/NE HOTELS.

Gordon's Inverkeilor Long-standing, yet smart rooms; food with flair. Report: 928/TAYSIDE.

The following all have 1 tick:

The Horseshoe Inn nr Peebles Borders destination. Bistro/restaurant designed to impress. Rooms in old school behind. Report: 853/BORDERS.

Blar Na Leisg at Drumbeg House Drumbeg Artistic, historic and unbelievably picturesque surroundings. Report: 1043/HIGHLANDS.

Windlestraw Walkerburn Very special house discreetly overlooking Tweed Valley. Excellent dining. Report: 849/BORDERS.

Buccleuch & Queensberry Arms Hotel Thornhill Great bar and smart rooms in drive-through village N of Dumfries. Report: 811/SW HOTELS.

The Creel St Margaret's Hope, Orkney Long-established, great location, excellent good-value food. New owners at TGP. Report: 2244/ORKNEY.

Yann's Crieff Victorian mansion with 5 rooms above best bistro in the county. Report: 917/PERTHSHIRE.

The Mash Tun Aberlour Boutique-style rooms above pub in whisky country. Report: 1030/SPEYSIDE.

The Inn on the Tay Grandtully A made-over inn on the banks of the rushing River Tay. Great for kids. Report: 1178/INNS.

Creagan House Strathyre Rob Roy and Trossachs country. On the road W and to the islands. Report: 834/CENTRAL.

The Smiddy House Spean Bridge Comfy roadside inn; best casual food in Fort William area. Report: 1084/HIGHLANDS.

Wildings Hotel & Restaurant Maidens Huge local reputation for food; refurbished rooms overlook the sea. Report: 803/AYRSHIRE.

The Wheatsheaf Swinton, Berwickshire 12 all-different bedrooms above gastropub of long standing. Report: 1311/GASTROPUBS.

The Great Get-Away-From-It-All Hotels

1191 8/L23
14 ROOMS
LL
ATMOS
LOTS

Monachyle Mhor nr Balquhidder · www.mhor.net · 01877 384622
I have to declare this is one of my got-to-get-aways and I like to get away
often! Though only 11km from the A84 Callander-Crianlarich road as you follow a
thread of road along Loch Voilside with the Balquhidder Braes above, you know
you're leaving those urban blues behind. Once you're inside the old pink farmhouse
you could be in a boutique hotel in smart downtown anywhere, except your
window looks over the farm to big, beautiful countryside. Contemporary, calm and
sexy. 7 rooms in courtyard annexe, 6 (a bit smaller) in main building, 1 out back. All
completely gorgeous, especially the baths and bathrooms. A bar that locals and
visitors use. Tom Lewis on stoves (when he's not food festing, including their own
36/EVENTS) cooking up some of the best food in the North. Friendly, cosy,
inexpensive for this standard; a place to relax summer or winter. MM is the HQ,
perhaps, of what Tom, Dick and Madeleine have turned into the Mhor brand, which
includes **Mhor 84**, the 'motel' on the A84 20 mins away and a less expensive
get-away (831/CENTRAL) and the bakers and café in Callander (1433/BAKERS; 1362/
FISH & CHIPS). See also 1247/GLAMPING and perhaps there's Mhor to come!

1192 5/J17
19 ROOMS
DF
CLOSED JAN
NO KIDS
LL
LOTS

The Torridon Glen Torridon, nr Kinlochewe · www.thetorridon.
com · 01445 700300 Impressive former hunting lodge on lochside,
surrounded by the pick of the peaks of the Scottish mountains. Deluxe comfort and
taste in this family-run (the Rose-Bristows) baronial house with relaxed atmos: an
all-round Highland experience. Focuses on outdoor activities like clay-pigeon shoots,
kayaking, gorge-scrambling, mountain biking or fishing with 2 full-time guides/
instructors. Lots of walking possibilities nearby including the Torridon big 3: **Beinn
Alligin** (1957/MUNROS), Liathach right in front of the hotel and the easier Beinn Eighe.
This great hotel spawned some years ago a less expensive roadside option: **The
Torridon Inn** in adjacent block with own bar and bistro. An excellent budget choice.
Main hotel has elegant dining room under 3-rosette chef David Barnett (5-course
rustic but delicate fine-dining menu) who also oversees the inn menu. Fruit & veg
from their splendid Kitchen Garden. Nice afternoon tea after the exertions and a
fantastic malts bar for a dram in the dwindling day (see Whisky, p. 264).

1193 7/G23
11 ROOMS
DF
EASTER-OCT
L
LOTS

Tiroran House Mull · www.tiroran.com · 01681 705232 SW corner on
road to Iona from Craignure then B8035 round Loch na Keal (they say 35
mins, but good luck), or more scenic and sometimes scary via Salen.
1 hour Tobermory. Family-friendly small country house in fabulous gardens by the
sea, under conscientious owners Laurence and Katie Mackay. Near Iona and Ulva
ferry; you won't miss Tobermory. Excellent food from sea and organic kitchen
garden. Traditional rooms. Sea eagles fly over, otters flop in the bay.
EAT Though tucked away, this is top dining on Mull. 2/3 choice menu in refined
surroundings (the garden, the sea) and afternoon tea.

1194 8/P21
17 ROOMS
DF · L
MED.EX-LOTS

Dalmunzie Castle Spittal of Glenshee · www.dalmunzie.com ·
01250 885224 3km off Blairgowrie-Braemar road and near Glenshee skiing.
By riverside and surrounded by bare hills, this laird's house is warm and welcoming but
splendidly remote. Some great rooms, Michelin-mentioned dining, bar and 9-hole golf
course. Good aesthetic, comfy yet stylish. You wanna be here! See also 908/PERTHSHIRE.

1195 7/F23
17 ROOMS
NO TV
APR-OCT
LL · MED.EX

Argyll Hotel Iona · www.argyllhoteliona.co.uk · 01681 700334
Quintessential island hotel on the best of small islands just large enough to
get away for walks and explore (2198/ISLANDS). You can hire bikes (or bring). Abbey
is nearby (1878/ABBEYS). 3 lounges (1 with TV, 1 with sun) and 1 lovely suite (with
wood-burning stove). Good home-grown/made food from their organic garden.

1196 5/H20
4 ROOMS +
LODGE
NO PETS
APR–SEP
CHP

✓ **Doune Stone Lodge** Knoydart · www.doune-knoydart.co.uk · 01687 462667 On the wonderful and wild and remote peninsula of Knoydart and this great spot on the W tip overlooking a bay on the Sound of Sleat. They have own boats, so pick you up from Mallaig and drop you round the inlets for walking. Otherwise 10km from Inverie, the village with brilliant pub. The Bay Lodge mainly for groups (shared bathroom area), the 4 individual rooms are adjacent to the dining room. Fixed menu, home-made dinner to a high standard convivial and communal; wine list. Breakfast and packed lunch. An edge-of-the-wilderness labour of love.

1197 5/F17
8 ROOMS
EASTER–NOV
LL
MED.EX

✓ **Greshornish Country House** Skye · www.greshornishhouse.com · 01470 582266 Pronounced Gresh-nish. Off A850 Portree-Dunvegan road about halfway, then 6km along Loch Greshornish to delightful isolation. It's a long way to another good dinner but here by arrangement only (lovely menu from Greshornish Loch starters to impressive Scottish cheeseboard). Comfy, spacious, airy rooms presented with great taste (nice pics) by the Colquhouns. Log fires, billiard room, candlelit dinners. A superb retreat (available for exclusive use).

1198 8/Q21
10 ROOMS
NO PETS
L
CHP

✓ **Glen Clova Hotel** nr Kirriemuir · www.clova.com · 01575 550350 Well, not that near Kirriemuir: 25km N up the glen on B955 from Dykehead. Rooms surprisingly well appointed. Climbers' bar (till all hours). Superb walking (eg Loch Brandy and classic path to Loch Muick). A laid-back get-away though lots of families drive up on Sunday for lunch. Also has a bunkhouse (cheap) and 3 luxury lodges with hot tubs. Great value, great craic! Calmer, greener and more basic is **Prosen Hostel** at the head of Glen Prosen, probably the most beautiful and unspoiled of the glens. No pub, no interference (1155/HOSTELS).

1199 9/J30
11 ROOMS
DF · LL
ATMOS
MED.EX

✓ **Corsewall Lighthouse Hotel** nr Stranraer · www.lighthousehotel.co.uk · 01776 853220 20 mins from Stranraer (via A718 to Kirkcolm) and follow signs, but way up on the peninsula and as it suggests a hotel made out of a working lighthouse. Romantic and offbeat, but only OK food. Local attractions include Portpatrick, 30 mins by quiet back roads. Report: 817/SW HOTELS.

1200 5/H18
7 ROOMS
NO TV
DF · LL
MED.INX

✓ **Applecross Inn** Applecross · www.applecross.uk.com/inn · 01520 744262 At the end of the road (the Pass of the Cattle which is often snowed up in winter), you can really disappear here N of Kyle of Lochalsh and W of Strathcarron. After a spectacular journey, this waterside inn is a haven of hospitality. Buzzes all seasons. Rooms small and not so cheap but Judy Fish, a great team and a real chef, Robert Macrae, will look after you. Poignant visitor centre (2119/HISTORY), walled garden with café 2km, lovely walks (2027/WALKS) easily enough to keep you happy in faraway Applecross for days.

1201 7/K20
4 ROOMS
NO PETS
APR–OCT
L · CHP

✓ **Corriechoille Lodge** Spean Bridge · www.corriechoille.com · 01397 712002 3km from S Bridge via road by station. Lovely road and spectacularly situated; it's great to arrive. Justin and Lucy share their perfect retreat with you in house and 2 turf-covered chalets out back. Rooms simple. Set menu dinner. All home-made breakfast. All round serenity! Report: 1060/HIGHLANDS.

1202 5/N16
6 ROOMS + 3
COTTS
NO PETS · LOTS

✓ **Glenmorangie House** Cadboll, nr Fearn · www.theglenmorangiehouse. com · 01862 871671 On the little peninsula E of Tain off A9 (10km). Luxurious but laid-back mansion; house-party atmos with communal-style delectable dining. Owned by LVMH. Michelin award. Report: 1044/HIGHLANDS.

1203 7/L21
5 ROOMS
NO TV

Moor of Rannoch Hotel Rannoch Station · www.moorofrannoch.co.uk · 01882 633238 Beyond Pitlochry and the Trossachs and far W via Loch Tummel and Loch Rannoch (B8019 and B8846), a wonderful journey to the edge of Rannoch

DF	Moor and adjacent station (you could get the sleeper from London and be here for
MID FEB-OCT	breakfast. 4 trains either way each day via Glasgow). Literally the end of the road,
LL	they make much of their perfect isolation (no phone reception or Wi-Fi). Cosy,
MED.INX	wood-panelled rooms. A lovely wee restaurant with locally sourced suppliers. A
	great-value quintessential Highland inn. Superb walking and they hire bikes.

1204 3/D17
12 ROOMS
DF
MAR-JAN
MED.INX-EXP

Langass Lodge North Uist · www.langasslodge.co.uk · 01876 580285 On the A867 which runs through the middle of the Uists, 7km S of Lochmaddy, 500m from the road. Small, hideaway hotel with garden and island outlook, though the entrance ain't so lovely. Half of rooms in extension to stylish standard; others in hotel OK. Nice bar and very decent dining overlooking the garden, from where veg and salads come. Kid-friendly and you can bring the dog. Uists are wonderful to explore and there's prehistoric stuff nearby and a great short (2.5km) walk. 1809/ PREHISTORIC; 1566/BEACHES.

1205 5/K18
8 ROOMS
DF
L
MED.INX

Tomich Hotel Tomich, nr Drumnadrochit · www.tomichhotel.co.uk · 01456 415399 25km from Drumnadrochit. Fabulous **Plodda Falls** nearby (1594/ WATERFALLS). Cosy, well-run country inn in conservation village with bonus of use of swimming pool in lovely nearby steading. Faraway feel, surprising bar round the back where what's left of the locals do linger. Good base for outdoorsy weekend. Glen Affric across the way; this is the nearest good place to stay.

✓✓ **Glenapp Castle** nr Ballantrae Report: 1128/COUNTRY-HOUSE HOTELS.

✓✓ **Glenelg Inn** Glenelg Report: 1173/INNS.

✓✓ **The Three Chimneys** Colbost, Skye Reports: 1169/INNS; 2239/SKYE.

✓ **Mackay's** Durness Report: 1055/HIGHLANDS.

✓ **Knockinaam Lodge** Portpatrick Report: 809/SW HOTELS.

✓ **Broad Bay House** Lewis Report: 2242/HEBRIDES.

✓ **Balcary Bay** Auchencairn Report: 813/SW HOTELS.

▬▬▬ The Best Very Scottish Hotels

1206 4/K15
13 ROOMS
NO TV
ATMOS
CHP-MED.EX

✓✓ **The Ceilidh Place** Ullapool · www.ceilidhplace.com · 01854 612103 Off main street near port for the Hebrides. Inimitable Jean Urquhart's (and daughter Rebecca's) place which, more than any other in the Highlands, encapsulates Scottish traditional culture and hospitality. Caters for all sorts: hotel rooms are above (with a truly comfortable lounge – you help yourself to drinks) and a bistro/bar below often with live music and performance (ceilidh style). A bunkhouse across the way with cheap and cheerful accom and a bookshop where you can browse through the best of Scottish literature. There's nothing like coming back from a walk and sitting down with a book and a dram in the downstairs lounge. Though it was long ago that the Ceilidh Place put Ullapool on the must-visit map of Scotland, it has moved effortlessly with the times. Now and forever, as they say. More detail: 1054/HIGHLANDS.

1207 4/J14
5 ROOMS
NO PETS

✓✓ **The Albannach** Lochinver · www.thealbannach.co.uk · 01571 844407 2km up road to Baddidarach as you come from S into Lochinver on A837, at the bridge. Lovely 18th-century house in one of Scotland's

NO KIDS	most scenic areas, Assynt, where the mountains take your breath away
MAR-DEC	(1925/1927/HILLS). The Byre overlooks the croft, and 3 suites, bespoke rooms
LL	handcrafted by an irrepressible owner. The Penthouse and the Loft, with outside
LOTS	cliff-enclosed terrace. Great walk behind house to Achmelvich beach – otters on

the way – and the 'secret' beach nearby (1574/BEACHES). Non-res can, and should, eat. Fixed-menu dinner with Michelin star (not the only reason for coming here; Lesley's food has always been fab): it's nature on a plate. They keep bees as well as greenhouses and because they – Colin and Lesley – are so very Scottish, the hotel is too. Highland hospitality done rather well! All in all, a highly individual urban-boutique-hotel experience in a glorious landscape.

1208 8/L23 ✓✓ **Mhor 84** nr Balquhidder · www.mhor.net · 01877 384646
7 ROOMS   Determinably a motel on the busy A84 between Callander and the NW
DF   and in the heart of the Trossachs, this is the latest venture and adventure from the
ATMOS   Lewis family's Mhorification of the country life hereabouts (1191/GET-AWAY HOTELS;
MED.INX   1362/FISH & CHIPS; 1433/BAKERS). Their places all feed off each other. But this is the perfect realisation of friendly, sympatico, old-fashioned yet cool contemporary Scottish hospitality. Locals use the bar, school-room-type bistro – excellent food includes all the Scottish staples. A brazier burns on the road outside. Welcome to Mhor country! See 831/CENTRAL.

1209 5/H19 ✓✓ **Eilean Iarmain** Sleat, Skye · www.eileaniarmain.co.uk ·
12 ROOMS   01471 833332 Sleat area in S of Skye, this snug Gaelic inn nestles in the
4 SUITES   bay and is the classic island hostelry: the word 'location' comes very much to mind.
LL   Bedrooms in hotel best but garden rooms overby are quieter. The 2-floor suites in
ATMOS   adjacent steading are more expensive, like being in your own Highland cottage.
MED.EX   Food decent in dining room and with immersing atmos in the bar. Mystic shore walks. Gallery with selected exhibitions and shop by the quay (2172/SHOPS). The EI is very Highland and very Scottish, its voice is Gaelic, its charm subtly friendly; all totally engaging.

1210 6/Q19 ✓ **Kildrummy Castle Hotel** nr Alford · 01975 571288 60km W of Aberdeen
16 ROOMS   via A944 through some fine bucolic scenery and the green Don valley to this
ĽL   spectacular location with real Highlands aura. Well placed if you're on the Castle
EXP   Trail, this comfortable chunk of Scottish Baronial has the redolent ruins of Kildrummy Castle on the opposite bluff and a gorgeful of gardens between. Some rooms small; all very Scottish and a bit old style. Romantic in autumn when the gardens are good.

1211 7/J20 ✓ **Glenfinnan House Hotel** Glenfinnan · www.glenfinnanhouse.com ·
14 ROOMS   01397 722235 Off the Road to the Isles (A830 Fort William to Mallaig 1631/
NO TV   SCENIC ROUTES). The MacFarlanes have owned this legendary hotel in this historic
DF   house for 40 years (1900/CHARLIE); managers, the Gibsons keep it soundly
MAR-OCT   sympatico. Ongoing refurbishments retain its charm; the huge rooms remain yet
LL   are intimate and cosy with open fires. Impromptu sessions and ceilidhs in the bar,
ATMOS   especially on Thursdays. Eat in the bar or dining room. Fishing or dreaming on Loch
MED.INX-EXP   Shiel at foot of the lawn. Day trips to Skye and the small islands. Scotland the best!

1212 7/K28 ✓ **Savoy Park** 16 Racecourse Road, Ayr · www.savoypark.com ·
15 ROOMS   01292 266112 In a street and area of indifferent hotels this one, owned and
DF   run by the Henderson family for over 50 years, is a real Scottish gem. Many
MED.INX   wedding guests will agree. Period features, much oak, lovely garden; not too much tartan. The antithesis of a chain hotel, a warm, cosy, homespun atmos. And round one of the fireplaces: 'blessed be God for his giftis'.

✓✓✓ **Crieff Hydro** Crieff *The* Scottish family hotel. Report: 1133/KIDS.

✓✓ **George Hotel** Inveraray Happy memories of Scotland are made of this. Report: 775/ARGYLL.

✓ **Glengarry Castle** Invergarry In the Great Glen, lochside grounds. Centuries of history. Report: 1064/HIGHLANDS.

Stonefield Castle Hotel Tarbert Report: 789/ARGYLL.

Luxurious Isolation

1213 5/H20

✓✓ **Knoydart Hide** nr Inverie · www.knoydarthide.co.uk · 01687 460278 Knoydart near the village and part of Knoydart House (see the **Old Forge** 1286/GOOD PUBS), this is a to-die-for – or at least go-away-for – newly built (2014) high-spec, architect-designed cabin with deck, tub, sauna, fab views and perfect privacy. You'd call it a romantic retreat (honeymoons, etc). The pub is 5 mins away if you do fall out. Self-catering, or a cooked meal package is possible. Water taxi from Mallaig, then by Land Rover. Knoydart itself is the wild peninsula.

1214 3/E15
LL

✓✓ **Borve Lodge Estate** South Harris · www.borvelodge.com · 01859 550358 Off the A859 on the west of South Harris by the amazing beaches, 4 self-catering options, 2 traditional and comfortable, and 2 newly built to exceptional standards – 'The Rock House' (along the lines of Blue Reef, below, who established that there was a demand first), and the landmark 'Broch', a glass and stone tower of contemporary living and luxury. None of this was cheap to build or is cheap to rent but provided you're getting on quite well, it will be unforgettable!

In StB there's no category for self-catering accommodation – too much to choose from and not possible to try them out and then select the best but these cottages in exceptional locations are too special to go unmentioned.

1215 3/E16
LL

✓ **Blue Reef Cottages** South Harris · www.stay-hebrides.com · 01859 550370 1km from **Scarista House** (2224/ISLAND HOTELS) and overlooking the same idyllic beach (1568/BEACHES). 2 exceptional turf-roofed cottages, the first of the new wave of luxury-in-good-location lodges. For couples only, though the study could be another bedroom at a pinch. Stylish, good facilities, amazing view. Gourmet meals from lady nearby or eat at Scarista House. 2-day minimum stay in winter.

1216 8/S25
LL

✓ **Blue Cabin by the Sea** Cove · www.bluecabinbythesea.co.uk · 07849 058493/07768 990998 It's blue and it's 10m from its own little beach near perfect little Cove harbour in Berwickshire. You reach the cottage through a rock-cut smuggling tunnel and across the beach. Owned by Ben Tindall, the architect who did the Queen's Gallery at Holyrood Palace; we can expect a uniquely, even quirkily comfortable abode and perfect isolation. Sleeps 4.

1217 4/L13
L

✓ **Croft 103** nr Durness · www.croft103.com · 01971 511202 2 state-of-the-eco-art lochside cottages by the people who have Mackay's in Durness (10km along beautiful coast 1561/BEACHES). Hill and sea cottages overlooking **Loch Eriboll** (1614/LOCHS) with their own wind turbine and solar panels so carbon negative. Merging into the rocky, watery landscape with big, big windows, underfloor heating, outside tubs and high-tech appliances. Well... you'll never want to leave. One bedroom. Open AYR. £1200-£1500 a week.

1218 3/E14 **Beach Bay Cottage** Carnish, nr Uig, Lewis · www.beachbaycottage.co.uk ·
LL 07768 711881 Way out W to the Atlantic and the sunset, a new build – stone,
glass, turf roof, nestling into the hillside 150m above a truly spectacular beach
(1569/BEACHES). 180° windows, sauna, totally mod con. 2 bedrooms. Though
you're in seemingly splendid isolation, the rather good **Auberge** (2242/HEBRIDES)
is right next door for meals and further accom. From £1100.

Great Wild Camping Up North

*In StB we don't do caravans. In fact, because I spend a lot of time behind them
on Highland roads, WE HATE CARAVANS; ain't mad about campervans, either.
Wild camping is different, provided you are sensitive to the environment and
respect the rights of farmers. All sites are* LL *(location, location).*

1219 3/E16 ✓ **South Harris West Coast** S of Tarbert where the boat comes in. 35km to
Stornoway. Follow road and you reach some truly splendid beaches (eg **Scarista**
1568/BEACHES). You could treat yourself to dinner at **Scarista House** (2224/ISLAND
HOTELS). Gaze on your own private sunset and swim in a turquoise sea.

1220 3/E16 ✓ **Lickisto Blackhouse Camping South Harris** · 01859 530485 **East Coast**
(see 1625/SCENIC ROUTES) of South Harris, a beautiful natural campsite in
landscaped rough garden, not so wild because there are showers and a 180-year-
old blackhouse for warmth and wash-up facilities. Terraced pitches; also a couple
of yurts for hire. Unlikely as it may seem, there's a great caff nearby. Very
Hebridean, very Harris and very happy hens are here. (2242/HEBRIDES).

1221 7/F22 ✓ **Calgary Beach Mull** 10km from Dervaig, where there are toilets, picnic
tables and BBQs but no other facilities – this is classic wild camping but you
won't be alone. Sculpture trail, art gallery and a great café nearby (2141/ART
SPACES). Also on Mull, S of Killiechronan on the gentle shore of **Loch na Keal**, there
is nothing but the sky and the sea and you have it all to yourself. **Ben More** is in
the background (1958/MUNROS). Both sublime!

1222 7/K22 ✓ **Glen Etive nr Ballachulish & Glen Coe** One of Scotland's great unofficial
camping grounds. Along the road/river side in a classic glen (1587/GLENS)
guarded where it joins the pass into Glen Coe by the awesome Buachaille Etive
Mor. Innumerable grassy terraces and small meadows on which climbers and
walkers have camped for generations, and pools to bathe in (1659/SWIMMING).
Repair perhaps to the famous Kingshouse Pub, 2km from the foot of the glen,
though it has seen better days.

1223 7/J27 ✓ **Glen Rosa Arran** · 07985 566004 4km N from Brodick Pier via
Blackwaterfoot road, then by the 'cart track', 500m past the pretty village, a
serene meadow by the lazy river (choose pitch carefully), with very basic facilities.
Wood for fires. Goatfell above. Bliss but for the midges.

1224 7/F26 **Kintra Islay** Bowmore-Port Ellen road, take Oa turn-off, then look for sign on
the right 7km. A long beach one way, a wild coastal walk the other. Camping (and
room for a few campervans) on grassy strand looking out to sea; basic facilities in
farmyard – shower, toilet, washing machine.

1225 7/H20 **Lochailort** A 12km stretch S from Lochailort on the A861, along the southern
shore of the sea loch itself. A flat, rocky and grassy foreshore with a splendid
seascape and backed by brooding mountains. Nearby is Loch nan Uamh where

Bonnie Prince Charlie left Scotland for the last time (1899/CHARLIE). Once past the salmon farm laboratories, you're in calendar scenery; the excellent **Glenuig Inn** at the southern end is the pub to repair to (1174/INNS). No facilities except the sea.

1226 5/H19 **Glenelg** Near Glenelg village which is over the amazing hill from Shiel Bridge (1618/SCENIC ROUTES). Village has great pub, the **Glenelg Inn** (1173/INNS) and a shop. Best spots to camp are 2km from village on road to Skye ferry on the strand.

1227 4/K13 **Oldshoremore** nr Kinlochbervie 3km from village and supplies. Gorgeous beach (1565/BEACHES) and **Polin**, next cove. On the way to **Sandwood Bay** where the camping is legendary (but you have to carry everything 7km).

1228 1/J11 **Achmelvich** nr Lochinver Signed off the fabulous Lochinver-Drumbeg road (1621/SCENIC ROUTES) or walk from village 3km via Ardroe (a great spot to watch otters that have been there for generations). There is an official campsite adjacent horrible caravan park, but walk further N towards Stoer. The beach at **Port Alltan na Bradhan** with the ruins of the old mill is fabulous. Best sea-swimming on this coast. Directions: 1574/BEACHES.

Camping With The Kids

Caravan sites and camp grounds that are especially kid-friendly, with good facilities and a range of things to do (including a good pub).

1229 6/N19 ✓ **Glenmore Camp Site** nr Aviemore · www.campingintheforest.co.uk · 01479 861271 9km Aviemore on the road to the ski slopes, B970. Across the road from Glenmore Visitor Centre and adjacent to **Loch Morlich Watersports Centre** (2101/WATER SPORTS). Extensive grassy site on lochside with trees and mountain views. Loads of activities include watery ones, reindeer (1704/KIDS) and at the **Coylumbridge Hotel** (1147/KIDS) there's a pool and the Fun House, a separate building full of stuff to amuse kids of all ages. Shop at site entrance; café (does breakfast).

1230 5/H18 ✓ **Applecross Campsite** Applecross · www.applecross.uk.com/campsite · **APR–OCT** 01520 744268 First thing you come to as you approach the coast after a hair-raising drive over the *bealach*, the mountain pass. Grassy meadow in farm setting, 1km sea. Some wigwam wooden cabins (and trailers further in). Usual facilities; Flower Tunnel café for breakfast and a great café/restaurant along the bay (1078/HIGHLANDS). A green, grassy, safe landing.

1231 4/J15 ✓ **Port A Bhaigh Campsite** Altandhu, nr Achiltibuie · www.portabhaigh. co.uk · 01854 622339 Wild yet civilised camping on grassy sward gently sloping to a wee beach on one of Scotland's secretly celebrated foreshores with an immense and forever memorable view of the Summer Isles. Add the pub (who run the site), the **Am Fuaran** with its great grub and it would be hard to find a more perfect spot. Cruise to the isles, climb something, gaze at the sunset.

1232 4/L12 ✓ **Sango Sands** Durness · www.sangosands.com · 07838 381065 Great **APR–OCT** location overlooking sea in downtown Durness with everything you would want, including a pub (The Oasis, on a corner of the site). View only obstructed by campervans. Plenty to do round here (1561/BEACHES), Smoo Cave, Balnakeil Craft Village, etc. Well run and very friendly.

1233 7/H22 ✓ **Shieling Holidays** Craignure, Mull · www.shielingholidays.co.uk ·
APR–MID OCT   01680 812496 35km from Tobermory right where the ferry docks. Great views and a no-nonsense, thought-of-everything camp park. Self-catering shielings (carpeted cottage tents with heaters and en-suite facilities) or hostel beds. Loads to do and see (though mainly by car), including nearby **Duart Castle** (1762/CASTLES); and a pool at the Isle of Mull Hostel open to the plebs (1km). Eat here too or at the Craignure Inn.

1234 7/J28 ✓ **Seal Shore** Kildonan, Arran · www.campingarran.com · 01770 820320 In
APR–OCT   the S of the island, the emerging fun place to be, **Kildonan** (2240/ARRAN), with a long littoral to wander and open views to Pladda Island. Smallish, intimate greenfield site (40+) for campers and caravans. BBQ, dayroom and hotel adjacent for grub and pub. 'We're always in the UK top 20,' says Mr D, who will brook no nonsense from naughty kids or naughty parents. Sleep with the seals! Bus stop nearby.

1235 7/H21 ✓ **Resipole Farm** Loch Sunart, Ardnamurchan · www.resipole.co.uk ·
MAR–OCT   01967 431235 Arrive via Corran Ferry or from Mallaig or Fort William route via Lochailort (1632/SCENIC ROUTES). Extensive grassy landing on lochside with all mod cons including shop, dishwashers, washing machines. A bit caravan-cluttered, but quiet days in Ardnamurchan are all around you. Adventurous may kayak on the loch.

1236 5/H16 ✓ **Sands Holiday Centre** nr Gairloch · www.sandsholidaycentre.co.uk ·
APR–OCT   01445 712152 4km Gairloch (road to Melvaig) with island views, a large grassy park with dunes and its own long, sandy beach (1575/BEACHES). Separate camping area. 10 wooden wigwams named after islands. Kids' play area. Lots to do and see in Gairloch: a great pub, the **Old Inn** (1184/INNS); well-equipped shop, mountain bikes for hire; great camping in dunes plus walking, fishing, etc.

1237 4/J14 **Clachtoll Beach Campsite** nr Lochinver · www.clachtollbeachcampsite.
APR–SEP   co.uk · 01571 855377 Friendly grassy beach site in spectacular scenery (1622/ SCENIC ROUTES). The caravan part is a bit of a blot on the landscape but the beach is great. Camping, caravan hook-ups and chalets: all usual facilities in a great wild area.

1238 5/H20 **Camusdarach** nr Arisaig · www.camusdarach.co.uk · 01687 450221 Friendly,
MAR–OCT   natural campsite sheltered by big trees near splendid beach and looking onto the islands. It's on the Road to the Isles (1631/SCENIC ROUTES): turn left, signed Camusdarrach 6km after Arisaig, then 3km. Small (42 pitches); book in summer. Decent shower block. No shop; free-range eggs available. Beaches are the thing (1580/BEACHES).

1239 7/H23 **Roseview Caravan Park** Oban · www.roseviewoban.co.uk · 01631 562755
MAR–OCT · 3km out of Oban. Quiet, clean and friendly ground with stream running through. All sorts of extras such as undercover cooking area, BBQ, play park. No bar. No dogs. The **Oban Caravan & Camping Park** www.obancaravanpark.com · 01631 562425 is adjacent at Gallanachmore overlooking the sea and easier to find. Well-run C&C Club family site with shop and ducks! Both near the Kerrera ferry, the walks and the **Tea Garden** (797/OBAN).

1240 7/L24 **Cashel Caravan & Campsite** Rowardennan · www.campingintheforest.
MAR–OCT   co.uk · 01360 870234 Forestry Commission site on the quieter shores of Loch Lomond in Queen Elizabeth Forest Park. Jumbo pitches and pre-pitched tents. Excellent facilities including shop, takeaway and play area, and tons to do in the surrounding area which includes Ben Lomond and plootering on or by the loch.

1241 5/G18 **Sligachan** Skye · www.sligachan.co.uk · 01478 650204 The camp site you
JAN-DEC see at the major bend in the road on the A87 going N to Portree from the bridge
LL and the ferries. Sligachan is major hotel landmark and all its facilities include all-
day bistro/Seamus' bar (famous whisky list). Lovely site by river with many walks
from here. Free choice. Just pitch up and they'll come round. Laundry facilities.
Adventure playground by hotel and the adventure playground of Skye all around.

1242 5/F18 **Kinloch Campsite** Dunvegan, Skye · www.kinloch-campsite.co.uk ·
APR-OCT 01470 521531 Friendly, family-run grassy campsite on Glendale road by Dunvegan.
Not so caravan heavy; choose your own pitch from many. Good location for NW
Skye wanderings and eating-out options in Dunvegan, especially **Jann's Cakes** and
The Oyster Shed (2239/SKYE).

Glorious Glamping

1243 8/R25 ✓✓ **Lochhouses Farm** nr North Berwick · www.harvestmoonholidays.
NO PETS com · 07817 968985 From A1 S of Haddington, A198 to North Berwick
L past Tyninghame; Lochhouses signed on right. 1km to farmyard. 7 well-appointed
safari tents (can take 8) under trees and 7 treehouses (all with wood-burning
stoves and en-suite toilets) in beautiful farmland near beach. Fabulous light and a
microclimate of one of the driest places in Scotland. Shop, BBQ and cock-a-doodle
kids' corner. All mod glamping cons. Can hire for exclusive use.

1244 5/N19 ✓✓ **Inshriach** Rothiemurchus, nr Aviemore · www.inshriachhouse.
com · 01540 651341 In the grounds of this quirky Edwardian country
house (1273/HOUSE PARTIES) by the Spey, a range of wonderful woodland retreats: a
16-foot yurt (by Red Kite), a converted (1954 Commer) lorry, an 'isolated' bothy and
a Shepherd's Hut by the river. All are highly individual, comfy and quite beautiful,
especially The Bothy (part of a project funded by the Royal Scottish Academy), a
mile away, and the Hut by the March Pool, built by Tim Westman. Wood-burning
stoves, compost loos and the like; it's eco-heaven.

1245 6/P19 ✓✓ **Lazy Duck** nr Nethy Bridge · www.lazyduck.co.uk · 01479 821642
Beautiful setting and eco accom in heart of Cairngorm National Park. A
hut, a lodge, wee hostel and camping in whispering woods by the River Nethy.
Report: 1149/HOSTELS.

1246 8/N23 ✓ **Comrie Croft** nr Comrie · www.comriecroft.com · 01764 670140 On A85
Comrie-Crieff road, essentially a hostel (1148/HOSTELS) and camp ground but
they have 5 Swedish katas, canvas yurt-type things beautifully situated up the hill
in the woods. Wood stoves, platform to sleep, picnic tables. Millpond nearby and
superb walking. Bike hire (and sales) on premises. Shop, tearoom, trails; good
eating-out options in Comrie and Crieff (932/917/PERTHSHIRE).

1247 8/L23 ✓ **Lovestruck @ Monachyle Mhor** nr Balquhidder · www.mhor.net ·
L 01877 384622 11km from Balquhidder along Loch Voil. The irrepressible
Lewis family get on the glamping bandwagon and in this case it really is a (horse)
wagon, parked overlooking the amazing loch beneath the Braes a discreet distance
from their fabulous hotel (1191/GET-AWAY HOTELS), where you will want to eat and
hang out in the bar or lounge. Roomy this ain't but romantic – no question.
Veranda and wood stove. You will want to be in love!

1248 8/R24　**Yurts at Cambo** nr Crail & St Andrews · www.camboestate.com · 01333 450054 2 yurts in the grounds of Cambo House, a fabulous old crumbly mansion with B&B, self-catering and exclusive use (899/FIFE; 1280/HOUSE PARTIES). But it's those gardens and grounds you want to be in – these yurts among the trees. Basic but lovely. Café in the courtyard and beach nearby.

1249 7/F26　**Storm-Pods** Lagavulin, Islay · www.islay-pods.co.uk · 01496 300129 Along the road W of Port Ellen in the S of Islay, where the distilleries – Ardbeg, Laphroaig and Lagavulin – sit by the sea, these (currently 3) 'pods' are lodged discreetly into the bank overlooking the cove on a farm near a boatyard – all perfectly Islay. Close to one another but private. The delights of Port Ellen – a good pub, and food at the **Islay Hotel**, and 3km in the other direction, the **Ardbeg Distillery Café** (2241/ISLAY).

1250 9/Q28　**Ecopods** nr Port Appin · www.domesweetdome.co.uk · 07725 409003 On A828 between Oban and Fort William at the **Castle Stalker** café and viewpoint (1410/TEAROOMS). Jim and Nicola who have the café (and can give you breakfast) have built 2 (so far) futuristic dome structures (by Zendome of Berlin) full of light, space and mod cons in what they call a boutique retreat. Tucked away in the rhododendron and birch woods they have maximum privacy though none of the view. A very intimate hideaway, couples or real close friends only.

Real Retreats

1251 9/Q28
NO TV
LL
ATMOS
✓✓✓ **Samye Ling** nr Eskdalemuir · www.samyeling.org · 01387 373232 Bus or train to Lockerbie/Carlisle then bus (Mon-Sat 0871 200 2233) or taxi (01576 470480). Community consists of an extraordinary and inspiring temple not so incongruous in these Border wilds. The complex comprises main house (with some accom), dorm and guest-house blocks (many single rooms), Tibetan Tearooms and shop. Further up the hill, longer retreats in annexes. Samye Ling, a world centre for Tibetan Buddhism, is always under construction under the supervision of Tibetan masters, but they offer daily and longer stays and courses in all aspects of Buddhism, meditation, t'ai chi, yoga, etc. Daily timetable from prayers at 6am and work period. Breakfast/lunch; light supper at 6pm, all vegetarian. Busy, thriving community atmos. This is Buddhism, pure and simple. See also World Peace Centre (below).

1252 6/P17
✓✓✓ **Findhorn Community & Park** nr Forres · www.findhorn.org · 01309 690311 The world-famous and world-class spiritual community and foundation begun by Peter and Eileen Caddy and Dorothy Maclean in 1962, a village of caravans, cabins and brilliant houses on the way into Findhorn on B9011. Visitors can join the community as short-term guests, eating and working on-site but probably staying at recommended B&Bs. This sprawling, always-growing eco-village is fascinating and a joy just to pass through. Programme of courses and residential workshops in spiritual growth/dance/ healing, etc. Many other aspects and facilities available in a cosmopolitan and well-organised community. Excellent shop (1454/DELIS), pottery (2160/SCOTTISH SHOPS) and café – the **Blue Angel** (1326/VEGETARIAN); the Universal Hall has a great music and performance programme featuring many of Scotland's finest.

1253 6/P17
ATMOS
✓✓ **Pluscarden Abbey** between Forres & Elgin · www. pluscardenabbey.org Signed from the main A96 (11km from Elgin) in a sheltered glen south-facing with a background of wooded hillside, this is the only medieval monastery in the UK still inhabited by monks. It's a deeply calming place. The Benedictine community keep walled gardens and bees. 8 services a day in the

glorious chapel (1879/ABBEYS) which visitors can attend. Retreat for men (14 places) and women (separate, self-catering) with 2-week maximum and no obligatory charge. Write to the Guest Master, Pluscarden Abbey, by Elgin, IV30 8VA; no telephone bookings. Men eat with the monks (mainly vegetarian). Restoration/ building work always in progress (of the abbey and of the spirit).

1254 8/P23 ✓✓ **The Bield at Blackruthven** Tibbermore, nr Perth · www. bieldatblackruthven.org.uk · 01738 583238 Take Crieff road (A85) from Perth and A9/ring road past Huntingtower then left for Tibbermore. 2km. Bield is an old Scottish word for a place of refuge and shelter; also means to nurture, succour, encourage. All are possible here in this superbly well-managed, tasteful Christian retreat. A Georgian home with outbuildings containing accom, lounges, meeting rooms in 30 gorgeous garden acres, with a swimming pool, chapel (in old carpenter's workshop) and a surprisingly spacious barn laid out for events; they're always open. More like a country-house hotel but there are prayers, courses and support if you want it. No guests on Monday, so 6 days max. Very cheap for this level of comfort. It is beautiful, peaceful and contemporary. The Solas Festival is in mid-June, there are open days, concerts. Yet this is possibly Perthshire's best kept secret. Meals and self catering. Serenity!

1255 8/L24 ✓ **Lendrick Lodge** Brig o' Turk · www.lendricklodge.com · 01877 376263 On A821 scenic road through the Trossachs. Near road but in idyllic grounds with beautiful standing stones and gurgling river. An organised retreat and get-away-from-it-all yoga and healing centre. Yoga, reiki and shamanic teaching throughout year (they even do fire walking!). Can take up to 50 people and run 2 courses at the same time. Individual rooms and full board if required. River Retreat in separate building overlooking the river has a pool and 2 en-suite rooms.

1256 8/L23 ✓ **Dhanakosa** Balquhidder · www.dhanakosa.com · 01877 384213 3km village on Loch Voilside 9km from A84 Callander-Crianlarich road. Gentle Buddhist place with ongoing retreat programmes (Introductory or Regular; 1 week or weekends in winter). Guidance and group sessions. Yoga and t'ai chi. Meditation room. Rooms hold 2–6 and are en suite. Vegetarian food. Beautiful serene setting on Balquhidder Braes: you will 'radiate love'. Open day in June.

1257 7/J27 ✓ **The World Peace Centre** Holy Island · www.holyisle.org · 01770 601100 LL Take a ferry from Lamlash on Arran (ferry 01770 700463/600998) to find yourself part of a Tibetan (albeit contemporary) mystery. Escape from the madding crowd on the mainland and compose your spirit or just refresh. Built by Samye Ling abbots, this tiny Celtic refuge centre offers a range of activities to help purge the soul or restore the faith. Day trippers, holiday-breakers and all faiths welcome. Can accommodate 60. Conference/gathering centre. Must phone ahead. And there's a hill to climb (2216/ISLAND WALKS). Ferries very limited in winter.

1258 7/K26 **College of the Holy Spirit** Millport, Cumbrae · www.island-retreats.org · 01475 530353 Continuous ferry service from Largs (every 15 mins, and 30 mins in winter) then 6km bus journey to Millport. Off main street through a gate in the wall, into grounds of the **Cathedral of the Isles** (1847/CHURCHES) and another, more peaceful world. A retreat for the Episcopal Church since 1884. Available for groups but there are 16 comfortable rooms (5 en suite), with B&B. Also half/full board. Morning and night prayer each day, Eucharist on Sunday and delightful concerts in summer. Fine library. Bike hire available on island. See also (1374/CAFÉS).

1259 7/J24   **EcoYoga Centre** Ford, Argyll · www.ecoyoga.org · 01546 810259 In a sylvan, almost lochside setting, deep in glorious Argyll, reached by an unnumbered road from Ford off the A816, 20km N of Lochgilphead. On booking you'll get directions but, suffice to say, it's discreetly delightful here – when you find it. Off-grid electricity, wild swimming in the gorge, room to roam and superb food. I haven't stayed or sampled but Dana M, a regular retreater, world traveller and a bit of a foodie recommends their yoga courses highly. Other reports please.

The Best Spas

1260 8/Q25   ✓✓ **One Spa** Sheraton Grand Hotel, Edinburgh · www.onespa.com · 0131 221 7777 Considered the best spa in the city and on many national/ international lists, it's also one of the best things about the hotel which is centrally situated on Festival Sq opposite the Usher Hall (90/MAJOR HOTELS). As well as the usual (reasonably spacious) pool there's another which extends outdoors dangling infinity-style over Conference Sq behind the hotel. Decent gym. Exotic hydrotherapy and a host of treatments, with all the right unguents. Range of day and half-day tickets and gift vouchers available.

1261 8/R23   ✓✓ **The Kohler Waters Spa** The Old Course Hotel, St Andrews · www. oldcoursehotel.co.uk · 01334 468067 In the mega Old Course resort (892/FIFE), this beautifully designed leisure/treatment suite, though small, is another reason for staying. The spa was designed by the team who created the original Cow Shed at Babington House. Owners of the hotel, the Kohler Company, produce iconic kitchens and bathrooms in the US and own a slew of luxury resorts. In the main suite there's a 20m pool, monsoon showers, saunas, crystal steam rooms and treatment rooms; you will be perfectly pampered. Non-res welcome.

1262 8/P27   ✓✓ **Stobo Castle** Stobo, nr Peebles · www.stobocastle.co.uk · 01721 725300 Border baronial mansion 10km S of Peebles in beautiful countryside of towering trees and trickling burns. **Dawyck Gardens** nearby (1510/ GARDENS) and there are Japanese Water Gardens in the grounds. Mainly a hotel (51 rooms) but day visits possible; the spa is the heart of the pampering experience. Over 70 treatments. Not too much emphasis on exercise though a lovely pool. Different categories of rooms and suites; also lodges. Bespoke and every conceivable and currently fashionable treatment for men and women; all medical peculiarities accounted for. Decent dining: 'healthy', of course, but no denial of carbs or cream. Coffee shop/juice bar. White-towelled ladies lounge all over. Deals often available for days and half days.

1263 8/M26   ✓✓ **The Spa at Blythswood Square** Glasgow · www.blythswoodsquare. com · 0141 240 1662 In the basement of Glasgow's fab city centre hotel, a top spa and destination in itself. Hugely popular with Glasgow lasses for individual treatments and day packages using, among others, ishga products (natural, organic, Scottish). Great lighting, steam, sauna, jacuzzi-tastic; seductive and indulgent, as they say. Pure (as well as purifying) Glasgow.

1264 8/N24   ✓✓ **The Spa at Gleneagles** Gleneagles Hotel, Auchterarder · www. gleneagles.com/spa · 01764 694332 Naturally, the leisure suites here have always offered one of the best spa experiences. 20 treatment rooms, a plethora of therapists and built-in soothing atmos, it's practically irresistible with or without golf fatigue. Suites for men and women, vitality pool, heated beds and a long menu of tantalising treatments. Only branded ESPA in Scotland.

1265 7/L25 ✓✓ **The Spa at Cameron House on Loch Lomond** · www.qhotels.co.uk ·
01389 727647 The spa of **Cameron House** (496/HOTELS OUTSIDE
GLASGOW) is 4km along the road and lochside at the Carrick, the 18-hole golf course
(shuttle service). New building complex incorporates golf clubhouse facilities, shop
and recommended Claret Jug bar/restaurant. Very professional service. Many
treatment rooms and therapists; 3 different spa products in use. There's a pool, a
rooftop infinity pool, an outside (sheltered) deck, bar and restaurant. When you've
made enough dosh to afford this (or somebody treats you), just relax.

1266 7/J22 ✓ **The Spa at Isle of Eriska Hotel** Isle of Eriska Hotel, Ledaig · www.
eriska-hotel.co.uk · 01631 720371 The Isle of Eriska ('hotel/spa/island') is one
of Scotland's most comfy country-house hotels (1127/COUNTRY-HOUSE HOTELS), 20km
N of Oban. Apart from other activities and the usual indulgences there's a lovely spa in
the gardens overlooking the surprising 9-hole golf course. There's a 17m-pool and
well-equipped gym, the **Deck Restaurant** with terrace and treatment rooms using
ESPA and ishga products. Unlikely to be crowded; enjoy tranquillity.

1267 7/L24 ✓ **The Spa In The Walled Garden** Luss · www.lochlomond.com ·
01436 655315 The more leisurely side of Loch Lomond Golf Club, this
stunning contemporary spa suite (designed by Donna Vallone) is what it says on
the tin. Thermal suites, treatment and relaxation rooms open onto small, private
gardens and the walled garden itself with its fabulous glass houses, a visit to which
is relaxation in itself. ESPA products. Go on, you (possibly) deserve it!

For The Best House Parties

Rent these for families or friends and have to yourselves: exclusive use.

1268 8/R25
ATMOS ✓✓ **Greywalls** Gullane · www.greywalls.co.uk · 01620 842144 36km E of Edinburgh off A198 beyond Gullane towards North Berwick. Though a fabulous country house, Greywalls is still homely and available for exclusive use. Overlooks Muirfield, the championship course, and is close to several of Scotland's top courses. The Lutyens-designed manor house and the gardens attributed to Gertrude Jekyll are simply superb, especially in summer, and the public rooms are the epitome of taste and comfiness at all times. Dining c/o the Albert Roux team. The Colonel's House adjacent is also available (takes 8). 23 rooms in the hotel and lodges in the garden where dogs are welcome. £7k approximately; £1.2k for the House at TGP. This is house-party living as it's supposed to be.

1269 4/Q13
L
ATMOS ✓✓ **Ackergill Tower** nr Wick · www.amazingvenues.co.uk · 01955 603556 Deluxe retreat geared for parties and groups (mostly corporates) though 'leisure guests' can stay by the night (med.exp), and there are 3-day packages throughout the year. All-inclusive: means activities, atmospheric dinners (huge fires, candlelight); you may not always eat in the same place (they have the Smuggler's Inn for gastropub food). Outside, the wild coast. A perfect treat/retreat. Individual prices on request. You'll probably have to mingle.

1270 8/P20
LL ✓✓ **Mar Lodge Estate** nr Braemar · www.ntsholidays.com · 0844 493 2173 For exclusive use, there are several remarkable properties including apartments in the big hoose in the NTS-run, extensive 72,000-acre estate 15km from Braemar. Classic Highland scenery superb in any season; the upper waters of the Dee. Apartments in main mansion (takes 4–15) and 2 other houses. Public rooms including library, billiard room and ballroom can be hired separately. Expensive, of course, but not when divided between mates. And big wow factor. Live like the royals down the road, without the servants (unless you bring with). Otherwise, it's all sorted!

1271 1/R10
LLL ✓✓ **Balfour Castle** Shapinsay · www.balfourcastle.co.uk · 01856 711282 Lording it, though sympathetically so, over the 300 souls of Shapinsay (they built them a pub), this is as far as you can get in the UK to gracious living from your city or The City whence many guests will come (by plane or helicopter). Castle launch from Kirkwall or regular ferry. Up to 18 guests, unbridled luxury, dedicated chef, the esteemed Jean-Baptiste Bady. In summer, the light! 2244/ORKNEY.

1272 8/P24 ✓✓ **Myres Castle** nr Auchtermuchty · www.myrescastle.co.uk · 01337 828350 2km Auchtermuchty on Falkland road. Well-preserved castle/family home (Henry and Amanda Barge) in stunningly beautiful gardens, recent relandscaping and a new tented venue attached to the garden wall. High country life though at a very reasonable price. 10 rooms individually refurbished to exceptional standard. Formal dining room, evocative Victorian kitchen and impressive billiard room. The perfect setting for a bespoke friendly or family get-together; several selected caterers will feed you. Central to Fife attractions, Falkland and St Andrews. Takes 20.

1273 5/N19 ✓✓ **Inshriach House** nr Aviemore · www.inshriachhouse.com · 01540 651341 On B970 back road between Inverdruie and Feshiebridge, 8km S of Aviemore. Atmospheric, comfy, lived-in Edwardian country house with gorgeous public rooms, highly individual bedrooms, gardens and small estate. Close to spectacular **Loch an Eilean** (1609/LOCHS) and **Inshriach Nursery** (2191/GARDEN CENTRES) with its famous cakes and bird-watching, but loads to do round here. Self-catering or food from the **Old Bridge Inn** (1307/GASTROPUBS) nearby. Up to 17 can stay and there is uniquely fabulous eco-accommodation in the woody grounds (1244/GLAMPING). One of the most laid-back options on this page. They have fishing! Great wee festival, The Insider, in the grounds in June.

1274 5/N17 ✓ **Drynachan Lodge** nr Nairn · www.cawdor.com · 01667 402402 This fab 19th-century hunting lodge is on the Cawdor Estate S of Nairn. The castle is signed from all over (1758/CASTLES). While there are many cottages here for let this is the big house (sleeps 16) and was personally decked out by Lady Isabella Cawdor. Like all things on the estate it's done with great taste. Fully staffed and catered, it's like a hip shooting lodge. It'll cost ya.

1275 7/H14 ✓ **Lunga House** Ardfern, Argyll · www.lungahouse.co.uk · 01852 500237 Take Craobh Haven (marina) turn-off on the A816. Once had a boho-chic, Lunga-time reputation among those who know, this rambling big hoose is less crumbly of late and, though still old style, is perfect for parties, gatherings and mainly weddings. Great public space includes a ballroom. 18 bedrooms and many cottages. Here, you really can call it your own! Catering provided.

1276 7/K28 ✓ **Culzean Castle: Eisenhower Apartment** nr Maybole · www.nts.org.uk · LL 01655 884455 The second-floor apartment once stayed in by the wartime NTS Supreme Allied Commander in Europe and later president of the US. 6 suites and public rooms available singly or for exclusive use. Spectacular both in and out with great easy walking. Dinner can be provided; the grounds are superb (1755/CASTLES).

1277 3/E15 ✓ **Amhuinnsuidhe Castle** Harris · www.amhuinnsuidhe.com · ATMOS 01859 560200 N from Tarbert then W to faraway strand (directions: see 2211/ ISLAND WALKS). Staffed, fab food and gothic Victorian castle/shooting and fishing lodge (salmon arrive in a foaming mass at the river mouth). 12 bedrooms; mainly sporting and fishing weeks but individuals can join at certain times for mixed house party. Grand interiors and top fishing on 9 lochs and rivers. Expensive for exclusive use but everything – from ghillies to afternoon tea – is thrown in.

1278 7/K28 ✓ **Doonbrae House** Alloway · www.doonbrae.com · 01292 442466 In heart of unspoiled, well-kept village still evocative of Burns, whose birthplace, gardens and Tam o' Shanter graveyard are nearby. Opposite and part of Brig o' Doon Hotel, much favoured for weddings. This refurbished mansion is separate and you have it to yourself (group bookings only). Also 2 cottages. On Doon banks (to amble) in delightful gardens. Self-catering or eat at hotel. 5 suites.

1279 5/F17 ✓ **Greshornish Country House** Skye · www.greshornishhouse.com · 01470 582266 Comfy, artful country house to yourself; lovely rooms. Lochside in the middle of Skye. Report: 1197/GET-AWAY HOTELS.

1280 8/R24 ✓ **Cambo House and Gardens** nr Crail · www.camboestate.com · L 01333 450054 On Fife coast route, 14km from St Andrews. Rambling house, fabulous au naturel grounds, and garden famous for snowdrops and bulbs in spring 24/EVENTS. 5 B&B rooms, 4 apartments, 3 cottages, 2 'glamping' tents. A very special country-house experience awaits here; you make it what you will. Great walking, golfing and carousing opportunities. See also 899/FIFE.

1281 9/N30 ✓ **Cavens** Kirkbean · www.cavens.com · 01387 880234 Off A710 Solway Coast road 20km S Dumfries. Informal and well-appointed mansion in gorgeous grounds near beach. Sleeps up to 22 in house (16) and lodges. Great value compared to other grand manors. Angus's dinner-party cooking. 810/SW HOTELS.

1282 7/J24   **Castle Lachlan** Loch Fyne · www.castlelachlan.com · 01369 860669 For
       L   directions see Inver, the fab restaurant on the estate (791/ARGYLL). Stunning
setting in heart of Scotland scenery, the 18th-century ancestral home of the
Clan Maclachlan. Snooker room; all-weather tennis. Self-catering but dining can
be arranged. Sleeps '13 people comfortably' (more for dinner). £2-3k per week.
Sumptuous surroundings for rock stars and weddings and the like.

1283 4/H16   **Rua Reidh Lighthouse** Melvaig, nr Gairloch · www.stayatalighthouse.
      LL   co.uk · 01445 771263 End of the road 20km from Gairloch and remote and
dramatic, but, yes, you can have this lighthouse to yourself. The McLachlans make
you welcome in 4 rooms and the 3-roomed self-contained First Officer's Quarters
(by the week). Gairloch has good food/pub options but you arrange your own
catering. Plus the sea and the scenery! It can be wild.

    1284   **National Trust for Scotland** has many interesting properties they rent out
for weekends or longer. www.nts.org.uk or 0131 243 9331 for details. **The
Landmark Trust** also have 19 mostly fabulous properties in Scotland including
The Pineapple (1833/MONUMENTS), **Auchenleck House** in Ayrshire which sleeps
13 and the wonderful **Ascog House** or **Meikle House** on the Isle of Bute which
sleep 9 and 10 respectively. Phone 01628 825925 to get their beautiful handbook
(properties throughout the UK) or see www.landmarktrust.org.uk.

the Best

Good Food & Drink

Bloody Good Pubs

Pubs in Edinburgh and Glasgow are listed in their own sections. See also Real Ale & Gastropubs in following pages.

1285 7/K23
L
ATMOS
✓ **The Drover's Inn** Inverarnan · www.thedroversinn.co.uk ·
01301 704234 A famously Scottish drinking den/hotel, just N of Ardlui at the head of Loch Lomond and 12km S of Crianlarich on the A82. Smoky, low-ceilinged rooms, open ranges, whisky in the jar, stuffed animals in the hall and kilted barmen; slack though it sometimes seems, this is nevertheless the antithesis of the contrived Scottish tourist pub. Also see 839/CENTRAL.

1286 5/H20
LL
ATMOS
✓ **The Old Forge** Inverie, Knoydart · www.theoldforge.co.uk ·
01687 462267 A warm haven for visitors to this pristine peninsula. Suddenly you're part of the community; real ales and real characters, excellent pub grub. Pub for sale at TGP but the community will ensure its survival intact. Lunch & dinner. Evenings only in winter. Stay at fabulous luxe self-catering Knoydart House or their superb **Knoydart Hide** (1213/LUXURIOUS ISOLATION) or along the road (well, 10km) at **Doune Stone Lodge** (1196/GET-AWAY HOTELS) or in the adjacent 'Knoydart Snug' cottage or bunk nearer by (info@knoydart-foundation.com).

1287 7/K21
DF
L
ATMOS
✓ **Clachaig Inn** nr Glencoe · www.clachaig.com · 01855 811252 Deep in the glen itself down the road signed off the A82, 5km from Glencoe village. Both the pub with its wood-burning stoves and the lounge are woody and welcoming. Backdoor best for muddy boots or those averse to leather-studded sofas. Real ale and real climbers and walkers. Handy if you're in the hostel 2km down road or camping. Walking fuel food in bar/lounge and good, inexpensive accom, including lodges. Impressive plethora of ales and beer fests in May and October.

1288 8/S20
L
✓ **Marine Hotel** Stonehaven · www.marinehotelstonehaven.co.uk ·
01569 762155 Popular local on a great harbour with seats outside and always a crowd. 6 guest ales, big Belgian and wheat-beer selection, and their own brew – 6°N. Food till 9pm. Upstairs dining room overlooks the boat-bobbing bay. Same menu; local fish specials. Open all day.

1289 7/G22
✓ **Mishnish** Tobermory, Mull · www.themishnish.co.uk · 01688 302500
Though perhaps no longer the iconic island pub for craic and music culture, still a great bar (poshed up a bit). On the bay and on the money. Report: 2243/MULL.

1290 3/C20
LL
ATMOS
Castlebay Bar Castlebay, Barra · www.castlebay-hotel.co.uk · 01871 810223
Adjacent to Castlebay Hotel. A deceptively average-seeming but brilliant bar. All human life is here. More Irish than all the Irish makeovers on the mainland. Occasional live music including the – legend in their own lifetime – Vatersay Boys; conversations with strangers. Report: 2236/ISLAND HOTELS.

1291 5/J19
L
Cluanie Inn Glenmoriston · www.cluanieinn.com · 01320 340238 On A87 at head of Loch Cluanie 15km before Shiel Bridge on the long road to Kyle of Lochalsh (and Skye). A wayside inn with pub food, a restaurant and the (both bunkhouse and hotel) accommodation walkers want (1188/INNS). Good base for climbing/walking (especially the **Five Sisters of Kintail** 1975/WALKS). It's a cosy refuge.

1292 8/L27
ATMOS
Poosie Nansie's 21 Loudoun Street, Mauchline · 01290 550075 Main street of this Ayrshire village where Burns lived in 1788. This pub there then, those characters still there at the bar. Sport on the big TV. 4 of his children buried (yes, 4) in the churchyard opposite. A room in the pub left as was. The rest is here and now. Lunch & 6-8pm Fri/Sat. Otherwise the ale.

1293 9/M30   **The Murray Arms & The Masonic Arms** Gatehouse of Fleet 2 adjacent unrelated pubs that have always been a big part of this wee town's community. The Masonic has had the reputation for best food and many changes of management later, this is fair and it has the good atmos. Masonic symbols still on the walls of the upstairs rooms. The Murray Arms has a Burns *Scots Wha' Ha'e* connection and seems to survive on its history; it could do with a nudge into the 21st century now.

1294 5/L19   **Lock Inn** Fort Augustus · 01320 366302 Busy canalside (Caledonian Canal
     L   which joins Loch Ness in the distance) pub for locals and visitors. Good grub downstairs or up if you want (overlooking lock). Pub staples; reasonable malts. Food LO 9.30pm. Occasional live music. Boats go by very slowly.

1295 9/L31   **The Steampacket Inn** Isle of Whithorn · www.thesteampacketinn.biz ·
     LL   01988 500334 The hub of this atmospheric wee village at the end of the road
  ATMOS   south (1559/VILLAGES). On harbour that fills and empties with the tide. Great for ales and food. 7 inexpensive rooms upstairs. An all-round happy hostelry.

✓✓ **Glenelg Inn** Glenelg A pub for the village and those who make it over the Pass. A classic. Report: 1173/INNS.

✓✓ **Applecross Inn** Applecross Like the Glenelg above it serves its community and folk who come from everywhere to eat. Report: 1172/INNS.

Great Pubs For Real Ale

For Real Ale & Craft Beer pubs in Edinburgh, see p. 75, and in Glasgow, see p. 125.

1296 8/Q23   ✓ **Fisherman's Tavern** Broughty Ferry · www.fishermanstavern-
  ATMOS   broughtyferry.co.uk · 01382 775941 In 'The Ferry', but not too far to go from Dundee centre for great atmos and great collection of ales (6). In Fort St near the seafront. Regular IPAs and many guests. Low-ceilinged and friendly. Inexpensive accom adjacent and pub grub as you like (945/DUNDEE).

1297 8/N21   ✓ **Moulin Inn/Hotel** Pitlochry · www.moulinhotel.co.uk · 01796 472196
  ATMOS   4km uphill from main street on road to Bridge of Cally, an inn at a picturesque crossroads since 1695. Some rooms and (mixed) reputation for pub grub but loved for cosy bar and brewery out back from which comes Moulin Light, Ale of Atholl and 2 others (one of the first microbreweries).

1298 8/N25   **The Four Marys** Linlithgow · www.fourmarys-linlithgow.co.uk ·
     01506 842171 Main street near road up to Palace (1772/RUINS), so handy for a pint after schlepping around the historical attractions. Mentioned in most beer guides. 9 ales, usually guests. Beer festivals May and October. Notable malt whisky collection and popular locally for lunches (daily) and evening meals.

1299 8/M24   **The Lade Inn** Callander · www.theladeinn.com · 01877 330152 At Kilmahog, western approach to town, at the start of road into the Trossachs; a good place to stop. Inn brews its own (Waylade, Ladeback, Ladeout). Ale shop adjacent with well over 200 of Scotland's finest (noon-6pm). Big pub food operation (reports vary).

1300 5/H16   **The Old Inn** Gairloch · www.theoldinn.net · 01445 712006 Southern approach on A832 near golf course, an old inn across an old bridge; a goodly selection of malts and ales, including their own: Mike's Mild, Bees Knees and Blind Piper and other Scottish. Tourists and locals mix in season. Regular live music. Rooms above make this an all-round good reason to stop in Gairloch (1184/INNS).

The Best Gastropubs

Gastropubs in Edinburgh and Glasgow are listed in their own sections.

1301 8/L27
DF
ATMOS
✓✓ **The Sorn Inn** Sorn · www.sorninn.com · 01290 551305 Village main street, 8km E of Mauchline, 25km Ayr. Pub with rooms and big reputation for food. Restaurants and tables in bar. Family-run (the Grants with chef Craig Grant). Consistently classic, comforting food and steaks rarely come better than this – an exemplary rural gastropub experience and great value. 7 days.

1302 7/H26
MAR-OCT
✓✓ **The Kilberry Inn** nr Tarbert, Argyll · www.kilberryinn.com · 01880 770223 On the single-track B8024 that follows the coast of the Knapdale peninsula between Lochgilphead and Tarbert, halfway round, this is out on its own. A Michelin Bib Gourmand for over 10 years and a treat to eat. Clare Johnson is a great cook, all her ingredients properly sourced; the lounges have a smart, pubby ambience with relaxed, unobtrusive service led by Clare's bloke David. Make that journey (1633/SCENIC ROUTES) and discover Knapdale. Closed Mon.

1303 4/J15
APR-OCT
LL
✓✓ **The Summer Isles Hotel Bar** Achiltibuie · www.summerisleshotel. com · 01854 622449 The adjacent bar of this romantic hotel on the foreshore faces the isles and the sunset (1045/HIGHLANDS). All the superior qualities of their famous food operation available at less than half the price in the cosy bistro-like bar with tiny terrace; occasional traditional music. Great seafood and vegetarian. Apr-Oct lunch & dinner (bar Thu-Sun in winter).

1304 8/M24
DF
✓✓ **The Cross Keys** Kippen · www.kippencrosskeys.com · 01786 870293 Here forever in this quiet town off A811 15km W of Stirling. A while back Debby McGregor and Brian Horsburgh transformed this dependable pub for grub into a gastropub stopover anytime, not just for Sunday lunch or a weekend stay. 3 rooms upstairs, open fires, great food in bar or lounge. Seriously thought-over and sourced, and tempting (ambitious even) gastropub food. Some live music. Beer garden. Mon-Fri lunch & dinner. All day Sat & Sunday roast till 8pm.

1305 8/R24
L
ATMOS
✓✓ **The Ship Inn** Elie · www.shipinn.scot · 01333 330246 Pub on the bay at Elie, the perfect toon in the picturesque East Neuk of Fife (1557/ VILLAGES). New owners and major refurbishment 2015 into a restaurant with rooms. In summer a huge food operation upstairs and down (the former has good view). Same menu throughout; all home-made blackboard specials. On warm days the Beach Bar terrace overlooking the strand goes like Bondi. 7 days.

1306 8/R24
✓✓ **The 19th Hole** Earlsferry · www.19thhole.scot · 01333 330610 At the furthest point of Earlsferry from Elie on the Links Rd facing the golf course (follow the one-way system round). New 2015 as sister restaurant of The Ship Inn above, a great addition to eating out in Fife. Despite it not being easy to find, it was packed from the start. Classy, contemporary menu and presentation. Must book weekends. Cottagey layout. 7 days.

1307 5/N19
✓✓ **Old Bridge Inn** Aviemore · www.oldbridgeinn.co.uk · 01479 811137 Off Coylumbridge road at S end of Aviemore as you come in from A9 or Kincraig. 100m from main street by the river. Old like it says but one of those exemplary inn-like inns that completely takes you in! Excellent eclectic menu under chef Chris McCall. Cask ales, artisan beers; kids, skiers, walkers. Very much part of the local music scene, so it also rocks. Kids' menu. 7 days lunch & dinner. In summer, tables over road by the river. Hostel adjacent (1153/HOSTELS).

1308 8/R23 ✓ **The Grange Inn** St Andrews · www.thegrangeinn.com · 01334 472670
ATMOS   4km out of town off A917. This perennially popular country pub has built on its
long reputation under John and Carolyn Kelly. Superior gastropub fare; not large, so
book. Lunch Tue-Sun & dinner Tue-Sat.

1309 8/S26 ✓ **The Craw Inn** Auchencrow · www.thecrawinn.co.uk · 01890 761253
Off A1 near Reston and Eyemouth – actually 3km off the A1 and further than
they sign but near enough for a swift detour and the best place to eat between
Berwick and the Lothians: a real destination for great food (lovely pies) and amazing
wine in classic pub atmos. A great deck out the back. Go find! 7 days.

1310 4/J15 ✓ **Am Fuaran** Altandhu · www.amfuaran.co.uk · 01854 622339 Along from
LL   Achiltibuie, this pub has an elevated, elevating view of the Summer Isles from
its terrace. Inside is dark and pub-like and welcoming. Classic pub grub menu.
Home-made, locally sourced (especially seafood and salad leaves). 'How do they do
this so well so far from, well, anywhere', my companion asked. They also have a fab
wee campsite on the foreshore (1231/CAMPING WITH KIDS). 7 days lunch & dinner.

1311 8/S26 ✓ **The Wheatsheaf** Swinton · www.wheatsheaf-swinton.co.uk ·
01890 860257 A village hotel pub about halfway between Kelso and Berwick
(18km) on B6461. In deepest Berwickshire, owners Chris and Jan Winson serve up
the best pub grub you've had since England. Rooms in main building and cottages
with great dinner, B&B deals. An all-round good hostelry. 7 days.

1312 7/K28 ✓ **Souter's Inn** Kirkoswald · www.soutersinn.com · 01655 760653 On A77
between Girvan and Ayr. Contemporary and ambitious transformation of old
hotel and adjacent buildings to form a smart, modern complex that includes a
tearoom, deli/shop, ice-cream factory and bakers. Created by the estimable Costley
family (see Cochrane Inn below), the pub here offers their esteemed gastropub
menu with a Scottish emphasis. Restaurant open all day for snacks, hot meals –
the chocolates, the ice cream – the brand. All good stuff. 7 days.

1313 8/S21 ✓ **The Creel Inn** Catterline, nr Stonehaven · www.thecreelinn.co.uk ·
L   01569 750254 8km S Stonehaven, perching above the bay from where the
lobsters come. And lots of other seafood. Good wine; huge speciality beer selection.
Cove itself has a haunting beauty. Catterline is Joan Eardley (notable artist) territory.
It's also famous for this great atmospheric pub and its grub. 7 days lunch & dinner.

1314 7/L27 ✓ **Wheatsheaf Inn** Symington · www.thewheatsheafsymington.co.uk ·
01563 830307 2km A77. Pleasant village off the unpleasant A77 with this
busy coaching inn opposite the church. Folk come from miles around to eat (book
at weekends) honest-to-goodness pub fare in various rooms (roast beef every
Sunday). Menu on boards. Beer garden. 7 days lunch & dinner.

1315 4/K14 ✓ **Kylesku Hotel** nr Kylestrome · www.kyleskuhotel.co.uk · 01971 502231
MAR-NOV   Off A894 between Scourie and Lochinver. A hotel and pub with a great
LL   quayside location on Loch Glencoul, where boats leave for trips to see the 'highest
waterfall in Europe' (1602/WATERFALLS). Tanja's and Sonia's friendly bar/bistro, with
local fish and seafood including interesting specials, eg spineys (the tails of squat
lobsters) and their signature seafood platter, everything from waters within reach;
yum desserts. Mar-Nov lunch & dinner (food noon all day July/Aug). Cool spot!

1316 8/Q23 ✓ **The Ship Inn** Broughty Ferry · www.theshipinn-broughtyferry.co.uk ·
L   01382 779176 Excellent seafront snug pub with food in upstairs attic
ATMOS   and down (best tables at window upstairs). Famous for clootie dumpling, other

classic pub fare, not so very gastro but good for fish. There are sometimes dolphins in the estuary (binoculars available). 7 days lunch & dinner. See also: 956/DUNDEE.

1317 7/J26 ✓ **Smiddy Bar at the Kingarth Hotel** Isle of Bute · www.kingarthhotel. co.uk · 01700 831662 13km Rothesay, 4km after **Mount Stuart** (1814/ HOUSES). Good, friendly old inn serving probably the best pub food on the island. Blackboard menu and à la carte. Covered terrace; good for family feeding. The atmos is just right. Open AYR 7 days.

1318 8/L25 ✓ **Old Mill** Killearn · www.theoldmillkillearn.co.uk · 01360 550068 More than one inn in this village but this one on the main street is the cosy, friendly one and all that an old pub should be (old here is from 1774). Pub and restaurant. Log fires, brilliant for kids. Garden. New owners 2015. 7 days noon-9pm.

1319 8/R25 ✓ **Goblin Ha' Hotel** Gifford · www.goblinha.com · 01620 810244 In twee village in East Lothian heartland, it is named after a faery place in the nearby woods, and serves a very decent pub lunch and supper (7 days) in lounge and pub, conservatory, terrace and beer garden. Nice rooms above (878/LOTHIANS).

1320 8/R25 ✓ **Waterside Bistro** Haddington · www.watersidebistro.co.uk ·
L   01620 825674 On the banks of the River Tyne near **Lamp of the Lothians** (1860/CHURCHES). This great multi-chambered gastropub makes the most of its great riverside location. Report: 889/LOTHIANS.

1321 7/L27 **Cochrane Inn** Gatehead · www.cochraneinn.com · 01563 570122 Part of the Costley hotel empire (802/AYRSHIRE). A trim and cosy ivy-covered, very inn-like inn – most agreeable. On A759 Troon to Kilmarnock and 2km A71 Kilmarnock-Irvine road. A bugger to get to (locals know how), but excellent gourmet pub with huge local reputation; must book weekends. Mon-Fri lunch & dinner, Sat/Sun all day.

1322 8/M24 **Lion & Unicorn** Thornhill · www.lion-unicorn.co.uk · 01786 850204 Since 1635! On A873 off A84 road between M9 and Callander, near Lake of Menteith in the Trossachs. On main road through the village. They come from miles around for pub grub and sizzling steaks. 3 cosy dining areas, open fires and garden. Changing menu (including a gluten-free one), not too fancy, just nice. 7 days lunch & dinner.

1323 8/L24 **The Byre** Brig o' Turk · www.byreinn.co.uk · 01877 376292 Off A821 at Callander end of the village by Loch Achray. Country inn in deepest Trossachs. Basic pub grub in cosy, firelit rooms with outside decks in summer. Inexpensive wine list. Can walk from here to **Duke's Pass** (1630/SCENIC ROUTES).

1324 9/J30 **The Crown** Portpatrick · www.crownportpatrick.com · 01776 810261
L   Popular, busy pub on harbour with tables outside in summer and everywhere else (it's huge!). Light, airy conservatory. Freshly caught fish their speciality. 12 simple rooms above. Locals and Irish who sail over. Lunch & LO 9.30pm.

1325 9/N30 **The Anchor Hotel** Kippford · www.anchorhotelkippford.co.uk ·
LL   01556 620205 A defining pub of this popular coastal village on the 'Scottish Riviera'. The plate of sauce sachets lets you know this ain't gastro territory but it's hearty and old style with a huge throughput in bar and lounges and especially outside tables. Overlooking a tranquil cove and the sunset. 7 days.

 The Boat Inn Aboyne A hotel, local and all-in destination. Eat on the Dee. Report: 977/NE HOTELS.

The Best Vegetarian Restaurants

There are many vegetarian restaurants in Edinburgh p. 55 and Glasgow p. 115. And these:

1326 6/P17
<£15

✓ **Blue Angel at Findhorn Community** Findhorn · **01309 690110** You will go a long way in the North to find real vegetarian food, so it may be worth the detour from the main A96 Inverness–Elgin road to Findhorn and the famous community (1252/RETREATS), where there is a great deli (1454/DELIS) and this vibrant caff by the 'Universal Hall'. Very pleasant garden terrace. 7 days till 5pm and evenings if event in the hall (hot food till 3pm).

1327 6/P17
£15-25

✓ **The Bakehouse** Findhorn · www.bakehousecafe.co.uk · **01309 691826** Same neck of the woods as Blue Angel (above); its owners loosely connected. Not strictly vegetarian either but lots of vegetarian choice; all ethical and 'slow'. Bread and cakes from the bakery behind. Lovely, conscientious cookery. 7 days 10am-4pm (open longer in summer).

1328 5/G17
<£15

✓ **Ellishadder Art Café** Skye · www.ellishadderartcafe.co.uk · **01470 562734** 25 mins N of Portree on Staffin road. Signed near the Kilt Rock and 250m off the road at the crofting museum. Small cottage gallery and caff with simple menu of savoury tarts, soup and cakes, all home-made. Easter-Oct weekdays.

1329 7/J26
<£15

✓ **Musicker** Rothesay · www.musicker.co.uk · **01700 502287** Beside the castle, up from the ferry. Great pastries, paninis and soup, Best coffee in town. And the ginger cake! Totally vegetarian! Nice books, old juke box, newspapers, bluesy: jazz CDs for sale. Friendly, relaxed. Loyal clientele. Mon-Sat 10am-5pm.

1330 8/R28
ATMOS
<£15

✓ **Damascus Drum** Hawick · www.damascusdrum.co.uk · **07707 856123** One of the notable cafés of the Borders (867/BORDERS), Chris Ryan's bookshop and haven of civilisation is not strictly vegetarian but is mostly, and it gets a tick a) coz it's quirky and good and b) for sticking it out in this least favourite of towns where men and rugby and meat still rule. Coffee/cake, hot dish of the day, bagels and borek (sic). Great atmos. Mon-Sat 9am 5pm.

✓ **Woodside** nr Ancrum On B6400 near Monteviot House, a tearoom in a walled garden (1513/GARDENS). Organic, simple food. Report: 1386/TEAROOMS.

The Best Vegetarian-Friendly Places

HIGHLANDS
The Ceilidh Place Ullapool Report: 1054/HIGHLANDS.
Café One Inverness See *Best Places To Eat In Inverness*.
The Three Chimneys Colbost, Skye Report: 2239/SKYE.
Café Arriba Portree, Skye Report: 2239/SKYE.
Skye Pie Café Culnacnoc Report: 2239/SKYE.
Mountain Café Aviemore Report: 1086/HIGHLANDS.
Riverside Bistro Lochinver Report: 1093/HIGHLANDS.
Old Pines nr Spean Bridge Report: 1063/HIGHLANDS.
The Smiddy House Spean Bridge Report: 1084/HIGHLANDS.
Plockton Shores Plockton Report: 1079/HIGHLANDS.

NORTH EAST
Food Story Aberdeen Report: 1001/ABERDEEN.
Milton Restaurant Crathes Report: 989/NE RESTAURANTS.
Rendezvous @ Nargile Aberdeen Report: 1019/ABERDEEN.
Buchanan's Banchory Report: 987/NE RESTAURANTS.

ARGYLL & ISLES
Argyll Hotel Iona Report: 1175/INNS.
St Columba Hotel Iona Report: 2243/MULL.
Inver Strathlachlan, Loch Fyne Report: 791/ARGYLL.
The Green Welly Stop Tyndrum Report: 1382/TEAROOMS.
Julie's Coffee House Oban Report: 797/OBAN.
Kilmartin House Café Kilmartin, nr Lochgilphead Report: 1402/TEAROOMS.
Kerrera Tea Garden Isle of Kerrera Report: 797/OBAN.

FIFE & LOTHIANS
Pillars of Hercules nr Falkland Report: 1396/TEAROOMS.
Ostler's Close Cupar Report: 903/FIFE.
The Vine Leaf St Andrews See *Where To Eat* in St Andrews.
Livingston's Linlithgow Report: 890/LOTHIANS.

CENTRAL
Monachyle Mhor nr Balquhidder Report: 1191/GET-AWAY HOTELS.
Mhor 84 nr Balquhidder Report: 831/CENTRAL.
T. Ann Cake Dundee Report: 957/DUNDEE.
Jute at Dundee Contemporary Arts Dundee Report: 947/DUNDEE.
The Parlour Dundee Report: 961/DUNDEE.
Malabar Dundee Report: 959/DUNDEE.
88° Kirriemuir & Forfar Report: 933/PERTHSHIRE.
Jam Jar Bridge of Allan Report: 841/CENTRAL.
The Hideaway Bridge of Allan Report: 845/STIRLING.

SOUTH & SOUTH WEST
Marmions Melrose Report: 862/BORDERS.
Osso Peebles Report: 861/BORDERS.
Whitmuir, the Organic Place Lamancha, nr Peebles Report: 865/BORDERS.
Saffy's Ayr Report: 808/AYR.
Thomas Tosh Thornhill Report: 2168/SHOPS.

The Best Seafood Restaurants

1331 8/R24
£25-35

✓✓ **East Pier** East Shore, St Monans · www.eastpier.co.uk ·
01333 405030 James Robb's converted shed by the slipway in sleepy St Monans, where East Neuk shellfish (some smoked on the premises) is served box-fresh upstairs in the café or out on the roof overlooking the ever-changing sea. Weekends only in winter. 7 days Jun-Aug, with dinner Fri/Sat. Real plates; great little wine list. Fortunate for Fife that James and Kilp have fetched up on this shore.

1332 4/P12
LL
£25-35

✓✓ **Captain's Galley** Scrabster · www.captainsgalley.co.uk · ·
01847 894999 In the Galley there is a very firm and sure hand on the tiller. This is the place to eat on the N coast and a reputation built on total integrity with a conservation, sustainability and slow-food ethos throughout. Chef/ proprietor Jim Cowie and his missus know exactly where everything comes from: salad from their polytunnel and daily-landed fish from the boats and bay is all personally selected (and from a 50-mile radius). Those crabs actually choose Jim's creels. Menu short (usually 4 choices) and to the point, as are opening hours. Dinner only. Best book: this restaurant wins many awards and this entry virtually unchanged over 2 editions – it's all still true!

1333 7/G22
L
£25-35

✓✓ **Café Fish** Tobermory · www.thecafefish.com · 01688 301253 The upstairs café/restaurant on the corner of the famously picturesque bay, one of the best and least assuming in the land. Here, seafood really does come straight off the boat (*The Highland*) and into the tiny kitchen. Absurdly good value, laid-back, sympatico service. Definitely best to book. Report: 2243/MULL.

1334 7/J21
MAR-OCT
L
£25-35

✓✓ **Lochleven Seafood Café** North Ballachulish · www. lochlevenseafoodcafe.co.uk · 01855 821048 Leave the A82 at N Ballachulish, 15km S of Fort William, then 7km on B863 down the side of Loch Leven to this shellfish tankery, shop and bright, airy restaurant. A la carte of scallops, mussels, clams, lobster, crab and specials. Excellent wine list. Reciprocal products, such as Spanish cookware, from places they export to. Best food in the area.

1335 7/K27
L
£25-35

✓✓ **MacCallums of Troon Oyster Bar** Troon · www.maccallumsoftroon. co.uk · 01292 319339 On the quayside 3km from centre. Follow signs for ferry, past the woodpiles and fish market. Red-brick building with discreet sign, so eyes peeled. MacCallums here on their home quay, with James in the kitchen, literally over the tanks where langoustines lurk. Lovely fish (big on oysters and catch of the day), great atmos, unpretentious. They keep it admirably simple. Tue-Sat lunch & dinner. Sun lunch only. John's adjacent fish 'n' chip shop is the best in the west (1351/FISH & CHIPS).

1336 8/R25
L
<£15

✓ **Lobster Shack** North Berwick · www.lobstershack.co.uk · 07910 620480 It is a shack, it is on the quayside; takeaway and a few outside tables, by the people with the **Nether Abbey Hotel** (876/LOTHIANS). Box-fresh, wok-fresh. Lobster and the like. The Edinburgers love it, so they popped up in **The Dome** (378/EDINBURGH PUBS). Shack open only in summer months.

1337 8/R23
LL
£25-35

✓ **The Seafood Restaurant** St Andrews · www.theseafoodrestaurant. com · 01334 479475 In a landmark position overlooking the Old Course and bay, this glass-walled pavilion is a top spot in the town and for a sunset supper is hard to beat. Great wines, their own beers, nice puds but mainly fish pure and simple (usually 1 meat option). 7 days lunch & dinner.

1338 8/R24 ✓ **Craig Millar @ 16 West End** St Monans · www.16westend.com ·
L
£25-35
01333 730327 Title sounds like a cosmo upmarket bistro in a city somewhere but this is a street up from the harbour in a quiet East Neuk Village. It is smart though and a destination dinner. Conservatory and terrace overlooks sea, waves lap, gulls mew, etc. Superb, out-of-the-way setting. Chef/proprietor Craig Millar rattles the pans. Seasonal menu, lunch Wed-Sun & dinner Wed-Sat. Together with the East Pier (above), St Monans is seafood central.

1339 7/H23 ✓ **The Waterfront** Oban · www.waterfrontoban.co.uk · 01631 563110 On
£25-35
the waterfront by the station and upstairs, a light, airy room (formerly the Seaman's Mission) above the busy bar, both serving some of the best seafood around in an authentic setting – it's part of a small chain of diverse, very well-sussed places to eat. Specials change daily. The fish leap upstairs and onto your plate; oysters and scallops (hot or cold) a speciality. Good chips, by the way! Wait for the ferry here. Open AYR. 7 days lunch & dinner.

1340 7/H23 ✓ **Ee-Usk** Oban · www.eeusk.com · 01631 565666 Landmark new-build on
L
£25-35
the N pier by the hospitable Macleods (adjacent an Italian restaurant in a similar building which they also run – the Piazza). A full-on seafront caff with urban-bistro feel, great views and fish from that sea. Goes like a ferry; deft service. Good wee wine list. 7 days lunch & dinner.

1341 8/S20 ✓ **The Tolbooth** Stonehaven · www.tolbooth-restaurant.co.uk ·
LL
£25-35
01569 762287 On a corner of the harbour, long one of the best restaurants in the area, in a great setting (reputedly the oldest building in town) under chef Craig Somers. Upstairs bistro, a light room with windows overlooking the beach. Harbour no longer landing much fish but fishermen from here and Gourdon do supply crab, langoustine, great lobster and the odd halibut. In summer, this sea still hoaches with mackerel. Fresh, simple and decent value. Closed Mon.

1342 5/F17 ✓ **Lochbay Restaurant** Stein, Skye · www.lochbay-restaurant.co.uk ·
LL
ATMOS
£25-35
01470 592235 12km N Dunvegan; A850 to Portree, B886 Waternish peninsula coastal route. A scenic Skye drive leads you to this small cottage at end of the village row, where David and Alison Wilkinson made a reputation for their simply sublime seafood. At TGP this now new Skye foodie destination overlooking the water has been taken over by ex-Three Chimney's Michelin chef Michael Smith; we can expect very good grub. Times TBC.

1343 7/K23 ✓ **Loch Fyne Oysters** Loch Fyne · www.lochfyne.com · 01499 600482
£15-25
On A83 the Loch Lomond to Inveraray road, 20km Inveraray/11km Rest and Be Thankful. Landmark roadside restaurant and all-round seafood experience on the way out west. Though Loch Fyne Seafood is a huge UK chain, this in 1978 was home to the original aquaculture (and not actually in the chain after a management buy-out). People come from afar for the oysters and the smokery fare, especially the kippers. Spacious and with many banquettes though somewhat refectory-ish! Well-chosen wine and whisky. Same menu all day. Shop sells every conceivable packaging of salmon and other Scots produce.

1344 7/K26 ✓ **The Catch @ Fins** Fairlie, nr Largs · www.fencebay.co.uk ·
£15-25
01475 568989 On main A78 S of Fairlie a seafood bistro and smokery, and probably the best place to eat for miles in either direction. Simple, straightforward good cookin' (the original team are back), the wine list similarly to the point. Nice conservatory; and geraniums. Tue-Sun lunch & dinner. Farmers' market here last Sunday of the month.

1345 7/J26 ✓ **The Seafood Cabin** Skipness · www.theseafoodcabin.co.uk ·
LL 01880 760207 Adjacent Skipness Castle, signed from Claonaig where the
<£15 CalMac ferry from Lochranza arrives. Sophie James's famous wee cabin with
outdoor seating and indoor options in perfect spot for their fresh and local seafood,
snacks and cakes. Mussels come a little further (Loch Etive). Smoked stuff from
Arran. Jun-Sep 11am-7pm. Closed Sat.

1346 9/J30 **Campbell's** Portpatrick · www.campbellsrestaurant.co.uk · 01776 810314
£15-25 Friendly, harbourside restaurant in much visited Portpatrick. Some meat dishes,
but mainly seafood. Every day their own boat brings back crab and lobster (and sea
bass and pollock). Tue-Sun lunch & dinner. Closed Jan & Mon.

1347 7/J21 **Crannog Restaurant** Fort William · www.crannog.net · 01397 705589
L Long-established landmark and destination restaurant. Nice, bright contemporary
£15-25 setting, not only great seafood but a real sense of place in this rainy town. They do
cruises from adjacent pier. 7 days lunch & dinner.

1348 4/K13 **Shorehouse Restaurant** Tarbet, nr Scourie · 01971 502251 Charming
LL conservatory restaurant on cove where boats leave for **Handa Island** reserve
£15-25 (1713/BIRDS). Julian catches your seafood from his boat and Jackie cooks it; they
have the Rick Stein seal of approval. Home-made puds. Located at end of beautiful
unclassified road off the A894 between Laxford Bridge and Scourie (5km); best
phone to check openings. Apr-Sep: Mon-Sat noon-8pm. Closed Sun.

1349 5/H18 **Kishorn Seafood Bar** Kishorn · www.kishornseafoodbar.co.uk ·
MAR-NOV 01520 733240 Conveniently located and long-established on A896 at Kishorn
£25-35 on the road between Lochcarron (Inverness) and Shieldaig near the road over the
hill to Applecross (1619/SCENIC ROUTES). Fresh local seafood in a roadside diner:
Kishorn oysters, hand-dived scallops, squat lobsters. Applecross crab; lobsters in a
tank out back. Light and bright, courtesy of the ebullient Viv Rollo. Busy, so book.

1350 7/J22 **The Pierhouse Hotel** Port Appin · www.pierhousehotel.co.uk ·
LL 01631 730302 At the end of the minor road and 3km from the A828 Oban-Fort
£15-25 William road in Port Appin village right by the tiny pier where the passenger ferry
leaves for Lismore; the setting is everything. A hotel and restaurant with bar.
Ingredients from local suppliers: oysters, mussels, crab. The Cullen skink and the
platters! Lively atmos, wine and the wow view. Report: 1180/INNS.

✓✓ **Applecross Inn** Applecross At the end of the road. Seafood and classic
fish 'n' chips. Report: 1200/GET-AWAY HOTELS.
✓ **Silver Darling** Aberdeen On the harbour in an ethereal location. Best in the
NE. Report: 1007/ABERDEEN.
✓ **The Oyster Shed** Skye Report: 2239/SKYE.

▬▬ The Best Fish & Chip Shops

For Edinburgh listings see p 54; for Glasgow see p 114.

1351 7/K27 ✓✓ **The Wee Hurrie** Harbour Road, Troon · www.maccallumsoftroon.
L co.uk · 01292 319340 Famed and fabulous, the Wee Hurrie is part of
MacCallums oyster and fish restaurant (see 1335/SEAFOOD for directions because
it's a fair walk from the town centre). Big range of fresh daily fish displayed and to
select. Light tempuras, even salads to go. Tue-Sun noon-8pm (9pm Fri/Sat). Best
in the west, we still say!

1352 8/S20 ✓✓ **The Bay** Stonehaven · www.thebayfishandchips.co.uk · 01569 762000 On the prom towards the open-air pool (2091/OPEN-AIR POOLS), just look for the queue almost always there. They really do come from miles away (and to Aunty Betty's ice-cream shop next door). All is cooked to order. You wait and walk on the front – perfect! The Bay wins many awards. 7 days.

1353 7/H23 ✓✓ **Fish & Chips in Oban** Oban has declared itself the Seafood Capital of Scotland, with good seafood restaurants but also these 4 great chip shops. All are in George St near the bay, with sit-in caffs adjacent. **Nories** at 86 has been here over 50 years. They are uncompromising about the lard but they do great F&C (noon-11pm). They've recently opened a shiny newcomer, the **Oban Bay Fish Bar** at 34, right on the bay itself; same deal and lard again but a bigger caff (11.30am-9.30pm). **Oban Fish & Chip Shop** is the fancy newcomer at 116 with coley, hake and home-made fishcakes, along with sustainable haddock and cod. They do use vegetable oil (11.30am-11pm). A poll of Obanites and the longer queues suggest this is *the* top takeaway. The **George Street Fish & Chip Shop** (number 15) behind the Caledonian Hotel is bright and fresh, with definitely the smartest sit-in. They do use beef dripping and keep the menu small. 7 days 10.30am-11pm. Wherever you go, Oban's waterfront is the perfect place to scoff 'em.

1354 8/Q24 ✓ **Fish & Chips in Fife** Apart from the estimable Valente's in Kirkcaldy and the much-vaunted **Anstruther Fish Bar** (in the Lard section; see below), Fife has other less celebrated but damned good fish 'n' chip shops. **The Wee Chippy** in Anstruther is on the harbour W of the AFB. Open till 10pm. There are also 2 others, including **The Waterfront** on this waterfront and, along the road, the better-kept secret: the **Pittenweem Fish & Chip Bar**, a door in the wall at the end of the High St next to the clock tower. 6-10pm (Sun from 5pm). Closed Mon.

1355 7/J26 ✓ **West End** Rothesay · www.westendcafebute.co.uk · 01700 503596 Remains a Rothesay must-do and always a queue. Only haddock but a wide range of other fries and fresh pizza. Closed Mon.

1356 6/T19 ✓ **The Ashvale** Aberdeen, Elgin, Inverurie, Ellon, Banchory, Brechin · www.theashvale.co.uk Original restaurant (1985) at 42-48 Great Western Rd (always rammed); 3 other city branches. Restaurant/takeaway à la Harry Ramsden (stuck to dripping for long enough but changed to vegetable oil in '09). Various sizes of haddock, sole, plaice. Home-made stovies, etc, all served fresh so you do wait. From noon but hours vary.

1357 4/K15 **Seaforth Chippy** Ullapool · www.theseaforth.com · 01854 612122 Part of Seaforth Hotel, which has upstairs seafood bistro, but probably best to stick to fish and chips and walk the harbour. Some question in Ullapool whether it's the Seaforth or the **Sea Fresh** or the one round the corner, but I'll stick with this. Chips often pale but fish don't get any fresher. 7 days till 10pm (8.30pm in winter).

1358 9/N29 **Balmoral** Balmoral Road, Dumfries · 01387 252583 Seems as old and essential as the Bard himself (actually 100 years!). Using rapeseed oil, it's the best chip in the south. Out the Annan road heading E, 1km from centre.

1359 7/G22 L **The Fish & Chip Van aka The Fishermen's Pier** Tobermory By the clock on Fisherman's Pier, this van has almost achieved destination-restaurant status. Always a queue. Fresh and al fresco. Summer 12.30-9pm. Closed Sun in winter.

1360 8/S20 **The Square** Stonehaven · 01569 763234 As Sandy's, it was the established Stoney chipper, and still is always busy despite interlopers (see The Bay, below). 7 days noon-10pm. Big haddock like the old days.

AND THESE THAT STICK TO LARD

1361 8/Q24 ✓✓ **Valente's** Kirkcaldy Ask directions or satnav to this superb chippy in E of town (not the high street one); worth the detour and the queue when you get there. They also make ice cream. At 73 Hendry Rd (01592 203600). Closed Wed.

1362 8/M24 ✓✓ **Mhor Fish** Callander · www.mhor.net · 01877 330213 A destination on the Trossachs food map, courtesy of the ambitious and industrious Lewis family of **Monachyle Mhor** (1191/GET-AWAY HOTELS). Unprepossessing frontage but here, Dick Lewis adds a fresh fish counter and general panache but doesn't tamper with the basic product: the fish tea with seasonally sourced fish and great chips. Fish here is to love and there are brilliant burgers from meat from their farm. They use dripping but they can tell you why. Noon-9pm. Takeaway later.

1363 6/T18 ✓ **The Dolphin Café** Peterhead · 01779 478595 By the harbour, where the fish come from, so you don't get closer to the source than this. Serving the fishermen (from 5am), as well as us; it's a community thing. The cold North Sea outside (no, we wouldn't want to go there). 5am-7pm, from 11am Sat. Closed Sun.

1364 6/T19 ✓ **Dolphin Fish & Chips** Aberdeen · 01224 644555 Despite the pre-eminence of the Ashvale in Aberdeen, many swear by this small, always busy place just off Union St. Many hangovers in the queue. Till 1am (4am Fri/Sat).

1365 8/R22 ✓ **Peppo's Harbour Chip Bar** Arbroath · 01241 872373 By the harbour where those fish come in. Fresh as that and chips in dripping. Peppo was here in 1951; John and Frank Orsi carry on the family tradition of feeding the hordes. 7 days.

1366 8/Q24 ✓ **The Anstruther Fish Bar** Anstruther · www.anstrutherfishbar.co.uk · 01592 261215 On the front (1557/VILLAGES). Often listed as the best fish 'n' chips in Scotland/UK/Universe and the continuous queue suggests that either: a) we want to believe that; or b) they may be right. Sit in (paper plates) or walk round the harbour and decide for yourself. There's also the ice cream. 7 days.

1367 8/T26 ✓ **Giacopazzi's** Eyemouth · www.giacopazzis.co.uk · 01890 750317 By the big wooden boat in this real working harbour. A caff and takeaway with the catch on its doorstep. For over 100 years, the home of the now oft cited Eyemouth-landed haddock and their award-winning ice cream. Takeaways eaten on boat-filled harbour, probably attended by very pushy gulls. 7 days 9am-8pm (till 9pm Fri/Sat). Upstairs to flashier **Oblo's Bistro** (01890 752527), a bar, restaurant and deli. Sun-Thu 10am-midnight, till 1am Fri/Sat.

1368 5/N19 ✓ **Harkai's** Aviemore · www.harkai.co.uk · 01479 810430 On main street at S end as you come in from A9. Aka **The Happy Haggis**. Here for decades with a big local reputation. A long way from the sea but this a chipper (and café) that takes itself seriously (although no obvious sustainable fish policy, local sourcing or any of that malarkey). Harkai's is also in Kingussie. 7 days.

Great Cafés

For cafés in Edinburgh, see p. 66–67, Glasgow, p. 118–19.

1369 5/M18 ✓✓ **Castle Restaurant** Inverness · 01463 230925 On road that winds up to the castle from the main street, near the tourist office and the hostels. No pandering to tourists here, but this great caff has been serving chips (home-made from local potatoes) with everything for 40 years. Pork chops, perfect fried eggs, prawn cocktail to crumbles. They work damned hard. In Inverness or anywhere nearby, you'll be pushed to find better-value grub than this (but see below). New owners, the MacKinnons, but all is well – no change. Closed Sun.

1370 5/M18 ✓✓ **Girvans** Inverness · www.girvansrestaurant.co.uk · 01463 711900 A different proposition to the Castle (above), more of the moment – more perhaps a restaurant, but the atmos is of a good, unpretentious caff serving everything from omelettes to full-blown comfort meals. Great all-day Sunday breakfast. Tempting cream-laden cakes. Always busy but no need to book. I never go to Inverness without going here. 7 days.

1371 7/K23 ✓ **The Real Food Café** Tyndrum · www.therealfoodcafe.com · 01838 400235 On the main A82 just before the junction Oban/Fort William. May appear like a chip shop but this is good food for the road, conscientiously prepared and seriously sourced. Fish 'n' chips probably best but burgers, breakfasts, pies – all home-made. Lounge with wood-burning stove. Birds to watch. Cardboard plates apart, this is a good pit stop! 7 days.

1372 4/K15 ✓ **The Tea Store** Ullapool · www.theteastore.co.uk · 01854 612995 In the street parallel to and one up from the waterfront. Excellent, unpretentious café serving all-day fry-ups and other snacks. Great home baking including those strawberry tarts in season. Best caff in Ullapool. 7 days. Winter hours vary.

1373 8/N24 ✓ **Allan Water Café** Bridge of Allan · www.allanwatercafe.co.uk · 01786 833060 The main street, beside the eponymous bridge. Worth coming over from Stirling (8km) for a takeaway or a seat in the caff (a steel-and-glass extension somewhat lacking in charm) for great fish 'n' chips and the ice cream (1452/ICE CREAM). In BoA the AWC has long been a must! 7 days 8am-8.30pm.

1374 7/K26 ✓ **The Ritz Café** Millport · 01475 530459 See Millport, see the Ritz. Since 1906
L (though pure 1960s) and now in its fourth generation, the classic café on the
ATMOS Clyde. A short ferry journey away (from Largs, continuous; then 6km), an essential part of any visit to this part of the coast, and Millport is not entirely without charm. Toasties, rolls, the famous hot peas. Excellent ice cream (especially with melted marshmallow). Something of 'things past'. 7 days 10am-9pm (in season).

1375 7/J26 ✓ **Ettrick Bay Café** Bute · 01700 500223 End of the road from Port
L Bannatyne near Rothesay. In the middle of the bay and the beach looking over to Arran/Kintyre – this is the caff with the view. Here forever, a family fixture from seaside days gone by. Honest, home-made menu including their famous garlic mussels and Alec's rather large cakes. 7 days 10am-5pm. Cash only.

1376 8/Q24 ✓ **Campbell's** Falkland · www.campbellscoffeehouse.com · 01337 858738 At The Cross, i.e. the main square, in this, the most pleasant village in Fife, with its Palace (1756/CASTLES) and walks (1946/HILL WALKS). Busy caff with home baking and hot dishes. A cuppa and a cake when you need it. 7 days.

The Best Tearooms & Coffee Shops

For Edinburgh, see p. 63–65, for Glasgow, p. 116–18.

1377 8/R25 ✓✓ **Falko** Gullane · www.falko.co.uk · 01620 843168 Main street of genteel village on corner crossroads. A bakery/coffee shop (the bakery is actually in Edinburgh) that calls itself a *konditerei* because those gorgeous cakes and breads are German, Austrian and Swiss, and they change with the seasons (Stollen comes in October). Soup and wonderful bread. The cakes are simply irresistible – I know, I've tried to resist! Master baker and proprietor Falko in command. Wed-Sun daytime only.

1378 6/R20 ✓✓ **Finzean Tearoom** Finzean · www.finzean.com · 01330 850710 The tearoom and farm shop of the Finzean (pronounced Fing-in) estate on back road between Aboyne and Banchory, a very worthwhile detour. Great food, great views. Report: 1464/FARM SHOPS. Mon-Sat 9am-5pm, Sun from 11am.

1379 8/P23 ✓✓ **Small Talk** Perth · 01738 634770 Unobtrusive online (no website) and on the street but this is the best kind of a 'traditional' tearoom. All home-made and to order: maccy cheese (same recipe for 18 years), mince & tatties, stovies, great scones and cakes, signature cheesy 'Dutch' eggs. Lovely and twee, meticulously managed (proprietor George Sinclair) and goes like a fair all day. May have to book. The best carrot cake! 7 days 9.30am-5.30pm.

1380 7/G22 ✓✓ **Glengorm Farm Coffee Shop** nr Tobermory, Mull · www. EASTER-OCT glengormcastle.co.uk · 01688 302321 First right on Tobermory-Dervaig road (7km). Organic food served in well-refurbished stable block. Soups, cakes, staples (maccy cheese, steak pie), specials and delicious salads from their famous garden (they supply other Mull restaurants). All you need after a walk in the grounds of this great estate (2243/MULL; 2214/ISLAND WALKS) ...and the *best* cappuccino on Mull. 7 days.

1381 9/M29 ✓✓ **Kitty's Tearoom** New Galloway · 01644 420246 Main street of town in the forest. Absolutely splendid. Sylvia Brown's steady hand in the kitchen. Lovely teas, lovely china, lovely cakes! Conversation. Great salads. High tea 4-6.30pm very popular, including 'a roast'. All this but you must take cake. It's an Alan Bennett world. 11am-5pm (6.30pm Sat/Sun). Closed Mon.

1382 7/K23 ✓✓ **The Green Welly Stop** Tyndrum · www.thegreenwellystop.co.uk · L 01838 400271 On A82, a strategically placed natural pit stop and all-round super services on the drive to Oban or Fort William (just before the road divides), with a Scottish produce shop, a gas station, a snack stop which does pizzas, and a self-service restaurant: great home-made comfort food. Food prepared to order, excellent cakes and puds, fresh OJ and fast, friendly service. Shops stuffed with everything kind of Scottish. Opening hours vary.

1383 5/N19 ✓✓ **The Potting Shed** nr Aviemore · www.inshriachnursery.co.uk · NO DOGS 01540 651287 On the B970 between Kincraig and Inverdruie on the MAR-OCT Coylumbridge/ski slopes road out of Aviemore. This is a garden centre (2191/ GARDEN CENTRES) and an enchanting and remarkable place to watch birds (1720/ BIRDS) from the tiny tearoom windows, but it's also a mecca for cakes – endless, heavenly cakes. Much walking required to burn this lot off but these Borrowmans bake the crème de la crème. Wed-Sun 10am-5pm.

1384 6/R20 ✓✓ **The Black-Faced Sheep** Aboyne · www.blackfacedsheep.co.uk · 01339 887311 Near main Royal Deeside road through Aboyne (A93) and Mark and Sylvi Ronson's excellent coffee shop/gift shop is well-loved by locals (and regulars from all over) but is thankfully missed by the bus parties hurtling towards Balmoral. Home-baked breads and cakes. Light specials and good coffee. Their love affair with Italy means specially sourced and imported wines (excellent exclusive house red) and olive oil. 10am-5pm, Sun from 11am. Fascinating furniture and objets, way better than the usual knick-knacks.

1385 8/N22 ✓✓ **The Watermill** Aberfeldy · www.aberfeldywatermill.com · 01887 822896 Off Main St direction Kenmore near the **Birks** (2009/WALKS). Downstairs caff on riverside in a conserved mill. Much more than this, though: the top independent bookshop in the Highlands, a remarkable art gallery upstairs with Scottish artists and international print work for sale and Homer, a selective, always-interesting homes-and-gardens shop (they have opened another Homer in Howe St, Edinburgh). Waiter service in busy caff with inside and terrace seating. Soups, quiches, home baking. 10am-5pm (Sun from 11am). Signed from all over. The Watermill has led the Aberfeldy revival!

1386 8/R27 ✓ **Woodside (aka Birdhouse Tearoom)** nr Ancrum · www.
L woodsidegarden.co.uk · 01835 830315 On B6400 off A68 at Ancrum turn-off. The caff in the shack at the back of the Woodside Garden Centre in the walled garden of **Monteviot House** (1513/GARDENS). Simple, delicious, mostly organic and locally sourced home baking: soup, sandwiches, quiche and cakes. Outside tables on sheltered lawn. Check for weekend evening meals with great chefs; a local foodie treat. Mar-Oct: 9am-5pm; Nov-Feb 10am-4pm.

1387 5/M17 ✓ **Couper's Creek** Cromarty · www.sutorcreek.co.uk · 01381 600729 Not far (in this small, perfectly presented town) from the Fox's original home: the pizza and seafood restaurant **Sutor Creek** (1080/HIGHLANDS). This daytime coffee shop, which also sells great wee Highland gifts, does soups, salad and sandwiches really well. Fab ice-cream concoctions. Cromarty great to visit for many reasons (1552/VILLAGES), now this. 7 days 10am-5pm.

1388 6/S20 ✓ **Raemoir Garden Centre** Banchory · www.raemoirgardencentre.co.uk · 01330 825059 On A980, the Deeside road through town, about 3km to a garden centre that has grown into a house-and-gardens megastore. Self-service caff with salad bar, quiches, etc, and cream-laden cakes (though not a good coffee machine) and beyond the packed emporium a waitress-service restaurant with extensive menu and more cakes. Always packed; it's a phenomenon. 7 days.

1389 8/S27 ✓ **The Terrace Café** Floors Castle, Kelso · www.roxburghe.net ·
L 01573 225714 Top garden tearoom inside and out an old outbuilding that forms one side of the estate walled garden (2187/GARDEN CENTRES) some distance from the castle (1822/HOUSES). Good, home-made, unpretentious hot dishes and baking: home-cured ham, salads and irresistible cakes and puds and pies. Shop with deli stuff. And the terrace: bliss. 7 days 10am-4pm, hot food till 2.30pm, then toasties. Open AYR.

1390 7/G22 ✓ **The Glass Barn at Sgriob-Ruadh Farm** nr Tobermory, Mull · www.
isleofmullcheese.co.uk · 01688 302627 On the road to Dervaig 2km from town, a fab barn at the heart of the farmyard-smelling farm and dairy, where they turn thousands of litres of milk into the famous Mull cheddar. Hard to be precise about what's on offer here or when, but drop by for something unique and authentic, even on your way to/from Glengorm (above). See 1483/CHEESES.

1391 8/N22 ✓ **Legends & The Highland Chocolatier** Grandtully · www.
highlandchocolatier.com · 01887 840775 Main street of village on the Tay
where rivers are as busy with rafters as the road with traffic. Gifts and, even in the
now·crowded chocolate-making world, Iain Burnett's famously good home-made-
chocolate shop (widely recognisable and available). Through the back a good
tearoom for light snacks, home-made stuff, great tea list and of course hot
chocolate. 7 days 10am-5pm.

1392 3/E14 ✓ **Loch Croistean Coffee Shop** nr Uig, Lewis · 01851 672772 Further W than
L all the rest (30 mins from Stornoway by A8110), Marianne Campbell's homely
oasis in an unforgiving landscape. Further on, the amazing beaches and the sunset,
here home-made, lovely food (the soda bread and soup). Closed Sun.

1393 8/L24 ✓ **Brig o' Turk Tearoom** Brig o' Turk · www.brigoturktearoom.co.uk ·
FEB-NOV 01877 376283 On the A821 Callander to Aberfoyle main sightseeing and
walking route through the Trossachs (1630/ROUTES; 1612/LOCHS; 1933/HILLS), a
must-stop, delightful and historic (it was featured in the original 1959 film *The 39
Steps*), where Csaba and Veronika Brünner dispense great restaurant-style food
(including their signature goulash – they are Hungarian) and cakes. Closed Wed.

1394 7/L25 ✓ **Three Sisters Bake** www.threesistersbake.co.uk · Quarrier's Village,
nr Bridge of Weir · 01505 228087 & Killearn · 01360 550116 The original
in the truly remarkable and always uplifting Quarrier's Village (quarriers.org.uk) and in
the village hall in Killearn; both villages great to walk in/around. The sisters (Gillian,
who wrote a tome), Nichola and Linsey are all involved in the purveying of lovely food
from 'brekkie' to tea. Quiche, tartlets, soda bread sandwiches. Both 7 days.

1395 5/M20 ✓ **Laggan Coffee Shop** nr Laggan · www.potterybunkhouse.co.uk ·
01528 544231 On A889 from Dalwhinnie on A9 that leads to A86, the road W
to Spean Bridge and Kyle. Lovely Linda's road sign points you to this former pottery,
craft shop and bunkhouse (1156/HOSTELS). Great home baking, scones, soup,
sarnies and *the* most yummy cakes. Near great spot for forest walks and river
swimming (1662/SWIMMING). Open AYR.

1396 8/P24 ✓ **Pillars of Hercules** nr Falkland · www.pillars.co.uk · 01337 857749
Rambling, rustic tearoom on organic farm on A912 2km from village towards
Strathmiglo and the motorway. Excellent, homely place and fare; and ethical.
Home-made cakes, soup, hot dishes, etc. They also have a bothy and you can camp
around them. See also 1473/FARM SHOPS. Very wholefoodie ambience. 7 days.

1397 9/M30 ✓ **The Schoolhouse** Ringford · 01557 820250 On A75 10km W of Castle
Douglas. A busy road and a perennially busy food stop where passers-by and a
legion of regulars love fresh, home-made cooking done with integrity and
commitment. It's all made here (except the bread). Can take away. 10am-6pm.
Closed Wed (except Jul/Aug).

1398 9/L30 ✓ **Caffs in Wigtown** Scotland's booktown and home of the **Wigtown Book**
DF **Festival** 70/EVENTS. **Reading Lasses** 01988 403266 This tiny caff at the back of
one of the main bookshops is a rest and respite from all that browsing. 2-lovely-wifey
operation with named, locally sourced ingredients, soup and pies, salad leaves from
garden and home-made cakes. Can be as packed as a bookshelf. 7 days daytime only.

1399 9/L30 **Beltie Books** www.beltiebooks.co.uk · 01988 402730 'Beltie' after the Belted
Galloway cow. More home cooking and caking; garden. Wed-Mon daytime only.

1400 9/L30 **Café Rendezvous** 01988 402074 Top of main street. More restaurany than
those above, hot meals. And no books. Good though. 7 days daytime only.

1401 8/R26 ✓ **Flat Cat Gallery Coffee Shop** Lauder · www.flatcatgallery.co.uk · 01578 722808 Opposite Eagle Hotel on Market St. Speeding through Lauder (don't: speed cameras) you might miss Annette and Jacquie's cool coffee spot and serious gallery. Always interesting work, including furniture from Harestanes down the road; and ethnic things. Soup and sandwiches, home baking. 7 days till 5pm.

1402 7/H24 ✓ **Kilmartin House Café** Kilmartin, nr Lochgilphead · www.kilmartin.
MAR-DEC org · 01546 510278 Attached to early peoples' museum (2124/HISTORY) in Kilmartin Glen and on main road N of Lochgilphead. Worth swinging in here from road or glen walk for home-made, conscientiously prepared light food. Down steps to bright conservatory with pastoral outlook. Organic garden produce. Good vegetarian choices and creative cooking. 7 days. Hot food till 3pm, cakes till 5pm & dinner Thu-Sat in summer.

1403 6/N17 ✓ **Logie Steading** nr Forres · www.logie.co.uk · 01309 611733 S of town towards Grantown (A940) – 10km. Or from Carrbridge via B9007. See 2001/WALKS (Randolph's Leap). In a lovely spot near the River Findhorn, a courtyard of fine things (2144/SCOTTISH SHOPS) and the de Oliveiras' **Olive Tree Tearoom** – home bakes, burgers, fish cakes, tartlets; sound local sourcing. Hot food till 3pm. Tables in the courtyard. All in, a vital place to visit. 7 days. Winter hours vary.

1404 8/Q27 ✓ **No1 Peebles Road Coffee House** Innerleithen · www.no1peeblesroad. coffee · 01896 830873 Address and statement, perhaps. Well, they are the number one coffee house in these parts with Steampunk (the estimable) coffee, baking and freshly made snacks. Craig Anderson and Emma Jane Perry have quickly established a fuel stop on the bikeathon between Glentress and Traquair. It has the right vibe! 8am-4pm (till 6pm Sat/Sun). Closed Tue/Wed.

1405 8/M24 ✓ **Buttercup Café** Doune · www.buttercupcafe.co.uk · 01786 842511 Great wee town tearoom in Doune main street, where home-made means home-made (though Mackie's ice cream). From the best breakfast hereabouts through hot and salad lunches to afternoon tea, this is worth a detour from the A84 Callander–Stirling road. 7 days.

1406 8/P22 ✓ **Spill the Beans** Dunkeld · 01350 728111 A great wee tearoom just where you need it in this town so good to wander. Fiona MacPhail gets it right with her mega-cakes, soups and sandwiches. Some outside tables. You will need to walk this lot off!

1407 8/P24 **The Powmill Milkbar** nr Kinross · 01577 840376 On A977 Kinross (on the M90, junction 6) to Kincardine Bridge road, a real milk bar and real slice of Scottish craic and cake. Apple pie, moist fly cemeteries, big meringues: an essential stop on any Sunday run hereabouts (but open every day). Hot meals, great old-style salads. Local girls! Good place to take kids. Unreconstructed nostalgia. 7 days. Then: 1983/WALKS.

1408 5/J17 **Whistle Stop Café** Kinlochewe · 01445 760423 This 'amazing find' hasn't got a tick because I have to admit I never found it myself. Somehow my travels in Torridon have not taken me the village hall, where this caff has revived and delighted so many walkers and fellow travellers. Home-made, right-on, welcoming in summer and wood-burning stove in winter. Go find!

1409 5/H16 **Bridge Cottage Café** Poolewe · 01445 781335 In village and near **Inverewe Gardens** (1500/GARDENS), a cottage, right enough, with crafts/pictures upstairs and parlour teashop down. Salads, soups, baked potatoes, big cakes (yum Victoria sponge); nearby produce. Neighbouring artists; the Inmans' shop and support local. Thu-Tue 10.30am-4.30pm. Weekends only in winter.

1410 7/J22 **Castle Stalker View** **Portnacroish** · www.castlestalkerview.co.uk ·
L 01631 730444 On A828 Oban-Fort William about halfway. Modern build café/
gift shop with soup 'n' salad menu and home baking. Breakfast till 11.30am. Nice
people so a popular local rendezvous as well as passers-through. Extraordinary view
(1655/VIEWS) and in the woods, **Ecopods** (1250/GLAMPING). Mar-Oct 9.30am-
5.30pm. Winter Thu-Sun 10am-4pm. Closed Jan.

1411 7/L24 **The Coach House** **Luss** · 01436 860341 Long after the soap *Take The High Road*,
which was set here ended, this village still throngs with visitors happy with twee.
Rowena Ferguson's caff goes like a proverbial fair. Not all home-made but good
soups and quiches. Big tea selection, lashings of cream. Some outside seating.
Nice loos. 7 days 10am-5pm.

1412 7/J23 **Robin's Nest** **Taynuilt** · www.robinsnesttearoom.co.uk · 01866 822429
Off A85 (to Bonawe 2129/HISTORY). For over 20 years, tiny home-baking caff with
unusual soups and snacks as well as the good WRI kind of cakes. 7 days 9am-5pm.
Thu-Sun in winter.

1413 7/H24 **Crinan Coffee Shop** **Crinan** · www.crinanhotel.com · 01546 830261 Run by
LL the hotel people (774/ARGYLL) in this fascinating village for yachties and anyone
with time to while away. The café overlooks canal basin with boats always going
through. Excellent cakes, bread and scones. Easter-Oct daytime only.

1414 4/J16 **Maggie's Tearoom** **Dundonnell** · 01854 633326 On A832 in Wester Ross, the
road to Inverewe Gardens and Gairloch. Not Maggie but the wonderful Ishbel. This
well-placed bistro and craft shop in a roadside cottage, though small inside, has a
great deck and garden. Home-made hot dishes, salads, bakes. Apr-Oct. Closed Sun.

1415 8/P27 **Laurel Bank** **Broughton** · www.laurelbanktearoom.co.uk · 01899 830462
On A701 near Biggar. Strung-out cottage tearoom, bistro and bar, local, friendly
and a tad traditional under Ally McGrath from **Osso** (861/BORDERS). Home baking
and Broughton Ales. 9am-11pm in summer. Winter hours may vary.

1416 8/R24 **The Cocoa Tree Shop & Café** **Pittenweem** · www.pittenweemchocolate.
DF co.uk · 01333 312682 Near end of the high street, a chocolate emporium and
through the back a busy tea/coffee/choc room with hot snacks, soups, crêpes,
cakes and, naturally, hot choco. Sympatico. An excellent brownie! 7 days daytime.

1417 8/R24 **Crail Harbour Tearoom** **Crail** · www.crailharbourgallery.co.uk ·
01333 451896 In cute little Crail, a tearoom where you need it on the road going
down to the harbour. Gallery with pics from the owner. Lovely, sheltered terrace
overlooking the shore. Dressed crab from harbour, herring and dill, flaky salmon
and cakes. Perfect! 7 days daytime only. Closed Jan.

1418 9/M29 **The Smithy** **New Galloway** · www.thesmithy-newgalloway.co.uk ·
MAR-OCT 01644 420269 This village has long been a tearoom terminus because of Kitty's
(above) but the Smithy has a brilliant location by the burn, with outside terrace
(the Briggs have been by this bridge for 7 years) and there's home baking, soups,
omelettes. 7 days 10am-5pm.

1419 7/H24 **Crafty Kitchen** **Ardfern** · 01852 500303 Down the Ardfern B8002 road (4km)
from A816 Oban-Lochgilphead road, the classier yachty haven of the Craignish
peninsula. More kitchen craft than crafty craft: great home-made cakes and special
hot dishes emerge along with superior salads. Tue-Sun daytime only. Weekends
only Nov/Dec. Closed Jan-Mar.

1420 6/R20   **Platform 22** Torphins · 01339 882807 Torphins is a wee place on the A980 8km N of Banchory. This sweet tearoom 150m up from the crossroads on the B993 to Inverurie is on the site of a former railway station. Emma (cakes 'n all) and David Pattullo work damned hard in the pottery studio/gallery and in the community. Their weekly market on Wednesdays (10am-2pm) in the garden runs AYR. Grub good and home-made, lunch keeps going till 5pm.

1421 7/J24   **Brambles** Inveraray · www.inverarayhotel.com · 01499 302252 A busy little unpretentious tearoom there where you want it, in the main street of Argyll's historic town on Loch Fyne. Home baking, 'butties', light meals; locals also mingle. 7 days daytime only in season.

1422 4/M15   **Pier Café** Lairg · www.pier-cafe.co.uk · 01549 402971 On the lochside (Loch Shin) on the left of the main road N to Tongue – a grass bank and tiny pier. All gorgeous on a summer's day. Home-made and well-sourced from Sutherland's larder. Welcome on the long haul north. Daytime only. Closed Mon & Jan.

1423 8/R25   **1650** 76 High Street, Dunbar · 01368 862870 In middle of main street, near the John Muir Visitor Centre. Rhona Bell's essential coffee shop. She makes everything: breakfast, patisserie, shortbreads. A good stopover on the 'Way'. Mon-Sat.

1424 5/M17   **The Pantry** Cromarty · 01381 600455 In great wee town in Black Isle 45km NE of Inverness (1552/VILLAGES) on corner of Church St. Excellent home baking, soups and a decent cup of coffee. Easter-end Oct daytime only. Closed Fri.

✓✓ **Gloagburn Farm** Tibbermore Report: 1463/FARM SHOPS.

✓✓ **Jessie's Kitchen** Broughty Ferry Report: 946/DUNDEE.

✓✓ **Steampunk** North Berwick Report: 883/LOTHIANS.

✓ **The Corn Kist** Milton Haugh, nr Arbroath Report: 1467/FARM SHOPS.

✓ **Walled Garden Restaurant** Applecross Report: 1078/HIGHLANDS.

✓ **The Hideaway** Bridge of Allan Report: 845/STIRLING.

✓ **The Woodhouse** nr Kippen Report: 1474/FARM SHOPS.

The Best Afternoon Teas

1425 8/M26 ✓ **The Hidden Lane Tearoom** Glasgow · www.thehiddenlanetearoom.com · 0141 237 4391 Beyond Kelvingrove under an arch at the west end of Argyle St where there are many other coffee shops and grazing places, to the end of a backstreet lane which is pure Glasgow, a truly hidden but once found, oft-revisited tearoom. Old style and very new style at the same time. With a new Kirsty but still the great old cakes turned out miraculously from a tiny kitchen. Tier of tea noon-5pm, otherwise 10am-5pm (Sat 6pm). Not so hidden anymore!

1426 8/R25 ✓ **Greywalls** Gullane · www.greywalls.co.uk · 01620 842144 The Lutyens manor house and Gertrude Jekyll gardens at this country-house hotel 40 mins E of Edinburgh is the perfect setting for genteel afternoon tea. It's a Roux restaurant (873/LOTHIANS) so expect well-thought-out, smartly delivered niceties, with comfy lounges, the gorgeous gardens; and croquet! 2.30-5pm.

1427 8/Q25
ATMOS ✓ **Prestonfield** Edinburgh · www.prestonfield.com · 0131 668 3346 This superlative country-house hotel and restaurant on the edge of the city (93/BOUTIQUE HOTELS), the epitome of gracious living; ideal prospect for a proper tea. An art piece of knitted cakes in the hallway may also put you in the mood. A number of sumptuous lounges and locations, tea options and, of course, champagne. 2-7pm. In town, another of James Thomson's esteemed establishments, The Tower (0131 225 3003) above and adjacent to the museum, serves tea 2.30-5.30pm; wonderful views of the Old Town from the terrace.

1428 6/N17 ✓ **Boath House** Auldearn, nr Nairn · www.boath-house.com · 01667 454896 On A96 3km east, this is one of the great country-house hotels of the north, on the food map of Scotland for Charlie Lockley's Michelin magic; he also knocks out a top afternoon tea! You can bet it's rather good but the point of coming here for your scone and cake is that. And then there's the grounds, walled garden and lakeside are a joy to walk in before or after. So this is a civilised way to pass an afternoon in the (sometimes) summer (on the terrace), blowy autumn (in the trees) or blazing fireside winter. Even online it's irresistible. 1036/HIGHLANDS.

1429 8/Q25 ✓ **Palm Court at The Balmoral Hotel** Edinburgh · www.thebalmoralhotel.com · 0131 556 2414 The grande dame of afternoon tea in the Palm Court beyond the foyer of Edinburgh's landmark hotel. Urbane and soothing (a harpist on the balcony). A cake stand with all you would expect, though not cheap at £35 (with champagne from £50) at TGP. Noon-5pm (you get 2 hours). Book! See 84/MAJOR HOTELS.

1430 7/K20
L **The Smiddy House** Spean Bridge · www.smiddyhouse.com · 01397 712335 On A82 14km N of Fort William. Guest house and hugely popular bistro with big local reputation that (pre-booked) does a specially made afternoon tea in a cosy afternoon-tea-type parlour. Bakewell tart, whisky cake, fruit tarts and an eclectic range of teas. Climb something, then treat yourself (possibly with champagne)! 1084/HIGHLANDS.

1431 8/M26 **The Tearooms** Glasgow · www.thebutterflyandthepig.com · 0141 243 2459 The less pub-like, more tearoom-like tearoom of **The Butterfly and The Pig** (717/BAR FOOD) somewhat sips the zeitgeist but on ever-changing style-driven Bath St, this is a more reflective space. From breakfast to supper but it's in afternoon and high-tea sessions that it comes into its own. 8.30am-5pm.

Mhor 84 nr Balquhidder They've thought of everything at this 'motel' on the A84. Drop by for afternoon tea all afternoon. Goodies from their bakery in Callander (see below) and those meringues! Report: 831/CENTRAL.

The Best Scotch Bakers

1432 8/Q23 ✓✓ **Fisher & Donaldson** Dundee, St Andrews & Cupar · www. fisheranddonaldson.com Main or original branch in main square, Cupar, and a kind of factory outlet up by Tesco, 3 in Dundee (12 Whitehall St, 300 Perth Rd and 83 High St) and 13 Church St, St Andrews. Superior contemporary bakers along traditional lines (born 1919). Surprising (and a pity) that they haven't gone further but they do supply selected outlets with pastries and most excellent Dr Floyd's bread which is as good as anything in the 'artisan' world. Sample also their yum yums, coffee trees, other breads and signature mini apple and rhubarb pies. Dundee Whitehall and Cupar have good tearooms (958/DUNDEE) and the factory one is fab.

1433 8/M24 ✓✓ **Mhor Bread** Callander · www.mhor.net · 01877 339518 W end of main street in busy touristy town. Here forever but taken on by Dick of the food-loving Lewis family of **Monachyle Mhor** (1191/GET-AWAY HOTELS) so those pies, cakes, the biggest, possibly the best, tattie scones and sublime doughnuts in Scotland have all been thrust into the 21st century; your picnic on the Braes is sorted and our favourite Trossachs pit stop! Adjacent café does bake stuff plus sandwiches, omelettes and always, the scone. 7 days.

1434 5/M17 ✓ **Cromarty Bakery** Cromarty · 013810 600388 For some, a reason to visit this picturesque seaside town. A wee shop but an abundance of speciality cakes, organic bread, rolls and pies, baked daily on premises. Top oatcakes! Also tea, coffee, hot savouries and takeaway. Stick to the traditional and the stodge though they use old-style ersatz cream. They have also expanded to Fortrose and produce is available elsewhere, eg the Storehouse at Evanton. Closed Sun.

1435 4/J14 ✓ **Riverside Bistro, The Lochinver Larder** Lochinver · www.piesbypost. co.uk · 01571 844356 On way into town from Ullapool, etc. A bistro/ restaurant mostly and rightly famous for their brilliant pies from takeaway counter. Huge variety of savoury and fruit from traditional to exotic. Rapid turnover; always freshly baked. And irresistible puds. Ready sustenance or merely indulgence; you can also get 'em by post. 7 days. Pie shops popping up all over the UK; these are streets ahead and wisely they haven't expanded – they're the best!

1436 8/Q23 **Goodfellow & Steven** Dundee, Perth & Fife · www.goodfellowscakes.co.uk The other bakers in the Fife/Dundee belt (not a patch on Fisher & Donaldson, but hey). G&S have several branches. Good commercial Scotch baking, with the kind of cakes that used to be a treat.

1437 8/R23 **JM Bakery** Carnoustie (main branch) · 01241 859530, · also in Monifieth & Arbroath · www.jmbakery.co.uk Specialising in wedding and designer cakes, the Robbs are also purveyors of bread and traditional savoury and sweet things. They do well at the Scotch Pie Championships and are famous for their rolls. Keeping the craft alive! Closed Sun.

1438 7/G22 **Tobermory Bakery** Tobermory · 01688 302225 In the middle of the postcard houses and shops around Tobermory Bay, this is very much the island bakery. Bread, pies, quiches and an array of old-style fancies and cakes including the bright yellow pineapple jobs. Some deli stuff. 7 days daytime only.

1439 6/P17 **The Bakehouse** Findhorn · 01309 691826 The bakery behind the excellent Bakehouse café (1077/HIGHLANDS) where David Boyle turns out a huge range of breads, scones etc. to supply the caff, the deli and the Findhorn community (1454/ DELIS) and other places further and wide. Ryes, spelt, gluten-free and from French country to focaccia. Until the caff opens at 10am you can buy from the bakery door.

1440 8/Q22   **McLaren's** Forfar · www.mclarenbakers.co.uk Also in Kirriemuir. Best in town for the famous Forfar bridie, a large, meaty shortcrust pasty hugely underestimated as a national delicacy. It's so much better than the gross and grossly overhyped Cornish pasty but it has never progressed beyond its (beefy) Angus heartland; one of the best copies is the home-made bridie that can be found in the café at **Glamis** (1760/CASTLES). 8am-4.15pm. Closed Sun & Thu afternoon. In Forfar, the other bakery **Saddler's** is better for cakes.

1441 8/M26   **Waterside Bakery** Strathaven · 01357 521260 Alexander Taylor's oldest in Scotland (1820) bakery in Strathaven. Some people say Taylors is one of the reasons for living here. OK, they do good breads, croissants, bics and cakes and the Flour Store Gallery is upstairs – you wouldn't find that at Greggs. Closed Sun (though caff adjacent open).

1442 8/P23   **Murray's** Perth · 01738 624633 In Perth and far and wide they know that Murray's Scotch pies are the business. Baked continuously from early till afternoon; there's often a queue. Their sausage rolls, and plain and onion bridies are also top, followed possibly with a perfect pineapple cake. Closed Sun.

1443 8/R25   **The Bakery** Dunbar · www.thebakerydunbar.co.uk · 01368 238178 Dunbar can do with all the good food it can get, so this community co-operative is a welcome 'social' enterprise. Artisan bread, cakes, patisserie. I suppose it matters who makes it but the standard is high and it's all a very good thing. There are over 800 shareholder members. Tue-Sat.

1444 8/N23   **Campbell's Bakery** www.campbellsbakery.com · Crieff · 01764 652114 & Comrie · 01764 679944 On the main streets and across from the main square in Crieff. Traditional bakers, family run; great window displays by Ailsa herself. Soup, coffees and all they make. Great pies, strawberry cakes and the fudge doughnuts. Crieff: 6am-5pm; Comrie: 7am-4.30pm. Closed Sun.

The Best Ice Cream

1445 8/Q25   ✓✓ **Luca's** 32-38 High Street, Musselburgh · www.s-luca.co.uk · 0131 665 2237 Queues out the door in the middle of a Sunday afternoon in February are testament to the enduring popularity of this much-loved ice-cream parlour. The classic flavours (vanilla, choc and strawberry) and many flashier arrivistes and a plethora of sorbets. In basic and always busy café through the back, The Olympia; you may also have to wait there too. Mon-Sat 9am-10pm, Sun 10.30am-10pm. For many, Luca's is simply the best, and folk come from Edinburgh (14km), though there is a branch in town at 16 Morningside Rd (319/CAFFS). Café upstairs more pizza/pasta and sandwiches. 7 days 9am-10pm. Luca's (wholesale) spreading everywhere 287/KIDS.

1446 9/M31   ✓✓ **Cream o' Galloway** Rainton, nr Gatehouse of Fleet · www. creamogalloway.co.uk · 01557 814040 A75 take Sandgreen exit 2km then left at sign for Carrick. Originally a dairy farm producing cheese, now you can watch them make the creamy concoctions that you find all over. Nature trail, fab kids' adventure-play area (1696/KIDS; they could spend a day here) and decent organic-type café and Burger Barn with Galloway beef. And there's a dogs-run-free field and a beach at **Sandgreen** (1583/BEACHES). Closed Nov-Jan.

1447 8/R23 ✓ **Jannetta's** St Andrews · www.jannettas.co.uk · 01334 473285 Family firm since 1908. There are two Jannetta's, but the one to adore is at top end South St. Look for the queue. Once only vanilla, then Americans at the Open asked for other flavours. Now there are over 50, sorbets and frozen yoghurt and numerous awards. Pastel pink café serves family fare; outside tables. 7 days.

1448 8/Q27 ✓ **Caldwell's** Innerleithen · 01896 830382 & Peebles · 01721 729005 The original (best) in Innerleithen, a ribbon of a town between Peebles and Galashiels. 2011 was their centenary – yes, they've been making ice cream since 1911. Purists may bemoan the fact that they've exploded into flavours in the 21st century, but their vanilla is still best. Many jars of sweeties. And get the hours: 6am-7.30pm (5pm in winter). Peebles: 7 days 10am-5pm.

1449 8/Q25 ✓ **Mary's Milk Bar** Edinburgh · www.marysmilkbar.com At west end of the Grassmarket, Mary's (for it is she) artisan gelateria – ice cream for the Instagram generation (you gotta get snapped cone in hand with the castle behind you). 10 or so flavours of a contemporary flava: salted caramel, of course. It's made through the back; there's often a big queue. Tue-Sat 11am-7pm, Sun noon-6pm.

1450 9/P30 ✓ **Drummuir Farm** Collin, nr Dumfries · www.drummuirfarm.co.uk · 01387 750599 5km off A75 (Carlisle/Annan) road E of Dumfries on B724 (near Clarencefield). A real farm producing real ice cream – still does supersmooth original and honeycomb, seasonal specials; on a fine day, sit out and chill. Indoor and outdoor play areas. Easter-Sep daily till 5.30pm; Oct-Dec Sat/Sun till 5pm.

1451 8/Q23 **Visocchi's** Broughty Ferry · www.visocchis.co.uk · 01382 779297 Originally from St Andrews; ice-cream makers for 75 years with legendary caff in Kirriemuir (now no longer connected). So here in Dundee's seaside suburb, a trusty tratt with home-made pasta, as well as the peach melba and a perfectly creamy vanilla. On a sunny day you queue! Closed Mon (unless it's hot). Also: 960/DUNDEE.

1452 8/N24 **Allan Water Café** Bridge of Allan · www.allanwatercafe.co.uk · 01786 833060 In early editions of this book this was an old-fashioned café in an old-fashioned town in the main street (since 1902). Fabulously good fish 'n' chips and ice cream. Now it's taken over the whole block and has a glass-and-metal extension; the ice cream has many new flavours. Plus ça change – this ice cream will run and run. 7 days 8am-8.30pm (LO). From 9am Sun.

The Really Good Delis

For Edinburgh and Glasgow delis, see p. 71 and p. 120.

1453 5/L18 **Corner on the Square** Beauly · www.corneronthesquare.co.uk · 01463 783000 On said corner of the square. For locals and passers-through, perhaps mainly because of its sit-in coffee-shop fare, including great baking, quiches, scones, soups, etc. But also Gary Williamson's well-cared-for cheeses, Cromarty bakes (1434/BAKERS) and a great eclectic wine selection. Open till 9pm weekends in summer for supper.

1454 6/P17 **Phoenix Findhorn Community** Findhorn · www.phoenixshop.co.uk Serving the eco-village (1252/RETREATS) and wider community and pursuing a conscientious approach long before it was de rigueur, this is an exemplary and very high-quality deli worth the detour from A96 Inverness-Elgin road. Packed and carefully selected shelves; as much for pleasurable eating as for healthy. Best organic fruit and veg in the NE. The excellent **Bakehouse** café in Findhorn itself owned by folk who used be here; superb ethical eats (1077/HIGHLANDS). Their breads on sale here. Till 6pm (weekends 5pm).

1455 8/N23 **2 Damned Fine Delis in Crieff: McNee's** www.mcneesofcrieff.co.uk · 01764 654582 Near the town clock. Deli/bakers/chocolatiers. More like an old-fashioned grocer and they make things: great home baking and ready-made meals, home-roasted meats; some sweety and Italian stuff creeping in... Open 7 days. **J.L. Gill** www.scottishproduce.co.uk · 01764 652396 West end, near turn to Crianlarich. And the real McCoy, here over 70 years. Judicious choice of provisions: honey, 10 kinds of oatcakes, lotsa whisky and wine. This genuine old-style, still the best style. Closed Sun.

1456 6/Q18 **Spey Larder** Aberlour · www.speylarder.com · 01340 871243 In deepest Speyside. Beautiful old shop (1864), spacious and full of great, often local produce (honeys, bread, game in winter, Speyside chanterelles and, of course, whisky). Nice cheese counter. Friendly provisioners are here. Closed Sun.

1457 8/R28 **Turnbull's** Hawick · 01450 372020 & Galashiels · 01896 750577 · www. turnbullshop.com By 'The Horse' in main street, a much-needed shot in the foodie arm in a town which waited a long time for olive oil to drip into the diet. Now this attractive, eclectic deli/café supplies the lot, makes life better and has expanded to Galashiels, with a more eating-in focus. Tables in Hawick a bit cramped for soup/salad/sandwich menu but where else would you go (perhaps **Damascus Drum** 867/BORDERS)?

1458 5/M18 **Oil & Vinegar** Inverness · www.oilvinegar.co.uk · 01463 240073 Near the train station. Does exactly what it says on the tin and bottle – olives and the stuff that goes with olives. A culinary treat in a town with good restaurants but not a lot on the foodie front. Closed Sun.

1459 8/R22 **E&O Fish** East Grimsby, Arbroath On road to harbour. Wholesalers of fish, the door in the wall with the queue outside is their retail 'shop', where they purvey that great Scottish delicacy – the smokie (smoked haddock) and other smoked fish and kippers. This is the place to go. 7am-7pm, Sat/Sun from 8am.

1460 3/F14 **Good Food Boutique** Stornoway · www.thegoodfoodboutique.co.uk · 01851 701394 It's small, it's good and it's food, and kind of essential in downtown Isle of Lewis. Big cheese counter, local bread, great takeaway sandwiches and nibbles. Closed Sun.

1461 8/P23   **Provender Brown** Perth · www.provenderbrown.co.uk · 01738 587300 As we might expect, a decent deli in the city where several good restaurants reside, there's a big farmers' market (first in Scotland) and many folk aren't short of a bob or two. Good for olives, vacuum-packed products and cheese. Closed Sun.

✓✓ **Pillars of Hercules** nr Falkland Organic grocers with tearoom (1396/ TEAROOMS) and outstanding farm shop and deli.

✓✓ **I.J. Mellis** St Andrews, Aberdeen, as well as Edinburgh and Glasgow. The cheese guy and other epicurean delights. See www.mellischeese.net.

▆▆▆▆▆ The Really Good Farm Shops

1462 9/N30   ✓✓ **Loch Arthur Creamery & Farm Shop** Beeswing, nr Dumfries · www. locharthur.org.uk · 01387 259669 Run by Camphill Trust, this is the genuine article once tucked away in a working dairy farm with a strong organic agenda, now a destination for SW foodies and anyone who cares about what they eat. Since the new building, it's a real honeypot!. Great bakery (the best bread, cakes and pies), famous organic veg, highly regarded cheeses and the UK's tastiest granola. Meats and eggs. From Beeswing take New Abbey road 1km. Closed Sun.

1463 8/P23   ✓✓ **Gloagburn Farm & Coffee Shop** Tibbermore, nr Perth · www.
☕   gloagburnfarmshop.co.uk · 01738 840864 Off A85 Perth-Methven and Crieff road from A9 and ring road at Huntingtower, signed Tibbermore (Tibbermore also signed off A9 from Stirling just before Perth). Through village, second farm on right: a family (the Nivens') farm shop (it all started with a free-range egg) with ducks on the pond and Tamworth pigs out back – excellent fresh produce and, inside, a deli and expanded café where food (hot dishes, cakes, etc.) is exemplary. Lovely eggy things and a signature soufflé. Hot and other food till 5pm. Vacuum-packed meats, frozen meals, fruit 'n' veg, home-made bread and their own oats. A destination place only 15 mins from Perth. Open 7 days AYR.

1464 6/R20   ✓✓ **Finzean Farm Shop & Tearoom** Deeside · www.finzean.com ·
☕   01330 850710 On the S side of the river on B976 between Banchory and Aboyne on the Farquharson family's Finzean estate. Kate and Catriona's foodie haven, a showcase for local suppliers, in glorious open countryside with views to the hills from the terrace. Local and carefully sourced produce beautifully presented fresh and frozen. Meat and game from the estate. Cool cookbooks. Hot dishes till 3pm. Cakes that don't rely on cream, and the mother-in-law's Victoria sponge. Open 7 days. See 1378/TEAROOMS.

1465 8/R24   ✓✓ **Ardross Farm** nr Elie · www.ardrossfarm.co.uk · 01333 331400 Between St Monans and Elie on the A917 Fife coastal route. East Neuk farm shop, an all-round highly selective provisioner of home-farm produce, including grass-fed, 21-day hung beef and a vast array of seasonal dug vegetables (over 50 varieties, with 7 types of hand-sown potatoes!), Fiona's pies, ready-made meals. The Pollock family have been here over a century and they're big supporters of UK farm produce as well as their own. Open 7 days.

1466 8/P26   ✓✓ **Whitmuir, the Organic Place** Lamancha, nr Peebles · www.
☕   whitmuirtheorganicplace.co.uk · 01968 661147 All-round foodie destination and fully realised good-life emporium, with shop, art gallery and café/ restaurant. Farm supplies own beef, lamb, pork, eggs and up to 32 different veg and fruit. Own butchery. A light, well-run place with good attitude. Only 40 mins from Edinburgh. Open daytime (though occasional foodie evenings).

1467 8/R22 ✓✓ **Milton Haugh Farm Shop** Carmyllie · 01241 860579 Off A92
🖥 Dundee-Arbroath road at Carnoustie, follow Forfar road then signs.
Enormously popular faraway farm on B961. Great range of fruit and veg, meats and
selected deli fare with own-label meals, jams, etc. Many different oatcakes.
Excellent Corn Kist Coffee Shop with home-made cakes, soups and specials; from
far and wide you come. 7 days.

1468 6/T19 ✓ **The Store** nr Foveran · www.thestorecompany.co.uk · 01358 788083
🖥 Off A90 at Foveran (1km), this beautiful farm shop is a food-lovers' haven and
a base for the Booth family (in their fourth generation), their Aberdeen Angus
(well-hung and tender) operation and their lovely caff with outside seating.
Vacuum-packed meats, cooked meals and the stuff including fruit and veg to go
with them. Oh, and there's also a hairdresser's! 7 days 10am-5pm.

1469 8/P25 ✓ **Craigie's Farm** nr South Queensferry · www.craigies.co.uk ·
🖥 0131 319 1048 Take the South Queensferry exit from dual carriageway N from
Edinburgh, A90 to Forth Road Bridge. Farm is signed 2km. Like many on these
pages, these guys saw the potential in farm shopping and grew rapidly from a PYO
farm on the edge of town to a visitor magnet. You can still PYO strawbs and rasps
and other soft fruit (Jun-Aug) but there's a self-service caff and an emporium of
food. Best is their own butchery section but the real attraction is to sit on a terrace
taking tea and cake overlooking rows and fields of fruit like vineyards in France
while the city shimmers in the distance. Open AYR 9am-5pm.

1470 9/N30 ✓ **Kilnford Barns Farm Shop** Dumfries · www.kilnford.co.uk ·
01387 253087 Edge of town on a roundabout of the A75 heading to
Stranraer. Built around a farm (actually supplied by 3), known for its Beltie (the
Belted Galloway) beef, but also pigs, this is a major farm shop emporium and café.
Around a courtyard, probably the best local/seasonal food provisioner in/around
Dumfries. Open 7 days.

1471 8/R25 ✓ **Fenton Barns Farm Shop** nr Drem · www.fentonbarnsfarmshop.com ·
🖥 01620 850294 Off A1 on A198, then signed by Dirleton, Mhairi and Roy's
country stores/caff is on craft parklet, an old airfield complex. They also look after
St Giles' Cathedral coffee shop in Edinburgh – they never flag (though now they
occasionally go on holiday). Organic meats, free-range eggs, home-made pies,
soups, terrines, selected fruit and veg, Roy's great coffee and their home-made
just-about-everything coffee shop in the back. 884/LOTHIANS. Open 7 days.
The Gosford Bothy Farm Shop nearby (Edinburgh side of Aberlady) is especially
good for meats, pies etc. At entrance to the lovely walk in the **Gosford Estate**
(1821/HOUSES). Also 7 days. A Haddington venture on the cards 2016/17.

1472 8/R25 ✓ **Knowes Farm Shop** nr East Linton · www.knowesfarmshop.co.uk ·
01620 860010 Close to A1 on A198 to North Berwick, just before
Tyninghame. A row of farm cottages converted into a spacious food store. Organic
veg and herbs, home-made pâtés, pavlova. Lots of eggs; many, many chickens in
the field and PYO. Open 7 days. They supply many other farm shops, restaurants,
etc, with their excellent 'sun and dung' home-grown veg. Real integrity here.

1473 8/P24 ✓ **Pillars of Hercules** nr Falkland · www.pillars.co.uk · 01337 857749 On
🖥 A912 2km from town towards Strathmiglo and motorway. A pillar of the
organic community and a more ethical way of life. Grocers with tearoom (1396/
TEAROOMS) on farm/nursery where you can PYO herbs and flowers. Always fruit/
veg and great selection of dry goods that's a long way from Sainsbury's and here
long before the organic boom spread all over this country road; they have a bothy
and camping. Open 7 days.

1474 8/M24 ✓ **The Woodhouse** nr Kippen · 01786 870156 New-build contemporary farm shop/deli and airy café, with outside terrace on the Lamb family farm, easily found on the long, straight A811 Stirling to Loch Lomond road at the first (Stirling-side) crossroads to Kippen and Thornhill. Cheese counter and Kippen butchers, local bread. The caff with salads, tortes and a roast of the day. A busy little food and fuel stop! Open 7 days.

1475 8/Q23 ✓ **Cairnie Fruit Farm (and Maze)** nr Cupar · www.cairniefruitfarm.co.uk · 01334 655610 A truly a(maze)ing conversion of a fruit farm into major family attraction (1688/KIDS) demonstrating if nothing else the inexorable rise of the strawberry. This and other berries can be picked, purchased and eaten in all manner of brilliant cakes, with other farm produce and snack food. Main thing though is the kids' area outside. Apr-Oct. Maze: Jul-Oct. Farm is 4km N of Cupar on minor road past the hospital or 3km from main A92, signed near Kilmany.

1476 8/R23 **Allanhill** nr St Andrews · www.allanhill.co.uk · 01334 477998 6km out of town off Anstruther/Crail road A917 past the **Grange** (1308/GASTROPUBS). Simple farm shop mainly and café with tables in the field. Kids' stuff includes animals, hay bales. Great views to St Andrews Bay. Known for excellent soft fruits including the elusive blueberry and '1000 tonnes of strawberries'. Tearoom has excellent strawberry cakes and a top scone. May-Sep.

1477 8/Q24 **Muddy Boots** Balmalcolm · www.muddybootsfife.com · 01337 831222 On A914 from A92 S of Cupar, a farm shop with kitchen and crafts and integrity over their produce; with a full-on activities play barn for kids. Their home-grown fruit and veg is high quality (the *best* raspberries) and they're keen to educate and inspire kids into good country practice (1689/KIDS). Open 7 days AYR.

▪▪▪▪▪ Where To Find Scottish Cheeses...

The delis on p. 71, 120 and 257-58 will have good selections (especially Valvona's in Edinburgh).

1478 8/Q25 ✓✓ **I.J. Mellis** Edinburgh, Glasgow, St Andrews & Aberdeen · www.
8/M25 mellischeese.net A real cheesemonger. Smell and taste before you buy.
8/R23 Cheeses from all over the UK in prime condition. Daily and seasonal specials.
6/T19 Reports: 357/EDINBURGH DELIS; 668/GLASGOW DELIS.

1479 8/M25 ✓✓ **George Mewes** Glasgow · www.georgemewescheese.co.uk · 0141 334 5900 The Byres Rd magnet for anyone with an epicurean taste: cheese as it should be seen, smelled and eaten. Scottish selection is just that – a judicious selection (ie, when they're ripe and ready). Report: 669/DELIS. Opened in Edinburgh late 2015 (358/DELIS).

1480 8/R23 ✓✓ **The Old Cheese Shop** St Andrews · www.oldcheeseshop.co.uk · 01334 477355 Down a close in mid-section of South St, oddly near I.J. Mellis (see above). An all-round cheese shop not obvious from the street, though with tables in the courtyard. Alex and Caroline Nite clearly love what they sell and do. Cheese & wine nights, artisan beers, honey from the Botanic Gardens and cheese at its very best, including up to a dozen Scottish. Tue-Fri 10am-5.30pm, Sat till 5pm. Phone ahead for times on Sun/Mon.

1481 8/P25 ✓ **Herbie of Edinburgh** Edinburgh · www.herbieofedinburgh.co.uk · 0131 332 9888 Excellent selection – everything here is the right stuff. Great bread, bagels, etc, from independent baker, home-made hummus and Scottish cheeses. You never get a Brie or a blue here in less than perfect condition.

1482 8/P22 ✓ **McDonald's Cheese Shop** Rattray, nr Blairgowrie · 01250 872493 Long-established emporium of cheese (80 varieties – though not specialising in Scottish – selected by owner Caroline Robertson): great blues, 'crumblier' and especially Swiss. You can buy a whole wheel of Gruyère. Closed Mon.

1483 7/G22 ✓ **Sgriob-Ruadh Farm** Mull · www.isleofmullcheese.co.uk · 01688 302627
L Head out on road to Dervaig, take turning for Glengorm (great coffee shop; 1380/TEAROOMS) and watch for sign and track to farm. Past big glass barn where they live in some kind of blissful bohemia and follow path to distant doorway into the cheese factory and farm shop (though all there is usually are lovely shit-covered fresh eggs and the cheddar, their new blue and a bit of sausage). **The Glass Barn** tearoom is a must (1390/TEAROOMS). Honesty box when nobody is around.

1484 5/M17 ✓ **The Cheese House** Cromarty · www.cromartycheese.com · 01381 600724 In the old police station. Boutique cheese shop in lovely Cromarty (1552/VILLAGES), with a Dutch connection, so those familiar and the farmers' cheeses, along with local (Highland Fine Cheeses, and the organic vegetarian ones from Connage Cheeses at Ardersier), Humphrey Errington, and the Mulls (above). The biscuits and chutneys to go with.

1485 7/J27 **Arran Cheese Shop** nr Brodick · www.arranscheeseshop.co.uk · 01770 302788 5km Brodick, road to castle and Corrie. Excellent selection of their own (the well-known cheddars) but many others especially crowdie, Camembert, Brie, Arran white (like Cheshire) and award-winning blue. Selected others. See them being made. Mon-Sat 9am-5pm, from 10am Sun.

1486 5/H18 **West Highland Dairy** Achmore, nr Plockton · www.westhighlanddairy. co.uk · 01599 577203 Charming and shuffly Mr and Mrs Biss still running their great farm dairy shop, selling their own cheeses (goats' and cows' milk), yoghurt, ice cream, cranachan cheesecake. Signed from village. Highland sylvan setting but no cows in sight. You can learn to make cheese here – they do courses. If you're making the trip specially, phone first to check they're open (usually 10am-4.30pm).

1487 8/Q23 **The Cheesery** Dundee · www.thecheesery.co.uk · 01382 202160 In Exchange St where there are good caff/restaurants (see Dundee p. 174-77), Dorothy Hegarty's cheese place is a foodie oasis in downtown Dundee. Scottish, continental, artisan. Tue-Fri 9.30am-5.30pm, Sat till 5pm.

✓✓ **Loch Arthur Creamery** Beeswing, nr Dumfries Off A75, A711 to New Abbey. Their own superlative cheeses and one of the best farm shops/ delis in and off the land. Report: 1462/FARM SHOPS.

✓✓ **House of Bruar** nr Blair Atholl Roadside superstore. Report: 2166/ SHOPS.

Whisky: The Best Distillery Tours

There are many distilleries (and tours of them); some more atmospheric and interesting than others. These are the best.

1488 7/F25 ✓✓ **The Islay Malts** Plenty to choose from on this island where whisky rules the waves:
Caol Ila (Mon-Fri, tour times vary Feb-Nov; 01496 302769); the wholly independent **Bruichladdich** (01496 850221); and
Kilchoman, the brand new Wills kid, daily tours, with great café; 2241/ISLAY (01496 850156).
In the S near Port Ellen, 3 of the world's great malts all in a row on a mystic coast. The distilleries here look like distilleries should.

LLL **Lagavulin** (01496 302749) and **Laphroaig** (01496 302418) offer fascinating tours where your guide will lay on the anecdotes as well as the process and you get a feel for the life and history as well as the product of these world-famous places. At Laphroaig there are enhanced (cost and effect) tours especially on Friday. AYR.
Ardbeg (01496 302244) is perhaps the most visitor-oriented and has a really good café (2241/ISLAY) and makes the most of its (dark olive) brand. All these distilleries are in settings that entirely justify the romantic hyperbole of their advertising. Worth seeing from the outside as well as the factory floor.
Bowmore (01496 810441) has a slick operation with peat-bog standard and more expensive Craftsman's Tours. Open AYR.

1489 6/Q17 ✓ **Strathisla** Keith · www.chivas.com · 01542 783044 Oldest working
ATMOS distillery in the Highlands, literally on the strath of the Isla River; methinks the most evocative atmos of all the Speyside distilleries. Tastefully reconstructed, this is a very classy halt for the malt. Used as the heart of Chivas Regal, the Strathisla though not commonly available is still a fine dram. You wait for a tour group to gather; there's a dram at the beginning and the end.

1490 6/P18 ✓ **The Glenlivet** Minmore · www.theglenlivet.com · 01340 821720
APR-OCT Starting as an illicit dram celebrated as far S as Edinburgh, George Smith
LL licensed the brand in 1824 and founded this distillery in 1858, registering the already mighty name so anyone else had to use a prefix. After successions and mergers, independence was lost in 1978 when Seagrams took over. Now owned by Pernod Ricard. The famous Josie's Well, from which the water springs, is underground. Small parties and a walk-through which is not on a gantry make the tour satisfying and as popular, especially with Americans, as the product. Excellent reception centre (tours every 20 mins) with bar/restaurant (food average) and shop; the tour on the website's so good, you probably don't need to go at all, though you won't then get a dram in those hallowed surroundings. 7 days.

1491 6/Q18 ✓ **Glenfiddich** Dufftown · www.glenfiddich.com · 01340 820373 Outside
LL town on A941 to Craigellachie by Balvenie Castle ruins. Well-lubricated tourist
🖫 operation and the only distillery where you can see the whole process from barley to bar (well, not the bottlery). The only major distillery that's free (including dram). Still very much family run (their story on the walls), they sponsor the Spirit of Scotland awards. Also runs artists-in-residence scheme with changing exhibitions in summer; gallery by car park (01340 821565). AYR. Good restaurant.
On the same road you can see a whisky-related craft that hasn't changed. **Speyside Cooperage** is 1km from Craigellachie. See those poor guys from the gantry (no chance to slack). Open AYR Mon-Fri 9.30am-4.30pm. Good coffee shop.

1492 8/N21
L ✓ **Edradour** nr Pitlochry · www.edradour.com · **01796 472095** Picturesque and as romantic as you can imagine the smallest distillery in Scotland to be, producing single malts for blends since 1825 and limited quantities of the Edradour (only 12 casks a week then laid for 10 years, so not easy to find; see website for stockists) as well as the House of Lords' own brand. Guided tour of charming cottage complex every 20 mins. 4km from Pitlochry. Mid-Apr to mid-Oct, Mon-Sat.

1493 5/F18
L **Talisker** Carbost, Skye · www.discovering-distilleries.com/talisker · **01478 614308** From Sligachan-Dunvegan road (A863) take B8009 for Carbost and Glen Brittle along the S side of Loch Harport for 5km. Skye's only distillery; since 1830 they've been making this classic after-dinner malt from barley and the burn that runs off the Hawkhill behind. A dram before the informative 40-min tour. Good visitor centre. Apr-Oct 9.30am-5pm (check winter times). Great gifts nearby (2159/SCOTTISH SHOPS). Nice pub for grub and music nearby: the Old Inn at Carbost.

1494 8/Q26 **Glenkinchie** Pencaitland, nr Edinburgh · www.discovering-distilleries. com/glenkinchie · **01875 342012** Only 25km from city centre; one of the most accessible distilleries. Founded in 1837 in a pastoral place watered from the Lammermuirs, 3km from village, with its own bowling green – a trip to the country and a whisky tour! State-of-the-art visitor centre. 7 days AYR.

1495 1/Q10 **Highland Park** Kirkwall, Orkney · www.highlandpark.co.uk/visit · **01856 874619** 2km from town on main A961 road S to South Ronaldsay. The whisky is great and the award-winning tour one of the best. The most northerly whisky in a class and a bottle of its own. You walk through the floor maltings and you can touch the warm barley and fair smell the peat. Good combination of the industrial and the traditional. Best check website for times.

1496 8/Q25 **Scotch Whisky Heritage Centre** Edinburgh · www. scotchwhiskyexperience.co.uk · **0131 220 0441** On Castlehill, on last stretch to castle (you cannot miss it). Not a distillery of course, but a visitor attraction to celebrate all things a tourist can take in about Scotland's main export. Shop has huge range. 7 days 10am-5pm (extended hours in summer).

THE BEST OF THE SPEYSIDE WHISKY TRAIL

1497 6/Q17 **Glen Grant** Rothes · www.glengrant.com · **01340 832118** In Rothes on the A941 Elgin to Perth road. Not the most picturesque but a distillery tour with an added attraction, viz. the gardens and orchard reconstructed around the shallow bowl of the glen of the burn that runs through the distillery: there's a lime-tree-lined walk (15 mins) and delightful Dram Pavilion. Now owned by Campari, you will be immersed in the history as well as the process with a word from the founder in a replica of his study and then 2 tastings before you leave. Mon-Sun 9.30am-5pm, except Nov-Mar noon-5pm on Sun.

1498 6/P18 **Cardhu (or Cardow)** Cardow · www.discovering-distilleries.com/cardhu · **01340 872555** Off B9102 from Craigellachie to Grantown through deepest Speyside, a small if charming distillery with its own community, a millpond, picnic tables, etc. Owned by Diageo, Cardhu is the 'heart of Johnnie Walker' (which, amazingly, has another 30 malts in it). Open AYR Mon-Fri (7 days Jul-Sep). Hours vary.

1499 6/P17 **Benromach** Forres · www.benromach.com · **01309 675968** Signed from A96 at Forres. The smallest working distillery so no bus tours or big tourist operation. Human beings with time for a chat. Rescued by Gordon & MacPhail and reopened 1999. A great introduction to whisky. May-Sep 9.30am-5pm (& Sun Jun-Aug only noon-4pm). Winter 10am-4pm.

Whisky: The Best Malts Selections

EDINBURGH

✓✓ **Scotch Malt Whisky Society** www.smws.com · 0131 220 2044 Your search will end here. More a club (with membership), and top restaurant.

Bennets Bar Report: 368/UNIQUE PUBS.

Kay's Bar Report: 373/UNIQUE PUBS.

The Bow Bar Report: 386/ALES.

Cadenhead's www.wmcadenhead.com · 0131 556 5864 The shrine.

Canny Man's Report: 173/GASTROPUBS.

The Malt Shovel www.taylor-walker.co.uk · 0131 225 6843 Unpretentious pub.

Blue Blazer Report: 390/ALES.

Whiskirooms Report: 250/SCOTTISH.

GLASGOW

✓✓ **The Pot Still** www.thepotstill.co.uk · 0141 333 0980 450 different bottles of single malt. And proud of it.

Bon Accord Report: 706/ALES.

The Lismore Report: 704/UNIQUE PUBS.

Ubiquitous Chip Restaurant, bistro and great bar on the corner. Report: 502/ TOP-END DINING.

Ben Nevis Report: 705/UNIQUE PUBS.

REST OF SCOTLAND

✓✓ **The Torridon** nr Kinlochewe Classic Highland hotel bar with 360 malts shelf-by-shelf. And the mountains! Report: 1192/GET-AWAY HOTELS.

✓✓ **Clachaig Inn** Glencoe Over 100 malts to go with the range of ales and the range of thirsty hillwalkers. Report: 1287/GOOD PUBS.

✓✓ **The Oystercatcher** Portmahomack Gordon Robertson's exceptional malt (and wine) collection in far-flung village. Report: 1094/HIGHLANDS.

✓ **Forss House Hotel** nr Thurso Hotel on N coast. Often a wee wind outside; warm up with one of 300 well-presented malts. Report: 1052/HIGHLANDS.

✓ **The Quaich Bar at The Craigellachie Hotel** Whiskies arranged around cosy bar of this essential Speyside hotel, the river below. Report: 1028/SPEYSIDE.

✓ **Lochside Hotel** Bowmore, Islay · www.lochsidehotel.co.uk · 01496 810244 More Islay malts than you ever imagined in a friendly local.

✓ **Knockinaam Lodge** Portpatrick Comfortable country-house hotel; good Lowland selection includes the local Bladnoch. Report: 809/sw HOTELS.

✓ **The Piano Bar at the Glenmoriston Townhouse** Inverness Easy-to-decipher malt list in superior, stylish surroundings. Report: 1039/HIGHLANDS.

✓ **The Drover's Inn** Inverarnan Classic hostelry with around 75 drams to choose and the right atmos to drink them in. Kilty barmen. Report: 1285/GOOD PUBS.

✓ **The Anderson** Fortrose Amazing collection of over 250 malts (and beers) in atmospheric, small-town hotel bar. And great food! Report: 1058/HIGHLANDS.

✓ **Ardanaiseig Hotel** Loch Awe A dram's a must after dinner in the bar looking over the lawn to the loch. Report: 1132/COUNTRY-HOUSE HOTELS.

✓ **Sligachan Hotel** Skye · www.sligachan.co.uk · 01478 650204 On A87 (A850) 11km S of Portree. Nearly 400 malts in Seamus' huge cabin bar. Good ales, including their own (the Cuillin Brewery is here).

✓ **Gordon & MacPhail** Elgin · www.gordonandmacphail.com · 01343 545110 The whisky provisioner and bottlers of the *Connoisseurs Choice* brand you see all over. From humble beginnings over 100 years ago they now supply their exclusive and rarity range to the world. Closed Sun.

✓ **The Whisky Shop Dufftown** www.whiskyshopdufftown.co.uk · 01340 821097 The whisky shop in the main street (by the clock tower) at the heart of whisky country. Within a few miles of numerous distilleries, this place stocks all the products (including many halfs). Open 7 days.

Loch Fyne Whiskies Inveraray · www.lochfynewhiskies.com · 01499 302219 On Main Street (A83), a shop with 400 malts, quaichs, etc.

Robbie's Drams Ayr · www.robbieswhiskymerchants.com · 01292 262135 Robin Russell's impressive emporium. Bottle or case.

the
Best
Outdoor Places

The Best Gardens

1500 5/H16
L
ADMISSION
▣
NTS

✓✓ **Inverewe** **Poolewe** · **www.nts.org.uk** · **01445 712952** 80km S of
Ullapool on A832. World-famous gardens on a Loch Ewe promontory.
Beginning in 1862, Osgood Mackenzie made it his life's work and since then people
have come from all over the world to admire his efforts. Helped by the ameliorating
effect of the Gulf Stream, the wild garden became the model for many others. The
walled garden is beyond immaculate: if you were a flower or vegetable, you'd want
to be here sheltered, nurtured and inclined to the southern sun (terrace best
viewed from the top path by James Reid bench). Guided tours to get the most out
of this vast garden or go in the evening when it's quiet! Shop, visitor centre. Café
(Mar-Oct; great space, food less so) 10am-4.30pm; hot meals till 3pm. Gardens AYR
till dusk.

1501 7/K25
MAR-OCT
L
ADMISSION
▣

✓✓ **Benmore Botanic Garden** **nr Dunoon** · **www.rbge.org.uk** ·
01369 706261 12km on A815 to Strachur. An outstation of the Royal
Botanic in Edinburgh, gifted to the nation by Harry Younger in 1928, but the first
plantations date from 1820. Marked walks through formal gardens, woody grounds
and pinetum where the air is often so sweet and spicy it seems like the elixir of life
(I said this in my first edition – it's still true). Redwood avenue, terraced hill sides,
views; a garden of different moods and fine proportions. Good walk, **Puck's Glen**,
nearby (2004/WALKS). Café and shop open AYR (closed Mon/Tue).

1502 6/S20
L
ADMISSION
▣
NTS

✓✓ **Crathes** **nr Banchory** · **www.nts.org.uk** · **01330 844525** 25km W of
Aberdeen, just off A93. One of the most interesting tower houses (1826/
HOUSES) surrounded by terrific topiary and walled gardens of inspired design and
tranquillity (though you're unlikely to have any part of it to yourself). Keen
gardeners will be in their scented heaven. The Golden Garden (after Gertrude Jekyll)
works particularly well and there's a wild garden beyond the old wall that many
people miss. A very *House & Garden* experience, though in summer it's stuffed with
people as well as plants. Grounds and Courtyard Café open AYR.

1503 9/N29
ADMISSION

✓✓ **The Garden of Cosmic Speculation** **Holywood, Dumfriesshire** ·
www.charlesjencks.com I hesitate to include this extraordinary garden
by the landscape artist Charles Jencks because it's only fully open to the public for
one day a year in early May (through the Scotland's Gardens Scheme). But it is too
remarkable not to include. Laid out in 1988, this extraterrestrial garden of
landforms, sculptures, bridges, terraces and architectural works around Portrack,
the artist's Georgian farmhouse, remains both a memorial to Jencks's wife Maggie
Keswick (who gave her name to the Maggie Cancer Caring Centres) and a place of
national importance. Also by Jencks, in the same district and much more accessible
is the **Crawick Multiverse** (2133/ART SPACES).

1504 8/P26
LL
ATMOS
ADMISSION

✓✓ **Little Sparta** **nr Dunsyre** · **www.littlesparta.org.uk** · **07826 495677**
Near Biggar off A702 (5km), go through village then signed. House, in bare
hill country, the home of conceptual artist and national treasure, Ian Hamilton
Finlay, who died 2006. Gardens lovingly created over years, full of thought-
provoking art/sculpture/perspectives (over 250 separate artworks). Unlike
anywhere else. A privilege to visit but it is fragile; no dogs or little kids. 700m walk
from car park. Jun-Sep: Wed/Fri/Sun 2.30-5pm, but check the website (and note
satnav instructions). New lovely book 2015: *Little Sparta*.

1505 8/L28
ADMISSION
✓✓ **Dumfries House** nr Cumnock · www.dumfries-house.org.uk ·
01290 425959 On the A70 25km E of Ayr. The house, grounds and
gardens have been transformed following the intervention of Prince Charles and
the Prince's Trust. There's the building itself, a great café, restaurant and many
ways to walk. Several garden areas, including the flagship Walled Garden. Gardens
under extensive development at TGP but we can be sure that what will emerge and
mature will be a wonder and a wandering, probably for generations. Check website
for times.

1506 8/N23
ADMISSION
✓✓ **Drummond Castle Gardens** Muthill · www.
drummondcastlegardens.co.uk · 01764 681433 Near Crieff. Signed
from A822, 2km from Muthill, then up an avenue of fabulous trees to the most
exquisite formal gardens, viewed first from the terrace by the house. A boxwood
parterre of a vast St Andrew's Cross in yellow and red (especially antirrhinums and
roses), the Drummond colours, with extraordinary sundial centrepiece; 5 gardeners
keep every leaf in place. 7 days Easter & May-Oct 1-5pm (last admission). House
not open to public.

1507 9/J31
L
ADMISSION
✓✓ **Logan Botanical Garden** nr Sandhead · www.rbge.org.uk ·
01776 860231 16km S of Stranraer by A77/A716 and 2km on from
Sandhead. Remarkable outstation of the Edinburgh Botanics, among sheltering
woodland in the mild SW. Compact and full of pleasant southern surprises. Less
crowded than other exotic gardens. Walled, woodland gardens and the Tasmanian
Creek. The Gunnera Bog is quite extraterrestrial. Coffee shop decent. Mar-Oct:
7 days 10am-5pm. Sun in Feb 10am-4pm for the snowdrops.

1508 7/J24
ADMISSION
NTS
✓✓ **Crarae** Inveraray · www.nts.org.uk · 01546 886614 16km SE on A83
to Lochgilphead. Most gorgeous of the famed gardens of Argyll; peaceful
in any season. The wooded banks of Loch Fyne with the gushing Crarae burn are as
lush as the Himalayan gorges, where many of the plants originate. Follow the
footsteps of plant-hunters and pandas! Open AYR 9.30am-dusk. Visitor centre
Apr-Oct. Walks 0.5-2km.

1509 4/N15
LL
ADMISSION
✓✓ **Dunrobin Castle Gardens** Golspie · www.dunrobincastle.co.uk ·
01408 633177 On A9 1km N of town. The Versailles-inspired gardens that
sit below the opulent Highland chateau of the Dukes of Sutherland (1771/CASTLES).
Terraced, parterred and immaculate, they stretch to the sea. 30 gardeners once
tended them, now there are 4 but little has changed since they impressed a more
exclusive clientele. Castle Apr-Oct 10.30am-last admission 4pm (5pm Jun-Aug).
Garden gate open later.

1510 8/P27
ADMISSION
✓✓ **Dawyck Gardens** nr Stobo · www.rbge.org.uk · 01721 760254 On
B712 Moffat road off A72 Biggar/Peebles road, 2km from Stobo. An
outstation of the Edinburgh Botanics, though tree planting here goes back
300 years. Sloping grounds around the gurgling Scrape burn which trickles into the
Tweed. Landscaped woody pathways for meditative walks. Famous for shrubs, blue
Himalayan poppies and Douglas Firs. Rare Plant Trail and great walk on 'The John
Buchan Way' nearby, 2km off Stobo Rd before Dawyck entrance. Visitor centre with
café (home-made food) and shop. Apr-Sep 10am-6pm (closes earlier in winter).

1511 9/K30
ADMISSION
✓ **Glenwhan** nr Glenluce, nr Solway Coast · www.glenwhangardens.co.
uk · 01581 400222 Signed from A75 and close to more famous **Castle
Kennedy** (also very much worth a visit), this the more edifying labour of love.
Up through beechy (and in May) bluebell woods, and through backyards to
horticultural haven, teased from bracken and gorse moorland from 1979.

Open moorland still beckons at the top of the network of trails through a carefully planted but wild botanical wonder. Many seats for contemplations; some sculpture. Gardens and tearoom Easter-Sep 10am-5pm. Honesty box Oct.

1512 9/M30
ADMISSION
NTS

✓ **Threave** nr Castle Douglas · www.nts.org.uk · 01556 502575
64 acres of magnificent Victorian landscaping in incomparable setting overlooking Galloway coastline. Gardeners should not miss the walled kitchen garden; horticulturally inspiring and daunting. Garden is part of a vast estate, which includes the castle and a wildfowl reserve. Various walks: a circular Estate Walk 4km with spur (2km return) to the castle. Threave is a bat reserve. You can hire a bat detector with deposit and return next day. Centre open 10am-dusk (other access points for estate AYR).

1513 8/R27
ADMISSION
💬

✓ **Monteviot House Garden & Woodside Garden Centre** nr Ancrum & Jedburgh · www.monteviot.com · 01835 830380 Off A68 at Ancrum, the B6400 to Nisbet (3km), first there's Woodside on left (Victorian walled garden for the house; separate but don't miss) then the mainly formal gardens of the house (home of the Marquess of Lothian); terraced to the river (Teviot). All extraordinarily pleasant. Woodside has an organic demonstrations section, other events and a great tearoom (1386/TEAROOMS; 2192/GARDEN CENTRES). House: Jul (not Mon) 1-4.15pm (last entry). Gardens: Apr-Oct noon-4pm (last entry).

1514 7/J23
HONESTY BOX

✓ **Angus's Garden** Taynuilt · www.barguillean.co.uk 5km from village (22km from Oban on the A85) along the Glen Lonan road. Take first right after Barguillean Farm. A garden laid out by the family who own the farm in memory of their son Angus, a reporter killed reporting on the war in Cyprus. On the slopes around Angus's Loch, brimful of lilies and ducks and (rescued) swans. Informal mix of tended and uncultivated (though wild prevails), a more poignant remembrance is hard to imagine as you while an hour away in this peaceful place. 9am till dusk.

1515 8/Q25
L

✓ **Dr Neil's (Secret) Garden** Edinburgh · www.drneilsgarden.co.uk · 07849 187995 Not quite the secret it was (sorry!) but this garden can still feel like your private demesne on the shores of Duddingston Loch. End of the road through Holyrood Park just past Duddingston church; enter through manse gates. Turn right. At end of the manse lawn a corner gate leads to an extraordinary terraced garden bordering the loch. With wild Arthur's Seat above, you can feel you're in Argyll. The labour of love of Claudia Poitier and volunteers, this is an enchanting corner of the city. 7 days 10am till dusk. The skating minister of the Raeburn painting took off from the restored tower here.

1516 7/H24
ADMISSION
NTS

✓ **Arduaine Garden** nr Kilmelford · www.nts.org.uk · 01852 200366
28km S of Oban on A816, one of Argyll's undiscovered arcadias gifted to the NTS who in the current climate struggle to keep it open (in winter get tickets at the hotel). The creation of this (micro) climate in which the rich, diverse vegetation flourished, was influenced by Osgood Mackenzie of Inverewe (above) and its restoration is a testimony to the 20 years' hard labour of the famous Wright brothers. Enter/park by **Loch Melfort Hotel** (779/ARGYLL), gate 100m. Until dusk.

1517 9/M30
ADMISSION

✓ **Cally Gardens** Gatehouse of Fleet · www.callygardens.co.uk · 01557 815029 Off A75 at Gatehouse and through the gateway to **Cally Palace Hotel** (1146/KIDS), this walled garden is signed off to the left before you reach the hotel. Built in the 1770s as the kitchen garden of the big house, it was rescued in 1987 by Michael Wickenden, who transformed it into a haven for gardeners and meticulously gathered, introduced, nurtured and recorded herbaceous plants (over 3,000), many you won't find anywhere else. Serious stuff though not suburban neat and tidy. Easter-Sep. Closed Mon & weekday mornings.

1518 7/G26
ADMISSION

✓ **Achamore Gardens** Gigha · **www.gigha.org.uk/gardens** · **01583 505275** 1km from ferry. Walk or cycle (bike hire by ferry); an easy trip. The garden around the island's big hoose, once of the Horlick family and at TGP about to be turned into a boutique hotel. Lush tropical plants mingle with early-flourishing rhoddies (Feb-Mar): all due to the mild climate and the devotion of a long roll call of gardeners. 2 marked walks (40 mins/2 hours) start from the walled garden (green route takes in the sea view of Islay and Jura). Density and variety of shrubs, pond plants and trees revealed as you meander in this enchanting spot. Leaflet guides at entrance. Open AYR dawn to dusk. Honesty box. See 2204/ISLANDS.

1519 6/S20
ADMISSION
NTS

✓ **Drum Castle Rose Garden** nr Banchory · **www.nts.org.uk** · **01330 700334** 1km from A93. In the grounds of Drum Castle (the Irvine ancestral home, though nothing to do with my Irvines 1769/CASTLES), a superb walled garden that pays homage to the rose and encapsulates 4 centuries of its horticulture. 4 areas (17th-20th centuries). Fabulous, Jul/Aug especially. Open Mar-Oct 11am-4.15pm (last entry).

1520 7/J26
ADMISSION

Ascog Hall Fernery Rothesay · **www.ascogfernery.com** · **01700 503461** Outside town on road to **Mount Stuart** (1814/HOUSES), worth stopping at Ascog Hall, its small garden and sunken Victorian Fern House, rescued and restored in 1997. Green and lush and dripping! Easter-Oct 10am-5pm. And don't miss Rothesay's Victorian men's loos (which women can visit, too); they are not small.

1521 8/R27
ADMISSION
NTS

Priorwood Melrose · **www.nts.org.uk** · **01896 822493** Next to Melrose Abbey, this tranquil secret garden behind high walls specialises in growing flowers and plants for drying. Picking, drying and arranging continuously in progress. Samples for sale. Run by enthusiasts on behalf of the NTS, they're always willing to talk stamens with you. Includes a historical apple orchard with trees through the ages. Mon-Sat 10am-5pm; Sun 1-5pm. Closed 4pm winter. A superior shop with flowers and veg from nearby Harmony Garden, where they hold the book festival (43/EVENTS).

1522 8/Q27
L
ADMISSION

Kailzie Gardens Peebles · **www.kailziegardens.com** · **01721 720007** On B7062 Traquair road. Spacious, well-kept walled garden with informal glasshouses and perfect hedges. Informal woodland gardens all eminently strollable. Old-fashioned roses, wilder bits. Courtyard teashop and deli. Kids' corner and ospreys (Apr-Aug). Fishing ponds. Apr-Oct 11am-5.30pm (less access winter).

1523 6/S18
ADMISSION
🖵
NTS

Pitmedden Garden nr Ellon · **www.nts.org.uk** · **01651 842352** 35km N of Aberdeen, 10km W of A92. Formal French gardens recreated in 1950s on site of Sir Alex Seton's 17th-century ones. The 4 great parterres, 3 based on designs for Holyrood Palace gardens, are best viewed from the terrace. Charming farmhouse museum seems transplanted. For lovers of symmetry and an orderly universe (but there is a woodland walk with wildlife garden area). May-Sep 10am-5pm (last entry).

1524 6/R19

Pittodrie House nr Inverurie · **www.macdonaldhotels.co.uk** · **01467 681444** An exceptional walled garden in the grounds of **Pittodrie House Hotel** at Chapel of Garioch (978/NE HOTELS). Different gardens compartmentalised by hedges. 500m from house and curiously unvisited by many of the guests, this secret and sheltered haven is both a kitchen garden and a place for meditations and reflections (and those wedding photos); chances are you'll have this haven to yourself.

1525 7/K24
ADMISSION

Ardkinglas Woodland Cairndow · www.ardkinglas.com Off the A83 Loch Lomond-Inveraray road. Through village to signed car park and these mature woodlands in the grounds of Ardkinglas House on the southern bank near the head of Loch Fyne. Fine pines include 'the tallest tree in Britain'. Magical at dawn or dusk. 2km **Loch Fyne Oysters** (1343/SEAFOOD), where there is also the Tree Shop garden centre, especially good for trees and shrubs.

1526 5/J18
ADMISSION

Attadale Gardens Strathcarron · www.attadalegardens.com · 01520 722603 On A890 from Kyle of Lochalsh and A87 just S of Strathcarron. Lovely West Highland home (to the Macphersons) and these delightful gardens near Loch Carron. Exotic specials, water gardens, collected sculpture, great rhoddies May/Jun. Nursery and kitchen garden. Fern and Japanese gardens. Good café/restaurant **The Carron** 1095/HIGHLANDS nearby. Apr-Oct 10am-5.30pm. Closed Sun.

1527 7/J21

Ard-Daraich Hill Garden Ardgour · www.arddaraich.co.uk · 01855 841384 3km S Ardgour at Corran Ferry on A861 to Strontian. A private (50 years), labour of love hill and wild garden where you are at liberty to wander. Shores of Loch Linhe with views of Ben Nevis and Glen Coe – you could be in the Himalayas. Once the home of Constance Spry. Tending to the ericaceous (i.e. specialising in rhoddies), shrubs, trees; birdsong! Open AYR 7 days. 3 lovely rooms to stay over; home-garden produce.

1528 8/M26

The Hidden Gardens 25a Albert Drive, Glasgow · www.thehiddengardens. org.uk · 0141 433 2722 This garden oasis in the asphalt jungle of Glasgow's southside was created in the disused wasteland behind The Tramway performance and studio space, a project of environmental theatre group NVA working with landscape architects City Design Co-operative, this is a very modern approach to an age-old challenge – how to make and keep a sanctuary in the city! It's ageing gracefully. Nice caff (664/KIDS). Opening hours vary. Closed Mon.

✓✓✓ **Royal Botanic Garden** Edinburgh Report: 427/ATTRACTIONS.

✓ **Mount Stuart** Report: 1814/HOUSES.

Botanic Gardens & Kibble Palace Glasgow Report: 731/ATTRACTIONS.
Kildrummy Castle Hotel Report: 1210/SCOTTISH HOTELS.
Stonefield Castle Hotel Report: 789/ARGYLL.
Castle of Mey Report: 1757/CASTLES.
Cawdor Castle Report: 1758/CASTLES.
Brodick Castle Report: 1761/CASTLES.
Dunvegan Castle Report: 1763/CASTLES.
Manderston Report: 1816/HOUSES.
Floors Castle Report: 1822/HOUSES.

Learn more about all these gardens and many others in 'Scotland for Gardeners' by Kenneth Cox, published by Birlinn.

The Best Country Parks

1529 9/N28
ADMISSION
✓✓ **Drumlanrig Castle** Thornhill · www.drumlanrigcastle.co.uk · 01848 331555 On A76, 7km N of Thornhill in the west Borders, in whose romance and history it's steeped, much more than merely a country park; spend a good day, both inside the castle (summer only; check website) and in the grounds. Apart from *that* art collection (Rembrandt, Holbein and you may remember the Leonardo got stolen) and the courtyard of shops, the delights include a wee tearoom, an adventure playground and regular events programme. Main outdoor focus is on extensive trails for walking (4) and cycling (7) up to 15km round the estate lochs and silvery Nith. Open Apr-Sep 10am-5pm.

1530 7/L26
L
✓ **Muirshiel** nr Lochwinnoch · www.clydemuirshiel.co.uk · 01505 614791 Via Largs (A760) or Glasgow (M8, junction 29 A737 then A760 5km S of Johnstone). N from village on Kilmacolm road for 3km then signed. Muirshiel is name given to wider area but park proper begins 6km on road along the Calder valley. Despite proximity to the conurbation, this is a wild and enchanting place for walks, picnics, etc. Trails marked to waterfall and summit views (Windy Hill an easy 2km). Extensive events programme. Go look for hen harriers. See also 747/WALKS. Escape!

1531 8/R25 **John Muir Country Park** nr Dunbar · www.eastlothian.gov.uk · 01620 827459 Named after the 19th-century conservationist who founded America's national parks (and the Sierra Club), and who was born in Dunbar (his birthplace is now an interactive museum at 126 High St and the start of The John Muir Way, which runs across Central Scotland to Helensburgh). This swathe of coastline to the W of the town (partly known locally as Tyninghame) is an important estuarine nature reserve but is good for family walks and beachcombing. Various entry points: main one is from Dunbar roundabout on A1 back towards North Berwick, then A1087, 1km; by clifftop trail from Dunbar; or from car park on road into Dunbar from W at West Barns.

1532 7/L25
ADMISSION
Finlaystone Estate Langbank · www.finlaystone.co.uk · 01475 540505 A8 to Greenock, Houston direction at Langbank, then signed. Grand mansion home to chief of Clan MacMillan set in formal gardens in wooded estate. Lots of facilities, craft shop, leafy walks, walled garden and rather good tearoom. Apr-Sep daily until 5pm; Oct-Mar till 4pm. An all-round get oot o' the house experience and kinda vital!

1533 8/S27 **Hirsel Country Park** Coldstream · www.dandaestates.co.uk · 01555 851536 On A697, N edge town (direction Kelso). 3,000 acres the grounds of Hirsel House (not open to public). 2-4km walks through farmland and Dunglass Woods including lovely languid lake. Museum, tearoom (7 days) and craft units at the Homestead.

1534 8/N25 **Muiravonside Country Park** nr Linlithgow · www.falkirkcommunitytrust. org · 01324 590900 4km SW of Linlithgow on B825, or signed from junction 4 of M9 Edinburgh/Stirling. Former farm estate and a park just where you need it, with 170 acres of woodland walks, parkland, picnic sites and a visitor centre for school parties or anyone else with an interest in birds, bees and badgers. Ranger service; guided walks (01324 506119). Great place to walk off that lunch at the not-too-distant **Champany Inn** (279/BURGERS & STEAKS). Apr-Sep 8am-8pm (Oct-Mar till 5pm).

✓✓ **Culzean Castle Park** Ayrshire Superb. Report: 1755/CASTLES.

✓✓ **Haddo House** nr Ellon Beautiful grounds. Report: 1815/HOUSES.

Mugdock Country Park nr Glasgow Vast. Report: 743/WALKS.

Tentsmuir nr Tayport Estuarine; John Muir, on Tay. Report: 1748/RESERVES.

Kelburn Country Centre Largs Report: 1685/KIDS.

The Best Town Parks

1535 8/Q25 ✓✓ **Princes Street Gardens** Edinburgh On S side of Princes St. This former loch, drained when the New Town was built, divided by the Mound, was wrested from the landlords to become a pleasure ground for 'the people' in perpetuity. The eastern half has pitch and putt, Winter Wonderland and the **Scott Monument** (470/VIEWS) and, well, Christmas; the western has its much-photographed fountain, open-air café, space for locals and tourists to sprawl on the grass when sunny, the Ross Bandstand – heart of **Edinburgh's Hogmanay** (83/EVENTS) and the International Festival's fireworks concert (60/EVENTS). Workers on lunch, senior citizens on benches, dazed tourists: all our lives are here. Till dusk. And as I often rediscover: **The Meadows** is also an exceptional asset to the city.

1536 6/S19 ✓✓ **Hazlehead Park** Aberdeen · www.aberdeencity.gov.uk Via Queens Rd, 3km centre. Extraordinary park where the Aberdonians' mysterious gardening skills are magnificently in evidence. Many facilities including a maze, pets' corner, tearoom and there are lawns, memorials and botanical splendours aplenty, especially azalea garden in spring and roses in summer. Sculpture and serenity!

1537 6/T19 ✓ **Duthie Park** Aberdeen · www.aberdeencity.gov.uk Riverside Dr along River Dee from the bridge carrying main A92 Stonehaven road. The other large well-kept park with duck pond, bandstand, hugely impressive summer rose gardens, carved sculptures and the famous David Welch Winter Garden of subtropical palms/ferns and home to one of the UK's biggest collections of cacti.

1538 8/P25 ✓ **Pittencrieff Park** Dunfermline · www.fifedirect.org.uk Extensive park alongside the abbey and palace ruins, gifted to the town in 1903 by Carnegie. Open areas, glasshouses pavilion (more a function room) but most notably a deep verdant glen crisscrossed with pathways. Great kids' play area. Lush, full of birds, good after rain.

1539 8/N23 ✓ **MacRosty Park** Crieff · www.pkc.gov.uk On your left as you leave Crieff for Comrie and Crianlarich; for parking ask locally. A perfect green place on sloping ground to the River Earn (good level walk – Lady Mary's Walk) with tearooms, innovative kids' area, mature trees and superb bandstand. A fine old park.

1540 8/Q24 **Beveridge Park** Kirkcaldy · www.fifedirect.org.uk Also in Fife, another big municipal park with a duck and boat pond, wide-open spaces and many amusements (eg bowling, tennis, putting, plootering). **Ravenscraig**, a coastal park on the main road E to Dysart, is an excellent place to walk. Great prospect of the firth and its coves and cruise.

1541 8/R28 **Wilton Lodge Park** Hawick · www.scotborders.gov.uk Hawick not overfull of visitor attractions but it does have a nice park with facilities and diversions enough for everyone, eg the civic gallery, rugby pitches (they like rugby a lot in Hawick), a large kids' playground, a seasonal café and lots of riverside walks by the Teviot (you can smell the river banks). Lots of my school friends lost their virginity in the shed here. All-round open-air recreation centre. South end of town by A7. PS: the shed is still there.

1542 9/P28 **Station Park** Moffat · www.visitmoffat.co.uk On your right as you enter the town from the M74. Well-proportioned people's park; boating pond (with giant swans) main feature. Annan water alongside offers nice walking. Notable also for the monument to Air Chief Marshall Hugh Dowding, Commander in Chief during the Battle of Britain. 'Never... was so much owed by so many to so few'.

1543 8/L27 **Dean Castle Park** Kilmarnock · www.deancastle.com A77 S first turn-off for Kilmarnock then signed; from Ayr A77 north, 3rd turn-off. Surprising green and woody oasis in suburban Kilmarnock; lawns and woods around restored castle and courtyard. Urban farm, adventure playground, caff.

1544 9/M30 **Garries Park** Gatehouse of Fleet Notable for its tiny perfect garden which you enter under an arch from the village main street. A wee gem, especially for its large flowers. Leads to bigger public space (and woody walk 2.5km round S side of village), but pause in the garden and smell those roses. **Murray Arms** (1293/GOOD PUBS) or **Galloway Lodge Preserves** (822/SW RESTAURANTS) for pub and grub.

1545 8/L26 **Rouken Glen & Linn Park** Glasgow Both on S side of river. Rouken Glen via Pollokshaws/Kilmarnock Rd to Eastwood Toll then right. Visitor area with info centre, garden centre, a café, kids' play area and woodland walks. Linn Park via Aikenhead and Carmunnock road. It's a journey but worth it; this is one of the undiscovered Elysiums of a city which boasts over 60 parks. Activities, wildlife walks, kids' nature trails, horse-riding and Alexander 'Greek' Thomson's **Holmwood House**; open Easter-Oct (NTS).

1546 8/Q23 **Camperdown Park** Dundee · www.camperdownpark.com Calling itself a country park, Camperdown is a splendid recreational breathing space for the city and hosts a plethora of distractions – a golf course, a wildlife complex with a great kids' play area (1695/KIDS), and the neoclassical Victorian mansion house, **Camperdown House**, may be open in summer for posh afternoon tea (972/ DUNDEE) and events, especially the **Dundee Flower and Food Festival** (68/ EVENTS). Situated beyond Kingsway, the ring-route; go via Coupar Angus turn-off. Best walks across the A923 in **Templeton Woods** (2020/WALKS).

1547 6/P17 **Grant Park** Forres · www.moray.gov.uk Frequent winner of the Bonny Bloom competitions (a board proclaims their awards) and, with its balance of ornamental gardens, open parkland and woody hill side, this is obviously a carefully tended rose. Good municipal facilities such as pitch and putt, playground. Cricket in summer and topping topiary. Through woods on Cluny Hill to the Nelson Tower for exercise and view.

1548 8/N25 **Callendar Park** Falkirk · www.falkirkcommunitytrust.org Park on edge of town centre, signed from all over. Overlooked by high-rise blocks and near a busy road system, this is nevertheless a beautiful green space with a big hoose (heritage museum with exhibitions), woods and lawns. You can't help feeling they could do with it here. See also **The Kelpies and the Helix** (4/ATTRACTIONS).

The Most Interesting Coastal Villages

1549 5/H18
L
✓ **Plockton** nr Kyle of Lochalsh · www.plockton.com A Highland gem 12km over the hill from Kyle, clustered around inlets of a wooded bay on Loch Carron. Cottage gardens down to the bay and palm trees! Great walks over headlands. Plockton Inn and on the front the Plockton Hotel have rooms and pub grub (1067/HIGHLANDS); there's also the estimable **Plockton Shores** (1079/HIGHLANDS). **www.calums-sealtrips.com** are a treat (seals and dolphins almost guaranteed). It's not hard to feel at one with this village (as generations do).

1550 6/R17
LL
✓ **Moray Coast Fishing Villages** From Spey Bay (where the Spey slips into the sea) to Fraserburgh: some of Scotland's best coastal scenery with interesting villages in cliff/cove and beach settings. See 1563/BEACHES for the best. Especially notable are **Portsoy**, with 17th-century harbour (and see 48/EVENTS); **Sandend**, with its own beach and a fabulous one nearby at **Sunnyside**; **Pennan**, famous from the film *Local Hero*; **Gardenstown**, with a walk along the water's edge to **Crovie** (pronounced Crivee), the epitome of a coast-clinging community (near **Troup Head** 1732/BIRDS); and **Cullen**, a village on the main road with accom and a great wide beach.

1551 1/Q10
✓ **Stromness** Orkney Mainland 24km from Kirkwall and a different kettle of fish. Hugging the shore and with narrow streets and wynds, it has a unique atmos: both maritime and oddly European. Some of the most singular shops you'll see anywhere and the Orkney folk going about their business. Park near harbour and walk down the cobbled main street if you don't want to scrape your paintwork. Great art gallery (2244/ORKNEY; 2140/GALLERIES).

1552 5/M17
✓ **Cromarty** nr Inverness At end of road across Black Isle from Inverness (45km NE); does take longer than you think (well, 30 mins). Village with dreamy times-gone-by atmos, without being twee. Lots of kids running about and a pink strand of beach. Delights to discover include: the East Kirk, plain and aesthetic with countryside through the windows behind the altar; Hugh (the geologist) Miller's cottage/Courthouse Museum (2125/HISTORY); **Couper's Creek** and **The Pantry** (1387/1424/TEAROOMS); **Cromarty Bakery** (1434/BAKERS); a perfect wee restaurant **Sutor Creek** (1080/HIGHLANDS); the shore and cliff walk (2031/WALKS); the Pirates' Cemetery and, of course, the obliging dolphins (1734/DOLPHINS).

1553 8/N25
NTS
Culross nr Dunfermline · www.nts.org.uk By A994 from Dunfermline or junction 1 of M90 just over Forth Road Bridge (15km). Old centre conserved and restored by NTS. Mainly residential and not awash with craft and coffee shops. More historical than quaint; a community of careful custodians lives in the white and yellow red-pantiled houses. Footsteps echo in the cobbled wynds. Palace and Town House open Easter-Oct noon-5pm, weekends Sep/Oct. Interesting back gardens and lovely church at top of hill (1851/CHURCHES).

1554 7/G22
L
Tobermory Mull Postcard/calendar village with painted houses round the bay, but also the main town of Mull. Ferry port for Ardnamurchan, but main Oban ferry is 35km away at Craignure. Usually a bustling harbour front with quieter streets behind; a quintessential island atmos. Some good inexpensive hotels (and quayside hostel) well situated to explore the whole island and a great fish restaurant. See 2243/MULL; 1166/HOSTELS; 1333/SEAFOOD.

1555 7/F26   **Port Charlotte** Islay A township on the Rhinns of Islay, the western peninsula. By A846 from the ports, Askaig and Ellen, via Bridgend, then A847. Rows of whitewashed, well-kept cottages along and back from shoreline. Great wee museum (www.islaymuseum.org), a restaurant, Yan's Kitchen (both Mar-Oct) and the lovely **Port Charlotte Hotel**, with bar and dining room. Town beach and the one between Port Charlotte and Bruichladdich (the war memorial nearby). Quiet and charming, not merely quaint. See 2241/ISLAY; 2227/ISLAND HOTELS.

1556 9/N30   **Rockcliffe** nr Dumfries 25km S on Solway Coast road, A710. On the Scottish Riviera, the rocky part of the coast around to **Kippford** (2025/WALKS). A good rock-scrambling foreshore though not so clean, the village with few houses, and repair to the **Anchor** (1325/GASTROPUBS) in Kippford.

1557 8/R24   **East Neuk Villages** www.eastneukwide.co.uk The quintessential quaint wee fishing villages along the bit of Fife that forms the mouth of the Firth of Forth. **Crail, Anstruther, Pittenweem, St Monans** and **Elie** have different characters and attractions, especially Crail (1417/TEAROOMS) and Pittenweem harbours; Anstruther is main centre and home of **Fisheries Museum** (2130/HISTORY) (see also 1366/FISH & CHIPS; 1716/BIRDS); St Monans for seafood (1331/1338/SEAFOOD); and perfect Elie (1305/1306/GASTROPUBS; 2054/GOLF). Also St Andrews, p. 166-68. Cycling good, traffic in summer not.

1558 8/P25   **Aberdour** Between Dunfermline and Kirkcaldy, 10km E from junction 1 of M90 or go by train from Edinburgh (frequent service: Dundee or Kirkcaldy); delightful station. Walks round harbour and to headland, **Silver Sands** beach 1km (465/BEACHES).

1559 9/L31   **Isle of Whithorn** www.isleofwhithorn.com Strange faraway village at end of the road, 35km S of Newton Stewart, 6km Whithorn (1806/PREHISTORIC). Mystical harbour where low tide does mean low, saintly shoreline, a sea angler's pub, the **Steampacket** – very good pub grub (1295/GOOD PUBS). Ninian's chapel round the headland underwhelming but you pass the poignant memorial to the *Solway Harvester*. Everybody visiting IoW seems to walk this way.

1560 7/J27   **Corrie** Arran · www.visitarran.com Last but not least, the bonniest bit of
      LL   Arran (apart from Kildonan and the glens and the rest), happily reached by bike from Brodick (10km). Many walks from here, including **Goat Fell** (1928/HILLS), but nice just to sit or potter on the foreshore. Hotel has never quite been up to expectations. Animal sculptures on the foreshore and even the boats in the slips of harbours are aesthetic.

Fantastic Beaches & Bays

*All those listed below are in **L**, **LL** and **LLL** settings, obviously.*

1561 4/L12 ✓✓ **Pete's Beach** nr **Durness** The One of the many great beaches on the North Coast (see below) that I've called my own. The hill above it is called Ceannabeinne; you find it 7km E of Durness. Coming from Tongue it's just after where Loch Eriboll comes out to the sea and the road hits the coast again (there's a lay-by opposite). It's a small perfect cove flanked by walls of coral-pink rock and shallow turquoise sea. Splendid from above (land rises to a bluff with a huge boulder) and from below. Revisiting many times in several aspects (of weather and light), it's never short of magnificent. There's a great coastal walk to the **Ceannabeinne Township** (2033/WALKS) nearby. All in all, this is the coast with the most (great beaches!). Don't tell me there's a better one than this!

1562 7/F24 ✓✓ **Kiloran Beach** **Colonsay** 9km from quay and hotel, past Colonsay House (8km circular walk); parking and access on hill side. Often described as the finest beach in the Hebrides, it doesn't disappoint though it can change character. Craggy cliffs on one side, negotiable rocks on the other, tiers of grassy dunes between. Do go to the end! The island was once bought as a picnic spot. This beach was probably the reason why.

1563 8 ✓✓ **Moray Coast** Many great beaches along coast from Spey Bay to Fraserburgh, notably **Cullen** and **Lossiemouth** (town beaches), and **New Aberdour** (1km from New Aberdour village on B9031, 15km W of Fraserburgh) and **Rosehearty** (8km W of Fraserburgh), both quieter places for walks and picnics. 2 of the great secret beaches on this coast are:
Sunnyside nr **Sandend** where you walk past the incredible ruins of Findlater Castle on the clifftop (how did they build it? A place, on its grassed-over roof, for a picnic) and down to a cove which on my sunny day was simply perfect. Signed (Findlater) from A98. Take a left from Sandend 16km W of Banff, follow road for 2km. Park in the farmyard. Walk from here past dovecote, 1km to cliff, then left from the ruin viewpoint. See also 1779/RUINS; 2029/WALKS.
Cullykhan Bay E of Gardenstown signed from the coast road (200m to small car park). A small beach but great littoral for beach scrambling and full of surprises (1923/ENCHANTING PLACES).

1564 7/G28 ✓✓ **Machrihanish** nr **Campbeltown** Foot of the Kintyre peninsula 10km from Campbeltown. Walk N from Machrihanish village or golf course, or from the car park on A83 to Tayinloan and Tarbert at point where it hits/leaves the coast. A joyously long strand (8km) of unspoiled orange-pink sand backed by dunes and facing the 'steepe Atlantic Stream' all the way to Newfoundland (2060/GOLF). Great accom and eats at **Machrihanish Dunes** (786/ARGYLL).

1565 4/K12 ✓✓ **Sandwood Bay** **Kinlochbervie** This mile-long sandy strand with its old Stack is legendary but there's the problem: too many people like us come here and you may have to share its glorious isolation. Inaccessibility is its saving grace: it's a 7km walk from the sign off the road at Balchrick (near the cattle grid), which is 6km from Kinlochbervie; allow 3-4 hours return plus time there. More venturesome is the walk from the north and **Cape Wrath** (2023/WALKS). Go easy and go in summer!

1566 3/D18 ✓✓ **South Uist** Deserted but for birds, an almost unbroken strand of beach running for miles down the W coast; the machair is best in early summer (follow the Machair Way). Take any road off the spinal A865; usually less than 2km.

Good spot to try is turn-off at Tobha Mòr 25km N of Lochboisdale; real blackhouses and a chapel on the way to the sea. Listen to the birds – this is as far away as you can get from Shoreditch High Street.

1567 7/F26 ✓✓ **Saligo, Machir Bay & The Big Strand Islay** The first two are bays on NW of island via A847 road to Port Charlotte, and B8018 past Loch Gorm. Wide beaches; remains of war fortifications in deep dunes, Machir perhaps best for beach bums but Saligo is one of the most pleasingly aesthetic beaches... anywhere. The Big Strand on Laggan Bay: along Bowmore–Port Ellen road take Oa turn-off, follow Kintra signs. There's camping and great walks in either direction, 8km of glorious sand and dunes (contains the Machrie Golf Course). All these are airy ambles under a wide sky. See 2059/GOLF; 2021/WALKS.

1568 3/E16 ✓✓ **Scarista Beach & the Beaches of South Harris** On road S of Tarbert (20km) to Rodel. Scarista is so beautiful that people get married here. Hotel over the road is worth staying just for this, but is also a great retreat (2224/ ISLAND HOTELS), and there's the hard-to-get-into island luxury cottages (1215/ HEBRIDES). Golf on the links (2061/GOLF). This coast has many extraordinary beaches, including **Luskentyre** and **Northton**, and the great **Temple Café** (2242/ HEBRIDES). Ask here about the machair walk to Toe Head. You may want to camp (1219/WILD CAMPING). It's magnificent here in early evening. The sun also rises.

1569 3/G13 ✓ **The Beaches of Lewis** Perhaps less celebrated than Harris (above), there are numerous enchanting beaches on the Lewis coast; apart from the odd surfie, you've likely to have the strand to yourself. Around **Uig** in the W via A8011, especially Timsgary/Ardroil, the beaches are legendary. Great hotel, the **Auberge**, and (separate) bistro and top **Loch Croistean Coffee Shop** on the way (2242/ HEBRIDES). Big sunsets! For the beach at the N end (of the Hebrides), **Port Nis**: keep driving (some interesting stops on the way 1150/HOSTELS; 2112/HISTORY) until you get to this tiny bay and harbour down the hill at the end of the road. Anthony Barber's Harbour View Gallery full of his own work (which you find in many other galleries and even on postcards) is worth a visit (Mon-Sat 10am-5pm). For refreshment with a brilliant view, there's The Beach Café. 3 more secret spots via the B895 15km NW of Stornoway (past Broad Bay) are at the long strand at **Tolsta** and further, at the end of the road, **Traigh Mhor** and the bridge to nowhere, exquisite **Ghearadha** (pronounced Gary).

1570 4 ✓ **North Coast** W of Thurso are some of Britain's most unspoiled and unsung beaches. But no beach bums and no Beach Boys. There are many great little coves, you choose; but those to mention are: **Strathy** and **Armadale** (35km W Thurso), **Farr** and **Torrisdale** (48km), the latter gets the mentions but Farr is far easier to reach, **Coldbackie** (65km) and **Balnakeil** by Durness, 1km W after the craft village (2147/SHOPPING). My favourite (in the far west) is elevated to the top of this category.

1571 4/K13 ✓ **Oldshoremore nr Kinlochbervie** The beach you pass on the road to Balchrick, only 3km from Kinlochbervie. It's easy to reach and a beautiful spot: the water is clear and perfect for swimming, and there are rocky walks and quiet places. **Polin** 500m north, is a cove you might have to yourself (1227/WILD CAMPING).

1572 7/J26 ✓ **Ostal Beach/Kilbride Bay Millhouse, nr Tighnabruaich** 3km from Millhouse on B8000 signed Ardlamont (not Portvadie, the ferry), a track to right before white house (often with a chain across to restrict access). Park and walk 1.5km, turning right after lochan. You arrive on a perfect white sandy crescent known locally as Ostal and, in certain conditions, a mystical place to swim and picnic. **Arran's north coast** is like a Greek island in the bay. **Ettrick Bay on Bute** is another good beach with the view and a brilliant wee café (1375/CAFÉS).

1573 8/R22 ✓ **Lunan Bay** nr Montrose 7km from main A92 road to Aberdeen and 5km of deep red crescent beach under a wide northern sky. The **But 'n' Ben** in Auchmithie, is an excellent place to start or finish (931/PERTHSHIRE) and good approach (from south), although **Gordon's** restaurant at Inverkeilor is closer (928/PERTHSHIRE). You can climb up to the Red Castle. Lunan is often deserted. The **Lunan Bay Diner** is at the car park – it's OK! 100m to the beach. **St Cyrus** N of Montrose (a nature reserve) also a lovely littoral to wander. Walk 2km S of village.

1574 4/J14 ✓ **The Secret Beach** nr Achmelvich From Achmelvich car park going N, it's the next proper bay round, or easier: Lochinver–Stoer/Drumbeg road (1621/SCENIC ROUTES); lay-by on right 3km after Achmelvich turn-off, 250m beyond sign for Cathair Estate. Park on the right, cross the road and walk towards the sea (20 mins) following stream (a sign points to Mill). The path is well defined – you step over the old mill stones. Called **Port Alltan na Bradhan**, it's the site of an old mill (grinding wheels still there), perfect for camping and the best sea for swimming in the area. And pretty special.

1575 5/H16 ✓ **Gairloch** A beach I missed until one (rare in 2011) sunny July afternoon when lots of people, but not (and I imagine never) too many, were lying on this perfect curve of sand, a sheltered bay of Loch Gairloch and swimming in its shallow, shimmering, non-wavy water. There's a tranquil old graveyard behind (1877/GRAVEYARDS) and the green golf course beside. Parking and toilets. The longer Big Sand is 4km W by the campsite (1236/CAMPING WITH KIDS). I go back.

1576 7/G25 **Lowlandman's Bay** Jura Not in itself a beach but a rocky foreshore with ethereal atmos; great light and space (lovely **Corran Sands** are adjacent; ask directions locally). Only seals break the spell. Go right at 3-arch bridge to first group of houses (Knockdrome), through yard on left and right around cottages to track to Ardmenish. After deer fences, bay is visible on your right, 1km walk away.

1577 3/C20 **Vatersay** Outer Hebrides The tiny island joined by a causeway to Barra. Twin crescent beaches on either side of the isthmus, one shallow and sheltered visible from Castlebay, the other an ocean beach with more rollers. Dunes/machair; safe swimming. Poignant memorial to a 19th-century shipwreck in the Ocean Bay and another (on the way here) to a plane crash during the war; the wreckage is still there. There's a helluva hill between Barra and Vatersay if you're cycling.

1578 3/C19 **Seal Bay** Barra 5km Castlebay on W coast, 2km after Isle of Barra Hotel through gate across machair where road right is signed Allathasdal a Deas (after a sandy then a rockier cove). A flat, rocky Hebridean shore and skerries where seals flop into the water and eye you with intense curiosity. The more beach-type beach is next to the hotel that you pass on the way.

1579 8/R23 **West Sands** St Andrews As a town beach, this is hard to beat; it dominates the view to west. Wide swathe not too unclean and sea just about swimmable. Golf courses behind. Consistently gets the blue flag, but beach buffs may prefer **Kinshaldy** (1748/RESERVES) or **Kingsbarns** (10km S on Crail road), where there is a great beach walk taking in the **Cambo Estate** (gorgeous garden and woods 899/FIFE) and skirting the great Kingsbarns Golf Course. Or lovely **Elie** (28km S).

1580 5/H20 **Sands of Morar** nr Mallaig 70km W of Fort William and 6km from Mallaig by a good road, these easily accessible beaches may seem overpopulated on summer days and the S stretch nearest to Arisaig may have one too many caravan parks, but they go on for miles and there's enough space for everybody. The sand's supposed to be silver but in fact it's a very pleasing pink. Lots of rocky bits for exploration. One of the best stretches (the bay before the estuary) is Camusdarach, signed from the main road (where *Local Hero* was filmed); further from the road, it is quieter and a very good swathe of sand. **Traigh**, the golf course makes good use of the dunes (2074/GOLF).

1581 7/F23 **The Bay at the Back of the Ocean** Iona Easy 2km walk from the ferry from Fionnphort, S of Mull (2243/ISLANDS) or bike hire from store on your left as you walk into the village (01681 700321). Mostly track: road straight up from the pier, left at the village hall, uphill to Maol Farm and then across the machair. John Smith, who is buried by the abbey, once told me this was his favourite place. 2 great inexpensive hotels on Iona, the **Argyll** and **St Columba** (1139/KIDS).

1582 4/N16 **Dornoch (& Embo Beaches)** The wide and extensive sandy beach of this pleasant town at the mouth of the Dornoch Firth famous for its golf links (2049/GOLF). 4km N, Embo Sands starts with ghastly caravan city, but walk N towards Golspie. Embo is twinned with Kaunakakai, Hawaii. We can dream!

1583 9/J30 **3 Beaches in the far South West** Off A77 before Portpatrick signed Dunskey Gardens in summer, follow road signed Killantringan Lighthouse (dirt track). Park 1km before lighthouse or walk from Portpatrick following the Southern Upland Way. Beautiful bay for exploration. **Sandhead Beach** A716 S of Stranraer. Shallow, safe waters of Luce Bay (8km of sands). Perfect for families (in their damned caravans). And newly discovered by *StB* in 2015: **Sandgreen**, off the A75 by Gatehouse of Fleet, signed and go past **Cream o' Galloway** (1696/KIDS) 3km. Lovely wee beach, then the rough road to a southern secret (1623/SCENIC ROUTES).

The Great Glens

All those listed below are in L, LL *and* LLL *settings, obviously.*

1584 5/K18 ✓✓✓ **Glen Affric** nr Drumnadrochit · www.glenaffric.org Beyond Cannich at end of Glen Urquhart A831, 20km from Drumnadrochit on Loch Ness. The 'Glen of a Thousand Whispers', a dramatic gorge that strikes westwards into the wild heart of Scotland. Superb for rambles (1978/GLEN WALKS), expeditions, Munro-bagging (beyond Loch Affric) and even just tootling through in the car. Shaped by the Hydro Board, Loch Beinn a'Mheadhain adds to the drama. One of the best places in Scotland to appreciate the beauty of Scots pine. Cycling good (bike hire in Cannich and at the campsite) as is the detour to Tomich and **Plodda Falls** (1594/WATERFALLS). Stop at **Dog Falls** (1668/SWIMMING) but do go to the end of the glen.

1585 8/M22 ✓✓✓ **Glen Lyon** nr Aberfeldy One of Scotland's crucial places historically and geographically, much favoured by fishers/walkers/Munro-baggers. Wordsworth, Tennyson, Gladstone and Baden-Powell all sang its praises. The Lyon is a classic Highland river tumbling through corries, gorges and riverine meadows. Several Munros are within its watershed and rise gloriously on either side. Road all the way to the lochside (30km). Eagles soar over the more remote tops at the head of the glen. The **Post Office Tearoom** halfway round at Bridge of Balgie, does a roaring trade (closed Wed; weekends only in winter) and **Fortingall House** on the way in is very good, if expensive (922/PERTHSHIRE).

1586 7/K21 ✔✔ **Glen Nevis   Fort William** Often in film shoots, and easy to see why. Ben Nevis is only part of the magnificent scenery. Many walks and convenient facilities (1603/WATERFALLS; 1974/WALKS). West Highland Way emerges here. Visitor centre; cross river to climb Ben Nevis and the walkers' **Ben Nevis Inn** (1099/FORT WILLIAM). A couple of caffs so-so but they're there. This dramatic glen is a national treasure.

1587 7/K22 ✔✔ **Glen Etive   nr Ballachulish & Glen Coe** Off from more exalted Glen Coe and the A82 at Kingshouse, as anyone you meet there will tell you, this truly is a glen of glens. Treat with great respect while you make it your own. (1222/WILD CAMPING; 1659/SWIMMING).

1588 4/M16 **Strathcarron   nr Bonar Bridge** You drive up the N bank of this Highland river from the bridge outside Ardgay (pronounced Ordguy) which is 3km over the bridge from Bonar Bridge. Road goes 15km to Croick and its remarkable church (1858/CHURCHES). The river gurgles and gushes along its rocky course to the Dornoch Firth and further up there are innumerable places to picnic, swim and stroll. Heavenly here on the warm days we long for.

1589 8/Q21 **The Angus Glens: Glen Clova**, **Glen Prosen** and **Glen Isla** Isla for drama, Clova for walkers, Prosen for the soul. All via Kirriemuir. Isla to the W is a woody, approachable glen with a deep gorge, on B954 near Alyth (1604/WATERFALLS) and the cosy **Glenisla Hotel** (1185/INNS). Others via B955, to Dykehead then road bifurcates. Both glens stab into the heart of the Grampians. Minister's Walk goes between them from behind the kirk at Prosen village over the hill to B955 before Clova village (7km). Glen Clova is a walkers' paradise, especially from Glendoll 24km from Dykehead; limit of road with the Ranger Centre. Viewpoint. Jock's Road to Braemar and the Capel Mounth to Ballater (both 24km). **Clova Hotel** (923/PERTHSHIRE) with famous Loops of Brandy walk (2 hours, 2-B-2); stark and beautiful. **Prosen Hostel** at end of the road is a serene stopover (1155/HOSTELS). The Museum of the Glens in Kirriemuir is sweet and has a surprising homage to AC/DC (no, really!).

1590 9/L29 **Glen Trool   nr Newton Stewart** 26km N by A714 via Bargrennan which is on the **Southern Upland Way** (1967/LONG WALKS). A gentle wooded glen within the vast Galloway Forest Park (one of the most charming, accessible parts). Visitor centre 5km from Bargrennan. Pick up a walk brochure and walk. Many options (1901/BOD). Start of the **Merrick** climb (1936/HILLS).

1591 8/N23 **The Sma' Glen   nr Crieff** Off the A85 to Perth, the A822 to Amulree and Aberfeldy. Sma' meaning small, this is the valley of the River Almond where the Mealls (lumpish, shapeless hills) fall steeply down to the road. Where the road turns away from the river, the long distance path to Loch Tay begins (28km). Sma' Glen, 8km, has good picnic spots, but they get busy and midgy in summer.

1592 5/L18 **Strathfarrar   Struy** Rare unspoiled glen accessed from A831 leaving Drumnadrochit on Loch Ness via Cannich (30km), or S from Beauly (15km). Signed at Struy, it's a hike (25km) in to tackle the celebrated Munros. For vehicular access check www.mcofs.org.uk before you set off. 2km to the gate, then 22km to the head of glen past Loch Monar. Good climbing, walking, fishing. No overnight stays. The real peace and quiet!

The Most Spectacular Waterfalls

One aspect of Scotland that really is improved by rain. All the walks to these falls are graded 1-A-1 unless otherwise stated (see p. 12 for walk codes).

1593 5/J19 · 2-C-3 · NTS ✓✓ **Falls of Glomach** www.nts.org.uk 29km E of Kyle of Lochalsh off A87 near Shiel Bridge via Strath Croe to bridge. Walk starts other side; there are other ways (eg from the S.Y. Hostel in Glen Affric) but this is most straightforward. Allow 5/7 hours for the pilgrimage to one of Britain's highest falls (370ft). Path is steep, can be wet, with mist and low cloud. Glomach means gloomy and you might feel so, peering into the ravine; from precipice to pool, it's 200m. Vertigo factor and sense of achievement both fairly high. But don't get lost! Consult www.walkhighlands.co.uk or locally. Ranger service 01599 511231.

1594 5/K19 ✓✓ **Plodda Falls nr Tomich** · www.glenaffric.org A831 from Loch Ness to Cannich (20km), then 7km to Tomich, a further 5km up mainly woodland track to car park. 400m walk down through woods of Scots pine and ancient Douglas Fir to one of the most enchanting woodland sites in Britain and the Forestry Commission's vertiginous viewpoint over the 150m fall into the churning river below. Pools excellent for swimming. The 'Tweedmouth Trail' is an easy 2.3km loop. Freezes into winter wonderland. Good hotel in village (1073/HIGHLANDS).

1595 8/N21 ✓ **Falls of Bruar nr Blair Atholl** Close to the main A9 Perth-Inverness road, 12km N of Blair Atholl near **House of Bruar** shopping experience (2166/SHOPS). Consequently, the short walk to lower falls is very consumer-led but less crowded than you might expect. The lichen-covered walls of the gorge below the upper falls (1km) are less ogled and more dramatic. 2.3km circular path well marked; steep/rocky in places. Tempting to swim on hot days (1667/SWIMMING).

1596 7/J27 · 1-B-1 ✓ **Glenashdale Falls Arran** 3.5km walk from bridge on main road at Whiting Bay. Signed up the burn side, but uphill and further than you think, so allow 2 hours (return). Series of falls in a rocky gorge in the woods with paths so you get right down to the brim and the pools. Swim here, swim in heaven! There's another waterfall walk, **Eas Mor**, further S off the A841 at the second Kildonan turn-off.

1597 5/K16 ✓ **Corrieshalloch Gorge/Falls of Measach** Junction of A832 and A835, 20km S of Ullapool. A dramatic approach is from the car park on the A832 Gairloch road. Staircase to swing bridge from whence to consider how such a wee burn could make such a deep gash. Very impressive. There's another viewpoint 100m over the bridge and a longer walk from the car park. A must-stop on the way to/from Ullapool.

1598 8/P28 ✓ **The Grey Mare's Tail between Moffat & Selkirk** On the wildly scenic A708. About halfway, a car park and signs for waterfall. 8km from **Tibbie Shiels Inn** (refreshments! but not recommended for food). The lower track takes 10/15 mins to a viewing place still 500m from falls; the higher, on the other side of the Tail burn, threads between the austere hills and up to Loch Skene from which the falls overflow (45/60 mins). Then do the circular trail above you for an all-round satisfying day in the Borders. Mountain goats scamper.

1599 8/N27 ✓ **The Falls of Clyde New Lanark** · www.scottishwildlifetrust.org.uk Dramatic falls in a long gorge of the Clyde. New Lanark, the conservation village of Robert Owen, the social reformer, is signed from Lanark. A curious village, a mighty river. The path to the power station is about 1km, the route more interesting after it, a 1km climb to the first fall (Cora Linn) and another 1km to the next (Bonnington Linn). One of the mills is a decent family hotel, with some rooms (and 8 'waterhouses' overlooking the river). The strange uniformity of New Lanark is oddly poignant when the other tourists have gone home. When the river is full, the Falls are amazing.

1600 7/G22   **Eas Fors Mull** On the Dervaig to Fionnphort road 3km from Ulva Ferry; a series of cataracts tumbling down on either side of the road. Easily accessible from small car park on left going S (otherwise unmarked). There's a path down the side to the brink where the river plunges into the sea. On a warm day swimming in the sea below the fall is a rare exhilaration.

1601 5/G17   **Lealt Falls Skye** Impressive torrent of wild mountain water about 20km N of
2-C-2   Portree on the A855. Look for sign: River Lealt. There's a car park on a bend on right (going N). Walk to grassy ledges and look over or go down to the beach.
Kilt Rock, a viewpoint much favoured by bus parties, is a few km further (you look over and along the cliffs). This road is great for drop-in food (**Ellishadder Art Café, The Small & Cosy Teahouse** and **Skye Pie** Café 2239/SKYE), especially the latter at the Glenview. Also...
Eas Mor Glen Brittle near end of road. 24km from Sligachan. A mountain waterfall with the wild Cuillin behind and views to the sea. Approach as part of a serious scramble or merely a 30-min Cuillin sampler. Start at the Memorial Hut, cross the road, bear right, cross burn and then follow path uphill.

1602 4/K14   **Eas A' Chual Aluinn Kylesku** Britain's highest waterfall (638ft), near the head
2-C-3   of Glencoul, is not easy to reach. Kylesku is between Scourie and Lochinver off the main A894, 20km S of Scourie. There are 2-hour cruises May-Sep (01971 502231) from outside the hotel (1085/HIGHLANDS). Falls are a rather distant prospect but the cruise will do you good; baby seals an added attraction Jun-Aug. There's also a track to the top of the falls from 5km N of the Skiag Bridge on the main road (4-6 hours return); get directions locally. The water freefalls for 200m, which is 4 times further than Niagara (take pinch of salt here). You'll need a head for heights, good footwear (track is often wet) and a map (folk do get lost — check the number of marker cairns).

1603 7/K21   **Steall Falls Glen Nevis, Fort William** Take Glen Nevis road at the roundabout
3-A-3   outside town centre and drive to the end (16km) through glen. Start from the second and final car park, following marked path uphill through the woody gorge with River Ness thrashing below. Glen eventually and dramatically opens out and there are great views of the long veils of the falls. Precarious 3-wire bridge for which you will also need nerves of steel. You can cross further down or see the falls from a distance. 3km walk, 1.5-2 hours.

1604 8/Q22   **Reekie Linn Alyth** 8km N of town on back roads to Kirriemuir on B951 between Bridge of Craigisla and Bridge of Lintrathen. A picnic site and car park on bend of road leads by 200m to the wooded gorge of Glen Isla with precipitous viewpoints of the defile where Isla is squeezed and falls in tiers for 100ft. Walk further along the glen and look back.

1605 8/M22   **Falls of Acharn nr Kenmore** 5km along S side of Loch Tay on an unclassified road. Walk from just after the bridge going W in township of Acharn; falls are signed. Steepish start then 1km up side of gorge; waterfalls on other side. Can be circular route. Splendid trees!

1606 5/L17 **Falls of Rogie** nr **Strathpeffer** · www.ullapool.co.uk Car park on A835 Inverness-Ullapool road, 5km Contin/10km Strathpeffer. Accessibility makes short walk (250m) quite popular to these hurtling falls on the Blackwater River. Bridge (built by the Territorial Army) and salmon ladder (they leap in summer). Woodland trails 1-3km marked, include a circular route to Contin (2017/WALKS).

1607 4/M15 **Falls of Shin** nr **Lairg** · www.fallsofshin.co.uk 6km E of town on signed road, car park and falls nearby are easily accessible. Not quite up to the splendours of others here, but one of the best places in Scotland to see Atlantic salmon battling upstream (May-Nov; best late summer). Adventure playground across the road.

The Lochs We Love

All those listed below are in L, LL *and* LLL *settings, obviously.*

1608 5/J16 ✓✓ **Loch Maree** A832 between Kinlochewe and Gairloch. Dotted with islands covered in Scots pine, one hiding some of the best examples of Viking graves and apparently a money tree in their midst. Easily viewed from the road which follows its length for 15km. Beinn Eighe rises behind you and the omniscient presence of Slioch is opposite. Aultroy Visitor Centre (5km Kinlochewe), fine walks from lochside car parks, among the largest original Scots pine woodlands in the West Highlands. See 1743/RESERVES. The hotel and a GH, opposite each other on the lochside road, are recommended (1192/GET-AWAY HOTELS).

1609 5/N19 ✓✓ **Loch an Eilean** 4km Inverdruie off the Coylumbridge road from Aviemore. Car park and info board. An enchanted loch in the heart of the Rothiemurchus Forest (2005/WALKS for directions). You can walk right round the loch (5km, allow 1.5 hours). This is classic Highland scenery, a calendar landscape of magnificent Scots pine. Very special. Then cake and birds (1383/TEAROOMS).

1610 5/J20 ✓ **Loch Arkaig** 25km Fort William. An enigmatic loch long renowned for its fishing. From the A82 beyond Spean Bridge (at the **Commando Monument** 1836/MONUMENTS) cross the Caledonian Canal, then on by single-track road through the Clunes Forest and the Dark Mile past the Witches' Pool (a cauldron of dark water below cataracts) to the loch. Bonnie Prince Charlie came this way before and after Culloden; one of his refuge caves is marked on a trail.

1611 8/L24 ✓ **Loch Achray** nr **Brig o' Turk** The small loch at the centre of the Trossachs between **Loch Katrine** (on which SS *Sir Walter Scott* and smaller *Lady of the Lake* sail 3/4 times a day; the morning one stops at the end of the loch. 01877 376316) and **Loch Venachar**. The A821 from Callander skirts both Venachar and Achray. Many picnic spots and a fishing centre and the **Venachar Lochside Café**, though better is the **Brig o' Turk Tearoom** (1393/TEAROOMS). Ben Venue and Ben A'an rise above: great walks (1930/HILLS) and views. A one-way forest road goes round the other side of Loch Achray through Achray Forest (enter and leave from the Duke's Pass road between Aberfoyle and Brig o' Turk). Trail details from forest visitor centre 3km N Aberfoyle. Bike hire at Loch Katrine (01877 376366), Callander or Aberfoyle – best way to see the lochs.

1612 8/L24 **Glen Finglas Reservoir** **Brig o' Turk** And while we're on the subject of lochs in the Trossachs (see above) here's a great one to walk to. Although it's man-made it's a real beauty, surrounded by soft green hills and the odd burn bubbling in. Approach from car park of the new stark visitor centre on the A821 before Brig o' Turk (3 & 5km circular walks), or from Brig o' Turk itself (1km), then join trails.

It's about 5km to the head of the loch and 18km on the Mell Trail round the hill or 12km to Balquhidder: a walk across the heart of Scotland (1981/GLEN & RIVER WALKS). Ranger board gives details.

Brig o' Turk Tearoom is great (1393/TEAROOMS) or, nearby, **The Byre** (1323/GASTROPUBS).

1613 8/Q20 **Loch Muick nr Ballater** At head of road off B976, the South Dee road at Ballater. 14km up Glen Muick (pronounced Mick) to the car park and visitor centre and 1km to the lochside. **Lochnagar** rises above (1961/MUNROS) and walk also begins here for Capel Mounth and **Glen Clova** (1589/GLENS). 3-hour walk around loch; any number of ambles. The lodge where Vic met John is at the furthest point (well, it would be). Open aspect; grazing deer. Ranger: 01339 755059.

1614 4/L13 **Loch Eriboll North Coast** 90km W of Thurso. The long sea loch that indents into the North Coast for 15km and which you drive right round on main A838 (40 mins). Deepest natural anchorage in the UK, exhibiting every aspect of lochside scenery including, alas, fish cages. Ben Hope stands near the head of the loch and there is a perfect beach (my own private Idaho) on the coast (1561/BEACHES). The people who have Mackay's in nearby Durness now have 2 luxury, high-spec eco-lodges overlooking the loch at Laid (1217/LUXURIOUS ISOLATION) and halfway up the W bank is the extraordinary art garden of **Lotte Glob** (2137/GALLERIES). Walks from Hope.

1615 9/M30 **Loch Ken between Castle Douglas & New Galloway** Loch Ken: it was a while before I got it. So many times I hurtled up both sides (it's long and thin). Maybe it was the perfect spring day and it shimmered and lots of people were boating and surfing and hanging out and it's clear that this is the loch of life here. Marina, holiday park and **Galloway Activity Centre** (2102/WATER SPORTS; coffee shop) all thrive on its banks. Then there's New Galloway. Many trails (and deer) around. And the glorious kites!

1616 5/H20 **Loch Morar nr Mallaig** 70km W of Fort William by A850 (a wildly scenic but smooth route). Morar village is 6km from Mallaig. A single-track road leads from the coast to the loch (500m) then 5km to Bracora. It's the prettiest part with wooded islets, small beaches, lochside meadows and bobbing boats. The road stops at a turning place but a track continues from Bracorina to Tarbet and it's possible to connect with a boat and sail back to Mallaig on Loch Nevis (check locally). Boat hire on the loch: Ewan MacDonald 01687 462520. Loch Morar, joined to the coast by the shortest river in Britain, also has the deepest water. There is a spookiness about it and just possibly a monster called Morag.

Loch Lomond The biggest, not the bonniest, with major visitor centre and retail experience, **Lomond Shores**, at S end near Balloch. Report: 1/ATTRACTIONS.
Loch Ness The longest; and the monster. Report: 3/ATTRACTIONS.

All those listed below are in L, LL and LLL settings, obviously.

1617 7/K22
ATMOS
✓✓✓ **Glen Coe** www.glencoe-nts.org.uk The A82 from Crianlarich to Ballachulish is a fine drive, but from the extraterrestrial Loch Ba onwards, there can be few roads anywhere that bring you into direct contact with such imposing scenery. After Kingshouse and Buachaille Etive Mor on the left, the mountains and ridges rising on either side of Glen Coe proper invoke the correct usage of the word 'awesome'. The visitor centre sets the topographical and historical scene. (1287/GOOD PUBS; 1973/WALKS; 1889/BATTLEGROUNDS; 1914/ENCHANTING PLACES; 1168/HOSTELS).

1618 5/H19
✓✓ **Shiel Bridge–Glenelg** The switchback road that climbs from the A87 (Fort William 96km) at Shiel Bridge over the hill and down to the coast opposite the Sleat Peninsula in Skye (short ferry to Kylerhea 6/JOURNEYS). As you climb you're almost as high as the surrounding summits and there's the classic view across Loch Duich to the Five Sisters of Kintail. Coming back you think you're going straight into the loch! It's really worth driving to Glenelg (1808/PREHISTORIC; 1226/WILD CAMPING; 1173/INNS), to Arnisdale and Loch Hourn (16km).

1619 5/H18
✓✓ **Applecross** www.applecross.uk.com 120km from Inverness. From Tornapress near Lochcarron for 18km. Leaving the A896 seems like leaving civilisation; the winding ribbon heads into monstrous mountains and the high plateau at the top is another planet. It's not for the faint-hearted and Applecross is a relief to arrive in with its campsite and the faraway, famed **Applecross Inn** (1200/GET-AWAY HOTELS). Also see 1078/HIGHLANDS; 1230/CAMPING. This awesome road rises 2,000 feet in 6 miles. See how they built it at the **Applecross Heritage Centre** (2119/HISTORY).

1620 5/J17
✓✓ **Glen Torridon** A896 between Kinlochewe and Torridon with staggering views along the route of the 3 mighty Torridon mountains: Beinn Eighe Liathach and Beinn Alligin. There are various starts along this road – enquire and all other information at the NTS Countryside Centre at the Diabaig turn-off. Excellent two-tier accom at **The Torridon** (1192/GET-AWAY HOTELS) and a SYHA tents-only campsite adjacent the Centre. There is much to climb and clamber over here; or merely be amazed. See also 1637/VIEWS.

1621 4/K14
✓✓ **Lochinver–Drumbeg–Kylesku** The coast road N from Lochinver (35km) is marvellous, essential Assynt. Actually best travelled north-south so that you leave the splendid vista of Eddrachilles Bay and pass through lochan, moor and even woodland, touching the coast again by sandy beaches (at Stoer a road leads 7km to the lighthouse and the walk to the **Old Man of Stoer**, 2024/WALKS) past the wonderful **Secret Beach** (1574/BEACHES) and approach Lochinver (possible detour to Achmelvich) with a classic long view of Suilven. Take tea 'n' cake at the tea garden **Little Soap 'n' Candles** in Drumbeg (Apr-Oct). Or stock up at the remarkable **Drumbeg Stores** (2169/SHOPS). There's a brilliant restaurant with rooms at **Drumbeg House** (1043/HIGHLANDS). Get your pies in Lochinver (1093/HIGHLANDS). The Drumbeg viewpoint S of the village is worth a stop 'n' gaze.

1622 4/J15 ✓ **Lochinver-Achiltibuie** S of Lochinver, Achiltibuie is 40km from Ullapool; so this is the route from the north; 28km of winding road/unwinding Highland scenery; through glens, mountains and silver sea. Known locally as the 'wee mad road' (it is maddening if you're in a hurry). Passes **Achin's Bookshop** (2171/SHOPS, alas for sale at TGP), the path to Kirkaig Falls and the mighty Suilven. Near Achiltibuie there's one of Scotland's most uplifting views (1640/VIEWS).

1623 9/M31 ✓ **The Islands of Fleet** Galloway Only discovered this enchanting coastal track (it's not really a road) and the hut village – Carrick – (not even on the map) in 2015. Off A75 by Gatehouse of Fleet, signed for **Cream o' Galloway** (1696/KIDS), then to Sandgreen (6km from main road). 200m before Sandgreen and its beach 1583/BEACHES, take the track towards the sea at a corner. Follow this round the hidden coves, headlands, dunes and the shacks always looking out to the islets in Fleet Bay. There's a spooky derelict church and great views before eventually coming back to life in Borgue. Go find!

1624 7/J25 ✓ **Rothesay-Tighnabruaich** A886/A8003. The most celebrated part of this route is the latter, the A8003 down the side of Loch Riddon to Tighnabruaich along the hill sides with the breathtaking views of Bute and the Kyles (can be a lot of vegetation in summer – there's one good lay-by/viewpoint) but the whole way, with its diverse aspects of lochside, riverine and rocky scenery, is supernatural. Includes short crossing between Rhubodach and Colintraive. Great hotels/ restaurants in Tighnabruaich (783/784/ARGYLL; 1176/INNS).

1625 3/E16 ✓ **The Golden Road** South Harris The main road in Harris follows the W
ATMOS coast, notable for bays and beaches (1568/BEACHES). This is the other, winding round a series of coves and inlets with offshore skerries and a treeless, rocky hinterland: classic Hebridean landscape, especially Finsbay. **Skoon Art Café** nearby (2242/HEBRIDES). Great campsite (1219/CAMPING). Tweed is woven; visit and buy (2183/TWEED).

1626 5/G19 **Sleat Peninsula** Skye The unclassified road off the A851 (main Sleat road) especially coming from south, i.e. take road at Ostaig near Gaelic College (good place to stay nearby 2239/SKYE); it meets the coast after 9km. Affords rare views of the Cuillins from a craggy coast. Returning to 'main' road S of Isleornsay, pop into the great hotel pub there, **Eilean Iarmain** (2239/SKYE).

1627 8/R27 **Leaderfoot-Clintmains** nr St Boswells The B6356 between the A68 and the B6404 Kelso-St Boswells road. This small road, busy in summer, links Scott's View and **Dryburgh Abbey** (1882/ABBEYS; find by following abbey signs) and Smailholm Tower, and passes through classic Border/Tweedside scenery. 500m walk to the Wallace Statue is signed. Don't miss **Irvine's View** if you want to see the best of the Borders (1638/VIEWS).

1628 8/P20 **Braemar-Linn Of Dee** 12km of renowned Highland river scenery along the upper valley of the (Royal) Dee. The Linn (rapids) is at the end of the road and the mighty Dee is squeezed until it is no more than 1m wide, but there are river walks and the start of the great Glen Tilt walk to Blair Atholl (1977/GLEN & RIVER WALKS). Deer abound. The whole road between Ballater and Braemar is fit for a queen and all.

1629 5/L19 **Fort Augustus-Dores** nr Inverness The B862 often single-track road that follows and latterly skirts Loch Ness. Quieter and more interesting than the main W bank A82. Starts in rugged country and follows the straight road built by Wade to tame the Highlands. Reaches the lochside at Foyers and goes all the way to Dores

(15km from Inverness) and popular pub for grub, the **Dores Inn** (01463 751203). Fabulous untrodden woodlands near Errogie (marked) and the spooky graveyard adjacent Boleskin House where Aleister Crowley did his dark magic and Jimmy Page of Led Zeppelin may have done his. 35km total; worth taking slowly.

1630 8/L24 **The Duke's Pass, Aberfoyle–Brig o' Turk** Of the many roads through the Trossachs, this one is spectacular though gets busy; numerous possibilities for stopping, exploration and great views. Good viewpoint 4km from Loch Achray Hotel, above road and lay-by. One-way forest road goes round Loch Achray and 2 other lochs (Drunkie and Venachar). Good hill walking starts (1930/1931/1932/HILLS) and Loch Katrine regular daily sailings (2km) Apr-Oct (01877 376316). Bike hire at Loch Katrine (01877 376366), Aberfoyle and Callander. Best food stop: **Brig o' Turk Tearoom** 1393/TEAROOMS.

1631 7/H20 **Glenfinnan–Mallaig** www.road-to-the-isles.org.uk The A830, aka the Road to the Isles. Through some of the most impressive and romantic landscapes in the Highlands, splendid in any weather (it does rain a bit) to the coast at the **Sands of Morar** (1580/BEACHES). This is deepest Bonnie Prince Charlie country (1900/CHARLIE) and demonstrates what a misty eye he had for magnificent settings. A full-throttle bikers' dream. The road is shadowed by the West Highland Railway, an even better way to enjoy the scenery (5/JOURNEYS).

1632 7/H21 **Lochailort–Acharacle** Off from the A830 above at Lochailort and turning S on the A861, the coastal section of this great scenery is superb especially in the setting sun, or in May when the rhoddies are out. **Glenuig Inn** is a 'green' and improved pub to stop over and eat (1174/INNS). This is the road to the **Castle Tioram** shoreline, which should not be missed (1775/RUINS); and glorious Ardnamurchan.

1633 7/H26 **Knapdale: Lochgilphead–Tarbert** B8024 off the main A83 follows the coast for most of its route. Views to Jura are immense (and on a clear day, Ireland). Not much happens here but in the middle in exactly the right place is the superb **Kilberry Inn** (1171/INNS; 1302/GASTROPUBS). Take it easy on this very Scottish 35km of single track. Short walk to the Coves 3km from Kilberry.

1634 8/N22 **Amulree–Kenmore** Unclassified single-track and very narrow road from the hill-country hamlet of Amulree to cosy Kenmore signed Glen Quaich. Past Loch Freuchie, a steep climb takes you to a plateau ringed by magnificent (far) mountains to Loch Tay. Steep descent to Loch Tay and Kenmore. You may have to open and close the gates. Great walk from car park on left 1km before Kenmore.

1635 8/N23 **Muthill–Comrie** Pure Perthshire. A route which takes you through some of the best scenery in central Scotland and ends up (best this way round) in Comrie with bar/restaurants and other pleasures (909/932/PERTHSHIRE; 1669/SWIMMING). Leave Muthill (pronounced Mew-thil) and the **Barley Bree** (1170/INNS) by Crieff road turning left (2km) into **Drummond Castle** grounds up a glorious avenue of beech trees (gate open 1-5pm). Visit garden (1506/GARDENS); continue through estate. At gate, go right, following signs for Strowan. First junction, go left following signs (4km). At T-junction, go left to Comrie (7km). Best have a map or GPS, but if not, who cares? It's all bonnie!

The Classic Views

For views of and around Edinburgh and Glasgow see p. 88 and p. 133-34. No views from hill or mountain tops are included here.

1636 5/G17 ✓✓✓ **The Quirang** Skye Best approach is from Uig direction taking the right-hand unclassified road off the hairpin of the A855 above and 2km from town signed Staffin via Quirang (more usual approach from Staffin side is less of a revelation). View (and walk) from car park, the massive rock formations of a towering, contorted ridge. Solidified lava heaved and eroded into fantastic pinnacles. Fine views also across Staffin Bay to Wester Ross. See also 2220/ISLAND WALKS. **Ellishadder Art Café, The Small & Cosy Teahouse** and **Skye Pie Café** 2239/SKYE.

1637 5/J16 ✓✓✓ The views of **An Teallach** and **Liatach** An Teallach, that great favourite of Scottish hill walkers (40km S of Ullapool by the A835/A832), is best viewed from the side of Little Loch Broom or the A832 just before you get to Dundonnell (1414/TEAROOMS). The classic view of the other great Torridon mountains (**Beinn Eighe**, pronounced Ben-A, and **Liathach** together, 100km S by road from Ullapool) in Glen Torridon (1620/SCENIC ROUTES) 4km from Kinlochewe. This viewpoint is not marked but it's on the track around Loch Clair which is reached from the entrance to the Coulin estate off the A896 (small lay-by), Glen Torridon road (be aware of stalking). Park outside gate; no cars allowed, 1km walk to lochside. These mountains have to be seen to be believed.

1638 8/R27 ✓✓ **Irvine's View** St Boswells The full panorama from the Cheviots to the Lammermuirs. This the finest view in southern Scotland. It's only a furlong further than the famed Scott's View (see below): cross the road from **Scott's View** lay-by through the kissing gate, veering left uphill across rough pasture till you reach the double track. Head up till the track divides and take the right, lesser path. You'll see the fallen standing stone where I would like my bench. The telecoms masts aren't pleasant but turn your back on them and gaze across the beautiful Borders to another country... you know, England. Excellent café/bookshop/deli in St Boswells **Main Street Trading Co** (859/BORDERS).

1639 5/G18 ✓✓ From **Raasay** www.raasay.com There are several fabulous views looking over to Skye from Raasay, the small island reached by ferry from Sconser (2196/ISLANDS). The panorama from Dun Caan, the hill in the centre of the island (444m) is of Munro proportions, producing an elation incommensurate with the small effort required to get there. Start from the road to the North End or ask at the rebuilt **Raasay House**, with its café, comfy rooms and great view from the lawn (2239/SKYE).

1640 4/J15 ✓✓ **The Summer Isles** Achiltibuie · www.summer-isles.com The Summer Isles are a scattering of islands seen from the coast of Achiltibuie, the lounge of the **Summer Isles Hotel** (1045/HIGHLANDS), the terrace of the **Am Fuaran** bar (1310/GASTROPUBS) and visited by boat from Ullapool. But the best place to see them and the stunning perspective of this western shore is on that road to Altandhu (has other spellings). Best approach is: from Achiltibuie, veer left through Polbain, on and through Altandhu, past turning for Reiff and Blairbuie, then 500m ascending inland. There's a bench (which should have my name on it) and a path (sign for Viewpoint) 50m to little plateau with many cairns and this one of the ethereal views of Scotland. On this same road 500m round the corner, the distant mountains of Assynt all in a row: 2 jaw-dropping perspectives of the Highlands in 5 minutes.

1641 7/K24 ✓✓ **The Rest and Be Thankful** On A83 Loch Lomond-Inveraray road where it's met by the B828 from Lochgoilhead. In summer the rest may be from driving stress and you may not be thankful for the camera-toting masses, but this was always one of the most accessible, rewarding viewpoints in the land. Surprisingly, none of the encompassing hills are Munros but they are nonetheless dramatic.

1642 6/P17 ✓ **Califer nr Forres** 7km from Forres on A96 to Elgin, turn right signed for Pluscarden, follow this road for 5km back towards Forres. You are unaware how high above the coastal plain you are and the lay-by is discreetly located. When you walk across a small park with young memorial trees you are rewarded with a truly remarkable sight – down across Findhorn Bay and the wide vista of the Moray Firth to the Black Isle and Ben Wyvis. There is often fantastic light on this coast.

1643 5/G19 ✓ **Elgol Skye** End of the road, the B8083, 22km from Broadford. The classic view of the Cuillin from across Loch Scavaig and of Soay and Rum. Cruises (Apr-Oct) in the *Bella Jane* (0800 731 3089) or *The Misty Isle* (Apr-Oct, not Sun 01471 866288) to the famous corrie of Loch Coruisk, painted by Turner, romanticised by Walter Scott. A journey you'll remember. There are great Cuillin views also from the Glenbrittle Rd.

1644 8/Q23 ✓ **The Law Dundee** Few cities have such a single good viewpoint. To N of the centre, it reveals the panoramic perspective of the city on the estuary of the silvery Tay, with its emerging exciting waterfront. Route to Law Rd not easy to follow but walk from town or satnav/Google.

1645 6/N18 **Dulsie Bridge nr Nairn** 16km S of Nairn by the A939 to Grantown, this locally revered but otherwise secret beauty spot is imbued with history. Follow B9007 from Ferness then the signed unclassified road. Park on S side and walk 200m for the best view of the remarkable arched bridge over the charming Findhorn river. Built in 1755, it survived the 'Muckle Spate' of 1829, when the river rose by 40ft. Other walks nearby 2001/WALKS.

1646 7/G21 **Camas Nan Geall Ardnamurchan** 12km Salen on B8007. Coming especially from the Kilchoan direction, a magnificent bay appears below you, where the road first meets the sea. Almost symmetrical with high cliffs and a perfect field (still cultivated) in the bowl fringed by a shingle beach. Car park viewpoint; there is a path down. Amazing Ardnamurchan!

1647 5/K20 **Glengarry** 3km after Tomdoun turn-off on A87, Invergarry-Kyle of Lochalsh road. Lay-by/viewfinder. An uncluttered vista up and down loch and glen with not a house in sight (pity about the salmon cages). Distant peaks of Knoydart are identified, but not Loch Quoich nestling spookily and full of fish in the wilderness at the head of the glen. Gaelic-named mountains on the board. Bonnie Prince Charlie passed this way. Great hotel at Invergarry (1064/HIGHLANDS).

1648 8/R27 **Scott's View St Boswells** Off B6404 St Boswells to Kelso road (follow Dryburgh Abbey signs). The View, old Walter's favourite (the horses still stopped there long after he'd gone), is 4km along the road (**Dryburgh Abbey** 3km further 1882/ABBEYS). Magnificent sweep of his beloved Border country, but only in one direction. If you cross the road and go through the kissing gate you approach **Irvine's View** (see above... and beyond).

1649 8/R27 **Peniel Heugh** nr Ancrum On the subject of great views in the Borders, look no further than this – sentinel of the Borders. Report: 1830/MONUMENTS.

1650 8/N21 **Queen's View** Loch Tummel, nr Pitlochry 8km on B8019 to Kinloch Rannoch. Car park and 100m walk to rocky knoll where pioneers of tourism Queen Victoria and Prince Albert were 'transported into ecstasies' by view of Loch Tummel and **Schiehallion** (1953/MUNROS), though the view was named after Isabella, the first wife of Robert the Bruce. Their view was flooded by a hydro scheme after World War II; more recently it spawned a whole view-driven visitor experience. Well, it... makes you wonder!

1651 8/L23 **The Rallying Place of the Maclarens** Balquhidder Short climb from behind the church (1873/GRAVEYARDS) along the track 150m then signed Creag an Tuirc, steep at first. Superb view down Loch Voil, the Balquhidder Braes and the real Rob Roy Country and top bar/restaurant on the A84 on your descent, **Mhor 84** (831/CENTRAL) by the **Monachyle Mhor** people (where you could treat yourself and stay 1191/GET-AWAY HOTELS).

1652 7/L25 **Duncryne Hill** Gartocharn Gartocharn is between Balloch and Drymen on the A811 and this view was once recommended by writer and outdoorsman Tom Weir as 'the finest viewpoint of any small hill in Scotland'. Turn up Duncryne road at the E end of village and park 1km on left by a small wood (a sign reads Woods Reserved for Teddy Bears). The hill is only 470ft high and easy, but the view of Loch Lomond and the Kilpatrick Hills is superb.

1653 4/M13 **Tongue** From the causeway across the kyle, or better, follow the minor road to Melness, Talmine and the **Craggan Hotel** (1096/HIGHLANDS) on the W side, look S to Ben Loyal or N to the small islands. There's a lovely, lonely graveyard after the causeway.

1654 8/N25 **Cairnpapple Hill** nr Linlithgow Volcanic geology, Neolithic henge, east of Scottish agriculture, the Forth plain, the bridges, Grangemouth industrial complex and telecoms masts: not all pretty, but the whole of Scotland at a glance. For directions see 1801/PREHISTORIC.

1655 7/J22 **Castle Stalker View** Portnacroish Near Port Appin on main A828 Oban-Fort L William road. On right going south, the view has been commandeered by the CSV Café (1410/TEAROOMS) which ain't bad (closed in evenings) but viewpoint can be accessed at all times 50m away from car park. Always impressive, in certain lights the vista of Port Appin, the castle in the fore and Loch Linnhe, is ethereal. There are ecopods here if you want to stay (1250/GLAMPING).

1656 8/R28 **Carter Bar** English Border, nr Jedburgh On the A68 Edinburgh-Newcastle road, the last and first view in Scotland just happens to be superb. The Border hill country spread out before you for many long miles. The tear in my eye is not because of the wind, but because this was the landscape of my youth and where I spent my lightsome days. In 2014, I was privileged to give 'The Address' to the Redeswire Stone – the last skirmish between the Scots and English in 1575. It's 200m E of the car park.

1657 4/P12 **Dunnett Head** between Thurso & John o' Groats More sense of place than Jo'G and it is the most northerly part of the British mainland. Part of extensive RSPB reserve, there are happily more birds than sightseers. View to island of Stoma, Hoy and Orkney Mainland; and those cliffs. A walk (2032/WALKS), and nearby **Mary-Ann's Cottage** (2123/HISTORY) and the venerable **Castle of Mey** (1757/CASTLES) are all on or just off the A836 which takes you here.

The Great Wild Swimming Holes

Take care when swimming in rivers; don't ever take them for granted. Watch the kids. Most of these places are traditional local swimming and picnic spots where people have swum for years but rivers continuously change their course and their nature. Wearing sandals or old sports shoes is a good idea.

1658 5/F18 ✓✓ **The Fairy Pools Glen Brittle, Skye** On that rare hot day, this is one of the best places on Skye to go; swimming in several clear, deep pools with the massif of the Cuillins around you. One pool has a stone bridge you swim under. Head off A863 Dunvegan road from Sligachan Hotel then B8009 and Glenbrittle road. 7km down just as road begins to parallel the glen itself, you'll see a river coming off the hills. Park in lay-by on right. 1-2km walk. Swim with the fairies!

1659 7/K22 ✓✓ **The Pools in Glen Etive** Glen Etive is a wild, enchanted place where people have been camping for years to walk and climb in Glen Coe area. There are many grassy landings at the river side as well as these perfect pools for bathing. The first is about 5km from the main road, the A82 at Kingshouse, but just follow the river and find your own. Take midge cream for evening wear. Lots.

1660 5/N19 ✓✓ **Feshiebridge** At the bridge itself on the B970 between Kingussie and Inverdruie near Aviemore. 4km from Kincraig. Great walks here into Glen Feshie and in nearby woodland; under bridge a perfect spot for Highland swimming. Go down to left from south. Rocky ledges, clear water. One of the best but cold even in high summer. Further pools nearby and a sculpture trail. Brilliant tearoom further along this road at Inshriach (1383/TEAROOMS).

1661 8/N22 ✓✓ **Rumbling Bridge & The Braan Walk nr Dunkeld** Excellent stretch of cascading river with pools, rocky banks and ledges. Just off A9 heading N opposite first turning for Dunkeld, the A822 for Aberfeldy, Amulree (signed Crieff/Crianlarich). Car park on right after 4km. Connects with forest paths (the Braan Walk) to the **Hermitage** (2010/WALKS) – 2km. Fab picnic and swimming spot though take great care. This is the nearest Highland-type river to Edinburgh (about 1 hour). Tearoom in Dunkeld (1406/TEAROOMS).

1662 5/M20 ATMOS ✓✓ **Strathmashie nr Newtonmore** On A86 Newtonmore-Dalwhinnie (on A9) to Fort William road 7km from Laggan, watch for Forest sign. Car parks on either side of the road; the Druim an Aird car park has finder boards. Great swimming spot, but often campers. Viewpoints, waterfall, pines. If people are here and you want privacy, there are great forest walks and follow the river; there are many other great pools. **Laggan Coffee Shop** does rather good cakes. 5km towards the A9 (1395/TEAROOMS).

1663 7/K23 ATMOS ✓✓ **Rob Roy's Bathtub The Falloch Falls, nr Inverarnan** A82 N of Ardlui and 3km past the **Drover's Inn** (1285/GOOD PUBS). Sign on the right (Picnic Area) going north. Park, then follow the path. Some pools on the rocky river course but 500m from car park you reach the main falls and below a perfect round natural pool 30m across. There's an overhanging rock face on one side and smooth slabs at the edge of the falls. Natural suntrap in summer (if there is a summer), the water Baltic at all times.

1664 5/K19 ✓✓ **Below Plodda Falls nr Tomich** About 30km from Drumnadrochit on Loch Ness via the lovely village of Tomich (1073/HIGHLANDS). Short walk to the well-signposted falls (1594/WATERFALLS) and these serene pools in a spectacular woodland setting.

1665 8/P27 ✓ **Neidpath Peebles** 2km from town on A72, Biggar road; sign for castle. Park by Hay Lodge Park and walk upriver or down the track to the castle (now closed) or the lay-by 100m beyond. Idyllic setting of a broad meander of the Tweed, with medieval Neidpath Castle, a sentinel above. Two pools (3m deep in average summer) linked by shallow rapids which the adventurous chute down on their backs. Usually a rope-swing on the oak tree at the upper pool. Also see 1993/GLEN & RIVER WALKS. TAKE CARE.

1666 6/N17 ✓ **Randolph's Leap nr Forres** Spectacular gorge on the mythical Findhorn which carves out some craggy scenery on its way to a gentle coast. This no-longer secret glade and fabulous swimming hole are behind a wall on a bend of the B9007 (see 2001/WALKS for directions) S of Forres and Nairn and near **Logie Steading**, a courtyard of good things (a board there gives directions) and refreshment (1403/TEAROOMS). One Randolph or Alistair as the new tale tells, may have leapt here; we just bathe and picnic under the trees.

1667 8/N21 ✓ **Falls of Bruar nr Blair Atholl** Just off A9, 12km N of Blair Atholl. 250m walk ☕ from **House of Bruar** car park and shopping experience (2166/SHOPS) to lower fall (1595/WATERFALLS) where there is an accessible large deep pool by the bridge. Cold, fresh mountain water in a woody gorge. The proximity of the retail experience can make it all the more... naturally exhilarating.

1668 5/K18 **Dog Falls Glen Affric** Halfway along Glen Affric road from Cannich before you come to the loch, a well-marked picnic spot and great place to swim in the peaty waters surrounded by the Caledonian Forest (with trails). Birds well sussed to picnic potential – your car covered in tits and cheeky chaffinches – Hitchcock or what? (1978/GLEN & RIVER WALKS). Falls (rapids really) to the left. The more spectacular **Plodda Falls** (1594/WATERFALLS) are nearby.

1669 8/M23 **Near Comrie www.comrie.org.uk** 2 great pools of different character near the neat little town in deepest Perthshire. **The Linn**, the town pool: go over humpback bridge from main A85 W to Lochearnhead, signed The Ross. Take left fork then after 2km there's a parking place on left. River's relatively wide, very pleasant spot. For more adventurous, **Glenartney**, known locally as The Cliffs: go over bridge, the Braco road after 3km signed Glenartney, past Cultybraggan training camp (no longer in use) and then MoD range on left just before the end-of-the-road sign (200m after boarded-up cottage on right, 5km from Comrie). Park and walk down to river in glen. What with the twin perils of the Army and the Comrie Angling Club, you might feel you have no right to be here, but you do, and this stretch of river is marvellous. Respect the farmland. Follow the road further for picnic spots. Comrie has a great pub/hotel bistro (909/PERTHSHIRE) and the **Deil's Cauldron** (932/PERTHSHIRE). And 1444/BAKERS.

1670 7/K26 **Greeto Falls Gogo Glen, Largs** Well known locally so ask to find Flatt Rd. At top there's a car park and you follow the beautiful Gogo Glen path, past Cockmalane Cottage. Superb views of the Clyde. 3 pools to choose from in the Gogo Burn near the bridge. Walk can extend to the mast (4km return). You can also start from the main road near the ferry.

1671 7/J26 **North Sannox Burn Arran** Park at the North Sannox Bridge on the A841 (road from Lochranza to Sannox Bay) and follow the track W to the deer fence and tree line (1km). Just past there you will find a great pool with small waterfall, dragonflies and perhaps even an eagle or two wheeling above.

1672 7/H23   **Swimmers' Quarry** Easdale Cross to Easdale on the wee boat (5-min continuous service); see 2115/HISTORY for details. Do visit the museum and the Puffer pub but go beyond scattered houses, following paths to slate quarries full of seawater since 1881 with clear water like an enormous hotel swimming pool. The L-shaped one with its little bench is easiest; the water can be blue like the Aegean.

1673 8/M24   **The Scout Pool & The Bracklinn Falls** Callander The latter are a Callander must-see, easy-to-find (signposted from S end of Main St, up hill to golf course then next car park up on right – from there it's a 2km walk). The Scout Pool is a traditional swimming hole on same river, the fabulously named Keltie Water, it's a summer thing only. Follow road further 2km from Bracklinn car park till road goes on through iron gate. Park on right. Downhill 150m cross wooden bridge then follow river path to right 250m. Access to huge pool dammed by giant boulders. A beautiful secret spot in the woods.

1674 9/L30   **The Otter's Pool** New Galloway Forest A clearing in the forest reached by a track, the Raiders' Road, running from 8km N of Laurieston on the A762, for 16km to Clatteringshaws Loch. The track is only open March to October and gets busy. It follows the Water of Dee and halfway down the road – the Otter's Pool. A bronze otter used to mark the spot (it got nicked) and it's a place mainly for kids and paddling; but when the dam runs off it can be deep enough to swim. Road closes dusk. 2015/WALKS.

1675 8/R27   **Ancrum** www.ancrum.com A secret place on the quiet Ale Water (out of village towards Lilliesleaf, 3km out 250m from farm sign to Hopton – a recessed gate on the right before a bend and a rough track that locals know). A buttercup meadow, a Border burn, a surprisingly deep pool to swim. Go to left of rough vegetation in defile, going downhill follow fence on your right. Cross further gate at bottom (only 100m from road). Arcadia awaits beyond the meadow. In Ancrum there's a great pub, The Cross Keys, for ale and excellent food and nearby, with an approach via the A698 to Hawick, there's **Born in the Borders**, an all-round retail and refreshment farmyard with its own brewery (2148/SHOPPING).

1676 8/N24   **Paradise** Sheriffmuir, nr Dunblane A pool at the foot of an unexpected leafy gorge on the moor between the Ochils and Strathallan. Here the Wharry Burn is known locally as 'Paradise' or contradictorily the **Devil's Bucket**. Take road from 'behind' Dunblane or Bridge of Allan to the Sheriffmuir Inn; go downhill (back) towards BoA. Park 1km after humpback bridge. Head for the pylon nearest the river and you'll find the pool. Only midges (or rain) will infiltrate your paradise.

1677 6/Q20   **Potarch Bridge & Cambus o' May** on The Dee 2 places: the first by the reconstructed Victorian bridge (and near the hotel) 3km E of Kincardine O'Neil. Cambus another stretch of river E of Ballater (6km). Locals swim, picnic on rocks, etc, and there are forest walks on the other side of road. The brave jump off the bridge at Cambus (in wetsuits). Great tearooms nearby: the **Black-Faced Sheep** in Aboyne (1384/TEAROOMS) and see below.

1678 6/R20   **The Feugh** The Water of Feugh is the largest tributary of the Dee, with famous falls on the B974 2km S of Banchory, where there is a restaurant/café. Further along the road towards Aboyne, there are tracks in the beautiful Forest of Birse and, I'm told, some brilliant secret pools. I heard this from folk at the tearoom/ farm shop on the nearby **Finzean** Estate (1464/FARM SHOPS), which you should certainly visit. It's only 3/4km from the pools. They'll tell you how to find them.

Good Places To Take Kids

CENTRAL

1679 8/P25   ✓✓✓ **Edinburgh Zoo** Corstorphine Rd · www.edinburghzoo.org.uk · 0131 334 9171 4km W of Princes St. A large and long-established zoo which is always evolving and where the natural world from the poles to the plains of Africa is ranged around Corstorphine Hill. Enough huge/exotic/ghastly creatures and friendly, amusing ones to fill an overstimulated day. The Budongo Trail chimp enclosure is first class. The penguins do their famous parade at 2.15pm. The beavers are brill, the koalas are cool as... then there are the Pandas (time-ticketed, you should book in advance). Tian Tian may or may not be pregnant, but we so hope so. Shop stocked with PC toys and souvenirs. Café. Open AYR (even on Christmas Day!), 7 days, Apr-Sep 9am-6pm, reduced hours in winter.

✓✓✓ **Riverside Museum** By Clydeside Expressway, Glasgow & **National Museum of Scotland** Chambers Street, Edinburgh World-class and fun and awe. Reports: 723/418/ATTRACTIONS.

✓✓ **Our Dynamic Earth** Holyrood Road, Edinburgh · www.dynamicearth.co.uk · 0131 550 7800 Edinburgh's major kids' attraction. Report: 424/ATTRACTIONS.

✓✓ **Museum of Childhood** 42 High Street, Edinburgh · www.edinburghmuseums.org.uk · 0131 529 414242 An Aladdin's cave of toys for all ages. Report: 432/ATTRACTIONS.

1680 8/R25   ✓✓ **East Links Family Park** Dunbar · www.eastlinks.co.uk · 01368 863607 Off the A1 and A199 (East Linton to Dunbar road) by the entrance to the John Muir Country Park (well-signed). An easy-going, non-high-tech animal farm and activity centre with inside and outside play areas, go-karts, a train, climbing walls and lots of obliging animals. 7 days 10am-5pm. Combine with **Foxlake** (below) nearby for older kids.

1681 8/R25   ✓ **Foxlake Adventures** www.foxlake.co.uk · 01620 860657 & **Reboot Disc Golf** www.rebootdiscgolf.com · nr Dunbar Two related outdoorsy fun things on a lake in a wood on the A199 4km E of Dunbar. At Foxlake you get on a wetsuit, hook on a cable and go wakeboarding. Off the same car park you take to the woods and throw frisbees. This is what we do with our leisure time. Kids love it and (on Foxlake) more daring dads. Mar-Dec 9am-dusk. Good caff.

1682 8/Q25   ✓ **Edinburgh Butterfly Farm & Insect World** nr Dalkeith · www.edinburgh-butterfly-world.co.uk · 0131 663 4932 On A7 signed Eskbank/Galashiels from ring road (1km). Part of a garden-centre complex. Beauty and the beasties in a creepy-crawly world: delightful butterflies but kids are more impressed by the glowing scorpions, locusts, iguanas and other assorted uglies. Red-kneed tarantula not for the faint-hearted. 7 days, 9.30am-5.30pm (10am-5pm in winter).

1683 8/P25   ✓ **Gorgie City Farm** Edinburgh · www.gorgiecityfarm.org.uk · 0131 337 4202 A working farm on busy road in the heart of the city. Friendly domestic animals and people, garden, great playground and café. Open summer 9.30am-4.30pm (4pm in winter). Free. Green and fluffy in the concrete jungle.

1684 8/M26   ✓ **Glasgow Science Centre** Pacific Quay · www.glasgowsciencecentre.org · 0141 420 5000 One of Glasgow's most flash attractions. State-of-the-art interactive landmark tower and IMAX. Report: 728/ATTRACTIONS.

1685 7/K26   ✓ **Kelburn Country Centre** Largs · www.kelburnestate.com ·
L   **01475 568685** 2km S of Largs on A78. Riding school, gardens, woodland walks up the Kelburn Glen and a visitor section with shops/exhibits/cafés. Oh, and a music festival! Wooden stockade for clambering kids; indoor playbarn with quite scary slides. Falconry displays (those long-suffering owls). The Plaisance indeed a pleasant place and the Secret Forest beckons. The graffiti art is... well, something else! 7 days Apr-Oct 10am-6pm, winter 10am-4pm. Stock up on ice cream at **Nardini's** famous caff (806/AYRSHIRE).

1686 8/R25   **Yellowcraigs** nr Dirleton Beautiful beach 35km E of Edinburgh via A1, the A198,
LL   though Dirleton village then right, for 2km. Lovely, scenic strand and dunes (464/BEACHES). Treasure Island play park in the woods is great for kids. Activity and sea air! **Luca's** on the way for ice cream (1445/ICE CREAM).

1687 8/Q25   **The Edinburgh Dungeon** 31 Market St · www.thedungeons.com ·
0131 240 1000 Slick but très contrived experience takes you through a ghoulish history of Scottish nasties. Hammy of course, but kids will love the monorail. Opening times vary.

✓✓ **Falkirk Wheel** Falkirk Report: 4/ATTRACTIONS.

FIFE & TAYSIDE

1688 8/Q23   ✓✓ **Cairnie Fruit Farm & Maze** nr Cupar · www.cairniefruitfarm.co.uk ·
☕   **01334 655610** Leave town by minor road from main street heading past the hospital; signed (4km) or from main A92; signed near Kilmany (3km). A fruit and farm shop/café (1475/FARM SHOPS); hugely popular due to extensive play area using farm materials to amuse kids and get them countrified. This is the Tayside equivalent of Cream o' Galloway (below), this time built around the strawberry rather than the ice cream. The annually seeded maze in the maize field is major. There's strawberries for tea and other very good grub. Apr-Oct 10am-5pm (9.30am-5.30pm Jul/Aug).

1689 8/Q24   ✓ **Muddy Boots** www.muddybootsfife.com · **01337 831222** Balmalcolm on
☕   A914 S of Cupar. Like Cairnie above this is where kids can go wild in the country but this is no manufactured experience. The goats love being goats; similarly the asparagus. Playbarn and playfields: biking sledging, jumping (possibly for joy). Great café. Mon-Sat 9am-5pm, Sun from 10am.

1690 8/P25   ✓ **Deep Sea World** North Queensferry · www.deepseaworld.com ·
01383 411880 The aquarium in a quarry which may be reaching its swim-by date. Habitats are viewed from a conveyor belt where you can stare at the fish as diverse divers teem around and above you. Maximum hard sell to this all-weather attraction – the shark capital – but kids like it even when they've been queueing for aeons. Cute seals and sharp sharks! Café is fairly awful, but nice views. Open AYR. 7 days 10am-5pm; weekends till 6pm (last entry 1 hour before).

1691 8/Q23   ✓ **Dundee Science Centre** Dundee · www.dundeesciencecentre.org.uk ·
01382 228800 Greenmarket across roundabout from Discovery Point and adjacent **DCA** (2132/GALLERIES). Purpose-built indoor infotainment, this is an innovative and interactive games complex with a message. 7 days 10am-5pm. Average visit time 2-3 hours.

1692 8/Q23 ✓ **Verdant Works** Dundee · www.rrsdiscovery.com · **01382 309060** Near
🖥 Westport. Heritage museum that recreates workings of a jute mill. Sounds
industrial, but is brilliant for kids and grown-ups. Report: 2110/HISTORY.

1693 8/R23 **Craigtoun Park** St Andrews · www.friendsofcraigtoun.org.uk ·
01334 473666 3km SW of St Andrews on the Pitscottie road (enter via Dukes Golf
Course). An oasis of fun: bouncy castles, trampolines, putting, crazy golf, boating
lake, a train through the grounds, adventure playgrounds and glasshouses. A
perfect day's amusement especially for nippers. Opening hours vary through the
year. Entrance charge covers all attractions.

1694 8/M23 **Auchingarrich Wildlife Park** nr Comrie · www.auchingarrich.co.uk ·
L **01764 679469** 4km from main street over bridge and signed or via Braco
off the M9. Conscientious corralling in the Perthshire hills of fluffy, hairy and
feathered things, all friendly. Some exotic creatures but mostly familiar. Adventure
playground, flying fox. All on a very informal and approachable scale. 7 days 10am-
5.30pm.

1695 8/Q23 **Camperdown Park** Dundee · www.camperdownwildlifecentre.com ·
01382 431811 Large park just off ring road (Kingsway and A923 to Coupar Angus)
with wildlife centre and nearby play complex. Animal-handling at weekends. Over
80 species: porcupines to pine martens and the odd wallaby. Open AYR. Centre
10am-4.30pm, earlier in winter (1546/PARKS).

SOUTH & SOUTH WEST

1696 9/M31 ✓✓ **Cream o' Galloway** Rainton, nr Gatehouse of Fleet · www.
creamogalloway.co.uk · **01557 814040** There is something inherently
good about a visitor attraction based on the incontrovertible fact that human
beings love ice cream, especially with a 'pure and simple' message. Organic café,
burger barn, herb garden, karting and fab adventure playground in the woods, part
of 5km of child-friendly nature trails. Let's hear it for cows! Open summer
10am-6pm, winter till 5pm. Allow a few hours. Report: 1446/ICE CREAM. And then
Sandgreen 1583/BEACHES.

1697 7/L27 ✓ **Kidz Play** Prestwick · www.kidz-play.co.uk · **01292 475215** Off main
street at Station Road, past station to beach and to right. Big-shed soft play
area for kids. Everything the little blighters will like in the throwing-themselves-
around department. Shriek city. Babies-12. 7 days 9.30am-6pm.

1698 8/Q27 ✓ **Kailzie Gardens** Peebles · www.kailziegardens.com · **01721 720007**
L All-round family destination 4km from Peebles on B7062, with fishing lochan,
osprey-watching (Apr-Aug) though birds are 2km away (as the osprey flies) and the
marvellous, serene, well-tended gardens (walled and wild); perfectly hedged.
Apr-Oct 11am-5.30pm; gardens only, winter.

1699 8/Q27 **Bowhill** nr Selkirk · www.bowhillhouse.co.uk · **01750 22204** 4km from
MAR-SEP Selkirk on the A708 Moffat-Selkirk road. Bowhill House and Estate, though not
offering itself as a kids' 'attraction', is a lovely, woody place for family walking,
messing about and getting to feel the trees. Adventure playground. Guided
tours only of House (check website), with its world-class art collection. Further
down the road St Mary's Loch and the **Grey Mare's Tail** (1598/WATERFALLS) for
more outdoors.

1700 8/M25 **Palacerigg Country Park** Cumbernauld · www.northlanarkshire.gov. uk · 01236 720047 6km SE of Cumbernauld off A801, 40 mins from Glasgow. 740 acres of parkland; ranger service, nature trails, picnic area and kids' farm with rare breeds; the longhouses. Golf course and putting green. Changing exhibits about forestry, conservation, etc. Open AYR 7 days; daylight hours. Café.

✓✓ **Drumlanrig Castle** Thornhill Report: 1529/PARKS.

NORTH EAST

1701 6/S17 ✓ **Macduff Marine Aquarium** www.macduff-aquarium.org.uk · 01261 833369 On the seafront E of the harbour, a family attraction for this Moray Firth port. Small but underrated, perhaps because nearby Banff gets more tourist attention, though **Duff House** (2139/GALLERIES) gets fewer visitors than this child-friendly sea-life centre. All fish seem curiously happy with their lot, content to educate and entertain. Open AYR 10am-5pm (last admission 4.15pm). Check winter hours.

1702 6/S20 ✓ **The Den & The Glen** Maryculter, nr Aberdeen · www.denandtheglen. co.uk · 01224 732941 Fibreglass fantasy land in verdant glen 16km S of Aberdeen via B9077, the South Deeside road, a nice drive. Characters from every fairy tale and nursery story dotted around 20-acre park. Their fixed manic stares give them a spooky resemblance to people you know. Older kids may find it tame: no guns, no big technology but nice for little 'uns. Indoor play area and quite wonderful gardens. 7 days, 9.30am-5.30pm (4.30pm last admission), weather permitting.

1703 6/T18 **Aden** Mintlaw · www.adencountrypark.org.uk Pronounced Ah-den. Country park just beyond Mintlaw on A950 16km from Peterhead. Former grounds of mansion with walks and organised activities and events. Farm buildings converted into Farming Heritage Centre, café, etc. Adventure playground. Open AYR.

HIGHLANDS & ISLANDS

1704 6/N19 ✓ **Cairngorm Reindeer Herd** Glenmore, nr Aviemore · www. cairngormreindeer.co.uk · 01479 861228 At Glenmore Forest Park 12km Aviemore along Coylumbridge Rd, 100m behind Glenmore visitor centre. Stop at centre (shop, exhibition) to buy tickets and follow the guide in your vehicle up the mountain. From here, a 20-min walk. Real reindeer aplenty in authentic free-ranging habitat (when they come down off the cloudy hillside in winter with snow all around it's very real); they're so... small. 90-min trip. 11am AYR and 2.30pm in summer. Wear suitable footwear; phone if weather looks threatening.

1705 5/N19 ✓ **Leault Farm** nr Kincraig · www.leaultworkingsheepdogs.co.uk · 01540 651402 On A9 but easier to find from a sign 1km S of Kincraig on B9152. Working farm with daily sheepdog trials showing an extraordinary facility with dogs and sheep (and ducks). A great spectacle, totally authentic in this setting. Usually 4pm May-Oct (possibly other times). Closed Sat. Sometimes pups to love.

1706 6/N19 ✓ **Landmark Park** Carrbridge · www.landmarkpark.co.uk · 01479 841613 A purpose-built family outdoor activity centre with much to throw yourself into, AV displays and shopping. Great for kids messing about in the woods on slides, in a maze, etc, in a large adventure playground, Microworld or (especially squealy) the Wildwater Coaster. Fire Tower may be too much for granny but there are fine forest views. 7 days 10am-6pm (5pm in winter, 7pm mid-Jul to mid-Aug). Disappointing caff. Great in autumn!

1707 5/N19 The Highland Wildlife Park Kincraig · www.highlandwildlifepark.org.uk · 01540 651270 On B9152 Aviemore-Kingussie. Large drive-through reserve run by Royal Zoological Society with wandering herds of deer, bison, etc, and pens of other animals. Some in habitats, but also cages. Cute, vicious little wildcats! Victoria, a real polar bear, and a couple of endangered snow leopards arrived 2015. Does feel much more natural than a zoo in this swathe of Highland Scotland. Must be time to bring back bears, let the wolves go free and liven up the caravan parks. Open 10am-5pm (Jul/Aug 6pm, winter 4pm).

1708 5/M20 Highland Folk Museum Newtonmore · www.highlandfolk.com ·
MAR-OCT 01540 673551 Just outside town on the A86 to Kingussie and 10 mins from the A9. Historical Highlandish and folksy, but a lovely, interesting place to take kids. Thatched cottages, places to run around, adventure park. 10,000 new old items arrived in 2014!

1709 7/F26 Islay Wildlife Information & Field Centre Port Charlotte · www.islaynaturalhistory.org · 01496 850288 Fascinating, hands-on wildlife centre, activities and day trips. Excellent for getting kids interested in wildlife. Then go find it! Guided rambles c/o the Islay Natural History Trust. Jun-Sep 10.30am-4.30pm.

1710 7/J22 The Scottish Sealife Sanctuary Oban · www.visitsealife.com/oban · 01631 720386 16km N on the A828. On the shore of Loch Creran, one of the oldest British waterworlds, still in there with the fishes. 'Environmentally conscientious', they rescue seals and turtles and house numerous aquatic beasties. Various aquaria, all kinds of fish going round, multi-level viewing otter enclosure and the seal thing. Feeding times posted: almost a theatrical show. Café/shop/adventure playground. 10am-4pm.

1711 7/G21 Nàdurra Visitor Centre Ardnamurchan · www.nadurracentre.co.uk · 01972 500209 A861 Strontian, B8007 Glenmore 14km. Photographer Michael McGregor's award-winning interactive exhibition (under different owners). Kids enjoy, adults impressed. A walk-through of wildlife including live pine martens (if you're lucky), herons and CCTV of more cautious creatures. Tearoom. Apr-Oct. Check website for hours.

1712 5/N19 Loch Insh Kincraig · www.lochinsh.com · 01540 651272 Watersports centre (2100/WATER SPORTS) but much more on B970 2km from Kincraig (near Kingussie and the A9). Beautiful loch and mountain setting, 2 small beaches and gentle water. Lots of instruction available, wildlife boat trips, biking possibilities and small adventure playground. Good café and terrace overlooking loch: the Boathouse. All-round active day out; there are chalets to stay longer.

The Best Places To See Birds

See p. 304-305 for Wildlife Reserves, many of which are good for bird-watching. All those listed below are in L, LL and LLL settings.

1713 4/K13 ✓✓ **Handa Island** nr Scourie, Sutherland · www.scottishwildlifetrust. org.uk Take the boat from Tarbet Pier 6km off A894 5km N of Scourie or from Scourie itself (both 07780 967800) and land on a beautiful island run as a nature reserve by the Scottish Wildlife Trust. Boats (Apr-early Sep though fewer birds after Aug) are continuous depending on demand. Crossing 30 mins. Small reception hut and 2.5km walk over island to cliffs which rise 350m and are layered in colonies, 200,000 strong: fulmars, shags and the UK's largest colony of guillemots. Allow 3-4 hours. Though you must take care not to disturb the birds, you'll be eye to eye with seals and bill to bill with razorbills. Eat at the seafood café on the cove when you return (1348/SEAFOOD). Mon-Sat. Last return 5pm.

1714 9/P30
LL
ADMISSION ✓✓ **Caerlaverock** nr Dumfries · www.wwt.org.uk · 01387 770200 17km S on B725 near Bankend, signed from road. The WWT Caerlaverock Wetlands Centre is an excellent place to see whooper swans, barnacle geese in their 30-thousand and more (countless hides, observatories, farmhouse viewing tower). Has Fairtrade café as well as farmhouse-style accom with a variety of basic rooms (and a badger feeding station). More than just birds too: natterjack toads, badgers, so not just for twitchers. The Sir Peter Scott hide is pure entertainment. Centre open AYR, 7 days 10am-5pm.

1715 7/F22 ✓✓ **Lunga & The Treshnish Islands** off Mull · www.hebrideantrust.org Sail from Iona or Fionnphort or Ulva ferry on Mull to these uninhabited islands on a 5/6-hour excursion which probably takes in Staffa and Fingal's Cave. Best time is May-July when birds are breeding. Talk of pufflings not making it because parents can't find sand eels seems premature here. Some trips allow 3 hours on Lunga. Razorbills, guillemots and a carpet of puffins oblivious to your presence. This is a memorable day. Boat trips (Ulva Ferry 08000 858786; or 01681 700358 from Fionnphort) from Iona or Oban. Trips dependent on sea conditions.

1716 8/R24 ✓✓ **Isle of May** Firth of Forth Island at mouth of Forth off Crail/Anstruther reached by daily boat trips from Anstruther harbour (*The May Princess* (07957 585200; www.anstrutherpleasurecruises.co.uk). Apr-Sep times dependent on tides). Trip 45 mins; allows 3 hours ashore. Or quicker, smaller *Osprey Rib* (07473 631671; www.isleofmayboattrips.co.uk). Can reserve the day before. Island (including isthmus to Rona) 1.5km x 0.5km. Info centre and resident wardens. See guillemots, razorbills and kittiwakes on cliffs and shags, terns and thousands of puffins. Most populations increasing. This place is strange as well as beautiful. The puffins in early summer are, as always, engaging.

1717 8/R25 ✓✓ **The Bass Rock** off North Berwick · 01620 892838 Temple of gannets. A guano-encrusted massif sticking out of the Forth: their largest island colony in the world. Davie Balfour was imprisoned here in RLS's *Catriona* (aka Kidnapped II). A variety of weather-dependent boat trips available Easter-Sep, including landings and safaris (which sell out first). Extraordinary birds, extraordinary experience. For daily trips on *The Sula*: www.sulaboattrips.co.uk, 01620 880770 or enquire at the Seabird Centre (below).

1718 8/P22 ✓✓ **Loch of the Lowes** nr Dunkeld · www.scottishwildlifetrust.org.uk · 01350 727337 4km NE Dunkeld on A923 to Blairgowrie or walk from Dunkeld main street (2.5km). Superbly managed (Scottish Wildlife Trust) site with double-floored hide (always open) and other hide (same hours as visitor centre) and permanent binoculars. Main attractions are the captivating ospreys (from early Apr-Aug). Nest 100m over loch and clearly visible. Their revival (over 250 pairs now in UK) is well documented, including diary of movements, breeding history, etc. Also the near-at-hand endless fascination of watching wild birds, including woodpeckers, and red squirrels feeding outside the picture window is a real treat. Great walks nearby (1984/GLEN & RIVER WALKS) including to the other loch (Ordie).

1719 6/N19 ✓✓ **Loch Garten** nr Boat of Garten · www.nnr-scotland.org.uk · 01479 831476 3km village off B970 into Abernethy Forest. Famous for the ospreys and signed from all round. Best Apr-Jun. 2 car parks: the first has nature trails through Scots pine woods and around loch; other has visitor centre with the main hide 250m away: TV screens, binoculars, other wild-bird viewing and informed chat. Here since 1954, that first pair have done wonders for local tourism – in fact, they and the RSPB and the army of determined volunteers practically invented ecotourism! Och, but they are magnificent.

1720 5/N19 ✓✓ **Inshriach Nursery** nr Aviemore · www.inshriachnursery.co.uk A (very good) garden centre and superb tearoom, **The Potting Shed** (1383/ TEAROOMS), but also one of the best places to watch wild birds who swarm round the feeders hanging in the woods over the gorge. Has been voted the most popular UK site by RSPB members. Red squirrels and great cakes are other good reasons for going. Mar-Oct 10am-5pm. Closed Mon/Tue.

1721 8/Q25 ✓ **The Scottish Ornithologists' Club House** nr Aberlady · www.the-soc. org.uk · 01875 871330 A198 on the left going into Aberlady from Edinburgh, opposite Gosford Estate. Not a bird-watching site per se (though between the Lagoon and the Seabird Centre, below, and near Aberlady Reserve 2km), but an archive, library and resource centre for lovers of Scottish birds. Light modern building looks across bay to reserve. Art exhibitions; much to browse. Bird-watching for beginners courses. Friendly staff. The Society published the definitive *The Birds of Scotland*. Open 10am-4pm (noon-6pm weekends in summer). Go in October, late afternoon, when the geese come in over Aberlady Bay (best viewed from Kilspindie Golf Club road).

1722 8/Q25 ✓ **The Lagoons** Musselburgh On E edge of town behind the racecourse (follow road round, take turn-off signed Race Course Parking) at the estuarine mouth of the River Esk. Waders, sea birds, ducks aplenty and often interesting migrants on the mudflats and wide littoral. The Lagoons are man-made ponds behind with hide and attract big populations (both birds and binocs), though surprisingly 'concrete'. This is the nearest diverse-species area to Edinburgh (15km) and is one of the most significant migrant stopovers in the UK.

1723 8/S20 ✓ **Fowlsheugh** nr Stonehaven · www.rspb.org.uk · 01346 532017 8km S of Stonehaven and signed from A92 with path from Crawton. Sea-bird city on 2km of red sandstone cliffs up to 200 feet high; take great care. 80,000 pairs of 6 species especially guillemots, kittiwakes, razorbills and also fulmars, shags, puffins. Possible to view the birds without disturbing them and discern the layers they occupy on the cliff face. Best seen May-July and best to go by bike!

1724 7/F25 ✓ **Loch Gruinart, Loch Indaal** Islay RSPB reserve. Take A847 at Bridgend then B8017 turning N and right for Gruinart. The mudflats and fields at the head of the loch provide winter grazing for huge flocks of Barnacle and Greenland geese. They arrive, as do flocks of fellow bird-watchers, in late Oct. Hides and good vantage points near road. Don't miss beautiful **Saligo Bay** (1567/BEACHES). The Rhinns and the Oa in the south also sustain a huge variety of birdlife.

1725 1/P10 ✓ **Marwick Head** Orkney Mainland · www.rspb.org.uk 40km NW of Kirkwall, via Finstown and Dounby; take left at Birsay after Loch of Isbister, cross the B9056 and park at Cumlaquoy. A 4km circular walk. Spectacular sea-bird breeding colony on 100m cliffs and nearby at the Loons Reserve, wet meadowland, 8 species of duck and many waders. Orkney sites include the Noup cliffs on Westray, North Hill on Papa Westray and Copinsay, 3km E of the mainland.

1726 7/G23 **Isle of Mull** www.rspb.org.uk Sea eagles. Very successful reintroduction of these magnificent eagles; a hide with CCTV viewing. By appointment only. Site changes every year. Mull claims the highest breeding density of golden eagles in Europe.

1727 8/R25 **Scottish Seabird Centre** North Berwick · www.seabird.org · 01620 890202 Award-winning, interactive visitor attraction near the harbour overlooking Bass Rock and Fidra (above). If you don't want to go out there, video and other state-of-the-art technology makes you feel as if the birds are next to you. Viewing deck for dramatic perspective of gannets diving (140km per hour!). Café and shopping, where puffins prevail. 10am-6pm (4pm winter/5.30pm weekends).

1728 8/S22 **Montrose Basin Wildlife Centre** www.montrosebasin.org.uk · 01674 676336 1.5km S of Montrose on A92 to Arbroath. Accessible Scottish Wildlife Trust centre overlooks estuarine basin hosting residents and migrants. Good for twitchers, kids. Autumn geese. Visitor centre Mar-Oct daily 10.30am-5pm. Call for winter hours.

1729 4/N13 **Forsinard Flows Nature Reserve** www.rspb.org.uk · 01641 571225 44km from Helmsdale on the A897, or train stops on route to Wick/Thurso. RSPB (proposed World Heritage site) reserve, acquired after public appeal. 19,000 hectares of the Flow Country and its birds: divers, plovers, merlins and hen harriers (nest watch in visitor centre). Guided walks and trails. Reserve open AYR; visitor centre Apr-Oct 9am-5.30pm.

1730 8/Q22 **Loch of Kinnordy** Kirriemuir · www.rspb.org.uk · 01577 862355 4km W of town on B951, an easily accessible site with 3 hides overlooking loch and wetland area managed by RSPB. Geese in late autumn, gulls aplenty. You may see the vanishing ringlet butterfly. Good deli/café in Kirriemuir (933/TEAROOMS).

1731 6/T17 **Strathbeg** nr Fraserburgh · www.rspb.org.uk · 01346 532017 12km S off the A952 Fraserburgh-Peterhead road, signed Nature Reserve at Crimond. Wide, shallow loch close to coastline, a 'magnet for migrating wildfowl'. Marsh/fen, dune and meadow habitats. In winter 30,000 geese/widgeon/mallard/swans and occasional rarities like cranes and egrets. 20% of the world's pink-footed geese drop by. Binoculars in visitor centre (8am-6pm, dusk in winter) and 3 hides.

1732 6/S17 **Troup Head** between Macduff and Fraserburgh, Moray Firth · www.rspb. org.uk · 01346 532017 Near the cliff-clinging villages of Crovie and *Local Hero* Pennan on the coastal B9031. Fantastic airy walk from the former (2030/WALKS) or (closer) directly from the road signed for Northfield following RSPB signs for 2km, then a 1.5km stroll from car park. Puffins, kittiwakes, the whole shebang; and dolphins.

Where To See Dolphins, Whales, Porpoises & Seals

The coast around the north of Scotland has some of the best places in Europe to view whales and dolphins and seals. Boat trips/sealife cruises get you closer but these are the coastal locations for the best sightings. Dolphins are most active on a rising tide, especially May-September.

MORAY & CROMARTY FIRTHS (near Inverness)
The population of bottlenose dolphins in this area is about 190. They can be seen all year (mostly Jun-Sep).

1733 5/M18 **The Dolphins & Seals of the Moray Firth Centre** 01463 731866 Just N of Kessock Bridge on A9. Underwater microphones pick up chatterings of dolphins and porpoises. There's always somebody there to explain. Up-to-date list of recent sightings and all cruises available. Jun-Sep. They also run a wildlife centre at Speybay at the mouth of the Spey, S of the Moray Firth, off A96 between Mosstodloch and Fochabers on B9014. 01343 820339. Apr-Oct.

1734 5/M17 **Cromarty** Any vantage around town is good, especially South Sutor for coastal walk, and an old lighthouse cottage has been converted into a research station run by Aberdeen University. **Chanonry Point, Fortrose**, through the golf course, E end of point beyond lighthouse is the *best* place to see dolphins from land in Britain. Occasional sightings can also be seen at **Balintore**, opposite Seaboard Memorial Hall; **Tarbert Ness** beyond **Portmahomack**, end of path through reserve further out along the Moray Firth possible at **Burghead**, **Lossiemouth** and **Buckie**, **Spey Bay** and **Portknockie**. Also check the Dolphin Space Programme, an accreditation scheme for boat operators: www.dolphinspace.org.

THE NORTH WEST
On the west coast, especially near **Gairloch** the following places may offer sightings of orcas, dolphins and minke whales, mainly in summer.

1735 4/H16 **Rubha Reidh** nr Gairloch 20km N of Melvaig (unclassified road). Near Carn Dearg Youth Hostel W of Lonemore. Where road turns inland is good spot.

1736 5/H17 **Red Point of Gairloch** By B8056 via Badachro round Loch Gairloch. High ground looking over North Minch and S to Loch Torridon. Harbour porpoises often seen from all along this coast.

1737 4/H15 **Greenstone Point** north of Laide Off A832 (unclassified road) through Mellon Udrigle round Gruinard Bay. Harbour porpoises Apr-Dec, minke whales May-Oct.

1738 5/F16 **Rubha Hunish** Skye The far NW finger of Skye. Walk from Duntulm Castle or Flodigarry. Dolphins and minke whales in autumn.

OTHER PLACES
1739 2/V5 **Mousa Sound** Shetland 20km S of Lerwick (1797/PREHISTORIC).

1740 7/F21 **Ardnamurchan** The Point The most westerly point (and lighthouse) on this wildly beautiful peninsula. Go to end of road or park near Sanna Beach and walk round. Sanna Beach worth going to just to walk the strand. Visitor centre; tearoom.

Great Wildlife Reserves

These wildlife reserves are not merely bird-watching places. Most of them are easy to get to from major centres; none requires a permit.

1741 8/S25
NTS

✓✓ **St Abb's Head** www.nts.org.uk · 01890 771443 9km N of Eyemouth and 10km E of main A1. Spectacular cliff scenery (2026/WALKS), a huge sea-bird colony, rich marine life and varied flora. Good view from top of stacks, geos and cliff face full of serried ranks of guillemot, kittiwake, razorbill, etc. Hanging gardens of grasses and campion. Behind cliffs, grassland rolls down to the Mire Loch and its varied habitat of bird, insect, butterfly life and vegetation. Surprisingly good art gallery (2155/SHOPS) and NTS interpretation centre in a row of cottages by car park. 1/2/3km walks marked. Disabled access to the Lighthouse on tarmac road behind the cottages. Coffee shop at the car park. New Inn in Coldingham (3km) for decent pub grub (01890 771315) and 2 good caffs in St Abbs village (a sweet harbour) 2km down the road.

1742 6/T18

✓✓ **Sands of Forvie & Ythan Estuary** Newburgh · www.nnr-scotland. org.uk · 01358 751330 25km N Aberdeen. Cross bridge outside Newburgh on A975 to Cruden Bay and park. Path follows Ythan estuary, bears N and enters the largest undisturbed dune system in the UK (though see below). Dunes in every aspect of formation. Collieston, a 17/18th-century fishing village, is 5km away. These habitats support the largest population of eiders in Britain (especially Jun) and huge numbers of terns. It's easy to get lost here, so get lost! Some wish the same would happen to Donald Trump who has turned the adjacent dune system into a habitat only for golfers.

1743 5/J17

✓ **Beinn Eighe** Pronounced Ben-A. Bounded by the A832 S from Gairloch and A896 W of Kinlochewe, this first National Nature Reserve in Britain includes remaining fragments of old Caledonian pinewood on the S shore of Loch Maree (largest in West Highlands) and rises to the rugged tops with their spectacular views and varied geology. Excellent wood and mountain trails with starts on both roads – from A832 on Loch Maree side there are woodland strolls. Starts to the Beinn (easier) and to the mighty Liathach are from the A896 Glen Torridon road (1637/VIEWS; 1620/SCENIC ROUTES). Hotel/GH (1192/GET-AWAY HOTELS). Great café (1408/TEAROOMS).

1744 7/H24 **Scottish Beaver Trial** www.scottishbeavers.org.uk In the Knapdale Forest W of Lochgilphead, off the Tayvallich road (B8025) to the Barnluasgan car park and information centre. Introduced in 2009, the trial has been 'an outstanding success', and on a 5km circular walk, there is much evidence of their activity. Early morning and evening there is a good chance of sightings. Their story to be continued.

1745 8/R25 **John Muir Country Park** nr Dunbar · www.eastlothian.gov.uk · 01620 827459 Vast park between Dunbar and North Berwick named after the Dunbar-born father of the conservation movement. Includes estuary of the Tyne; part of the park is also known as Tyninghame, and see 462/BEACHES. Diverse habitats: cliffs, sand spits and woodland. Many bird species. Crabs, lichens, sea and marsh plants. Enter at E extremity of Dunbar at Belhaven, off the B6370 from A1; or off A198 to North Berwick. Or better, walk from Dunbar by clifftop trail (2km+). You could of course walk to Helensburgh (215km) on the John Muir Way!

1746 7/L26 **Lochwinnoch** www.rspb.org.uk · 01505 842663 30km SW of Glasgow via M8 junction 28A then A737 past Johnstone onto A760. Also from Largs 20km via A760. Reserve just outside village on lochside and comprises wetland and woodland habitats. A serious nature centre, incorporating an observation tower. Hides and marked trails; and a birds-spotted board. Shop and coffee shop. Events programme. Good for kids. Visitor centre open 10am-5pm.

1747 5/N20 **Insh Marshes** Kingussie · www.rspb.org.uk · 01540 661518 4km from town along B970 (past **Ruthven Barracks** 1788/RUINS), 2,500 acres of Spey floodplain run by RSPB. Trail (3km) marked out through meadow and wetland and a note of species to look out for (including 6 types of orchid, 7 'red list' birds and half the UK population of goldeneye). Also 2 hides (250m and 450m) high above marshes, vantage points to see waterfowl, birds of prey, otters and deer. A National Nature Reserve since 2003.

1748 8/R23 **Tentsmuir** between Newport & Leuchars · www.tentsmuir.org · 01382 553962 North tip of Fife at the mouth of the Tay, reached from Tayport or Leuchars via the B945. Follow signs, taking road that winds for 4km over flat then forested land. Park (car park closes 9pm in summer, dusk in winter) and cross dunes to broad strand. Walks in both direction: W back to Tayport, E to Leuchars. Also 4km circular walk of beach and forest. Hide 2km away at Ice House Pond. Seals often watch from waves and bask in summer. Lots of butterflies. Waders aplenty and, to the east, one of UK's most significant populations of eider. Most wildfowl offshore. (Ranger: 07985 707593).

1749 8/P24 **Loch Leven Nature Reserve, aka Vane Farm** Loch Leven, Kinross · www. rspb.org.uk · 01577 862355 RSPB reserve on S shore of Loch Leven, beside and bisected by B9097 off junction 5 of M90. Easily reached visitor centre with observation lounge and education/orientation facilities. Hide nearer lochside reached by tunnel under road. Nature trail on hill behind through heath and birchwood (2km circular). Steep, but has the vista. Good place to introduce kids to nature watching. Centre 10am-5pm. Hides always open (and there are ospreys).

1750 3/C17 **Balranald** North Uist · www.rspb.org.uk · 01463 715000 W coast of North Uist reached by the road from Lochmaddy, then the Bayhead turn-off at Clachan Stores (10km north). This most western, most faraway reach is one of the last redoubts of the disappearing corncrake. Catch its calling while you can.

1751 8/M24 **Flanders Moss** nr Thornhill · www.nnr-scotland.org.uk · 01786 450362 This curious swathe of the Forth valley on the road between Thornhill and Kippen (1km rough track from B822 to car park) is a much-revered and well-interpreted... bog, a kind of micro ecosystem. It's a 'raised bog' and there's a raised walkway around it (1km) and an impressive tower to overlook it. Wet-loving wildlife includes adders, dragonflies and a host of other insects and the birds who feed on them. Then there's the history. This place is a bit of an oddity, central but not overrun. Good grub in Kippen and Thornhill (1304/1322/GASTROPUBS). A very satisfactory afternoon can be had around here.

the
Best
Historical Places

The Best Castles

NTS *National Trust for Scotland. Hours vary. Admission.*
HS *Historic Scotland. Standard hours are: Apr–end Sep, 7 days 9.30am–6pm.*
Winter hours vary. Admission.

1752 8/N24
LLL
ADMISSION
HS

✓✓✓ **Stirling Castle** www.stirlingcastle.gov.uk · 01786 450000
Dominating town and plain, this, like Edinburgh Castle, is worth
the hype and history. More aesthetically pleasing, it is, like Edinburgh, a
timeless attraction that withstands the waves of tourism as it did the centuries
of warfare for which it was built. It does seem a very civilised billet, with
gorgeous frescoes, peaceful gardens and cannon-studded rampart walks from
which the views are excellent, including the aerial view of the ghost outline of
the King's Knot Garden (the Cup and Saucer, as they're known locally). Includes
the Renaissance Palace of James V and the Great Hall of James IV restored to full
magnificence. Some rock legends have played here and there are many dinners.
Unicorn Café is average.

1753 8/Q25
LLL
ADMISSION
HS

✓✓✓ **Edinburgh Castle** www.edinburghcastle.gov.uk · 0131 225 9846
City centre. Impressive from any angle and all the more so from
inside. Despite the tides of tourists and time, it still enthrals. Superb perspectives
of the city and of Scottish history. Stone of Destiny and the Crown Jewels are
the Big Attractions. Café and restaurant (superb views) with efficient but
uninspiring catering operation; open only castle hours and to castle visitors.
Report: 417/ATTRACTIONS.

1754 6/N17
ADMISSION
NTS

✓✓ **Brodie Castle** nr Nairn · www.nts.org.uk · 01309 641371 6-7km
W of Forres off main A96. More a (Z-plan) tower house than a castle,
dating from 1567. In this century and like Cawdor nearby, the subject of family
feuding – now resolved and under the calming influence of the NTS, its guides
discreetly passing over any unpleasantness. With a minimum of historical
hokum, this 16/17th-century, but mainly Victorian, country house is furnished
from rugs to moulded ceilings in excellent taste. Every picture (very few gloomies)
bears examination. The nursery and nanny's room, the guest rooms, indeed all
the rooms, are eminently habitable. Wonderful library. Tearoom and informal
walks in grounds. An avenue leads to a lake; in spring the daffodils are famous.
Apr-Oct and last tour (register on arrival) at 3.30pm (4pm Jul/Aug). Closed Fri/Sat
May/Jun and Oct. Grounds open AYR till sunset.

1755 7/K28
LL
ADMISSION
NTS

✓✓ **Culzean Castle** nr Maybole · www.nts.org.uk · 01655 884455
Pronounced Cullane. 24km S of Ayr on A719. Difficult to convey here the
scale and the scope of the house and the country park. Allow some hours especially
for the grounds. Castle is more like a country house and you examine from the
other side of a rope. From the 12th century but rebuilt by Robert Adam in 1775, a
time of soaring ambition, its grandeur is almost out of place in this exposed clifftop
position. It was designed for entertaining, and the oval staircase is magnificent.
Wartime associations (especially with President Eisenhower and you can stay in
these suites 801/AYRSHIRE) plus the enduring fascination of the aristocracy.
560 acres of grounds including clifftop walk, formal gardens, walled garden, Swan
Pond (a must) and Happy Valley. Harmonious home farm is visitor centre with
exhibits and shop, etc. Caff could be better. Open Mar-Oct 10.30am-5pm. Park
open AYR. Many special events.

1756 8/Q24
ADMISSION
NTS

✓✓ **Falkland Palace** www.nts.org.uk · 01337 857397 Middle of farming Fife, 15km from M90 junction 8. Not a castle at all, but the hunting palace of the Stewart dynasty. Despite its recreational rather than political role, it's one of the landmark buildings in Scottish history and in the 16th century was the finest Renaissance building in Britain. They all came here for archery, falconry and hunting boar and deer on the Lomonds; and for Royal Tennis which is displayed and explained. Still occupied by the Crichton-Stewarts, the house is dark and rich and redolent of those days of 'dancing and deray at Falkland in the Grene'. Mar-Oct 10am-5pm. Sun 1-5pm. Plant shop and events programme. Great walks from village (1946/HILL WALKS; 1990/GLEN & RIVER WALKS). See also 1396/TEAROOMS.

1757 4/Q12
L
ATMOS
ADMISSION
☕

✓✓ **Castle of Mey** nr Thurso · www.castleofmey.org.uk · 01847 851473 Actually near John o' Groats (off A836), castles don't get further-flung than this. Stunted trees, frequent wind and a wild coast but the Queen Mother famously fell in love with this dilapidated house in 1952, filled it with things she found and was given and turned it into one of the most human and endearing of the Royal (if not all aristocratic) residences. Guides tell the story and if you didn't love her already, you will when you leave. Lovely walled garden and animal centre in converted granary with farm animals including North Country sheep – great for kids. A top tearoom. Mey cattle and produce (cottage pie and crumble). Charles and Camilla still visit. May-Sep (closed 2 weeks early Aug). Castle 10am-4pm.

1758 5/N17
ADMISSION
☕

✓ **Cawdor Castle** Cawdor, nr Nairn & Inverness · www.cawdorcastle. com · 01667 404674 The mighty Cawdor of Macbeth fame. Most of the family clear off for the summer and leave their romantic yet habitable and yes... stylish castle, sylvan grounds and gurgling Cawdor Burn to you. Pictures from Claude to Craigie Aitchison, a modern kitchen as fascinating as the enormous one of yore. Even the tartan passage is nicely done. The burn is the colour of tea. An easy drive (25km) to Brodie (above) means you can see 2 of Scotland's most appealing castles in one day. Courtyard café. 9-hole golf course. These gardens are gorgeous. May-early Oct, 7 days 10am-5pm (last admission).

1759 8/N21
ADMISSION

✓ **Blair Castle** Blair Atholl · www.blair-castle.co.uk · 01796 481207 Impressive from the A9, the castle and the landscape of the Dukes of Atholl (present Duke not present); 10km N of Pitlochry. Hugely popular; almost a holiday-camp atmos. Numbered rooms chock-full of 'collections': costumes, toys, plates, weapons, stag skulls, walking sticks – so many things! Upstairs, the more usual stuffed apartments including the Jacobite bits. Walk in the policies (includes Hercules Garden with tranquil ponds); catch The Whim. Apr-Oct 9.30am-4.30pm (last admission) daily.

1760 8/Q22
LL
ADMISSION

✓ **Glamis** Forfar · www.glamis-castle.co.uk · 01307 840393 8km from Forfar via A94 or off main A929, Dundee-Aberdeen road (turn-off 10km N of Dundee, a picturesque approach). Fairy-tale castle (pronounced Glawms) in majestic setting. Seat of the Strathmore family (Queen Mum spent her childhood here) for 600 years; every room an example of the interior of a certain period. Guided tours (continuous/50 mins long). Restaurant/gallery shop haven for tourists (and for an excellent bridie 1440/BAKERS). Apr-Oct 10am-5.30pm; last entry 60 mins before. Italian Gardens and nature trail well worth 500m walk. A 'Prom' concert is held mid-July.

1761 7/J27
ADMISSION
NTS

✓ **Brodick Castle** Arran · www.nts.org.uk · 01770 302202 4km from town (bike hire 01770 302377). Impressive, well-maintained landmark castle, exotic formal gardens and extensive grounds. **Goat Fell** (1928/HILLS) in the background and the sea through the trees. Dating from 13th century and until the 1950s the home of the Dukes of Hamilton. An over-antlered hall leads to liveable rooms with portraits and heirlooms, an atmos of long-ago afternoons. Tangible sense of relief in the kitchens now the entertaining is over. Robert the Bruce's cell less convincing. Easter-Oct; check hours. Marvellous grounds open AYR (and Goat Fell).

1762 7/H23
LL
ADMISSION
🖪
Duart Castle Mull · www.duartcastle.com · 01680 812309 A fabulous setting for the 13th-century ancestral seat of the Clan Maclean and home to Sir Lachlan and Lady Maclean. Quite a few modifications over the centuries as methods of defence grew in sophistication but with walls as thick as a truck and the sheer isolation of the place it must have doomed any prospect of attack from the outset. Now a happier, homelier place, the only attacking that gets done these days is on scones and cake in the superior tearoom. Apr: Sun-Thu 11am-4pm. May-Oct: 10.30am-5.30pm. Diverse event programme in summer months.

1763 5/F17
ADMISSION
Dunvegan Castle Skye · www.dunvegancastle.com · 01470 521206 3km Dunvegan village. Romantic history and setting, though more baronial than castellated, the result of mid-19th-century restoration that incorporated the disparate parts. The castle and the 30,000-acre estate now presided over by the 30th MacLeod of MacLeod with the task of repairing the roof, etc, from the controversial disposal of the Cuillin. Your visit also helps. Necessary crowd management leads you through a series of rooms where the Fairy Flag, displayed above a table of exquisite marquetry, has pride of place. Gardens, perhaps lovelier than the house, down to the loch; boats leave the jetty to see the seals. Busy café, The Macleod Tables (though food disappointing; instead, go to **Jann's** in the village 2239/SKYE). Open Apr-Oct 10am-5.30pm. Loch cruises from the jetty.

1764 5/J18
LLL
ADMISSION
Eilean Donan Dornie · www.eileandonancastle.com · 01599 555202 On A87, 13km before Kyle of Lochalsh. A calendar favourite, often depicted illuminated. Inside is a generous portion of history (American size). The Banqueting Hall with its Pipers' Gallery must make for splendid dinner parties for the Macraes. Much military regalia among the bric-a-brac, but also the impressive Raasay Punchbowl partaken of by Johnson and Boswell. Mystical views from ramparts as well as the more ersatz human story below the stairs. Mar-Oct 10am-5pm; open from 9am Jul/Aug.

1765 8/N22
ADMISSION
Castle Menzies nr Aberfeldy · www.menzies.org · 01887 820982 In Tay valley with spectacular ridge behind (**Walks In The Weem Forest**, part of the Tummel Valley Forest Park; separate car park). On B846, 5km W of Aberfeldy, through Weem. The 16th-century stronghold of the Menzies (pronounced Mingiss), one of Scotland's oldest clans. Sparsely furnished with odd clan memorabilia, the house nevertheless conveys more of a sense of Jacobite times than many more brimful of bric-a-brac. Bonnie Prince Charlie stopped here on the way to Culloden. Open farmland situation, so manured rather than manicured grounds. No tearoom but tea and Tunnocks and now many options in Aberfeldy. Apr-Oct 10.30am-5pm, Sun 2-5pm.

1766 8/P23
ADMISSION
Scone Palace nr Perth · www.scone-palace.co.uk · 01738 552300 Pronounced Skoon. On A93 road to Blairgowrie and Braemar. A 'great house', the home to the Earl of Mansfield and gorgeous grounds. Famous for the Stone of Scone (aka The Stone of Destiny) on which the kings of Scots were crowned, and the Queen Vic bedroom. Maze and pinetum. Many contented animals greet you and a plethora of peacocks. Annual Game Fair, horse trials and antique fair. The Rewind Music Festival late July, a more recent rewinding of the clock. Apr-Oct 7 days 9.30am-5pm (last admission). Winter hours check website.

1767 8/R24
ADMISSION
NTS

Kellie Castle nr Pittenweem · www.nts.org.uk · 01333 720271 Major castle in Fife. Dating from 14th century and restored by Robert Lorimer, his influence evidenced by magnificent plaster ceilings and furniture. Notable mural by Phoebe Anna Traquair. The gardens, nursery and kitchen recall all the old Victorian virtues. The old-fashioned roses still bloom for us. Check website for opening hours.

1768 6/R19
ADMISSION
NTS

Craigievar nr Banchory · www.nts.org.uk · 0844 493 2174 15km N of main A93 Aberdeen-Braemar road between Banchory and Aboyne. A classic tower house, perfect like a porcelain miniature. Random windows, turrets, balustrades. Set among sloping lawns and tall trees. Limited access to halt deterioration means you are spared the shuffling hordes. Tours only; check website for hours. No caff.

1769 6/S20
ATMOS
ADMISSION
NTS

Drum Castle (the Irvine Ancestral Home) nr Banchory · www.nts.org.uk · 01330 700334 Please forgive this, the longest entry in this section. 1km off main A93 Aberdeen-Braemar road between Banchory and Peterculter and 20km from Aberdeen centre. For 24 generations this has been the seat of the Irvines. My ain folk! 4 times I've signed the visitor book and each time have wandered through the accumulated history hopeful of identifying with something. Gifted to one William De Irwin by Robert the Bruce, it combines the original keep (the oldest intact tower house in Scotland), a Jacobean mansion and Victorian expansionism. Hugh Irvine, the family 'artist', whose extravagant self-portrait as the Angel Gabriel raised eyebrows in 1810, does seem like my kind of chap; at least more interesting than most of my soldiering forebears. Give me a window seat in that library! Grounds have an exceptional walled rose garden (Easter-Oct 11am-4.15pm 1519/GARDENS). Jul/Aug: 7 days 11am-4pm (last admission), Mar-Jun: Thu-Mon, winter Sat/Sun. Tower can be climbed for great views. Some pleasant walks from the car park. New gallery space showing (until Mar 2017) excellent contemporary art from Aberdeen Art Gallery.

1770 6/Q20
LL
ADMISSION

Balmoral nr Ballater · www.balmoralcastle.com · 01339 742534 On main A93 between Ballater and Braemar. Limited house access (ie only the ballroom: public functions are held here when They're in residence and some corporates). Grounds (open Apr-Jul) with Albert's wonderful trees are more rewarding. For royalty rooters only, and if you like Landseers... Crathie Church along the main road has a good rose window, an altar of Iona marble. John Brown is somewhere in the old graveyard down track from visitor centre, the memorial on the hill is worth a climb for a poignant moment and view of the policies. Crathie services have never been quite the same Sunday attraction since Di and Fergie on a prince's arm (bring it on, Wills and Kate). 7 days from end March to end July.

1771 4/N15
LL
ADMISSION

Dunrobin Castle Golspie · www.dunrobincastle.co.uk · 01408 633177 The largest house in the Highlands, the home of the Dukes of Sutherland who once owned more land than anyone else in the British Empire. It's the first Duke who occupies an accursed place in Scots history for his inhumane replacement, in these vast tracts, of people with sheep. His statue stands on Ben Bhraggie above the town (1835/MONUMENTS). Living the life of imperial grandees, the Sutherlands transformed the castle into a *château* and filled it with their obscene wealth. Once there were 100 servants for a house party of 20 and it had 30 gardeners. Now it's a leisure industry. The gardens are beyond fabulous (1509/GARDENS). The castle and separate museum are open Mar-Oct, 10.30am-4.30pm (5pm Jun-Aug), Sun from noon.

Crathes nr Banchory Reports: 1502/GARDENS; 1826/HOUSES.
Fyvie Aberdeenshire Report: 1825/HOUSES.

The Most Interesting Ruins

HS *Historic Scotland. Standard hours: Apr-end Sep 7 days 9.30am-5.30pm. Oct-Mar Mon-Sat 9.30am-4.30pm. Some variations; call 0131 668 8831 to check. Most HS properties carry admission.*
Membership: 0131 668 8600, any manned sites or www.historic-scotland.gov.uk

1772 8/N25
HS
✓✓✓ **Linlithgow Palace** www.historic-scotland.gov.uk ·
01506 842896 Impressive from the M9 and from the southern approach to this most agreeable of West Lothian towns, but don't confuse the magnificent Renaissance edifice with St Michael's Church next door, topped with its controversial crown and spear spire. From the Great Hall, built for James I, King of Scots, with its huge adjacent kitchens, and the North Range with loch views, you get a real impression of the lavish lifestyle of the court. Not as busy as some HS attractions on this page but it is fabulous. King's Fountain restoration added to the palace appeal. A music fest, 'Party at the Palace', is held in early Aug.

1773 9/P30
LL
🗅
HS
✓✓ **Caerlaverock** nr Dumfries · www.historic-scotland.gov.uk ·
01387 770200 17km S by B725. Follow signs for Wetlands Reserve (1714/BIRDS) but go past road end (can walk between). Fairy-tale fortress within double moat and manicured lawns, the daunting frontage being the apex of an unusual triangular shape. Since 1270, the bastion of the Maxwells, the Wardens of the West Marches. Destroyed by Bruce, besieged in 1640. The whole castle experience is here and the Power of the Lawn. Café and another 7km away in Glencaple.

1774 8/S20
LL
✓ **Dunnottar Castle** nr Stonehaven · www.dunnottarcastle.co.uk ·
01569 762173 3km S of Stonehaven on the coast road just off the A92. Like Slains further north, the ruins are impressively and precariously perched on a clifftop. Historical links with Wallace, Mary, Queen of Scots (the odd night) and even Oliver Cromwell, whose Roundheads besieged it in 1650. The Crown Jewels of Scotland were once held here. 400m walk from car park. Can walk along clifftop from Stonehaven (2km) or take 'The Land Train' (enquire locally). Open AYR.

1775 7/H21
L
ATMOS
✓ **Castle Tioram** nr Acharacle · www.tioram.org Pronounced Cheerum. A romantic ruin where you don't need the saga to sense the place. 5km from A861 just N of Acharacle signed Dorlin. 5km then park by Dorlin Cottage. Serenely beautiful shoreline then walk across a short causeway. Musical beach at nearby Kentra Bay (2028/WALKS). A great hike, 'the Silver Walk', starts here (8km).

1776 6/P17
HS
✓ **Elgin Cathedral** Elgin · www.historic-scotland.gov.uk · 01343 547171
Follow signs in town centre. Set in a meadow by the river, a tranquil corner of this busy market town, the scattered ruins and surrounding graveyard of what was once Scotland's finest cathedral. The nasty Wolf of Badenoch burned it down in 1390, but there are some 13th century and medieval renewals. The octagonal chapterhouse is especially revered, but this is an impressive and evocative slice of history. HS have made great job of restorations. Tower can be climbed. Around the corner, there's a biblical garden planted with species mentioned in the Bible. Gardens open Apr-Sep, 9.30am-5.30pm (4.30pm in winter & closed Thu/Fri).

1777 6/Q19
L
ATMOS
HS
✓ **Kildrummy Castle** nr Alford · www.historic-scotland.gov.uk ·
01975 571331 15km SW of Alford on A97 near the hotel (1210/SCOTTISH HOTELS) and across the gorge from its famous gardens. Most complete 13th-century castle in Scotland, an HQ for the Jacobite uprising of 1715 and an

evocative site. Here the invitation in the old HS advertising to 'bring your imagination' is truly valid. Apr-Sep 9.30am-5.30pm. Now head for the gardens (400m).

1778 3/C20 ✓ **Kisimul Castle** Isle of Barra · www.historic-scotland.gov.uk ·
LLL 01871 810313 The medieval fortress, home of the MacNeils that sits on a
HS rocky outcrop in the bay 200m offshore. Originally built in the 11th century, it was burnt in the 18th and restored by the 45th chief, an American architect, but was unfinished when he died in 1970. An essential pilgrimage for all MacNeils, it is fascinating and atmospheric for the rest of us, a grim exterior belying an unusual internal layout – a courtyard that seems unchanged and rooms betwixt renovation and decay. Open 7 days Easter-Oct and has a gift shop. Last boat 4.30pm.

1779 6/R17 ✓ **Findlater Castle** Moray Coast Ruin of a marvellous castle on a mystical
LLL coast. On the way to **Sunnyside** (1563/BEACHES). Signed off A98 Banff-Inverness (3km): park in farmyard, pass the impressive doocot; you don't see the castle until walking through the cornfields. The 13th–15th-century ruin is built into the promontory, fortified by nature. A board at the clifftop viewpoint depicts it in its glory – but how did they build it? This is a ruin of ruins though intriguingly you can't really reach it.

1780 8/R21 **Edzell Castle** Edzell · www.historic-scotland.gov.uk · 01356 648631 3km
HS village off main street, signed. Pleasing red sandstone ruin in bucolic setting – birds twitter, rabbits run. The notable walled parterre Renaissance garden created by Sir David Lindsay way back in 1604 is the oldest-preserved in Scotland. The wall niches are nice. Lotsa lobelias! Mary, Queen of Scots was here (she so got around). Gate on the road is closed at night.

1781 5/M17 **Fort George** nr Inverness · www.historic-scotland.gov.uk · 01667 460232
HS On promontory of Moray Firth 18km NE via A96 by Ardersier. A vast site – one of the most outstanding artillery fortifications in Europe. Planned after Culloden as a base for George II's army and completed 1769, it remains unaltered and allows a very complete picture. May provoke palpitations in the nationalist heart, but it's heaven for militarists and altogether impressive (don't miss the museum). It's hardly a ruin, of course, as still occupied by the Army. 7 days 9.30am-4/5.30pm.

1782 7/H23 **Dunollie Castle** Oban · www.dunollie.org · 01631 570550 Just outside town
via Corran Esplanade towards Ganavan. An iconic ruin under restoration recently, becoming part of a new historic attraction – The Laird's House Museum – but mainly worth a visit for views of the bay and its 'enchanting' woodlands.

1783 7/H25 **Tarbert Castle** Tarbert, Argyll · www.tarbertcastle.info Strategically and
dramatically overlooking the sheltered harbour of this epitome of a West Highland port. It's for the timeless view rather than an evocation of tangible history (Robert the Bruce connected) that it's worth finding the way up. Access from Harbour Rd.

1784 7/K23 **Kilchurn Castle** Loch Awe · www.historic-scotland.gov.uk Romantic ruin at
L the head of awesome Loch Awe, reached by a 1km walk from the car park off the
HS main A85 5km E of Lochawe village. You go under the railway line. A very pleasant spot for loch reflections; and your own. Apr-Sep.

1785 8/R23 **St Andrews Cathedral** St Andrews · www.historic-scotland.gov.uk ·
HS 01334 472563 The ruins of the largest church in Scotland before the Reformation, a place of great influence and pilgrimage. St Rule's Tower and the jagged fragment of the huge West Front, in their striking position at the convergence of the main

streets and overlooking the sea, are remnants of its great glory. Find a great photographic book: *St Andrews A Portrait of a City* by Adamson & Macintyre. 7 days AYR.

1786 8/Q26
HS
Crichton Castle nr Pathhead · www.historic-scotland.gov.uk · 01875 320017 3km W of A68 at Pathhead (28km S of Edinburgh) or via A7 turning east, 3km S of Gorebridge. Massive Border keep dominating the Tyne valley in pristine countryside. Open Apr-Sep, Mon-Wed & Sat, 9.30am-5pm (last entry). Nearby is the 15th-century collegiate church. 500m walk from Crichton village. Good picnic spots below by the river though may be overgrown in summer.

1787 8/R25
LL
HS
Tantallon Castle North Berwick · www.historic-scotland.gov.uk · 01620 892727 5km E of town by coast road; 500m to dramatic clifftop setting with views to Bass Rock (1717/BIRDS). Dates from 1350 with massive curtain wall to see it through stormy weather and stormy history. The Red Douglases and their friends kept the world at bay. Wonderful beach nearby (461/BEACHES). Open AYR.

1788 5/M20
L
HS
Ruthven Barracks Kingussie · www.historic-scotland.gov.uk · 01667 460232 2km along B970 and visible from A9, especially at night when it's illuminated. These former barracks built by the English Redcoats as part of the campaign to tame the Highlands after the first Jacobite rising in 1715, were actually destroyed by the Jacobites in 1746 after Culloden. It was here that Bonnie Prince Charlie sent his final order, 'Let every man seek his own safety', signalling the absolute end of the doomed cause. Life for the soldiers is well described and visualised. Open AYR.

1789 5/L18
LLL
HS
Urquhart Castle Drumnadrochit · www.historic-scotland.gov.uk 28km S of Inverness on A82. The classic Highland fortress on a promontory overlooking Loch Ness visited every year by bus loads and boat loads of tourists. Photo opportunities galore among the well-kept lawns and extensive ruins of the once formidable stronghold of the Picts and their scions, finally abandoned in the 18th century. Visitor facilities almost cope with demand.

1790 8/M24
HS
Doune Castle Doune · www.historic-scotland.gov.uk Follow signs from centre of village which is just off A84 Callander-Dunblane road. Overlooking the River Teith, the well-preserved ruin of a late 14th-century courtyard castle with a great hall and another draughty room where Mary, Queen of Scots once slept. Is a location for many films (famously *Monty Python and the Holy Grail*) and TV series (*Game of Thrones* and *Outlander*). Nice walk to the meadow begins on track to left of castle; you can swim from the riverbank. Good view from the top but a narrow, steep climb. **Buttercup Café** in the village is good (1405/TEAROOMS).

1791 6/T18
LL
ATMOS
Slains Castle nr Cruden Bay 32km N of Aberdeen and 2km W of Cruden Bay, from car park (Meikle Partans) on bend of the A795. You see its craggy outline then walk 1km. Obviously because of its location, but also because there's no reception centre/postcard shop or proper signposts, this is a ruin that talks. Your imagination, like Bram Stoker's (who was inspired after staying here, to write *Dracula*), can be cast to the winds. The seat of the Earls of Erroll, it has been gradually disintegrating since the roof was removed in 1925. Once, it had the finest dining room in Scotland. The waves crash below, as always. Be careful!

1792 8/S27
L
Hume Castle Hume This imposing, well-preserved ruin sits above the road and the countryside between Greenlaw and Kelso. Its impressive walls here since the 18th century from a 13th-century fortification. Marvellous views across the Merse as far as the English border.

The Best Prehistoric Sites

HS *Historic Scotland. Standard hours: Apr-end Sep 7 days 9.30am-5.30pm; Oct-Mar 9.30am-4.30pm. Local and winter variations.*

1793 1/P10
L
ADMISSION
HS

✓✓✓ **Skara Brae** Orkney Mainland · www.historic-scotland.gov. uk · 01856 841815 32km Kirkwall by A965/B9655 via Finstown and Dounby. Excellent visitor and orientation centre. Can be a windy (500m) walk to this remarkable shoreline site, the subterranean remains of a compact village 5,000 years old. It was engulfed by a sandstorm 600 years later and lay perfectly preserved until uncovered by the laird's dog after another storm in 1850. Now it permits one of the most evocative glimpses of truly ancient times in the UK.

1794 1/Q10
FREE
HS

✓✓ **The Standing Stones of Stenness** Orkney Mainland · www. historic-scotland.gov.uk Together with the **Ring of Brodgar** and the great chambered tomb of **Maes Howe**, all within 18km of Kirkwall, these are as impressive ceremonial sites as you'll find anywhere. From same period as Skara Brae. The individual stones and the scale of the Ring are very imposing and deeply mysterious. The burial cairn is the finest megalithic tomb in the UK. 500m walk from the visitor centre. Guided tour only. Note: tunnel entry is only 1m high! Seen together, they stimulate even the most jaded sense of wonder.

1795 3/F14
FREE
▢
HS

✓✓ **The Callanish Stones** Lewis · www.historic-scotland.gov.uk · 01851 621422 24km from Stornoway. Take Tarbert road and go right at Leurbost. The best preserved and most unusual combination of standing stones in a ring around a tomb, with radiating arms in cross shape. Predating Stonehenge, they were unearthed from the peat in the mid-19th century and are the Hebrides' major historical attraction. Other configurations nearby. At dawn and dusk, hardly anyone else is there. Visitor centre has a good caff (2242/HEBRIDES).

1796 5/M18
ATMOS
FREE
HS

✓ **Clava Cairns** nr Culloden · www.historic-scotland.gov.uk · 01667 460232 Here long before the most infamous battle in Scottish and other histories; another special atmos. Not so well signed but continue along the B9006 towards **Cawdor Castle**, that other great historical landmark (1758/CASTLES), taking a right at the Culloden Moor Inn; follow signs for Clava Lodge holiday homes, picking up HS sign to right. Chambered cairns in a grove of trees. They're really just piles of stones but the death rattle echo from 5,000 years ago is perceptible to all, especially when no one else is there. Remoteness probably inhibits New Age attentions and allows more private meditations in this extraterrestrial spot.

1797 2/V5
LL
FREE
HS

✓ **Mousa Broch** Shetland · www.historic-scotland.gov.uk · 01856 841815 On island of Mousa off Shetland mainland 20km S of Lerwick. To see it properly take the Mousa Boat www.mousa.co.uk 07901 872339 from Sandsayre Pier. Takes 15 mins. Isolated in its island fastness, this is the best-preserved broch in Scotland. Walls are 13m high (originally 15m) and galleries run up the middle, in one case to the top. Solid as a rock, this example of a uniquely Scottish phenomenon would have been a very des res. Also **Jarlshof** in the S next to Sumburgh airport has remnants and ruins from Neolithic to Viking times – 18th century, with especially impressive wheelhouses.

1798 8/M22 ✓ **Crannog Centre** Kenmore, nr Aberfeldy · www.crannog.co.uk On S
ADMISSION Loch Tay road 1km Kenmore. Superb reconstruction of Iron Age dwelling (there
are several under the loch). Credible and worthwhile archaeological project, great
for kids: conveys history well. Displays in progress and human story told by
pleasant costumed humans. Open Apr-Oct 10am-5.30pm. Great waterfall walk at
Acharn, 2km (1605/WATERFALLS). Eat Aberfeldy (941/PERTHSHIRE).

1799 7/H24 ✓ **Kilmartin Glen** nr Lochgilphead · www.historic-scotland.gov.uk An
HS important, easily accessible area. Possibly start 2km S of Kilmartin and 1km
(signed) from A816 and across road from car park, 2 distinct stone circles from a
long period of history between 3000-1200 BC. Story and speculations described
on boards. Pastoral countryside and wide skies. Look for the 'cup and saucer'!
There are apparently 150 other sites in the vicinity (c. 800 'ancient monuments'),
and an excellent museum and café (2124/HISTORY; 1402/TEAROOMS). Guided tours
of the glen leave from here. See also **Dunadd** (1934/HILLS) for a perspective of the
whole area.

1800 1/Q12 ✓ **Tomb of the Eagles** Orkney Mainland · www.tomboftheeagles.co.uk ·
ATMOS 01856 831339 33km S of Kirkwall at the foot of South Ronaldsay; signed from
ADMISSION Burwick. A relatively recent discovery, the excavation of this cliff cave is on private
land. You call in at the visitor centre first and they'll tell you the story. There's a
2km walk then you go in on a skateboard – no, really! Allow time; ethereal stuff.
Mar-Oct 9.30am-5.30pm (by appointment Nov-Feb).

1801 8/N25 **Cairnpapple Hill** nr Linlithgow · www.historic-scotland.gov.uk ·
ADMISSION 01506 634622 Approach from the Beecraigs road off W end of Linlithgow main
HS street. Go past the Beecraigs turn-off and continue for 3km. Cairnpapple is
signed. Astonishing Neolithic henge and later burial site on windy hill with views
from Highlands to Pentlands. Atmosphere made even more strange by the very
21st-century communications mast next door. Cute visitor centre! Summer only
9.30am-5.30pm but can be accessed any time.

1802 9/L30 **Cairnholy** between Newton Stewart & Gatehouse of Fleet · www.
FREE historic-scotland.gov.uk 2km off main A75. Signed from road. A mini-Callanish
HS of standing stones around a burial cairn on very human scale and in a serene
setting with another site (with chambered tomb) 150m up the farm track. Excellent
view – sit and contemplate what went on 4,000–6,000 years ago. I have it on good
authority that this is a great place to watch the sunrise over the Solway Firth.

1803 8/R21 **The Brown and White Caterthuns** Kirkton of Menmuir, nr Brechin & Edzell ·
L www.historic-scotland.gov.uk 5km uphill from war memorial at Menmuir,
FREE then signed 1km: a steep pull. Lay-by with obvious path to both on either side of
HS the road. White easiest (500m uphill). These Iron Age hill top settlements give
tremendous sense of scale and space and afford an impressive panorama of the
Highland line. Colours refer to the heather-covered turf and stone of one and the
massive collapsed ramparts of the White. Sit here for a while and picture the Pict.

1804 4/Q13 **The Grey Cairns of Camster** nr Wick · www.historic-scotland.gov.uk ·
FREE 01667 460232 20km S of Wick, a very straight road (signed for Cairns) heads
HS W from the A9 for 8km. The cairns are instantly identifiable near the road and
impressively complete. The 'horned cairn' is the best in the UK. In 2,500 BC these
stone-piled structures were used for the disposal of the dead. You can crawl inside
them if you're agile (or at night, brave). There are many other sights signed off the
A9/99 but also interesting and nearby is:

1805 4/Q14   **Hill o' Many Stanes** nr Wick · www.historic-scotland.gov.uk · 01667 460232
FREE   Aptly named place with extraordinary number of small standing stones; 200 in 22
rows. If fan shape was complete, there would be 600. Their very purposeful layout
is enigmatic and strange.

1806 9/L31   **The Whithorn Story** Whithorn · www.whithorn.com Excavation site (though
ADMISSION   not active), medieval priory, shrine of St Ninian, visitor centre and café. More than
enough to keep the whole family occupied – enthusiastic staff. Christianity? Look
where it got us: this is where it started in Scotland. Also 1559/VILLAGES. Easter-Oct.

1807 8/M25   **Bar Hill** Twechar, nr Kirkintilloch A fine example of the low ruins of a Roman
FREE   fort on the Antonine Wall which ran across Scotland for 200 years early AD. Great
place for an out-of-town walk (754/VIEWS).

1808 5/H19   **The Brochs** Glenelg · www.historic-scotland.gov.uk · 01667 460232 110km
HS   from Fort William. Glenelg is 14km from the A87 at Shiel Bridge (1618/SCENIC
ROUTES). 5km from Glenelg village in beautiful Glen Beag. The 2 brochs, Dun
Trodden and Dun Telve, are the best preserved examples on the mainland of these
mysterious 1st-century homesteads. Easy here to distinguish the twin stone walls
that kept out the cold and the more disagreeable neighbours. Brilliant pub (food
and rooms) in village (1173/INNS).

1809 3/D17   **Barpa Langass** North Uist 8km S of Lochmaddy, visible from main A867 road,
FREE   like a stone hat on the hill (200m walk). A squashed beehive burial cairn dating
from 1,000 BC, the tomb of a chieftain. It's largely intact and the small and nimble
can explore inside, crawling through the short entrance tunnel and down through
the years. Nice hotel nearby (1204/GET-AWAY HOTELS) where a circular walk starts,
taking in this site and the loch (direction board 2.5km).

1810 6/S19   **Aberdeenshire Prehistoric Trail: East Aquhorthies Stone Circle** nr
FREE   Inverurie · www.historic-scotland.gov.uk · 01667 460232 4km from Inverurie.
HS   Signed from B993 from Inverurie to Monymusk. A circle of pinkish stones with
2 grey sentinels flanking a huge recumbent stone set in the rolling countryside of
the Don Valley. **Bennachie** over there, then as now (1943/HILLS)!

1811 6/S18   **Loanhead of Daviot Stone Circle** nr Inverurie · www.historic-scotland.gov.uk
ATMOS   Head for the village of Daviot on B9001 from Inverurie; or Loanhead, signed off
FREE   A920 road between Oldmeldrum and Insch. The site is 500m from top of village.
HS   Impressive and spooky circle of 11 stones and one recumbent from 4,000/5,000
BC. Unusual second circle adjacent encloses a cremation cemetery from 1,500 BC.
Remains of 32 people were found here. Obviously, an important place. God knows
what they were up to.

1812 6/R19   **Tomnaverie Stone Circle** nr Tarland and Aboyne · www.historic-scotland.
gov.uk · 01667 460232 Less visited or even known than the above so here
you really are likely to take in its mystery and the panoramic view of bucolic
Aberdeenshire and distant Lochnagar without distraction. An easily imaginable
circle from 2,500 BC: a long time then! Leave A93 near Aboyne Academy for
Tarland, 6km just before the town, 300m uphill walk from car park.

Great Country Houses

NTS *National Trust for Scotland. Hours vary. Admission.*
HS *Historic Scotland. Standard hours: Apr–end Sep 9.30am–5.30pm;*
Oct–Mar 9.30am–4.30pm. Some local variations. All charge admission.
☕ *signifies notable café.*

1813 8/R27 ✓✓ **Abbotsford** nr Melrose · www.scottsabbotsford.com ·
01896 752043 The beautiful home built by Sir Walter Scott and lived in until his death. Scott was once the world's most successful novelist and the man who practically invented the romantic image of Scotland and, in so doing, tourism. A recent major makeover returned the house to its original splendour – it's exactly as he left it, and the gardens are pristine and peaceful. Lovely aspect overlooking the Tweed, all strollable and it's on the Borders Abbeys Way (www.bordersabbeysway.com). Excellent interpretation and exhibition building as you arrive with Ochiltree's café/restaurant above – a terrace offers a first aerial view of the policies. 10am–4/5pm.

1814 7/K26 ✓✓ **Mount Stuart** Bute · www.mountstuart.com · 01700 503877
L   Unique Victorian Gothic house; echoes 3rd Marquess of Bute's passion for
ATMOS   mythology, astronomy, astrology and religion. Amazing splendour in intimate and
☕   romantic atmos. Italian antiques, notable paintings, fascinating detail with humorous touches. Equally grand gardens with fabulous walks, sea views. Stylish visitor centre/café and coffee shop, as well as curated artworks in the wooded grounds. Apr–Oct 11.30am–4pm. Best check whether a day for hourly guided tours or free-flow admission. Grounds 10am–6pm. Allow a bit of time here.

1815 6/S18 ✓✓ **Haddo House** nr Ellon, Aberdeenshire · www.nts.org.uk ·
L   01651 851440 Designed by William Adam for the Earl of Aberdeen, the
☕   Palladian-style mansion itself by guided tour only (must book) but the serenely
NTS   superb grounds open always. Not so much a house, more a leisure land in the best possible taste, grounds with bluebells, wild garlic and autumn trees, a pleasant café, estate shop and gentle education. Grand house, full of things; the basements are the places to ponder. Glorious window by Burne-Jones in the chapel. Occasional afternoon teas followed by evening service: heaven (May–Oct)! Limited programme of other events. Gardens AYR till sunset.

1816 8/S26 ✓✓ **Manderston** Duns · www.manderston.co.uk · 01361 883450
LL   Off A6105, 2km down Duns-Berwick road. Swan song of the Great
ATMOS   Classical House, one of the UK's finest examples of Edwardian opulence. *The Edwardian CH* of TV fame. The family still lives here. Below stairs as fascinating as up (the famous silver staircase!); sublime gardens (do see the woodland garden across the lake and the marble dairy). May–Sep, Thu/Sun 1.30pm–4.15pm (last entry). Gardens 11.30am–dusk AYR.

1817 8/Q27 ✓✓ **Traquair** Innerleithen · www.traquair.co.uk · 01896 830323
I   3km from A72 Peebles-Galashiels road. Archetypal romantic Border retreat steeped in Jacobite history (ask about the Bear gates). Human proportions, liveability and lots of atmos. An enchanting house, a maze (20th century) and tranquil duck pond in the garden. Traquair ale still brewed. 1745 cottage tearoom, pottery and candlemaking. Apr–Oct House 11am–5pm (Oct 11am–4pm, Nov weekends only). Cool events programme, including main Traquair Fair and Festival of Literature & Thought, both Aug.

1818 8/Q25
✓✓ **Newhailes House** Musselburgh · www.nts.org.uk · 0131 653 5599
Well signed from Portobello end of Musselburgh (3km). NTS flagship
NTS time-capsule project stabilising the microcosm of 18th-century history
encompassed here and uniquely intact. Great rococo interiors, very liveable,
especially library. A rural sanctuary near the city: parklands, shell grotto, summer
house. Easter and May-Sep, Thu-Mon, noon-5pm. Tours last 1 hour 15 mins. Book:
0844 493 2125.

1819 8/L28
✓✓ **Dumfries House** nr Cumnock · www.dumfries-house.org.uk ·
HS 01290 425959 One of the finest Palladian mansions in the country saved
for the nation by a consortium led by Prince Charles (and £5M from the Scottish
Government). The 750 acres and 18th-century apartments with their priceless
Chippendale furniture and pristine artefacts are to open to the public, as are the
emerging landscaped gardens (1505/GARDENS). Great walks in the grounds, café,
guest house (799/AYRSHIRE) and restaurant. Check website for hours.

1820 8/T26
✓ **Paxton** nr Berwick · www.paxtonhouse.co.uk · 01289 386291 Off B6461
to Swinton and Kelso, 5km from A1. Country park and Adam mansion with
Chippendales and Trotters; the picture gallery is a National Gallery outstation.
80 acres of woodlands to walk. Good adventure playground. Restored Victorian
boathouse and salmon fishing museum on the Tweed. Red-squirrel hide. Event
programme including indoor and outdoor performance; in September, a Regency
Ball. Tours (1 hour) every 45 mins, end Mar-Oct 10am-5pm. Garden 10am-sunset.

1821 8/Q25
✓ **Gosford House** nr Aberlady · www.gosfordhouse.co.uk · 01875 870808
On A198 between Longniddry and Aberlady, Gosford estate is behind a high
wall and strangely stunted vegetation. Imposing house with centre block by Robert
Adam and the wing you visit by William Young who did Glasgow City Chambers.
The Marble Hall houses the remarkable collections of the unbroken line of Earls of
Wemyss. Priceless art, informally displayed. Phone for opening times and tours.
Walk in the superb grounds AYR. Park by the Bothy farm shop/café signed.
Edinburgh side of Aberlady (car park closes 5pm).

1822 8/S27
LL **Floors Castle** Kelso · www.roxburghe.net · 01573 223333 More vast mansion
than old castle, the ancestral home of the Duke of Roxburghe, overlooks with
imposing grandeur the town and the Tweed. 18th-century with later additions.
You're led round lofty public rooms past family collections of fine furniture,
tapestries and porcelain. Priceless; spectacularly impractical. Excellent garden
centre (2187/GARDEN CENTRES) and tearoom, **The Terrace Café** (1389/TEAROOMS),
and another by the house. Apr-Oct 10.30am-5pm. Tours 01573 227660.

1823 8/R27 **Mellerstain** nr Gordon/Kelso · www.mellerstain.com · 01573 410225 Home
of the Earl of Haddington, signed from A6089 (Kelso-Gordon) or A6105 (Earlston-
Greenlaw). One of Scotland's great Georgian houses, begun by William Adam in
1725, completed by Robert. Outstanding decorative interiors (the ceilings are *sans
pareil*) especially the library and spectacular exterior 1761; it is truly a stately home.
Easter weekend and May-Sep Fri-Mon. Courtyard teahouse 11.30am-4.30pm and
beautiful gardens 11.30am-5pm.

1824 8/R26 **Thirlestane** Lauder · www.thirlestanecastle.co.uk · 01578 722430 2km
off A68. Castellated/baronial seat of the Earls and Duke of Lauderdale and family
home of the Maitlands. Extraordinary staterooms, especially plasterwork; the
ceilings must be seen to be believed. The nurseries (with toy collection), kitchens
and laundry are more approachable. Adventure playground. Quiet meadow.
Opening times vary.

1825 6/S18 **Fyvie** Aberdeenshire · www.nts.org.uk · 01651 891266 40km NW of
🖥 Aberdeen, an important stop on the Castle Trail which links the great houses of
NTS Aberdeenshire. Before opulence fatigue sets in, see this pleasant baronial pile
first. Lived-in until the 1980s, it feels less remote than most. 13th-century origins,
Edwardian interiors. Fantastic roofscape and ceilings. Restored racquets court and,
yes, bowling alley. Good tearoom. Tree-lined acres; lochside walks. Apr-Oct noon-
5pm; Sat-Wed July/Aug daily 11am-5pm. Grounds AYR.

1826 6/S20 **Crathes** nr Banchory · www.nts.org.uk · 01330 844525 25km W of Aberdeen
L on A93. In superb gardens (1502/GARDENS), a fairy-tale castle: a tower house which
🖥 is actually interesting to visit. Up and down spiral staircases and into small but
NTS liveable rooms. Timed tickets, one-way system. The notable painted ceilings and
the Long Gallery at the top are all worth lingering over. 350 years of the Burnett
family are ingrained in this oak. Apr-Oct 10.30am-4.45pm; till 3.45pm winter. Last
entry 45 mins before. Big event programme. Grounds AYR 9.30am-dusk. Go Ape
playground. Courtyard tearoom and nearby 989/NE RESTAURANTS.

✓✓ **Drumlanrig** Thornhill The art! The courtyard, the park. Report:
1529/PARKS.

Great Monuments, Memorials & Follies

These sites are open at all times and free unless otherwise stated.

1827 7/F27 ✓✓ **The American Monument** Islay · www.islayinfo.com On the SW
1-A-2 peninsula of the island, known as the Oa (pronounced Oh) 10km from Port
II Ellen. A monument to commemorate the shipwrecks nearby of 2 American ships,
ATMOS the *Tuscania* and the *Otranto*. The obelisk overlooks this sea – which is often beset
by storms – from a spectacular headland, the sort of disquieting place where you
could imagine looking round and finding the person you're with has disappeared.
Take road from Port Ellen past Maltings marked Mull of Oa, then 8km. Signed off
the road. Park, then a spectacular 1.5km clifftop walk to monument. Can do 6km
round trip. Birdlife good in Oa area (RSPB reserve).

1828 8/N24 ✓✓ **Wallace Monument** Stirling · www.nationalwallacemonument.com ·
LL 01786 472140 Visible for miles and with great views, though not as
dramatic as Stirling Castle. Approach from A91 or Bridge of Allan road. 150m walk
from car park (or minibus) and 246 steps up. Victorian gothic spire marking the
place where Scotland's great patriot swooped down upon the English at the Battle
of Stirling Bridge. Mel Gibson's *Braveheart* increased visitors mid 90s. Thankfully,
the recent makeover has consigned Mel to history! In the 'Hall of Heroes' the
heroines section requires a feminist leap of the imagination. The famous sword is
very big. Clifftop walk through Abbey Craig woods is worth detour. Monument open
daily AYR. Caff not great. Nice woodland walks.

1829 5/F16 **The Grave of Flora Macdonald** Skye Kilmuir on A855, Uig-Staffin road, 40km
ADMISSION N of Portree. A 10ft-high Celtic cross supported against the wind, high on the ridge
overlooking the Uists from whence she came. Long after the legendary journey, her
funeral in 1790 attracted the biggest crowd since Culloden. The present memorial
replaced the original, which was chipped away by souvenir hunters. Dubious
though the whole business may have been, she still helped to shape the folklore of
the Highlands.

1830 8/R27 **Peniel Heugh** nr Ancrum Pronounced Pinal-Hue. An obelisk visible
LL for miles and on a rise offering some of the most exhilarating views of the
Borders. Also known as the Waterloo Monument, it was built on the Marquess
of Lothian's estate to commemorate the battle. It's said that woodland on
the slopes around represents the positions of Wellington's troops. From A68
opposite Ancrum turn-off on B6400, go 1km past Monteviot Gardens up steep,
unmarked road to left (cycle sign; monument not marked) for 150m; sign says
Vehicles Prohibited, etc. Park, walk up through woods. Great organic caff nearby
(1386/TEAROOMS).

1831 8/R25 **The Hopetoun Monument** Athelstaneford, nr Haddington · www.
L eastlothian.gov.uk The 30m needle atop a rare rise in East Lothian (Byres Hill)
and a great vantage point from which to view the county from the Forth to the
Lammermuirs and Edinburgh over there. Off A6737 Haddington to Aberlady road
on B1343 to Athelstaneford. Car park and short climb. Tower usually open and
viewfinder boards at top but take a torch; it's a dark climb (132 steps). Good gentle
ridge walk east from here.

1832 8/P25 **The Tower at the House of the Binns** nr Linlithgow · www.nts.org.uk Off
NTS A904 W from the access road at the Forth Road Bridge. This is the perfect chess-
piece castle or tower that sits so proudly on the horizon with its saltire blowing
behind the NTS-managed House of the Binns. The austere house, home of the
Dalyell family since 1612 (including Our Tam who asked the famous West Lothian
Question) ain't intrinsically interesting (Jun-Sep, Sat-Wed 2-5pm) but the view of
the Forth from the tower, which was built for a bet and cost £29 10 shillings, is
splendid. Park by the house and walk 250m. Grounds open AYR till 7pm/dusk.

1833 8/N25 **The Pineapple** Airth · www.landmarktrust.org · 01628 825925 From Airth
N of Grangemouth, take A905 to Stirling and after 1km the B9124 for Cowie. It
sits on the edge of a walled garden at the end of the drive. 45ft high, it was built
in 1761 as a garden retreat by an unknown architect and remained 'undiscovered'
until 1963. How exotic the fruit must have seemed in the 18th century, never
mind this extraordinary folly. Grounds open AYR. Oddly enough, you can stay here
(2 bedrooms, Landmark Trust). The gardens are kept by NTS (National Trust for
Scotland) and there's a figure-of-eight walk that takes in Dunmore village and the
River Forth.

1834 4/L12 **John Lennon Memorial** Durness In a garden created in 2002 (a BBC *Beechgrove
Garden* project) amazing in itself surviving these harsh, very northern conditions,
an inscribed slate memorial to JL who for many years as a child came here with
his aunt for the hols. 'There are places I'll remember all my life' from *Rubber Soul*.
Who'd have thought that song (*In My Life*) was about here? There's also a piece by
national treasure, ceramic artist **Lotte Glob** (2137/GALLERIES). Garden upkept by
volunteers.

1835 4/N15 **The Monument on Ben Bhraggie** Golspie Atop the hill (pronounced Brachee)
L that surmounts the town, the domineering statue and plinth (over 35m) of the
dreaded first Duke of Sutherland; many have campaigned to have it demolished;
yet it survives. Climb from town fountain on marked path. The hill racers go up in
mins but allow 2 hours return. His private view along the NE coast is superb (1771/
CASTLES; 1509/GARDENS) and for background 2117/HISTORY.

1836 7/K20 **The Commando Monument** nr Spean Bridge On prominent rise by the A82
L Inverness to Fort William road where the B8004 cuts off to Gairlochy 3km N of
Spean Bridge. Commemorates the Commandos who gave their lives in the Second
World War and who trained in this area. Spectacular visa and poignant memorial
garden to troops lost in more recent conflicts, including the Iraq and Afghan wars.

1837 7/H23 **McCaig's Tower or Folly** Oban Oban's great landmark on Battery Hill built
L in 1897 by McCaig, a local banker, to give 'work to the unemployed' and as a
memorial to his family. Built from Bonawe granite, it's like a temple or coliseum
and time has mellowed whatever incongruous effect it may have had originally.
The views of the town and the bay are magnificent and it's easy to get up from
several well-signed points in town centre.

1838 6/Q20 **The Victoria Memorial to Albert** Balmoral Atop the fir-covered hill behind the
L house, she raised a monument, the **Albert Cairn**, whose distinctive pyramid shape
can be seen peeping over the crest from all over the estate. Desolated by his death,
the broken-hearted widow had this memorial built in 1862 and spent so much time
here, she became a recluse; the British Empire trembled. Path begins at shop on
way to Lochnagar distillery, 45 mins up, 460 feet above sea level. Forget **Balmoral**
(1770/CASTLES), all the longing and love for Scotland can be felt here, the great
estate laid out below.

1839 6/S18 **The Prop of Ythsie** nr Aberdeen 35km NW of city near Ellon to W of A92, or
L pass on the Castle Trail since this monument commemorates one George Gordon
of Haddo House nearby, who was prime minister 1852-55 (the good-looking guy in
the first portrait you come to in the house 1815/HOUSES). Tower visible from all of
rolling Aberdeenshire and there are reciprocal views should you take the easy but
unclear route up. On B999 Aberdeen-Tarves road (Haddo–Pitmedden on the Castle
Trail) and 2km from entrance to house. Take road for the Ythsie (pronounced Icy)
farms, car park 100m. Don't miss the stone circle nearby.

1840 9/L30 **Murray's Monument** nr New Galloway Above A712 road to Newton Stewart
L about halfway between. A fairly austere needle of granite to commemorate a
'shepherd boy', one Alexander Murray, who rose to become a professor of Oriental
Languages at Edinburgh University in the early 19th century. A 10-min walk up for
fine views of Galloway Hills; pleasant waterfall nearby. Just as he, barefoot...

1841 8/R27 **Smailholm Tower** nr Kelso & St Boswells · www.historic-scotland.gov.uk ·
L 01573 460365 The classic Border tower which inspired Walter Scott; plenty of
ATMOS history and romance in a bucolic setting. Picnic or whatever. Good views from its
ADMISSION crags. Near main road B6404 or off smaller B6937 – well signposted. Open Apr-Sep
HS 9.30am-6.30pm. But fine to visit at any time (1627/SCENIC ROUTES).

Scott Monument Princes Street, Edinburgh Report: 470/VIEWS.

The Most Interesting Churches

*Generally open unless otherwise stated; those marked * have public services.*

1842 8/Q26 ✓✓✓ ***Rosslyn Chapel** Roslin · www.rosslynchapel.com · 0131 440 2159
L 12km S of Edinburgh city centre. Take A702, then A703 from ring-route
ATMOS road, marked Penicuik. Roslin village 2km from main road and chapel 500m from
village crossroads above Roslin Glen. Medieval but firmly on the world map because
of *The Da Vinci Code*. Grail seekers have been coming forever but now a whole
experience – chapel, tour, visitor centre, coffee and gift shop – is available. No
doubting the atmos in this temple to the Templars and all holy meaningful stuff in a
Foucault's Pendulum sense. But a special place. Recent major restoration. A working
Episcopalian church. Mon-Sat 9.30am-4.30pm (last admission), noon-4.15pm Sun
(last admission). Walk in the glen (450/WALKS). Coffee shop.

1843 7/K23 ✓✓ ***St Conan's Kirk** Loch Awe · www.stconanskirk.org.uk ·
LL 01838 200298 A85 33km E of Oban. Perched among trees on the side of
ATMOS Loch Awe, this small but spacious church seems to incorporate every ecclesiastical
architectural style. Its building was a labour of love for one Walter Campbell who
was perhaps striving for beauty rather than consistency. Though modern (begun by
him in 1881 and finished by his sister and a board of trustees in 1930), the result is
a place of ethereal light and atmos, enhanced by and befitting the inherent
spirituality of the setting. There's a spooky carved effigy of Robert the Bruce, a cosy
cloister and the most amazing flying buttresses. Big atmos.

1844 1/R11 ✓✓ **The Italian Chapel** Lamb Holm, Orkney · www.visitorkney.com ·
LL 01856 872856 8km S of Kirkwall at Lamb Holm, the first causeway on the
ATMOS way to St Margaret's Hope. In 1943, Italian PoWs transformed a Nissen hut, using
the most meagre materials, into this remarkable ornate chapel completed at the
end of the war in 1945. The meticulous *trompe l'œil* and wrought-iron work are a
touching affirmation of faith. Open AYR, daylight hours. At the other end of the
architectural scale, **St Magnus Cathedral** in Kirkwall is a great edifice, but also
imbues spirituality.

1845 8/M25 ✓✓ **Queen's Cross Church** 870 Garscube Road, Glasgow · www.
ADMISSION mackintoshchurch.com · 0141 946 6600 Set where Garscube Rd
becomes Maryhill Rd at Springbank St. C.R. Mackintosh's only church. Fascinating
and unpredictable in every part of its design. Some elements reminiscent of
Glasgow School of Art (built in the same year 1897) and others, like the tower,
evoke medieval architecture. Bold and innovative, now restored and functioning as
the headquarters of The Mackintosh Society. Apr-Oct: Mon-Fri 10am-5pm;
Nov-Mar: Mon, Wed, Fri 10am-4pm. No services. See 768/MACKINTOSH.

1846 9/N28 ✓ ***Durisdeer Parish Church** nr Abington & Thornhill · www.
L scotlandschurchestrust.org.uk Off A702 Abington-Thornhill road and 3km
ATMOS off the Edinburgh road, near **Drumlanrig** (1529/PARKS). If I lived near this delightful
village in the hills, I'd go to church more often. It's exquisite and the history of
Scotland is in the stones. The Queensberry marbles (1709) are displayed in the
north transept (enter behind church) and there's a cradle roll and a list of ministers
from the 14th century. The plaque to the two brothers who died at Gallipoli is
especially touching. Covenanter tales are writ on the gravestones.

1847 7/K26 ✓ ***Cathedral Of The Isles** Cumbrae · 01475 530006 Frequent ferry service
from Largs is met by bus for 6km journey to Millport. Lane from main street by
Newton pub, 250m then through gate. The smallest cathedral in Europe, one of

Butterfield's great works (other is Keble College in Oxford). Here, small is outstandingly beautiful and absolutely quiet except Sundays in summer when there are concerts. Can stay (1258/RETREATS); see also 1374/CAFÉS.

1848 6/Q19 ✓ **The Chapel at Migvie** nr Tarland and Aboyne An extraordinary tiny chapel on a farm in the midst of Aberdeenshire, hardly known, rarely visited. And yet when you open the door (and wait) the lights go on to reveal a Tardis-like space somewhere between a crypt and an art gallery. Local artists working with glass, stone, paint and poetry have created this homely homage by Philip Astor, in memory of his mum and dad. Wonderfully affecting. To find this very secret place head N from Dinnet on the A93 halfway between Ballater and Aboyne, past the signed **Burn o' Vat** (1921/ENCHANTING PLACES) on the A97 for 12km, Migvie, a farming hamlet, 2km E. You'll see it, then you'll get it! It's always open.

1849 3/E16 HS **St Clement's** Rodel, South Harris · www.historic-scotland.gov.uk Tarbert 40km. Classic island kirk in Hebridean landscape. Go by the **Golden Road** (1625/SCENIC ROUTES). Simple cruciform structure with tower, which the adventurous can climb. Probably influenced by Iona. Now an empty but atmospheric shell, with blackened effigies and important monumental sculpture. Goats in the churchyard graze among the headstones of all the young Harris lads lost at sea in the Great War. There are other fallen angels on the outside of the tower. Decent family hotel adjacent (2242/HEBRIDES).

1850 3/D19 ***St Michael's Chapel** Eriskay, nr South Uist/Barra · 01878 700305 That rare example of an ordinary modern church without history or grand architecture, which has charm and serenity and imbues the sense of well-being that a religious centre should. The focal point of a relatively devout Catholic community who obviously care for it. Overlooking the Sound of Barra. Edifying whatever your religion.

1851 8/N25 HS ***Culross Abbey Church** www.historic-scotland.gov.uk Top of Forth-side village of interesting buildings and windy streets (1553/VILLAGES). Worth hike up hill (signed; ruins adjacent) for views and for this well-loved and cared-for church. Great stained glass (see Sandy's window); often full of flowers.

1852 8/M24 HS ***Dunblane Cathedral** www.dunblanecathedral.org.uk · 01786 825388 Huge nave of a church, charmingly asymmetrical, built around a Norman tower (from David I) on the Allan Water and restored 1892. The wondrously bright stained glass is mostly 20th century. The poisoned sisters buried under the altar helped change the course of Scottish history. A contemplative place! Summer concerts and once when I was there our Andy (Murray) got married.

1853 6/T19 ***St Machar's Cathedral** Aberdeen · www.stmachar.com · 01224 485988 The Chanonry in Old Aberdeen off St Machar's Drive about 2km from centre. Best seen as part of a walk round the old village within the city occupied mainly by the university. The cathedral's fine granite nave and twin-spired West Front date from 15th century, on site of 6th-century Celtic church. Noted for heraldic ceiling and 19/20th-century stained glass. Seaton Park adjacent has pleasant Don-side walks and there's the old Brig o' Balgownie. Church open daily 9.30am-4.30pm.

1854 8/R27 ***Bowden Kirk** nr Newtown St Boswells Signed from A68 (the A699), 500m off the main street. Beneath the **Eildons** (1947/HILL WALKS) in classic rolling Border country, an atmospheric 17th-century kirk of 12th century origin. Beautiful setting in one of southern Scotland's prettiest villages. Sun service 9.30am. Eat in Melrose or St Boswells, p. 158–59.

1855 8/S26 **Fogo Parish Church** Fogo, nr Greenlaw Go find this sweet historic church by the Blackadder, the quintessential Berwickshire river. 17th century from 12th century origins: lairds' lofts, box pews. Rural, and spiritual; be alone.

1856 8/Q25 ***The East Lothian Churches** Aberlady, Whitekirk, Athelstaneford &
8/R25 Garvald 4 charming churches in bucolic settings; quiet corners to explore and reflect, though sadly these churches are not usually open. Easy to find. All have interesting local histories and in the case of Athelstaneford, a national resonance: a vision in the sky near here inspired the flag of Scotland, the saltire. The spooky Doocot Heritage Centre behind the church explains. Aberlady is my favourite, Garvald a days-gone-by village with pub.

1857 8/P25 **Abercorn Church** nr South Queensferry Off A904. 4km W of roundabout at Forth Bridge, just after village of Newton, Abercorn is signed. 11th-century kirk nestling among ancient yews in a sleepy hamlet, untouched since Covenanter days. St Ninian said to have preached to the Picts here and though hard to believe, Abercorn was once on a par with York and Lindisfarne in religious importance. Church always open. Walk in woods from corner stile or the Hopetoun Estate.

1858 4/L16 **Croick Church** Bonar Bridge · www.croickchurch.com 16km W of
L Ardgay, just over the river from Bonar Bridge and through the splendid glen of
ATMOS **Strathcarron** (1588/GLENS). This humble and charming church is remembered for its place in the story of the Highland Clearances. In May 1845, 90 folk took shelter in the graveyard around the church after they had been cleared from their homes in nearby Glencalvie. Not allowed even in the kirk, their plight did not go unnoticed and was reported in *The Times*. The harrowing account is there to read, and the messages they scratched on the windows. Sheep graze all around then and now.

1859 8/L26 ***Thomas Coats Memorial Church** Paisley · www.paisley.org.uk Built by Coats (of thread fame), an imposing edifice, sometimes called the Baptist cathedral of Europe. A monument to God, prosperity and the Industrial Revolution. Viewing by arrangement 0141 587 8992. Sun service 11am.

1860 8/R25 ***The Lamp Of The Lothians St Mary's Collegiate** Haddington · www. stmaryskirk.co.uk Signed from east main street. A beautiful town church on the River Tyne, with good stained glass and interesting crypts and corners. Obviously at the centre of the community, a lamp as it were, in the Lothians. Tours, brass rubbings (Sat). Summer concert season. Coffee shop and gift shop. Don't miss the ancient orchard and St Mary's Pleasance medicinal garden: contemplate your condition. Daily and Sun service.

1861 8/P22 ***Dunkeld Cathedral** www.dunkeldcathedral.org.uk In town centre by lane to the banks of the Tay at its most silvery. Medieval splendour among lofty trees. Notable for 13th-century choir and 15th-century nave and tower. Parish church open for edifying services and other spiritual purposes. Lovely summer recitals.

1862 7/J20 **St Mary & St Finnan Church** Glenfinnan · www.glenfinnanchurch.org · 01687 450223 On A830 Fort William–Mallaig Road to the Isles (1631/SCENIC ROUTES), a beautiful (inside a bit crumbly; roof recently repaired) Catholic church in a spectacular setting. Queen Vic said she never saw a lovelier or more romantic spot (though she said that a lot). Late 19th century. Open daily, Sun mass 1pm.

St Giles' Cathedral Edinburgh Report: 433/ATTRACTIONS.

Glasgow Cathedral/University Chapel Report: 726/ATTRACTIONS.

The Most Interesting Graveyards

1863 8/M26
LL
ATMOS

Glasgow Necropolis www.glasgow.gov.uk The vast burial ground at the crest of the ridge, running down to the river, that was the focus of the original settlement of Glasgow. Everything began at the foot of this hill and, ultimately, ended at the top where many of the city's most famous (and infamous) sons and daughters are interred within the reach of the long shadow of John Knox's obelisk. Generally open dawn till dusk, but best if you can get the full spooky experience to yourself (possibly best not alone – though there is now CCTV). Tours: 0141 287 5064.

1864 8/Q25
ATMOS

Edinburgh Canongate Kirkyard On left of Royal Mile going down to Palace. Adam Smith and the tragic poet Robert Fergusson revered by Rabbie Burns (who raised the memorial stone in 1787 over his pauper's grave) are buried here in the heart of Auld Reekie on the Heritage Trail. Tourists can easily miss this one. **Greyfriars,** a place of ancient mystery, famous for the wee dog who guarded his master's grave for 14 years, for the plundering of graves in the early 18th century for the Anatomy School and for the graves of Allan Ramsay (prominent poet and burgher), James Hutton (the father of geology), William McGonagall (the 'world's worst poet') and sundry serious Highlanders. Annals of a great city are written on these stones. **Dean Cemetery** is an Edinburgh secret; my New Town lips are sealed.

1865 7/G25

Isle of Jura: Killchianaig graveyard in the north Follow road as far as it goes to Inverlussa, graveyard is on right, just before hamlet. Mairi Ribeach apparently lived until she was 128. **In the south at Keils** (2km from road N out of Craighouse, bearing left past Keils houses and through the deer fence), her father is buried and he was 180! Both sites are beautiful, isolated and redolent of island history, with much to reflect on, not least the mysterious longevity of the inhabitants and that soon many of us may live this long.

1866 5/L18

Chisholm Graveyard nr Beauly Last resting place of the Chisholms and 3 of the largest Celtic crosses you'll see anywhere in a secret, atmospheric woodland setting. 15km W of Beauly on A831 to Struy after Aigas dam and 5km after golf course on right-hand side; 1km before Cnoc Hotel opposite Erchless Estate and through a white iron gate on right. Walk 150m on mossy path. Sublime!

1867 5/J19
LL

Clachan Duich nr Inverinate A beautiful stonewalled graveyard at the head of Loch Duich just S of Inverinate, 20km S of Kyle of Lochalsh. A monument on a rise above, a ruined chapel and many, many Macraes, this a delightful place to wander with glorious views to the loch and the mountains.

1868 7/J21

Eilean Munde nr Ballachulish The island and graveyard in Loch Leven around the chapel of St Fintan Munnu who travelled here from Iona in the 7th century; the church was rebuilt in the 18th. Notable apart from mystery and history because of the Stewarts buried here and also the Macdonalds and Camerons who maintained it despite their conflicts. You'll need a wee boat or kayak, probably from Lochaber Watersports at **Isles of Glencoe Hotel** (1138/KIDS).

1869 7/H28

Campbeltown Cemetery One of the nicest things about this end-of-the-line town is the cemetery. At the end of a row of posh houses, the original merchant and mariner owners of which will be interred in the leafy plots next door. Still in use after centuries of commerce and seafaring, it has crept up the terraces of a steep and lush overhanging bank. The white cross and row of WW2 headstones are affecting. **Royal Hotel** for sustenance (786/ARGYLL).

1870 7/K28 **Kirkoswald Kirkyard** nr Maybole & Girvan On main road through village between Ayr and Girvan. The graveyard around the ruined kirk and famous as the burial place of the characters in Burns' most famous poem, *Tam o' Shanter*. A must for Burns fans and famous-grave seekers with Souter Johnnie and Kirkton Jean buried here. **Souter Johnnie** himself gives his name to the restaurant and pub across the road: a great grub stop (1312/GASTROPUBS).

1871 8/Q26 **Humbie Churchyard** Humbie, East Lothian 25km SE of Edinburgh via A68 (turn-off at Fala). Deep in the woods with the burn besides, this is as reassuring a place to be buried as you could wish for; if you're set on cremation, come here and think of earth. I wrote this 25 years ago; these decisions come closer.

1872 8/R27 **Ancrum Churchyard** nr Jedburgh The quintessential country churchyard; away from the village (2km along B6400), by a lazy river (the Ale Water) crossed to a farm by a humpback bridge and a chapel in ruins. Elegiac and deeply peaceful. Great river swimming spot nearby (1675/SWIMMING). The Ancrum Cross Keys for excellent food and ale.

1873 8/L23 **Balquhidder Churchyard** Chiefly notable as the last resting place of one Rob Roy MacGregor who was buried in 1734 after causing a heap of trouble hereabouts and raised to immortality by Sir Walter Scott and then Michael Caton-Jones (the movie). Despite well-trodden path, setting is poignant. Sunday evening concerts have been held in the kirk Jul/Aug (check locally). Nice walk from back corner to the waterfall and then to **Rallying Place** (1651/VIEWS). Great long walk to **Brig o' Turk** (1981/GLEN & RIVER WALKS). Refresh at **Mhor 84** (831/CENTRAL).

1874 8/N24 **Logie Old Kirk** nr Stirling A crumbling chapel and an ancient, lovingly restored graveyard at the foot of the Ochils. The wall is round to keep out the demons, a burn gurgles beside and there are some fine and very old stones going back to the 16th century. Take road for Wallace Monument off A91, then first right. The old kirk is 500m beyond the new. The interpretation board is sponsored by the enigmatic-sounding Sons of the Rock. Continuing on this steep narrow road (then right at the T-junction) takes you onto the **Ochils** (1948/HILL WALKS).

1875 4/P14 **Tutnaguail** Dunbeath There are various spellings of this enchanting cemetery 5km from Dunbeath, Neil Gunn's birthplace. Found by walking up the strath he describes in his book *Highland River* (1908/LITERARY PLACES). With a white wall around it, this graveyard, which before the Clearances once served a valley community of 400 souls, can be seen for miles. Ask at heritage centre for route or see www.dunbeath-heritage.org.uk.

1876 8/Q23 **Birkhill Cemetery** Dundee Opened in 1989. Part of the city's Templeton Woods across the road (to Coupar Angus from the dual carriageway) from **Camperdown Park** (1546/PARKS; 2020/WALKS), this well-laid-out cemetery is a revelation. No other graveyard on these pages seems so well kept and well used. Garlands of flowers on the graves. Aesthetic and reflective. Many Islamic graves and a woodlands burial section beyond.

1877 5/H16 **Gairloch Old Graveyard** On the left as you arrive in Gairloch from the S by the golf course (where you park). Looking over the lovely bay and beach (1575/BEACHES), a green and tranquil spot to explore. Osgood Mackenzie of **Inverewe Gardens** (1500/GARDENS) is buried in the bottom-right corner (facing the sea) under a simple Celtic cross, wild ferns behind, among many other Mackenzies.

The Great Abbeys

NTS *National Trust for Scotland. Hours vary. Admission.*
HS *Historic Scotland. Standard hours are: Apr-end Sep Mon-Sat 9.30am–5.30pm. Oct-Mar 9.30am–4.30pm. Local variations.*

1878 7/F23
ATMOS
HS

✓✓ **Iona Abbey** www.historic-scotland.gov.uk · 01681 700512 This hugely significant place of pilgrimage for new age and old age pilgrims and tourists alike is reached from Fionnphort, SW Mull, by frequent CalMac Ferry (a 5-min crossing). Walk 1km. Here in 563 AD St Columba began his mission for a Celtic church that changed the face of Europe. Cloisters, graveyard of Scottish kings and, marked by a modest stone, the inscription already faded by the weather, the grave of John Smith, the patron saint of New Labour. Ethereal, clear light through the unstained windows may illuminate your contemplations. Great sense of being part of a universal church and community. Regular services. Good shop (2161/SCOTTISH SHOPS) and nearby galleries. Residential courses and accom (MacLeod Centre adjacent, 01681 700404). For many, this is best thing on or off Mull.

1879 6/P17
ATMOS

✓✓ **Pluscarden Abbey** between Forres & Elgin · www.pluscardenabbey.org · 01343 890257 The oldest abbey monastic community still working in the UK in one of the most spiritual of places. Founded by Alexander II in 1230 and being restored since 1948. Benedictine services (starting with Vigil and Lauds at 4.30am through Prime-Terce-Sext-None-Vespers and Compline at 7.50pm) open to the public. The ancient honey-coloured walls, brilliant stained glass, monks' Gregorian chant: the whole effect is a truly uplifting experience. The bell rings down the valley. Services aside, open to visitors 4.30am–8.30pm. See also 1253/RETREATS.

1880 8/L26

✓✓ **Paisley Abbey** www.paisleyabbey.org.uk · 0141 889 7654 In the town centre. An abbey founded in 1163, razed (by the English) in 1307 and with successive deteriorations and renovations ever since. Major restoration in the 1920s brought it to present-day cathedral-like magnificence. Exceptional stained glass (the recent window complementing the formidable Strachan East Window), an impressive choir and an edifying sense of space. Sunday services are superb, especially full-dress communion and there are open days and concerts. Abbey open AYR Mon-Sat 10am-3.30pm. Café/shop.

1881 8/R28
HS

✓✓ **Jedburgh Abbey** www.historic-scotland.gov.uk · 01835 863925 The classic abbey ruin; conveys the most complete impression of the Border abbeys built under the patronage of David I in the 12th century. Its tower and remarkable Catherine window are still intact. Excavations have unearthed a 12th-century comb. It's now displayed in the excellent visitor centre which brilliantly illustrates the full story of the Abbey's amazing history. Best view from across the Jed in the Glebe. My home town; my abbey! Check HS for hours.

1882 8/R27
ATMOS
HS

✓✓ **Dryburgh Abbey** nr St Boswells · www.historic-scotland.gov.uk · 01835 822381 One of the most evocative of ruins, an aesthetic attraction since the late 18th century. Sustained innumerable attacks from the English since its inauguration by Premonstratensian Canons in 1150. Celebrated by Sir Walter Scott, buried here in 1832 (with his biographer Lockhart at his feet), its setting, among huge cedar trees on the banks of the Tweed is one of pure historical romance. 4km A68. See also 1648/VIEWS. Hotel adjacent not what it was. Eat at **Main Street**, St Boswells (859/BORDERS).

1883 9/N30 **Sweetheart Abbey** New Abbey · www.historic-scotland.gov.uk ·
HS 01387 850397 12km S by A710. The endearing and enduring warm red sandstone abbey in the shadow of Criffel, so named because Devorguilla de Balliol, devoted to her husband (he of the Oxford college), founded the abbey for Cistercian monks and kept his heart in a casket which is buried with her here. No roof, but the tower is intact. The Abbey Cottage tearoom has good comforting food and even its own cookbook (so-so gift shop). Gaze at the ruins while eating your soup and cake.

1884 8/R27 **Melrose Abbey** www.historic-scotland.gov.uk · 01896 822562 Another
HS romantic setting, the abbey seems to lend class to the whole town. Once again built by David I (what a guy!) for Cistercian monks from Rievaulx from 1136. It once sustained a huge community, as evinced by the widespread excavations. There's a museum of abbey, church and Roman relics; soon to include Robert the Bruce's heart, recently excavated in the gardens. Tempting Tweed walks start here. Nearby caff better of late and numerous good food options in Melrose, p. 158–59.

1885 8/R22 **Arbroath Abbey** www.historic-scotland.gov.uk · 01241 878756 25km N
HS of Dundee. Founded in 1178 and endowed on an unparalleled scale, this is an important place in Scots history. It's where the Declaration was signed in 1320 to appeal to the Pope to release the Scots from the yoke of the English (you can buy facsimiles of the yellow parchment; the original is in the Scottish Records Office in Edinburgh – oh, and tea towels). It was to Arbroath that the Stone of Destiny (on which Scottish kings were traditionally crowned) was returned after being 'stolen' from Westminster Abbey in the 1950s and is now at Edinburgh Castle. Great interpretation centre before you tour the ruins.

▬▬▬ The Great Battlegrounds

NTS *National Trust for Scotland. Hours vary. Admission.*

1886 5/M18 ✓✓ **Culloden** nr Inverness · www.nts.org.uk · 0844 493 2159 Signed
ATMOS from A9 and A96 into Inverness and about 8km from town. This
NTS state-of-the-art visitor centre puts you in the picture, then there's a 10-min rooftop perspective or a 40-min through-the-battlefield walk. Positions of the clans and the troops marked out across the moor; flags enable you to get a real sense of scale. If you go in spring you see how wet and miserable the moor can be (the battle took place on 16 April 1746). No matter how many other folk are there wandering down the lines, a visit to this most infamous of battlefields can still leave a pain in the heart. Centre opening times vary but generally 9am-5.30pm. Ground open at all times for more personal Cullodens.

1887 8/N24 ✓✓ **Bannockburn** nr Stirling · www.battleofbannockburn.com ·
NTS 01786 812664 4km town centre via Glasgow road (it's well signposted) or junction 9 of M9 (3km), behind a sad hotel, a spanking new state-of-the-art visitor centre, where you can actually play the game of Battle. Some visitors might be perplexed as to why 24 Jun 1314 was such a big deal for the Scots and, apart from the 50m walk to the flag-pole and the huge statue, there's not a lot doing in the field. But the battle against the English did finally secure the place of Robert I (the Bruce) as King of Scots, paving the way for the final settlement with England 15 years later. The best place to see the famous wee burn is from below the magnificent Telford Bridge. Controversies still rage among scholars: on many aspects but nobody would question now its significance. In 2014, a festival 'Bannockburn Live', in which I had a hand, commemorated its 700 years.

1888 5/G18   **Battle of the Braes** Skye 10km Portree. Take main A850 road S for 3km then left, marked Braes, for 7km. Monument is on a rise on right. The last battle fought on British soil and a significant place in Scots history. When the Clearances, uninterrupted by any organised opposition, were virtually complete and vast tracts of Scotland had been depopulated for sheep, the Skye crofters finally stood up in 1882 to the Government troops and said enough is enough. A cairn has been erected near the spot where they fought on behalf of 'all the crofters of Gaeldom', a battle which led eventually to the Crofters Act which has guaranteed their rights ever since. At the end of this road at Peinchorran, there are fine views of Raasay (which was devastated by clearances) and Glamaig, the conical Cuillin, across Loch Sligachan. Great B&Bs, **Peinmore House** and **Canowindra**, at the start of Braes road (2239/SKYE B&BS).

1889 7/J21   **Glen Coe** Not much of a battle, of course, but one of the most infamous
LLL   massacres in British history. Much has been written (John Prebble's *Glencoe*
ATMOS   and others) and a discreetly located visitor centre provides audiovisual scenario. Macdonald monument near Glencoe village and the walk to the more evocative Signal Rock where the bonfire was lit, now a happy woodland trail in this doom-laden landscape. Many other great walks. See 1914/ENCHANTING PLACES; 1287/ GOOD PUBS.

1890 1/Q11   **Scapa Flow** Orkney Mainland & Hoy · www.scapaflow.co.uk · 01856 791300 Scapa Flow, surrounded by various of the southern Orkney islands, is one of the most sheltered anchorages in Europe. Hence the huge presence in Orkney of ships and personnel during both wars. The Germans scuttled 54 of their warships here in 1919 and many still lie in the bay. The *Royal Oak* was torpedoed in 1939 with the loss of 833 men. Much still remains of the war years: the rusting hulks, the shore fortifications, the Churchill Barriers and the ghosts of a long-gone army at Scapa and Lyness on Hoy. Evocative visitor centre, museum and naval cemetery at Lyness. Open Mar-Oct.

1891 8/R27   **Lilliard's Edge** nr St Boswells On main A68, look for Lilliard's Edge Caravan Park 5km S of St Boswells; park and walk back towards St Boswells to the brim of the hill (about 500m), then cross rough ground on right along ridge, following tree-line hedge. Marvellous view attests to strategic location. 200m along, a cairn marks the grave of Lilliard who, in 1545, joined the Battle of Ancrum Moor against the English 'loons' under the Earl of Angus. 'And when her legs were cuttit off, she fought upon her stumps'. An ancient poem etched on the stone records her legendary... feet. Hardly anyone goes/finds this place. If you do, let me know and I'll buy you lunch.

1892 8/N21   **Killiecrankie** nr Pitlochry The first battle of the Jacobite Risings where, in July
NTS   1689, the Highlanders lost their leader Viscount (aka Bonnie) Dundee, but won the battle, using the narrow Pass of Killiecrankie. One escaping soldier made a famous leap. Well-depicted scenario in visitor centre; short walk to 'The Leap'. Battle viewpoint and cairn is further along road to Blair Atholl, turning right and doubling back (3km from visitor centre). You get the lie of the land from here. Many good walks and the lovely **Killiecrankie Hotel** (913/PERTHSHIRE) for rest, refreshments and excellent food.

Mary, Charlie & Bob

HS Historic Scotland. Standard hours are: Apr-end Sep 7 days 9.30am–5.30pm. Oct-Mar 9.30am-4.30pm; and winter variations.

MARY, QUEEN OF SCOTS (1542–87)
Linlithgow Palace Where she was born. Report: 1772/RUINS.
Holyrood Palace Edinburgh And lived. Report: 421/ATTRACTIONS.

1893 8/M24 **Inchmahome Priory** Port of Menteith · www.historic-scotland.gov.uk
LL Priory ruins on the Isle of Rest in Scotland's only lake. Here the infant queen spent
HS her early years cared for by Augustinian monks. A short boat journey. Signal the
ferryman by turning the board to the island, much as she did. Apr-Oct 7 days. Last
trip 4.15pm (Oct till 3.15pm). **Lake Hotel** adjacent for great food (835/CENTRAL).

1894 8/R28 **Mary, Queen of Scots' House** Jedburgh In gardens via Smiths Wynd off main
street. Historians quibble but this long-standing museum claims to be *the* house
where she fell ill in 1566 but still made it over to visit the injured Bothwell at
Hermitage Castle 50km away. Tower house in good condition; displays and well-
told saga. Me and my brother used to play tennis in the garden. Mar-Nov 9.30am-
4.30pm, Sun 10.30am-4pm.

1895 8/P24 **Loch Leven Castle** nr Kinross · www.historic-scotland.gov.uk Well signed!
L The ultimate in romantic penitentiaries; on the island in the middle of the loch;
visible from the M90. Not much left of the ruin to fill the fantasy, but this is where
Mary spent 10 months in 1568 before her famous escape and final attempt to get
back the throne. Sailings Apr-Oct 10am-4.15pm last sailing (Oct 3.15pm), from pier
at the National Game Angling Academy (Pier Bar/café serves as you wait) in small
launch from Kirkgate Park. 7-min trip, return as you like.

1896 9/M31 **Dundrennan Abbey** nr Auchencairn · www.historic-scotland.gov.uk Mary
HS got around and there are innumerable places where she spent the night. This was
where she spent her last one on Scottish soil, leaving next day from Port Mary
(nothing to see there but a beach, 2km along the road skirting the sinister MoD
range, the pier long gone). The Cistercian abbey (established 1142) which harboured
her on her last night is now a tranquil ruin.
'In my end is my beginning,' she said, facing her execution 19 years later.

1897 8/R25 Her 'death mask' is displayed at **Lennoxlove House** nr Haddington · www.
lennoxlove.com; it does seem small for someone who was supposedly 6 feet tall!
Lennoxlove on road to Gifford. Apr-Oct Wed/Thu/Sun 1.30-4pm.

BONNIE PRINCE CHARLIE (1720–88)
1898 3/D19 **Prince Charlie's Bay or Strand** Eriskay The uncelebrated, unmarked and
L quietly beautiful beach where Charlie first landed in Scotland to begin the Jacobite
Rebellion. Nothing much has changed (except the pier for Barra ferry is adjacent)
and this crescent of sand with soft machair and a turquoise sea is still a special
place. 1km from township heading south; approach from township, not by the new
ferry road. 2206/ISLANDS.

1899 5/H20 **Loch Nan Uamh, The Prince's Cairn** nr Arisaig Pronounced Loch Na Nuan.
L 7km from Lochailort on A830 (1631/SCENIC ROUTES), 48km Fort William. Signed
ATMOS from the road (100m lay-by), a path leads down to the left. This is the traditional
spot where Charlie embarked for France in September 1746, having lost the battle
and the cause. The rocky headland also overlooks the bay and skerries where he'd

landed in July the year before to begin the campaign. This place was the beginning and the end and it has all the romance necessary to be utterly convincing. Is that a French ship out there in the mist? The movie still awaits.

1900 7/J20   **Glenfinnan** www.visitglenfinnan.co.uk Here he raised his standard to rally the
LL clans to the Jacobite cause. For a while on that day in August 1745 it looked as if few
NTS were coming. Then pipes were heard and 600 Camerons came marching from the valley (where the viaduct now spans). That must have been one helluva moment. It's thought that he actually stood on the higher ground but there is a powerful sense of place and history here. The visitor centre has an excellent map of Charlie's path through Scotland – somehow he touched all the most alluring places! Climb the tower or take the long view from Loch Shiel (1631/SCENIC ROUTES). Nice church 1km (1862/CHURCHES); notable hotel and bar (1211/SCOTTISH HOTELS).

Culloden nr Inverness Report: 1886/BATTLEGROUNDS.

ROBERT I, THE BRUCE (1274–1329)

1901 9/L29   **Bruce's Stone** Glen Trool, nr Newton Stewart 26km N by A714 via Bargrennan (8km to head of glen) on the **Southern Upland Way** (1967/LONG WALKS). The fair **Glen Trool** is a celebrated spot in Galloway Forest Park (1590/GLENS). The stone is signed (200m walk) and marks the area where Bruce's guerrilla band rained boulders onto the pursuing English in 1307 after routing the main army at Solway Moss. Good walks, including to **Merrick** which starts here (1936/HILLS).

1902 8/N24   **Bannockburn** nr Stirling The climactic battle in 1314, when Bruce decisively whipped the English and secured the kingdom (though Scotland was not legally recognised as independent until 1329). The scale and even the excitement of the skirmish can be visualised in the fancy (new 2014) visitor centre. See 1887/BATTLEGROUNDS.

1903 8/R22   **Arbroath Abbey** www.historic-scotland.gov.uk · 01241 878756 Not much
HS of the Bruce trail here, but this is where the famous Declaration was signed that was the attempt of the Scots nobility united behind him to gain international recognition of the independence they had won on the battlefield. What it says is stirring stuff; the original is in Edinburgh. Great interpretation centre. 9.30am-5.30pm.

1904 8/P25   **Dunfermline Abbey Church** www.dunfermlineabbey.co.uk Here, some
HS tangible evidence: his tomb. Buried in 1329, his remains were discovered wrapped in gold cloth when the site was being cleared for the new church in 1818. Many of the other great kings, the Alexanders I and III, were not so readily identifiable (Bruce's ribcage had been cut to remove his heart). With great national emotion he was reinterred under the pulpit. The church (as opposed to the ruins and Norman nave adjacent) is open Easter-Oct, winter for services. Great café in **Abbot House** through graveyard (2114/HISTORY). Look up and see Robert carved on the skyline.

1905 8/R27   **Melrose Abbey** www.historic-scotland.gov.uk On his deathbed Bruce asked
HS that his heart be buried here after it was taken to the Crusades to aid the army in their battles. A likely lead casket thought to contain it was excavated from the chapter house and it did date from the period. It was reburied here and is marked with a stone. Let's believe in this!

The Important Literary Places

1906 7/K28 **Robert Burns (1759–96)** Alloway, Ayr & Dumfries · www.robertburns. org A well-marked heritage trail through his life and haunts in Ayrshire and Dumfriesshire. **Alloway**: A good start with the (NTS) restoration of **Burns Cottage** www.burnsmuseum.org.uk and 1km away, the state-of-the-art **Museum**. Here, the bard has a legacy and interpretive centre worthy of his international stature and appeal (2106/HISTORY). Both open 7 days 10am-5pm, 5.30pm Apr-Sep. Also in Alloway, the Auld Brig o' Doon and the Auld Kirk where Tam o' Shanter saw the witches dance are evocative, and the Monument and surrounding gardens are lovely. Elsewhere: **Ayr**: The Auld Kirk off main street by river; graveyard with diagram of where his friends are buried; open at all times. **Dumfries**: The house where he spent his last years and mausoleum 250m away at back of a kirkyard stuffed with extravagant masonry. His howff in Dumfries, the **Globe Inn**, is very atmospheric – established in 1610 and still going strong (829/DUMFRIES). 10km N of Dumfries on A76 at **Ellisland Farm** (home 1788–91) possibly the most interesting site. The farmhouse with genuine memorabilia, eg his mirror, fishing rod, a poem scratched on glass, original manuscripts. There's his favourite walk by the river where he composed *Tam o' Shanter* and a strong atmos about the place. Open 7 days summer, closed Sun/Mon in winter. **Poosie Nansie's**, the pub he frequented in Mauchline, is a must (1292/GOOD PUBS). **Brow Well near Ruthwell** on the B725 20km S of Dumfries and near **Caerlaverock** (1714/BIRDS), is a quieter place, a well with curative properties where he went in the latter stages of his illness.

1907 8/S21 **Lewis Grassic Gibbon (1901–35)** Arbuthnott, nr Stonehaven · www. grassicgibbon.com Although James Leslie Mitchell left the area in 1917, this is where he was born and spent his formative years. Visitor centre (01561 361668; Mar-Oct 7 days 10am-4.30pm) at the end of the village (via B967, 16km S of Stonehaven off main A92) has details of his life and can point you in the direction of the places he writes about in his trilogy, *A Scots Quair*. The first part, *Sunset Song*, as depicted in the Terence Davies 2015 film, is generally considered to be one of the great Scots novels and this area, the **Howe of the Mearns**, is the place he so effectively evokes. Arbuthnott is reminiscent of 'Kinraddie' and the churchyard 1km away on the other side of road (the Kirk of St Ternan) still has the atmosphere of that time of innocence before the war which pervades the book. His ashes are here in a grave in a corner; the inscription: 'the kindness of friends/the warmth of toil/ the peace of rest'. From 1928 to when he died 7 years later, at the age of only 34, he wrote an incredible 17 books. From the Kirk go downhill to right, the wooden bridge over the Bervie: the Mearns as was.

1908 4/P14 **Neil Gunn (1891–1973)** Dunbeath, nr Wick · www.neilgunn.org.uk Scotland's foremost writer on Highland life, perhaps still not receiving the recognition he deserves, was brought up in this North East fishing village and based 3 of his greatest yarns here, particularly *Highland River*, which must stand in any literature as a brilliant evocation of place. The **Strath** in which it is set is below the house (nondescript, next to the shop) and makes for a great walk (1992/GLEN & RIVER WALKS). Commemorative statue by the harbour, not quite the harbour you imagine from the books. The excellent heritage centre (www.dunbeath-heritage.org.uk) depicts the Strath on its floor and has all info. Gunn also lived for many years near **Dingwall** and there is a memorial on the back road to Strathpeffer and a wonderful view in a place he often walked (on A834, 4km from Dingwall).

1909 8/P27   **James Hogg (1770–1835)** St Mary's Loch, Ettrick The Ettrick Shepherd who wrote one of the great works of Scottish literature, *The Private Memoirs and Confessions of a Justified Sinner*, was born, lived and died in the valleys of the **Yarrow** and the **Ettrick**, some of the most starkly beautiful landscapes in Scotland. **St Mary's Loch** on the A708 28km W of Selkirk: there's a commemorative statue looking over the loch and the adjacent and supernatural seeming Loch of the Lowes. On the strip of land between is **Tibbie Shiels** pub (and hotel), once a gathering place for the writer and his friends (e.g. Sir Walter Scott) though for food not so recommendable. Across the valley divide (11km on foot, part of the **Southern Upland Way** 1967/LONG WALKS), or 25km by road past the Gordon Arms, Yarrow, is the remote village of **Ettrick**, another monument and his grave (and Tibbie Shiels') in the churchyard.

1910 8/R27   **Sir Walter Scott (1771–1832)** Abbotsford, Melrose No other place in Scotland (and few anywhere) contains so much of a writer's life and work. This was the house he rebuilt from the farmhouse he moved to in 1812 in the countryside he did so much to popularise. The house, even recently lived in by his descendants, is now a major Borders tourist attraction (1813/HOUSES), sympathetically restored with an excellent visitor centre and café. Pleasant grounds and topiary and walks by the Tweed which the house overlooks. His grave is at **Dryburgh Abbey** (1882/ABBEYS). There are monuments to Walt famously in Edinburgh (470/VIEWS) and in George Square, Glasgow. Mar-Sep.

1911 8   **Robert Louis Stevenson (1850–94)** Edinburgh Though Stevenson travelled widely – lived in France, emigrated to America and died and was buried in Samoa – he spent his first 30 years in Edinburgh. He was born and brought up in the New Town, living at **17 Heriot Row** from 1857–80 which is still lived in (not open to the public). Most of his youth was spent in this newly built and expanding part of the city in an area bounded then by parkland and farms. Both the Botanics (427/ATTRACTIONS) and **Warriston Cemetery** are part of the landscape of his childhood. However, his fondest recollections were of the **Pentland Hills** and, virtually unchanged as they are, it's here that one is following most poignantly in his footsteps. The cottage at **Swanston** (a delightful village with some remarkable thatched cottages reached via the city bypass/Colinton turn-off or from Oxgangs Rd and a bridge over the bypass; the village nestles in a grove of trees below the hills and is a good place to walk from), also the ruins of **Glencorse Church**. A pleasant walk in Colinton Dell (**Water of Leith** 444/WALKS) can include **Colinton Parish Church**, where Stevenson often visited his grandfather, who was the minister. In 2013 a statue of RLS as a child was installed here. **The Writers' Museum** at Makars' Court has exhibits (and of many other writers). The **Hawes Inn** in South Queensferry where he wrote *Kidnapped* has had its history obliterated in brewery makeovers.

1912 8   **J.K. Rowling (b.1965)** Edinburgh · www.jkrowling.com Scotland's most successful and revered writer ever as the creator of Harry Potter, was famously an impecunious single mother scribbling away in Edinburgh coffee shops. The most mentioned is opposite the Festival Theatre and is now **Spoon** (144/BRASSERIES); the **Elephant House** (312/TEAROOMS) and makes the most of a tenuous connection. Harry Potter country as interpreted by Hollywood can be found at **Glenfinnan** (1900/CHARLIE) and **Glen Coe**, especially around the **Clachaig Inn** (1189/INNS).

1913 8   **Irvine Welsh (b.1958), Alexander McCall Smith (b.1948), Ian Rankin (b.1960) and Val McDermid (b.1955)** have an international readership, homes in Edinburgh and all have their haunts.

The Most Enchanting Places

1914 7/J21
2-B-2
LLL
ATMOS
The Lost Valley Glen Coe The secret glen where the ill-fated Macdonalds hid the cattle they'd stolen from the Lowlands and which became (with politics and power struggles) their undoing. A narrow wooded cleft takes you between the imposing and gnarled 3 Sisters hills and over the threshold (God knows how the cattle got there) and into the huge bowl of Coire Gabhail. The place envelops you in its tragic history, more redolent perhaps than any of the massacre sites. Park on the A82 6.5km from the visitor centre (300m W of the infamous Jimmy Savile bungalow) by the road (always cars parked here). Follow clear path down to and across the River Coe. Ascend keeping burn to left; 1.5km further up, it's best to ford it. Allow 3 hours. See also 1889/BATTLEGROUNDS.

1915 1/Q13
LL
The Whaligoe Steps Ulbster 10km S of Wick. 100m to car park by an unsigned road off the A99 at the (modern) telephone box near sign for the Cairn of Get. Short walk from the car park at the end of cottage row to this remarkable structure hewn into sheer cliffs, 365 steps down to a grassy platform – the Bink – and an old fishing station. From 1792, creels of cod, haddock and ling were hauled up these steps for the merchants of Wick and Lybster. Consider these labours as you follow their footsteps in this wild and enchanting place. No rails and can be slippy. Take great care!

1916 8/Q25
Under Edinburgh Old Town Visit Mary King's Close, a medieval street under the Royal Mile closed in 1753 (**The Real Mary King's Close** www.realmarykingsclose. com; 0845 070 6244); and the Vaults under South Bridge – built in the 18th century and sealed up around the time of the Napoleonic Wars (**Mercat Tours** www.mercattours.com; 0131 225 5445). History underfoot for unsuspecting tourists and locals alike. Glimpses of a rather smelly subterranean life way back then. It's dark during the day, and you wouldn't want to get locked in.

1917 1/P10
LL
Yesnaby Sea Stacks Orkney Mainland · www.visitorkney.com A clifftop viewpoint that's so wild, so dramatic and, if you walk near the edge, so precarious that its supernaturalism verges on the uneasy. Shells of lookout posts from the war echo the melancholy spirit of the place. ('The bloody town's a bloody cuss/No bloody trains, no bloody bus/And no one cares for bloody us/In bloody Orkney' – first lines of a poem written then, a soldier's lament). Near Skara Brae, it's about 30km from Kirkwall and way out west. Follow directions from **Marwick Head** (1725/BIRDS).

1918 5/F17
LLL
ATMOS
The Fairy Glen Skye A place so strange, it's hard to believe that it's merely a geological phenomenon. Entering Uig on the A855 (becomes A87) from Portree, there's a turret on the left (Macrae's Folly) by the Uig Hotel. Take road on right marked Balnaknock for 2km and you enter an area of extraordinary conical hills which, in certain conditions of light and weather, seems to entirely justify its legendary provenance. Your mood may determine whether you believe they were good or bad fairies, but there's supposed to be an incredible 365 of these grassy hillocks, some 35m high – well, how else could they be here?

1919 5/M18
ATMOS
HS
Clava Cairns nr Inverness Near **Culloden** (1886/BATTLEGROUNDS) these curious chambered cairns in a grove of trees near a river in the middle of 21st-century nowhere. This spot can make you feel a glow or goose pimples (1796/PREHISTORIC).

1920 5/M17 **The Clootie Well** between Tore on the A9 & Avoch Spooky place on the road
ATMOS towards Avoch and Cromarty 4km from the roundabout at Tore, N of Inverness.
Easily missed, though there is a marked car park on the right side of the road going
east. What you see is hundreds of rags or clouts: pieces of clothing hanging on the
branches of trees around the spout of an ancient well where the wearer might be
healed. They go way back up the hill behind and though some may have been here
a long time, this place seems to have been commodified like everywhere else so
there's plenty of new socks and t-shirts with messages. It's weird!

1921 6/Q20 **Burn o' Vat** nr Ballater · www.visitdeeside.org.uk This impressive and rather
L spooky glacial curiosity on Royal Deeside is a popular spot and well worth the short
walk. 8km from Ballater towards Aberdeen on main A93, take B9119 for Huntly for
2km to the car park at the Muir of Dinnet nature reserve – driving through forests
of strange spindly birch. Some scrambling to reach the huge 'pot' from which the
burn flows to Loch Kinord. SNH visitor centre. Forest walks, 1.3km circular walk
to Vat, 6km to loch. Can be busy on fine weekends, supernatch when you find it
deserted.

1922 9/N29 **Crichope Linn** nr Thornhill A supernatural sliver of glen inhabited by water
ATMOS spirits of various temperaments (and midges). Now I haven't been for a while so
please let me know if these directions are inaccurate. Take road for Cample on A76
Dumfries to Kilmarnock road just S of Thornhill; at village (2km) there's a wooden
sign so take left for 2km. Discreet sign and gate in bank on right is easy to miss, but
park in quarry 100m further on. Take care – can be very wet and very slippy. Gorge
is a 10-min schlep from the gate. We saw red squirrels! **Durisdeer Church** nearby
is also enchanting (1846/CHURCHES).

1923 6/S17 **Hell's Lum Cave** nr Gardenstown, Moray Firth Coast Locally popular but
LL still secret beach picnic and combing spot E of Gardenstown off the B9031 signed
for Cullykhan Bay. From car park (200m from main road), you walk down to bay
and can see on left a scar on the hill which marks the lum, approached along the
shoreline possibly via a defile known as the Devil's Dining Room. Lots of local
mythology surrounds this wild and beautiful spot. In the cave itself you hear what
sounds like children crying.

1924 8/R24 **Dunino Den** Strathvithie, nr Crail A reader, Ian Smith, alerted me to this
ancient, sacred and mysterious place off the B9131 in deepest Fife. There's a
church which probably occupies a stone circle site (some stones dated AD 800).
A pathway by the graveyard leads to a promontory above the Kinaldy Burn. The
pools here are reputedly where the druid priests made human sacrifices to appease
the gods. Steps lead to a narrow gorge – The Den – where a Celtic cross has been
carved into the rock face. Well, who knows!

The Necropolis Glasgow Report: 1863/GRAVEYARDS.
Loanhead of Daviot Stone Circle nr Inverurie Report: 1811/PREHISTORIC.

the
Best
Strolls, Walks
& Hikes

Favourite Hills

Popular and notable hills in the various regions of Scotland but not including Munros or difficult climbs. Always best to remember that the weather can change very quickly. Take an OS map on higher tops. See p. 12 for walk codes.

1925 4/K14
2-C-3

✓✓ **Suilven** Lochinver From close or far away, this is one of Scotland's most awe-inspiring mountains. The 'sugar loaf' can seem almost insurmountable, but in good weather it's not so difficult. Route from Inverkirkaig 5km S of Lochinver on road to Achiltibuie, turns up track by Achin's Bookshop (2171/SHOPS) on the path for the Kirkaig Falls; once at the loch, you head for the Bealach, the central waistline through an unexpected dyke and follow track to the top. The slightly quicker route from the N (Glencanisp) following a stalkers' track that eventually leads to Elphin, also heads for the central breach in the mountain's defences. Either way it's a long walk in; 8km before the climb. Allow 8 hours return. At the top, the most enjoyable 100m in the land and below – amazing Assynt. 731m. Take OS map.

1926 4/J15
2-B-3

✓✓ **Stac Pollaidh/Polly** nr Ullapool This hill described variously as 'perfect', 'preposterous' and 'great fun'; it certainly has character and rising out of the Sutherland moors on the road to Achiltibuie off the A835 N, demands to be climbed. Route everyone takes is from the car park by Loch Lurgainn 8km from main road. The last lap to the pinnacles is exposed and can be off-putting. Best half-day hill climb in the North. 613m. Allow 3-4 hours return.

1927 4/K14
2-B-3

✓✓ **Quinag** nr Lochinver Pronounced Koonyag. Like Stac Polly (above), this Corbett has amazing presence and seems more formidable than it actually is. Park off the A894 – great views from several viewpoints N of Kylesku – where great seafood awaits (1315/GASTROPUBS). An up-and-down route can take in 6 or 7 tops in your 5-hour expedition (or curtail). Once again, awesome Assynt!

1928 7/J27
2-B-2

✓ **Goat Fell** Arran Starting from the car park at Cladach 3km from town, or from Corrieburn Bridge S of Corrie further up the coast (12km). A worn path, a steady climb, rarely much of a scramble; a rewarding afternoon's exertion. Some scree and some view! 874m. Usually not circular. Allow 5 hours. Brodick for refreshments.

1929 7/K24
2-B-3

✓ **The Cobbler (aka Ben Arthur)** Arrochar Perennial favourite of Glasgow hillwalkers and, for sheer exhilaration, the most popular of the Arrochar Alps. A motorway path ascends from the A83 on the other side of Loch Long from Arrochar (park in lay-bys near Succoth road end; there are always loads of cars) and takes 2.5-3 hours to traverse the up 'n' down route to the top. Just short of a Munro at 881m, it has 3 tops, of which the N peak is the simplest scramble (central and S peaks for climbers). Where the way is not marked, consult.

• •

5 MAGNIFICENT HILLS IN THE TROSSACHS

1930 8/L24
2-B-3

✓ **Ben Venue & Ben A'an** 2 celebrated tops in the Highland microcosm of the Trossachs around Loch Achray; strenuous but not difficult and with superb views. Ben Venue (729m) is more serious; allow 4-5 hours return. Start from Kinlochard at Ledard or more usually from Loch Katrine corner, the car park before Loch Achray Hotel. Ben A'an (pronounced An), 454m, starts with a steep climb from the main A821 near the same corner before the Tigh Mor timeshare apartments. An awesome stone staircase leads to an easy scramble at top. Allow 2-3 hours. Very busy on fine days. The café at Brig o' Turk is great (1393/TEAROOMS).

1931 8/L23
2-B-3

Ben Shian Strathyre Another Trossachs favourite and not taxing. From village main road (the A74 to Lochearnhead), cross bridge opposite Munro Inn (being refurbished at TGP), turn left after 200m then path to right at 50m a steep start through woods. Overlooking village and views to Crianlarich and Ben Vorlich (see below). 600m. 3 hours return. **Broch Café** in the village (you'll go past it) for refreshments 10am-4pm.

1932 8/L24
1-B-1

Doon Hill The Fairy Knowe, Aberfoyle Legendary hillock in Aberfoyle, only 1 hour up and back, so a gentle elevation into faery land. The tree at the top is the home of the People of Quietness; one local minister had the temerity to tell their secrets (in 1692) and paid the price thereafter. Go round it 7 times and your wish will be granted, go round backwards at your peril (you wouldn't, would you?). From main street take Manse Rd by garden centre. 1km past cemetery, then signed.

1933 8/L24
2-B-3

Ben Ledi nr Callander Another Corbett (879m, seems higher than it is) with the Trossachs spread before you as you climb. W from town on A84 through Pass of Leny. First left over bridge to car park. Well-trodden path, ridge at top. Return via Stank Glen then follow river. Allow 4 hours. **The Lade Inn** for (one of 200) beers, anyone (1299/REAL-ALE PUBS)?

• •

1934 7/H24
1-A-1
HS

✓ **Dunadd** Kilmartin Halfway from Kilmartin on A816. Less of a hill, more of a lump, but it's where they crowned the kings of Dalriada for half a millennium. Rocky staircases and soft, grassy top. Stand there when the Atlantic rain is sheeting in and... you get wet, presumably like the kings did. Or when the light is good you can see the glen and distant coast. **Kilmartin House Museum** nearby for info and great food (2124/HISTORY; 1402/TEAROOMS).

1935 9/N30
2-A-2

Criffel New Abbey, nr Dumfries 12km S by A710 to New Abbey, which Criffel dominates. It's only 569m, but seems higher. Exceptional views from top as far as English lakes. Granite lump with brilliant outcrops of quartzite. The annual race gets up and back to the Abbey Arms in under an hour; you can take it easier. Start 3km S of village, turn-off A710 100m from one of the curious painted bus shelters signed for Ardwell Mains Farm. Over there the Solway shimmers.

1936 9/L29
2-B-3

Merrick nr Newton Stewart Go from bonnie Glen Trool via Bargrennan 14km N on the A714. **Bruce's Stone** is there at the start (1901/BOB). The highest peak in southern Scotland (843m), it's a strenuous though straightforward climb, a grassy ridge to the summit and glorious scenery. 6 hours.

1937 8/R25
BOTH 1-A-1

North Berwick Law The conical volcanic hill, a beacon in the East Lothian landscape. **Traprain Law** nearby (signed from A1), is higher, easy and celebrated by rock climbers, but has major prehistoric significance as a hill fort citadel of the Goddodin and a definite aura. NBL is also simple and rewarding – leave town by Law Rd, path marked beyond houses. Car park and picnic site. Views 'to the Cairngorms'(!) and along the Forth. Famous whalebone at the top.

1938 8/R28
2-A-2

Ruberslaw Denholm, nr Hawick This smooth hummock above the Teviot valley affords views of 7 counties, including Northumberland. Millennium plaque on top. At 424m, it's a gentle climb taking about 1 hour from the usual start at Denholm Hill Farm (private land, be aware of livestock). Leave Denholm at corner of green by post office and go past war memorial. Take left after 2km to farm. One fine day I will climb this hill!

1939 8/N27 **Tinto Hill** nr Biggar & Lanark A Clyde Valley landmark and favourite climb in
2-A-2 South/Central Scotland with easy access to start from Fallburn on the A73 near
Symington, 10km S of Lanark. Park 100m behind Tinto Hills farm shop. Good,
simple track there and back though it has its ups and downs before you get there.
Braw views. 707m (it's a Graham). Allow 2.5 hours.

1940 7/L24 **Conic Hill** Balmaha, Loch Lomond An easier climb than the Ben up the
2-A-2 road and a good place to view it from, Conic, on the Highland fault line, is one
of the first Highland hills you reach from Glasgow. Stunning views also of Loch
Lomond from its 361m peak. Ascend through woodland from the corner of
Balmaha (the visitor centre) car park. Watch for buzzards and your footing on the
final crumbly bits. Easy walks also on the nearby island, **Inchcailloch** (2008/
WALKS). 1.5 hours up.

1941 8/N21 **Ben Vrackie** Pitlochry Small mountain, magnificent views. **Moulin Inn** to
2-A-2 return to for pub grub (1297/REAL-ALE PUBS). Woods, moorland, a loch and a bit of
a steep finish (at 841m, it's a Corbett). For the start, take A924 from Moulin (1.5km
uphill from Pitlochry), going straight ahead when the road turns left to the car park
300m further on. Track well signed and obvious. 4 hours.

1942 8/P23 **Kinnoull Hill** Perth Various starts from town and A85, eg Manse Rd. The wooded
1-A-1 ridge above the Tay with its tower and incredible views to S from the precipitous
cliffs. Surprisingly extensive area of hill side (Coronation Rd, Deuchny Hill) common
and it's not difficult to get lost. The leaflet/map from Perth tourist information
centre helps. Local lurve spot after dark (that Quarry car park).

1943 6/R19 **Bennachie** nr Aberdeen The pilgrimage hill, an easy 528m often busy at
2-B-2 weekends but never disappoints. Various trails take you to 'the Taps' from
3 main car parks. (1) From the Bennachie Centre (01467 681470): 3km N of
Inverurie on the A96, take left to chapel of Garioch (pronounced Geery), then left
(it's signed). (2) 16km N of Inverurie on the A96, take the B9002 through Oyne,
then signed on left – picnic here among the pines. (3) The Donview car park 5km
N of Monymusk towards Blairdaff – the longer, gentler walk in. All car parks have
trail-finders. From the fortified top you see what Aberdeenshire is about. 2 hours.
Bennachie's soulmate, **Tap o' Noth**, is 20km W. Easy approach via Rhynie on A97
(then 3km).

1944 3/C20 **Heaval** Barra The mini-Matterhorn that rises above Castlebay is an easy and
2-B-2 rewarding climb. At 383m, it's steep in places but never over-taxing. You see 'the
road to Mingulay'. Start up hill through Castlebay, park behind the new-build house
and find path via Our Lady, Star of the Sea. 1.5 hours return.

▆▆▆ Hill Walks

*The following ranges of hills offer walks in various directions and more than
one summit. They are all accessible and fairly easy. See p. 12 for walk codes.*

1945 5/G18 **Walks on Skye** Obviously many serious walks in and around the **Cuillin** (1962/
MUNROS; 1971/WALKS), but almost infinite variety of others. Can do no better than
read a great book, *50 Best Routes on Skye and Raasay* by Ralph Storer (available
locally), which describes and grades many of the must-dos. Other pocket guides
from tourist office.

1946 8/P24
3-10KM
CIRC
XBIKES
2-A-2

Lomond Hills nr Falkland The conservation village lies below a prominent ridge easily reached from the main street especially via Back Wynd (off which there's a car park). More usual approach to both East and West Lomond, the main tops, is from Craigmead car park 3km from village towards Leslie trail-finder board. The celebrated Lomonds (aka the Paps of Fife), aren't that high (West is 522m), but they can see and be seen for miles. Also: easy start from radio masts 3km up road from A912 E of Falkland. 1376/CAFÉS and pubs in the village.

An easy rewarding single climb is **Bishop Hill**. Start 100m from the church in Scotlandwell. A steep path (150m down main road) veers left and then there are several ways up. Allow 2.5 hours. Great view of Loch Leven and a good swathe of Central Scotland. Sheep tracks down to Kinnesswood (park a second car to save walk back). Gliders overhead from the airstrip below.

1947 8/R27
3KM
CIRC
XBIKES
1-A-2

The Eildons Melrose The 3 much-loved hills or paps visible from most of the central Borders and easily climbed from the town of Melrose which nestles at their foot. Leave main square by road to station (the Dingleton road); after 100m a path begins between 2 pebble-dash houses on the left. You climb the smallest first, then the highest central one (422m). You can make a circular route of it by returning to the golf course. Allow 2 hours. Good pub and food options in Melrose; p. 158–59.

1948 8/N24
2-40KM
SOME CIRC
XBIKES
1/2-B-2

The Ochils Usual approach from the 'hillfoot towns' at the foot of the glens that cut into their south-facing slopes, along the A91 Stirling-St Andrews road. Alva, Tillicoultry and Dollar all have impressive glen walks easily found from the main streets where tracks are marked (1982/GLEN WALKS). Good start near Stirling from the Sheriffmuir road uphill from Bridge of Allan about 3km, look for pylons and a lay-by on the right (a reservoir just visible on the left). Usually other cars here. A stile leads to the hills which stretch away to the east for 40km and afford great views for little effort, eg from Dumyat (3 hour return) though the highest point is Ben Cleugh at 721m. Swimming place nearby is 'Paradise' (1676/SWIMMING).

1949 8/R26
5-155KM
SOME CIRC
MTBIKES
1/2-B-2

The Lammermuirs The hills SE of Edinburgh that divide East Lothian's rich farmlands from the Borders' Tweed valley. Mostly high moorland but there's wooded gentle hill country in the watersheds of the southern rivers and spectacular coastal scenery between Cockburnspath and **St Abb's Head** (1741/RESERVES; 2026/WALKS). Eastern part of the **Southern Upland Way**, follows the Lammermuirs to the coast (1967/LONG WALKS). Many fine walks begin at Whiteadder Reservoir car park (A1 to Haddington, the B6355 through Gifford), then 10km to a mysterious loch in the bowl of the hills. Also, the 10km 428m Priestlaw Hill circuit to the south and the Sparleton Hill loop, 10km, 465m, and around Abbey St Bathans (head off A1 at Cockburnspath): through village to Toot Corner (signed 1km) and off to left, follow path above valley of Whiteadder to Edinshall Broch (2km). Further on, along river (1km), is a swing bridge and a fine place to swim. Circular walks possible; ask in village. **The Yester Estate** near Gifford is nearer Edinburgh and a good foothill option (455/WALKS).

1950 5/L17
3KM
CIRC
XBIKES
1-A-2

Knockfarrel Dingwall to Strathpeffer A walk (around 8km) between the two towns N of Inverness along the ridge between the A834 and A835 that includes Knockfarrel, an Iron Age fort site on a raised plateau with views of the valleys, Loch Ussie and the Cromarty Firth. Non-taxing, hugely rewarding and damned pleasant. Find starts in either town or drive to Knockfarrel from the A835 Dingwall-Contin road off the A9, turning at the sign for the red kites. Go past kite turn-off to the T-junction, turn left and 500m further, finish on a rough track to the car park.

1951 8/S27 **The Cheviots** Not strictly in Scotland but they straddle the border and Border history. Many fine walks start from Kirk Yetholm (such as the Pennine Way stretching 400km S to the Peak district and **St Cuthbert's Way** 1970/LONG WALKS), including an 8km circular route of typical Cheviot foothill terrain. Many walking guides available at Border tourist centres. Most forays start at Wooler 20km from Coldstream. Cheviot itself (815m) is a boggy plateau; Hedgehope via the Harthope Burn more fun. In 2014 I was privileged to give 'The Redeswire Address' at the Redeswire Stone by **Carter Bar** (1656/VIEWS).

Campsie Fells nr Glasgow Report: 744/WALKS OUTSIDE GLASGOW.
The Pentlands nr Edinburgh Report: 448/WALKS OUTSIDE EDINBURGH.

Some Great Easy Munros

There are almost 300 hills in Scotland over 3,000ft as tabled by Sir Hugh Munro in 1891. Those selected here have been chosen for their relative ease of access both to the bottom and thence to the top. Tackle only what is within your range of experience and ability. All these offer rewarding climbs. None should be attempted without proper clothing (especially boots) and sustenance. You may also need an OS map or GPS thing. Never underestimate how fast weather conditions can change in the Scottish mountains.

1952 7/L24 **Ben Lomond** Rowardennan, Loch Lomond Many folks' first Munro, given proximity to Glasgow (soul and city). It's not too taxing a climb and has rewarding views (in good weather). 2 main ascents: the tourist route is easier, from toilet block at Rowardennan car park (end of road from Drymen), well-trodden all the way; or 500m up past Youth Hostel, a path follows burn – the Ptarmigan Route. Steeper but quieter, more interesting. Circular walk possible. 974m. 3 hours up.

1953 8/M22 **Schiehallion** nr Kinloch Rannoch Fairy Hill of the Caledonians and a bit of a must (though very busy). New path c/o John Muir Trust over E flank. Start Braes of Foss car park 10k from KR. 10km walk, ascent 750m. 5 hours. 1083m.

1954 8/P21 **Carn Aosda** Glenshee Very accessible, starting from Glenshee ski car park; follow ski tow up. Ascent only 270m of 917m, so bag a Munro in an hour. Easier still, take chairlift to Cairnwell, take in peak behind and then Carn Aosda – and you're doing three Munros in a morning (cheating, but hey). The Grampian Highlands unfold. Another easy (500m to climb) Munro nearby is **Carn an Tuirc** from the A93.

1955 5/M20 **Meall Chuaich** Dalwhinnie Starting from verge of the A9 S of Cuaich at Cuaich cottages. Ascent only 623m, though the total walk is 14km. Follow aqueduct to power station then Loch Cuaich. An easily bagged 951m.

1956 5/J16 **An Teallach** Torridon Sea-level start from Dundonnell on the A832 S of Ullapool. One of the most awesome Scots peaks but not the ordeal it looks. Path well trodden; great scrambling opportunities for the nimble. Peering over the pinnacle of Lord Berkeley's Seat into the void is a jaw-drop. Take a day. Nice coffee shop called **Maggie's** near start/finish (1414/TEAROOMS). 1,062m.

1957 5/H17 **Beinn Alligin** Torridon The other great Torridon trek. Consult regarding start at NTS Countryside Centre on corner of Glen Torridon–Diabeg road. Car park by bridge on road to Inveralligin and Diabeg, walk through woods over moor by river. Steepish pull up onto the Horns of Alligin. You can cover 2 Munros in a circular route that takes you across the top of the world. 985m. Then you could tackle **Liathach** (trickier; **Beinn Eighe**, also from a start on Glen Torridon road, probably easiest).

1958 7/G23 **Ben More** Mull The cool, high ben sits in isolated splendour, the only Munro bar the Cuillin not on the mainland. Sea-level start from the bridge over the Scarisdale river on the coast road B8035, 5km SW of Gruline, that skirts the southern coast of Loch Na Keal, then a fairly clear path through river gorge and rocky landscape. Tricky near the top but there are fabulous views across the islands. 966m. Allow 6/7 hours.

1959 4/L13 **Ben Hope** nr Tongue The most northerly Munro and many a bagger's last; also a good one to start with. Steep and craggy with splendid views, the approach from the south is relatively easy and takes about 5 hours there and back. Go S from Hope (on the A38) on the unclassified road to Strathmore. 927m.

1960 5/L17 **Ben Wyvis** nr Garve Standing apart from its northern neighbours, you can feel the presence of this mountain from a long way off. North of main A835 road Inverness-Ullapool and very accessible from it, park 6km N of Garve (48km from Inverness) and follow marked path by stream and through the shattered remnants of what was once a forest (replanting in progress). Leave the dereliction behind; the summit approach is by a soft, mossy ridge. Magnificent 1,046m.

1961 8/Q20 **Lochnagar** nr Ballater Described as a fine, complex mountain, its nobility and mystique apparent from afar, not least Balmoral Castle. Approach via Glen Muick (pronounced Mick) road from Ballater to car park at Spittal of Glen Muick at the loch (1613/LOCHS). Path to mountain well signed and well trodden. 18km return, allow 6-8 hours. Steep at top; the loch supernatural. Apparently on a clear day you can see the Forth Bridge. 1,155m.

1962 5/G19 **Bla Bheinn** Skye Pronounced Blahven. The magnificent massif, isolated from the other Cuillin, has a sea-level start and seems higher than it is. The *Munro Guide* describes it optimistically as 'exceptionally accessible'. It has an eerie jagged beauty and – though some scrambling is involved and it helps to have a head for exposed situations – there are no serious dangers. Take B8083 from Broadford to Elgol through Torrin, park 1km S of the head of Loch Slapin, walking W at Allt na Dunaiche along N bank of stream. Bla Bheinn is an enormously rewarding climb. Rapid descent for scree runners, but allow 8 hours. 928m.

1963 8/M22 **Ben Lawers** Killin & Aberfeldy The massif of 7 summits, including 6 Munros that dominate the N side of Loch Tay, are linked by a 12km twisting ridge that only once falls below 800m. If you're very fit, you can do the lot in a day starting from the N or Glen Lyon side. Have an easier day of it knocking off Beinn Ghlas then Ben Lawers from the Lawers car park, 5km off the A827. 4/5 hours. **Ben Lawers Hotel** on N Loch Tay/Killin but eat Aberfeldy.

1964 8/M22 **Meall Nan Tarmachan** The part of the ridge W of Lawers (above), which takes in a Munro and several tops, is one of the easiest Munro climbs and is immensely impressive. Start 1km further on from Lawers car park down 100m track and through gate. Slog to start. 12km walk, climb 800m, allow 6 hours.

Long Walks

These walks require preparation, maps, good boots, etc. Don't carry too much. Sections are always possible. See p. 12 for walk codes.

1965 7/K23
2-B-3

✓ **The West Highland Way** www.west-highland-way.co.uk The 150km walk which starts at Milngavie 12km outside Glasgow and goes via some of Scotland's most celebrated scenery to emerge in Glen Nevis before the Ben. The route goes like this: Mugdock Moor-Drymen-Loch Lomond-Rowardennan-Inversnaid-Inverarnan-Crianlarich-Tyndrum-Bridge of Orchy-Rannoch Moor-Kingshouse Hotel-Glen Coe-The Devil's Staircase-Kinlochleven. The latter part from Bridge of Orchy is the most dramatic. **The Bridge of Orchy Hotel** (01838 400208; 1177/INNS Best; not cheap!) and the rather shabby **Kings House** (01855 851259) are both historic staging posts, as is the **Drover's Inn**, Inverarnan (839/CENTRAL). When booking accom allow time for fatigue; don't carry a lot. **START** Officially at Milngavie (pronounced Mill-guy) Railway Station (regular service from Glasgow Central, also buses from Buchanan St Bus Station), but actually from Milngavie shopping precinct 500m away. However, the countryside is close. From other end on Glen Nevis road from roundabout on A82 N from Fort William. The Way is well marked; there's a good *Official Pocket Companion* or download from website.

1966 5/K18
2-C-3

✓ **Glen Affric** In enchanting Glen Affric and Loch Affric beyond (1978/GLEN & RIVER WALKS; 1584/GLENS; 1668/SWIMMING), some serious walking begins on the 32km Kintail trail. Done either west-east starting at Morvich, 2km from A87 near Shiel Bridge, or east-west starting at the Affric Lodge 15km W of Cannich. Route can include one of the approaches to the **Falls of Glomach** (1593/WATERFALLS).

1967 9/P28
2-B-3

The Southern Upland Way 350km walk from Portpatrick across the Rhinns of Galloway, much moorland, the Galloway Forest Park, the wild heartland of southern Scotland, then through **James Hogg** country (1909/LITERARY PLACES) to the gentler east Borders and the sea at Pease Bay (official end, Cockburnspath). Route is Portpatrick–Stranraer–New Luce–Dalry–Sanquhar–Wanlockhead–Beattock–St Mary's Loch–Melrose–Lauder–Abbey St Bathans. The first and latter sections are the most obviously picturesque but highlights include Loch Trool, the Lowther Hills, St Mary's Loch, Traquair, Melrose and the River Tweed. Usually walked west to east, the Southern Upland Way is a formidable undertaking... Info from **Ranger Service** (01835 824000). **START** Portpatrick by the harbour and up along the cliffs past the lighthouse. Or Cockburnspath. Map is on side of shop at the Cross.

1968 6/Q18
1-A-3

The Speyside Way A long-distance route which generally follows the valley of the River Spey from Buckie on the Moray Firth coast to Aviemore in the foothills of the Cairngorms, with side spurs to Dufftown up Glen Fiddich (7km) and to Tomintoul over the hill between the River Avon (pronounced A'rn) and the River Livet (24km). The main stem of the route largely follows the valley bottom, criss-crossing the Spey several times – a distance of around 100km, and is less strenuous than Southern Upland or West Highland Ways. The Tomintoul spur has more hill-walking character and rises to a great viewpoint at 600m. Throughout the walk you are in whisky country with opportunities to visit **Cardhu**, **Glenlivet** and other distilleries nearby (1498/1490/WHISKY). Info from **Ranger Service** (01343 557046). **START** Usual start is from Spey Bay 8km N of Fochabers (from Buckie adds another 8km); the first marker is by the banks of shingle at the river mouth.

1969 8/Q22
2-B-3

The Cateran Trail Named after the Caterans who were marauding cattle thieves, this 100k hike crosses their old stamping ground, the splendid hills and glens of Angus and Perthshire. Circular (100km) from a start at Blairgowrie and 4/5 days to complete; there are also 5 sections: Blairgowrie-Bridge of Cally-Glenshee-Glen Isla-Alyth. Good inn options on the way (1185/1186/INNS). All in splendid country, this is a well-thought-out route.

1970 8/S27
2-A-3

St Cuthbert's Way From Melrose in the Borders (where St Cuthbert started his ministry) to Lindisfarne on Holy Island off Northumberland (where he died) via St Boswells-Kirk Yetholm-Wooler. 100km but many sections easy. Bowden-Maxton and a stroll by the Tweed especially fine. Check local tourist centres. Causeway to Holy Island a treat at the end.

▬▬ Serious Walks

None of these should be attempted without OS maps, equipment and preparation. Hill or ridge walking experience may be essential.

1971 5/G19
3-C-3

The Cuillin Mountains Skye Much scrambling and, if you want it, serious climbing over these famously unforgiving peaks. The Red ones are easier and many walks start at the **Sligachan Hotel** on the main Portree-Broadford road. Every July there's a hill race up Glamaig; the conical one which overlooks the hotel. Most of the Black Cuillin including the highest, Sgurr Alasdair (993m), and Sgurr Dearg, 'the Inaccessible Pinnacle' (978m), can be attacked from the campsite or the youth hostel in Glen Brittle. Good guides are *Introductory Scrambles from Glen Brittle* by Charles Rhodes, or *50 Best Routes in Skye and Raasay* by Ralph Storer, both available locally, but you will need a map. (2/ATTRACTIONS; 1163/HOSTELS; 1601/WATERFALLS; 1962/MUNROS; 1658/SWIMMING).

1972 7/K22
3-C-3

Aonach Eagach Glen Coe One of several possible major expeditions in the Glen Coe area and one of the world's classic ridge walks. Not for the faint-hearted or the ill-prepared. It's the ridge on your right for almost the whole length of the glen from Altnafeadh to the road to the **Clachaig Inn** (rewarding refreshment). Start from the main road. Car park opposite the one for the **Lost Valley** (1914/ENCHANTING PLACES). Stiff pull up then the switchback path across. There is no turning back. Scary pinnacles two-thirds over, then one more Munro and the knee-trembling, scree-running descent. On your way, you'll have come close to heaven, seen Lochaber in its immense glory and reconnoitred some fairly exposed edges and pinnacles. Go with somebody good as I once did. (1617/SCENIC ROUTES; 1287/GOOD PUBS; 1168/HOSTELS; 1889/BATTLEGROUNDS).

1973 7/K22
3-C-3

Buachaille Etive Mor Glen Coe In same area as above and another of the UK's best high-level hauls. Not as difficult or precarious as the Eagach and long loved by climbers and walkers, with stunning views from its several false summits to the actual top with its severe drops. Start on main Glen Coe road. 5km past King's House Hotel. Well-worn path. Allow 6/7 hours return. 1022m.

1974 7/K21
2-B-3

Ben Nevis Start on Glen Nevis road, 5km Fort William town centre (by bridge opposite youth hostel or from visitor centre) or signed from A82 after Glen Nevis roundabout. Both lead to start at Achintee Farm and the **Ben Nevis Inn** (handy afterwards 1099/FORT WILLIAM). This, 'The Mountain Path', is the most popular and safest route. Allow the best part of a day (and we do mean the best – the weather can turn quickly here). For the more interesting and tougher arete route, allow

8/9 hours. There are accidents on this mountain even with experienced climbers so take great care. It is the biggest, though not perhaps the best; you can see 100 Munros on a clear day (i.e. about once a year). You climb it because... you have to. 1,344m.

1975 5/J19 **The Five Sisters of Kintail & The Cluanie Ridge** Both generally started from
3-C-3 A87 along from **Cluanie Inn** (1291/GOOD PUBS) and they will keep you right; usually walked east to west. Sisters is an uncomplicated but inspiring ridge walk, taking in 3 Munros and 2 tops. It's a hard pull up and you descend to a point 8km further up the road (so arrange transport). Many side spurs to vantage-points and wild views. The Cluanie or S ridge is a classic which covers 7 Munros. Starts at inn; 2 ways off back onto A876. Both can be walked in a single day (Cluanie allow 9 hours).
From Morvich off A87 near Shiel Bridge another long-distance walk starts to **Glen Affric** (1966/LONG WALKS).

1976 6/N19 **Glenmore Forest Park** From Coylumbridge and Loch Morlich; 32km through
3-C-3 the **Rothiemurchus Forest** (2005/WALKS) and the famous **Lairig Ghru**, the ancient right of way through the Cairngorms which passes between Ben Macdui and Braeriach. Ascent is over 700m and going can be rough. This is one of the great Scottish trails. At end of June the Lairig Ghru Race completes this course east-west in 3.5 hours, but generally this is a full-day trip. The famous shelter, Corrour Bothy between Devil's Point and Carn a'Mhaim, can be a halfway house. Near Linn of Dee, routes converge and pass through the ancient Caledonian Forest of Mar. Going east-west is less gruelling and there's Aviemore to look forward to!

Glen & River Walks

See also Great Glens, p. 280–81. Walk codes are on p. 12.

1977 8/N21 ✓ **Glen Tilt** Blair Atholl A walk of variable length in this classic Highland
UP TO 17KM glen, easily accessible from the old Blair Rd off main Blair Atholl road near
CIRC Bridge of Tilt Hotel, car park by the (very) old bridge. Trail leaflet from park office
XBIKES and local tourist information centres. Fine walking and unspoiled scenery begins
1-B-2 only a short distance into the deeply wooded gorge of the River Tilt, but to cover the circular route you have to walk to Gilbert's Bridge (9km return) or the longer trail to Gow's Bridge (17km return). Begin here also the great route into the Cairngorms leading to the Linn of Dee and Braemar, joining the track from Speyside which starts at **Feshiebridge** (1660/SWIMMING) or **Glenmore Forest** (2011/LONG WALKS).

1978 5/J19 ✓ **Glen Affric** Cannich, nr Drumnadrochit Easy short walks are marked
5/8KM and hugely rewarding in this magnificent glen well known as the first
CIRC stretch in the great east-west route to Kintail (1966/LONG WALKS) and the **Falls**
BIKES **of Glomach** (1593/WATERFALLS). Starting point of this track into the wilds is at
1-B-2 the end of the road at Loch Affric; there are many short and circular trails indicated and in Forestry Commission's free guide, locally available. Track closed in stalking season. Easier walks in famous Affric forest from car park at **Dog Falls**, 7km from Cannich (1668/SWIMMING). Waterfalls and spooky tame birds. Good idea to hire bikes at Drumnadrochit or Cannich (01456 415364). See also 1584/GLENS.

1979 4/J14 ✓ **Glen Canisp and the Inver River** Lochinver An enchanting river and
6KM woodland walk, with a middle section up an easy hill. Following a broad sweep
CIRC round the back of Lochinver. Best from N to S starting on the bridge at the junction
XBIKES of the road to Baddidarach, on fisherman paths along the river, among beautiful
1-B-2 mixed trees with some Scots pine. Well maintained and signed, you ascend 75m to
fine views with Suilven presiding, and back into the village via Canisp Lodge. Don't
forget the pies at the **Riverside Bistro** (1093/HIGHLANDS).

1980 8/M24 ✓ **The Darn Walk** A perfect, easy walk in any season following the Allan Water
4KM between Bridge of Allan and Dunblane. Sometimes on the banks, at others
XCIRC high above; the river in different aspects totally endears itself. The path crosses two
1-B-1 tumbling tributaries, the Wharry Burn and Cock's Burn. Not circular, so two cars
needed or the bus, or conveniently, the train. Starts by BoA station at the bridge,
Henderson St to Blairforkie Dr – 500m, then a gap in the wall and a sign for
'Dunblane 2.5 miles'. Enter Dunblane across the golf course. Allow 2 hours one
way. **Jam Jar** café in BoA for refuel (841/CENTRAL).

1981 8/L24 ✓ **Glen Finglas and Balquhidder to Brig o' Turk** Easy amble through the
18KM heart of Scotland via **Glen Finglas** (1612/LOCHS) from the car park on the A821
XCIRC with a handy pub (1323/GASTROPUBS) and a great tearoom (1393/TEAROOMS). Long
XBIKES walk not circular so best to arrange transport. Usually walked starting at
2-B-2 Balquhidder graveyard (1873/GRAVEYARDS), then Ballimore and past Ben Vane to
the reservoir and Brig o' Turk. B o' T and A821 start offers some great walk options.

1982 8/N24 ✓ **Dollar Glen** Dollar The classic fairy glen in central Scotland, positively
3KM + TOPS hoaching with water spirits, reeking of ozone and euphoric after rain. 20km by
CIRC A91 from Stirling or 18km from M90 at Kinross junction 6. You walk by the Burn of
XBIKES Care and the Burn of Sorrow. Start at side of the volunteer-run museum or golf
1-A-2 club, or further up road (signed Castle Campbell) where there are 2 car parks, the
top one 5 mins from castle. The castle at head of glen is open 7 days last entry
5.30pm (Oct-Mar till 4pm) and has boggling views. There's a circular walk back
(3km) or take off for the Ochil Tops, the hills surrounding the glen. There are also
first-class walks up the glens of the other hillfoot towns, Alva and Tillicoultry which
also lead to the hills (1948/HILL WALKS).

1983 8/N24 ✓ **Rumbling Bridge** nr Dollar Formed by another burn off the Ochils, an easier
3KM short figure-of-eight walk in a glen with something of the chasmic experience
CIRC and added delight of the unique double bridge (built 1713). At the end of one of
XBIKES the walkways under the bridge you are looking into a Scottish jungle landscape
1-A-1 as the Romantics imagined. Near Powmill on A977 from Kinross (junction 6, M90)
then 2km. Up the road is The **Powmill Milkbar** (1407/TEAROOMS) serving very
traditional home-made food for over 40 years. It's 5km W on the A977. Open
7 days till 5pm (6pm weekends). Damage and repairs to bridge ongoing 2015.

1984 8/P22 ✓ **Loch Ordie** nr Dunkeld Not a walk through a specific glen or riverside but
16KM one which follows many burns past lochs and ponds, skirts some impressive
CIRC hills and is all in all a splendid and simple hike through glorious country almost
BIKES Highland in nature but close to the Central Belt. Loch Ordie is halfway on a loop
1-A-2 that starts at a bend on the A923 Blairgowrie road on left about 7km from Dunkeld
after the turn-off for Loch of the Lowes or signed from Butterstone 7km (and can
combine with walk to Loch of the Lowes 3km). Deuchary Hill, the highest here at
509m, can be climbed on a non-circular path from the main circuit. This is one of
the best, most scenic walks in Perthshire. Mostly level.

1985 8/Q21 ✓ **Glen Clova Walks** Most walked of the Angus glens. Many start from end at Acharn, especially W to Glen Doll (ranger centre for orientation, etc). Also enquire at **Glen Clova Hotel** (1198/GET-AWAY HOTELS) – 2-hour Loops of (Loch) Brandy walk starts here – and repair there afterwards (great walkers' pub). Easy, rewarding walks!

1986 8/R23 ✓ **The Lade Braes** St Andrews Unlike most walks on these pages, this cuts
BIKES through the town itself following the Kinness Burn. But you are removed from
1-A-1 all that! Start at Westport at the traffic lights just after the garage on Bridge St or (marked) opposite 139 South St. Trailboard and signs. Through Cockshaugh Park (side spur to Botanics on opposite bank) and the leafy glen and green sward at the edge of this famously fine town. Ends in a duck pond. You pass the back gardens of some very comfortable lives.

1987 5/M17 ✓ **The Fairy Glen** Rosemarkie On the Black Isle. On the main A832, the road
BIKES to Cromarty, 150 metres after the Plough Inn on the right, a car park and
1-A-1 information board. Beautiful, easy 3km walk with gorge, 2 waterfalls and some great birdlife. Can finish on Rosemarkie beach to picnic and look for dolphins. Some superb trees. Eat in **Cromarty** (1552/VILLAGES).

1988 8/L24 **Loch Ard Walks** nr Aberfoyle Pleasant Trossachs ambles through mixed
2-7KM forestry by Loch Ard and other lochans. Start around Milton on the B829 3km W of
CIRC · 1-A-1 Aberfoyle. Trailboards. Wildlife abounds. Good family outing.

1989 8/N23 **River Earn** Perthshire An easy riverside amble in Perthshire between Crieff
8KM and Muthill. Not circular so two cars best or bus. I'd recommend starting at Crieff,
XCIRC from the corner of the Stuart Crystal Visitor Centre, on the road between the
XBIKES towns. Follow the yellow arrow waymarkers and take care not to miss the one in
1-B-1 Sallyardoch Wood near the end. No effort and an unsung beautiful river to follow. Great food at **The Barley Bree** in Muthill (1170/INNS) is your reward.

1990 8/Q24 **Falkland** Fife If you're in Falkland for the Palace (1756/CASTLES) or the tearoom
3KM (1396/TEAROOMS), add this amble up an enchanting glen to your day. Go through
CIRC village then signed Cricket Club for Falkland Estate and School (an activity centre)
XBIKES – car park just inside gate (with map) – and gardens are behind it. Glen and
1-A-2 refurbished path up the macadam road are obvious. Gushing burn, waterfalls - you can even walk behind one! You can take to the hill. Couple of OK pubs.

1991 4/N15 **The Big Burn Walk** Golspie A non-taxing, perfect glen walk through lush diverse
6KM woodland. 3 different entrances including car park marked from A9 near Dunrobin
CIRC Castle gates but most complete starts beyond Golspie Inn and Sutherland
XBIKES Stonework at the end of the village. Go past derelict mill and under aqueduct
1-B-1 following river. A supernature trail unfolds with ancient tangled trees, meadows, waterfalls, cliffs and much wildlife. 3km to falls, return via route to castle woods for best all-round intoxication.

1992 4/P14 **The Strath at Dunbeath** The glen or strath so eloquently evoked in Neil
5KM Gunn's *Highland River* (1908/LITERARY PLACES), a book which is as much about
XCIRC the geography as the history of his childhood. Starting below the row of cottages
XBIKES on your left after the flyover going N near the much older Telford Bridge. A path
1-B-1 follows the river for many miles. A leaflet from the Dunbeath Heritage Centre points out places on the way as well as map on its entire floor. It's a spate river and in summer becomes a trickle; hard to imagine Gunn's salmon odyssey. It's only 500m to the broch, but it's worth going into the hinterland where it becomes quite mystical (1875/GRAVEYARDS).

1993 8/Q27
5/12KM
CIRC
XBIKES
1-A-1

Tweedside Peebles The riverside trail that follows the Tweed from town (Hay Lodge Park) past Neidpath Castle (1665/SWIMMING) and on through classic Border wooded countryside crossing river either 2.5km out (5km round trip), or at Manor Bridge 6km out (Lyne Footbridge, 12km). *Walking in the Scottish Borders* and many Tweedside trail guides. Other good Tweedside walks between Dryburgh Abbey and Bemersyde House grounds (1627/SCENIC ROUTES) and at Newton St Boswells by the golf course. Great pub-grub/tearoom options in Melrose, p. 158–59, and **Main Street Trading**, St Boswells (859/BORDERS).

1994 8/L27
3/5KM · CIRC
XBIKES
1-A-1

Failford Gorge nr Mauchline Woody gorge of the River Ayr. Start from bridge at Ayr end of village on B743 Ayr-Mauchline road (4km Mauchline). Easy, marked trail. Pub in village. Particularly notable for food is the **Sorn Inn** near Mauchline (1301/GASTROPUBS). All bucolic Ayrshire at its best.

1995 8/M23
3/5KM · CIRC
XBIKES
1-A-1

Glen Lednock nr Comrie Walk from Comrie or take the car further up to monument or drive further into glen to reservoir (9km) for more open walks. From town take right off main A85 (to Lochearnhead) at the excellent **Deil's Cauldron** bar/restaurant (932/PERTHSHIRE). Walk and Deil's Cauldron (waterfall and gorge) are signed after 250m. Walk takes less than 1 hour and emerges on road near Lord Melville's monument (climb for great views back towards Crieff, about 25 mins). Other walks up slopes to left after you emerge from the tree-lined gorge road. There's also the start of a hike up Ben Chonzie, 6km up glen at Coishavachan. This is one of the easiest Munros (931m) with a good path and great views, especially to NW.

1996 6/R17
1-A-1

Bridge of Alvah Banff Details: 2016/WALKS, mentioned here because the best bit is by the river and the bridge itself. The single-span crossing was built in 1772 and stands high above the river in a sheer-sided gorge. The river below is deep and slow. In the right light it's almost Amazonian. Walk takes 1.5 hours from **Duff House** (2139/GALLERIES). There's a picture of Alvah upstairs in the collection.

1997 8/R21
2KM
XCIRC
XBIKES
1-A-1

The Gannochy Bridge & The Rocks of Solitude nr Edzell 2km N of village on B966 to Fettercairn. There's a lay-by after bridge and a wooden door on left (you're in the grounds of the Burn House). Through it is another world and a path above the rocky gorge of the River North Esk (1km). Huge stone ledges over dark pools. You don't have to be alone (or maybe you do).

1998 7/J23
10KM
CIRC
BIKES
1-A-1

Near Taynuilt A walk combining education with recreation. Start behind **Bonawe Iron Furnace** (2129/HISTORY) and go along the river side to a suspension bridge and thence to Inverawe Smokehouse (open to the public; café). Walk back less interesting but all very nice. Best not to park in Bonawe car park (for HS visitors, and it closes at 6pm).

1999 9/L29
1-B-2

Glen Trool nr Newton Stewart A simple non-clambering, well-marked route round Loch Trool. A circular 8km but with many options. And a caff at the visitor centre. 1590/GLENS.

Woodland Walks

2000 7/G21

✓✓ **Ardnamurchan** For anyone who loves trees (or hills, great coastal scenery and raw nature), this far-flung peninsula is a revelation. Approach from S via Corran ferry on A82 S of Fort William or N from Lochailort on A830 Mallaig-Fort William road (1631/SCENIC ROUTES) or from Mull. Many marked and unmarked trails (see Ariundle below) but consult online or locally. To visit Ardnamurchan is to fall in love with Scotland again and again. Woods especially around Loch Sunart. Good family campsite at **Resipole** (1235/camping with kids) and lovely food at Lochaline (1075/highlands).

2001 6/N17
1-4KM
CIRC
XBIKES
1-A-2

✓ **Randolph's Leap** nr **Forres** On the B9007. Spectacular gorge of the gorgeous Findhorn river lined, with beautiful beech woods and a great place to swim or picnic (1666/swimming), so listen up. Go **either**: 10km S of Forres on the A940 for Grantown, then the B9007 for Ferness and Carrbridge. 1km from the sign for **Logie Steading** (2144/scottish shops) and 300m from the narrow stone bridge, there's a pull-over place on the bend. The woods are on the other side of the road. **Or**: take the A939 S from Nairn or N from Grantown and at Ferness take the B9007 for Forres. Approaching from this direction, it's about 6km along the road; the pull over is on your right. This is one of the sylvan secrets of the North. Trailboard at site and at Logie Steading from which it's a 3.5km walk return, so you could simply head for here; there's a great café.

2002 7/J23
2-8KM
CIRC
XBIKES
2-A-2

✓ **Lochaweside** Unclassified road on N side of loch between Kilchrenan and Ford, centred on Dalavich. Illustrated brochure available from local hotels around Kilchrenan and Dalavich post office, describes 6 walks in the mixed, mature forest all starting from car parking places on the road. 3 starting from the Barnaline car park are trail-marked and could easily be followed without a guide. Avich Falls route crosses River Avich after 2km with falls on return route. Inverinan Glen is always good. The timber trail from the Big Tree/Cruachan car park 2km S of Dalavich takes in the loch, a waterfall and it's easy on the eye and foot (4km). The track from the car park N of Kilchrenan on the B845 back to Taynuilt is less travelled but also fine. Pub at Kilchrenan.

2003 7/J24
3KM
CIRC
XBIKES
1-A-1

✓ **Inveraray Castle Estate** I don't actually list Inveraray in Best Castles in *StB*, but the gardens and especially the woodland walks on the estate are superb in any season. Two main routes to follow, one around the policies and another up to the folly (not more than an hour) for great views. Castle (or its tearoom with pictures from *Downton's* Scottish episode, which was filmed here). Apr–Oct, grounds AYR. There's also a good tearoom in the village 1421/tearooms and the estimable **George Hotel** 775/argyll.

2004 7/K25
3KM
CIRC
XBIKES
1-B-1

✓ **Puck's Glen** nr **Dunoon** Close to the gates of the **Younger Botanic Garden at Benmore** (1501/gardens) on the other side of the A815 to Strachur 12km N of Dunoon. A short, exhilarating woodland walk from a convenient car park. Ascend through trees then down into a fairy glen, follow the burn back to the road. Some pools to be swum.

2005 5/N19
1-B-2

✓ **Rothiemurchus Forest** nr **Aviemore** The place to experience the magic and the majesty of the great Caledonian Forest and the beauty of Scots pine. Approach from B970, the road that parallels the A9 from Coylumbridge to Kincraig/Kingussie. 2km from Inverdruie near Coylumbridge follow sign for Loch an Eilean; one of the most perfect lochans in these or any woods. Loch circuit 5km (1609/lochs). Info, sustenance and shopping at the Rothiemurchus visitor centre at Inverdruie (**Druie**, their café daytime only) or at the superb **Potting Shed** at Inshriach (1383/tearooms).

2006 5/M20
3KM
CIRC

✓ **Uath Lochans** Rothiemurchus A less frequented place and a very fine walk in the same neck of the woods as one of several around Glen Feshie. Off the B970 road between Kincraig and Coylumbridge/Aviemore signed Glen Feshie, 2km

XBIKES

1-A-1

to car park on the right. 3 walks marked around the lochans, all a dawdle. Best take you around Farleitter Crag with views over the treetops (red route is not as long as it says, maybe 1.5 hours). Repair to **The Potting Shed** at Inshriach (1383/ TEAROOMS).

2007 7/H21

5KM

CIRC

MTBIKES

1-B-2

✓ **Ariundle Oakwoods** Strontian 35km Fort William via Corran Ferry. Walk guide brochure at Strontian visitor centre. There are many walks around Loch Sunart and Ariundle. Rare oak and other native species. You see how very different Scotland's landscape was before industrialisation. Start over town bridge, turning right for Polloch. Go on past Ariundle Centre, with good home baking in Kate Campbell's café, and park. Walks are well marked.

2008 7/L24

3KM

CIRC

1-A-2

✓ **Inchcailloch Island** Loch Lomond Surprisingly large island near Balmaha, criss-crossed with easy, interesting woodland walks (<1km) with the loch always there through the trees. A pleasant afternoon option is to row there from Balmaha Boatyard (£10 a boat at TGP). They also run a regular ferry; 01360 870214.

2009 8/N22

3.5KM

CIRC

XBIKES

1-A-2

The Birks o' Aberfeldy Circular walk through oak, beech and the birch (or birk) woods of the title, easily reached and signed from town main street (1km). Steep-sided wooded glen of the Moness Burn with attractive falls especially the higher one spanned by bridge where the 2 marked walks converge. This is where Burns 'spread the lightsome days' in his eponymous poem. Excellent tearoom and all-round life enhancer, **The Watermill**, back in town (1385/TEAROOMS) and the **3 Lemons** (941/PERTHSHIRE). Allow 2 hours.

2010 8/N22

1-3KM

CIRC

XBIKES

1-A-1

The Hermitage, Dunkeld On A9 2km N of Dunkeld. Popular, easy, accessible walks along glen and gorge of River Braan with pavilion overlooking the falls and, further on, Ossian's Cave. Also uphill Craigvinean walks starts here to good viewpoint (2km). Several woody walks around Dunkeld/Birnam – there's a good leaflet from the tourist information centre. 2km along river is **Rumbling Bridge**, a deep gorge, and beyond it great spots for swimming (1661/SWIMMING). Good tearoom in Dunkeld (1406/TEAROOMS).

2011 6/N19

Glenmore Forest Park nr Aviemore Along from Coylumbridge (and adjacent Rothiemurchus) on road to ski resort, the forest trail area centred on Loch Morlich (sandy beaches, good swimming, water sports). Visitor centre has maps of walk and bike trails and an activity programme. Glenmore Lodge (01479 861256) is Scotland's Outdoor Training Centre and well worth a visit. They know a thing or two about walking!

2012 7/J22

<1-5KM · CIRC

MTBIKES

1-B-1

Sutherland's Grove Barcaldine 10km N of Oban on the A828. Accessible and easy walking where paths are well signed (maps usually available in the car park). Notable for splendid Douglas firs (from 1870), gorge and waterfalls. 5 walks from <500m to 5km.

2013 8/M24

2 OR 4KM

CIRC

XBIKES

1-A-1

Above the Pass of Leny Callander A walk through mixed forest (beech, oak, birch, pine) with great Trossachs views. Start from main car park on A84 4km N of Callander (Falls of Leny are on opposite side of road, 100m away). Various options marked and boarded where marshy. Another short but glorious walk is to the **Bracklinn Falls** – signed off E end of Callander Main St; start by the golf course (1km; see also 1673/SWIMMING). Also loop to the Crags (adding another 2km).

2014 8/M21

2-15KM

CIRC

Loch Tummel Walks nr Pitlochry Mixed woodland N of Loch Tummel, reached by the B8019 from Pitlochry to Rannoch. Visitor centre at **Queen's View** (1650/ VIEWS), 01796 473123; and walks in the Allean Forest which take in some historical sites (a restored farmstead, standing stones) start nearby (2-4km). There are many other walks in area: the Forestry Commission brochure is worth following (available from visitor centre and local tourist information centres).

2015 9/L29 **The New Galloway Forest** Huge area of forest and hill country with every type of trail including part of **Southern Upland Way** from Bargrennan to Dalry (1967/LONG WALKS). Visitor centres at Kirroughtree (5km Newton Stewart) and Clatteringshaws Loch on the Queen's Way (9km New Galloway). Glen and Loch Trool are very fine (1590/GLENS); the Retreat Oakwood near Laurieston has 5km trails. **Kitty's** in New Galloway has great cakes and tea (1381/TEAROOMS). There's a river pool on the Raiders' Road (1674/SWIMMING). One could ramble on...

2016 6/R17 **Duff House** Banff Duff House is the major attraction around here (see 2139/
7KM GALLERIES), but if you've time it would be a pity to miss the wooded policies and the
CIRC · XBIKES meadows and riverscape of the Deveron. To the Bridge of Alvah where you should
1-A-2 be bound is about 7km return; 1.5 hours return. See 1996/GLEN & RIVER WALKS.

2017 5/L17 **Torrachilty Forest & Rogie Falls** nr Contin & Strathpeffer Enter by old bridge
1-4KM just outside Contin on main A835 W to Ullapool or further along (4km) at Rogie
CIRC Falls car park. Shame to miss the falls (1606/WATERFALLS), but the woods and gorge
XBIKES are pleasant enough if it's merely a stroll you need. **Ben Wyvis** further up the road
1-A-2 is the big challenge (1960/MUNROS).

2018 6/N19 **Abernethy Forest** nr Boat of Garten 3km from village off B970, but hard to miss because the famous ospreys are signposted from all over (1719/BIRDS). Nevertheless this woodland reserve is a tranquil place among native pinewoods around Loch Mallachie with dells and trails. Many other birdies twittering around your picnic. They don't dispose of the midges.

2019 6/Q17 **Fochabers** On main A96 about 3km E of town are some excellent woody and winding walks around the glen and Whiteash Hill (2-5km). Further W on the **Moray Coast Culbin Forest**: head for Cloddymoss or Kintessack off A96 at **Brodie Castle** 12km E of Nairn (1754/CASTLES). Acres of Sitka (spruce) in a sandy coastal forest. Worth going to **The Bakehouse** in Findhorn for sustenance (1077/HIGHLANDS).

2020 8/Q23 **Templeton Woods** Dundee Extensive and atmospheric woodlands on the edge of Dundee just beyond the Kingsway dual carriageway, turning 3km on Coupar Angus road after Camperdown Park. Many trails to walk or bike; visitor centre. Red squirrels and roe deer may scamper. **Birkhill Cemetery** on the way in is a joy (1876/GRAVEYARDS).

Dumfries House Cumnock Wooded policies, farmland and extensive new gardens in development. Report: 1505/GARDENS.

Coastal Walks

2021 7/F26 ✓✓ **Kintra** Islay On Bowmore-Port Ellen road take Oa turn-off: 2km to
XCIRC Kintra turn-off, then 4km. Park in old farmyard by campsite (1224/WILD
XBIKES CAMPING). A fabulous beach (1567/BEACHES) runs in opposite direction and a
2-B-2 notable golf course behind it (2059/GOLF). You are invited to 'Walk on the Wild Side' along N coast of the Mull of Oa, an area of diverse beauty with a wonderful shoreline. The walk to the **American Monument** is also spectacular (1.5km or 6km circular 1827/MONUMENTS).

2022 6/T18 ✓✓ **The Bullers of Buchan** nr Peterhead 8km S of Peterhead on A975 Cruden Bay road. Park and walk 100m to cottages. To the N is the walk to Boddam and Longhaven Nature Reserve along dramatic cliffs and S past **Slains Castle** (1791/RUINS). The Bullers is at start of walk, a sheer-sided hole 75m deep with outlet to the sea through a natural arch. Walk round the edge, looking down on layers of birds (who may try to dive-bomb you away); it's a wonder of nature on an awesome coast. Take great care (and a head for heights).

2023 4/K12 ✓✓ **Cape Wrath & The Cliffs of Clo Mor** Britain's most northwesterly point reached by ferry from 1km off A838 4km S of Durness; a 10-min crossing then 40-min minibus ride to Cape. Ferry holds 12 and runs Apr-Sep (call for times: 01971 511246) or ferryman direct (07719 678729): John Morrison on his boat for 30 years. At 280m Clo Mor are high though not the UK's highest. For cliffs, ask to be put off the bus (which goes to the Stevenson lighthouse) and reduce the walk to 3km. The caff here **Ozone**, is always open (I've never been). Around 8 trips a day, weather and MoD range permitting. Bikes are OK. Easter-Sep. In other direction, the 28km to Kinlochbervie is one of Britain's most wild and wonderful coastal walks. Beaches include **Sandwood** (1565/BEACHES). While in this area: **Smoo Cave** 2km E of Durness is worth a visit.

2024 4/J14 ✓ **Old Man of Stoer** nr Lochinver Easy, exhilarating and spectacular walk to
1-B-2 the dramatic 70m sandstone sea stack. Start at lighthouse off unclassified road 14km N Lochinver. Park and follow sheep tracks; cliffs are high and steep. 7km round trip; 2/3 hours. Then find the **Secret Beach** (1574/BEACHES).

2025 9/N30 ✓ **Rockcliffe to Kippford** An easy and can be circular stroll along the 'Scottish
1-A-2 Riviera' through woodland near the shore (2km) past the Mote of Mark, a Dark Age hill fort with views to Rough Island. The better clifftop walk is in the other direction to Castlehillpoint. No tearoom now but the famed waterside pub, **The Anchor**, is in Kippford (1325/GASTROPUBS).

2026 8/R25 ✓ **St Abb's Head** Among the most dramatic coastal scenery in southern
5-10KM Scotland, scary in a wind, rhapsodic on a summer's day. Extensive wildlife
CIRC reserve and trails through coastal hills and vales to cliffs. Best to park at visitor
XBIKES centre on St Abbs village road 3km from A1107 to Eyemouth and follow route
1-B-2 (1741/RESERVES). 30 mins to cliffs, walks marked 1/2/3km. Nice caff, interpretation centre, gallery (2155/SHOPS). Decent pub grub at **New Inn**, Coldingham and 2 good caffs in St Abbs village (2km).

2027 5/H18 **Applecross** This far peninsula is marvellous for many reasons (1619/SCENIC ROUTES) and there are fine walks in and around Applecross Bay foreshore including river and woodland strolls. See *Walks on the Applecross Peninsula*, available locally.

2028 7/H21 **Singing Sands** Ardnamurchan 2km N of Acharacle, signed for Arevegaig. 3km
10KM RETURN to Arevegaig and park before wooden bridge (gate may be locked). Cross wooden
XCIRC bridge, following track round side of Kentra Bay. Follow signs for Gorteenorn, and
BIKES walk through forest track and woodland to beach. As you pound the sands they
1-B-1 should sing to you whilst you bathe in the beautiful views of Rum, Eigg, Muck and Skye (and just possibly the sea). Check at tourist information centre for directions and other walks booklet. 'Beware unexploded mines', it says.

2029 6/R17 **East From Cullen** Moray Coast This is the same walk mentioned with reference
8KM · XCIRC to **Sunnyside** (1563/BEACHES), a golden beach with a fabulous ruined castle
XBIKES (**Findlater**) that might be your destination (1779/RUINS). There's a track E along
1-A-1 from harbour. 2 hours return. A superb coastline.

2030 6/S17   **Crovie-Troup Head** Moray Coast Another Moray Coast classic that takes in the extraordinary cliff-clinging village of Crovie and the bird-stacked cliffs of the headland. Start at car park and viewpoint above Crovie 15km E of Banff off B9031. Park and walk to end of village, then follow path to Troup Head. 5km return. Shorter walk (1.5km) from RSPB car park 2km off B9031 E of Crovie/Gardenstown, signed for Northfield. Big sky and sea and birdlife.

2031 5/M17   **The South Sutor** Cromarty The walk, known locally as 'The 100 Steps' though
5KM   there are a few more than that, from Cromarty village (1552/VILLAGES; 1424/
CIRC   TEAROOMS; 1080/HIGHLANDS) round the tip of the S promontory at the narrow
XBIKES   entrance to the Cromarty Firth. E of village past bowling green then up through
1-A-1   woods to headland. Good bench! Go further to top car park and viewpoint panel.
Perhaps return by road. You may see dolphins in that sea!

2032 4/Q12   **St John's Point & Scotland's Haven** East Mey, nr John o' Groats A short, secret
2KM   walk between Thurso and John o' Groats on this northernmost headland. Prince Charles
CIRC   walks here. Brilliant views to Dunnet Head and S Orkney. Follow signs then pass the
XBIKES   **Castle of Mey** (1757/CASTLES). After 2km turn left. Park at cottages and go through long
1-B-2   gate at the bend of the road, finding a path to right of the gorse heading for the sea. You
don't see the stacks, the Men of Mey where the 5 tides meet, till you're almost there.
Following track to right mostly carved out of heather you arrive at a narrow, steeply
banked cove called Scotland's Haven. A perfect shelter! Then back. 1 hour.

2033 4/L12   **Ceannabeinne Township Trail** nr Durness This is the walk near my favourite
1KM · CIRC   beach (1561/BEACHES), 7km E of Durness. There's a lay-by; marker boards direct
XBIKES   you on the path, relating the story of the township abandoned in 1842. A short, life-
1-B-2   enhancing stroll through history (the 'Durness Riots!') and splendid coastal scenery.

2034 8/R24   **The Fife Coastal Path and The Chain Walk** Elie Adventurous headland
2-B-2   scramble at the W end of Elie (and Earlsferry). Britain's only Via Ferrata? Go to end
of the road then by path skirting golf course towards headland. Hand- and footholds
carved into rock with chains to haul yourself up. Emerge by Shell Bay Caravan Park.
Watch tide; don't go alone. **The 19th Hole** is a must-eat (1306/GASTROPUBS).

2035 7/J26   **Cock of Arran** Lochranza This round trip usually starts at Lochranza castle, a
2-B-2   breathtaking coastal trail round the N end of the island (see 2215/ISLAND WALKS).
Great for twitchers, ramblers, fossil hunters and geologists. Strong boots advisable.
Approximately 4 hours, around 12km.

2036 1/P11   **Island Coasts** See Fantastic Walks in the Islands, p. 382–84, but also these
5/F19   3 spectacular walks:
5/F18   **Duirinish** coast on **Skye**, a long (8-12 hours) route with some of the best coastal
architecture in the UK: sea arches, waterfalls, stacks. For starts, consult locally.
Minginish coast, also on **Skye**, with views to the small isles, Hebrides and the
Cuillin with fantastic geology and sea eagles above. 6-8 hours.
The Old Man of Hoy from Rackwick on Hoy. 10km of epic coast. Ferry from
Stromness then minibus.

2037 8/Q23   **Broughty Ferry Esplanade** This is a very different walk/stroll from others on these
3KM   pages, no wild coast here but nonetheless an engaging and pleasant pursuit only
XCIRC   20 mins from Dundee centre. Head to the front (The Tay Estuary Waterfront) in 'The
1-A-1   Ferry' (many good food and drink options, see p. 174–76) towards the castle. Beyond is
'The Esplanade' and a 3km easy, breezy beach walk to Monifieth. Highlights are the
Barnhill Rock Garden, the 'swimming zone' – they are proud of this beach – and the
customary beverage stop at the **Glass Pavilion** (963/DUNDEE). There may be dolphins!

the
Best
Outdoor Activities

Scotland's Great Golf Courses

Those listed open to non-members and available to visitors at most times unless stated. Handicap certificates may be required.

AYRSHIRE

2038 7/K28
LLL
✓✓✓ **Trump Turnberry** www.trumpturnberry.com · 01655 331000 Ailsa (championship) set to re-emerge upgraded in June 2016 and Kintyre courses. Possible by application, cheaper if you're at the hotel (798/AYRSHIRE). Among the UK's top 3 courses: superb. Golf academy a great place to learn. Let's not talk of Trump here.

2039 7/K27
✓✓ **Royal Troon** Old Course · www.royaltroon.co.uk · 01292 311555 One of the great links courses. Staying at Marine Highland Hotel (01292 314444) helps to get on. Easier is the **Portland Course** (also 01292 311555) across the road from Royal (shorter, more sheltered). Closed Oct-Apr. And 804/AYRSHIRE for the adjacent **Piersland House Hotel**.

2040 8/L25
✓ **Gailes Links** www.gaileslinks.co.uk · 01294 311649 Superb championship links course. Near Troon and Prestwick above and below, 5km S of Irvine off A78.

2041 7/L27
Old Prestwick www.prestwickgc.co.uk · 01292 477404 Original home of The Open and 'every challenge you'd wish to meet'. Hotels opposite cost less than a round. Unlikely to get on at weekends (Sat members only).

EAST LOTHIAN

2042 8/R25
✓✓ **Gullane No.1** www.gullanegolfclub.com · 01620 842255 One of 3 varied courses surrounding charming village on links and within driving distance (35km) of Edinburgh. **Muirfield** is nearby, but you need an introduction. Gullane is OK most days except Sat/Sun. (Handicap required for no.1 only – under 24 men, 30 ladies). No.3 best for beginners. Visitor centre acts as clubhouse for non-members on 2/3. Clubhouse for members/no.1 players only.

2043 8/R25
LL
✓✓ **North Berwick East & West** www.northberwickgolfclub.com · 01620 895040/892135 East (officially the Glen Golf Club) has stunning views. A superb clifftop course and not too long. West is the third-oldest course in the world and more taxing (especially the classic Redan), used for Open qualifying. In UK top 30 and world top 100 courses, this is a very fine links.

2044 8/Q25
Musselburgh Links www.musselburgholdlinks.co.uk · 0131 653 5122 The original home of golf (recorded here in 1672), but this local-authority-run 9-hole links is not exactly top turf and is enclosed by Musselburgh Racecourse. Nostalgia still appeals though. **Royal Musselburgh** (01875 810276; www.royalmusselburgh.co.uk) nearby for the serious game. Dates to 1774, fifth-oldest in Scotland. On both you play through history.

NORTH EAST

2045 8/R23
✓✓ **Carnoustie** www.carnoustiegolflinks.co.uk · 01241 802270 3 good links courses; even possible (with handicap certificate) to get on the **Championship Course** (though weekends difficult). Every hole has character. **Buddon Links** is cheaper and relatively quiet. Combination tickets available. A well-managed and accessible course, increasingly a golfing must.

2046 6/T19 ✓ **Murcar Links** Aberdeen · www.murcarlinks.com · 01224 704354
Getting on **Royal Aberdeen** Course is difficult, but Murcar is a testing alternative, a seaside course 6km N of centre off Peterhead road signed at roundabout after Exhibition Centre. Handicap certificate needed. Other municipal courses include charming 9-hole at Hazlehead (in an excellent 3-course complex).

2047 6/T18 ✓ **Cruden Bay** nr Peterhead · www.crudenbaygolfclub.co.uk ·
LL 01779 812285 On A975 40km N of Aberdeen. Designed by Tom Simpson and ranked 54th in the world, a spectacular links course with the intangible aura of bygone days. Quirky holes epitomise old-fashioned style. Weekends difficult to get on.

2048 5/N17 ✓ **Nairn** www.nairngolfclub.co.uk · 01667 453208 Traditional seaside links, L one of the easiest championship courses to get on. Good clubhouse, friendly folk. Nairn Dunbar across town also has good links. Handicap certificate required.

2049 4/N16 ✓ **Royal Dornoch** www.royaldornoch.com · 01862 810219 Sutherland LL championship course laid out by Tom Morris in 1877. Has been declared 5th best course in the world outside the US, but not busy or incessantly pounded. No poor holes. Stimulating sequences. Probably the most northerly great golf course in the world – and not impossible to get on. Sister course the **Struie** also a treat.

2050 6/T19 ✓ **The Trump Golf Course** Balmedie · www.trumpgolfscotland.com ·
01358 743300 Surrounded by controversy as well as a uniquely special sand-dune system, Donald Trump's 'best golf course in the world' opened 2014 manicured and managed as you'd expect. There will end up being wind farms in the sea out there, but some feel Trump's protest against this potential blot on this horizon was hypocritical.

FIFE

2051 8/R23 ✓✓✓ **St Andrews** www.standrews.com · 01334 466666 The home and L Mecca of golf and the largest golf complex in Europe. Old Course most central and celebrated. Application by ballot the day or year before (handicap certificate needed) or buy an 'Old Course Experience'. For Jubilee (1897, upgraded 1989) and Eden (1914, laid out by Harry S. Colt paying homage to the Old with large, sloping greens), apply the day before or in advance (01334 466718). Similar arrangements for the New Course (1895, some rate the best); probably has easiest access. Less demanding are new Strathtyrum and Balgove (upgraded 9-hole for beginners, not advance bookable) courses. All 6 courses contiguous and in town. The new Castle Course is a 320-acre clifftop course for all abilities (no handicap needed, open Mar-Nov) and the Dukes Course (part of Old Course Hotel) 3km away is a great alternative to the links. Reservations (and ballot). There's a whole lot of golf to be had – get your money out!

2052 8/R24 ✓✓ **Kingsbarns** www.kingsbarns.com · 01334 460860 Between Crail and L St Andrews, one of Fife's newest and Scotland's best courses. In all top rankings. Challenging and a beautiful location on a secret coast. Not cheap.

2053 8/Q24 ✓ **Ladybank** www.ladybankgolf.co.uk · 01337 830814 Best inland course in Fife; Tom Morris-designed again. Very well kept and organised. Good facilities. Tree-lined and picturesque. Hosts Open qualifying rounds.

2054 8/R24 **Elie** www.golfhouseclub.co.uk · 01333 330301 Splendid open links kept in top condition; can be windswept. The starter has his famous periscope and may be watching you. Adjacent 9-hole course, often busy with kids, is fun (01333 330955).

2055 8/R24   **Crail** www.crailgolfingsociety.co.uk · 01333 450686 **Balcomie Links** originally designed by that legendary Tom Morris (again), or **Craighead Links** new sweeping course. All holes in sight of sea. Not expensive; easy to get on.

2056 8/Q24   **Lundin Links** www.lundingolfclub.co.uk · 01333 320202 Challenging seaside course used as Open qualifier. Some devious contourings. In the village there is also a separate 9-hole course, Lundin Ladies, the oldest ladies' golf club in the world, open to all (01333 320832).

ELSEWHERE

2057 8/N24   ✓✓✓ **Gleneagles** www.gleneagles.com · 0800 389 3737 Legendary
     LL   golf the mainstay of Perthshire resort complex (2057/COUNTRY-HOUSE HOTELS). 3 courses: PGA Centenary, designed by Jack Nicklaus, which hosted the 2014 Ryder Cup, and the King's and Queen's Courses.

2058 8/S27   ✓✓ **Roxburghe Hotel Golf Course** nr Kelso · www.roxburghe.net · 01573 450333 Only championship course in the Borders. Designed by Dave Thomas along banks of River Teviot. Part of the Floors Castle estate. Open to non-res. Bar/lounge/clubhouse. See also 848/BORDERS.

Good Golf Courses In Great Places

2059 7/F26   ✓ **Machrie** Islay · www.machrie.net · 01496 302310 7km Port Ellen. Worth
     LL   going to Islay just for the golf. The Machrie (Golf) Hotel undergoing major refurbishment at TGP; reopening 2018. Old-fashioned course to be played by feel and instinct. Splendid, often windy isolation. The notorious 17th, Iffrin (it means Hell), vortex shaped from the dune system of marram and close-cropped grass, is one of many great holes. 18 holes.

2060 7/G28   ✓ **Machrihanish** www.machgolf.com · 01586 810213 & **Machrihanish**
     LL   **Dunes** nr Campbeltown · www.machrihanishdunes.com · 01586 810000 Among the dunes and links of the glorious 8km stretch of the **Machrihanish Beach** (1564/BEACHES). The Atlantic provides thunderous applause. See 786/ARGYLL.

2061 3/E16   ✓ **Harris Golf Club** Scarista, Isle of Harris · www.harrisgolf.com ·
     LLL   01859 550226 Phone number is for the secretary but no need to ring: just turn up on the road between Tarbert and Rodel and leave £20 in the box. First tee commands one of the great views in golf and throughout this basic but testing course, you are looking out to sea over **Scarista Beach** (1568/BEACHES) and bay. The sunset may put you off your swing. 9 holes.

2062 3/C19   ✓ **Askernish** South Uist · www.askernishgolfclub.com · 01878 700628 Another superb Hebridean dunes and machair course first laid out by Tom Morris in 1891, rescued and reopened in 2008. 'One of the most natural golf courses in the world'. 18 holes.

2063 9/N30   ✓ **Southerness** Solway Firth · www.southernessgolfclub.com ·
     L   01387 880677 25km S of Dumfries by A710. A championship course on links on the silt flats of the firth. Despite its prestige, visitors do get on. Start times available 10am-noon and 2-4pm. There are few courses as good as this at these prices. Under the wide Solway sky, it's pure – southerness.

2064 8/P22 ✓ **Rosemount** Blairgowrie · www.theblairgowriegolfclub.co.uk · 01250 872622 Off A93, S of Blairgowrie. An excellent, pampered and well-managed course in the middle of green Perthshire, an alternative perhaps to Gleneagles, usually easier to get on and rather cheaper.

2065 6/N19 ✓ **Boat of Garten** www.boatgolf.com · 01479 831282 Challenging, picturesque course in town where ospreys have been known to wheel overhead. Has been called the Gleneagles of the North; certainly the best around, though not for novices. 18 holes.

2066 5/M16 ✓ **Tain** www.tain-golfclub.co.uk · 01862 892314 & **Brora** www.broragolf.
L co.uk · 01408 621911 2 northern courses that are a delight to play on. Tain designed by Tom Morris in 1890. Brora stunning, with good clubhouse, hotel (1046/HIGHLANDS) and coos on the course. With Royal Dornoch (above), they're a roving-golfer must.

2067 5/H16 **Gairloch** www.gairlochgolfclub.co.uk · 01445 712407 As you enter town from
L S on A832, it overlooks the bay and a perfect, pink, sandy beach (1575/BEACHES). Small clubhouse with honesty box out of hours. Not the most agonising course; and on a clear day with views to Skye, you can forget agonising over anything. 9 holes.

2068 9/M29 **New Galloway** www.nggc.uk · 01644 420737 Local course on S edge of this fine wee toon. Almost all on a slope but affording great views of Loch Ken and the Galloway Forest behind. No bunkers and only 9 short holes, some well steep but exhilarating play. Easy on, except Sun. Just turn up.

2069 8/R28 **Minto** Denholm · www.mintogolf.co.uk · 01450 870220 9km E of Hawick. Spacious parkland in Teviot valley. Best holes 3rd, 12th and 16th. **Vertish Hill** www.hawickgolfclub.com · 01450 372293 · **Hawick** A more challenging hill course. Both among the best in Borders. 18 holes. Best holes 2nd and 18th.

2070 8/R25 **Gifford** www.giffordgolfclub.com · 01620 810591 Dinky 9-hole inland course on the edge of a charming village, by-passed by the queue for the big East Lothian courses and a guarded secret among regulars. Generally OK, but phone starter (above) for availability. I was touched when they wrote to thank me for this entry a few editions back. *Golf World* once called it 'the best 9 holes in Scotland'.

2071 5/L17 **Strathpeffer** www.strathpeffergolf.co.uk · 01997 421219 Very hilly (we do mean hilly) course full of character and with exhilarating Highland views. Small-town friendliness. You play up there with the gods and other old codgers. 18 holes.

2072 6/P17 **Elgin** www.elgingolfclub.com · 01343 542338 1km from town on A941 Perth road. Many memorable holes on moorland/parkland course in an area where links may lure you to the coast (**Nairn, Lossiemouth**). 18 holes.

2073 4/L12 **Durness** www.durnessgolfclub.org · 01971 511364 The most northerly golf
LL course on mainland UK, on the wild headland by Balnakeil Bay, looking over to Faraid Head. The last hole is over the sea. Only open since 1988, it's already got cult status. 2km W of Durness. 9 holes.

2074 5/H20 **Traigh** Arisaig · www.traighgolf.co.uk · 01687 450337 A830 Fort William-
LL Mallaig road, 2km N Arisaig. Pronounced Try and you should. The islands are set out like stones in the sea around you and there are 9 hilly holes of fun. Has been called 'the most beautiful 9 holes in the world'.

The Best Cycling

EASY CYCLING

2075 8/S27

✓✓ **The Borders** The Borders with its gentle hills, river tracks and low urbanisation has been paving the cycleway both for mountain biking (see below) and for more leisurely and family pursuits. Good linkage and signage and many routes, eg the 4 Abbeys, the Tweed Cycleway, the Borderloop and individual trails. **Glentress,** by Innerleithen, now a top cycling hub. '**Tweedlove**' is an international love of cycling festival in late May (34/EVENTS). Cycling guides and downloads widely available. There's ample choice for all abilities and ages. See also 7 Stanes (below).

2076 6/Q18
20KM
CAN BE CIRC

✓ **Speyside Way: Craigellachie-Ballindalloch** The cycling part of the Way (1968/LONG WALKS), with great views; it's flat and there are no cars. Goes past distilleries. Circular by return on minor roads.
START Craigellachie, by rangers' office.

2077 8/L24
11KM
CAN BE CIRC

✓ **The Trossachs** nr Aberfoyle & Callander · www.trossachs.co.uk Many low-level lochside trails and long-distance routes, including the West Loch Lomond Cycle Path and Sustrans Route 7. Good runs are Aberfoyle–Callander (20km, all off-road) and the Loch Ard Circle from Aberfoyle going W (signed Inversnaid Scenic Route) or Loch Katrine to Callander. Bike hire Loch Katrine, Callander, Aberfoyle.

2078 7/K26

✓ **Cumbrae** For an adventurous day out, take ferry from Largs (every 15 mins, 30 mins in winter) to beautiful Cumbrae (and visit the classic **Ritz** 1374/CAFÉS). 4 or 5 routes around the island. One a stiff pull to a great viewpoint. Others stick to sea level. Consult locally. Circular with extension to Barbay Hill, 15km. All these roads are quiet.

2079 8/M25
55KM
CIRC

Forth & Clyde Canal, Glasgow–Falkirk Wheel East out of the city, urban at first then nice in the Kelvin Valley; Kilsyth Hills to the north. Falkirk Wheel 4/ATTRACTIONS.
START The Maryhill Locks, Maryhill Rd. And check the brilliant hire project www.nextbike.co.uk/en/ in Glasgow.

2080 9/L30
15KM
CAN BE CIRC

Glentrool nr Newton Stewart Two routes from visitor centre (1590/GLENS; 1901/BOB). Deep in the forest and well signed. Briefly joins public road. The 7 Stanes sections can be difficult (see below).
START Glentrool Visitor Centre off A714. Bike hire at **Kirroughtree** and network of trails listed from here (see below).

2081 8
12KM
CIRC

Edinburgh Trails There is a vast network of cycle and towpaths especially N of the New Town. Another good run is to Balerno from Union Canal towpath in Lower Gilmore Place. End at Balerno High School.

2082 5/N19
20KM
CIRC

Loch an Eilean nr Aviemore Lots of bike tracks here in the Rothiemurchus Forest. This one goes past one of Scotland's most beautiful lochs (1609/LOCHS) and you can go further to Loch Insh via Feshiebridge and around Glen Feshie.
START Signed from B970 at Coylumbridge.

MOUNTAIN BIKING

2083 8, 9

✓✓ **7 Stanes** Borders & South West · www.7stanes.com Ambitious and hugely popular network of bike trails in S of Scotland, different lengths and abilities in each of 8 places. Include **Glentress/The Tweed Valley** (see below),

Newcastleton, Forest of Ae, Dalbeattie, Mabie, Glentrool (see above), and **Kirroughtree** (see above). Routes at all levels. Built by bikers. Many challenges. Good signage throughout.

2084 8/Q27 ✓✓ **Glentress Forest** nr Peebles · www.glentressforest.com
Meticulously constructed mountain-bike trails. Well signed and well used from 2 car park starts in this hugely popular national cycling centre, with café, shop (Alpine Bikes) and many facilities, including showers, 'Roompods' to stay in. Many food and drink options in Peebles and Innerleithen, p. 158–59. Trails for all levels, plenty of flowing descents and drops. The serious downhill stuff is nearby at **Traquair** where the **7Stanes** cross-country route also starts (see above).

2085 8/M26 ✓ **Cathkin Braes Country Park** Glasgow Host of the 2014 Commonwealth Games mountain bike competition. Car park at the top of the park is a good starting point to the trails, which offer technical biking and great views.

2086 7/K21 ✓ **Nevis Range** nr Fort William · www.nevisrange.co.uk Hosts the Mountain Bike World Cup on the Witch's Trails. For downhill adrenaline junkies take the gondola up. It's not all hardcore; there are terrain and routes to suit all. Pinemarten café at car park and Snowgoose Restaurant & Bar 650m up the mountain. Bike hire Nevis Range, Inverlochy. For more downhill action head to **Glencoe Mountain Resort**.

2087 9/L29
25KM
CIRC
Clatteringshaws nr Glentrool (see above). Various routes around Clatteringshaws Loch in the Galloway Forest and Hills. Most are easy, but some serious climbs and descents. Visitor centre has tearoom.

2088 6/R20
25KM
CIRC
Glen Tanar Royal Deeside · www.glentanar.co.uk Good way to encounter this beautiful glen in the shadow of Mount Keen. Quite difficult in places. **START** Tombae on the B976 opposite junction of A97 and A93.

2089 5
XCIRC
Great Glen, Fort William-Loch Lochy Easy at first on the Caledonian Canal towpath. Later it gets hilly with long climbs. Great views. **START** Neptune's Staircase at Banavie near Fort William.

2090 8
25KM
CIRC
Perthshire & Angus, Glenfernate-Blair Atholl Beautiful Highland trail that takes in forests, lochs and **Glen Tilt** (1977/GLEN & RIVER WALKS). Mainly rough track. Follow directions from tourist information centre leaflets. **START** On the A924 14km E of Pitlochry, 500m E of school.

The Only Open-Air Swimming Pools

2091 8/S20 ✓ **Stonehaven Outdoor Pool** Stonehaven · www.stonehavenopenairpool. co.uk · 01569 762134 The Friends of Stonehaven Outdoor Pool won the day (eat your hearts out North Berwick) and saved a great pool that goes from length to strength. Fabulous 1930s Olympic-sized heated salt-water pool (85ft). Midnight swims from 10pm Jul/Aug on Wednesdays (is that cool, or what?). Jun-Sep only: 10am-7.30pm (10am-6pm weekends). Heated salt-water heaven. And **The Bay** nearby (1352/FISH & CHIPS).

2092 7/K25 ✓ **Gourock Bathing Pool** Gourock · 01475 213122 The only other open-air (proper) pool in Scotland that's still open – historic and recently refurbished. On coast road S of town 45km from Glasgow. 1950s-style leisure. Heated (to 29°C), so it doesn't need to be a scorcher, but can get chock-a-block). May-Oct weekdays until 7.30/8pm, weekends 4.30pm.

2093 4/Q13 ✓ **The Trinkie** Wick On S side of town, follow cliff walk up from harbour or by car through housing estate. 2km. Not an organised set-up but a pool sluiced and filled by the sea within a natural formation of rocks. A bracing stroll, never mind immersion. Needs TLC. Wickers also go to the North Baths near the harbour (Wick side) and opposite the wee lighthouse. 2 rare open-air swim spots in the far north: midnight midsummer swimming, anyone?

2094 7/G22 **The Bathing Pool** Glengorm Estate, Mull A pool sluiced and filled by the sea by an Iron Age fort on the headland of this beautiful estate 7km N of Tobermory off the Dervaig road. Some seaweed fringing but once it was filled with white sand and they say one day it may be restored. In the meantime, for swimming baggers and the like. 45 mins from the best coffee shop on Mull (1380/TEAROOMS) and you can stay and lord it up in the castle (2243/MULL). Watch for cows on the way!

2095 8/R23 **The Step Rock Pool** St Andrews Shallow bathing pool between West Sands and East Sands beaches below the Aquarium and the **Seafood Restaurant** (1337/ SEAFOOD). Since 1903 when the gentlemen used to swim here naked, a shallow alternative to the colder sea and more recently the East Sands Leisure Centre. Costumes advised these days.

Especially Good Watersports Centres

2096 8/R24 ✓ **Elie Watersports** Elie · www.eliewatersports.co.uk · 01333 330962 Great beach location in totally charming wee town where there's enough going on to occupy non-watersporters. Easy lagoon for first timers and open season for inexperienced users. Wind-surfers, kayaks, water-ski. Also mountain bikes and inflatable 'biscuits'. See also 1305/1306/GASTROPUBS; 2054/GOLF.

2097 7/K26 ✓ **Scottish National Watersports Centre** Cumbrae · www. nationalcentrecumbrae.org.uk · 01475 530757 Frequent ferry from Largs (centre near ferry terminal so 5km Millport) then learn how to pilot things that float. Scotland's premier instructor facility. You need to book – call them, then bob about doon the watter. Great range of courses. 2-bunkroom accom available.

2098 8/P25 ✓ **Port Edgar** South Queensferry · www.portedgarwatersports.com · 0131 331 3330 End of village between the Road Bridge and the new bridge. Major marina, water sports centre. Berth your boat, hire dinghies (big range). Big tuition programme for kids and adults including canoes. Home to Port Edgar Yacht Club.

2099 8/M26 ✓ **Strathclyde Country Park** www.visitlanarkshire.com · 01698 402060
Major water sports centre 15km SE of Glasgow and easily reached from Central
Scotland via M8 or M74 (junction 5 or 6). 200-acre loch and centre with instruction
on sailing, canoeing, windsurfing, water-skiing. Hire canoes, Lasers and Wayfarers,
windsurfers and trimarans. Olympic-standard rowing (as seen in Commonwealth
Games).

2100 5/N19 ✓ **Loch Insh** Kincraig · www.lochinsh.com · 01540 651272 On B970, 2km
from Kincraig towards Kingussie and the A9. Marvellous loch site launching
from gently sloping dinky beach into the shallow forgiving waters of Loch Inch. Hire
of canoes, dinghies and windsurfers as well as rowing boats; river trips. Archery and
mountain biking. An idyllic place to learn anything. Watch the others and the
sunset from the balcony restaurant, the Boathouse. Chalets and apartments.
Sports Apr-Oct 9.30am-5.30pm.

2101 6/N19 ✓ **Loch Morlich Watersports Centre** nr Aviemore · www.lochmorlich.
com · 01479 861221 By Glenmore Forest Park, part of the plethora of outdoor
activities hereabouts (skiing, walking, etc). This is the loch you see from Cairngorm
and just as picturesque from the woody shore. Surprising coral-pink beach! Canoes,
kayaks, rowing boats and dinghies with instruction in everything. Evening hire
possible. Coffee shop up top. Good campsite adjacent (1229/CAMPING WITH KIDS).

2102 9/M30 ✓ **Galloway Activity Centre** Loch Ken, nr Castle Douglas · www.lochken.
co.uk · 01556 502011 15km N on A713 to Ayr. Dinghies, wind-surfers,
canoes, kayaks, tuition, biking. Also the Climbing Tower (so you zip-wire and take
that leap of faith). Mountain biking, Laserquest and archery. All this by a serene and
forgiving loch by the Galloway Forest (1615/LOCHS). Phone for times and courses.
Open Mar-Nov. Café Apr-Oct.

▰▰▰ The Best Surfing Beaches

It's true: Scotland has some of Europe's best surfing beaches.

2103 3/4 ✓✓ **North Coast: Thurso** Surf City. Some say the best surfing in Europe.
Waves in town at river mouth. Steep barrelling. **E of Thurso: Torrisdale**
and **Farr Bay**. **Isle of Lewis** Go N of Stornoway, off Barvas, N of just about
anywhere. Leave the A857 and your day job behind.

2104 7/D22 ✓ **West Coast: Isle of Tiree** Exposed to all the Atlantic swells, gorgeous little
7/G28 Tiree ain't just great for windsurfing. Stay at Millhouse, self-catering hostel.
Machrihanish Near Campbeltown at the foot of the Mull of Kintyre. Long strand
to choose from (1564/BEACHES). Clan Skates in Glasgow (0141 339 6523) has
up-to-date info.

2105 8/S25 ✓ **East Coast: Pease Bay** S of Dunbar near Cockburnspath on the A1. The
8/R25 nearest surfie heaven to the capital. The not-very-nice caravan site has parking
6/T19 and toilets. Very consistent surf; popular. Info and surf school from **Momentum**;
6/T17 07796 561615. Many other beaches here on E Lothian/Berwickshire coast, including
Coldingham and **Belhaven**. **Nigg Bay** S of Aberdeen and **Lunan Bay** (1573/
BEACHES), N of Aberdeen, around Fraserburgh (the broch). Info from Granite Reef
01224 252752.

the
Best
Consuming
Passions

For Edinburgh museums, see p. 79-82; Glasgow museums, see p. 128-130.
☕ *signifies notable café.*

2106 7/K28
☕ ✓✓ **Robert Burns Birthplace Museum** Alloway, Ayr · www.
burnsmuseum.org.uk · 01292 443700 Here in douce wee Alloway, the
restored cottage where Burns was born and the brilliant contemporary museum/
gallery/coffee shop, an appropriate paean to his memory, an evocation of his times
and works and both interesting and fun places to visit. Cottage is a row of rooms
with set pieces and slightly unnerving voiceovers, the museum has state-of-the-art
and technology exhibits exploring not just the well-kent and comic aspects (*Tam o'
Shanter, Auld Lang Syne*, the Kilmarnock Edition) but the wider implications of his
national significance and a modern translation of his influence. Serene gardens, red
roses as you enter; café. A world-class encomium! Open AYR. 10am-5pm (5.30pm
Apr-Sep). Caff much better than before.

2107 8/R25
☕ ✓✓ **National Museum of Flight** nr Haddington · www.nms.ac.uk ·
0300 123 6789 3km from A1. In the old complex of hangars and Nissen
huts by East Fortune, an airfield dating to World War I with a large collection of
planes from gliders to jets and especially wartime memorabilia respectfully
restored and preserved. Inspired and inspiring displays; not just boys' stuff. Marvel
at the bravery and sense the unremitting passage of time. From East Fortune the
airship R34 made its historic Atlantic crossings. Concorde is indeed an 'experience':
hugely impressive outside, claustrophobic in (especially queueing to leave). But did
David Frost and Joan Collins ever join the Mile High Club? Annual air show mid-July.
Recent 'hangar developments'. 7 days 10am-5pm (4pm in winter).

2108 7/H23
✓✓ **Atlantic Islands Centre** Isle of Luing · www.atlanticislandscentre.
com · 01852 314096 Great contemporary building telling the story of
Luing and the Slate Islands. A superb day out only 40 mins from Oban: take scenic
B844 12km S of Oban, then the B8003 at the fork for the ferry at Cuan (also 12km),
every half hour (fewer in winter), 3 mins on board. Fine walking but best by bike
(hire nearby 01852 314274) or car. Orientation/interpretation then explore the
island. Café has great community baking. See also Easdale below.

2109 8/R24
ATMOS ✓✓ **The Secret Bunker** nr Crail · www.secretbunker.co.uk ·
01333 310301 The nuclear bunker and regional seat of government in the
event of nuclear war: a twilight labyrinth beneath a hill in rural Fife so vast, well
documented and complete, it's both fascinating and chilling. Few museums are as
authentic or as resonant, even down to the claustrophobic canteen with bad food.
Makes you wonder what 300 people would have made of it, incarcerated there,
what the Cold War was all about and what secrets the MoD is brewing these days
for the wars yet to come. Mar-Oct 10am-5pm (last entry).

2110 8/Q23
☕ ✓✓ **Verdant Works** Dundee · www.rrsdiscovery.com · 01382 309060
West Henderson's Wynd near Westport. Award-winning heritage museum
that for once justifies the accolades. The story of jute and the city it made.
Immensely effective high-tech and designer presentation of industrial and social
history. Excellent for kids. Almost continuous guided tour. Café. 7 days 10am-6pm;
winter Wed-Sat till 4.30pm and closed Mon/Tue. Every Sun from 11am.

2111 4/Q13
✓✓ **Wick Heritage Centre** Bank Row, Wick · www.wickheritage.org ·
01955 605393 Amazing volunteer-run civic museum, jam-packed with
items about the sea, town and that hard land. Upstairs and downstairs, stretching

halfway along the street. Few places have so much meticulously gathered that lovingly portrays and evokes the spirit of a place. The much-used words 'secret gem' are entirely appropriate here. They got a Queen's Award but somebody should give these ladies MBEs or something. Easter-Oct 10am-last entry 3.45pm. Closed Sun.

2112 3/F13
ATMOS
HS

✓ **The Blackhouse at Arnol** Lewis · www.historic-scotland.gov.uk · 01851 710395 A857 Barvas road from Stornoway, left at junction for 7km then right through township for 2km. A blackhouse with earth floor, bedboxes and central peat fire (no chimney hole), occupied by the family and their animals. Remarkably, this house was lived in until the 1960s. Smokists may reflect on that peaty fug. Open AYR. 9.30am-5.30pm (4.30pm in winter, Oct-Feb). Closed Sun.

2113 4/P15
⌗

✓ **Timespan** Helmsdale · www.timespan.org.uk Far-northern town, where a historic strath comes down to the sea, was a special place (presumably) then and now. This museum and arts centre records and cleverly presents this, well, span of time. Makes you think! Great wee café by the bridge in its geology garden. Don't miss **Mirage** (1083/HIGHLANDS), and in keeping with the time thing, the fascinating **20th Century Collectables** (2173/SHOPS). Centre open Mar-Oct 10am-5pm (reduced winter hours).

2114 8/P25

✓ **The Abbot House** Dunfermline · www.abbothouse.co.uk Maygate in town centre historic area. Very fine conversion of ancient house showing the importance of this town as a religious and trading centre from this millennium to medieval times. Encapsulates history from Margaret and Bruce to the Beatles. One of the few tourist attractions where 'award-winning' is a reliable indicator of worth. Café, tranquil garden; gate to graveyard and abbey. 7 days 9.30am-4.30pm. Excellent coffee shop by ladies who can cook and bake.

2115 7/H23
LL
ATMOS

✓ **Easdale Island Folk Museum** www.easdalemuseum.org On Easdale, an island/township reached by a 5-min (continuous) boat service from Seil 'island' at the end of the B844 (off the A816, 18km S of Oban – you just press the button and it comes!). Something special about this grassy hamlet of whitewashed houses on a rocky outcrop which has a tearoom/bar, **The Puffer** (01852 300022; www.pufferbar.com), a gallery and a craft shop, and this museum across the green. The history of the place (a thriving slate industry erased one stormy night in 1881, when the sea drowned the quarry 1672/SWIMMING) is brought to life in displays from local contributions. Easter-Sep 11am-5pm.

2116 2/V5
L
ATMOS

✓ **Shetland Museum & Archives** Lerwick · www.shetland-museum.org .uk · 01595 695057 Impressive, landmark, purpose-built contemporary space developed from what remained of the Lerwick waterfront. 60,000 Images bringing the story of these fascinating islands to life. Also the **Up-Helly-Aa** story (21/ EVENTS)! **Hays Dock Café/Restaurant** worth a visit in its own right. And **The Mareel** 2245/SHETLAND. 7 days 10am-5pm (Sun from noon).

2117 4/M12
L

✓ **Strathnaver Museum** Bettyhill · www.strathnavermuseum.org.uk · 01641 521418 On N coast 60km W of Thurso in a converted church which is very much part of the whole appalling saga, a graphic account of the Highland Clearances told through the history of this fishing village and the strath that lies behind it whence its dispossessed population came; 2,500 folk were driven from their homes – it's worth going up the valley (from 2km W along the main A836) to see (especially at Achenlochy) the beautiful land they had to leave in 1812 to make way for sheep. Detailed leaflet of Strath to follow by car and foot. Find the poignant and beautiful **Rosal Clearance Township** about 6km from A836 via B871, 45-min walk from the car park. Café on roadside by museum for sustenance. Museum Apr-Oct Mon-Sat 10am-5pm.

2118 6/P18 ✓ **Knockando** nr Aberlour, Speyside · www.knockandowoolmill.org.uk · 01340 810345 On the B9102 off the A95 below Grantown and Keith, well signposted. Lovingly restored cottage woolmill complex in woody, watery Speyside setting. With reactivated Victorian machinery, this mill has been continuously running for over 200 years and all its history is here. You can still buy their products or just sit in wonder by the stream. Café Mar-Oct, 7 days 10am-4pm. Check winter times.

2119 5/H18 ✓ **Applecross Heritage Centre** www.applecrossheritage.org.uk Along
L the strand from the **Walled Garden** (1078/HIGHLANDS) and **Applecross Inn** (1200/GET-AWAY HOTELS) adjacent the lovely church built on an ancient monastery, a well-designed building and lay-out of the story of this remarkable, end-of-the-world community. Reading room with comfy chairs! 10am-4pm. Not weekends in winter.

2120 6/T17 ✓ **The Museum of Scottish Lighthouses** Fraserburgh · www.
L lighthousemuseum.org.uk · 01346 511022 At Kinnaird Head near the harbour. A top attraction, so signed from all over. Purpose-built and very well done. Something which may appear of marginal interest made vital. In praise of the prism and the engineering innovation and skill that allowed Britain once to rule the seas (and the world). A great ambition (to light the coastline) spectacularly realised. *At Scotland's Edge* by Allardyce and Hood is well worth taking home, as is Bella Bathhurst's *The Lighthouse Stevensons*. 10am-5pm (last tour 4pm).

2121 5/H18 ✓ **Bright Water Visitor Centre & Gavin Maxwell House** Eilean Ban, Skye ·
LL www.eileanban.org · 01599 530040 You don't have to be a Maxwell fan,
🖳 *Ring of Bright Water* reader or otter-watcher to appreciate the remarkable restoration of this fascinating man's last house on the island under the Skye Bridge. Skye is a natural haven and the Stevenson Lighthouse superb. The centre supports a number of natural heritage and wildlife projects. Contact centre for guided tours of the cottage, the lighthouse and the hide (otters not guaranteed but quite likely). Book and meet at Otter Gate on the bridge. Apr-Sep, Mon-Fri 2pm.

2122 7/J21 **West Highland Museum** Cameron Square, Fort William · www. westhighlandmuseum.org.uk · 01397 702169 Off main street in listed building. Good refurbishment yet retains mood; the setting doesn't overshadow the contents. 7 rooms of Jacobite memorabilia, archaeology, wildlife, clans, tartans, arms, etc, all effectively evoke the local history. Great oil paintings line the walls, including a drawn battle plan of Culloden. The anamorphic painting of Charlie isn't so bonnie, but a still fascinating snapshot. 10am-5pm (4pm in winter). Closed Jan/Feb and Sun.

2123 4/P12 **Mary-Ann's Cottage** Dunnet · www.caithness.org On N coast off A836 from Thurso to John o' Groats, signed at Dunnet; take the road for Dunnet Head. Lived in till 1990 by Mary-Ann Calder, 3 generations of crofters are in these stones. But not nostalgic or heritage-heavy, just an old lady's house, the near present and past and still the geraniums! Compare to that other old lady's house 10 mins up the road (**Castle of Mey** 1757/CASTLES). Open Jun-Sep 2-4.30pm.

2124 7/H24   **Kilmartin House Museum** nr Lochgilphead · www.kilmartin.org ·
01546 510278 N of Lochgilphead on A816. Centre for landscape and archaeology
interpretation – so much to know of the early peoples and Kilmartin Glen is
littered with historic sites. Intelligent, interesting, run by a small independent
trust. Excellent organic-ish café (1402/TEAROOMS) and bookshop without the usual
tat. Some nice Celtic carvings. Mar-Oct 10am-5.30pm daily; 11am-4pm Nov/Dec.
Guided tours of the Glen in summer. Closed Jan/Feb.

2125 5/M17   **Cromarty Courthouse Museum** Church St · www.cromarty-courthouse.org.
uk · 01381 600418 Housed in an 18th-century courthouse this award-winning
museum uses moving, talking models to bring to life a courtroom scene and
famous Cromarty figures to paint the varied history of this special town (1552/
VILLAGES). Noon-4pm. Closed Fri/Sat. **Hugh Miller's Birthplace** is next door.
Born in 1802 and best known as the father of geology, he was remarkable in
many ways and this tells his singular story. Apr-Sep noon-5pm. Oct Tue, Thu/Fri.

2126 5/F16   **Skye Museum of Island Life** Kilmuir · www.skyemuseum.co.uk ·
01470 552206 On A855 Uig-Staffin road 32km N of Portree. The most
authentic of several converted cottages on Skye where the crofter's life is
recreated for the enrichment of ours. The small thatched township includes
agricultural implements and domestic artefacts, many illustrating an improbable
fascination with the royal family. **Flora Macdonald's Grave** nearby (1829/
MONUMENTS). Apr-Oct 9.30am-5pm. Closed Sun.

2127 7/J24   **Auchindrain** nr Inveraray · www.auchindrain.org.uk · 01499 500235 8km
W of town on A83. A whole township reconstructed to give a very fair impression
of both the historical and spatial relationship between the cottages and their
various occupants. Longhouses and byre dwellings; their furniture and their ghosts.
Tearoom. 7 days. Apr-Oct 10am-5pm.

2128 7/J24   **Inveraray Jail** www.inverarayjail.co.uk The story of Scottish crime and
punishment told in 'award-winning' reconstruction of courtroom with cells, where
waxwork miscreants and their taped voices bring local history to life. Guided
Peterhead tours can't be far off. Open summer 9.30am-6pm (winter 10am-5pm).

2129 7/J23   **Bonawe Iron Furnace** Taynuilt · www.historic-scotland.gov.uk At its zenith
HS   (late 18th-early 19th century), this ironworks was a dark, brutal, fire-breathing
monster. Now, all is calm as the gently sloping grassy sward carries you around
from warehouse to foundry and to the shores of Loch Etive and the pier, where the
finished product was loaded onto ships for the purpose of empire-building (with
cannonballs). Apr-Sep daily until 5.30pm.

2130 8/R24   **Scottish Fisheries Museum** Anstruther · www.scotfishmuseum.org ·
01333 310628 In and around a cobbled courtyard overlooking the old fishing
harbour in this busy East Neuk town. Excellent evocation of traditional industry still
alive (if not kicking). Impressive collection of models and actual vessels including
those moored at adjacent quay. Crail and Pittenweem harbours nearby for the full
picture (and fresh crab/lobster). Open AYR. 10am-5.30pm, Sun 11am-5pm (closed
4.30pm in winter). 1366/FISH & CHIPS a must!

The Special Galleries & Art Spaces

For Edinburgh, see p. 83; Glasgow, p. 135. ☕: notable café.

2131 8/P25 ✓✓ **Jupiter Artland** Wilkieston · www.jupiterartland.org ·
ADMISSION   01506 889900 W of Edinburgh. Not a public gallery as such but a
☕ world-class open-air artland assembled by Robert and Nicky Wilson in the groves
and gardens of their home, Bonnington House. In an unfolding story, some of the
UK's leading artists have been commissioned to produce site-specific work for you
to discover: Andy Goldsworthy, Anthony Gormley, Anish Kapoor and an enormous
landform by Charles Jencks which you pass through when you arrive; and many
others. This is art exposure and extraordinary patronage on a grand scale. There are
temporary exhibitions in the courtyard gallery. Workshops and courses. Best get
directions from the website. Allow 3 hours on site. Book online. May-Sep, Thu-Sun.
Lovely courtyard caravan caff.

2132 8/Q23 ✓✓ **Dundee Contemporary Arts** Dundee · www.dca.org.uk ·
☕   01382 432000 State-of-contemporary-art gallery (by award-winning
architect Richard Murphy) with great café (947/DUNDEE), designer shop and
cinema. It once transformed the cultural face of Dundee and it is often worth
travelling to/from the Central Belt if you're interested in cutting-edge
contemporary art. Well used, well loved! Bring on the V&A!

2133 8/M28 ✓✓ **Crawick Multiverse** nr Sanquhar · www.crawickmultiverse.co.uk
             The latest major project by renowned landscape artist Charles Jencks (see
1503/GARDENS), privately funded on land of the Duke of Buccleuch estates. This
beautiful massive invention of stone and earth and grass has all the hallmarks of
his work, transforming an opencast coalmine into an enduring and edifying public
space. Just N of the village after the school then right on the B740, 1.5km from
Sanquhar station. The **Blackaddie Hotel** is excellent for food (820/SW
RESTAURANTS).

2134 8/P23 ✓ **The Fergusson Gallery** Perth · www.museumsgalleriesscotland.org.uk
            In distinctive round tower (a former waterworks). The assembled works on two
floors of J.D. Fergusson (1874-1961) and his partner Margaret Morris. Though he
spent much of his life in France, he had an influence on Scottish art and was
pre-eminent among The Colourists. It's a long way from Perth to Antibes 1913 but
these pictures are a draught of the warm south. May-Oct Tue-Sat 10am-5pm &
Sun noon-4.30pm.

2135 8/Q24 ✓ **Kirkcaldy Museum & Art Gallery** www.onfife.com · 01592 583206 Near
            railway station, but ask for directions (it's easy to get lost). One of the best
galleries in central Scotland; recently refurbished. Splendid introduction to the
history of 19th/20th-century Scottish art. Lots of Colourists/McTaggart/Glasgow
Boys. And Sickert to Redpath. And famously the only public collection in Scotland
showing Scotland's best-selling artist: one Jack Vettriano who was a Fife lad.
Kirkcaldy doesn't get much good press but this and the parks (1540/PARKS) are
worth the journey (plus **Valente's** 1361/FISH & CHIPS). 7 days till 5pm. Café.

2136 9/M31 ✓ **Hornel Gallery** Kirkcudbright · www.nts.org.uk · 01557 330437 Hornel's
NTS   (Broughton) house is a fabulous evocation with a collection of his work and
atelier as was. 'Even the Queen was amazed'. Beautiful, atmospheric garden
stretches to the river. Apr-Oct noon-5pm. Garden AYR. The **Jessie M. King House**,
now a B&B is 100m down the same road towards the Tolbooth.

2137 4/L13 ✔ **Lotte Glob's Gallery and Garden** Loch Eriboll · www.lotteglob.co.uk ·
01971 511727 In Laid, on western shore of Loch Eriboll and the main road N
to Durness, you enter through the Glob-like gateposts into Lotte's extraordinary
world, her distinctive ceramic works of art perfectly at home in this wild
landscape. Studio and gallery (but more a trail of rough tracks). Just wander, it is
uniquely special!

2138 6/P17 ✔ **Moray Art Centre** Findhorn · www.morayartcentre.org · 01309 692426
Part of the Findhorn Community/Foundation/park and eco-village. Another
very good reason for visiting this life-affirming place. Fascinating building by Randy
Klinger (2007) in keeping with the creative and ingenious architecture all around
you with an interesting programme of exhibitions and workshops. Tue-Sat; check
online for details.

2139 6/R17 ✔ **Duff House** Banff · www.duffhouse.org.uk · 01261 818181 Nice walk and
⚏ easy to find from town (it's a major attraction). Important outstation of the
National Galleries of Scotland in meticulously restored Adam house with
interesting history and spacious grounds. Ramsays, Raeburns, portraiture of mixed
appeal and an El Greco. Go further up the Deveron for a pleasant stroll (2016/
WALKS). Nice tearoom. Opening times online or ring to check.

2140 1/Q10 ✔ **The Pier Arts Centre** Stromness, Orkney · www.pierartscentre.com ·
01856 850209 On main street (1551/VILLAGES), a gallery on a pier which could
have come lock, stock and canvases from Cornwall. Permanent St Ives-style
collection assembled by one Margaret Gardiner: Barbara Hepworth, Ben Nicholson,
Paolozzi and others shown in a sympatico environment with the sea outside.
Important early-20th-century pictures complemented by work of recent
contemporaries. Partners with the Tate. A rare treat! Tue-Sat 10.30am-5pm.

2141 7/F22 **Calgary Art In Nature** Calgary, Isle of Mull · www.calgaryartinnature
⚏ .co.uk Contemporary artwork and sculpture to be found on a trail through the
woods adjacent to the wonderful beach at Calgary Bay on the far W coast of Mull
and an exhibition gallery space. The project of Matthew Reade who ran the Calgary
Farmhouse Hotel (the great **Café at Calgary Arts** remains, Easter-Nov), the 1km
trail is fun rather than thought provoking, but it's a great idea, nice for kids in one
of the best of places.

2142 6/T19 **Aberdeen Art Gallery** Schoolhill, Aberdeen · www.aagm.co.uk ·
01224 523700 Major gallery with temporary exhibits and eclectic and significant
permanent collection from Impressionists to 19th and 20th century British
and Scottish and contemporary artists. Closed at TGP for refurbishment;
reopening 2018.

2143 8/R22 **Hospitalfield** Arbroath · www.hospitalfield.org.uk · 01241 656124 An arts
centre in a historic (Arts & Crafts) house, 400m from the A92, S of the centre (at
McDonald's), with artists in residence. The collection and interiors are fascinating
(the legacy of artist and collector Patrick Allan Fraser (1812–1890)). Only open Wed
2-5pm. The café in the walled garden is also open Sat 2-5pm. Hospitalfield curated
Scotland's 'pavilion' at the Venice Biennale 2015.

signifies notable café.

2144 6/N17

✓✓ **Logie Steading** nr Forres · www.logie.co.uk · 01309 611378 In beautiful countryside 10km S of Forres signed from A940 Forres-Grantown road. Near pleasant woodlands and brilliant picnic spots (2001/WALKS), with lovely walled garden around the big house nearby (Apr-Dec). Much better than your usual crafty courtyard to visit and browse. Includes Giles Pearson's Country Furniture, the Cordy Hedge Gallery of contemporary art, a farm shop and the **Olive Tree Café**, a home-baking tearoom with integrity. Seems fitting as the estate was built with the fortune of the guy who invented the digestive biscuit! 1403/TEAROOMS. 7 days.

2145 5/N16

✓ **Anta Factory Shop** Fearn · www.anta.co.uk · 01862 832477 Off B9175 from Tain to Nigg ferry, 8km through Hill of Fearn, at disused airfield. Shop with adjacent pottery. Also in Edinburgh and London. Anta is a classy brand: distinctively but not too tartan. Fabrics; rugs and throws. You can commission furniture to be covered in their material. Pottery tour by arrangement. Shop. Open summer daily 9.30am-5.30pm (Sun 10am-5pm). Ring for winter hours. Pottery Mon-Fri only. Nice café shuts 4pm.

2146 5/N16

✓ **Tain Pottery** www.tainpottery.co.uk Off the A9 just S of Tain (opposite side of A9 to road signed for Anta at Fearn; see above). Big working pottery, big stuff and often big, perhaps OTT design, hand-painted and very popular (they do the National Trust for Scotland and are stocked all over the UK). Daily in summer, 9am-6pm (Sat/Sun 10am-5pm). Closed Sun in winter.

2147 4/L12

✓ **Balnakeil** Durness From Durness and the A836 road, take Balnakeil and Faraid Head road for 2km W. Founded in the 1960s in what one imagines was a haze of hash, this craft village is still home to downshifters and creatives, i.e. talented people. Paintings, pottery, print-making, glass, wood and jewellery in prefab huts where community members work and hang out (the site was an early-warning station). **Cocoa Mountain** (01971 511233) make here their heavenly thin chocolate you get all over the north and in Auchterarder, and have a chocolate bar open AYR (9am-6pm; 11am-4pm in winter).

2148 8/R27

✓ **Born in the Borders** nr Jedburgh · www.bornintheborders.com · 01835 830495 On the A698 Hawick-Jedburgh off the A68 Edinburgh road. Transformed farmyard on the Teviot with a deli, shop, café and microbrewery. Takes 'Borders' literally, so provisions from Northumberland in the deli. A well-run, good-looking new Borders stop and shop (and eat). Microbrewery open for look-see, Dark Horse, Foxy Blonde, etc, on the shelves. 7 days 10am-5pm. Dinner Thu-Sat is one of the best in the Borders!

2149 8/Q24

✓ **Maspie House Gallery** Falkland · www.maspiehousegallery.com · 01337 857735 Small up and downstairs gallery near The Cross in downtown Falkland, Fife's most pleasant village to visit (1756/CASTLES; 1990/WALKS; 1376/CAFÉS). John McLaren shows work from his own talented family and other local artists, and he has 'the eye', so some interesting pictures in various mediums, and ceramics. Closed Mon-Tue. 2-bedroom B&B adjacent.

2150 4/J14 ✓ **Highland Stoneware** Lochinver & Ullapool · www.highlandstoneware .com On road to Baddidarach as you enter Lochinver on A837; and on way N beyond Ullapool centre. A large-scale pottery business including a shop/warehouse and open studios that you can walk round (Lochinver is more *engagé*). Similar to the ceramica places you find in the Med, but less terracotta: rather, painted, heavy-glazed stoneware in set styles. Many broken plates adorn your arrivals. Great selection, pricey, but you may have luck in the Lochinver discount section. Mail-order service. 9am-6pm weekdays, and Sat in summer.

2151 8/R24 ✓ **Crail Pottery** Crail · www.crailpottery.com At the foot of Rose Wynd, signposted from main street (best to walk). In a tree-shaded Mediterranean courtyard and upstairs attic, a cornucopia of brilliant and useful things. Open 9am-5pm (weekends from 10am). Don't miss the harbour nearby, one of the most romantic neuks in the Neuk. Good tearoom on way to harbour (1417/TEAROOMS).

2152 8/N21 ✓ **MacNaughton's** Pitlochry · www.macnaughtonsofpitlochry.com On main street corner, this the best of many. A vast, old-fashioned family-owned outfitter (no longer the MacNaughtons) with acres of tartan attire including obligatory tartan pyjamas and dressing gowns! Make their own cloth; 9m kilts made in 6-8 weeks. This is the real McCoy. 7 days till 5.30pm (4pm Sun).

2153 8/Q25 ✓ **Kinloch Anderson** Edinburgh · www.kinlochanderson.com A trek from uptown but firmly on the tourist trail and so much better than the High St, i.e. the tartan-tainted Royal Mile. Independent, family-run company since 1868, they are experts in Highland dress and all things tartan; they've supplied *everybody*. They design and manufacture their own tartans, have a good range of men's tweed jackets; even rugs. Mon-Sat 9am-5.30pm.

2154 8/R27 ✓ **Harestanes Countryside Centres** nr Jedburgh Off A68 at Ancrum, the B6400 to Nisbet. Farm steading complex on Monteviot Estate (1513/GARDENS) with café/exhibition/superior crafts including the excellent **Buy Design** showing beautiful furniture, ceramics, glass and Mary's Dairy (she even makes the cones for the ice cream). Easter-Oct 10am-5pm. Event programme and walks (get Harestanes Path leaflet at the visitor centre). Best tearoom 1km down the road at **Woodside** (1386/TEAROOMS).

2155 8/S25 **Number Four** St Abbs · www.numberfourgallery.co.uk · 01890 771111 It's the number 4 cottage in the row by the car park and interpretation centre at the start of the walks to glorious **St Abb's Head** (2026/1741/WALKS; RESERVES). This very personal 'art and craft gallery' is perhaps much better than it has to be. Thrives because of the good taste and judgement of Jenny and all-round artist Chris. Hard not to find something here to adorn or enhance your life. From £10 to £1,000. Open AYR. Thu-Sun 10am-5pm, Jan/Feb 10am-4pm.

2156 6/N17 **Brodie Countryfare** between Nairn & Forres · www.brodiecountryfare. com By A96 near **Brodie Castle** (1754/CASTLES). One of those drive-in one-stop consumer experiences full of brands, full of people. Deli food, a fairly upmarket womenswear boutique and every crafty tartanalia of note. Spacious self-serve restaurant gets as busy as a motorway café; naturally you have to walk through everything else to get there. 7 days till 5.30pm (5pm in winter).

2157 6/S20 **The Milton** www.miltonart.com · 01330 844664 & **The Wee Boorachie** www.theweeboorachie.co.uk · Crathes Separate art and craft enterprises in a courtyard around the **Milton Brasserie** on the main A93 Deeside Road at the entrance to **Crathes House and Garden** (989/NE RESTAURANTS; 1826/HOUSES;

1502/GARDENS). Art Gallery has many harbours and sunsets but also some good work by notable artists such as Peter Goodfellow and Laurence Broderick, and ceramics. Craft shop more gifty but the Wee Boorachie has some surprises. The Milton: 10am-5pm, Sun from 11am.

2158 5/F17 **Edinbane Pottery** Skye · www.edinbane-pottery.co.uk 500m off A850 Portree (22km) to Dunvegan road. A great working pottery where the various processes are often in progress. Wood-fired and salt-glazed pots of all shapes and for every purpose. Mon-Fri 9am-6pm; 7 days Easter-Oct.

2159 5/F17 **Skye Silver** Colbost · www.skyesilver.com 10km Dunvegan on B884 to Glendale. Long-established and reputable jewellery made and sold in an old Skye schoolhouse in a distant corner; **Three Chimneys** restaurant and **Red Roof** café nearby (2239/SKYE). Well-made, Celtic designs, good gifts. Mar-Oct 7 days.

2160 6/P17 **Findhorn Pottery** Findhorn, nr Forres · www.findhornpottery.com Deep in both the Findhorn Community (since 1971) and the spreading park, it's more than interesting to wander through the eco-village to this long-standing pottery and shop. 3 potters work away here (including Brian Nobbs who helped to build it) and their ware is for sale. It's the real deal! Apr-Oct 10.30am-5.30pm (from noon Sun). From 1pm Nov-Mar (closed Mon/Tue). They never stop turning.

2161 7/F23 **Iona Abbey Shop** Iona Via CalMac ferry from Fionnphort on Mull. Crafts
HS and souvenirs across the way in separate building. Proceeds support a worthy, committed organisation. Christian literature, tapes, etc. but mostly artefacts from nearby and around Scotland. Celtic crosses much in evidence, but then this is where they came from! Also on the way to and from the abbey, **Aosdana** gallery (jewellers) and **Oran Creative Crafts** in restored steadings are good to browse.

2162 9/M30 **Galloway Lodge Preserves** Gatehouse of Fleet · www.gallowaylodge.
co.uk On High St, same building as the PO. Packed with local jams, marmalades, chutneys and pickles. Scottish pottery by Scotia Ceramics, Highland Stoneware and Dunoon. Good presents and jam for you. 10am-5pm. Self-service coffee shop, home-made and old-style – good for mum, gran and bairns! See 822/sw RESTAURANTS.

2163 7/J21 **Crafts & Things** nr Glencoe village · www.craftsandthings.co.uk ·
01855 811325 On A82 between Glencoe village and Ballachulish, across from Loch Leven. Long here, an eclectic mix, perhaps more things than crafts. Mind, body and mountain books and reasonably priced knit/outerwear. Good coffee shop doing salads, sandwiches, Luca's ice cream and home baking, with local artists' work on walls. Open 7 days AYR until 5.30pm.

The Very Special Shops

2164 6/S19 ✓✓ **Hammerton Store** Aberdeen · www.hammertonstore.co.uk ·
01224 324449 On road W to Deeside somewhere in a suburb. Susan Watson's love affair with Aberdeen and life. Not only a deli, more a superior provisioner where essentials include art, travelling rugs, cool pottery, cookery books and mine. Susan properly selects and sources everything. Provenance is not an idle gesture – she goes to Gigha and brings back the halibut! Tables outside where you can snack and reflect how nice it would be to have a place like this in your neighbourhood. There are a lot of artisan gins in that cabinet to get through. 7 days 8am-6.30pm, Sat/Sun 9am-5.30pm.

2165 8/R27 ✓✓ **Main Street Trading Company** St Boswells · www.
mainstreetbooks.co.uk · 01835 824087 On Main St just off A68.
All-round very good thing for the Borders: a well-thought-out and browsable
bookshop and café on the street, with excellent home-made food (859/BORDERS)
and, across a courtyard, a deli and 'home shop', with Scottish and elsewhere gifts
and interesting stuff for yourself. Bill and Roz Delaney and a great team have
created a distinctive and new Borders attraction (next best thing to the railway!).
Closed Mon.

2166 8/N21 ✓✓ **House of Bruar** nr Blair Atholl · www.houseofbruar.com
LL   Extraordinarily successful countryside mall, a courtyard emporia if not
☕ euphoria. The shopaholic honey pot on A9 N of Blair Atholl. In the various floors
and chambers they sell an enormous range of clothes, textiles and anything you
might need for the home, garden or body. Not just any old brand either but top end
and selective. It really can claim to be the Harrods of the North. The vast food
section sells the best of Scottish everything and there's always a queue at the
self-service café with tables in and out. There often seems more folk here than in
Pitlochry. Strategically placed where you want to stop on the A9, Bruar is the very
best of the roadside retail explosion. Falls nearby for non-retail therapy (1602/
WATERFALLS). 7 days 9am-5pm.

2167 8/N22 ✓ **The Highland Chocolatier** Grandtully · www.highlandchocolatier.com
☕   Part of **Legends** coffee shop (1391/TEAROOMS), Iain Burnett's chocolateria is a
Perthshire destination in itself. A splurge of artisan chocolate-makers in recent
years but Iain's meticulously crafted and beautifully presented individual and boxed
chocs are in a class of their own. Indulge. 10am-5pm. 7 days.

2168 9/N29 ✓ **Thomas Tosh** Thornhill · www.thomastosh.com · 01848 331553 Near
the crossroads in E Morton St. Mr T. Tosh was a local guy lang syne, not the
proprietor of this lofty emporium in an old parish hall, in the often sped-through
but delightful toon of Thornhill. Great taste here in all manner of essential and gifty
things, ceramics, furniture and especially books. I hope to see this one here. The
café does great home baking, soups, coffee. Licensed. Mon-Sat 10am-5pm. Go
shop and stop!

2169 4/K14 ✓ **Drumbeg Village Stores** www.drumbegstores.co.uk · 01571 833235 On
L   the single-track road that runs from Kylesku to Lochinver, halfway along
amidst some of the most spectacular scenery in Scotland (1621/SCENIC ROUTES), an
exceptional store in tiny Drumbeg township. Over 700 items in stock, a great deli
selection, local produce, fruit 'n' veg in the adjacent shack. Bringing a whole new
dimension to the 'shop local' mantra, at least they're unlikely to ever get Tescoed.
Teahouse – Little Soap and Candles – opposite.

2170 5/H16 ✓ **Hillbillies and the Mountain Coffee Co.** Gairloch · 01445 712316 In the
☕   middle of the straggly town amidst great coastal (and mountain) scenery a
bookshop/coffee shop totally at one with its location and the people who
appreciate it. Inspired selection of outdoor, thought-provoking and just good
books. Maps, great stuff for presents and the caff with bagels, soup and great tea
and coffee list. Been here a while, this place, but gets better. 9am-6pm. Closed
Dec-Feb.

2171 4/J14 ✓ **Achin's Bookshop** Lochinver · 01571 844262 At Inverkirkaig 5km from
☕   Lochinver on the 'wee mad road' to Achiltibuie (1622/SCENIC ROUTES).
Enduring, unexpected haven of books in the back of beyond providing something to

read when you've climbed everything or are unlikely to climb anything except the mount of knowledge. Outdoor wear too and hats. Path to Kirkaig Falls and Suilven begins at the gate. Easter-Oct 7 days; 9.30am-6pm (winter Mon-Sat 10am-5pm). Café 10am-5pm, summer only. **Note:** This national book treasure for sale at TGP. Phone if coming from far.

2172 5/H19 ✓ **Floraidh** Skye · www.floraidhskye.co.uk · 01471 833347 Sleat peninsula
LL adjacent the landmark **Eilean Iarmain Hotel** (2239/SKYE), more or less on the quayside of this mystic cove. Hand-made, stylish clothes in tweed and wool mainly but also silk and linen; a bespoke boutique in the best of taste. Easter-Oct. Closed Sun.

2173 4/P15 ✓ **20th Century Collectables** Helmsdale · www.20thcentury-collectables. co.uk · 07796 018243 Main street near **Mirage** (1083/HIGHLANDS) and **Timespan**, the interesting trip-through-time heritage centre (2113/HISTORY). Whereas here you rummage and browse through 20th-century memorabilia, bric-a-brac, clothes, jewellery, ornaments and yes, collectables. *StB* doesn't do antique or vintage shops but Euan Gibson's eye and enthusiasm make this shop off the northern road to nowhere remarkable. Who would expect a bit of camp this far from Brighton? Admirably avoids tartanalia. Happen by! Open AYR.

Where To Buy Good Scottish Woollies

2174 6/P17 ✓✓ **Johnston's Cashmere Centre** Elgin (the HQ), also St Andrews & Hawick · www.johnstonscashmere.com Johnston's is, as they say, one of the last of the Mohicans actually making textiles in Scotland. They are 'the only British mill to transform fibre to garment' (yarns spun at their factory in Elgin and made into garments in the Borders). They stock their own ranges including couture cashmere, many of which are sold internationally as well as other quality brands. This extensive mill shop, the high-quality and classy 'home' section, heritage centre and café is a serious visitor attraction hereabouts. The jumpers, bunnets and cardies are more classic than cool but they won't fall apart and they ain't made in China. Lovely garden adjacent the pulsating mill with free tours Mon-Fri (30 mins) from the wool store through dyeing, pearling, spinning and weaving into their cloth and scarves. You will want to buy something! Mon-Sat 9am-5.30pm, Sun 10am-5pm. Near the Cathedral (1776/RUINS).

2175 2/V5 ✓ **Jamieson & Smith: The Shetland Wool Brokers** Lerwick · www. shetlandwoolbrokers.co.uk · 01595 693579 If you love wool and woollies, come here. Purchasers of 80% of the wool produced on Shetland, they sustain the crofters and textile industry. Available online but go and see the fleeces coming in one door and the coloured yarn going out the other. Check hours.

2176 1/Q10 ✓ **Judith Glue** www.judithglue.com Kirkwall, Orkney · 01856 874225 & Bridge St, Inverness · 01463 248529 Opposite the cathedral in Kirkwall. Distinctive hand-made jumpers, the runic designs are signature. Also the individual Highland and Orkney ceramics and jewellery, condiments and preserves. Landscape prints of Orkney are by twin sister, Jane. See also (2244/ORKNEY). Mon-Sat 9am-6pm (longer hours in summer), Sun from 11am.

2177 8/Q25 ✓ **Belinda Robertson** 13a Dundas St, Edinburgh · www.belindarobertson. com · 0131 557 8118 Queen of commissioned cashmere not so much couture as once was but more accessible in her Edinburgh showroom and at **Fenton Barns**, the artisan farmyard, shop and café (1471/FARM SHOPS). Part of the collection is still made in Hawick. Closed Sun.

2178 6/P18 ✓ **Knockando** nr Aberlour · www.knockandowoolmill.org · 01340 810345 Cottage woolmill complex with original machinery. Weavers, spinning. Products for sale. Report: 2118/HERITAGE.

2179 3/E16 ✓ **The Harris Tweed Company** www.harristweedco.co.uk · 01859 511108 At Grosebay on the **Golden Road**, 10km S of Tarbert (1625/SCENIC ROUTES). A shop, not large, with selected tweedy and woolly apparel well presented, and probably the most upmarket of the emporiums on the Isles. Closed Sun.

2180 5/G19 **Ragamuffin** Armadale Pier, Skye · 01471 844217 On the pier, so one of the first or last things you can do on Skye is rummage through the Ragamuffin store and find a nice knit. Every kind of jumper and some crafts in this Aladdin's cave within a new-build shed; including tweedy things and mad hats. 7 days 9am-6pm (Sun 10am-5pm). Also in **Edinburgh's Royal Mile**.

2181 8/Q27 **Lochcarron Visitor Centre** Selkirk · www.lochcarron.co.uk If you're in Galashiels (or Hawick) which grew up around woollen mills, you might expect to find a good selection of woollens you can't get everywhere else; and bargains. Well, no. Loch Carron used to be in Gala but here is a big attraction with award-winning mill tours, exhibits, an OK mill shop and a coffee shop. 9am-5pm. Closed Sun. No mill tours Fri/Sat.

2182 8/R28 **Hawick Cashmere** Hawick · www.hawico.com · 01450 371221 Factory in Hawick since 1874, with visitor centre beside the river on Arthur St. Also shops in Gleneagles and Edinburgh. 'State-of-the-art colours and designs'. Not only, but mostly cashmere. Mon-Sat 9.30am-5pm.

▬▬▬ Harris Tweed

2183 3/E15 **Harris Tweed & Knitwear** Tarbert & Plocrapool · www. harristweedandknitwear.co.uk · 01859 502040 Catherine Campbell's warehouse and shop in Tarbert and croft/shop. Exhibition in the Old School on the Golden Road 5km S of Tarbert, an homage to Marion Campbell, the doyenne of croft-based weaving. Bales of tweed in Tarbert with knitwear and clothing at the adjacent shop and in the schoolhouse. Closed Sun.

2184 3/E15 **Luskentyre Harris Tweed** No 6, Luskentyre · www.luskentyreharristweed. co.uk · 01859 550261 2km off W coast on main road S to Rodel by the beautiful beach. Donald John Mackay's place is notable for its bolder-coloured tartan tweed and for the fact that Nike and Savile Row come here too. 9.30am-6pm Closed Sun.

2185 3/F14 **Lewis Loom Centre** Stornoway · 01851 704500 Main street, far from Harris but near the tourists. Cloth and clothes. Demos and displays. Closed Sun.

Not Just Garden Centres, More A Way Of Life

☕ signifies notable café. Others may have cafés that have not been recommended.

2186 8/P25
✓✓ **Dougal Philip's New Hopetoun Gardens** nr South Queensferry ·
☕   www.newhopetoungardens.co.uk · 01506 834433 On the A904. The ever-expanding and meticulously nurtured prize bloom of Scottish garden centres sprawling aesthetically among trees with many different zones and demonstration gardens (including Oriental and Scottish). Everything you could ever grow or put in a Scottish garden. Acres of accessories; big pots; statuary of every age. Orangery tearoom has verdant views and tasty home-made stuff. Open AYR 10am-5.30pm. Tearoom closes 4.30pm. Adjacent farm shop run by the estate, not Dougal.

2187 8/S27
✓✓ **Floors Castle** Kelso · www.roxburghe.net 3km outside town off
☕   B6397 St Boswells road (garden centre has separate entrance to main visitors' gate in town). Set among lovely old greenhouses within walled gardens some distance from house, it has a showpiece herbaceous border, plant centre and a great coffee shop, **The Terrace** (1389/TEAROOMS), and patio. 'Very good roses'. Lovely kids' lawn. Centre is open AYR. 10am-5pm. See also 1822/HOUSES.

2188 8/P23
✓✓ **Glendoick** Glencarse, nr Perth · www.glendoick.com ·
☕   01738 860205 Take slip road off the A85, 10km from Perth, in the fertile Carse of the Tay. A large family-owned garden centre long a destination; adjacent, their famous rhododendron and azalea gardens on which they have written many books. Well laid out, friendly and informed staff. Lovely pagoda garden. The (Cox) family house 2km up the road open for snowdrops (Feb) and rhoddies and azaleas (Apr to mid-Jun) and is remarkable. Nice coffee shop with some home baking, hot meals; big on soups. Good bookshop their 'Food Library' including Kenneth's own splendid book (see Best Gardens, p. 267–71) and mine. You could spend hours here! 7 days till 5.30pm, 5pm winter.

2189 8/Q23
✓ **Turriff's** Broughty Ferry · www.turriffs.com · 01382 778488 How did I
☕   miss this great wee nursery/farm shop/garden centre in all previous editions of *StB*? It's been here for decades. Maybe because it's deep in the Dundee suburbs, though only a few minutes from the main road into 'The Ferry' off Victoria Rd. In the garden, around a lovely old mansion, which now houses on its ground floor **Jessie's**, a superb tearoom (946/DUNDEE). It's a rambly, slightly shambly but nevertheless horticultural haven, merging into both the uncultivated and the precisely cultivated suburban landscape. An experience and still in the family. 8am-5pm (4.30pm Sat) & 10am-4pm Sun.

2190 7/J22
✓ **Kinlochlaich Garden** Appin · www.kinlochlaichgardencentre.co.uk ·
01631 730342 On main A28 Oban-Fort William road just N of Port Appin turn-off, the West Highlands' largest nursery/garden centre. Set in a large walled garden filled with plants and veg soaking up the climes of the warm Gulf Stream. The Hutchisons nurture these acres enabling you to reap what they sow. With an array of plants on offer it's like visiting a friend's garden and being able to take home your fave bits. Charming cottages and apartments. For the treehouse, book well ahead. 7 days 9.30am-5.30pm (dusk in winter).

2191 5/N19 ✓ **Inshriach Nursery** nr Aviemore · www.inshriachnursery.co.uk ·
01540 651287 On B970 between Kincraig and Inverdruie (which is on the
Coylumbridge ski road out of Aviemore), a nursery that puts others in the shade.
John and Gunn Borrowman carrying on (and developing) the horticulture of Jack
Drake (from 1930s) and John Lawson (1949). Specialising in alpines and bog plants
but with neat beds of all sorts in the grounds (and a wild garden) of the house by
the Spey and frames full of perfect specimens. This is a potterer's paradise, though
perhaps now overshadowed in a superlative sense by **The Potting Shed**, with its
famously good cakes and superb bird-viewing gallery (1383/TEAROOMS; 1720/
BIRDS). Mar-Oct 7 days 10am-5pm.

2192 8/R27 ✓ **Woodside** nr Ancrum · www.woodsidegarden.co.uk · 01835 830315 On
B6400 off A68 opposite Ancrum turn-off just past **Harestanes** (2154/
SCOTTISH SHOPS) and before **Monteviot** (1513/GARDENS), this is the walled garden
of the big hoose that overlooks the Teviot. Beautiful, quiet place with displays,
events and organic agenda. They really care about their plants and yours. Best
tearoom around in a wooden cabin in corner (1386/TEAROOMS). 7 days 10am-5pm.
Walk starts here to **Peniel Heugh** and the view (1830/MONUMENTS).

2193 6/S20 ✓ **Raemoir Garden Centre** Banchory · www.raemoirgardencentre.co.uk
On A980 off main street 3km N of town. A garden centre that grew into a
massive roadside emporium à la House of Bruar except that this is a side road in
Deeside. Still it's packed with people and the stuff they browse and buy. Café and
restaurant are a destination in themselves (1388/TEAROOMS). Somewhere there are
plants! 7 days 9am-6pm. Café till 5.30pm, restaurant till 4pm.

2194 9/M30 ✓ **Cally Gardens** Gatehouse of Fleet · www.callygardens.co.uk ·
01557 815029 An extraordinary assemblage of herbaceous perennials in a
gorgeous walled garden. Comprehensive sales online but a must to visit (1517/
GARDENS).

2195 8/R25 **Smeaton Nursery Gardens** East Linton · www.smeatonnurserygardens.
co.uk · 01620 860501 2km from village on North Berwick road (signed Smeaton).
Up a drive in an old estate is this walled garden going back to early 19th century.
Wide range; good for fruit (and other) trees, herbaceous, etc. Nice to wander round,
an additional pleasure is the Lake Walk halfway down the drive through a small
gate in the woods. 1km stroll round a secret finger lake in magnificent mature
woodland (10am-dusk, 458/WALKS). Mon-Sat 9.30am-4.30pm; Sun 10.30am-
4.30pm. Laid-back tearoom.

the
Best

The Islands

The Magical Islands

2196 5/G18 ✓✓ **Raasay** A small car ferry (car useful, but bikes best) from Sconser (between Portree and Broadford) on Skye takes you to this, the best of places. The distinctive flat top of Dun Caan presides over an island whose history and natural history is Highland Scotland in microcosm. The village Inverarish, with rows of mining-type cottages, is 1km from the new jetty which is by the 'big house', home to the excellent outdoor centre. Rising from the ashes of a fire which gutted most of it in 2009, **Raasay House** is also a hotel, café/bar, restaurant and library, and hosts a full activity programme for groups or individuals (2239/SKYE). The views from the lawn, or the viewpoint above the House, or better still from Dun Caan with the Cuillin on one side and Torridon on the other, are exceptional (2210/ISLAND WALKS). There's a ruined castle, a secret rhododendron-lined loch, seals, otters and eagles. Many walks on hill, shore or woods; free guides at the House or ferry to show you where! Find 'Calum's Road' and read the book. Much to explore, spend a day or days, but go quietly here.
Regular CalMac ferry from Sconser on Skye.

2197 7/G25 ✓✓ **Jura** Small regular car ferry from Port Askaig on Islay or from Tayvallich takes you to a different world. Jura is remote, scarcely populated and has an ineffable grandeur indifferent to the demands of tourism. Ideal for wild camping and there's a great hotel and pub (2234/ISLAND HOTELS) in the only village (Craighouse) 12km from ferry at Feolin on the 'Long Road' Also in Craighouse, **The Antlers** is open in season for sustenance (2241/JURA). Walking guides available at the hotel and essential, especially for the Paps, the hills that maintain such a powerful hold over the island. Easiest climb is from Three Arch Bridge; allow 6 hours. Evans Walk, starting 1km N of the bridge is easier, still boggy. The distillery where The Jura comes from is not as beautiful as the drink it produces: tours www. jurawhisky.com. Corryvreckan whirlpool is another lure but you may need a 4WD to get close; impressiveness depends upon tides. Barnhill, Orwell's house where he wrote *1984*, isn't open but there are many fascinating side tracks: the wild W coast; around Loch Tarbert; and the long littoral between Craighouse and Lagg. (Also 1576/BEACHES; 1865/GRAVEYARDS). With the one 'Long' road and over 5,000 deer, the sound of silence is everything And ask locally about 'T on the Beach' (Lussa Beach in the north) – a real treat.
CalMac (0800 066 5000) 7 days, 5-min service from Port Askaig. Passenger-only ferry from Tayvallich to Craighouse twice daily Easter to Sep (07768 450000). For bike hire in Craighouse, ask at the hotel.

2198 7/F23 ✓✓ **Iona** 150,000 visitors a year, but Iona still enchants (as it did the Colourists and centuries of pilgrims), especially if you can get away to the **Bay at the Back of the Ocean** (1581/BEACHES) or sit in one of the many gardens. Or stay: **Argyll Hotel** best 01681 700334 (1195/GET-AWAY HOTELS); **St Columba Hotel** near the abbey has more rooms and its own lovely garden 01681 700304 (2243/MULL); or B&B. Abbey shop and nearby galleries (2161/SCOTTISH SHOPS). Pilgrimage walks on Tuesday (10am from St John's Cross). Bike hire from Finlay Ross shop (01681 700357) and Seaview Guest House at Fionnphort (01681 700235) if you're staying in the village. Everything about Iona is benign; even the sun shines here when it's raining on Mull and corncrakes thrive while elsewhere they disappear.
Regular 15-min CalMac service from Fionnphort till 6pm, earlier in winter (0800 066 5000).

2199 7/F24 ✓✓ **Colonsay** www.colonsay.org.uk Accessible to day-trippers but time ashore is short so you need to arrange accom. The (7 x 16km) island is a haven of wildlife, flowers and beaches (1562/BEACHES) and a serene and popular stopover. 250m from the ferry, the eponymous hotel is congenial, convenient and way better than you might expect (2231/ISLAND HOTELS). Great bar; self-catering units nearby. Some holiday cottages and many B&Bs (check Colonsay website); camping not encouraged. Bar meals and supper at the hotel and Pantry at the pier. A wild 18-hole golf course and bookshop – yes, a bookshop adjacent (summer 3-5.30pm, closed Sun). Semi-botanical gardens at Colonsay House, with Garden Café adjacent, and fine walks, especially to Oronsay (2217/ISLAND WALKS). Don't miss the house at Shell Beach which sells oysters and honey.
CalMac from Oban (or Islay). Crossing takes just over 2 hours. Times vary.

2200 5/G20 ✓✓ **Eigg** www.isleofeigg.net Run by a community (heritage) trust, this small, perfectly formed island seems in robust health, with the first wind/water and solar-powered electricity grid in the world, and a growing, proactive population that many other islands would (and possibly will) die for. A wildlife haven for birds and sealife; otters, eagles and seal colonies. There's a friendly tearoom at the pier: home baking, licensed (boat hours only in winter); evening meals in summer. The irrepressible Sue Kirk runs the shop and Lageorna, which has a restaurant (01687 460081). There's also a B&B at Kildonan (01687 482446), a GH, and lovely cabins at Tigh an Sithean (01687 460049), near the Singing Sands (with other good walks). Check website for other B&Bs. **Glebe Barn** is a brill wee hostel 01687 315099 (1161/HOSTELS). Great walk to An Sgurr, an awesome perch on a summer's day (2223/ISLAND WALKS). Great events programme, including a summer music fest and in alternate years, 2016/18, The Howlin' Fling.
CalMac (from Mallaig) 0800 066 5000 or better, from Arisaig. Arisaig Marine (01687 450224) every day except Thu in summer. Phone for other timings. No car ferry. Day trips to Rum and Muck. Bike hire 07855 363252.

2201 5/F20 ✓✓ **Rum** www.isleofrum.com The large island in the group S of Skye, off the coast at Mallaig. The CalMac ferry plies between Canna, Eigg, Muck and Rum but not too conveniently and it's not easy to island-hop and make a decent visit (but see below). Rum, the most wild and dramatic, has an extraordinary time-warp mansion in Kinloch Castle, which is mainly a museum (guided tours tie in with boat trips). Of all heritage sites in the islands, this is a must to visit. Rum is managed by Scottish Natural Heritage and there are fine trails, climbs, bird-watching spots. 2 simple walks are marked for the 3-hour visitors, but the island reveals its mysteries more slowly. The Doric temple mausoleum to George Bullough, the industrialist whose Highland fantasy the castle was, is a 9km (3-hour) walk across the island to Harris Bay. Sighting the sea eagles (the first to be reintroduced into the UK) may be one of the best things that happens to you all summer. *CalMac ferry from Mallaig direct (twice a week) or via Eigg (2 hours 15 mins). Better from Arisaig (Murdo Grant 01687 450224), summer only (can get 3 hours ashore).*

2202 3/A15 ✓✓ **St Kilda** www.kilda.org.uk There's nothing quite like St Kilda,
NTS anywhere. By far the most remote and removed of the islands here, it is an expedition to reach and one of a physical, cultural and spiritual nature. A spectacular World Heritage site, run by NTS, it occupies a special place in the Scottish heart and soul. Now much more accessible, with several day-trip options, you will be among many photographers, birdwatchers, archaeologists and divers (very clear waters); then you leave! No catering on the island.
To visit: Kilda Cruises (www.kildacruises.co.uk) 01859 502060 from Leverburgh, Harris, and from Uig on Skye 07836 611699.

2203 7/E22 ✓ **Isle of Tiree** www.isleoftiree.com It is an isle, not just an island – flat, with lovely sand and grass and the weather's usually better than the mainland. High sun levels and a bit of wind does keep away the midges. Lots of outdoor activities: famously, windsurfing, but kayaking, bird-watching and other gentle pursuits. The **Scarinish Hotel** (www.tireescarinishhotel.com) is friendly, local and loved and there's another, the **Tiree Lodge Hotel** (www. tireelodge.co.uk), there are 3 guest houses, a wee hostel (01879 220435), a campsite and a couple of decent restaurants: amazing, really, in 30 square miles. Tiree has a unique character different to the islands on this page. But you may long for trees.
Daily flights from Glasgow (www.flybe.com; Tiree airport 01879 220456) and Stornoway & CalMac ferries from Oban (daily in summer, about 4 hours).

2204 7/G26 ✓ **Gigha** www.gigha.org.uk Romantic small island off Kintyre coast with classic views of its island neighbours. Easy mainland access (20-min ferry) contributes to an island atmos without a feeling of isolation (and yippee, no caravans!). Like Eigg, Gigha was bought by the islanders, so its fragile economy is dependent on your visit. The island is run by a heritage trust. **Achamore Gardens** (1518/GARDENS) are a big attraction (the house itself soon to be a boutique hotel at TGP) and the **Gigha Hotel** (2238/ISLAND HOTELS) provides comfortable surroundings. All very relaxed and friendly. The **Boathouse Café** (www.boathousegigha.co.uk) by the ferry for lunch and dinner is superb under Gordon McNeill (Mar-Sep: 01583 505123). 3 B&Bs. Many trails and tracks; ask locally for leaflet. Bike, kayak hire, etc, by the ferry 01786 506520. Double Beach where the Queen once swam off the royal yacht; two crescents of sand either side of the N end of Eilean Garbh isthmus.
CalMac ferry from Tayinloan on A83, 27km S of Tarbert (Glasgow 165km). One an hour in summer, fewer in winter.

2205 7/F22 ✓ **Ulva** www.isleofulva.com Off W coast of Mull; boat leaves Ulva Ferry on B8073 26km S of Dervaig. Idyllic wee island with 5 well-marked walks including to the curious basalt columns similar to Staffa, or by causeway to the smaller island of Gometra; plan routes at the **Boathouse** interpretive centre and tearoom (with Ulva oysters, home-cooked food 9am-4.30pm Easter-Sep, not weekends, except Sun Jun-Aug). Sheila's (thatched) Cottage faithfully restored tells the Ulva story. No accom though camping can be arranged (01688 500264). A charming Telford church has services 4 times a year. Ulva is a perfect day away from the rat race of downtown Tobermory (and everywhere else)!
All-day 5-min service (not Sat; Sun summer only) till 5pm. Ferryman (01688 500226).

2206 3/D19 ✓ **Eriskay** www.visitouterhebrides.co.uk Made famous by the sinking nearby of the SS *Politician* in 1941 and the salvaging of its whisky cargo, later immortalised by Compton Mackenzie in *Whisky Galore* (remake due 2016/17), this Hebridean gem has all the idyllic island ingredients: perfect beaches (1898/CHARLIE), a lovely church, **St Michael's** (1850/CHURCHES), a hill to climb, a pub (called The Politician and telling the story round its walls; it sells decent pub food all day in summer), and the causeway to South Uist (the road cuts a swathe across the island). Limited B&B and no hotel, but camping is OK if you're discreet. Eriskay and Barra together – the pure island experience. (Also 2242/ HEBRIDES).
CalMac ferry from Barra (Ardmhor) 40 mins: 5 a day in summer, winter hours vary.

2207 3/F15 **The Shiants** www.shiantisles.net 3 magical, uninhabited (save for 250,000 birds) tiny islands off E coast of Harris. Read about them in one of the most detailed accounts (a love letter) to any small island ever written: *Sea Room* by Adam Nicolson, the guy who owns them. There's a bothy and it's possible to visit by visiting first his website or www.hebridean-whale-cruises.co.uk out of Gairloch.

2208 7/H22 **Lismore** www.isleoflismore.com Sail from Oban (car ferry) or better from Port Appin 5km off the main A828 Oban-Fort William road, 32km N of Oban; there's a seafood bar/restaurant/hotel (1350/SEAFOOD) to sit and wait. A road runs down the centre of the island (heritage centre and a rather good café halfway), till 4pm in season though check (01631 760020). There are many hill and coastal walks; even the near end round Port Ramsay feels away from it all. History, natural history and air. Island bike hire from Port Appin (01631 730391). **Kerrera** is also a great excursion from Oban (ferry from Gallanach, 10 mins along the coast, takes only a few minutes) and another more peaceful world. Great **Tea Garden** (797/OBAN) and bunkhouse, a castle and walks.
CalMac service from Oban, 4 or 5 times a day (2 on Sun). From Port Appin (32km N of Oban) several per day, 5 mins. Last back 8.15pm; 9.45pm Fri & Sat; 6.35pm winter, but check (01631 562125).

2209 7/F22 **Staffa** For many, a must, especially if you're on Mull. The geological phenomenon
NTS of Fingal's Cave and Mendelssohn's homage are well known. But it's still impressive. Several boat-trip options, many including the Treshnish Islands.
Trips from Mull (08000 858786). From Iona/Fionnphort (01681 700338 or 01681 700358). From Oban (01631 730686).

Isle of Luing A small (6km-long) fascinating island reached by regular ferry (takes cars) 24km S of Oban. See 2108/HISTORY.

CalMac www.calmac.co.uk · 0800 066 5000

▇▇ Fantastic Walks In The Islands

For walk codes, see p. 12.

2210 5/G18 **Dun Caan** Raasay Still one of my favourite island walks – to the flat top of a
10KM magic hill, the one you see from most of the E coast of Skye. Take ferry (2196/
XCIRC ISLANDS). Walk guides at ferry or **Raasay House** (hotel, café, activity centre 2239/
XBIKES SKYE). Routes via old iron mine, near Inverarish village or shorter from road to N
2-B-2 end. Amazing views – the island enchants.

2211 3/E15 **Glen Uladail** North Harris Take B887 W from N of Tarbert (on A859) almost to
12KM RETURN the end (where at Hushinish there's a good beach), but go right (towards the power
XCIRC station) before the big house (1277/HOUSE PARTIES). Park here or further in and
XBIKES walk to dam (3km from road). Take right track round reservoir and left around the
2-B-2 upper loch. Over the brim you arrive in a wide, wild glen; an overhang 2km ahead is said to have the steepest angle in Europe and is favoured by extreme climbers. Go quietly; if you don't see deer and eagles here, you're making too much noise on the grass. On the way, 7km from the main road turn-off at **Meavaig**, there's a car park – a track leads up Glen Meavaig 2km to the North Harris Eagle Observatory. The longest single path in the Western Isles – **Meavaig to Bogha Glas** (16km) is also here. Glen Langdale is spectacular.

2212 3/G14   **Walks on Lewis** 2 coastal walks in the N of Lewis. **Tolsta Head** via B895 NE of
3-11KM   Stornoway and its continuation to the car park of **Traigh Mhor** (1569/BEACHES).
CIRC   Head for the cliffs of the Head; walk combines magnificent sands, big cliffs and
XBIKES   impressive sea stacks. **The Butt of Lewis** from Port Nis (2242/HEBRIDES) going
2-B-2   N as far as you can get in the Hebrides. Start at the cemetery by Eoropaidh Beach.
A fine, airy walk on mainly grassy paths, heading first for the Stevenson lighthouse.
Can shorten to 3km or do fuller circuit.

2213 7/G23   **Carsaig** Mull In S of island, 7km from A849 Fionnphort–Craignure road
15/20KM   near Pennyghael. 2 walks start at pier: going left towards Lochbuie for a
XCIRC   spectacular coastal/woodland walk past Adnunan Stack (8km); or right towards
XBIKES   the imposing headland where, under the cliffs, the Nuns' Cave was a shelter
2-B-2   for nuns evicted from Iona during the Reformation. Nearby is a quarry whose
stone was used to build Iona Abbey and much further on (12km Carsaig), at
Malcolm's Point, the extraordinary Carsaig Arches carved by wind and sea (take
great care!).

2214 7/G22   **Glengorm Estate** nr Tobermory, Mull Old, accessible estate 7km N of
3KM   Tobermory off Dervaig road with 3 easy-to-find-and-follow routes. Good map in
CIRC   coffee shop (1380/TEAROOMS), one of the best in this land for sustenance before
XBIKES   and after (it can get windy on the headlands). Walks vary from less than 30 mins
2-B-2   (the Flat Rock), through 1 hour (the Fort and bathing pool 2094/OPEN-AIR POOLS) to
1.5 hours (to Mingary Point). If you stay in **Glengorm Castle** (2243/MULL) you can
do the lot at your ease.

2215 7/J26   **Cock of Arran** Lochranza Start and finish at Lochranza Castle following the signs
11KM   to the magnificent shoreline. Divers and ducks share the littoral with seals. Look
CIRC   for Giant Centipede fossil trail, and *Hutton's Unconformity* a big deal in the geology
XBIKES   world. Further on at opening of wall, pace 350 steps and turn left up to Ossian's
2-B-2   Cave. Path crosses Fairy Dell Burn and eventually comes out at Lochranza Bay.
Allow 4/5 hours and stout boots.

2216 7/J27   **Holy Isle** by Arran The small island that sits so greenly and serenely in Lamlash
6KM   Bay is 1km away by hourly ferry (less frequently in winter; 07970 771960). Holy Isle
CIRC   is known as the spiritual sanctuary and World Peace Centre project of **Samye Ling**
XBIKES   **Monastery** (1257/1251/RETREATS) but you can freely walk around the littoral and
2-B-2   easily to the top of the presiding single hill (Mullach Mòr). It's natural, beautiful and
spiritual; a walk to cherish.

2217 7/F24   **Colonsay** 2199/ISLANDS. From hotel or the quay, walk to Colonsay House and its
12 + 6KM   lush, overgrown intermingling of native plants and exotics (8km round trip); Garden
XCIRC   Café. Or to the priory on Oronsay, the smaller island. 6km to the Strand (you might
BIKES   get a lift with the postman) then cross at low tide, with enough time (at least 2
1-A-2   hours) to walk to the ruins. Allow longer if you want to climb the easy peak of Ben
Oronsay. Tide tables at hotel. Nice walk also from **Kiloran Beach** (1562/BEACHES)
to Balnahard Beach – farm track 12km return.

2218 5/G17   **The Trotternish Ridge** The 30km high-level ridge walk, as opposed to The
30KM   Quiraing and The Old Man of Storr (see below for both), also offers many shorter
XCIRC   walks without climbing or scrambling, but to take in the whole in a circular walk,
XBIKES   start at the **Lealt Falls** (1601/WATERFALLS) car park on the A855 Staffin road. See
p. 391 for great tearooms nearby.

2219 5/G17
9KM
CIRC
XBIKES
2-B-2
The Old Man of Storr Skye The enigmatic basalt finger visible from the Portree-Staffin road (A855). Start from car park on left, 12km from Portree. There's a well-defined path through afforestation towards the cliffs and a steep climb up the grassy slope to the pinnacle which towers 165ft tall. Great views over Raasay to the mainland. Lots of space and rabbits and birds who make the most of it but an increasingly popular pilgrimage so expect human company, too.

2220 5/G17
6KM
CIRC
XBIKES
2-B-2
The Quirang Skye See 1636/VIEWS for directions to start point. The strange formations have names (eg The Table, The Needle, The Prison) and it's possible to walk round all of them. Start of the path from the car park on the Uig–Staffin road is easy. At the first saddle, take the second scree slope to The Table, rather than the first. When you get to The Needle, the path to the right between two giant pinnacles is the easiest of the 3 options. From the top you can see the Hebrides. This place is supernatural; anything could happen. So be careful.

2221 5/G18
3KM
CIRC
XBIKES
1-A-1
Scorrybreac Skye A much simpler prospect than the above and more quietly spectacular but mentioned here because anyone can do it; it's only 3km and it's more or less in Portree. Head for **Cuillin Hills Hotel** off Staffin Rd out of town (2239/SKYE). Shoreline path signed just below hotel. Passes Black Rock where once Bonnie Prince Charlie left for Raasay, and continues round hill. Nice views back to the bright lights and pink houses of Portree.

2222 1/Q11
20/25KM
CIRC
MTBIKES
2-B-2
Hoy Orkney There are innumerable walks on the scattered Orkney Islands; on a good day, head to the N of Hoy for some of the most dramatic coastal scenery anywhere. Ferries from Houton. Stromness via Graemsay, met by a minibus or a car ferry from Houton E of Stromness with 20km drive to start of walk. Make tracks N or S from junction near Moaness pier and don't miss the landmarks, the bird sanctuaries and of course the Old Man himself if you've got the time (4 hours). See 2036/WALKS.

2223 5/G20
An Sgurr Eigg Unmissable treat on Eigg. Take to the big ridge. Not a hard pull; extraordinary views and island perspective from the top. 2200/ISLANDS. Start from the ferry pier, 3 hours.

The Best Island Hotels

This section excludes Skye which has its own hotel listings, p. 387–89.

2224 3/E16
6 ROOMS
NO TV
DF
MAR-DEC
LL
EXP
✓✓ **Scarista House** South Harris · www.scaristahouse.com · 01859 550238 21km Tarbert, 78km Stornoway. On the W coast famous for its beaches and overlooking one of the best (1568/BEACHES). Tim and Patricia Martin's civilised retreat and home from home. Fixed menu meals in dining rooms overlooking sea. No phones or other intrusions (though TV in the kitchen and Wi-Fi); many books. The golf course over the road is exquisite. Good family hotel but delightfully laid-back. Great suites.
EAT A fixed menu but the place to eat in these Hebrides. 4 courses; good value for this quality. Notify fads and diets. Open to non-res.

2225 7/G22
6 ROOMS
NO PETS
MAR-OCT
MED.EX
✓✓ **Highland Cottage** Tobermory, Mull · www.highlandcottage.co.uk · 01688 302030 Breadalbane St opposite Tobermory fire station. Street above harbour (from roundabout on road from Craignure). Small, comfy rooms named after islands. This is a well-run cottage-boutique; both cosy and chic. Small, maybe, but perfectly formed: relax into Jo Currie's simply delicious, easy-going fine dining. Dave your amiable host. They know good food and they know Mull.
EAT Where to eat on Mull. Fine without fuss in a perfect parlour. 2243/MULL.

2226 7/F26
11 ROOMS
DF
MED.INX

✓✓ **Bridgend Inn** Islay · www.bridgend-hotel.com · 01496 810212
Bridgend near Bowmore on the Port Askaig road. I love this comfortable roadside hostelry, long a fixture on the island by the A846/A847 crossroads and a gathering place for locals and visitors. Owned by Islay Estates, it has an easy-going bar (with food), a lounge for tea and timeless afternoons, and a dining room opening onto lovely gardens. Bedrooms in simple, good taste are inexpensive. A peaceful retreat from island life!

2227 7/F26
10 ROOMS
L
MED.INX

✓✓ **Port Charlotte Hotel** Islay · www.portcharlottehotel.co.uk · 01496 850360 The epitome of the comfy island inn. Modern, discreet approach to guests. Sea swishing below; very much at the heart of this fine whitewashed village (1555/VILLAGES). Good whisky choice, traditional music (Wed & Sun) and good grub in the bar; restaurant dining room (and same chef since the Allisons took over in 2008), with conservatory and sea-gazing terrace. Tourists in summer, twitchers in winter. The Allisons support local and Scottish artists and music and Grahame sings in the Gaelic choir. Connected!

2228 7/J27
8 ROOMS + 4
COTTS
DF
NO KIDS
MAR-OCT
EXP

✓ **Kilmichael House** nr Brodick, Arran · www.kilmichael.com · 01770 302219 On road to Brodick Castle/Corrie, take left at bend by golf course. 3km down track to this bucolic haven far (but only minutes) from bustling Brodick. Various hens, peacocks and geese may attend your arrival. Unapologetically old-style country house refined, so not great for kids. Rooms in house or garden courtyard – painstaking detail in food, service and surroundings. Also 4 cottages. All delightful.
EAT Still Arran's homespun fine-dining option. Anthony cooks.

2229 7/J27
22 ROOMS
MED.EX

✓ **Douglas Hotel** Brodick, Arran · www.thedouglashotel.co.uk · 01770 302968 The new esplanade: where the Ardrossan ferry comes in. The Douglas redefining Brodick for visitors, with attention to detail (well-chosen art, good lighting) and to service overseen by local owner. You're plugged in very comfortably. See also 2240/ARRAN.

2230 7/J27
13 ROOMS
MED.INX

✓ **Glenisle Hotel** Lamlash, Arran · www.glenislehotel.com · 01770 600559 There's a good choice of classy hotels in Arran and to urban standards (2240/ARRAN). This is exemplary and the quite groovy Glenisle also has the advantage of being in Lamlash (5km Brodick), so relaxing and buzzy at the same time. Overlooks bay and **Holy Island** (2216/ISLAND WALKS). Nice bar and restaurant and other good eating options nearby. Has a Michelin recommendation.

2231 7/F24
10 ROOMS
MAY-SEP
L
MED.EX

✓ **Colonsay Hotel** www.colonsayestate.co.uk · 01951 200316 Long-established, well run, and generally superb island hotel, 400m from the ferry on this island perfectly proportioned for short stays (2199/ISLANDS). The laird (and wife) and their partners have turned this into a contemporary destination hotel. Cool public rooms and buzzy bar (especially quiz nights). Mobiles only work in the garden. House and garden to visit and stunning beach 5km. On your bike.

2232 7/F26
13 ROOMS
DF
MED.EX

✓ **The Islay Hotel** www.theislayhotel.com · 01496 300109 In Port Ellen, in the south, on the corner where the ferry comes in. Completely refurbished by well-versed locals Roland, Kathleen and Ian with a kind of Islay crowdfunding community buy-in. This hotel and bar is close to all island matters and yet the public and bedrooms are light and contemporary, and you feel you could be on any mainland. Very close to the big 3 distilleries: Laphroaig, Lagavulin and Ardbeg.

2233 7/F26
7 ROOMS
MED.EX

✓ **The Harbour Inn** Islay · www.harbour-inn.com · 01496 810330 Now owned by Bowmore Distillery, this top island restaurant with rooms is 2 doors up from the harbour in the centre of the main town on lovely, quite lively Islay. Rooms contemporary and comfy, lounge with views and notable restaurant, especially seafood. Bar with malts and bar meals (LO 8.30pm). 4 cottages across the street.

2234 7/G25
17 ROOMS
NO TV
L
MED.INX

✓ **Jura Hotel** www.jurahotel.co.uk · 01496 820243 Craighouse, 12km from Islay ferry at Feolin. The island hub given a new lease of life by Andy and Cath McCallum and young obliging team. Bedrooms are simple and serviceable though not large and no TV. Bar for all local craic; they make visitors welcome. Grub here and all else you'll need (including Wi-Fi). Camping on their grassy field to the sea is free. See 2197/ISLANDS.

2235 7/F22
6 ROOMS
MED.INX-MED.
EX

✓ **Coll Hotel** www.collhotel.com · 01879 230334 Julie and Kevin Oliphant continue to win accolades for their exemplary island hotel and restaurant on Coll, which to my shame and frustration I have never visited (yes, J & K, I'm still relying on other reports). But I know it's got a nice garden, a deck overlooking the sea and the Gannet Restaurant, which is highly recommended. 4 rooms have the islands view. Coll is now designated a Dark Sky destination because of its very low light pollution – so look up! I imagine it's rather perfect! Coll is 2.5/3 hours from Oban. Ferries sail AYR.

2236 3/C20
15 ROOMS
LL
MED.INX

Castlebay Hotel Castlebay, Barra · www.castlebay-hotel.co.uk · 01871 810223 Prominent position overlooking bay and ferry dock. You see where you're staying long before you arrive. Old-style holiday hotel at the centre of Barra life. Perhaps upgrading would spoil its charm though the bedrooms have improved a tad. OK restaurant and bar meals. Adjacent bar, famed for craic and car culture, has more than a dash of the Irish (1290/GOOD PUBS) and a busy pool table. Sea view superior rooms worth the extra.

2237 3/C20
15 ROOMS
DF
APR-OCT
MED.INX

Isle of Barra Beach Hotel www.isleofbarrahotel.co.uk · 01871 810383 A 3km hop from Castlebay on Tangasdale Beach, a quiet, very island location with wide views from the spacious lounge. Accom on brilliant Barra is often hard to come by (demand exceeds supply), and though the hotel could benefit from some titivation, location's the thing; you might be lucky to get in here. Good reports for food. They have bikes.

2238 7/G26
12 ROOMS
MED.INX

The Gigha Hotel Gigha · www.gigha.org.uk · 01583 505254 A short walk from the ferry on an island perfectly proportioned for a short visit; easy walking and cycling. Residents' lounge peaceful, with dreamy views to Kintyre. Menu with local produce, eg Gigha prawns, scallops and the halibut. Island life without the remoteness. 2204/ISLANDS.

✓ **Argyll Hotel** Iona · 01681 700334 & **St Columba Hotel** Iona · 01681 700304 Reports: 1175/INNS; 2243/MULL.

The Best of Skye

2239 5/H19 **The Bridge** Unromantic but easy and free; from Kyle. The **Ferries** Mallaig–Armadale, 30 mins. Tarbert (Harris)–Uig, 1 hour 35 mins (CalMac, as Mallaig). **The Best Way to Skye** Glenelg–Kylerhea www.skyeferry.co.uk 5-min sailing. Continuous Easter–Oct. Winter sailings – check tourist information centre. Community run. See 6/JOURNEYS.

WHERE TO STAY

6 ROOMS
LOTS

✓✓ **The House Over-By at The Three Chimneys** www.threechimneys. co.uk · 01470 511258 At Colbost 7km W of Dunvegan by the B884 to Glendale. When Eddie and Shirley Spear transformed their house overby into the House Over-By, it was the first boutique-style accom in the Highlands. Refurbished and now many years later it's still a model of understated luxury in a wild and woolly place. Adjacent or just overby from their accolade-laden restaurant (in world's top lists). Separate dining room for a healthy breakfast transforms into a light conservatory lounge in the evening. Outside the sheep, the sea and the sky. **EAT** After the long hike across the courtyard or a drive from the rest of the world you deserve a treat! With new (since last edition) chef Scott Davies. See below.

19 ROOMS
DF
LOTS

✓✓ **Kinloch Lodge** Sleat · www.kinloch-lodge.co.uk · 01471 833333 Just S of Broadford, 55km Portree. The ancestral but not-at-all imposing home of Lord and Lady Macdonald, with newer build house adjacent adding 10 well-appointed rooms. Spacious, country drawing room. It's a family affair with Isabella and Tom in charge but Lady Mac is Claire Macdonald of cookery fame; her many books (and jam range) are for sale in the bar. The kitchen is down to Michelin-starred Marcello Tully and you can bet that dinner in the perfect Highland lodge dining room is an epicurean experience from soupçon to cheese flight finish. **EAT** At Lady Claire and Marcello's elegant table. See below.

12 ROOMS
4 SUITES
NO TV
LL
ATMOS
MED.EX

✓✓ **Eilean Iarmain** Sleat · www.eileaniarmain.co.uk · 01471 833332 60km S of Portree. Tucked into the bay, Lady Lucilla Noble's Gaelic inn, with its great pub and good dining, provides sympatico, comfortable base in S of the island. Their famously Gaelic approach to hospitality (no TVs except in the suites but there is Wi-Fi), gives this place the indefinable 'it'. It hasn't changed much and really doesn't have to. Bar is local craic central. 6 rooms in main hotel best value (garden rooms are in the house overby). Also 4 suites in steading – expensive but your Hielan' hame. Shop and gallery adjacent. You wander down to the quay for mobile phone reception; you don't want to go anywhere else. **EAT** Bar for atmos and grub; dining room for atmos and fine dinner.

22 ROOMS
DF
MED.INX-EXP

✓ **Raasay House** www.raasay-house.co.uk · 01478 660300 The 'big house' in a classic setting on Raasay, the best of islands (2196/ISLANDS), a short ferry from Sconser, halfway between Broadfoot and Portree. An ill wind and a fire razed most of the building in 2009, but it has been extensively and sympathetically restored into an all round Skye asset: hotel, café, restaurant, bar, library and quite brilliant activity centre. Many walks. 3 levels of room, including posh. Raasay will enfold you from here.

18 ROOMS
NO PETS
MED.EX

✓ **Duisdale House** Sleat · www.duisdale.com · 01471 833202 Only 4km up the road from Toravaig (below) nearer to Broadford, Ken Gunn and Anne Gracie's bigger hotel, refurbished boutique-style to a high standard (big wallpapers, luxe bathrooms). Hot tub on the garden deck; the gardens themselves quite gorgeous. Also the larger restaurant of the two; a little more casual. K&A love to sail and will take you out on the *Solus* most days 10.30am–4.30pm to see the seals, whales and Skye from a different perspective. Then back to a very congenial dry land and excellent staff who look after you.

EAT Either Toravaig (more intimate) or Duisdale – both excellent eats in the south.

9 ROOMS
NO PETS
MED.EX

✓ **Toravaig House Hotel** Sleat · www.skyehotel.co.uk · 01471 833231
Main road S from Broadford to Armadale. Ken and Anne's personally run hotel along with Duisdale above; two brilliantly positioned places to eat and stay on Skye. Small and charming with contemporary refurbished rooms and pleasing restaurant with fine understated dining. As above, you can get on the yacht and picnic over the sea.

14 ROOMS
NO PETS
MED.EX

✓ **Skeabost Country House Hotel** nr Portree · www.skeabosthotel.com ·
01470 532202 11km W of Portree on the A850, the Dunvegan road. Venerable Skye chateau, with stately interior refurbished and upgraded by the folk who have the Toravaig and the Duisdale (above). Conservatory, panelled dining room, original billiard room (and table), loads of public space and some sumptuous bedrooms. Exquisite grounds, including the babbling River Snizort (hotel has salmon rights for 8 miles and own ghillie) and a sweet little 9-hole (though can do 18) golf course.

11 ROOMS
NO TV
APR-OCT
MED.INX

✓ **Viewfield House** Portree · www.viewfieldhouse.com · 01478 612217
One of the first hotels you come to in Portree on the road from S (driveway opposite gas station); you need look no further. Individual, grand but comfortable, full of antiques and memorabilia, though not at all stuffy (purposefully, no TV); this historic and comfortable, rambling house is also one of the best value-for-money hotels on the island. Log fires; supper available if you want but you don't have to eat in. Croquet and I wonder if they have revived the grass tennis court. Track through the woods to town (15 mins). Hugh Macdonald is your congenial host.

20 ROOMS
MED.EX

Bosville Hotel Portree · www.bosvillehotel.co.uk · 01478 612846
Refurbished rooms and a place to eat at the top of the brae heading N from centre on the road to Staffin. Dulse & Brose restaurant (see below); urban standard of comfort and at the very heart of Portree.

8 ROOMS
MED.INX

Marmalade Portree · www.marmaladehotel.co.uk · 01478 611711 Leave from corner of main square up hill away from sea and keep going 1.5km. Unlikely, almost suburban location until you see the view (from gardens and 4 of the 8 rooms). Rooms above the busy bar/restaurant popular with locals, especially for pizza. Friendly staff (and friendly midges if you're out on the lawn in summer).

29 ROOMS
MED.INX

Cuillin Hills Hotel Portree · www.cuillinhills-hotel-skye.co.uk ·
01478 612003 On the edge of Portree (off road N to Staffin) near water's edge. Secluded mansion-house hotel with nice conservatory. Great views from most rooms and a superb terrace/lawn. Nice walk from garden (2221/ISLAND WALKS). Dining room/brasserie seems OK.

85 ROOMS
CHP

Sabhal Mòr Ostaig Sleat · www.smo.uhi.ac.uk · 01471 888000 Pronounced Sawal More Ostag. Part of the Gaelic College off A851 N of Armadale. Excellent inexpensive rooms (<£40) in modern build overlooking Sound of Sleat. Best in student holidays but rooms often available outwith. The penthouse is spectacular. Breakfast in bright café. Best deal on the island; you could also learn Gaelic.

11 + 7 ROOMS **APR-OCT** **MED.INX** **Flodigarry Hotel** www.hotelintheskye.co.uk · 01470 522203 In a glorious elevated setting looking over to Staffin Island in the far N of Skye (35km from Portree on A855, mostly single track road). Recommended in early editions of *StB*, this much-loved mansion hotel went through a patchy patch, but new Dutch owners are refurbishing rooms (6 have sea views) and the High Tide restaurant is building a good reputation. Flora MacDonald's (actual) cottage adjacent has 7 additional rooms.

11 ROOMS **MED.EX** **Broadford Hotel** Broadford · www.broadfordhotel.co.uk · 01471 822204 On left heading N out of Broadford. Long-established Skye hotel contemporised by the people who also own the Bosville and Marmalade (above) but mixed reviews of late. Decent, not overdone look to new rooms. Busy bar and bistro.

✓ **Greshornish Country House** Edinbane Report: 1197/GET-AWAY HOTELS.

4 EXCELLENT B&Bs ON SKYE

3 ROOMS **NO TV** **MED.INX** ✓ **The Glenview** by Staffin · www.glenviewskye.co.uk · 01470 562248 25km N of Portree on the A855 Staffin road just N of the **Lealt Falls** (1601/ WATERFALLS). Kirsty and Simon's lovely rooms, inn-like ambience and pies(!) in this old cosy roadhouse in the north. Simple, nice style and decor. No TV or phones (there is Wi-Fi). B&B only (that would be a very comfy B and an excellent B in the morning). During the day, there's the **Skye Pie Café**, one of the island's best drop-by eats (see below).

3 ROOMS **MED.EX** ✓ **The Spoons** Skeabost Bridge · www.thespoonsonskye.com · 01470 532217 15km from Portree off Dunvegan road, 1km at Aird Bernisdale, a purpose-built luxury B&B overlooking Loch Snizort. Marie and Ian Lewis love their house and what they do and you will, too. Small but all done beautifully. Egyptian cotton, lotsa neat touches, splendid breakfasts with crêpes, home-made bread, freshly-laid eggs. You'll be lucky to get in here, of course, so book ahead.

3 ROOMS **MED.INX** ✓ **Tigh An Dochais** Broadford · www.skyebedbreakfast.co.uk · 01471 820022 Signed and on road coming into Broadford from the south (the bridge and ferries). Stunning contemporary building by award-winning architects Dualchas, this long, light house makes the most of its location. Bedrooms open out to and practically merge with the (appropriately monochrome) littoral. Breakfast in upstairs lounge; bread home-made, etc. And as I have said before, this is a superb introduction to Skye.

4 ROOMS + 2 COTTS **APR-OCT** **MED.EX** ✓ **Peinmore House** Portree · www.peinmorehouse.co.uk · 01478 612574 Traditional manor house built round courtyard just outside Portree (250m off B883 Braes road, 3km S on Broadford road). Traditional and spacious, light, tasteful with Margaret Greer's sure touches: family pics, wonderful flower baskets round courtyard, big rooms, choice DVDs.
And daughter Georgie has built and opened another B&B behind: **Canowindra** 01478 613640; www.canowindraskye.co.uk. Contemporary with similar great attention to detail; this is B&B deluxe.

THE BEST RESTAURANTS ON SKYE

>£35 ✓✓ **The Three Chimneys** Colbost · www.threechimneys.co.uk · 01470 511258 7km W of Dunvegan on B884 to Glendale. There has been a lot of water under the Bridge but after 25 years of this book and their restaurant, Shirley and Eddie Spear's Three Chimneys, in a converted cottage on the edge of the best kind of nowhere, is still where you want to go in Skye. This was the first restaurant in Scotland to prove that it didn't matter where you were – if the food and atmos were right, people would find you. Many followed in their footsteps. Refurbished 2015 and with a new chef, Scott Davies, the Chimneys is reclaiming its place in Scotland's premier league. They shop local for everything (Skye supplies hugely improved following their example) from Glendale leaves to local langoustines. Fastidious, smart service with a strong kitchen team. It's a long road to Colbost but by the start of your starter you know why you came. They can recommend some B&Bs when their own rooms are (as usual) full. Lunch Mar-Nov, dinner AYR.

>£35 ✓✓ **Kinloch Lodge** Sleat · www.kinloch-lodge.co.uk · 01471 833333 In S on Sleat Peninsula, 55km S of Portree signed off the main Sleat road along a characterful track. The Macdonald family home and hotel offers a taste of the high life without hauteur; their pics and portraits surround you as you start with drinks in the drawing rooms and move to the elegant dining room. Lady Claire herself no longer in the kitchen, it's Michelin-starred chef Marcello Tully's food you come to adore. 5 courses (fixed menu, with 2-choice main, so flag up fads/diets) or 7-course 'tasting' and 'special'. Great écossais/français cheeseboard with flight option. It's an 'experience Skye through food' thing! Private dining, chef's table and Marcello's workshops. There's also afternoon tea.

£25-35 ✓✓ **Scorrybreac** Portree · www.scorrybreac.com · 01478 612069 Scorrybreac House is indeed a house in Bosville Terrace along from the hotel (see below). Small (8 tables) and widely thought to be just about perfect, this started as a pop-up by Calum Munro (son of Donnie, notable Scottish musician and man about Skye) but became the must-go eaterie. Simple approach but very fine cooking. Couple of good people, couple of (living) rooms. You're gonna have to book!

>£35 ✓ **Dulse & Brose** Portree · www.dulsebrose.com · 01478 612846 Long the place to eat at the top of the town, the restaurant of the Bosville Hotel, got a new name, a new look and just about new everything 2015. No longer fine dining but well-turned-out food in a bistro setting. Reports, please.

LL ✓ **Lochbay Restaurant** Stein · www.lochbay-restaurant.co.uk · ATMOS 01470 592235 12km N of Dunvegan off A850. Small, celebrated seafood bistro £25-35 taken over by Michael Smith at TGP. Much may change, but with a Michelin chef in the kitchen, it will be good. Report: 1342/SEAFOOD.

<£15 ✓ **The Oyster Shed** www.skyeoysterman.co.uk · 07762 436913 Paul the oyster farmer's farm shop and seafood takeaway, near the Talisker Distillery, also has tables, both inside and out. Oysters, naturally, and lobster, crab, langoustines and salmon platters. They do chips and you can BYOB. A foodie corner of Skye worth finding. 11am-5pm. Check times in winter.

<£15 ✓ **Café Arriba** Portree · www.cafearriba.co.uk · 01478 611830 Upstairs at the top of the road down to the harbour. A funky, bright, long-established and kinda boho caff on Skye with a view of the bay. Good bread/Green Mountain coffee/vegetarian. Eclectic home-made food changes daily. Cosmo cuisine and atmos. Does the trick. 7 days 7am-6pm.

<£15 ✓ **Skye Pie Café** www.skyepiecafe.co.uk · 01470 562248 25km N of Portree on the A855 to Staffin. The dining room of the lovely (now B&B) Glenview Hotel. Simon's mouthwatering pies, savoury, sweet and all scrumptious, served simply with healthy raw salads and 'wedges'. There's also soup. Occasionally there's a pop-up 'Supper Club'. It's a winner! Mar-Oct, Mon-Fri noon-4pm.

£15-25 **The Old School Restaurant** Dunvegan · www.oldschoolrestaurant.co.uk · 01470 521421 On main road away from castle, for over 30 years a perennially popular family-run bistro, much loved for local food and approach. All the favourites are here. Lunch, summer only Wed-Sun, dinner 7 nights AYR.

GREAT TEAROOMS ON SKYE

✓ **Red Roof Café Gallery** Glendale · www.redroofskye.co.uk · 01470 511766 Way out NW at Glendale (beyond the 3 Chimneys, above). Gareth and Iona's labour of love, the white bothy with the red roof, a gallery for Elly's work and a top wee tearoom, with home-made everything using the nearby seafood and the Glendale leaves. Live music Friday evenings. Locally loved; so will you. Easter-Oct 11am-5pm. Closed Sat & Mon.

✓ **Jann's Cakes** Dunvegan Main road out of village, A863 to Broadford. A wee shack really but where Jann (and Lewis) Dove turn out an amazing array of heavyish but heavenly home-made cakes, bread, chocolates, soup and yes, curries, tagines and other scrumptious and unlikely world food. If you love chocolate, you'll love Jann's cakes. This is a great wee find! Mar-Oct 10am-5pm, Nov/Dec/Feb 11am-3pm. Closed Sun.

✓ **The Small & Cosy Teahouse** Digg · www.smallandcosyteahouse.co.uk · 01470 562471 In the north, main road to Staffin; a small and happy teahouse. Conscientiously home-made bread and soup, cakes and a big variety of tea. An excellent prospect after a walk on the (Trotternish) ridge, Old Man of Storr, Quirang, etc. Noon-6pm. Easter-Oct. Closed Mon.

✓ **Ellishadder Art Café** www.ellishadderartcafe.co.uk · 01470 562734 250m off Portree/Staffin road near Kilt Rock, 25 mins N of Portree (there's a croft/museum on the corner). Maggie Quigley's small art gallery and lovely café in a white cottage serves savoury tarts, soup 'n' cakes, and is all vegetarian. Easter-Oct weekdays.

Caledonian Café Portree · www.caledoniancafe.co.uk · 01478 612553 On the main street. Simple, serviceable caff open long hours in summer for hungry tourists who don't want to cough up loadsa dosh to eat. Hot specials and usual caff fare. Home baking and busy with their home-made ice cream. 7 days 9am-9pm.

WHAT TO SEE

The Cuillin Mountains (2/ATTRACTIONS); **Raasay** (2196/ISLANDS), (2210/ISLAND WALKS); **The Quirang** (1636/VIEWS), (2220/ISLAND WALKS); **Old Man Of Storr** (2219/ISLAND WALKS); **Dunvegan** (1763/CASTLES); **Eas Mor** (1601/WATERFALLS); **Elgol** (1643/VIEWS); **Skye Museum Of Island Life** (2126/HISTORY); **Flora Macdonald's Grave** (1829/MONUMENTS); **Skye Silver, Edinbane Pottery** (2159/2158/SCOTTISH SHOPS); **Fairy Pools** (1658/SWIMMING); **Duirinish & Minginish** (2036/WALKS).

Tourist Information Centre Portree · 01478 612137 & **CalMac** www.calmac. co.uk · 0800 066 5000

2240 7/J27   **CalMac Ferry** Ardrossan–Brodick, 55 mins. 6 per day Mon-Sat, 4 on Sun. Ardrossan–Glasgow, train or road via A77/A71 1.5 hours. Claonaig–Lochranza, 30 mins. 9 per day (summer only). The best way to see Arran is on a bike. Hire: 01770 302077 or 01770 302377.

WHERE TO STAY

8 ROOMS
DF
NO KIDS
MAT-OCT
EXP

✓ **Kilmichael House** nr Brodick · www.kilmichael.com · 01770 302219
Individual and discreet mansion 3km from the main road and into the glen. Elegant interior and furnishings in house and courtyard rooms, antiques and rugs; the antithesis of both bland and bling. Still *the* place to fine dine on Arran, must book (2228/ISLAND HOTELS). Also self-catering cottages (AYR).

22 ROOMS
MED.EX

✓ **Douglas Hotel** Brodick · www.thedouglashotel.co.uk · 01770 302968
On the front where the ferry comes in, you can't miss it even at night, lit large. High quality and complete renovation of the old Douglas by returned local lad Sean Henry raising the game in Arran immeasurably. Contemporary design and fixtures throughout. With recent rearrangement of the bar, it all works. 2229/ISLAND HOTELS.

13 ROOMS
MED.INX

✓ **Glenisle Hotel** Lamlash · www.glenislehotel.com · 01770 600559
Timothy Billings and Geoffrey Dallamore's carefully refurbished and rethought hotel in Lamlash looking out to Holy Isle. Local stone, colour and texture in evidence in well-appointed bedrooms, bar and restaurant. Calm, efficient and friendly: a perfect stay in lovely Lamlash. Good bistro and outside terrace/garden overlooking the bay. See also 2230/ISLAND HOTELS.

28 ROOMS
(HOUSE) + 36
(SPA)
DF
MED.INX

✓ **Auchrannie** Brodick · www.auchrannie.co.uk · 01770 302234 Once an old mansion, now expanded into a holiday complex. House has best rooms, eats (Eighteen69 restaurant and bistro Brambles) and small pool. But the Spa Resort, like a Holiday Inn in the country, is perfect for families: good modern rooms, bigger pool and leisure facilities. Juice Bar here means Scottish 'juice'. Upstairs restaurant Cruize a bit Glasgow Airport but fits all sizes! Plenty indoors for Arran weather but also out: Arran Adventure Centre on hand.
EAT Eighteen 69's small plates a hit!

13 ROOMS
MED.INX

The Lagg Hotel Kilmory · www.lagghotel.com · 01770 870250 S of Arran 25km Brodick. In a rare sylvan setting with serene river terraces, Peter Bowers' old coaching inn; an almost olde English feel. Log fires, local reputation for food, great lounge bar, whisky and wine. A fine retreat. 500m to Kilmory Beach.

15 ROOMS
DF
L
MED.INX

Kildonan Hotel Kildonan · www.kildonanhotel.com · 01770 820207 In the S of the island (Brodick 16km) on a beautiful strand overlooking Pladda Island and lighthouse; Ailsa Craig spectral beyond. Great outside terrace (with big stones) for gazing out to sea. Some rooms so-so. Happy, popular bar with grub and conservatory dining room. Somehow it's a bit special.

S.Y. Hostel Lochranza Recently refurbished. Report: 1167/HOSTELS.
Glen Rosa Campsite 4km Brodick. Bucolic. 1223/WILD CAMPING.

THE BEST RESTAURANTS ON ARRAN

>£35   ✓ **Kilmichael House** nr Brodick The finest dining on Arran. See above.

<£15   ✓ **The Glenisle Bistro** Lamlash Civilised contemporary dining. See above.

£15-25 ✓ **Stags Pavilion** Lochranza · www.stagspavilion.com · 01770 830600
Adjacent to the golf course in Lochranza in the N of the island, locals make the
journey here from all over (you probably have to book). Rino Pisano brings an
Italian influence to a seasonal menu. Nice building (the former clubhouse), atmos
and garden. They also have a wee shop adjacent campsite. It's an island thing.

£15-25 ✓ **The Drift Inn** Lamlash · www.driftinnarran.com · 01770 600608 Just off
the main road, by the sea. Hugely popular pub for atmos and grub, probably
the most rockin' place to eat on the island (occasional live music). Some
imaginative combos and faves. Seaside garden. Food 7 days noon-11pm.

£15-25 ✓ **Douglas Hotel Bistro** Brodick Contemporary dining. (Microbrewery
planned at TGP). See above.

£15-25 **Brodick Bar & Brasserie** Brodick · www.brodickbar.co.uk · 01770 302169
Best bistro/pub food in Brodick by common consensus (there is also the Douglas
above). Goes like a fair and can feel like a canteen on summer evenings. Long
blackboard menu. Pizzas. Lunch & LO 9pm. Bar till midnight. Closed Sun.

£15-25 **Felicity's** Whiting Bay · www.felicitysarran.co.uk · 01770 700357 Restaurant
of the former Eden Lodge Hotel on the long front of Whiting Bay, 15km S of
Brodick. Felicity Young just makes everything: sandwiches to cakes to chargrilled
dishes and pizza. Tables overlook the bay. All-day lunch and then 5-9pm.

£25-35 **Trafalgar** Whiting Bay · www.thetrafalgar.co.uk · 01770 700396 On the
Shore Rd, the Trafalgar for 30 years has been where on Arran you go for your tea,
i.e. dinner. Nothing too fancy, mind, just the Kroners cooking up what we like.
Behind a welcoming display of well-kept flowers, their old-style dining room. The
best steaks! You'd better book. Evenings only (LO 8.30pm). Closed Nov-Mar.

WHAT TO SEE

NTS ✓ **Brodick Castle** 5km walk or cycle from Brodick. Impressive museum and
gardens. Tearoom. Flagship NTS property. Report: 1761/CASTLES.

2-A-2 **Goat Fell** 6km/5-hour great hill walk starting from the car park at Cladach near
castle and Brodick, or sea start at Corrie. Report: 1928/HILLS.

1-B-1 **Glenashdale Falls** 4km, but 2-hour forest walk from Glenashdale Bridge at
Whiting Bay. Steady, easy climb, sylvan setting. Report: 1596/WATERFALLS.

Arran Distillery In Lochranza. Visitor centre, tour and tasting of the Arran Single
Malt. 7 days. Winter hours vary (01770 830264).

Machrie Moor Standing Stones Off main coast road 7km N of Blackwaterfoot.
Various assemblies of Stones, all part of an ancient landscape. We lay down there.

Glen Rosa, Glen Sannox Fine glens: Rosa near Brodick 1223/WILD CAMPING;
Sannox 11km N.

Holy Island Walk. Report: 2216/ISLAND WALKS.

Tourist Information Centre Brodick · 01770 303774 & **CalMac** www.calmac.
co.uk · 0800 066 5000

2241 7 **CalMac Ferry** Kennacraig–Port Askaig: 2 hours; Kennacraig–Port Ellen: 2 hours 10 mins. Port Askaig–Feolin, Jura: (0800 066 5000) 5 mins, frequent daily. Passenger ferry from Tayvallich near Crinan, Easter-Sep: 07768 450000. **By Air** Flybe (0871 700 2000) Glasgow to Port Ellen Airport in S of Islay.

WHERE TO STAY

11 ROOMS
DF
MED.INX
✓✓ **Bridgend Inn** Islay · www.bridgend-hotel.com · 01496 810212 Middle of island on road from Port Askaig, 4km Bowmore. Superb roadside inn with good pub meals, dining and cosy rooms. See also 2226/ISLAND HOTELS.

10 ROOMS
L
MED.INX
✓✓ **Port Charlotte Hotel** Islay · www.portcharlottehotel.co.uk · 01496 850360 Restored Victorian inn and gardens overlooking sea in conservation village. Restful place and views. Good bistro-style menu. Eat in bar/conservatory or dining room. Top terrace on the sea. See also 2227/ISLAND HOTELS.

13 ROOMS
DF
MED.EX
✓ **The Islay Hotel** www.theislayhotel.com · 01496 300109 In Port Ellen, in the S of the island, and very close to the ferry terminal. A friendly contemporary hotel, restaurant and bar (2232/ISLAND HOTELS)..

7 ROOMS + 4
COTTS
MED.EX
✓ **The Harbour Inn** Bowmore, Islay · www.harbour-inn.com · 01496 810330 Harbourside inn with conservatory lounge, Schooner bar for seafood lunch and less formal supper, and dining room with Modern-British menu. Bedrooms vary but all mod and con. Now owned by Bowmore; more corporate feel. See also 2233/ISLAND HOTELS.

17 ROOMS
NO TV
L
MED.INX
✓ **Jura Hotel** Craighouse · www.jurahotel.co.uk · 01496 820243 The island hotel and all-round social centre does all you want it to (including free camping and use of their facilities). Good bar, decent grub. One of the friendliest and quietly contemporary hotels in the islands. Situated in front of the distillery by the bay. See also 2234/ISLAND HOTELS.

5 ROOMS
NO TV
DF · L
CHP
✓ **Ardlussa House** Jura · www.ardlussaestate.com · 01496 820323 Hard to be more far-flung than this: the Ardlussa Estate occupies the N of Jura and this lived-in family house is a welcome destination after a single-track journey (28km from Craignure) on the 'Long Road'. 5 rooms (2 with superb views), 8 bathrooms. Convivial dinner with all their own venison, pork, lobsters and garden veg. The Fletchers share their splendid wild backyard with you. No TVs in rooms, phone reception dodgy; this is real island life. George Orwell's house is on their land. Ask about 'T on the Beach' (they know everything about Jura). Kids run free.

Islay House Bridgend · www.islayhouse.co.uk · 01496 810702 Major refurbishment at TGP to turn Islay's big house into hopefully a top hotel.

5 ROOMS
NO PETS
NO KIDS
MED.EX
Kilmeny Country House nr Ballygrant, Islay · www.kilmeny.co.uk · 01496 840668 Margaret and Blair Rozga's top-class guest house just off the road 6km S of Port Askaig (the ferry). Though small, big attention to detail, great home-made food (dinner available Tue and Thu), house-party atmos and shared tables.

4 ROOMS
NO C/CARDS
MED.INX
Glenmachrie nr Port Ellen, Islay · www.glenmachrie.co.uk · 01496 300400 On A846 between Bowmore and Port Ellen near airport. The Whytes' award-winning farmhouse with everything just so (fluffy bathrobes, toiletries supplied, fruit bowl, a sweet on the pillow, and afternoon tea on arrival). Rachel will tell you where to go, eg dinner at her sister's guest house up the road (see below).

Glenegedale House nr Port Ellen, Islay · www.glenegedalehouse.co.uk · **01496 300400** Near the sister B&B Glenmachrie and opposite the airport. It would be hard to find a homelier airport hotel... than this luxury GH or a better breakfast. Top baking. Dinner on request.

Camping/Caravan Site Kintra Farm, Islay · www.kintrafarm.co.uk · **01496 302051** Off main road to Port Ellen; take Oa road, follow Kintra signs 7km. Jul-Aug. Grassy strand, coastal walks. 1224/WILD CAMPING.
Islay Youth Hostel Port Charlotte, Islay · www.syha.org.uk · **01496 850385**

THE BEST RESTAURANTS ON ISLAY & JURA

✓ **The Harbour Inn, Port Charlotte Hotel & Bridgend Inn** See above. Best bets for dinner.

£15-25 ✓ **Ardbeg Distillery Café** Islay · www.ardbeg.com 5km E of Port Ellen on the whisky road. Great local reputation for food. Beautiful room. Food home-made as are those Ardbegs. Most vintages and cool clothing to boot. Open Mon-Fri (7 days Jun-Aug) 10am-LO 4pm. Closed weekends in winter.

£15-25 **The Antlers** Craighouse, Jura · www.theantlers.co.uk · **01496 820123** Middle of the ribbon of village, an alternative to the hotel; bistro popular with locals and visitors. Daytime and evening (till 9pm); must book. Local seafood and craic. It is what you want, though not all home-made. Closed Mon. Check winter hours.

<£15 **Taste of Islay** Bowmore · www.bowmore.com · **01496 810491** On the corner by, and owned by the distillery in downtown Bowmore. Haven't tried and perhaps a little soulless, but a contemporary caff with appealing all-day menu. Closed Sun.

£15-25 **Seasalt** Port Ellen, Islay · www.seasalt-bistro.co.uk · **01496 300300** On main road. Sister of Yan's in Port Charlotte, this the better of the two; more Italian-flavoured (they do pizza) all-round dinner and takeaway. Not a bad port in a storm. Lunch & LO 8.30pm. Closed Mon.

<£15 **Kilchoman Distillery Café** Rockside Farm, Islay · www.kilchomandistillery .com · **01496 850011** The new distillery in the NW off the A847 from Bridgend (12km). This caff has much to like, especially the secret-recipe Cullen skink. Mon-Sat 10am-5pm (not Sat in winter).

WHAT TO SEE

Islay: The Distilleries especially Ardbeg (good café) and Lagavulin (classic settings), all by Port Ellen; **Bowmore** perhaps more convenient (1488/WHISKY); **Wildlife Info & Field Centre** at Port Charlotte; **American Monument** (1827/ MONUMENTS); **Oa & Loch Gruinart** (1724/BIRDS); **Port Charlotte** (1555/VILLAGES); **Kintra** (2021/WALKS); **Finlaggan**, the romantic, sparse ruin on island in Loch Finlaggan: last home of the Lords of the Isles. Off A846 5km S of Port Askaig. **Jura:** (2197/ISLANDS). **The Paps of Jura and Evans Walk**; **Killchianaig, Keils** (1865/GRAVEYARDS); **Lowlandman's Bay, Corran Sands** (1576/BEACHES).

Tourist Information Centre Bowmore · **01496 810254** & **CalMac** www. calmac.co.uk · **0800 066 5000**

The Best of The Outer Hebrides

2242 3   **CalMac Ferries** Ullapool-Stornoway, 2 hours 40 mins (not Sun). Oban/ Mallaig-Lochboisdale, South Uist and Castlebay, Barra, up to 6.5 hours. Uig on Skye–Tarbert, Harris (not Sun) or Lochmaddy, North Uist 1 hour 40 mins. Also Leverburgh, Harris–Berneray (not Sun) 1 hour.

By Air Flybe (0871 700 2000) from Inverness/Glasgow/Edinburgh. Otter to Barra/ Benbecula from Glasgow (1/2 a day).

WHERE TO STAY

6 ROOMS
NO TV
DF
MAR–DEC
LL · EXP

✓✓ **Scarista House** South Harris · www.scaristahouse.com · 01859 550238 20km S of Tarbert. Cosy haven near famous but often deserted beach; this celebrated retreat offers the real R&R and a lovely dinner. Also self-catering accom. Dog-friendly and kid-friendly – it's an all n' all. Report: 2224/ ISLAND HOTELS; 1136/KIDS.

EAT Intimate dining, probably best on Harris.

6 ROOMS
NO TV
DF
MAY–SEP
LLL
MED.INX

✓✓ **Baile-Na-Cille** Timsgarry, West Lewis · www.bailenacille.co.uk · 01851 672242 Near Uig 60km W of Stornoway. This is about as far away as it gets but guests return again and again to the Collins' house overlooking that incredible beach. Hospitable hosts allow you the run of their place – the books, the games room, the tennis court, walled flower garden and perhaps others of the many beaches near here in their boat. All home-made grub (bread, ice cream, etc) in communal dining room with amusing RAF overtones. Inexpensive, basic B&B but great value and especially good for families. 1135/KIDS.

EAT Beautiful beach view and a unique dining experience open to non-res.

4 ROOMS
L
MED.EX

✓ **Broad Bay House** Lewis · www.broadbayhouse.co.uk · 01851 820990 11km N of Stornoway on E of island on the sea via B895 to Back. High approval ratings for this. Purpose-built with big, light dining and lounge area and outside deck. Spacious, contemporary rooms with big TV, iPod docks, etc. Ian and Marion solicitous but discreet. Ian knows everywhere you might want to go and you'll want to stay a while in this chilled-out back of beyond. Top grub (with choice) and a decent wine list.

4 ROOMS
LL
MED.EX

✓ **Auberge** Carnish, by Uig, Lewis · www.aubergecarnish.co.uk · 01851 672459 Best part of an hour and way out W from Stornoway by A8011 but you are heading for the best part of Lewis. New-build, all-mod-con hotel and what is undoubtedly the farthest-flung French-influenced restaurant in the UK. Richard and Jo-Ann Leparoux have settled here and who wouldn't: that view, that beach! Well-appointed rooms with Jo's calming photographs. Also a lovely cottage overby.

EAT Informal restaurant; toujours la plage. The sunset is to dine for.

21 ROOMS
MED.INX

✓ **Hotel Hebrides** Tarbert, Harris · www.hotel-hebrides.com · 01859 502364 Contemporary boutique-style new-build hotel right by the pier where the boat comes in, so convenient and probably just what you want (the Harris Hotel below is perhaps cosier). Rooms, restaurant and bar are light, uncluttered modern. I'd say best contemporary hotel in the Hebrides!

23 ROOMS
NO PETS
MED.INX

✓ **Harris Hotel** Tarbert, Harris · www.harrishotel.com · 01859 502154 In the township near the ferry terminal, and like the Hebrides above, a good base for travels in North/South Harris. These quite different hotels are among the best in all the islands; way better than anywhere in Lewis. Variety of public rooms and diverse range of bedrooms (view/non-view, refurbished/non-refurbished, standard/superior), some of which are large and very nice. Friendly and well run. Food not a strong point, but adequate in the hotel-like dining room. Both bar and conservatory have better atmos.

9 ROOMS + 4 CHALETS
MED.INX

✓ **Borve Hotel** Borve, North Lewis · www.borvehousehotel.co.uk · 01851 850223 32km N of Stornoway on a mainly long, straight road to Port of Ness. Surprisingly contemporary though perhaps a little soulless hotel, with boutique-style rooms (not sure about the art), bar and restaurant which are busy with locals at weekends. The smartest stay north Stornoway way.

8 ROOMS DF MED.INX

✓ **Hamersay House** Lochmaddy, North Uist · www.hamersayhouse.co.uk · 01876 500700 A contemporary new-build hotel: being red, it stands out for miles and stands out also for the level of style and efficiency in these far-flung islands, where the beaches and the sky are immense. Leisure Club includes sauna/steam. Good brasserie. Same owners as Langass Lodge (see below).

24 ROOMS MED.INX-EXP

Royal Hotel Stornoway, Lewis · www.royalstornoway.co.uk · 01851 702109 The most central of the 3 main hotels in town, all owned by the same family. HS-1 bistro and Boatshed (probably best hotel dining). The **Cabarfeidh** (01851 702604) once more upmarket, needs TLC but may have the best bedrooms. These hotels are about the only places open in Lewis on Sun. The **Caladh Inn** (pronounced Cala) and its caff Eleven, are possibly best value. Eleven has popular self-service buffet. Best all-round is the Royal.

4 ROOMS + 2 COTTS DF L MED.INX

Rodel Hotel South Harris · www.rodelhotel.co.uk · 01859 520210 At the southern tip of Harris, the **Golden Road** (1625/SCENIC ROUTES) and Leverburgh (4km). Romantic because it's the end of the road but lovely setting in an old harbour and near evocative **St Clements** (1849/CHURCHES). Cosy and family-run. When I was there it was filled with flowers. They manage 3 fishing lochs, so cast away!

11 ROOMS NO PETS LL MED.INX

Polochar Inn South Uist · www.polocharinn.com · 01878 700215 S of Lochboisdale near Eriskay causeway (and ferry for Barra 2242/HEBRIDES). An inn at the rocky end of the Uists. Excellent value, good craic and the view/sunset across the sea to Barra. Rooms refurbished to an OK standard. The pub-grub menu uses local produce. LO 8.45pm.

LL

Isle of Barra Beach Hotel www.isleofbarrahotel.co.uk · 01871 810383 Fabulous setting, good restaurant. Report: 2237/ISLAND HOTELS.

Castlebay Hotel Castlebay, Barra · www.castlebay-hotel.co.uk · 01871 810223 Overlooks ferry terminal in the village so superb views. Decent dining, atmospheric bar. Reports: 2236/ISLAND HOTELS; 1290/GOOD PUBS.

L

Langass Lodge North Uist Report: 1204/GET-AWAY HOTELS.

Hostels Simple hostels within hiking distance. 2 in Lewis, 3 in Harris, 1 each in North and South Uist. Am Bothan at Leverburgh is independent and funky. **The Blackhouse Village** in North Lewis is exceptional (1150/HOSTELS).

THE BEST RESTAURANTS IN THE HEBRIDES

<£15 ✓ **Loch Croistean Coffee Shop** nr Uig, Lewis · 01851 672772 About 30 mins
LL from Stornoway on the road into the sunset, Marianne Campbell's schoolhouse
converted into a tasteful, laid-back tearoom and restaurant. Simple good food;
soup, sandwich and cake, all home-made, and lovely buffet suppers (Fri/Sat in
season). Noon-8pm Mon-Sat (Wed-Sat in winter). Closed Sun.

<£15 ✓ **Skoon Art Café** South Harris · www.skoon.com · 01859 530268 Near
the **Golden Road** (1625/SCENIC ROUTES) 12km S of Tarbert or follow the sign
off A859, then 4km to Geocrab (pronounced Jocrab). Andrew and Emma Craig's
café in a gallery (his work on the walls). All done well – interesting soups, great
home baking. Apr-Sep Tue-Sat daytime only; weekends in winter (or check).

<£15 ✓ **Temple Café** Northton, West Harris · 07876 340416 Just N of Leverburgh
and near the great W Harris beaches (including Northton Beach at the end of
the village strip 2km main road). Interesting new build using old stones and skills.
Home-made savoury and sweet things (including maybe pizzas), Gail and Reuben's
labour of love. Good soundtrack; social hub. Tue-Sun 10.30am-5.30pm, Thu/Fri/
Sun, dinner high season. And if you're camping or cottaging near here, check out
Croft 36 in Northton for seafood, home-made bread and veg.

£25-35 ✓ **Digby Chick** Stornoway, Lewis · www.digbychick.co.uk · 01851 700026
Undoubtedly and for almost 30 years, the place to eat in Stornoway and the
contemporary dining standard that no one else has matched. Seafood a speciality;
a solid reputation. Can't go wrong here. Mon-Sat lunch & LO 8.30pm.

£15-25 **Café Kisimul** Barra · www.cafekisimul.co.uk · 01871 810645 On the 'main
street' of Castlebay down to the quay and overlooking the 'castle' in the bay, a
surprising Indian (with some Italian dishes!) restaurant that's rather good. Not a
lot of choice on Barra so all the more welcome. Mar-Sep, 7 days lunch & dinner.
Weekends only in winter.

£15-25 **The Thai Café** Stornoway, Lewis · www.thai-cafe-stornoway.co.uk ·
01851 701811 Opposite police station. Though there are palms outside in the
sometimes rainswept street, you couldn't be further from Phuket. Mrs Panida
Macdonald's restaurant an institution here; you may have to book. Good atmos and
real Thai cuisine. Still a surprising find (the furthest Thai in the west?). **Bangla Spice**,
further up the street is also well thought of. Both lunch & LO 10pm. Closed Sun.

<£15 **Coffee Shops: An Lanntair Gallery** Stornoway, Lewis · www.lanntair.com
& **Callanish Visitor Centre** Callanish, Lewis · www.callanishvisitorcentre.
co.uk An Lanntair, an all-embracing arts and cultural centre, is a great rendezvous
spot and has a good view of the ferry terminal. Lunch & evening menu. The
Callanish caff is far better than most visitor centres. Open till 8pm in summer. See
also 1795/PREHISTORIC.

>£35 **Scarista House** South Harris · www.scaristahouse.com Dinner possible for
non-res. A 20-min Tarbert/45-min Stornoway drive for best meal in Harris, maybe
the Hebrides. Fixed menu. Book. See *Where to Stay*.

<£15 **First Fruits Tearoom** Tarbert, Harris · 01859 502439 Near tourist information
DF centre and ferry to Uig, Skye. Cottage cooking that hits the ferry-waiting spot. Good
atmos and everything home-made. Dinner Jul/Aug with BYOB, otherwise 10am-
4pm Apr-Sep.

£15-25　**Orasay Inn**　Lochcarnan, South Uist · www.orasayinn.com · 01870 610298
You don't get more remote than this but it's always packed. In summer you may
have to book days ahead (or weeks for accom). Midway between Lochmaddy and
Lochboisdale signed off the spinal A865, go 3km then left at the shrine. Then
500m. No, it ain't easy to find. Conservatory and bar serving good, home-cooked
comfort food and fresh seafood: cod, shellfish and 'witches'. Also 9 but ordinary,
inexpensive rooms. Open AYR, lunch & LO 9pm.

<£15　**The Anchorage**　Leverburgh, South Harris · 01859 520225　Sally Lessi's
all-round family restaurant/café/bar at the pierhead where the boat leaves for
Berneray and the Uists. Much better than your average terminal caff with most
stuff home-made and cooked to order. Friendly! Mar-Sep (weekends in winter)
noon-9pm. Closed Sun.

<£15　**Stepping Stone Restaurant**　Balivanich, Benbecula · 01870 603377　8km
from main A855. Nondescript building in ex- (though sometimes operational)
military air base. Served the Forces, now the tourists – it aims to please. 7 days
lunch & dinner (winter hours may vary). Menu changes through day.

£15-25　**North Harbour Bistro & Tearoom**　Scalpay · 01859 540218　20 mins (10km)
S of Tarbet but E to the Isle of Scalpay (by a bridge). George Lavery's good food
destination restaurant has garnered great reviews and feedback since it opened
2014. Cheffy, contemporary food, but small, so book for dinner. All-day menu till
9pm. Closed Sun. BYOB.

The Boatshed at The Royal Hotel　Stornoway & 'Eleven' at The Caladh Inn
(see above). Best hotel options and your **only decent Sunday option on Lewis**.

WHAT TO SEE
Eriskay & Mingulay (2206/ISLANDS); **Golden Road** (1625/SCENIC ROUTES);
Beaches At Lewis, South Harris and South Uist (1569/1568/1566/BEACHES);
Balranald Reserve (1750/RESERVES). **Scarista Golf** (2061/GOLF); **Surfing** (2103/
SURFING BEACHES). **St Clement's Church & St Michael's Church** (1849/1850/
CHURCHES); **Blackhouse of Arnol** (2112/HISTORY); **Barpa Langass & Callanish
Stones** (1809/1795/PREHISTORIC); **Harris Tweed** (p. 375).

Tourist Information Centre　Stornoway · 01851 703088
CalMac www.calmac.co.uk · 0800 066 5000

2243 7/H23   **CalMac Ferry** Oban-Craignure, 45 mins. Main route: 6 a day. Lochaline-Fishnish, 15 mins. 9-15 a day. Kilchoan-Tobermory, 35 mins. 7 a day (Sun in summer only). Winter sailings – call CalMac 0800 066 5000.

WHERE TO STAY

6 ROOMS   ✓✓ **Highland Cottage** Tobermory · www.highlandcottage.co.uk ·
NO PETS   01688 302030 Opposite fire station on street above the harbour. Like a
MAR-OCT   country house, well… a country cottage in town. A top dining room. Report: 2225/
MED.EX   ISLAND HOTELS.

11 ROOMS   ✓✓ **Tiroran House** www.tiroran.com · 01681 705232 A treat and a retreat
DF   way down in the SW of Mull near Iona. Light, comfy house in glorious
EASTER-OCT   gardens with excellent food and flowers. Sea eagles fly over. Report: 1193/GET-AWAY
L · LOTS   HOTELS.

4 ROOMS   ✓✓ **Strongarbh House** Tobermory · www.strongarbh.com ·
NO PETS   01688 302319 Behind and above the landmark Western Isles (see below),
NO KIDS   a smart and exceptional B&B – cosy library, a 'gallery space', afternoon tea on
MED.EX   arrival. Jane Wilde and Adrian Lear have built a taste oasis.

17 ROOMS   ✓ **Argyll Hotel** Iona · www.argyllhoteliona.co.uk · 01681 700334 Near
MED.EX   ferry and on seashore overlooking Mull on road to abbey. Laid-back, cosy
accom, home cooking, good vegetarian. Report: 1175/INNS.

5 ROOMS   ✓ **Glengorm Castle** nr Tobermory · www.glengormcastle.co.uk ·
EXP   01688 302321 Minor road on right going N outside Tobermory (6km) takes
you to this fine castle on a promontory set in an extensive estate which is yours to
wander (excellent walks 2214/ISLAND WALKS). Fab views over to Ardnamurchan,
little peaks to climb and a natural bathing pool (2094/OPEN-AIR POOLS). Spacious
bedrooms (old-style comfy) in family home (the Nelsons) – use the library,
complementary bar and grand public spaces. Loads of art, lawn and gardens.
Excellent self-catering cottages on estate. B&B only. And overby (1380/TEAROOMS).

12 ROOMS   ✓ **The Mishnish** Tobermory · www.themishnish.co.uk · 01688 302500
MED.INX   Rooms above the once legendary Mishnish Pub. It may have lost some of its
music and mystique but this is now a well-refurbished hotel, with a restaurant and
bar that still retain some of their vibe. One bedroom has a jacuzzi! The Mish now
and forever at the heart of the matter on Mull.

7 ROOMS   ✓ **The Bellachroy Hotel** Dervaig · www.thebellachroy.co.uk ·
DF   01688 400314 Dating from 1608 no less, this is a well-known watering hole
MED.EX   and hotel in the delightful village of Dervaig between Tobermory and the beautiful
beach (and sculpture trail) at Calgary. Christine Weaver and Anthony Ratcliff have
turned it into a notable gastropub and it's a good base for exploring Mull away from
the hubbub of Tobermory.

26 ROOMS   **Western Isles Hotel** Tobermory · 01688 302012 At the end of the bay high
above the harbour, this Tobermory landmark has one of the most commanding
positions of any hotel in Scotland with spectacular views from (some) rooms,
conservatory brasserie, dining room and especially the terrace. Despite this, the
WI has had a chequered recent history, changing hands, etc, and is for sale at TGP.
Somebody and TLC will hopefully finally fulfil its potential.

| 82 ROOMS | **Isle of Mull Hotel** Craignure · www.crerarhotels.com · 01680 812544 |
| MED.EX | Strung-out, low-rise hotel round Craignure Bay near the ferry from Oban (hotel can pick you up); hotel with the largest number of rooms on Mull. Decent rooms, spa and pool. Bit of a drive to an alternative restaurant (which you will want to find). |

15 ROOMS
DF
MED.INX

Tobermory Hotel Tobermory · www.thetobermoryhotel.com · 01688 302091 On the waterfront. Creature comforts, open fires, great outlook in the middle of the bay. 10 rooms to front, upper with coombed ceilings; all recently refurbished and contemporary. Related to Galleon Grill (see below) nearby, where (in winter) the dining room may be closed for dinner. Very much downtown Tobermory, this is an excellent place to locate for all Mull meanderings.

27 ROOMS
MID MAR-OCT
MED.INX

St Columba Hotel Iona www.stcolumba-hotel.co.uk 01681 700304 Shares some ownership and ideals of the Argyll (above) and nearby, on the road to the Abbey. Larger and more purpose-built than the Argyll, so some uniformity in rooms. Nice views; extensive lawn and organic market garden. Relaxing and just a little religious. Menu has good vegetarian options. Rooms include 9 singles.

S.Y. Hostel In Tobermory main street on bay. Report: 1166/HOSTELS.
Caravan Parks At Fishnish (all facilities, near ferry), Craignure and Fionnphort.
Camping Tobermory on the Dervaig Rd, Craignure (1233/CAMPING WITH KIDS). Calgary Beach and at Loch Na Keal shore (1221/WILD CAMPING).

THE BEST RESTAURANTS ON MULL

£25-35
L

✓✓ **Highland Cottage** Tobermory · www.highlandcottage.co.uk · 01688 302030 Informal but fine-ish dining on Mull and the local treat out so must book. All the niceties and Jo Currie's dab hand in the kitchen. See 2225/ISLAND HOTELS.

£25-35

✓✓ **Café Fish** Tobermory · www.thecafefish.com · 01688 301253 Jane McDonald and chef Liz McGougan's deliciously informal 'café' restaurant upstairs in the white building at the pier on corner of the bay. Bright, bustling upstairs room and terrace on the dock – Johnny's boat at the quayside supplies the shellfish, arriving around 4pm every day; they're wheeched upstairs. All else is properly sourced (they close in winter, partly because supplies cannot be guaranteed) and 'the only thing frozen are our fisherman'. God and St Peter alone know how they produce that long, diverse, imaginative menu from the tiny, tiny kitchen. Sensible wine list, nice puds. Lunch & 5.30-10pm (LO). Mar-Oct.

£25-35

✓✓ **Ninth Wave** nr Fionnphort · www.ninthwaverestaurant.co.uk · 01681 700757 In the S of Mull near the ferry for Iona (1.5 hours to Tobermory). This highly regarded off-the-road-and-map restaurant is the epitome of destination dining. Carla Lamont in the kitchen and the garden, John out front (in a kilt) and on the boat. The terroir supplies your table in this surprisingly contemporary croft conversion in the quiet deep south. Simple choice, fixed-price menu fine-dining style. Easter-Oct. Closed Mon/Tue. Dinner only. Book!

<£15

✓✓ **Glengorm Farm Coffee Shop** Excellent daytime eats outside Tobermory. The best casual daytime dining. Report: 1380/TEAROOMS. And see Tobermory Bakery, below.

£15-25

✓ **The Bellachroy Hotel** Dervaig · www.thebellachroy.co.uk · 01688 400314 Some might say The Bellachroy *is* Dervaig. Now a destination for lunch and dinner. Craft beers and good wine list, especially Bordeaux (see above).

<£15 ✓ **The Café @ Calgary Arts** 01688 400256 A great wee café just where you need it by the sculpture trail (2141/ART SPACES). Easter-Nov.

<£15 ✓ **The Glass Barn @ Sgriob-Ruadh Farm** www.isleofmullcheese.co.uk · 01688 302627 On the road to Dervaig (2km). A tearoom out on its own in the farmyard and dairy where they make the Mull cheddars. 1390/TEAROOMS.

£15-25 **The Galleon Grill** Tobermory · www.galleongrill.com · 01688 301117 Just off the main street behind the post office. Same folk have the Tobermory Hotel (above). Mainly steaks but also seafood. Could be in a city somewhere. Liked by locals and TripAdvisors. 5.30-9pm. Lunch at weekends.

£15-25 **Hebridean Lodge** Tobermory · www.hebrideanlodge.co.uk · 01688 301207 On the way into the town from Craignure and the south. Upstairs restaurant above picture-framers and gallery. Home cooking and bakery with good local reputation. Food 12.30-4pm (till 8pm Thu/Fri). Closed Sun.

<£15 **Tobermory Bakery** www.glengormcastle.co.uk · 01688 302225 Tom and Marjorie Nelson's Main St bakery-deli with quiches, salads and old-fashioned fancies. Related to gorgeous Glengorm. See 1380/TEAROOMS. 7 days.

<£15 **The Chip Van aka The Fishermen's Pier** Tobermory · 01688 302390 Tobermory's famous meals-on-wheels under the clock tower on the bay. Fresh, al fresco: usually a queue. However, they don't actually make those chips! Open 7 days in summer 12.30pm-9pm. Closed Sun in winter. Report: 1359/FISH & CHIPS.

WHAT TO SEE

Duart Castle 5km Craignure. Seat of Clan Maclean. Impressive from a distance, homely inside. Good view of clan history and from battlements. Tearoom (1762/ CASTLES). **Eas Fors** Waterfall on Dervaig to Fionnphort road. Very accessible series of cataracts tumbling into the sea (1600/WATERFALLS). **Ulva & Iona** (many references). **The Treshnish Isles** (Ulva Ferry or Fionnphort). Marvellous trips in summer (1715/BIRDS); walks from **Carsaig Pier** and on **Glengorm** estate (2214/ ISLAND WALKS); or up **Ben More** (1958/MUNROS); **Croig** and **Quinish** in north, by **Dervaig** and **Lochbuie** off the A849 at Strathcoil 9km S of Craignure: these are all serene shorelines to explore. **Aros Park** forest walk, from Tobermory, about 7km round trip.

Tourist Information Centre Craignure · 01680 812377 Open AYR. Tobermory · 01688 302182
CalMac www.calmac.co.uk · 0800 066 5000

2244 1   **Ferry** www.northlinkferries.co.uk · 0845 600 0449 Kirkwall: from Aberdeen – Tue, Thu, Sat, Sun, takes 6 hours; Stromness from Scrabster – 2/3 per day, takes 2 hours. John o' Groats to Burwick (01955 611353), 40 mins, up to 4 a day (May–Sep only). www.pentlandferries.co.uk from Gills Bay (near John o' Groats) to St Margaret's Hope (01856 831226) – 3 a day, takes 1 hour.
By Air www.flybe.com 0871 700 2000. To Kirkwall from Aberdeen, Edinburgh, Glasgow and Inverness.

WHERE TO STAY

✔✔ **Balfour Castle**   Shapinsay · www.balfourcastle.co.uk · 01856 711282 On Isle of Shapinsay, a fabulously appointed castle, grounds and top chef for exclusive use. Arrivistes arrive by helicopter or launch. Dream on, those of ordinary means! Report: 1271/HOUSE PARTIES.

10 ROOMS   **The Lynnfield**   Kirkwall · www.lynnfield.co.uk · 01856 872505 Holm Rd
MED.INX   adjacent to **Highland Park** (1495/WHISKY) and overlooking the town. Kirkwall's most comfy (though rooms old-style), sporting 4 stars and with good local reputation for food, wine and whisky. And congenial.

8 ROOMS   **Foveran Hotel**   St Ola · www.thefoveran.com · 01856 872389 A964 Orphir
NO PETS   road; 5km from Kirkwall. Scandinavian-style, low-rise hotel is a friendly, informal
MED.INX   place serving traditional food using local ingredients; separate vegetarian menu. Great value. Small but comfy and light rooms; garden overlooks Scapa Flow.

16 ROOMS   **Merkister Hotel**   Harray · www.merkister.com · 01856 771366 Overlooking
MED.INX   loch, N but midway (15 mins) between Kirkwall and Stromness. A fave with fishers and twitchers; handy for archaeological sites and possibly the Orkney hotel of choice. Rooms small and B&B-ish; good bar meals.

42 ROOMS   **Stromness Hotel**   Stromness · www.stromnesshotel.com · 01856 850298
CHP   Orkney's biggest hotel at the heart of the Orkney matter and overlooking the harbour. Rooms so-so but very good value. Even has lifts. Central and picturesque. Flattie Bar a wee gem. Victorian Garden behind.

3 ROOMS   **The Creel**   St Margaret's Hope · www.thecreel.co.uk · 01856 831311
MED.INX   Restaurant with rooms, once the best. New owners at TGP. Reports, please.

L   ✔ **Bis Geos Hostel & Cottages**   Westray · www.bisgeos.co.uk · 01857 677420 Hostel with 2 self-catering cottages. Traditional features and some luxuries.

✔ **The Barn**   Westray · www.thebarnwestray.co.uk · 01857 677214 Near Pierowall. 4-star self-catering hostel in renovated stone barn. Great views.
Kirkwall Peedie Hostel   Ayre Rd, Kirkwall · 01856 875477 On the front. Private bedroom (3), sleep 2 or 4, own keys.
S.Y. Hostels   Stromness · www.syha.org.uk · 01856 850589 Excellent location. **Kirkwall** · 01856 872243 The largest.
Other hostels at Hoy, North and South Ronaldsay, Birsay, Sanday.

THE BEST RESTAURANTS IN ORKNEY

£25-35 ✓ **Judith Glue Café Restaurant** Kirkwall · www.judithglue.com · 01856 874225 Can't miss it opposite St Magnus Cathedral. An eating-out place that serves and champions Orkney produce: the ale, the seafood, the cheese, Orkney ales, the Highland Park. JG long known for the knits and quality souvenirs (and puffin stuff). Home-made, blackboard menu. 7 days AYR; times vary.

>£35 ✓ **Balfour Castle** Shapinsay · www.balfourcastle.co.uk · 01856 711282 You can pop over to Shapinsay outwith their exclusive-use periods. Chef Jean Baptiste Bady cooking up the best meal in the far North; they'll collect you from Kirkwall Pier. Phone/email for details.

£25-35 **The Creel** St Margaret's Hope · www.thecreel.co.uk · 01856 831311 On South Ronaldsay, 20km S of Kirkwall and a great drive. An accolade-laden restaurant and long Orkney's finest. New owners at TGP.

£25-35 **Foveran Hotel** St Ola · www.thefoveran.com · 01856 872389 5km Kirkwall. Excellent views and OK, locally sourced food. See *Where to Stay*.

£25-35 **The Lynnfield** Kirkwall · www.lynnfield.co.uk · 01856 872505 Some say the best hotel meal in Kirkwall. See *Where to Stay*.

£15-25 **The Hamnavoe Restaurant** Stromness · 01856 850606 Off main street. Seafood is their speciality, especially lobster and crab. Apr-Oct: lunch weekends only, dinner Tue-Sun 6.30pm-9pm. Nov-Mar: open weekends only.

<£15 **Julia's Café & Bistro** Stromness · www.juliascafe.co.uk · 01856 850904 Home baking, blackboard and vegetarian specials opposite harbour. A favourite with the locals. Gets busy – fill yourself up before the ferry journey! Open AYR. Rare early opening. 7 days 9am-5pm (from 10am Sun). Phone for winter opening hours.

WHAT TO SEE

✓✓✓ **Skara Brae** 25km W of Kirkwall. Amazingly well-preserved 5,000-year-old village. Report: 1793/PREHISTORIC.

✓✓ **Standing Stones of Stenness, The Ring of Brodgar, Maes Howe** 18km W of Kirkwall on A965. Vibrations! Report: 1794/PREHISTORIC.

✓✓ **The Italian Chapel** 8km S of Kirkwall at first causeway. A special act of faith. Inspirational and moving. Report: 1844/CHURCHES.

The Old Man of Hoy On Hoy; 30-min ferry 2 or 3 times a day from Stromness. 3-hour walk along spectacular coast. Report: 2222/ISLAND WALKS.

Yesnaby Sea Stacks 24km W of Kirkwall. A precarious clifftop at the end of the world. Report: 1917/ENCHANTING PLACES.

Skaill House by Skara Brae · 01856 841501 17th-century mansion built on Pictish cemetery. Set up as it was in the 1950s; with Captain Cook's crockery in the dining room looking remarkably unused. Apr-Sep: 7 days 9.30am-6pm (or by appointment). Tearoom and visitor centre and HS link with Skara are adjacent.

St Magnus Cathedral (1844/CHURCHES); **Stromness** (1551/VILLAGES); **The Pier Arts Centre** (2140/GALLERIES); **Tomb of the Eagles** (1800/PREHISTORIC); **Marwick Head** and many of the smaller islands (1725/BIRDS); **Scapa Flow** (1890/BATTLEGROUNDS); **Highland Park Distillery** (1495/WHISKY).

Tourist Information Centre Kirkwall 01856 872856

2245 2   **Ferry** www.northlinkferries.co.uk · 0845 600 0449 Aberdeen-Lerwick: Mon, Wed, Fri – departs 7pm, 12 hours. Tue, Thu, Sat, Sun – departs 5pm (via Orkney). **By air** Flybe www.flybe.com 0871 700 0535. To Sumburgh from Aberdeen, Inverness, Glasgow and Edinburgh.

WHERE TO STAY

6 ROOMS   ✓ **Burrastow House** Walls · www.burrastowhouse.co.uk · 01595 809307
APR-OCT   40 mins from Lerwick. Most guides and locals agree this is the place to stay on
LL   Shetland. Peaceful Georgian house on a quiet bay with views to island of Vaila.
MED.INX   Wonderful home-made/produced food. Full of character with food (set menu; order day before), service. Rooms probably the best on the island.

22 ROOMS   ✓ **Busta House Hotel** Brae · www.bustahouse.com · 01806 522506
MED.INX   Pronounced Boosta. Historic country house at Brae just over 30 mins from Lerwick (1 hour airport). Elegant and tranquil. High standards. Comfy rooms named after islands. Excellent food; famously great malt selection.

23 ROOMS   ✓ **Scalloway Hotel** Scalloway · www.scallowayhotel.com · 01595 880444
DF   10km W of Lerwick on a picturesque waterfront the McKenzies have built a
MED.EX   strong reputation for food and comfy, contemporary rooms.
EAT Closest to a fine-dining dinner on Shetland.

35 ROOMS   **The Lerwick Hotel** www.shetlandhotels.com · 01595 692166 Short walk to
MED.INX   downtown Lerwick. Along with Kveldsro below (same ownership), probably the best in town. Brasserie restaurant.

6 ROOMS   **The Spiggie Hotel** Dunrossness · www.thespiggiehotel.co.uk ·
MED.INX   01950 460409 8km Sumburgh Airport, 32km Lerwick. Overlooks RSPB reserve of Spiggie Loch. Small, personally run country hotel. Especially good for bar meals.

33 ROOMS   **St Magnus Bay Hotel** www.stmagnusbayhotel.co.uk · 01806 503372 Far
MED.INX   away in the NW of the mainland 50km (50 mins) from Lerwick on the Hillswick coast, a distinctive, wooden-built (in 1900) hotel (renovation ongoing). Have to admit I still haven't been here but all reports are good; everyone calls it 'charming'.

6 ROOMS   **Westings, The Inn On The Hill** Whiteness · www.originart.eu/westings/ ·
MED.INX   01595 840242 12km from Lerwick. Breathtaking views down Whiteness Voe. Excellent base for exploring. Old-style bedrooms. Large selection of real ales. Campsite alongside.

S.Y. Hostel: Islesburgh House Lerwick · www.islesburgh.org.uk · 0345 293 7373 Beautifully refurbished and central. A 5-star hostel. Apr-Sep. **Camping Bods** (fisherman's barns). Cheap sleep in wonderful seashore settings. **The Sail Loft** at Voe; **Grieve House** at Whalsay; **Windhouse Lodge** at Mid Yell; **Voe House** at Walls; **Betty Mouat's Cottage** at Dunrossness; **Johnnie Notions** at Eshaness. Remember to take sleeping mats. Check tourist office for details: 01595 693434.

THE BEST RESTAURANTS IN SHETLAND

£25-35   ✓ **Burrastow House** Walls & **Busta House Hotel** Brae See above. The best meals in the islands. My Shetland reporters do go to Busta. **Spiggie and Scalloway Hotels** also good.

<£15 ✓ **Hay's Dock Café Restaurant** Lerwick · www.haysdock.co.uk · 01595 741569 Part of the Shetland Museum & Archive. Contemporary, beautiful space with great views of Lerwick Harbour. Excellent, all-day café, dinner.

<£15 ✓ **Mareel** Lerwick · www.mareel.org · 01595 745500 Landmark purpose-built entertainment and community centre on Lerwick waterfront, embedded in the natural and cultural landscape of Shetland. Great cinema, great café and bar. Daytime (from 10am, salads, sandwiches, the oatcakes) or evening menu till 9pm. Bar later. Lovely light through those windows here, in this, the Shetland hub.

<£15 ✓ **Frankie's** Brae · www.frankiesfishandchips.com · 01806 522700 Busta Voe and the marina great asset to Shetland eating out (or in). Takeaway and caff. Local seafood, home baking, sustainable fish policy. Many awards including No 1 in the National Fish & Chip Awards 2015. 9.30am-8pm. Sun from noon (closed Sun in winter).

<£15 **Fjara Café Bar** Lerwick · www.fjaracoffee.com · 01595 697388 Near Tesco, but on the wee peninsula jutting out into Brewick Bay – seal spotting territory. Simple home baking and local produce. Supper at night, including burgers. 8am-10pm (bar until midnight Fri/Sat).

<£15 **The Olive Tree** Lerwick · 01595 697222 Nice deli/café/takeaway in the Toll Clock Shopping Centre. Home-made stuff. Daytime only.

<£15 **The Peerie Shop Café** The Esplanade, Lerwick · www.peerieshop.co.uk · 01595 692816 Great shop and caff in downtown Lerwick, with home baking. A local delicacy! 9am-6pm. Closed Sun.

<£15 **The Mid Brae Inn** Brae · 01806 522634 32km N of Lerwick. Lunch & supper till 8.45pm (9.30pm weekends), 7 days. Big portions of filling pub grub.

WHAT TO SEE

✓ **Mousa Broch & Jarlshof** Report: 1797/PREHISTORIC. Also **Clickimin** broch.

✓ **Shetland Museum & Archives** Lerwick Report: 2116/HISTORY.

St Ninian's Isle Bigton 8km N of Sumburgh on West Coast. An island linked by exquisite shell-sand. Hoard of Pictish silver found in 1958 (now in Edinburgh). Beautiful, serene spot.

Scalloway 10km W of Lerwick, a township once the ancient capital of Shetland, dominated by the atmospheric ruins of Scalloway Castle.

Noup of Noss Isle of Noss off Bressay 8km W of Lerwick by frequent ferry to Bressay and then wee boat (also by boat trip direct from Lerwick; check tourist information centre); limited in winter. Spectacular array of wildlife.

Up-Helly-Aa www.uphellyaa.org Festival in Lerwick on the last Tuesday in January. Ritual with hundreds of torchbearers and much fire and firewater. Norse, northern and pagan. A wild time can be had. See 21/EVENTS.

Sea Races The Boat Race every midsummer from Bergen in Norway. Part of the largest North Sea international annual yacht race.

Bonhoga Gallery & Weisdale Mill www.shetlandarts.org · 01595 830400 Former grain mill housing Shetland's first purpose-built gallery. Good café.

Tourist Information Centre Lerwick · 01595 693434

Maps

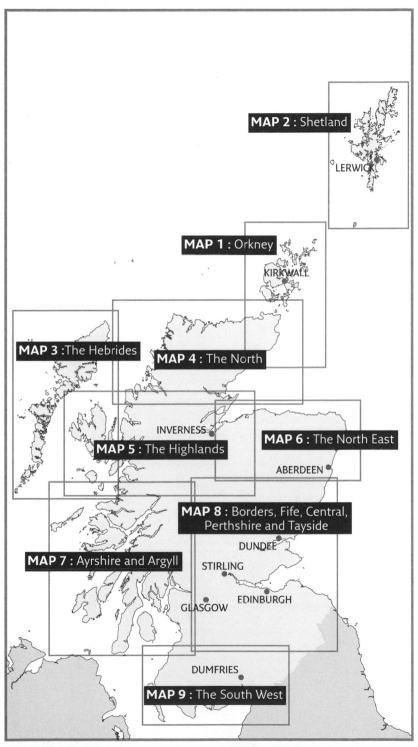

MAP 2 : Shetland

LERWICK

MAP 1 : Orkney

KIRKWALL

MAP 3 : The Hebrides

MAP 4 : The North

INVERNESS

MAP 5 : The Highlands

MAP 6 : The North East

ABERDEEN

MAP 8 : Borders, Fife, Central,
Perthshire and Tayside

DUNDEE

STIRLING

EDINBURGH

MAP 7 : Ayrshire and Argyll

GLASGOW

DUMFRIES

MAP 9 : The South West

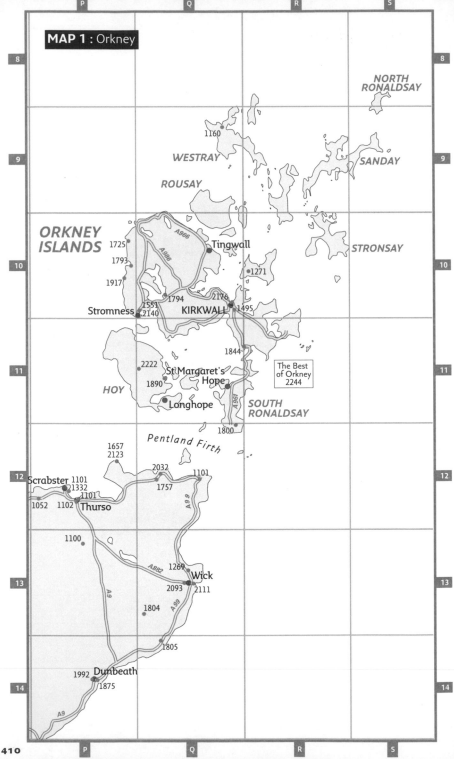

MAP 1 : Orkney

NORTH RONALDSAY

WESTRAY

1160

SANDAY

ROUSAY

STRONSAY

ORKNEY ISLANDS

1725
1793
1917

A966

A966

Tingwall

1271

1794
2176
1551
2140
1495
Stromness
KIRKWALL

1844

The Best of Orkney
2244

2222
1890
St Margaret's Hope

HOY

A961

Longhope
1800

SOUTH RONALDSAY

Pentland Firth

1657
2123
2032
1101
1757

Scrabster 1101
1332
1101
1052 1102 Thurso

A99

1100

A882
1269
Wick
A9
2093 2111

1804
A99

1805

1992 Dunbeath
1875

A9

410

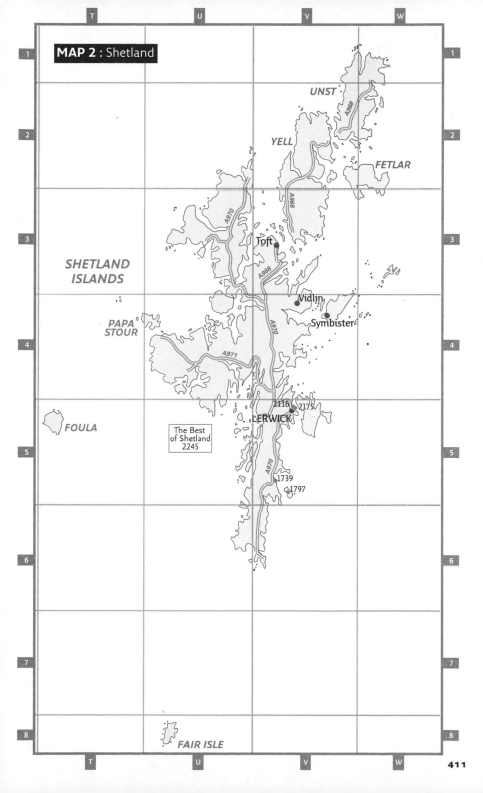

MAP 2 : Shetland

UNST

YELL

FETLAR

SHETLAND
ISLANDS

Toft

Vidlin

Symbister

PAPA
STOUR

A971

A970

2116 2175

LERWICK

FOULA

The Best
of Shetland
2245

1739
1797

A970

FAIR ISLE

411

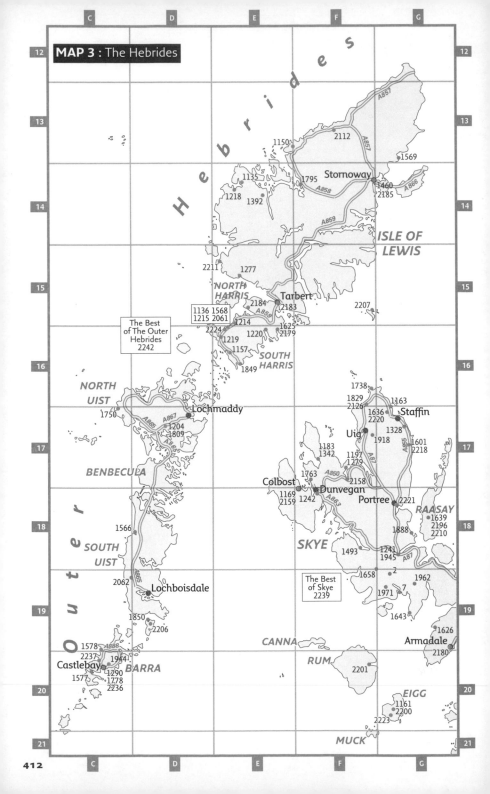

MAP 3 : The Hebrides

Hebrides

H e b r i d e s

C **D** **E** **F** **G**

12

13

2112

1150

1569

1135

1795

Stornoway

1218

1392

1460

2185

A857

A866

A858

14

**ISLE OF
LEWIS**

A859

15

2211

1277

2207

**NORTH
HARRIS**

2184

Tarbert

2183

1136 1568
1215 2061

1214

1625
2179

A859

2224

1220

1219

1157

16

1849

**SOUTH
HARRIS**

The Best
of The Outer
Hebrides
2242

**NORTH
UIST**

1738

1750

Lochmaddy

A867

A865

1204
1809

1829
2126

1163

1636
2220

Staffin

Uig

1328

1918

1601
2218

A855

BENBECULA

1183
1342

1197
1279

A87

O
u
t
e
r

1763

Colbost

2158

A850

1169
2159

1242

Dunvegan

A863

Portree

2221

17

RAASAY

1639
2196
2210

1566

1888

**SOUTH
UIST**

SKYE

1241
1945

A87

18

2062

Lochboisdale

1493

1658

2

The Best
of Skye
2239

1962

A865

1850

2206

1971

7

1643

1578

CANNA

Armadale

1626

2237

RUM

2180

1944

Castlebay

1290

BARRA

2201

4888

A888

1577

1778
2236

EIGG

1161
2200

2223

MUCK

19

20

21

412

C **D** **E** **F** **G**

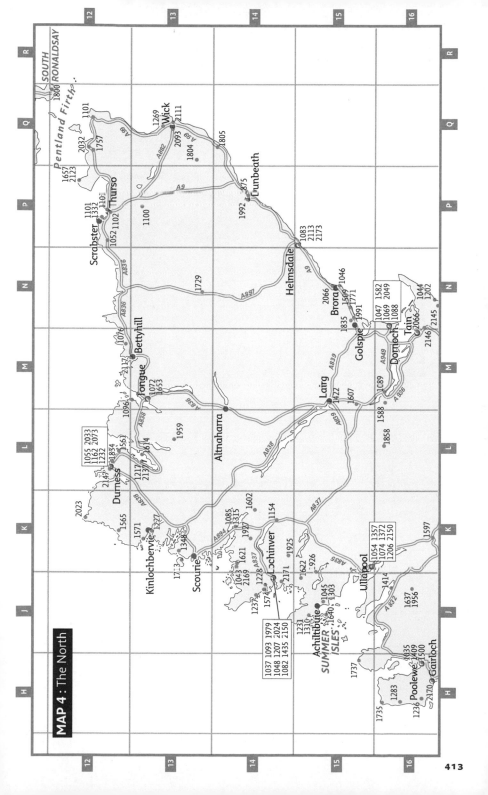

SOUTH RONALDSAY
1800

Pentland Firth

1657
2123

1101
2032
1757

1269
1804
2093
2111
Wick

1805

A99
A9
A882

Thurso
1101 1101
1332 1102
1052
Scrabster

1100

875
1992
Dunbeath

A9

1083
2113
2173
Helmsdale

A836

1729
A897

2066
Brora
1569 1046
835 1771
991
Golspie
Dornoch

1047 1582
1069 2049
1088

Tain
2066

1044
1202

2146 2145

A836

Bettyhill

1076
2417

Tongue
1096
1072
1653

A838

1959

Lairg
1422
1607

A839

1089

A949

A836

1588

1858

A897

1055 2033
1162 2073
1232

1834
1561
1614

2147

Durness

1217
2137

Altnaharra

A838

A836

A838

A837

2023

1565
1571
1227

Kinlochbervie

1348
173

Scourie

A894

1085
1315
1602

1927
1621

1154

1925

622
926

A835

Lochinver

1574
1228
171

1043
2169
1237

1231
1310
Achiltibuie
1640 1303
SUMMER
ISLES

1045

Ullapool
1414

1054 1357
1074 1372
1206 2150

1597

1037 1093 1979
1048 1207 2024
1082 1435 2150

1737

1637
1956

A832

1735

1236 Poolewe
2170
Gairloch
1409
1500

1035

1283

413

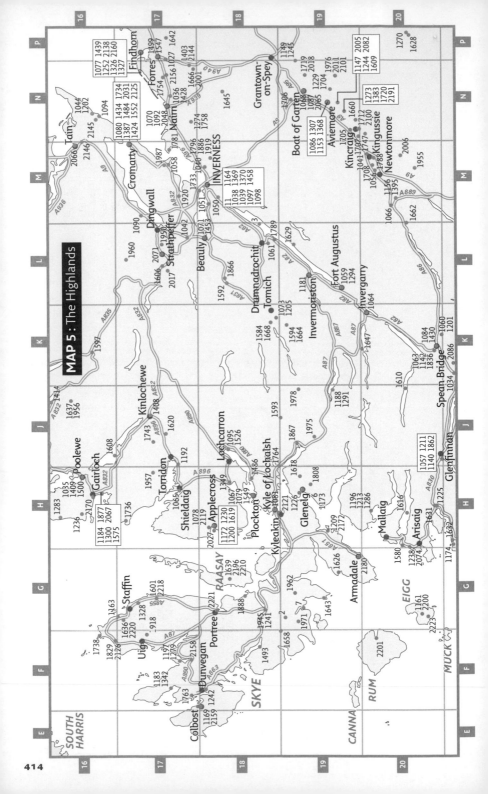

MAP 5 : The Highlands

414

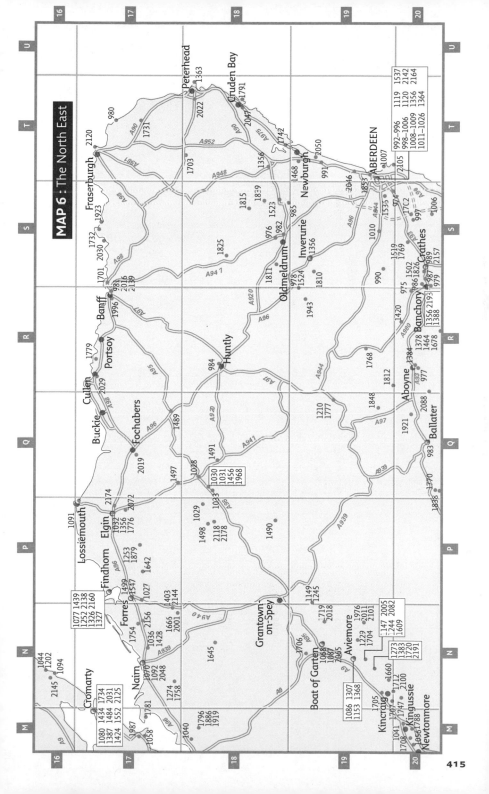

MAP 6 : The North East

415

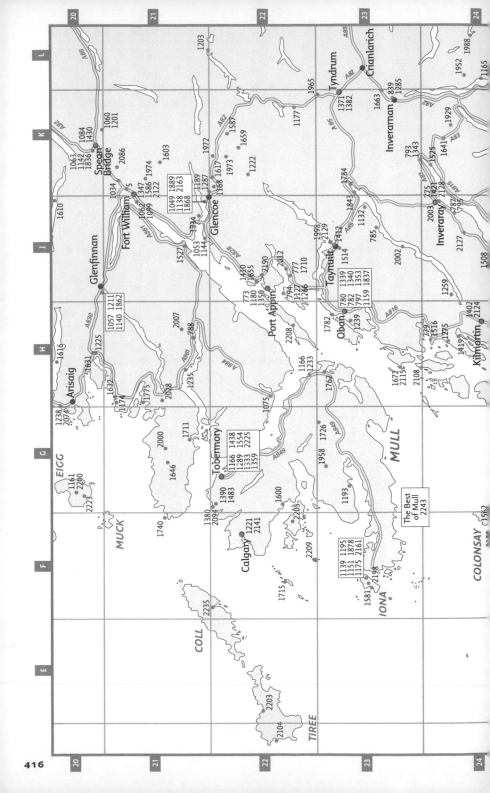

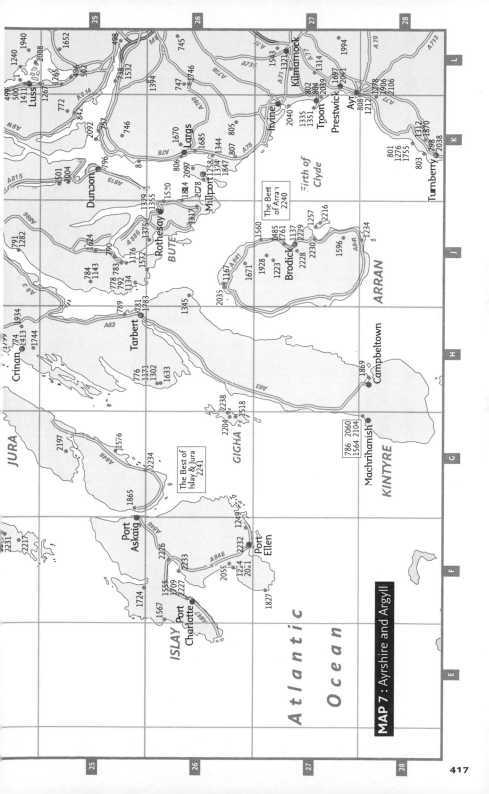

MAP 7 : Ayrshire and Argyll

417

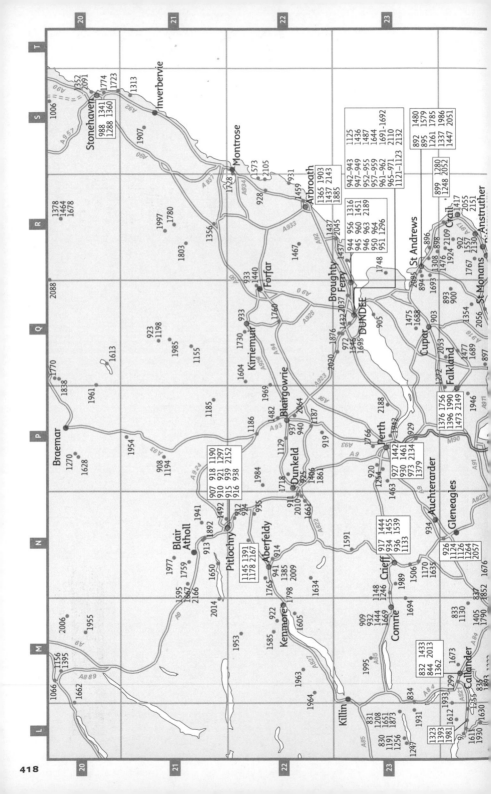

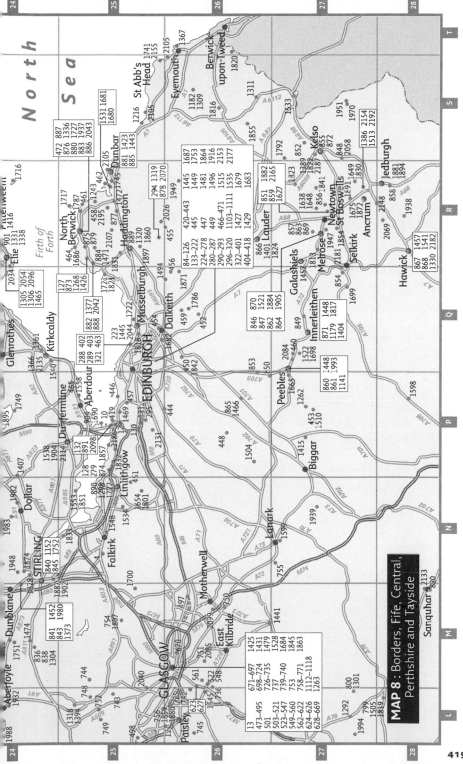

MAP 8 : Borders, Fife, Central, Perthshire and Tayside

419

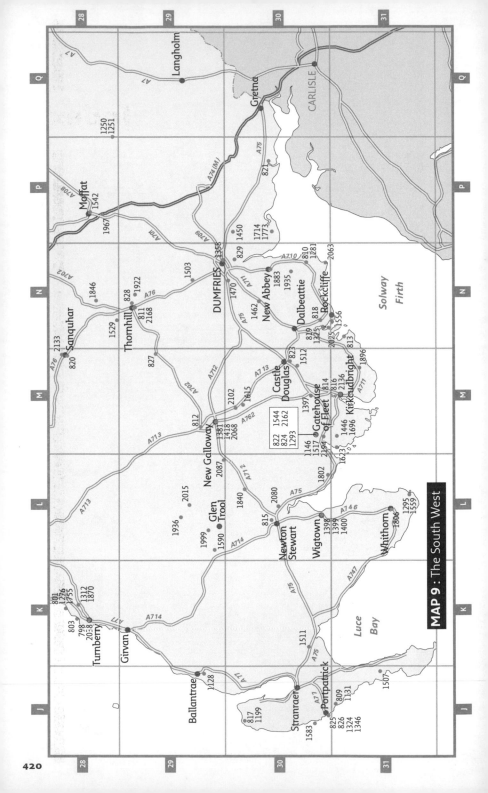

MAP 9 : The South West

420

Index

The numbers listed against index entries refer to the page on which the entry appears and not the entry's item number.

Scotland the Best ...at your fingertips

NOW AVAILABLE AS AN APP*

Whether you're planning a trip or out and about, you can instantly access over 2,300 of the best places to eat, sleep and visit.

Easily find the best
Quickly search by category, region or local area

Your personal guide
Every recommendation mapped and colour coded

Plan your trip
Bookmark your favourite places and share with friends

Download on the App Store

Collins

*Due to be released summer 2016